# FIEFS AND

MW01038887

# FIEFS AND VASSALS

*The Medieval Evidence Reinterpreted*

SUSAN REYNOLDS

CLARENDON PRESS · OXFORD

Oxford University Press, Walton Street, Oxford OX2 6DP
Oxford New York
Athens Auckland Bangkok Bombay
Calcutta Cape Town Dar es Salaam Delhi
Florence Hong Kong Istanbul Karachi
Kuala Lumpur Madras Madrid Melbourne
Mexico City Nairobi Paris Singapore
Taipei Tokyo Toronto
and associated companies in
Berlin Ibadan

Oxford is a trade mark of Oxford University Press

Published in the United States by
Oxford University Press Inc., New York

First published 1994
Reprinted 1994, 1995 (twice)
Published as a Clarendon Paperback 1996

British Library Cataloguing in Publication Data
Data available

Library of Congress Cataloging in Publication Data
Reynolds, Susan.
Fiefs and vassals: the medieval evidence reinterpreted / Susan Reynolds.
p. cm.
Includes bibliographical references and index.
1. Middle Ages—History. 2. Feudalism. I. Title.
D117.R49 1994 940.1—dc20 94-2428
ISBN 0-19-820458-2
ISBN 0-19-820648-8 (pbk)

Printed in Great Britain by
Bookcraft (Bath) Ltd
Midsomer Norton, Avon

*To Peggy Brown*

*Homage and fidelity*

# Acknowledgements

In the course of almost eight years of increasing obsession with fiefs, vassalage, and feudalism I have incurred many debts. First and foremost to the staffs of the British Library and the Institute of Historical Research, who have been kind and helpful far beyond their duty. Other debts are to those whose ears I have bent and who have listened and helped me in many ways. Right at the beginning the audience at a lecture at the Anglo-American Conference in 1985 produced several helpful and stimulating suggestions and so since then have seminars or societies at the universities of Birmingham, Cambridge, Delhi (South Campus), Jaipur, Michigan, Washington, and Western Washington, and at Boston College, Dartmouth College, Emory University, Goldsmith's College, and Harvard Law School. So did the members of the Battle conference of 1991. The paper I read there on 'Bookland, Folkland and Fiefs' was published in *Anglo-Norman Studies*, 14 (1992), and I am grateful to the editor, Dr Marjorie Chibnall, and the publishers, Boydell and Brewer, for permission to use it again: it forms part of chapters 3 and 8. One seminar above all has provided me with more than it is possible for me to acknowledge adequately: the convenors of the early medieval seminar at the Institute of Historical Research (now John Gillingham, Janet Nelson, Michael Clanchy, Wendy Davies, and Brenda Bolton) have made it combine friendliness with intellectual stimulus and rigour in a way that I could never have imagined before I joined it.

However unwieldy and perfunctory lists of names may seem I must mention some of the individuals who have helped me outside seminars. Working over fields in which I know so little I have been extremely lucky in having people to consult who know so much more about them. Paul Fouracre, Jane Martindale, and Janet Nelson have helped me with the Franks and early medieval France; Trevor Dean and Chris Wickham with Italy; Pauline Stafford and Patrick Wormald with Anglo-Saxon England; Tom Cain, Robin Fleming, Christopher Lewis, and Ann Williams with Domesday Book; Judith Green with twelfth-century England; and Joe Biancalana, Paul Brand, and Derek Keene with English law. Benjamin Arnold, Eckhard Müller-Mertens, and Timothy Reuter offered valuable suggestions about Germany, especially on bibliography. David D'Avray argued with me usefully about *de cuius feodo* (or *ad cuius feodum*) clauses. Mary MacRobert and Nigel Ramsay both gave me references for which I am grateful. Julia Walworth found my cover illustration for me. Kate

Gavron, Barbara Harvey, Vickie Macnair, and Janet Nelson all read parts, large or small, of the book and all offered kind encouragement as well as cogent criticism: even if I have not taken all their advice I think the result is clearer and has fewer mistakes than it would have had without them. Frances Goudge proof-read almost the whole book with me, Ella Goudge did the rest, and all their family helped us in different ways. Two people have, I think, read it all: Richard Jeffery of Oxford University Press who has once again been a wonderful copy-editor, and Peggy Brown, whose article on the 'Tyranny of a Construct' first made me worry about feudalism, and to whom I therefore dedicate this book.

# Contents

CONTENTS

# I

# THE PROBLEM OF FEUDALISM

## 1.1. *The nature of the problem*

FEUDALISM, to any members of the general public who ever refer to it, stands for almost any hierarchical and oppressive system. Bosses or landlords who bully their employees or tenants are being feudal. If they bully them fiercely they are worse: they are positively medieval. Medieval historians may dislike this hostile sidelight on their period but they are not on the whole much more precise in their use of the words feudal and feudalism. As E. A. R. Brown and C. van de Kieft both pointed out independently in 1974, feudalism can mean a lot of different things.[1] A good many medievalists have, however, continued to maintain that, whatever the difficulties of describing medieval society in general as feudal, there is a narrow, technical, more precise sense to feudalism which retains its utility. This is characterized by such words as 'the system of feudal and vassal institutions', *les liens féodo-vassaliques*, *i rapporti feudo-vassallatici*, or *das Lehnswesen*, for which I shall use the rather ugly and clumsy, but convenient, expressions feudo-vassalic relations or feudo-vassalic institutions.[2] Of course, no one agrees about just what these relations or institutions involved: some, for instance, think that either jurisdiction or military service or both were essential components, while others see either or both as peripheral or occasional.[3] Definitions, explicit or implied, also vary because some who propound or imply them assume that the character of an institution is determined by its origins, some rely on what is assumed to be its fully developed form, and yet others postulate some kind of ideal type or platonic form as lying behind empirical formations. The reference in the previous sentence to assumptions and

---

[1] Brown, 'Tyranny of a Construct'; van de Kieft, 'De feodale maatschappij'; cf. Ward, 'Feudalism'.

[2] e.g. Ganshof, *Feudalism*, pp. xvi–xvii; Brunner, '"Feudalismus": ein Beitrag', 156, 179–82; Le Goff, *La Civilisation*, 594; van Caenegem, 'Government, Law and Society', 198; cf. the survey by Cammarosano, 'Le Strutture feudali', 837–69.

[3] Jurisdiction was considered inessential by Ganshof, *Feudalism*, 156–8, but has been stressed in Italian historiography: Tabacco, 'Fief et seigneurie'; M. Tangheroni, 'La Sardegna prearagonese', 525–6. On military service, e.g. Stephenson, 'Origin and Significance of Feudalism'.

implications is not made lightly: those who define or discuss medieval feudalism seldom want to get bogged down in what I suspect they see as mere
matters of terminology which get in the way of concentration on Real
History.[4] Impatience with what is seen as mere theory or mere semantics
may be the reason why some discussions seem to slither from one sort of
implied definition to another, or focus at different points on ethos or *men-
talité*, politics, economy, or law, so that feudalism in its 'narrow sense'
sometimes broadens out to imply other senses too.[5] Recently it has become
customary to distinguish *féodalité*, or feudalism in the narrower, feudo-
vassalic sense of relations between lords and vassals within the noble class,
from *seigneurie* or manorialism, that is, relations between lords and peasants. As Brown and van de Kieft showed, this has not eliminated confusions, while it may raise some doubts about the extent to which a set of
institutions that concerned only the noble class, and was not, it seems,
essentially linked to the economic system, could have shaped a whole society.

   This book is concerned only with feudalism in its supposedly more precise sense. Its object is to establish how far vassalage and the fief, as they
are generally understood, constituted institutions which are definable,
comprehensible, and helpful to the understanding of medieval history. My
argument will be that in so far as they are definable and comprehensible
they are not helpful. Brown, in her seminal article of 1974, thought that
'feudal' had some meaning when it had specific reference to fiefs because
it was relatively easy to say what 'fief' meant.[6] As a result of work which
started under the inspiration of her article and has since been punctuated
by discussions with her, I shall argue that on that point she was too opti-
mistic. Fiefs and vassalage, as they are generally defined by medieval historians today, are post-medieval constructs, though rather earlier than the
construct of feudalism. Historians often refer to both fiefs and vassals when
neither word is in their sources. They sometimes refer to them in ways
that, irrespective of terminology, seem to me to distort the relations of
property and politics that the sources record. Even when the historians
follow the terminology of their documents and take pains to establish the
phenomena recorded, they tend to fit their findings into a framework of
interpretation that was devised in the sixteenth century and elaborated in
the seventeenth and eighteenth. Learned as were the scholars of those

---

   [4] Cammarosano, 'Le Strutture feudali', 846–7, cites examples. Cf. Lloyd, *Explanation*, 4.
   [5] Many recent formulations correspond more or less with J. O. Ward's 'focus VI', though
some slide into other foci: Ward, 'Feudalism'. On types of definition: Fischer, *Historians'
Fallacies*, 277–81.
   [6] Brown, 'Tyranny of a Construct', 1080, 1081, 1086.

times and much as we owe to them, they knew less than we know about the middle ages and much less about the differing ways that societies may be organized. We cannot understand medieval society and its property relations if we see it through seventeenth- or eighteenth-century spectacles. Yet every time we think of fiefs and vassals we do just that. Feudalism in its 'narrow sense' of relations within the noble class seems to me a much less important subject than feudalism in its Marxist sense, which involves not only relations between nobles and peasants but consideration of the whole economic structure of society and the reasons for economic and social change. At present, however, study of the broader subject seems to be impeded by its inheritance from the narrower one of the idea that fiefs and vassalage were central and defining institutions of medieval European society. In particular, the comparative use of feudalism in study of non-European societies, although generally conducted in what is intended to be a Marxist sense, is gravely hindered by a tendency to bring fiefs and vassals into the discussion in 'the Cinderella's slipper strategy' of trying to fit one whole society into a conceptual model derived from a quite different one.[7] That seems peculiarly unfortunate when the model was constructed so long ago at such an early stage of comparative social science.

## 1.2. *The historiography of feudalism*[8]

The eighteenth-century idea of the middle ages as the time of 'feudal government', 'feudal society', or the 'feudal system' was derived from discussions of the previous two centuries about 'feudal law'. From the early sixteenth century humanist scholarship in France was concerned with law, notably with the history of Roman law and its authority in France, and thus with the origin and authority of the feudal law or law of fiefs that had been studied in medieval universities along with Roman law.[9] This academic law about fiefs needs to be distinguished from the customary law of the middle ages that historians often call feudal law. It was based on a composite treatise, the *Libri Feudorum*, which had been compiled in Lombardy in the twelfth and early thirteenth centuries and remains one of the most extraordinarily neglected texts of the middle ages. It became attached to the books of Roman law in the thirteenth century and accumulated glosses and commentaries by many of the same academic lawyers who glossed and commented on the Corpus Juris Civilis. The resultant academic law of fiefs

---

[7] Jeffcott, 'Feudalism in China', 158; Reynolds, 'More about Feudalism'.
[8] This is to be much more fully discussed by E. A. R. Brown, from whose unpublished work I have profited greatly.
[9] Kelley, *Foundations*; Huppert, *Idea of Perfect History*, 40–1, 185–93.

was concerned only with the law about properties called fiefs, whose holders it called vassals. Its connection with the law actually practised in the
courts of the supposedly feudal kingdoms of medieval Europe was for the
most part rather tenuous and indirect. The university-trained lawyers
who, except in England, dominated higher courts from the fourteenth century on, occasionally introduced the terminology of fiefs and vassals that
they remembered from their university days into some legal documents.
Occasionally they used words and phrases from the literature of the law of
fiefs along with those from Roman law to make their arguments look better. The substance of property law and the procedures of the courts in
northern Europe were, however, not very seriously affected by the academic law of fiefs. In one respect court procedure and academic law became
more divided from each other just at the same time as knowledge of the
academic law was spreading: while writers on the law of fiefs continued to
discuss procedures using the judgement of peers (*judicium parium*), the
dominance of professional lawyers and judges in the courts of late medieval
Europe eliminated the collective judgement that had earlier been traditional and with which judgement by one's equals had originally been connected.[10]

The legal historians of sixteenth-century France quickly decided that
the academic law of fiefs had no authority in France.[11] Charles du Moulin
opened his discussion of the custom of Paris with a *titulus* on fiefs, which
he said belonged at the beginning because fiefs were the peculiar property
and creation of the ancient Franks. The Lombards learnt of fiefs from
them in *Germania* before taking them to Italy. That the *Libri* were merely
local custom, with no general authority, was shown, among other things,
by the notorious variations in feudal customs.[12] However hostile to
medieval writing on the law of fiefs the sixteenth-century French scholars
might be, their study of it and argument about it imprinted its vocabulary
and categories on their minds and the minds of their successors. That was
because the literature on it provided the framework they needed to make
the kind of sense they wanted of what seemed to them the shapeless chronicles of medieval history. It did so especially well when it was combined
with the idea of the Germanic or Gothic nations, and their distinctive contribution to European culture and history. The law of fiefs could be
explained as having originated in the law of all these barbarians, though

---

[10] See index: peers.
[11] Kelley, *Foundations*, on whom I largely rely, seems at times to conflate the academic law of
fiefs with customary law: some of the sixteenth-century scholars may have compared the two
more than my brief reading of some of them suggests.
[12] Du Moulin, *Opera*, i: *Commentarius*, 3–5, 21–2.

French scholars soon decided that it owed more to the Franks than to the Lombards, despite the Lombard origin of the work which inspired them even while they rejected its authority. The twelfth-century *Libri Feudorum* had included a brief piece of conjectural history to explain how benefices or fiefs had originated in grants by lords which had at first lasted only as long as the lords chose, then were extended to the life of the grantee, and were eventually made hereditary by the emperor Conrad II.[13] I shall argue that the properties of French (or any other) nobles had not been called fiefs before the thirteenth century, except in contexts where the word had a quite different meaning, but the sixteenth-century antiquaries could not know that. It was natural for them to assume that noble properties had always been called fiefs, as they were in their own time and in their texts. The *Libri Feudorum* thus seemed to provide an account of the origin of fiefs that offered both a hypothesis to guide research into medieval history and a framework for discussing the constitutional relations of king and nobles in the historians' present. The key place occupied by Conrad II in the original story could be filled well enough by a French king: Hugh Capet, for instance, would fit quite well. Remarks in the *Libri Feudorum* about the rights and obligations of vassals and the judgements they made as peers of their lords' courts were stimulating in the constitutional context. There is no doubt that the conjectural history of the *Libri Feudorum* did indeed serve as a very fruitful hypothesis. The relations of barbarian soldiers to their leaders were envisageable, with the help of Tacitus, as an early form of vassalage, while fiefs seemed a natural consequence of the barbarian settlements. With further research, a period of 'allodial' property was interposed, during which nobles had held their lands with full (alodial) rights, rather than as dependent fiefs.[14] The introduction of fiefs was postponed to the time of the Carolingians, while the stages by which they became hereditary were debated and connected to different episodes of French history. The framework and the terminology, however, survived all amendments—as they still do.

The contention of this book is that, while the sixteenth-century legal historians were right in their formal denial of the authority of the law of fiefs in France, and while they made very productive use of the hypotheses they nevertheless drew from it, their use of late medieval learning has misled medieval historians in several important ways ever since. Both the academic law of fiefs and the actual law practised in the courts of France were the creations of the later middle ages and of a culture of academic and

---

[13] Lehmann, *Consuetudines*, 8.

[14] Although the spellings 'allod, allodial' are more common in the literature, I use 'alod, alodial' throughout this book: see chapter 3 n. 1.

professional law and of professional, bureaucratic government that had
developed since the twelfth century. This cannot be appreciated until the
text of the *Libri Feudorum* is studied and related to the context of the customary law of property in eleventh- and twelfth-century Italy so that its
original character and purposes can be disentangled from those of the later
writings that were based on it.[15] My argument is that the law of property
embodied in the academic and professional law—what I shall call the
expert law—of the later middle ages did not develop out of the customary
law that governed noble property in the early middle ages, either in the way
that the sixteenth-century scholars supposed or in the various ways that
most historians of feudalism now seem to assume that it did. To some
extent, of course, it did develop out of earlier custom and law, but, in so
far as it did, it was from the custom and law created by the arrangements
made rather by great churches for the management of their lands than by
lay nobles for theirs. The relation between a bishop or abbot and the tenants of his church's land was different from the relation of a king or lord
and his warriors that is postulated by the idea of vassalage and the 'union
of vassal and fief'. The link between vassalage, as a relation that developed
from that between kings or other lords and their warriors, and fiefs, as
deriving from general grants of land made by lords in return for military
service, cannot therefore explain the origin of the complex of rules that
came to be understood as characteristic of 'feudal tenure'.

The concepts of vassalage and of the fief, moreover, as they have been
developed since the sixteenth century, originated in the work of the sixteenth-century scholars rather than in the late medieval texts they studied.
The texts talked about fiefs but they contained very little that amounted to
anything like a concept of the fief as a category of property that could be
distinguished from other sorts of property, let alone be seen as an organizing principle of government or society. Their authors were discussing the
law of fiefs, not property in general or the structure and bonds of society.
They sometimes explained the obligations of vassals—that is, fiefholders,
the only people they were interested in—in terms of gratitude to their lords
or of the noble obligation to military service, but these brief moralizing
rationalizations served a far more significant purpose in the works of sixteenth-century and later historians than they did in those of the medieval
lawyers. The idea of vassals as noble warriors who brought the ethos and
solidarity of the warrior band into the structures of medieval government,
who owed fidelity in return for the fiefs they were granted, and whose relation with their lords was contractual in a way that that of non-fiefholders

---

[15] A start on this is attempted in chapter 6.8.

was not—the whole idea, in short, of vassalage both as fiefholding and as the cement of medieval society—could be read between the lines of the texts of the law of fiefs, but only between the lines. It was the sixteenth- and seventeenth-century scholars who found it there.

The value of the law of fiefs for the study of history was soon appreciated outside France. In German universities it was studied in the seventeenth and eighteenth centuries alongside the thirteenth-century and later 'mirror' literature (*Sachsenspiegel*, *Schwabenspiegel*, etc.) on *Lehnrecht*, which gave further opportunities for deducing early medieval ideas and values from later literature and practice.[16] Before the end of the sixteenth century the Scottish lawyers Thomas Smith and Thomas Craig had taken up the subject, and in the seventeenth Henry Spelman brought it to England.[17] The law of fiefs, as interpreted and used by the French scholars, could be used in other countries, as it had been in France, to organize the past and provide arguments for the present so that ideas about it gradually spread to a wider public.[18] When what modern historians call 'feudal tenures' were abolished in England in 1660 the word 'feodall' was used only in an annexe to the act of parliament and only about titles to peerages.[19] By the late eighteenth century Francis Hargrave, editing the writings of the early seventeenth-century lawyer Edward Coke, marvelled at Coke's ignorance of what Hargrave called 'this interesting subject' and at the absence from Coke's *Institutes* of 'any thing like an historical illustration with the least reference to the *general* doctrine of feuds'. Without it, to Hargrave, it was 'scarcely possible to have a just and proper idea of our law of tenures, the greater part of which is founded on principles strictly feudal'.[20]

By the eighteenth century increasingly close and learned study of historical sources, combined with an increasing taste for abstraction and an increasing sense of the strangeness of the past, evoked a need to characterize and analyse medieval phenomena in general that found striking expression in the thirty-first book of Montesquieu's *L'Esprit des lois*. The way that so much historical study had started from the *Libri Feudorum* made it natural that historians should now characterize the whole of the middle ages as feudal. Feudal government and feudal society were the obvious counterparts of feudal law. Consequently, when Adam Smith and others in the Scottish Enlightenment developed the idea of different stages of

---

[16] Burmeister, *Studium*, 131–7; Brunner, 'Feudalismus, feudal', 339–40; Theuerkauf, *Land und Lehnswesen*, 88–122.

[17] Smith, 'Sir Thomas Smith'; Craig, *Jus Feudale* and *Scotland's Soveraignty*; Spelman, *Reliquiae*, 1–46, 216–21.

[18] Pocock, *Ancient Constitution*.

[19] *Statutes of the Realm*, v. 260 (12 Chas II, c. 24, cl. 10).

[20] Coke, *Institutes, part I*, iii: *Notes*, note on I. ii. 85.

history marked by differences in political economy, the agricultural stage (after the hunting and pastoral stages and before the commercial) was represented primarily by the middle ages, the age of feudal government. In Smith's description of feudal government the framework of the sixteenth-century discussions is still clearly visible. Feudal government had succeeded the alodial government of the barbarians when military *beneficia* became 'altogether hereditary, in which state they were called *feuda*'.[21] For Smith, feudal government in Britain had, it seems, already been effectively superseded, largely by the introduction of arts, commerce, and luxury.[22] To lawyers and intellectuals of the French Enlightenment it survived in France and would do so until *les droits féodaux et censuels* were abolished in 1789.[23] For the German, von Justi, common sense demanded the abolition of a system that shortage of cash had made necessary in a bygone age.[24] The French Revolution brought the package view of feudalism as a past stage of history to a wider public and accentuated the tendency to attribute to the middle ages whatever seemed most irrational and oppressive about the Ancien Régime, like the classification of society into distinct orders with a defined and legally privileged nobility. Ideas of progress suggested that such deplorable arrangements must have been archaic survivals. The package view of the middle ages as feudal and of feudalism as oppressive then got a new lease of life when Marx took it over, along with a newer version of the four-stage theory. He put new driving forces behind the beginning and end of what was now called simply feudalism, and concentrated on aspects of the middle ages that narrower or more romantic views had ignored or played down, but his knowledge of medieval history, despite wide reading, was still conditioned by the framework within which all scholars had seen it since the sixteenth century.[25]

The point of this rapid survey of the progress from sixteenth-century expositions of the law of fiefs to full-blown feudalism is to show how, while the idea of what was feudal expanded as the knowledge and interests of historians expanded, the fundamental concepts and the framework in which they were set remained virtually unaltered. Even Adam Smith and Marx did not change perceptions of what was feudal as much as they should have. For many non-Marxist medievalists (and even more oddly for a good many Marxists) feudalism still seems to inhibit post-Marxist—or post-Smithian—insights: society can apparently be changed

[21] Smith, *Lectures in Jurisprudence*, 249; cf. 14, 28–9, 49–55, 244–65; cf. Blackstone, *Commentaries*, ii. 44–58; Lieberman, *Province of Legislation*, 139–40.
[22] *Lectures in Jurisprudence*, 261.
[23] Sagnac and Caron, *Comités*, 172–81, 767–76; Mackrell, *Attack on Feudalism*.
[24] Cited by Brunner, 'Feudalismus, feudal', 340.
[25] Müller-Mertens, 'Zur Feudalentwicklung', 56–9; Levine, 'German Historical School'.

from the top by military conquest or royal patronage, as happened, supposedly, with the Norman Conquest of England. But how significantly
could the Normans have changed English society when they could not
change its economic base and when, moreover, they themselves, seen in a
wider comparative context than medieval historians before this century
could see them, had much the same economy, kinship system, religion,
legal system, and values in general as the pre-conquest English?

Ever since the sixteenth-century scholars borrowed the law of fiefs while
denying its authority in France, discussions of feudal law and feudal society have combined eclecticism with nationalist preoccupations in an extraordinarily unselfconscious way. Nearly everyone investigating supposedly
feudal phenomena, and especially those feudo-vassalic phenomena that
were the concern of the early scholars and are the subject of this book, has
tended to concentrate on one country or region while being ready to interpolate evidence or organizing concepts from elsewhere at every turn. Some
see the feudalism of their own area as the most typical or complete, some
stress its exceptional qualities, but none seems ready to question whether
the various phenomena are all part of the same thing. In England and
France feudalism, like the feudal law before it, is used to describe, and by
implication to explain, quite different situations. In seventeenth-century
England feudal law was first used to explain the origins of the monarchy's
rights over those who had come to be called tenants in chief. In France the
features of law which by the eighteenth century had come to seem most
archaic and oppressive and in need of historical explanation, and therefore
of an explanatory label, were the rights of nobles over peasants. As a result
feudalism in England has ever since been associated with a strong
central power, and particularly with military service, but not with noble
jurisdiction over peasants, while feudalism in France, as in Germany, has
been seen in terms of a weak monarchy and a nobility holding 'immunities'
of jurisdiction over their tenants—what is sometimes called feudal anarchy. These anomalies have stimulated much historical ingenuity but little
serious rethinking. Just as the image of feudal society was composed syncretically to fit a thousand years of the history of all Europe, so the vast
increase of knowledge about the middle ages has since then gone on being
accommodated syncretically to fit an image which changed by accretion
but not by radical revision. The middle ages have been taken as the time of
feudalism, and so whatever does not form part of the image of feudalism is
filtered out of the view or adapted to fit into the background.[26] Words

---

[26] I discussed the filtering out of important aspects of collective activity, for instance, in
Reynolds, *Kingdoms and Communities*.

which come from the Lombard *Libri Feudorum* are assumed to have central and technical significance, and medieval people are assumed to have thought in the categories derived over the centuries from those terms. If medieval sources use words we consider feudal then they meant by them what we mean. If they never use them they must have implied them.

The power of the feudal paradigm is demonstrated in the treatment of the so-called 'feudal aids'—dues paid to lords when they had extra expenses, such as the knighting of a son, the marriage of a daughter, or their own ransom or crusade. Although these aids have not been traced before the late eleventh century and although then and later they were taken (except in England) from non-fiefholding commoners rather than from noble fiefholders (and in England they were taken from both), this does not seem to have raised doubts about the origin of such aids in the primitive obligation of a vassal to render aid to his lord.[27] Neither evidence nor the lack of it nor alternative explanations, it seems, need to be considered.

Some historians defend the continued use of the construct of feudalism, whether used in its supposedly more narrow and precise sense or in any of its wider senses, as an ideal type which does not lose its utility merely because all the details of empirical forms do not correspond to it. Max Weber, the inventor of ideal types, certainly discussed feudalism as one of them, but even in his hands it is not a very convincing one. Ideal types, like Marx's social formations, seem to be most useful when they come in contrasted pairs.[28] Marxist feudalism is easiest to envisage when it is contrasted with capitalism, whereas Weber's contrast of his with patrimonialism and hereditary charisma is less clear. That is not only because a three-way comparison is more difficult. It is because, not surprisingly, since his ideas about it were based on information about medieval Europe derived from the historiographical tradition that I have described, his feudalism has too many defining characteristics.[29] Ideal types need to be reasonably simple, not only so that they can be contrasted, but so that they do not get cluttered up by characteristics which may be merely superficial epiphenomena that are not structurally related to each other. They are no use if they are merely bundles of characteristics that have been put together under a single label by successive generations of historians with different

---

[27] Though see chapter 7 n. 264 (though, for various reasons, none of the works cited there addresses the issue of origins) and chapter 9 n. 365.

[28] Weber, *Social and Economic Organization*, 152.

[29] Weber, *Economy and Society*, 255, 1070–1109. Among much literature on ideal types, the most appealing to medievalists may be Power, 'On Medieval History', and Watkins, 'Ideal Types and Historical Explanation'; cf. Leach, *Feudalism*, 7–11; Martindale, 'Sociological Theory'; Bendix and Berger, 'Images of Society'.

interests and different understandings of the past. We hold them together
in a bundle that we have tied up with the string of our ideas or words, but
this is only useful if there is some kind of core to which they are all
related.[30] That is particularly important if one is using feudalism to
compare different societies. Too many models of feudalism used for comparisons, even by Marxists, are still either constructed on the sixteenth-
century basis or incorporate what, in a Marxist view, must surely be
superficial or irrelevant features from it.[31] Even when one restricts oneself
to Europe and to feudalism in its narrow sense it is extremely doubtful
whether feudo-vassalic institutions formed a coherent bundle of institutions or of concepts that was structurally separate from other institutions
and concepts of the time. If one chooses to put them in a bundle it is a
modern bundle, held together by the string of our ideas—or the ideas of
past academic lawyers and historians—not by the essential interdepen-
dence of its contents. It is not just that all the phenomena and notions of
feudo-vassalic institutions never existed together anywhere, but that they
are too incoherent, too loosely related, and too imperfectly reflected in
medieval evidence to be envisaged as anything like an ideal type.

Some devotees of feudalism of one kind or another avoid the rigours of
ideal types by claiming that, all the same, we must have some generalizations. They are, of course, right, but generalizations are propositions that
can be verified or falsified, rather than abstract nouns that we use as labels
to save us from having to look at the contents of the bundle. It has been
suggested that the concept of feudalism may be used as what Abraham
Kaplan called a 'descriptive generalization' that may 'inform us of what
manner of creature we may expect to encounter on our travels without pur-
porting to lay bare the nature of the beast'. Kaplan, however, also said that
descriptive generalizations stem from fairly direct observations and are on
a low level of abstraction.[32] That does not apply to feudalism in any of its
senses. What the concept of feudalism seems to have done since the sixteenth century is not to help us recognize the creatures we meet but to tell
us that all medieval creatures are the same so that we need not bother to
look at them. Put another way, feudalism has provided a kind of protective
lens through which it has seemed prudent to view the otherwise dazzling
oddities and varieties of medieval creatures. The prescriptions of the lenses
can vary—feudal anarchy, military centralization and 'feudal incidents'
imposed on nobles, or a Marxist dominant mode of production—or we can

---

[30] An example of the discussion of feudalism as an ideal type without any 'core' or contrasted
type is Hall, 'Feudalism in Japan'.

[31] Reynolds, 'More about Feudalism'.

[32] Saltman, 'Feudal Relationships', 515; Kaplan, *Conduct of Enquiry*, 114.

have multifocals combining everything. However feudalism is defined, many medieval historians feel uncomfortable without their feudal sunglasses. Nicely shaded, the 'feudal anarchy' of eleventh-century France or fourteenth-century Germany can seem to belong to the same species as the system that formed the bastion of a strong central government in twelfth-century England or Sicily. For many historians who apparently think of feudalism in a feudo-vassalic, non-Marxist sense, monarchies can still count as feudal however much authority kings exercised over those of their subjects who were not their vassals, provided only that they exercised some over people who look like vassals according to some definition or other—and provided that the kings lived at the time which has already been labelled as the age of feudal monarchies. Some historians have left off their feudal spectacles and gone over to contact lenses: that is, they think no one will know that they are wearing them if they abjure the 'ism' and use the adjective feudal without defining it. Undefined, feudal sometimes seems to mean little more than medieval—as in feudal lord, feudal law, feudal government—much as it did in the eighteenth century.

One of the chief troubles with most discussions of feudalism in the narrow sense of feudo-vassalic institutions is that they tend to confuse words, concepts, and phenomena.[33] Historians who define fiefs generally say that they are defining the 'concept of the fief', but they nearly always start by discussing the word and its etymology and origins, while what they are really concerned with is neither the word nor the concept or notion that people may have in their heads when they use the word, but the phenomena that word and concept represent. The *word* fief is the normal translation of *feodum, feudum, fevum,* et cetera. These words were used in a variety of contexts and senses in the middle ages, so that they relate to rather different phenomena and presumably reflected a variety of concepts or notions in the minds of those who used them. The *concept* of the fief, as I have argued and as I hope will appear from my analysis of the medieval evidence, is essentially post-medieval: it is a set of ideas or notions about the essential attributes of pieces of property that historians have defined as fiefs, some of which may not appear in the sources under any of the words that we translate as fief. There is nothing wrong with that, any more than there is anything wrong with using our own words.[34] We may often legit-

---

[33] I am deliberately talking of words, concepts, and phenomena rather than signs, signifiers, and signified, partly because I think the terms are clearer and partly because I do not wish to use the terminology of a discussion (or should I say discourse?) in which I do not feel at ease. Although, when I originally worked out how the confusion of the three bedevils medieval history, I painstakingly reinvented the wheel, I am aware that others had invented it long before for use in other disciplines: survey in Lyons, *Semantics*, 95–114.

[34] See Maitland, *Township and Borough*, 21–2.

imately want to investigate the history of concepts or phenomena of which people in the past were not aware, like vitamin C deficiency or the doctrine of incorporation. But when the subject under investigation involves notions or attitudes held by people in the society concerned it is vital to distinguish whether a concept is ours or theirs. How far the ideas or notions about property that are involved in our concept of the fief correspond to any of the notions held by medieval people in any of several centuries, countries, and contexts when they used either that word or any other word is a subject that needs investigation. Lastly, after word and concept, there is the *phenomenon* of dependent noble or military tenure, with its varying conditions. Much of the discussion of fiefs, as of vassalage, seems to me to assume the identity of words with concepts, our concepts with medieval concepts, and all three with the phenomena. That is particularly dangerous with something like the medieval historian's concept of the fief, which embraces a whole lot of other concepts, similarly conflated with particular words, such as investiture, homage, or oaths of fidelity. How far each of these words had consistent meanings and how closely the phenomena they represent were connected with fiefholding is another problem which cannot be solved by imposing modern definitions of 'the concept of the fief' on the medieval evidence.

Of the trio, word, concept, and phenomenon, the least significant for the historian of society is the word. Starting our investigation of phenomena by focusing on particular words is a sixteenth-century habit that needs to be dropped. In one sense historians who work from written sources have to begin with words: they are all we have. But it may be more rewarding not to attempt definitions until after one has looked at usage and thought hard about what is being discussed (the phenomena) and about what may be implied about the notions of the time. If we start by discussing words we are liable to assume that words like *feudum* were used in the sense we expect unless the contrary is specified: many of the examples cited by Du Cange or Niermeyer are much less specific than the definitions they illustrate. Discussions of terminology, moreover, generally start from the assumption, not only that certain words are particularly significant for feudalism, but that such words have core or technical meanings and that these technical meanings were somehow more real and more significant than the others. To do this is to ignore how language works. Words used in real life, especially abstract nouns, do not have core meanings which are more central or more right than others. Dictionary makers deduce meanings from usage. They do not control usage. It varies from place to place, even from speaker to speaker, as well as from time to time. Words are used precisely or technically only within particular disciplines in which precision is necessary. In the context of property, political relations, or legal status and capacity, precise and consistent usage could come from lawyers, but it could be achieved over a wide area and long period only if they are professional lawyers working in a legal system which has acknowledged authorities, written documents in which authoritative pronouncements are recorded, and some system of publishing and enforcing those pronouncements. Even then, of course, laymen will continue to use words in ways which lawyers deplore, and their usage may get into the records which historians use.[35] Until after the twelfth century most of the medieval law of property, including the law of noble property, was customary law in which uniformity and consistency of vocabulary were impossible. After the twelfth century usage became more uniform within the various legal systems which evolved wherever governments could establish a hierarchy of courts with defined jurisdictions, but greater consistency within systems was accompanied by greater variation between them. The concept of the fief, like the concept of vassalage, awaited historians who thought they could understand the middle ages through understanding the phenomenon of the fief. It was not a bad idea, as far as it went, but it has not worked very well when it has taken the form of tracing the history of words and assuming that each word represented both a distinct concept and a consistent phenomenon.

## 1.3. *The plan of the book*

The object of this book is most emphatically not to prove that feudo-vassalic relations or institutions were less important than is generally thought, nor to trace their rise or say when and where they appeared, nor to judge which part of Europe was most truly feudal. These seem to me meaningless subjects. My object is to explore the relation between the modern concepts of the fief and of vassalage on the one hand and the evidence of property law and of social and political relations that I find in medieval sources on the other. I start in chapters 2 and 3 with attempts to say what seems to be involved in the modern concepts of vassalage and the fief respectively. For those who think of jurisdiction as a third defining element of feudo-vassalic relations I should point out that both here and in the rest of the book I deal with jurisdiction over free people as a variable accompaniment of property rights. No one will be contented with my attempts to characterize the modern concepts. Some will repudiate some

---

[35] For a characteristic illustration: Maitland, *Collected Papers*, ii. 305.

of the features I describe, some will think I have missed out vital features, some will say that the whole thing is a caricature. All I can say is that some kind of characterization seemed necessary as a starting-point and that I have tried to do my honest best. The greater part of the two chapters then looks at information about the middle ages and about other societies that was not available when the two concepts were invented: in chapter 2 ideas about medieval political and social attitudes against which the concept of vassalage needs to be evaluated, and in chapter 3 ideas about property that need to be considered if one is to evaluate the concept of the fief.

Chapters 4–9 deal with phenomena and words: that is to say, with a survey of what seems to me the most important evidence I have found about the law of free or noble property and the political and social relations associated with it. Fiefs will loom much larger than vassalage here, because, for reasons that will emerge in chapters 2 and 3, the concept of the fief seems to me to deserve much more attention than the comparatively vacuous concept of vassalage. My survey does not claim to be anything like comprehensive. I have deliberately omitted almost all of the vast and important subject of relations between lords and peasants—in other words the whole subject of feudalism in its Marxist sense. Such relations seem to be of only indirect relevance to the concepts of fiefs and vassalage as they have been understood since the sixteenth century. I have also, deliberately but regretfully, omitted large areas of Europe. The omissions I specially regret are Spain and—considering it as an honorary bit of western Europe—the kingdom of Jerusalem. I had intended to include both but my project turned out too big, too difficult, and too slow. Within each of the areas I have covered I have ignored a great deal of material: I have found most of the sources I cite through footnotes in secondary literature and I have read only a fraction of the relevant literature. I have also ignored a mass of local variations. I feel less ashamed about this when I consider how often close study of particular regions has not precluded the imposition of general or national stereotypes on local material. Although there was much mutual influence between my areas (as well as much variation within them) my determination to avoid the serendipitous eclecticism traditional in the history of feudalism forced me to consider them separately. The division I chose, though it may look teleological, has the advantage of enabling me to look at the way that some of the different national traditions of writing about feudalism have both produced different national views of apparently similar medieval phenomena and have prevented anyone from noticing a few apparently genuine medieval differences. My areas also correspond roughly to kingdoms which at one time or another had a significant degree of political unity. This played a significant part in shaping property law

in each of them and constitutes another argument for looking at them separately.

Most readers of this book will be more interested in one or at most two
of the areas and only part of the period it covers. I should, however, point
out that this is not a collection of separate essays. The argument is continuous. Chapters 2 and 3 set out the premises from which the later chapters
start. To avoid undue repetition, moreover, I have sometimes either cur-
tailed or omitted discussions in the later chapters of matters that I have
already covered earlier, notably in chapters 4 (on the Frankish kingdom)
and 5 (on the kingdom of France, 900–1100) and on which nothing
significantly different needs to be said in other connections. The
Carolingians and the 'feudal anarchy' of post-Carolingian France have
contributed so much to the image of feudalism that the importance of these
chapters is obvious. The contribution of the *Libri Feudorum* to the image
of feudalism in general has been so much underrated that the general
significance of chapter 6 (Italy) to the later chapters may need more
emphasis. It is impossible to understand both how French and German
property law developed in the later middle ages, and how the modern
image of feudalism has been distorted by unconscious reliance on the academic law of fiefs, if one does not look hard at the academic law and try to
understand how it arose and spread, and how it was related both to the
forms of professional law that developed in different countries and to the
realities of society and politics in each. Chapter 6, while it needs chapter 4
before it, is therefore essential to the later chapters, and particularly to
chapters 7 (France, 1100–1300) and 9 (the kingdom of Germany). England
too contributed several features to the image of feudalism, notably a stress
on military service and the hierarchy of tenure, the 'feudal aids', and wardship, so that chapter 8, which deals with it, is less detachable from the rest
than traditional ways of studying the middle ages might suggest.

# 2

# VASSALAGE AND THE NORMS OF MEDIEVAL SOCIAL RELATIONS

## 2.1. *The concept of vassalage*

BEFORE one can criticize the concept of vassalage as it is used in discussions of feudo-vassalic relations it is necessary to indicate as clearly as possible what it means there. This section is therefore intended to describe the main features of vassalage as it seems to be understood by those who use the word or who talk about vassals as a general category within medieval society. On occasion I shall note differences of opinion among those who use the concept, but I shall not at this stage say anything about those who reject it or criticize it radically. The first necessity is to get clear what it is that they or I reject. Clarity—or relative clarity—in this case may produce crudity and over-simplification, combining together views which some hold and others reject, but I do not intend to produce a caricature or straw man in order to make it easy to knock him down in later sections. In order to avoid clumsy repetitions I have not inserted phrases like 'some historians say', 'it seems to be generally thought', or 'vassals are (or have been) held to be this or that' in every sentence. The whole section must nevertheless be taken as a kind of indirect speech, even if it is more like rumour—and perhaps out-of-date rumour at that—rather than the accurate report of any one historian's views.

Historians use the words vassalage, *vassalité*, *Vasallität*, *vassallaggio*, et cetera to denote the relation between a lord and his free or noble follower—his vassal. Because the vassal was a free man they see the relation, although unequal, as having had a voluntary and reciprocal quality that distinguished it significantly from that of a lord with his peasant tenants or subjects. Mitteis went so far as to characterize Carolingian vassalage as a genuine partnership between equals, but that idea seems to be unusual.[1] The loyalties and obligations of vassalage are held to have been derived from those of the barbarian war-band, but these are obscure and I propose not to get involved in them here. It is generally agreed that by the end of

[1] Mitteis, *The State in the Middle Ages*, 56: he was presumably thinking of *pari suo* in *Formulae* 158 (Tours, 43): cf. Mitteis, *Lehnrecht*, 34.

the eighth century the *vassi* or *vassalli* of both the Frankish kings and other great men in their kingdom were free men who had entered into vassalage by a ritual known as commendation and by taking an oath of fidelity. Commendation and oath bound them to the service of their lords for life and they could normally leave only if the lord committed certain crimes against them. In return for the vassal's service the lord offered protection and some form or degree of maintenance, either by making the man a member of his household or by providing some kind of wage, whether in kind, in money, or in land.

Whatever the status of vassals or their predecessors before the eighth century, their status was by then rising. One reason for this was that the Carolingians bound counts, bishops, and other great men more closely to themselves by commendation so that they too became vassals. Vassalage thus became, in Ganshof's words, 'a coveted status, a mark of honour, at any rate where direct vassalage to the king was concerned and where the vassal obtained a benefice in return'.[2] Ganshof's reference to a benefice introduces the other reason for the rise in status of vassals. Not only the king but all lords with vassals were beginning to provide the maintenance that they owed to their vassals in the form of a landholding which became known as a benefice or fief. This marked a crucial stage in the creation of 'classic feudalism'. Scholarly opinion is divided on the date when vassals in general became fiefholders. Ganshof, for instance, thought that the 'union of benefice and vassalage' became general under the Carolingians, while Duby has argued that in the Mâconnais it did not happen until the eleventh century.[3] Benefices or fiefs were at first granted for life only, but later gained increasingly secure rights of inheritance. The new prosperity and independence that this brought to the humbler vassals confirmed their noble status and marked the beginning of what is often called the 'rise of the knights' and the growth of the ethos of chivalry. The conditions of fiefholding will be discussed in the next chapter, but here it must be noted that they are generally considered to have been shaped by the already established rights and obligations of vassalage. In the words of Heinrich Brunner, repeated by Mitteis, vassalage was the driving force (*der treibende Faktor*) in the history of feudalism.[4]

Because vassalage was, at least in theory, a freely contracted relation, and because the period when it emerged was one of formalism and ritual, every man who became a vassal is assumed to have undergone the ritual of com-

---

[2] Ganshof, *Feudalism*, 19.

[3] Ganshof, 'Note sur les origines de l'union' and other articles listed in the bibliography; Duby, *Société mâconnaise*, 151.

[4] Brunner, *Deutsche Rechtsgeschichte*, ii. 368; Mitteis, *Lehnrecht*, 16. Ganshof's 'Les Liens' and 'L'Origine', *passim* and esp. n. 1 in each, suggest that he agreed.

mendation, later alternatively known as homage (*hommage, Mannschaft, omaggio*). Bloch described how the prospective vassal commended himself or did homage. Sometimes but not invariably kneeling, he put his hands between the lord's hands and declared himself the 'man' of his lord. They then kissed, 'symbolizing accord and friendship. Such were the gestures—very simple ones, eminently fitted to make an impression on minds so sensitive to visible things—which served to cement one of the strongest social bonds known in the feudal era.'[5] Immediately after doing homage the vassal took an oath of fealty or fidelity. At first that was slightly less important, since similar oaths might be taken by subordinates who were not vassals, while an oath, as distinct from the rite of commendation, could be repeated and did not need any direct personal contact. For Kienast, homage without the physical contact of the lord's and vassal's hands would have been meaningless, while it was the ritual of homage or commendation that marked off vassalage from other, less close relations of subordination in the Carolingian age.[6] Later, however, after the rituals of vassalage had become established while Carolingian royal power had declined so that subjects in general ceased to take oaths of fidelity, homage and oath came to seem part of a single, indivisible rite almost everywhere.[7] One notable exception was north Italy, where commendation is rarely mentioned after the tenth century and the rite of homage seems to have been unknown or insignificant in the twelfth and thirteenth.[8]

The rite of commendation bound the lord to protect and maintain his vassal. Once vassals became tenants, the rights that went with the lord's duty gave him some control over the inheritance of the fief and protection or control of the tenant's widow and any minor heirs. These duties or rights, like the fiefholder's corresponding obligations, derived from the original relation of vassalage, which also explains why each heir had to renew homage on his succession and sometimes also on the succession of the lord. Even when the link between lord and vassal ceased to be merely personal and was 'territorialized' by the grant of fiefs, an element of personal commitment survived. The fiefholder's duties could at their simplest be expressed as honourable service, but they are often summarized as aid and counsel (*auxilium et consilium*), the aid being primarily military and the counsel being performed through attendance at the lord's court. Another way of summarizing the obligations of the vassal is to say that he was to be faithful: he owed fidelity or fealty. Magnou-Nortier distinguishes the general moral obligation to faith (*fides*) from oath-bound fidelity (*fidelitas*) and

[5] Bloch, *Feudal Society*, 145–6; cf. Le Goff, 'Rituel symbolique'.
[6] Kienast, *Vasallität*, 48.                    [7] Poly and Bournazel, *Mutation féodale*, 152.
[8] Brancoli Busdraghi, 'Formazione storica', 271–8.

sees the two as combined in the 'unilateral vassalic bond'.[9] Subjects who were not vassals were also required to be faithful and they too might be described in the Carolingian age as *fideles* but, as the bond of vassalage eclipsed other ties, the word *fidelis*, like the word 'man' (*homo*), became a synonym, or almost a synonym, for vassal. Fidelity—the bond of mutual fidelity between an individual lord and his individual follower—has been seen as the distinctive value of the feudal ethic, whether or not one derives it, or stresses its derivation, from the *Treue* of Germanic barbarians. A letter written by Bishop Fulbert of Chartres around 1020, which was later incorporated into the *Libri Feudorum*, is often cited as the best illustration of feudo-vassalic ideals. Asked by the duke of Aquitaine to write something about the nature of fidelity (*forma fidelitatis*), he replied that anyone who swore fidelity to his lord was obliged not to injure the lord, betray his secrets or fortresses, impede his justice or any business pertaining to the lord's honour, or cause him to lose his possessions. If the *fidelis* were to deserve the grant of a holding or fief (*casamentum*) he would have to go beyond these negative duties and faithfully give his lord aid and counsel. The lord in return should act in a corresponding way to his *fidelis*, lest he be censured for bad faith and perfidy.[10] The author of the twelfth-century English lawbook known as *Glanvill* maintained that the bond of fidelity deriving from lordship and homage (*dominii et homagii fidelitatis connexio*) ought to be mutual, so that the lord owes as much to the man as the man to the lord, saving only reverence.[11]

What made vassalage so important was that the time when it arose was one when, it is thought, there was no idea of the state and very little idea of impersonal, public obligations at all, and when kinship ties may have been becoming weaker. It was 'a state of society in which the main social bond [was] the relation between lord and man'.[12] Germanic barbarians did not have the Roman sense of *res publica*. Their loyalties were personal. Merovingian kings treated their kingdom as their own private property and, though the church kept alive some ideas of abstract good, people were only just beginning to think in terms of a 'transpersonal' state in the eleventh century. It was only with the twelfth-century Renaissance that ideas of the public good and public interest began to develop significantly.[13] Even in the great days of the Carolingian empire it was the personal bond, rather than high ideas of Christian empire, that worked: it was commendation that really bound counts to the king or emperor, while

---

[9] Magnou-Nortier, *Foi et fidélité*, 12; cf. Kienast, *Vasallität*, 23 n., 114; Poly and Bournazel, *Mutation féodale*, 108.

[10] Fulbert, *Letters and Poems*, no. 51.          [11] *Glanvill*, 107.

[12] Maitland, *Constitutional History*, 143.

[13] Beumann, 'Zur Entwicklung transpersonaler Staatsvorstellung'.

the oaths of fidelity that subjects at large had to take gained their force by seeming to create a personal bond with him.[14] But the king was too distant for the bond to hold. Inevitably, in the circumstances of the time, vassalage worked much more to the advantage of counts and other local lords: they could offer more effective protection to their vassals and their relations with them could be genuinely personal. As this suggests, while kings could make use of vassalage, they did so, not primarily as rulers of a kingdom or state, but as lords like any other lord. Vassalage was essentially a personal relation—what a modern sociologist might call an interpersonal, affective, dyadic relation. The element of affect is important. Men—vassals—were supposed to die for their lords. Boutruche pointed out that the union between lord and vassal could even, exceptionally, be expected to prevail over that between man and wife.[15] But the bond between lord and vassal did not supersede or undermine all other relations. Joint vassalage maintained the solidarity of the war-band among the vassals—a solidarity that is most famously exemplified in the Song of Roland, in which, incidentally, as Boutruche's remark might lead one to expect, Roland's betrothed plays a very minor part. Solidarity and sense of parity between vassals led to the 'judgement of peers' by which free and noble vassals gave counsel in their lord's court and joined in its judgements.

In practice, of course, obligations were not always fulfilled and the bond did not always hold. In the ninth and tenth centuries, partly because of the desire for benefices and partly because political troubles brought conflicts of loyalty, men began to commend themselves to more than one lord. Later, to cope with the problems of 'multiple vassalage', liege homage was introduced by which each vassal was supposed to have only one liege lord to whom he owed a single, primary loyalty and whose service took precedence over the others. In the mean time, during Bloch's 'first feudal age' before the late eleventh century, the competing claims of lords against each other and the conflicts between lords and vassals brought much disorder. That the values and norms of vassalage nevertheless retained a hold over people's minds, even when they were so often being betrayed and broken, is shown by the rules that emerged for ending the relation. Either side could end it legally if he had been betrayed by the other. By the twelfth century we know about a ritual for doing this.[16] By that time, however, as the 'second feudal age' developed, as abstract ideas of political obligation began to grow, and as something like states began to appear, the personal bond of vassalage was becoming less exclusively important. Hereditary rights in fiefs meanwhile undermined its personal and affective nature. The

---

[14] Ganshof, 'Charlemagne et le serment', 261, and 'Charlemagne et les institutions', 388–9.
[15] Boutruche, *Seigneurie et féodalité*, 177–8.                [16] Bloch, 'Les Formes'.

relation between lord and man was turning into a matter of property rights to be adjudicated, if necessary, in the increasingly formal courts of law that characterized the period. Nevertheless most kings and princes had significantly restricted authority over their vassals' vassals and little direct contact with them. Kings were still overlords or suzerains rather than sovereign rulers in the modern sense. Many of the traditional values of vassalage survived. The relation with their immediate lords was what counted with many vassals, so that a vassal was likely to side with his immediate lord against the king or an intermediate overlord if they came into conflict with each other. In the words of the thirteenth-century French jurist, John de Blanot, 'the man of my man is not my man'.[17]

## 2.2. *Some problems of the concept*

The first problem is terminological. References to *vassi* or *vassalli* are not nearly so common in the sources as one might suppose from reading modern works on medieval history.[18] They occur frequently in Carolingian documents and were exported by Frankish conquerors to Italy and Germany, while contemporary contacts and influences produced a few occurrences in England. From the tenth century on, however, while both Latin words continued to be used in Italy, they gradually went out of use in France and Germany, and did not return until they were brought back from Italy by lawyers trained in the academic law of fiefs. From the thirteenth century the occurrence of forms of 'vassal' in deeds, governmental documents, or legal texts in both countries seems to indicate the spread of the new academic law. In England, where legal education was different, the word remained rare throughout the middle ages. Meanwhile, to judge from literary texts, it passed into the vernacular in France without any necessary connotation of a specific relation to either lord or land. In the Song of Roland it generally seems to mean something like 'man of valour' and the same kind of sense looks likely in other texts.[19] Here the point that needs to be emphasized is that, when vassals are mentioned in modern works about the history of northern Europe between about 1000 and 1300, in

[17] Acher, 'Notes', 160. On John, see index: John de Blanot.

[18] References for most of the statements about the middle ages in this section will be given in later chapters. Those for particular words can be found through the entries for those words in the index.

[19] *Song of Roland*, ii. 256; Dufournet, *Cours*, 142–51, where the editor derives quite different uses from his study of the poem from those he takes on trust from secondary works about 'la réalité vassalique'. Cf. Bertrand de Bar-sur-Aube, *Girart de Vienne*, 318 (note to l. 1297), 404 (where the glossary suggests that *vasal* . . . 'proprement' meant vassal and only by extension 'homme noble en général'; cf. ibid.: '*vavasore* . . . proprement: homme pourvu d'un arrière fief; par extension: vassal en général').

translations of texts from that time, or in comments or indexes made by editors of texts, the sources nearly always use non-committal pronouns (*cum suis, ad suos,* etc.) or words like *fideles* or *homines. Fidelis* and *homo* may on some occasions have been used to mean much the same thing as historians mean by vassal, but both had other uses, and non-committal uses, that can also be found in contemporary sources. The idea that, when a king or noble called subordinates his men or his faithful men, their relation to him was that which historians call vassalage depends on acceptance of the premiss that vassalage was the most important, or only, political relation worth considering. The argument is circular. When Bishop Fulbert, in the letter mentioned earlier, talked of the obligations incurred under an oath of fidelity, he may have been thinking of them as incurred by someone we might now call a vassal, but he may have been thinking of other kinds of subordinate too. It does not seem right to say, as was said recently, that Fulbert used the words *fidelis* and *vassus* interchangeably and that a vassal was one who had sworn fidelity and held a fief. Fulbert does not use *vassus* in this letter or, I think, elsewhere, and he certainly makes it clear here that not all the *fideles* he was talking about had *casamenta* or *beneficia*.[20] We cannot be sure that we have got our ideas about vassalage right if we rewrite medieval texts in this way.

*Vavassor,* which is sometimes thought to mean the vassal of a vassal (subvassal, rear-vassal, *arrière-vassal*), was used in the intervening period both in France and England as well as Italy. Its derivation from *vassus vassorum* seems, however, to be late.[21] It does not seem to be established that its original meaning had anything to do with a position in a 'hierarchy of tenure'—a concept (as distinct from a phenomenon) that, as I shall argue, was itself a relatively late development. Vavassor may generally have denoted something more like a social status: a vavassor seems normally to have been part of noble, military society, though near the lower end of it. The status seems to have varied from place to place and time to time—not surprisingly, seeing the way that words acquire connotations from their context and use.[22] A word for any group will have different connotations of dignity or lowliness depending on the dignity or lowliness of the speaker and of the other groups with which the first is contrasted.

As for the word vassalage itself, forms like *vassaticum* and *vassallagium*

---

[20] I have not searched all his letters thoroughly, but he uses only *fideles* in nos. 9–10, 27, 42, 51, 83, 94, 100, and Behrends (who translates *fidelis* as 'vassal' in *Letters and Poems*) does not mention *vassus* or *vassallus* explicitly in his article 'Kingship and Feudalism'.

[21] The first suggestion I know of is Sainct Julien, *De l'Origine* (1581), 158, but this was found through Du Cange. There may well be earlier occurrences.

[22] Yver, 'Vavassor'; Coss, 'Literature and Social Terminology'; cf. Bertrand, *Girart de Vienne*, l. 1297.

occur occasionally, but in documentary sources they generally suggest something more like the holding or service of a *vassus* or *vassallus* than anything more general and abstract. In the Song of Roland *vasselage* seems to be the qualities appropriate to a vassal, like courage and loyalty.[23] Even in the more theoretical and normative writings of later medieval lawyers remarks about vassals and vassalage cannot be assumed to imply all the norms and values that have become embedded in post-medieval discussions of feudalism. If vassalage in anything like the sense given it by those who have written about feudo-vassalic relations since the sixteenth century had been as central to medieval life and had formed as distinct and well recognized a package as they suggest, might it not have been discussed more often and more explicitly?[24]

There are more serious problems than those of terminology. The concept of vassalage as outlined above suggests ideas about social structure and social evolution that must have looked better in the seventeenth, eighteenth, and even nineteenth centuries than they do in the light of late twentieth-century social sciences. The barbarians who invaded the Roman empire came from societies that were in some ways not unlike what are sometimes called 'tribal' societies in other parts of the world. To eighteenth- and nineteenth-century anthropologists these looked as strange and primitive as the people Tacitus called Germans did to him, but modern anthropologists see them rather differently. Students of late antique and early medieval barbarian history have revised some of the ideas about early 'Germanic' society that appeared at much the same time as ideas of feudalism developed.[25] As a result the supposed evolution of one into the other needs revision. The political organization of the barbarians immediately outside the empire must have been disturbed by Roman wars and machinations. Many of the bands who subsequently invaded may have been as culturally confused and politically incoherent as one would expect bands of uprooted guerrillas and their servants and camp-followers to be. Neither of these probabilities entitles us to suppose that the Germanic-speaking peoples were unaccustomed to life in settled agricultural societies with coherent social and political structures. Little as we know of the polities that the invaders came from or that survived outside the empire before they were converted to Christianity, it is questionable whether the only kinds of authority in barbarian society were those of sacral kings and the leaders of war-bands. It is also unlikely that barbarian societies were organized as exclusively, or almost exclusively, by kinship as is suggested by the

---

[23] *Song of Roland*, i. 208, 422–3; Dufournet, *Cours*, 151–5.
[24] Le Goff, 'Rituel', 359, notes the lack of systematic discussions of 'the rites of vassalage'.
[25] e.g. Wenskus, 'Probleme'; Murray, *Germanic Kinship Structure*.

proposition that vassalage arose because of the decay of kinship. Kinship and lordship are seldom mutually exclusive alternatives.[26] Finally, and perhaps most importantly, there is no reason to suppose that barbarians were incapable of distinguishing the good of individuals from the good of the community or were unaccustomed to any but the most direct interpersonal relations.

The distinction that is often drawn in discussions of early medieval society between public and private relations and obligations is at best confused—as is much talk of 'public' and 'private' within our own society—and at worst culture-bound and inappropriate.[27] It derives partly from a classification adopted within Roman law, which does not apply very well anywhere else, and partly from a belief that ideas of *res publica* were too intellectual and advanced for barbarians and developed only gradually during the middle ages. It seems to be thought, however, that, although barbarian societies outside the empire had largely interpersonal relations, they also had ideas of tribal welfare. The collapse of Roman bureaucracy and communications changed relations between rulers and subjects within Roman territory, while that of the Carolingian empire led to greater disorder in some, though not all, of its territories. But there is no evidence that the sense of public spirit disappeared at either stage. For what analogies are worth, the findings of social anthropologists suggest that in small, face-to-face societies such a sense may, by our standards, be suffocating. The difference between a king's private interest and his duty to the kingdom was not much discussed in academic terms before the twelfth century, because there was not much academic discussion, but the phrase *res publica* was in fact occasionally used well before the academic explosion of the twelfth century.[28] Irrespective of discussion and words, the public welfare and its difference from the ruler's welfare was probably recognized as well as it was, apparently, in traditional African societies—and perhaps better than in some modern ones.[29]

In examining a society without an extensive bureaucracy and without our habitual (though confused) distinctions between public and private, it is necessary to look carefully at what appear to be voluntary, affective relations. The characterization of early vassalage as a 'personal' relation raises a number of problems. Sometimes it derives from the belief that vassalage had originated in a 'familial' and aristocratic, rather than a political,

[26] La Fontaine, 'Land and the Political Community', 95–6, citing earlier work.
[27] Brunner, *Land und Herrschaft*, 102–25, 202–5. The problem of distinguishing governmental from property relations is discussed in chapter 3.
[28] Nelson, 'Kingship and Empire'; Reynolds, *Kingdoms and Communities*, 293, 325.
[29] Fortes, 'Ritual and Office', 58–60; Nelson, 'Legislation and Consensus', esp. n. 80; Reynolds, *Kingdoms and Communities*, 324–5.

system.[30] It is true that, in the earliest sources we have, *vassi* seem to be servants or dependants of fairly low status, but those we know most about were royal servants whose job was essentially to do with government: it was thus surely about politics, while everyone would presumably agree that the people whom historians call vassals and who they think held fiefs, sometimes with rights of jurisdiction, in the ninth century and later were part of some kind of political system. There is no reason to see their relations with their kings or lords as marked by having originated from an earlier relation that was more definably 'private' or 'personal'.[31] More important is the tendency to contrast 'personal' with 'territorial' relations. This is also ambiguous, since 'territorial' is a word to which medieval historians seem to attach a variety of connotations. The cases (as in 'territorial prince', 'territorial principality') in which it is used for units of government that are defined chiefly by not being kingdoms are not directly relevant here, though they are historiographically interesting. More important is the use that contrasts the originally purely 'personal' relation of lord and vassal with the 'territorial' relation that was created by the grant of fiefs. Still more important, because of the wide range of its implications, is the contrast between the early medieval kingdom or lordship that was held together by purely interpersonal bonds (what German historians call the *Personenverbandsstaat*) and the later 'territorial state', in which the government had authority over everyone within a fixed territory (*institutioneller Flächenstaat*).[32] The contrast here seems unsuitable for settled agricultural societies in which authority over people must imply authority over land. The definition of boundaries, the degree of 'institutional' or bureaucratic development, and the completeness of authority are matters of degree which do not fit well into a contrast between personal and territorial. A good many medieval historians do not merely distinguish the 'feudal state', with its personal bonds, from the modern administrative state. They prefer not to call medieval polities states at all. Since few who reject the word attempt any definition of the state that does not conflate it with modern state, nation state, or sovereign state, it is hard to know whether they do so because medieval kingdoms and lesser lordships lacked fixed boundaries, effective central authority, sovereignty (however defined), or modern technologies of communication. Most discussions, moreover, tend to confuse words (e.g. the use of *status* and its derivatives), concepts (the supposed modern concept of the state), and phenomena. A definition of the state as

[30] Le Goff, 'Rituel', 394.    [31] Lewis, *Social Anthropology in Perspective*, 359.
[32] Mayer, 'Ausbildung'; Reuter, *Germany*, 208; Kroeschell, *Deutsche Rechtsgeschichte*, i. 278, 298, gives a succinct summary, and cf. ibid. ii. 157–9 on the use of *Herrschaft* as an alternative to 'state'.

a phenomenon, however conceptualized by those within it, that will serve for comparative use seems desirable. I offer the following, which is based on Max Weber, with some modification: a state is an organization of human society within a fixed territory that more or less successfully claims the control (not the monopoly) of the legitimate use of physical force within that territory.[33] If one were to deny statehood on this definition to medieval kingdoms or lesser lordships in general, or even to those of the early middle ages, on grounds of the fluidity of their boundaries, the ineffectiveness of control within them, the autonomy, or partial autonomy, of lesser authorities within them, or their lack of sovereignty (however defined), one would have to deny it to a good many modern states as well.[34]

When medieval polities or societies are seen in terms of non-Marxist feudalism, a further implication of emphasis on the 'personal' nature of the bonds that held them together seems often to be that the relation of lord and vassal is thought of as close, affective, and interpersonal. It is surely misleading to define any widespread relation in terms of the sentiments it is supposed to embody. One would not define marriage by the mutual affection that husbands and wives are supposed to feel or by the promises they make in ceremonies that are enshrined in tradition. When a king or lord had many vassals his relations with each of them cannot have been all that close. If vassalage was widespread it would be diluted. It could not therefore be the strongest bond in a society. When it lasted through generations it must have become more formal. In such circumstances—indeed in most circumstances—it is likely to have been less affective and less mutual than modern ideas of feudo-vassalic relations suggest or even than the medieval texts themselves imply. It seems to be quite common for humans to represent obligatory and subordinate relations as more affective and interpersonal than they may appear to an analytical observer. Rulers find it useful to call on the devotion of subjects they have never met and probably care little about; literature is full of human-interest stories about encounters between kings and peasants; and medieval academics rationalized and moralized the obligations of tenants to landlords in terms of the military ideals they had been brought up to admire. All this may be an example of a dominant ideology at its conspiratorial work, but it is not clear that the subordinates always rejected it. People often like to represent their relations with distant superiors as personal and affective, and to think that the person at the top cares about them. That people in the middle ages were brought up to obedience and loyalty as well as other military virtues

---

[33] Weber, *From Max Weber*, 78 ('Politics as a Vocation'), Reynolds, *Kingdoms and Communities*, 323–4.

[34] For sovereignty in relation to layers of authority, see next section and chapter 3.3.

is highly relevant to the understanding of their society, but it does not mean that the society really depended only on a mass of individual, dyadic, interpersonal, and affective relations. The element of prescription in the sources needs analysis, not merely because prescription is not description and rules are always broken, but because the form and emphasis of the prescriptions may not reveal the full range or nature of the norms that mattered.

The idea that vassalage was essentially defined by its rituals of initiation also needs to be looked at rather more carefully now than seemed necessary when ideas of feudalism first developed. A society without printing or broadcasting needs to use its rituals to confirm and inculcate its values more urgently than does a modern society, but some of the traditional belief that ritual is the mark of 'primitiveness' derives from a primitive and culture-bound knowledge of other societies. We notice rituals more when they are strange to us.[35] Some of the apparently rigid ritualism of early medieval society turns out to be an illusion of crude evolutionary thought: it is hard now to see how anyone who had been in a modern lawcourt and read some of the reports of early medieval disputes could think that their procedures were more ritualized or rigid than ours.[36] It is, nevertheless, highly probable that most appointments to office, agreements to perform duties, or transfers of property in the middle ages required some kind of ritual, just as they do in literate societies. The problem is to know which occasions needed rituals, what the rituals were, and how far they were different from rituals used for other purposes. From the late seventh or early eighth century we have a formula for the initiation of an *antrustio*— *antrustiones* being generally taken as prototype vassals—but none for that of a *vassus*. From the Carolingian age there are many allusions to commendations and oaths and a few descriptions of famous cases of rites of submission which may or may not be typical of the rituals of routine vassalage. Since these examples included features such as kneeling and joining hands (though not kissing) that recur in the better-recorded rites of the twelfth century and later, and are sometimes alluded to in the intervening period, it may be right to see them as part of a continuous and coherent tradition.[37] All the same, the honesty of scholarship requires us to note the variations that occurred later (including, for instance, about kissing), and to admit that we have little if any idea what, if any, ceremony was under-

[35] Moore and Myerhoff, *Secular Ritual*, 3–24; Goody, 'Against "Ritual"'; Goffman, *Interaction Ritual*.
[36] Davies and Fouracre, *Settlement of Disputes, passim*; Reynolds, *Kingdoms and Communities*, 23–34.
[37] On kissing: Chénon, 'Le Rôle juridique'; Major, '"Bastard Feudalism" and the Kiss'.

gone either by the ordinary Carolingian *vassus* or by those whom historians call vassals in the post-Carolingian period.

Bare references to 'homage' or 'commendation' cannot be used to fill in the gaps in the evidence. Neither word always referred to a rite or ceremony: both could indicate the initiation of a range of different relations, or the relation itself, without any indication of a rite. Even when someone is said to have commended himself or been commended 'into the hands of' another, we cannot be sure that this implied the ceremony that Bloch described. Human beings use their hands a lot and use them in different ways. Sometimes, having language as well as hands, they refer to them in metaphors, as we know that they did in the middle ages.[38] Nor, even when we have evidence that suggests a ceremony, can we assume that it was peculiar to those whom we would consider vassals. People who look like peasants seem to have undergone rather similar rites on occasion. Given that anything to do with more important people is more likely to have got into surviving records, the comparative rarity of references to commendation or homage in connection with peasants is not evidence that people who used the words (or rather their vernacular equivalents) thought of their feudo-vassalic senses as more obvious or primary. In so far as ceremonies that involved touching or taking hands and swearing oaths seem to have been common in medieval society, and to have been practised through many social and political changes, it seems likely that they meant different things to different people at different times.[39] The rites of subordination or submission that people performed when they entered the service of a king or other lord, or when they received office or land from him, need to be studied, but they cannot be studied if they are lumped together as a single, uniform ceremony of commendation or homage that was peculiar to that relation and that we have already defined because we assume we have understood it.

The element of voluntary and individual contract in vassalage also needs more critical examination and analysis, especially since we have evidence of any kind of agreement, contract, or rite of initiation in only a minute fraction of cases before the twelfth century. Assuming a significantly common element in these and seeing it as distinctive of feudo-vassalic relations in general, while ignoring other contractual or possibly contractual relations of the time, looks peculiarly unwise when one looks at other stratified societies. Barrington Moore suggests that some kind of contract between rulers and subjects, dominant and subordinate groups, is implied or

---

[38] See Du Cange, *Glossarium*, v (1), 248–9; Du Cange's examples under *investitura*, listed by Le Goff ('Rituel', 415–19), include cases where land is being transferred with full rights, not in fief.
[39] Maurice Bloch, *Ritual, History and Power*, 79.

assumed to exist within all stratified societies, and that 'the first, perhaps most essential obligation of the ruler is protection, especially protection from foreign enemies'.[40] The idea of contract, however vaguely or explicitly articulated in myths, ceremonies, traditions, or formal constitutions, serves both sides. It puts pressure on rulers to behave, while it suits governments to depict their subjects, especially their more dangerous and powerful subjects, as serving willingly, and to make it a matter of honour, dignity, and freedom for them to do so. In many societies without powerful bureaucracies it is common to stress the element of mutual obligation in relations which in reality leave little room for manœuvre either on one side or on both.[41]

If it is true that medieval society was bound together by a mass of individual and explicit contracts between superiors and inferiors, rather than by the more common implied and collective contracts, then that would certainly make it distinctive, but to conclude that it was we would need to establish the prevalence of individual contracts and the absence of collective bonds. That has not yet been done. The suggestion, for instance, that all, or even most, of those who owed *commendisia*, *commenda*, *commanda*, et cetera in twelfth- and thirteenth-century France, or their ancestors, had, 'at least in principle', made some sort of individual submission or request for protection, is based on a priori ideas about the individual contractual basis of feudal ties in general and 'commendation' in particular. If people under *commendise* sometimes complained that their lord was not protecting them in return for the dues that he received from them, that need not imply that their relation was modelled on the feudo-vassalic contract.[42] It may show nothing more than a sense of the duties of government that is so common in traditional societies. One could, of course, argue that, while free peasants could have been put under *commendisia* without their consent, noble vassals would have expected to give it. But that only takes one back to the problem of drawing a line between those whom one considers to have been nobles and vassals and those that one does not: some of the people who are recorded as doing homage and taking oaths of fidelity before about 1200 look very unlike noble vassals.

It may be that most people whom we choose to call vassals before the

[40] Moore, *Injustice*, 20, and 15–25, 438, 503–11; cf. e.g. Cohen and Middleton, *Comparative Political Systems*, p. xiv and various of the essays, e.g. that of Beattie at pp. 361, 364–5; Mason, *Patterns of Dominance*, 16–19; Lewis, *Social Anthropology in Perspective*, 313–15.

[41] Mauss, *The Gift*, 3, 54–9; Gluckman, *Law, Politics and Ritual*, 48.

[42] Duparc, 'La Commendise'. The variations of meaning between *commendare* and *commandare* apparently started early (Du Cange, *Glossarium*, ii. 468, 471–2, 476; *OED*, iii. 539; Niermeyer, *Lexicon*, 212–17). Some of those who used both forms may from quite early have been thinking of *commendisia* in more coercive and less voluntary terms than modern ideas of feudal commendation imply.

thirteenth century had gone through a rite like what we call homage, made
some sort of individual profession of faith to someone, or were otherwise
bound by contract more than were the freer kinds of peasants, but the evidence for it is much weaker than traditional ideas about fiefs and vassals
suggest. The degree of freedom in any individual contract in a stratified
society is presumably affected by the social distance between the parties: in
the middle ages nobles and free men must generally have made terms with
their lords more freely than did peasants, but the terms must have varied
a lot. Even great men did not always have much choice about doing homage
to the king if they wanted to keep their position and property in his kingdom. Defending themselves against accusations of treason by saying they
had never done homage or sworn fidelity did not generally get them very
far. We not only have little evidence of the rites and contracts made
between kings or lords and the mass of their subordinates before the
twelfth or thirteenth centuries: we have no real evidence that people at the
time thought of society as bound together, or supposed to be bound
together, primarily by individual contracts of the kind presupposed by
modern ideas of medieval feudalism.

Fidelity, the supposed counterpart and consequence of the vassalic
bond, is as hard to make specific to feudo-vassalic relations as is the idea of
individual contracts. All stratified societies demand some kind of loyalty
and obedience from subordinates just as they demand or hope that rulers
will obey the rules and keep faith with their subjects. Although medieval
lawyers liked to derive the word *feudum* from *fidelitas*, the idea of fidelity
does not look very specific to feudo-vassalic relations any more than calling it *Treue* makes it look specific to Germanic tribes.[43] It was not only vassals who were supposed to be loyal and obedient—that is, to be *fideles*.
Different kinds of loyalty, service, and obedience were, of course,
demanded from different kinds of people. The investigation of these, comparing them with each other, and with the obligations imposed on people
in other societies, is not promoted by using words like fidelity, *Treue*, *fides*,
or *fidelitas*, as if they had obvious and established connotations or were
culture-specific.[44] Labels do not encourage analysis.

The biggest problem of all about the concept of vassalage, as about its
ceremonies, is that it is such a composite construct. It seems to have been
devised first from the study of the *Libri Feudorum* and the later academic
commentaries on it, in which vassals are simply fiefholders. Study of
Carolingian records, especially the capitularies or records of legislation,

---

[43] Kaminsky and Melton in Brunner, *Land and Lordship*, pp. xxviii, xxxiv, and nn. 58, 75.
[44] For early uses of *fides*, *fidelitas*, and *triuwa*: Green, *Carolingian Lord*, 67–9, 82, 117–26; cf.
Kroeschell, 'Die Treue'.

then confirmed the belief that the *Libri* reflected older arrangements, and that vassals, like fiefs, had originated in the early middle ages. A good deal of the idea of the values and norms of vassalage that has since been worked out comes in fact from the records of legislation recorded in Carolingian capitularies. Ganshof, for instance, like earlier scholars, often seems to treat the capitularies as embodying norms that were generally accepted at the time.[45] But the legislation in the capitularies often dealt with particular political circumstances and the references to *vassi* there were often, though not always, to royal *vassi*. There is sometimes no reason to assume that similar rules applied to the *vassi* of other lords or that what was forbidden in particular royal laws was generally considered wrong. It cannot be right to construct a general picture of something we call vassalage by bringing together all the rules of Carolingian legislation about *vassi* with the rules stated or implied by later academic lawyers, for whom vassals were simply the holders of a particular sort of property, and with observations on the behaviour of people in the intervening period whom historians choose to call vassals. How the change of political and social conditions in tenth- and eleventh-century France affected norms and values it is very hard to say, but imposing composite ideas of vassalage on the period—let alone on the same period in other countries where conditions were different—is not the way to find out. One cannot put together remarks about allegedly arbitrary behaviour of lords in the early eleventh century with the apparently greater rights enjoyed by people we call vassals a hundred years later so as to deduce either that rules were becoming stricter or that generally accepted ideas were changing. Nor is it right either to castigate or to excuse early eleventh-century counts whom the historian considers to have been vassals of the king for not fulfilling the obligations that historians have since attached to vassalage.[46]

It would be foolish to deny that components of the modern construct of vassalage and the values attached to it existed in the early middle ages: mutual loyalties between lords and their followers were clearly important, and in a good many cases the property of the subordinates was subject to controls or obligations to the lord. But we need to look more closely at the relations between superiors and inferiors in the context of other relations and values, both interpersonal and collective. Above all, I suggest, we need to get away from the word vassal, especially where it is not used in the sources. Our job is surely to try to distinguish and analyse the relations of the time, rather than to put crude labels on to them, or duck the issue by

---

[45] e.g. Ganshof, 'Les Liens', 159, 163–6; 'L'Origine', 56–9; Brunner, *Deutsche Rechtsgeschichte*, ii. 349–68; Stutz, *Herrenfall*, 65–9.

[46] Poly and Bournazel, *Mutation*, 147–54; Guillot, *Comte d'Anjou*, 14–18.

adding vague glosses to the label like 'men who were bound by some fairly honourable tie of subordination'.[47] The concept of vassalage, I suggest, conceals at least half a dozen different types of relation that need to be distinguished. They are those of ruler and subject, patron and client, landlord and tenant, employer and employed, general (or lesser commander) and soldier, and something like a local boss or bully and his victim. Distinctions between those who serve for wages, or for their keep, or just in hope of favours to come, also need to be made among those who might be considered either clients or employees.[48] There may well be other distinctions that I have not thought of, while any of these could, of course, be combined together, but they were not invariably combined. The idea of the 'union of vassal and fief' as introducing the age of 'classic feudalism' is at best little more than a neat but rather meaningless phrase. Mitteis was at pains to point out that even in the central middle ages there were vassals without fiefs and fiefs for which no personal services were owed.[49] To judge from the carefree way that historians use the word vassal, his reservations have been largely ignored.[50] 'Vassals' is used as a matter of course to refer to those they think held fiefs, but not only to them: it often seems to cover whole armies or any free subjects or subordinates of a lord.[51] If it were always used as generally as that, with no implication that the subordinates were bound by feudo-vassalic ties, the reader could adjust to it, but that is by no means the case. The idea of the 'union of vassal and fief' was useful because, providing it was not looked at closely and all distinctions between words, concepts, and phenomena were ignored, it served to bridge the gap between Charlemagne's grants of benefices and the stage when the academic lawbooks called fiefholders vassals. Historians could go on writing about medieval lords and vassals as they had since the seventeenth century without having to rethink what they meant or might be thought to imply.

My list of the possible contents of the relations subsumed under the word vassalage is intended for consideration, testing, and improvement.

[47] Reynolds, *Kingdoms and Communities*, 223, where the gloss is made even more inappropriate and meaningless by being attached to vavassors as well as vassals.

[48] Stephen Church suggested this to me in talking of his work on King John's knights in England.

[49] Mitteis, *Lehnrecht*, 129–34, 518–31.

[50] Ganshof, 'Note sur les origines', 174, mentions it but does not explore the implications. Bloch, *Feudal Society*, 169, and Faussner, 'Verfügungsgewalt', 404 n., seem exceptional. The 'landless vassals' in Bloch's example are, presumably, the knights who hold no fiefs from their liege lords, which leaves the exact character of their relation unclear: *Rec. Philippe Auguste*, no. 229.

[51] For an example, used in passing and with no detriment to the subject of the book: Southern, *Saint Anselm*, 8: Anselm's letter (*Epistolae*, col. 102) refers to his *parentes* as Humbert's *homines* and *consanguines*. The 'feudal imagery' referred to later (*Saint Anselm*, 221–7) and more significantly also seems to refer to more general or other relations of subordination (see esp. Anselm, *Opera*, ii. 118).

The words I have chosen are not intended to be precise or technical and there would be no point in elaborating precise definitions of them or looking for synonyms in the sources. The point is to suggest that, instead of starting from the premiss that we have a relation called vassalage and that we know what it meant, it might be more profitable to examine the evidence and see if we can identify what kinds of relation we have in any given case. Having distinguished the kind of relation that is at issue, or the combination of relations, we might then try to assess the element of coercion or control that entered into it. How great and how exclusive was the jurisdiction of the superior over the inferior and how far did it include coercive authority? Was it, in other words, a matter of political control and domination? We might also analyse relations according to the status of each party, the social distance between them, and the amount and type of personal contact that was involved both between the superior and his subordinates and between the subordinates themselves. Again, there may well be other points to investigate, but until we have done at least something along these lines I suggest that the words vassals and vassalage imply conceptual black holes that are liable to swallow up any historical scholarship that ventures into them.

## 2.3. A substitute for the concept of vassalage: some medieval norms and values

The values that historians traditionally associate with vassalage need, I suggest, to be seen in a wider context of other relations and other norms. Although I do not believe that all medieval people in all countries, periods, and parts of society shared the same attitudes, this section sets out what I consider to be broad cultural values that I think were probably quite widely shared, at least among those free men and nobles who are my concern here.[52] While, however, I believe that they shared a good many values and norms, I do not believe that their norms formed a simple, coherent, and consistent whole, any more than do the norms of other comparably complex societies. Norms always conflict: if they did not there would be less need for them and for the resolution of conflicts between individuals and groups. One major source of conflict in medieval society, apart from what people then called sin, was that medieval culture embodied a belief in hierarchy, obedience, and loyalty on the one hand and a belief in custom,

[52] Scott, *Domination*, offers useful cautions about the people at the bottom, though his suggestion about the discouragement of assemblies etc. (p. 63) does not suit medieval society while I am not sure I would know, in the medieval context, where to draw a line under the ruling class (p. 68).

immanent justice, mutuality of obligations, and collective judgement on the other.

Inequality in this world seems to have been the accepted premiss of almost all social and political thought in the middle ages. Medieval society was highly unequal. People owed obedience and loyalty to their immediate superiors or lords, and there does not seem to be any reason, beyond what derives from largely retrospective conjecture about Germanic barbarians, for supposing that that was the only or chief obedience and loyalty that they owed. Except in moments of acute crisis and breakdown, which may have been less common than old stereotypes of 'feudal anarchy' imply, there was always some kind of hierarchy of authority, however ramshackle, above that level. Typically its top was a king. Though the earliest barbarian kingdoms had too many kings to be called monarchies, kingdoms with single kings soon emerged. Where kingdoms went on being divided for a while, joint kings nevertheless normally divided their spheres of authority in such a way that each king stood at the top of some sort of political hierarchy or power structure. Throughout the middle ages it was a king, not some lesser kind of lord, who was the archetype of a ruler. Emperors were a cut above kings, and dukes or counts might in practice be more or less independent of them, but kingdoms were seen as the typical—indeed the highest natural—units of government and every kingdom was seen to need a king.[53] The normal structure was neatly expressed by that supposed theorist of feudo-vassalic values, Fulbert of Chartres. As he remarked, in what looks like an uncontroversial premiss for an argument, no kingdom could exist without three things: a land, a people, and a king.[54] All kingdoms, whether the king was described as king of a people or king of a land, involved both people and land. In agricultural societies power over people meant power, however indirect or mediated, over their land.

The assumption that kings were envisaged by contemporaries merely, or primarily, as overlords, seems to be just that: an assumption based on general ideas about feudalism.[55] It would be hard to prove from the evidence about most kingdoms most of the time. In the early middle ages kings had a different relation with their subjects from that which nobles had with their followers.[56] Legislation was always a matter for kings, and they legislated about the relations between nobles and their followers. Some who

---

[53] Nelson, 'Kingship and Empire'; Reynolds, 'Medieval *Origines Gentium*' and *Kingdoms and Communities*, 255–302, 319–23, 330–1.

[54] Fulbert, *Tractatus contra Judaeos*, 307. Cf. La Fontaine, 'Land and the Political Community', 95–6.

[55] Historians seem quite often to use 'overlord' for an immediate lord. This is confusing and, on the feudo-vassalic principles they seem to be following, tautological.

[56] See the analysis of oaths by Odegaard, 'Carolingian Oaths'.

did not issue formal law-codes nevertheless occasionally made quasi-legislative pronouncements in their judgements on particular cases with an authority that surely belonged to them as kings. For what words are worth, expressions like *superior dominus* seem to have been less common in medieval sources than in the later historical literature. Eike von Repgow, who wrote about Saxon law in the early thirteenth century, refers to the *superior dominus* or *overe herre* when he needs to refer to the lord with jurisdiction over the fiefholder's lord, while *superior dominus*, with *sovereyn seignour* as the French equivalent, was used in 1291 during the Scottish succession dispute to denote the relation between two kings.[57] 'Suzerain' seems to be late and may have come into use as a term of art in the late medieval or post-medieval law of fiefs.[58] I do not have the impression that any of these words was generally used before then to express a king's relations with his own subjects: he was simply king. Kings might refer to those they ruled as their men, their *fideles*, or their subjects (*subditi*). Many whom they needed to address were those whom historians call royal vassals or tenants in chief, but not all. The words clearly had wider scope, and if they applied to some who were the men, *fideles*, or subjects of lords below the king, that did not automatically mean that they were not the king's men too. The fact that the words *dominus* and *senior* were used both of kings and lesser lords need not mean that the king's authority or *dominium* was seen as similar to theirs. God was a *dominus*, but that did not make his *dominium* over the world comparable either to the political authority or to the mere property rights enjoyed by a human lord. *Senior*, for what such distinctions are worth, may emphasize status, while *dominus* has more connotations of power, but that may be fanciful. The differing terminologies that developed in different vernaculars might reflect political or social differences but it would probably be hard to prove.[59] The distinction between the king as king and as 'feudal lord', confidently as it is drawn in modern works, is hard to find in the sources before the age of academic and professional law, and is not always very obvious then.[60]

Balancing hierarchy on the other side of the equation of conflicting norms was justice. Both kings and other lords had obligations to those who were subject to them. Their obligations were not created by oaths or cere-

---

[57] Eike von Repgow, *Auctor vetus*, e.g. 75, 78 (I. 57, 71) and cf. *supremus dominus*, ibid. 112 (II. 69); id. *Sachsenspiegel Lehnrecht*, e.g. 45, 58 (25. 1, 38. 1) and *overste herre*, ibid. 34 (14. 3, 71. 6); *Edward I and the Throne of Scotland*, i. 121.

[58] It is not in Du Cange, Niermeyer, or Godefroy. The first example in Littré, *Dictionnaire*, vii. 644, is from Montesquieu. The examples in *OED*, xvii. 332 are modern, though see ibid. *sub* suzerainty for a fifteenth-century case.

[59] Ganshof presumably based his suggestion (*Feudalism*, 69–70) that *senior* was the general term and *dominus* 'rather rare' on the French vernacular usage.

[60] Niermeyer, *Lexicon*, 957, seems to read it into some of the sources listed under *senior*, no. 9.

monies, whether ecclesiastical or secular, though they were reinforced by them. Every ruler, everyone in a position of authority from the emperor or king down to the head of a household, was supposed to rule justly and according to custom. Every unit of government was assumed to be a community with its own customs and every ruler was supposed to consult with the senior members of the community about what was customary, right, and just. Those senior members who had the primary right and duty to declare the community's custom and advise its ruler were men who deserved respect for their high social status and wealth, and generally also for their age and the length—or supposed length—of time that their families had been prominent in the community. In a kingdom they would be its greatest nobles and landowners, together of course with bishops and abbots, but in a village they might well be no more than the more prosperous peasants: either way they should be consulted. Although for both normative and pragmatic reasons kings needed to pay more attention to great nobles than lords of villages did to peasants, the difference was one of degree. In neither case, moreover, was consultation of the great supposed to exclude care for the welfare of the less. It was the duty of the great men of a community to speak on behalf of the less. On important matters the wider the consultation was, the better—though there was, of course, no need to consult women, children, or servants. The idea of the 'judgement of peers', as embodying the collective judgement of one's fellow subjects rather than the unilateral judgement of one's ruler, did not originate from the relations of lords with their warriors but from the relations of all lords with all subjects. At this stage it did not necessarily mean that the king or lord did not join in the judgement: hierarchy and authority needed to be balanced by consultation, not negated.[61] Any ruler would meanwhile have closer links with individual subjects which would in practice impose greater obligations on both sides. These were often reinforced by individual agreements and oaths, but any ruler's primary obligation was supposed to be to the whole community he ruled. As for subjects, their obligation was to the powers that be, which were ordained by God.

Ideas of justice and custom made the obligations of rulers and subjects mutual, but ideas of hierarchy and obedience meant that the reciprocity was not equal. According to the thirteenth-century *Schwabenspiegel*: 'We should serve our lords for they protect us; if they do not protect us, justice does not oblige us to serve them,'[62] but both in preaching and in practice the emphasis on the duties of obedience and the sin of rebellion was strong. When the subjects of Merovingian, Carolingian, and many later kings had

[61] Cf. Weitzel, *Dinggenossenschaft*, 914–41.
[62] Quoted Brunner, *Land and Lordship*, 200.

to take oaths of fidelity to them they might hope that the king would protect them but the oaths did not normally go into that. A subject's infidelity
was liable to fierce punishment while, as Fulbert of Chartres saw it, a lord's
would incur censure.[63] It would have been a brave *vassus* (or one with
friends in a hostile kingdom near by) who would have tried to justify leaving the service of his king by accusing him of any of the offences that were
listed early in the eighth century as justifications for leaving a lord.[64] If a
ruler was unjust it was the job of the senior members of the community to
remonstrate with him. At what stage lawful remonstrance turned into lawful or unlawful rebellion posed problems that could never be resolved
within the traditional system of values. One thing was clear: the lower
down the hierarchy you were the less it was your business to resist or even
remonstrate. Submission did not save you from being caught up in a
conflict of loyalties and duties if those above you quarrelled. There is nothing very unusual about that: conflicts of loyalty and authority occur in most
societies.[65] When they happen people at the bottom are liable to suffer
whatever they do and whichever side wins. People at the middling level,
like those whom historians traditionally call vassals, subvassals, or rear-
vassals, have more opportunity to choose, but that gives them more problems, if perhaps less suffering. As and when medieval governments became
more systematic and effective, at whatever level that happened, choices
tended to be pre-empted in all but exceptional circumstances. In England,
for instance, the maxim that 'the man of my man is not my man' would
have been nonsensical if put in the mouth of the king, while the German
Eike von Repgow would have rejected it.[66] There can have been few places
or times in which the maxim was obviously true at every level. It was the
product of debate about real dilemmas, not a statement of an obvious truth.

Social status was clearly an important determinant of everyone's life
chances, including, naturally, the chances of the kind of people whom historians call vassals. Vassalage is generally seen as a relation between people
of noble, or at the very least free, status. Nobility and freedom, however,
were much less clearly and consistently defined during the middle ages
than they became later. We cannot understand the workings of the
undoubted inequalities of the period if we interpret them like those of
the Ancien Régime—let alone like those of textbook horror stories of the
Ancien Régime. I suggest that we can best approach medieval society by
seeing it as broadly divided into three categories—categories which, it

---

[63] Fulbert, *Letters and Poems*, no. 51.
[64] *Capit.* nos. 77 c. 16, 104 c. 8 (on its source cf. Ganshof, 'L'Origine', n. 52).
[65] Lewis, *Social Anthropology*, 313–19, 359.
[66] Eike von Repgow, *Sachsenspiegel Lehnrecht*, 34 (14. 3).

must be emphasized, are not intended to approximate to the 'three orders' of some medieval classifications to which historians have recently paid a good deal of attention. The threefold classification proposed here is an entirely artificial construct for the purposes of my argument, though my reason for proposing it is that I think it bears some relation to the medieval evidence as I see it. The first or top category contained those whom historians generally call nobles—or, in England, nobles and gentry. They—or the laymen among them—were the kind of people who wore swords, rode horses, cherished a military ethos, and did not push ploughs but lived off those who did. The higher clergy and monks belong in the same category because they too lived off the plough-pushers without (officially) wearing swords or thinking of themselves as soldiers, except of God. The bottom category consisted of the plough-pushers, or rather, more broadly, of those who worked with their hands and bodies, owed rents and services to the top group, and could generally be described as more or less unfree peasants. In between came another category that probably included a sizeable proportion of the population. By and large these people did not actually push ploughs themselves, but they were more closely concerned with getting their own livings than the first group and supervised their own plough-pushers more directly. Many of them owed rents and services of various kinds to people in the first category, but their rents and services were lighter and less demeaning than those of people in the bottom one. While some of them rode horses and all probably carried arms, they were not trained and brought up to think of fighting as their job, their horses were less good than those of the top category, and their arms were less effective and less valuable. Most people in this category would never have been called nobles, but many of them would at one time or another have been called free. Whatever they were called in surviving sources, many of them were free enough to make agreements, however unequal the bargain, about the services they would owe for their land, and then to take their complaints and disputes to courts not presided over by their lords. Some of them might be ranked by historians as peasants, but we have to remember that that word represents a modern construct almost as much as my classification does. The sources sometimes use the word *rusticus* or something similar, but in many cases it is their modern reader who decides who was a peasant.

The problem is not only that each of these categories, and especially the top and middle, was very wide and contained people who would not have considered themselves remotely equal in social or political terms, but that the boundaries between them are so vague. Medieval society in most areas and at most times looks like one of infinite gradations or layers rather than one of wide social gulfs. A simile that I once used of English urban society may be useful here, since it seems to apply almost as well to medieval society at large: the layers of society were more like those of a trifle than a cake: its layers were blurred, and the sherry of accepted values soaked through. Taking the whole of society, however, as distinct from that within little English towns, one has to see it as a very rich and deep trifle with a lot of layers. Similes and metaphors are dangerous because they are not falsifiable. This one is simply meant to illustrate and emphasize the point that the boundaries between nobles and peasants, or between free and unfree, were less clear than most discussions of fiefs and vassals imply. In the earlier middle ages legal and political conditions made it impossible for any definitions of nobility or freedom that anyone might make to be consistently maintained in individual lordships or kingdoms, let alone in 'feudal society' as a whole. Nobility was a matter of wealth, prestige, and life-style—and, of course, as we meet it in the sources, it lay in the eye of the beholder. The petty local scribe who listed witnesses to a charter might describe someone as noble who would be nothing of the kind to a royal clerk. In the absence of full and reliable records 'nobility of birth' or 'nobility of blood' might be equally subjective.

The uncertainties are illustrated by the story of Stabilis, who was a man 'of servile condition' according to the monk of Fleury who wrote it in the eleventh century, perhaps seventy years or so after it is supposed to have happened. Stabilis left his home close by the abbey and settled near Troyes, where he made his fortune. He did well enough to keep horses, hawks, hounds, and servants, to marry a noble wife, and to give up paying the dues (*census servitutis*) that the monks of Fleury thought he owed them. When the prior of a nearby dependency of the abbey tried to claim the dues Stabilis protested his liberty. The case came before the count of Troyes and an assembly of nobles, but Fleury's representative was apparently unable to produce any conclusive evidence. Stabilis tried to avoid the judgement of battle that was decreed, presumably because of his pretensions to nobility, by demanding an opponent of equally free status (*ingenuitas*). The abbey produced a champion who proclaimed himself free and of noble descent, but the duel was made unnecessary by the miraculous intervention of St Benedict, before which Stabilis capitulated.[67] The case suggests that it was difficult for a man to prove his freedom from a lordship which had a long arm to reclaim him and the prestige to persuade the élite of the relevant judicial assembly (with or without a miracle) to approve its claim. It also suggests that in this area at least there were no very clear rules

[67] Certain, *Miracles de Saint Benoît*, 218–21.

or tests for proving nobility or freedom, but that in the last analysis it was freedom, or rather unfreedom, that mattered at law.[68]

It is difficult to see how either nobility or freedom could have been defined at this period and in these conditions. Where wergelds (the values placed on people's lives according to their status) were in use, they could have provided a marker, but in England, where they still seem to have been used in the eleventh century, some contemporaries none the less thought of status in terms of wealth, standard of living, and particular obligations, rather than in terms of birth.[69] The rules they postulated also explicitly provided for social climbers. Doubts about nobility as a 'juridically defined status' do not mean that membership of a local élite was not useful at law: people locally thought of as noble would get better treatment from those who gave judgements on behalf of the local community. The provision in the emperor Frederick I's peace ordinance of 1152 that knights needed fewer people to help them clear themselves of charges of breaking the peace than did peasants probably reflected older, if less formal and consistent, practice.[70] People of yet higher rank, who not merely wore swords and rode war-horses but commanded others who did, had yet more legal advantages. They might be effectively in charge of the local application of custom and law. Depending on political circumstances, they might also rely to a large extent on being left alone by more powerful but distant lords. If the word noble were restricted to them it might be easier to say who was noble, but it would still not be very easy in the period before jurisdictions began to be properly classified and organized from above. In any case that is not how the word noble was generally used at the time. Before the thirteenth century at the earliest, anyone called noble in the sources may be said to have enjoyed a status which conferred legal privileges in so far as people locally thought of as noble would be likely to enjoy advantages in courts and assemblies. His advantages would come, however, from the power he wielded as an individual or from his membership of the élite that would be influential in courts and assemblies. That is a different matter from enjoying a legal privilege that belongs to a defined class or status group. One privilege that nobles do not seem to have enjoyed at this time was that of carrying arms, since that does not seem to have been regarded as a privilege or mark of status before the late middle ages. Peasants were more often called on to equip themselves for policing, defence, and

---

[68] For differing interpretations, as well as differing accounts of the source and content of the story: Arbois, *Hist. des ducs de Champagne*, i. 143; Bur, *Champagne*, 344; Flori, *L'Essor*, 55–6.

[69] Liebermann, *Gesetze*, i. 444, 456 (*Rectitudines, Gethinctho*).

[70] Some much earlier laws had related numbers of oath-helpers to the status of the accused, but others had not: *Leges Saxonum*, 56 (17); *Lex Frisionum*, 34–6 (1–13); Liebermann, *Gesetze*, i. 13–14, 50, 112–14, 464 (Wihtred 20–1, Alfred 4. 2, Ine 54, Ath. 1).

military service than prohibited from having or carrying their equipment, though, of course, they might be in trouble if they swaggered about like nobles with expensive and showy arms. When efforts were made to discourage arms-bearing in the interests of peace they were often directed at people of higher status as well as at peasants.[71] The anachronism of postulating rules about arms-bearing in a society where policing was a collective responsibility is matched by that of supposing that general rules about such matters could have been made or applied anyway.

The description of someone as free or unfree was in some ways as subjective and dependent on context in the earlier middle ages as the description of someone as noble. People were free or unfree from different things or to do different things at different times. Nevertheless, however variously and inconsistently the line between freedom and unfreedom was drawn, it seems to have needed to be drawn more frequently before the later middle ages than was the line between noble and non-noble. Stabilis was defeated because he was unfree. That he had claimed to be a noble made his impudence (as the monks saw it) all the worse, but it was the issue of freedom, not that of nobility that mattered. When freedom was a question of the right of individual peasants to leave their holdings, sell them, or resist the imposition of new dues, it was of practical concern both to them and to their lords. Being counted as free would mean first of all having the status to feel able to protest in one's lord's court and hope that people of higher status in the assembly would support one. After that it would mean being able to take one's case elsewhere. Members of my middle category would be more likely to achieve that than would members of my bottom category. But within that middle category were many people whose status must have been doubtful, though the doubts might only appear when, for instance, someone tried to leave or sell up or when the lord imposed dues that people were bold enough to resist.

Consistent definitions of both nobility and freedom depended on the reasonably consistent application of uniform rules. That came with the spread of more systematic and consistent law and of more systematic and bureaucratic government, whether at the level of a local lordship, a county or province, or a kingdom. In England the definition of freedom followed the establishment of a system of royal courts with wide jurisdiction in the later twelfth century. The royal courts were interested in prescribing tests for unfreedom because freedom was needed for access to the courts.[72] Nobility mattered less. Though English nobles naturally had many advan-

---

[71] See index: military service of peasants, and the sources cited (only for Germany) by Fehr, 'Das Waffenrecht'.

[72] Hyams, *Kings, Lords, and Peasants*.

tages and though earls and barons, for instance, began in the thirteenth century to claim to be judged only by their peers—that is, each other—the royal government was strong enough to be able to avoid granting them significant exemptions from general obligations. Elsewhere, although bureaucratic record-keeping and more expert law made definition more possible than it had been, more dispersed jurisdiction left decisions about freedom and unfreedom largely to local courts. The definition of nobility came under the eye of professional administrators and lawyers sooner than did that of freedom. In twelfth-century Italy academic lawyers decided that fiefholding implied nobility, and this idea was reinforced by the association that appeared there at much the same time between fiefholding and the possession of rights of jurisdiction. A similar link between fiefholding and nobility appeared north of the Alps, partly as a result of influence from academic law but partly because of the varying workings of government. In France the demands of the royal government were becoming heavy enough by the late thirteenth century to make people with the status and influence to claim privileges want to secure exemption from at least some of those demands. Since most people with status and influence were normally thought of as nobles, nobility became a qualification for privileges. Gradually rules began to be worked out and elaborated to decide who was noble.[73] In Germany royal demands for military service inadvertently forged a link between benefice-holding and military status in the twelfth century, even before the word *feodum* had come into general use, but political conditions there from the later thirteenth century on must have made the formulation of general rules about qualifications for nobility unnecessary. Late medieval nobles apparently dominated the assemblies (*Landtagen*) of the principalities in which they lived, and claimed, for instance, exclusive rights to conduct feuds, but decisions about the individuals who qualified for such privileges presumably still depended on the local sense of status rather than on anything that could be called legal definitions or rules of law.[74]

The attempts at definition at each level that we find from the thirteenth century on were made in quite different political and legal circumstances from those when nobles or free men had helped themselves and their friends to preferential treatment. Formal legal privileges were not the product of weak government—'feudal anarchy'—but of government over both great and small that was effective enough to invite demands for exceptional treatment. Status mattered equally in both the old world and the

---

[73] Contamine, *La Noblesse*, 32–5; cf. Larner, *Italy in the Age of Dante*, 83.
[74] Conze, 'Adel', 14–15; *Handwörterbuch*, i. 49–50.

new, but whereas in the old the general norms were vague and adaptable, so that each case could be decided according to custom or overweening power without questioning them, in the new there had to be much more argument. That may have made everyone more conscious and concerned about status. Other changes suggest the same thing. The word peers came to be used to describe, not only those who were called upon to defend each other from oppressive lords, but also privileged élites who were more equal than others. The consultative assemblies in which great men had formerly represented the whole community were now being divided into separate 'estates' that were supposed to represent separate status groups.[75] It is surely no accident that it was in this new world of professional law, professional government, and defined privileges that the nobility of vassals became established—at least in the lawbooks. It was the academic law of fiefs that first declared that fiefs were noble property.

It is true that even before the twelfth century some of the kinds of people whom historians call vassals would already have belonged in the top category of my classification. Some, however, would have belonged in the middle group. The *vassi* who were given benefices or fiefs under the Carolingians were presumably set on the way to nobility, however loosely understood, provided that their fiefs were big enough and provided they had security of tenure and not too many obligations. But, apart from these provisos, which are not negligible, Carolingian or post-Carolingian *vassi* who had been granted fiefs on royal or church land were only set on the way. Whether or not the tenants of benefices on the lands of the church of Milan in 1037 thought of themselves as nobles, which as sword-wearers and soldiers they may well have done, they paradoxically nevertheless lacked, or felt uncertain about, what one might consider the crucial rights of legal freedom—the right to judgement by their peers and appeal over the head of their lord if the verdict went against them. It was Conrad II's grant of those rights to the soldiers or knights (*milites*) who held benefices on royal or church land and whom historians call vassals (though he did not), that was later taken to mark the foundation of the academic law of fiefs. Conrad's ordinance came just as what is called 'the rise of the knights' or 'the rise of chivalry' was beginning in northern Europe, and has often been connected with it. People called *milites*, we are told, moved up into the noble class during the eleventh and twelfth centuries, largely or partly because they now achieved secure and heritable tenure of their fiefs.[76] The 'rise of the knights' may thus seem highly relevant to my topic. In spite of

[75] On estates as a later phenomenon: Reynolds, *Kingdoms and Communities*, 302–19.
[76] Flori, *L'Essor*, which also surveys the extensive literature on the topic. But see Barthélemy, 'La Mutation', 771.

that I propose to bypass it almost entirely, restricting myself to investigating the rights and obligations by which free men and nobles, including those called knights, held their land. Beyond that, the whole fascinating question of the development of the chivalric ethos lies outside the scope of this book, while questions about the use of particular words like *miles* and *nobilis* seem to me of only indirect relevance: some of the evidence cited for 'the rise of the knights' seems to be cited under the assumption that the words were used with more consistent and legal significance than seems to me probable.

So far as the rights and obligations of property are concerned, the issue of freedom, so far as it meant freedom to negotiate and to seek justice against one's lord, was more important in the centuries before professional government and law than the issue of nobility. In spite of that I shall say less than I should have liked about the problem of the borderlines between free and unfree. Problems about fiefs and vassals safely above the borderline provide more than enough material for this book on their own. All that can be done about the borderline is to suggest here how problematical it is and to point out that when I talk, as I shall, chiefly about those whom I shall lump together loosely as nobles and free men, while saying little about those whom I shall, even more loosely, call peasants or unfree peasants, the looseness of the categories and the difficulty of distinguishing them must always be borne in mind.

Methods of government changed during the middle ages as populations grew, economies developed, and literacy became more widespread. Forms of service and of subordination changed as a result. With more complex and more professional government and estate administration, more people earned their living by serving rulers and lesser lords in relatively distant and impersonal ways: there were more people who look to us more like civil servants (if not very like modern civil servants) than like household retainers. Many people would, however, be hard to assign to either side of the borderline between governmental and domestic service, while large numbers remained as courtiers, household servants, bodyguards, and so on throughout the period. They ranged from near equal friends or counsellors of the lord or ruler, who might be only occasionally at his court because they had lands of their own, down to menials with no home at all. Some served for their keep, some got wages, some relied on fees or favours from the public, and some simply hoped for land or loot in the future. Some perhaps served out of pure loyalty, though the feelings of all were probably mixed and variable. In spite of all the difficulties one would have in sorting out relations even if the evidence were better, it is clearly inadequate to lump all these people together as 'vassals'. The nature and norms of

clientage need much more investigation.[77] How far at any stage did relations of patronage coincide with property relations in the way suggested by
the model of feudo-vassalic society? How far did they coincide with governmental and jurisdictional relations?

   Where the concept of vassalage has been particularly misleading has
been in the suggestion that there was a period—whenever historians put it
for their respective areas—at which the 'union of fief and vassalage' altered
the general pattern of relations so that 'personal' relations were 'territorialized'. When some soldiers or other servants were given land they might
leave court—if they had been there—but others came in to replace them in
household retinues. Beyond the courtiers, servants, clients, and soldiers
there were many other free and noble subordinates and subjects of kings
and other great lords whose relations with their lords were always territorial in so far as power over people involved a measure of control over the
land they occupied. As I shall hope to show, however, the relations of most
lords or rulers and their free subjects were not, at least before the age of
professional law, seen in terms of a land nexus. The relation in which most
nobles and free men stood to their rulers was not that of fiefholders but of
subjects. Any of them, like all the courtiers, servants, and retainers, might
have to take oaths to their lords at various times and undergo ceremonies
to symbolize their subordination or their receipt of office or favours.
Whether or not the ceremonies were similar, the relations to the ruler of
all these different kinds of subject differed. Quite apart from their relations
with their lords they also all had other relations with other individuals and
above all with groups: their families and kinsmen, their neighbours, and
their colleagues and fellows in work and sociability. They were members
of local communities as much as they were 'vassals' of local lords, and they
were subjects of kingdoms as much as they were of kings.[78]

## 2.4. Conclusion

Nothing that I have said here is intended to cast doubt on the obvious
truths that interpersonal relations between powerful people in medieval
Europe mattered; that nobles placed a high value on the military virtues of
loyalty and courage; that ceremonies like the form of homage described by
Bloch were important symbols of the obligations of lord and man; that in

---

[77] For some useful comparisons with societies where clientage may be combined with other
relationships, e.g. Lloyd, 'Political Structure', esp. 91–2; Schmidt, *Friends, Followers and
Factions*; Eisenstadt and Roniger, *Patrons, Clients and Friends*; Maquet, *Power and Society*,
though his discussion is slightly hampered by the use of the kind of model of European feudalism that I am questioning.

[78] Reynolds, *Kingdoms and Communities, passim*.

an age of low literacy, few records, and poor communications, great men needed to use personal loyalties, ceremonies, and *ad hominem* rewards to maintain and extend their power over the land; and that, since rulers, nobles, and most free men lived off the work of a dependent peasantry, rulers could maintain, control, and reward their followers by delegating control over land and peasants to them. It also seems clear that, as collective activity became more organized, as bureaucracy developed, and as literacy increased the range and power of propaganda, so government relied less on direct interpersonal relations. I think, however, that we can best make sense of all the varying relations that we seem to find in the sources if we stop trying to fit them into the construct of vassalage or measuring their importance against vassalage. Studying medieval society or politics through vassalage will never get us further, because those who undertake it are almost bound to have decided what is there to be found. They are also almost bound to leave out great tracts of medieval life and values that scholars of past centuries did not know about and therefore could not put into their models of feudalism.

Vassalage itself is a term that no longer matches either the evidence we have available or the conceptual tools we need to use in analysing it. It is both too diffuse and too narrow—not surprisingly, since it survives from a primitive stage of the study of social relations. What we need to investigate are relations between rulers and subjects, superiors and inferiors, starting with such general and non-technical categories as these, rather than lords and vassals, until we see the categories that the sources impose. Any such general investigation, however, falls far outside the scope of this book. Where forms of the word vassal actually occur in the sources I have used, I shall discuss their significance.[79] Elsewhere I hope that what I say about the rights and obligations of property will suggest the categories of society on which governments relied and the nature of the relations between rulers and subjects. Otherwise, having concluded that vassalage is too vacuous a concept to be useful, I shall concentrate my attention primarily on fiefs, which raise much more substantial issues.

[79] See index: vassals.

# 3

# FIEFS AND MEDIEVAL PROPERTY RELATIONS

## 3.1. *The concept of the fief*

THIS section, like that on the concept of vassalage in the last chapter, is not a statement of what I believe but of what I take to be the general view taken by those who write about fiefs. As I explained more fully at the beginning of chapter 2, it must be read with that in mind. References to vassals, and in particular to fiefholders as vassals, that appear to ignore the arguments of that chapter are made here because the historians whose views I am trying to summarize very often refer to fiefholders as vassals.

Fiefs are generally taken to be units of property, normally though not always landed property, that were held with more restricted rights than historians consider normal in their own society. A fief was typically created in one of two ways. The most obvious was that a lord granted property, normally in land, to someone to hold in fief from him. Alternatively, someone surrendered to a lord property that he had formerly held as what is called an alod,[1] that is, as his own independent property, and received it back again as a fief. From the beginning of the middle ages peasants held their land with limited and subordinate rights, but the restriction of their rights was different from that of fiefs held by nobles or free men. Holdings that begin to look like fiefs appear first in the grants of land on restricted terms, known as benefices or *precaria*, that great churches began to make to nobles and free men quite early in the middle ages. The classic type of fief derives from the copying of this system by the Carolingians when they made grants of land to their vassals both from their own lands and from lands they took from churches for the purpose. At first the vassals held their benefices only for life or with very limited rights of inheritance, but quite soon they began to pass them on to their sons almost as a matter of course. At the same time the counts and other great men, who were also by now commended to the king or emperor as royal vassals, therefore also came to hold the lands attached to their offices (*honores*) as benefices and

---

[1] For the sake of consistency I have adopted this spelling throughout. It reflects earlier usage, though 'allod' became more common later in the age of professional law.

hoped to pass them on in the same way. With the collapse of the Carolingian empire it became even easier for them to do so: both their offices and the lands they held in benefice became in effect indistinguishable from their alodial family property. Meanwhile they and other great men who, with the decline of royal power, were now building up more or less independent lordships for themselves, granted out benefices or fiefs to their own vassals. The effective 'union of vassalage and benefice', though dated variously by different historians studying different areas, marked a most important stage in the emergence of feudo-vassalic institutions. Another important stage was that at which the inheritance of fiefs was formally accepted as a matter of right rather than of favour. Historians have sometimes seen the king of the west Franks and Emperor Charles the Bald as making a significant concession about the inheritance of counties in the Capitulary of Quierzy in 877, but lesser fiefs seem not to have become generally heritable until around the eleventh century. A landmark in the progress towards the general heritability of fiefs, at least in Italy and Germany, was the ordinance issued by the German emperor Conrad II in 1037 which granted security of tenure, protected by the judgement of their peers, to those who held benefices on royal or church land, together with the right to pass on their land to their sons and certain other male relatives.

The tenure of fiefs, it is said, although dependent, was honourable and free, and was even, in some formulations, restricted to nobles. The original purpose of Carolingian benefices was to provide military service. The services associated with fiefs continued typically to be military in contrast to the rents in money and kind and the more burdensome and non-military labour owed by peasants. Since fiefs were from the start granted to people who were already bound in vassalage, the grant of a fief was normally made by a ceremony of investiture that was derived from the commendation or homage and the oath of fidelity that initiated vassalage. The precise nature of the ceremonies varied: in some areas the word homage was not used, while in twelfth-century Italy, for instance, there were fiefs that did not owe fidelity. Exceptions like this are not, however, normally held to indicate a significant separation of vassalage and fief. The succession of a new lord normally required the renewal of homage, while, even after fiefs were firmly inherited, the heir to a fief would similarly have to do homage (or be invested). He or she might also have to make some kind of payment to the lord (relief, *relevium*, *rachat*, etc.) in order to take up the inheritance: though fiefs were thought of as suitable in principle only for those who would do military service, they were in practice sometimes inherited by women in default of male heirs. As all this suggests, fiefholding, like vassalage, was essentially contractual: the lord had to protect his

49

vassal, the fiefholder, and do justice to him in his court. The vassal had to fight for his lord and offer him counsel and aid, notably by paying certain customary 'feudal aids' when the lord faced exceptional expenses, like those involved in going on crusade, knighting his son, marrying off his daughter, or ransoming himself if he were captured in battle. If the vassal betrayed his lord or failed significantly in his duties his fief might be confiscated.

A fief needs to be contrasted not only with a peasant's more servile holding but with an alod, that is, an entirely independent holding not received by grant from a lord. It was as alods that nobles and free men—or some would say simply nobles[2]—held their land before the introduction of benefices or fiefs. The stage when fiefs replaced alods as the dominant form of property varied from place to place. For Ganshof it had happened in the Carolingian empire by the time the empire fell apart, although the two categories became confused during subsequent disorders. In what became the kingdom of France, though not in the east, the great fiefs of counts then became more or less alodialized. In spite of the effective independence of many French counties, however, historians continue to describe them as fiefs and generally see counts as bound, at least nominally, in vassalage to the king. Meanwhile the same relations survived, at least in principle, between the counts and their vassals. With the eleventh and twelfth centuries came a new stage in the emergence of fully feudalized states with the widespread conversion of alods into fiefs. There are no words in English either for the procedure of conversion or the fiefs that resulted, but Germans call the transaction a *Lehnsauftragung*, while *fiefs de reprise* and *feudi oblati* are used in French and Italian respectively for the resultant fiefs. Georges Duby put the 'union of vassal and fief' in the Mâconnais in the eleventh century. While some British scholars see the 'feudalization' of property starting in England before the Norman Conquest, all agree that after it anything like alods disappeared and were replaced by fiefs, which were normally held by nobles and knights in return for military service and by lesser free men by the tenure known as socage. It seems to be generally agreed that in the twelfth century the emperor Frederick I pursued a policy of feudalizing the property of his greater subjects in both Italy and Germany, though the decline of imperial power in the thirteenth century allowed some princely and noble alods to survive in Germany. With hereditary fiefs established as the norm, and alods left as anomalous enclaves, mostly (except perhaps in Germany) at a fairly low level, nearly everyone above the peasantry was now involved in relations of vassalage, so that

[2] e.g. Balon, *Structure*, 465, and *Fondements*, 50–72, 125.

landholdings formed a hierarchy—the 'hierarchy of tenure' or 'feudal pyramid'. At the top was the king or emperor; then came his immediate vassals or tenants in chief; and then those who may be called undertenants, subvassals, or rear-vassals, or sometimes vavassors, but to whom the generic title of 'vassals' is sometimes more particularly applied. There could be several layers of vassals above the peasants at the bottom, with each vassal in each layer owing duties both to his own immediate lord in respect of his own fief and to any vassals of his own to whom he had in turn granted a fief.

Irrespective of all the political and social corollaries of vassalage—military service, chivalry, and so on—the fundamental character of the fief reflects distinctive ideas of property. Rights of property in a fief were divided between lord and vassal. They may thus be contrasted with the ⟩ absolute property or 'ownership' that was enjoyed in a medieval alod, is reflected in Roman-law concepts of *dominium*, and is implicitly taken as normal by most modern writers. As Marc Bloch put it, 'in the whole feudal era . . . the word "ownership" (*propriété*), as applied to landed property (*un immeuble*), would have been almost meaningless'.[3] Harold Berman's more recent formulation seems to sum up the general view of those who follow Bloch in seeing the fief as embodying the characteristically medieval—or feudal—idea of property: 'Land, in fact, was not "owned" by anyone; it was "held" by superiors in a ladder of "tenures" leading to the king or other supreme lord. ("Tenure", derived from the Latin word *tenere*, "to hold", itself means "a holding").'[4]

There is another peculiarity in the feudal conception of property as it is generally understood: property in the middle ages was not clearly distinguished from government. That was partly because of the general lack of ⟩ distinction between private and public in the early middle ages. Some aspects of this lack were discussed in the previous chapter. So far as fiefs are concerned, the general view is that they carried rights and obligations that look to us governmental rather than proprietary. Partly this was because medieval nobles, whether they held alods or fiefs, normally had at least some jurisdiction over their peasant tenants. Lords, however, are also generally assumed to have had legal jurisdiction over their fiefholding vassals, at least to the extent that a vassal had to take any complaints or disputes about his fief to the court of his lord in the first instance. Judgement there was supposed to be given by the other vassals—the peers of the

---

[3] *Feudal Society*, 115 (*Société féodale*, i. 183).
[4] Berman, *Law and Revolution*, 312. The use of 'tenure' for a holding rather than a method of holding, hitherto apparently rare in English (*OED*), has recently come into writing about medieval history, perhaps from the French.

complainant. If the lord's court failed to do justice then a vassal was supposed to be able to complain to the overlord—that is, his lord's lord. How
it all worked in practice depended on political circumstances and the local
development of custom. While the general rule was that vassals or fiefholders came under their lord's private or quasi-private jurisdiction in feudal
matters (that is, regarding the tenure of their fiefs), fiefholding in many
areas had a wider impact on government and jurisdiction. When fiefs
became the standard form of noble property, criminal and other jurisdiction over peasants and anyone else within the fief that nobles often enjoyed
came in most countries to seem an integral part of fiefholding. In Italy, for
instance, the possession of the criminal and other jurisdiction known as *districtus* became associated with fiefs, so that Italian historians have traditionally identified the essential feudo-vassalic institutions not merely as
vassalage and fief or benefice but as vassalage, benefice, and immunity
(*immunità*).[5] 'Immunity' here is used by analogy from the grants of immunity from external jurisdiction that was granted as a special favour to
churches from the early middle ages, but in the case of Italian fiefs (or
benefices) it came to be not a special favour but a right inherent in fiefs as
such. Most historians who write about feudo-vassalic institutions in other
countries, or indeed about medieval society in general, see the connection
between fiefholding and jurisdiction as more variable than that, but nearly
all would agree that the lack of distinction between property and government, as we understand them, formed a significant element in the character of fiefholding and thus in medieval law and politics in general. These
two characteristics of the fief—the division of property rights in it and their
association with government—have been identified as distinctive and significant features of medieval society, reflecting distinctive and significant
features of medieval mentality, ever since the eighteenth century. It is
because they were embodied in fiefholding that the time when fiefs became
the dominant method of noble landholding—whenever and wherever they
did—is seen as a significant point in medieval history. The dominance of
fiefholding and its link with vassalage can be illustrated in various ways.
Robert Boutruche suggested that the alodholder, whatever his status, lay
outside the system of social relations that enclosed the medieval man.[6]
When money came into wider use in the eleventh and twelfth centuries and
kings and other lords wanted to make regular cash payments to their vassals rather than giving them land, they did it by granting annual sums
(money fiefs, *fiefs-rentes*) on similar terms to those that had become customary in fiefs of land.[7]

[5] Tabacco, 'Fief et seigneurie'.        [6] Boutruche, *Une société provinciale*, 21.
[7] Lyon, *From Fief to Indenture*.

## 3.2. *Ideas of property*

The first point to be made about the ideas of property that are reflected in the concept of the fief as it is sketched above is that they are found in many societies in which they coexist with a variety of other aspects of social organization, some of which look like those of medieval Europe and some of which do not. In a settled, agricultural, and hierarchical polity where there is no bureaucracy and little or no land market, it may be impossible to distinguish rulers from landlords, rights of property from rights of government, not because people confuse them but because the distinction does not exist.[8] There may be no difference to be noticed between rent and taxes or between services owed to a landlord and services to a ruler or government official. Some of the rights that we associate with property are also likely to be divided, so that people who are acting in what we would call a governmental or quasi-governmental capacity control the use that people under their authority make of the land they cultivate. Even where the hierarchy of government does not coincide with the layers of control over the exploitation of land no one may have thought of worrying about the difference or trying to explain it.[9] The customary law by which such societies are often ruled does not, in any case, encourage the conceptualization that such distinctions would require.

The conceptualization that lies behind the idea of 'ownership' that Bloch and Berman by implication contrast with feudal property is itself, moreover, rather primitive and culture-bound. 'Ownership' seems to mean something like absolute property, but absolute property exists nowhere except in the minds and polemics of those who are anxious to defend their rights either against governments or against those who claim conflicting rights. In England the supposedly peculiar character of 'feudal tenure' was first identified in the seventeenth and eighteenth centuries, just when arguments in defence of property were being formulated against the government and when landlords were trying to do away with the common rights that impeded the agricultural improvements (as they saw the matter) that they wanted to introduce on their estates.[10] Feudal property was seen in the light of current ideas and concerns. Its contractual character gave it an

---

[8] On the idea of confusion: Maitland, *Domesday Book and Beyond*, 224.

[9] Mair, *Introduction to Social Anthropology*, 137–42; Lowrie, 'Incorporeal Property'; Goody, *Death, Property and the Ancestors*, 284–303, and 'Feudalism in Africa?', esp. 10; Gluckman, *Ideas in Barotse Jurisprudence*, 75–112; Smith, 'Concept of Native Title'; Geertz, *Negara* , 66–7, 127, 175–7; La Fontaine, 'Land and the Political Community'.

[10] Cohen, *Law and the Social Order*, 41–68; Schlatter, *Private Property*; Minogue, 'Concept of Property'; Grey, 'Disintegration of Property', esp. 73; Whelan, 'Property as Artifice'; Kelley and Smith, 'What was Property?'; Thompson, *Customs in Common*, 159–68.

element of liberty that befitted what was seen as the uniquely free character of European civilization even in its archaic stages, but it was an incomplete and inadequate liberty. To those who argued for natural rights of
property, any inadequacies that were perceived in eighteenth-century
property law could be explained as survivals of feudal law from feudal society. Study of the academic law of fiefs, moreover, had started as part of the
study of Roman law. Once the difference between the two kinds of law had
been established, the contrast between the imperfect property in fiefs and
the supposedly absolute property of Roman law became glaring.[11] The
Justinianic separation of the law about persons from the law about things
may also, like the Roman law of occupancy, have favoured arguments that
property was a natural right of the individual, irrespective of others.[12]
According to rather more considered and less tendentious jurisprudence,
however, property rights must always be rights against other people.[13]
Property cannot be envisaged without some sort of social or governmental
recognition of the rights people claim in land or goods. In any society one's
property is that which the society recognizes and will in principle protect.
Property rights that are thought of as divided or are protected only by customary law are not necessarily less secure in practice than those that are
thought of as absolute and are protected by written constitutions or
statutes. Even in a *laissez-faire* capitalist society, and however little the man
in the street may like to recognize the fact, property is to some extent limited by social controls. Modern property rights are less absolute and more
liable to be divided and shared than those who stress the strange and
incomplete nature of feudal property seem to imply.[14] There are still landlords and tenants, who will share some rights and enjoy others against each
other and against outsiders, while they each have obligations to each other
and to outsiders, including both central and local government. An 'owner'
of property, in other words, does not have absolute rights over it. The distinction between 'ownership' or 'property' on the one hand and 'tenure' on
the other, or between 'owner' and 'tenant', is a distinction between
words—our words. In so far as it bears any relation to legal realities, they
are the realities of our particular legal system.

[11] Roman property rights seem to have been more divided in practice than they look in the
texts: Rodger, *Owners and Neighbours*, 1–2, 36–7; Donahue, 'Future of the Concept', esp. 35–6;
Frier, *Landlord and Tenant in Imperial Rome*, though rural estates worked by slaves would presumably not have given scope for the effective division of rights revealed by Frier.

[12] On confusions caused by the distinction between rights *in rem* and *in personam*: Hohfeld,
*Fundamental Legal Conceptions*, 69–91; Goody, *Death, Property and the Ancestors*, 288.

[13] Hohfeld, *Fundamental Legal Conceptions*, 69; cf. Moore, *Law as Process*, 70; Bloch,
'Property'.

[14] Hohfeld, *Fundamental Legal Conceptions*, 75–7, 96–7; Honoré, 'Ownership'; Becker,
*Property Rights*. For variations in modern systems: Merryman, 'Ownership and Estate'.

In trying to make sense of the norms and practice of property-holding by nobles and free men in medieval Europe, we cannot rely on residues of seventeenth- and eighteenth-century ideas, even if we label them 'feudal theory'. Serious modern students of comparative law and property do not see property in these terms.[15] As L. C. Becker puts it: 'property rights are typically aggregates of different sorts of rights and rights-correlatives.'[16] They need to be analysed. If we are to treat fiefs as something that one could call a category of property, which is what seems to be implied in the way that they are generally discussed, then we need to establish what were the rights and obligations of the properties that we call fiefs or that were called fiefs at the time, and how these rights and obligations differed from those of alods or peasant properties. We should also be prepared to look hard enough at property in our own society to be able to see in what respect the various forms of medieval property really differed from it. The discussions of A. M. Honoré, L. C. Becker, and Andrew Reeve have provided the material from which I have made up a check-list both of rights or claims and of liabilities or obligations of property that seems to me suitable for comparisons between different societies. My check-list contains the following rights (or claims) of property: the right to use and manage the thing concerned and the right to receive its produce or income; the right to pass it on to one's heirs and the right to alienate or dispose of it to others. The two last sometimes turn out to be in a sense contradictory, since the first of the pair creates expectations that the second may disappoint. There is also the question of the term, or absence of term, during which all the other rights and obligations exist and of what is commonly called the reversion: that is the right to take over property that lacks an owner.[17] Last but far from least, there is the right or claim to security, that is to the protection of one's title—in a sense the most fundamental and indispensable right of all. I shall consider these rights primarily from the point of view of the person or persons who appear to enjoy the primary right to use, manage, and

---

[15] e.g. works cited in previous note, and Reeve, *Property*; Munzer, *Theory of Property*; Moore, *Social Facts*, 38–40, 64–80; Goody, *Death, Property and the Ancestors*, 284–303; Gluckman, *Ideas*, 75–112. I have largely ignored what any of them says about European feudalism which is generally derived from the historiographical tradition that their own findings and arguments undermine.

[16] Becker, *Property Rights*, 21.

[17] I prefer to avoid the habitual use of 'reversion' (cf. Honoré's 'residuary character') as it reflects the idea that all property is derived from an original grantor to whom it 'reverts' (see *OED*, xiii. 826), which seems to derive from myths invented by later lawyers and historians. One right or claim I have not included is the right to exclude others, which is seldom absolute in the case of landed property and was often restricted in the middle ages by rights, for instance, to common pasture. I should have included it but can perhaps excuse the omission here, since it particularly affected the relations with peasant tenants that also fall outside this book, and the fiercest debates about it came after the period in which I am interested.

receive produce or income, noting any sharing or diminution of these rights where necessary and also noting the other rights enjoyed, or lacking, alongside.

In all societies the rights of property may be limited or regulated in some way, for instance by the degree to which one's use of property is exclusive or by the possibility of its confiscation in at least some circumstances, however restricted they may be and whatever the compensation that may be offered. Property may often be liable to be used to pay its owner's debts. It also always carries obligations, even if people within a society do not perceive the connection very clearly and some theorists of modern property rights play them down. In most societies there is an obligation not to use property in ways officially considered harmful. The property itself may be confiscated or put in execution to provide compensation for any harm it does. Property also normally carries some kind of obligation to taxation or service, even if, in quite a lot of relatively simple societies, dues or services seem to be conceived as voluntary or contractual gifts made by the property-holder rather than as obligations imposed on the property. Such conceptualizations are revealing of political ideas within the society, but we need to distinguish them—especially if the evidence of them is slight—from the conceptualizations that we impose. Heavy rents, taxes, or services, whether imposed directly on the property itself or not, reduce the rights of its holder to use, manage, and receive income from it, so that obligations constitute a reduction on rights. It is therefore not entirely logical to consider the two aspects separately. I nevertheless propose to do so since it makes for easier comparison and discussion of different combinations of rights and obligations.

Rights and obligations do not always come in solid packages. There is no reason to say that there are no true property rights in a society just because the packages—so far as they are done up together at all—are different from ours. The contents of the packages in each society need to be examined in context, not lumped into crude categories constructed by noticing only one or two kinds of right or obligation and sticking a label on the package so that we do not need to look inside. The rights and obligations attached to land or other forms of property are likely to vary within a single culture or society, especially if it is one as large and varied as that of medieval Europe. Finding what is in any package is made more difficult by the fact that few people, even when they write defences of property or compare the strange laws of other societies with their own, are concerned to work out anything like an analysis of all the rights and obligations of property even in a single society. For outsiders looking at a society the rights or obligations to be mentioned are likely to be those that look unfamiliar. For insiders what they are interested in and mention are the rights that they think are under threat and the obligations that are contested. If, like Locke and others in the eighteenth century whose ideas are still so influential, they see property under threat of taxation or confiscation, then they write about the absolute rights of property-holders against government. Documents of title and records of disputes from any society, particularly if they are not drawn up by professional lawyers (and even, sometimes, if they are), often omit information about a lot of items on my check-list and give a partial view of others. People who are bothered by the competing rights of their landlords or tenants will play them down and may imply that all property rights are of necessity undivided so that their own must be complete. If they want to sell property or give it away and are worried by the claims of their kin they will stress their free rights of disposition, while their kinsmen or heirs will stress the opposite.[18]

Apart from all problems of interpretation, medieval sources most of the time provide solid information about very few of the items on the checklist. The material in the following chapters has nevertheless been compiled on the basis that it is helpful to think about all the items and look for them. I have also added one item to the check-list which is not so important to theorists of property rights but which seems to me to be important in the medieval context. That is the question of title: the methods by which rights and obligations were supposed to be, or thought to have been, acquired, and the methods by which they were supposed to be transferred.

### 3.3. *A hypothesis about property law before 1100*

The norms that governed the rights and obligations of property before the twelfth century seem to have been more variable than is suggested by the contrast between alod, benefice or fief, and more or less unfree peasant property.[19] Something like the threefold division can certainly be discerned. While, in principle, people of high status had more rights in their property than people of low status and owed lighter and more honourable obligations, both nobles and lesser free men sometimes held property that churches or kings had granted to them with fewer rights and, sometimes, more obligations. Anomalies of many kinds were introduced by the working of political favour, power politics, the growth of a land market, and the drift of custom. All human life outside textbooks is full of anomalies,

[18] On questionable deductions about 'lineage property' from claims against alienation: La Fontaine, 'Land and the Political Community', 99–100.

[19] References to support most of the arguments put forward in this section and the next will be given in later chapters in which the arguments are set out in more detail for the countries concerned.

particularly human life under customary law. Customary law is real law by any but the most culture-bound standards. It has real normative force, but although perceived as old and fixed it is bound to vary from time to time as well as from place to place: the precedents followed are the precedents that are remembered and seem right at the time. Early medieval custom, moreover, like all law and all morality, embodied conflicting norms, while giving fewer opportunities for formal and authoritative discussion and resolution of conflicts of principle than professional law would later provide. Apparent statements of principle were often not rules of law but maxims that were stated just because there were doubts and disagreements— doubts and disagreements that may have been resolved differently the year before and would be resolved in yet another way the year after or in the next county.[20]

Much as there was in customary law that was common to wide areas of western Europe, the importance of land in agricultural economies meant that rules about it were peculiarly liable to vary according to both agricultural and political circumstances. They were also liable to be affected by the fundamental conflict, referred to in the last chapter, between hierarchy, obedience, and loyalty on the one hand and custom, immanent justice, mutuality of obligations, and collective judgement on the other. A man's claim to pass on his property to his children or other close kin was liable to frustrate the claim of a ruler to keep some control over land in the area he claimed to rule. All those whose land was protected by their rulers owed some obligations in return even if they thought of their rights in it as complete and whether or not anyone thought that those rights derived from a royal grant. The terms on which any particular estate was held must often have been uncertain. Even if it had originally been granted by a ruler or other lord, gratitude and a sense of obligation are perishable: the bond between grantor and grantee would erode as time and generations passed. Rulers hoped to maximize dues and controls, subjects hoped to secure maximum rights and minimum obligations. The normative working of custom turned any vindicated claim into a right by the mere passage of time. In these conditions I suspect that—to use the terminology of modern historiography—individual fiefs would tend with the passage of time to become assimilated to the condition of alods even while powerful rulers would be trying to assimilate alods to the condition of fiefs.

That terminology, however, is misleading. The Latin equivalents of the words benefice, fief, and alod were used less frequently and much less consistently before 1100—and indeed for some time later—than has generally

[20] Gluckman, *Law, Politics and Ritual*, 178–202; Moore, *Social Facts*, 38–40, and *Law as Process*, 169–70.

been appreciated by those who have concentrated on looking for the origins of the usage they expect and think significant. It would be pointless to try to give my alternative definitions of the words here: meanings must be derived from contexts, bearing in mind all the various kinds of rights and obligations that may be at issue. My attempt at that is therefore reserved for later chapters where a number of different definitions will emerge. What I have concluded from my investigations is that, while nobles and free men before the twelfth century might acknowledge that they held specific estates from churches (or more rarely from kings or other nobles) as fiefs, neither they nor anyone else applied the word to the main body of their inheritances, at least in anything like the sense in which it would later be used. In the only context in which it was applied to noble property or lordships in general it did not have any connotations of dependence or restricted rights.[21] Not until well after 1100 were the properties of nobles and other free men normally described as fiefs, nor did the word fief begin to denote anything like a consistent category of property—in so far, considering its aberrant use in England, as one can say that it ever did.

Before the twelfth century free men expected to hold their land as what I shall usually call full property: that is, they held it with what, irrespective of any obligations they owed, they thought of as full rights. Sometimes, chiefly in Frankish usage, the word alod was used to describe their holdings, sometimes *proprium*, sometimes *proprietas*, or *hereditas*, but the implication of full and complete rights is clear.[22] That does not mean, of course, that a noble's land was in reality his 'absolute property'. As Bloch pointed out, an alodholder's rights were restricted by his kin and by the tenants he might have below him. That includes his peasant tenants. Even the less free, provided they had holdings and can thus be reckoned as tenants, probably had some rights of property: that is, they used their land and took its produce subject to renders that were, probably, more or less effectively limited by custom. Tenant rights therefore, like tenant rights on a 'freehold' today, could constitute a fairly severe limitation on the rights of an owner of supposedly full property. In so far as Bloch implied that alodholders' rights were unlimited from above, moreover, that was misleading.[23] Wherever any semblance of government was maintained, the holder of what was thought of as full property had obligations to the ruler. Even the lands of churches normally owed some dues or services unless they had been explicitly exempted from them. While the obligations varied according to the status of the owner and the size of the estate or both, the rights

[21] See chapter 5.5.
[22] *Pace* Bloch, *Feudal Society*, 115 (*Société féodale*, i. 183), references to *proprietas* are common.
[23] *Feudal Society*, 171–2 (*Société féodale*, i. 264).

of a peasant holder of an alod or other full property seem in principle to have been the same as those of a noble, though a peasant would find it harder to maintain them. People with full property had some rights over their unfree or less free tenants that we might consider governmental rather than property rights. To have these the landowners did not need to be the kind of people who would generally be called noble, though they might seem so in comparison with their neighbours and tenants.

Authority over free men, especially free men with their own property, was another matter. Great churches were most likely to exercise it as an appurtenance of their property rights, because they were often granted what was called 'immunity' over their lands. This involved exemption from various dues and sometimes from external jurisdiction. Free men who held parts of a church's land might thus come under its jurisdiction, and some large ecclesiastical lordships extended their authority over property that might otherwise have been considered to carry full rights. Immunities, however, were grants of special privileges, whereas, according to many accounts of feudo-vassalic relations, the lord's exercise of jurisdiction over his vassals was a natural and normal consequence of their vassalage. There is no reason to doubt that early medieval lords must often have dealt with their followers' and subjects' disputes and misdoings in a more or less informal way, but it is doubtful that lords adjudicated disputes about the property of their free followers as a matter of course. That is because it is not at all clear that anyone except a king was normally supposed to exercise what we would consider governmental and coercive authority over free men who had full property rights without some sort of special authorization. Where a kingdom was big enough for the king to need to delegate local authority, as the Carolingians did to counts, the distinction between a noble's office and his own alods is generally clear, at least in principle. Whether this meant that the king could dismiss his counts at will and whether he also then confiscated their own property depended on custom and political circumstances. In conditions of customary law and poor communications kings were often content to leave their counts or other local officials a good deal of local autonomy, provided that they were loyal when it came to the pinch. That might allow counts to bully their lesser neighbours as well as to embezzle crown property, but it was only if the central government broke down that local bullying and embezzlement produced a complete confusion between their property and their governmental authority. The idea that from early on counts or other lay nobles received 'immunities' like those of the great churches and that this was the source of later political fragmentation—'feudal anarchy'— seems to be an over-simplification. Under the word 'immunity', which was, I think, seldom if ever used for lay jurisdictions before the twelfth century, it conflates together varying structures of local government and power in different centuries and different political circumstances.[24]

When lay lords in the aftermath of the Carolingian empire began to acquire independent jurisdiction over free men and their supposedly full property it seems at first to have been by the usurpation of what had been governmental authority rather than by the formal grant to them of 'immunities'. Whatever the structure of government that emerged in any area from the political order or disorder that became established during this period, the passage of time gave it legitimacy. That was an inevitable result of the working of customary law, fortified by the rights that attached to the exercise of governmental authority just as they attached to more obvious forms of property. Medieval government, like medieval society, came in layers. The king was supreme but not sovereign in the sense of being allowed to take and enforce decisions unilaterally. His obligation to justice and custom included a duty to respect the customary rights of his subjects, whether we would call them governmental or proprietary. His duty to protect the church and respect its rights was particularly strong. Churches held their property if anything more freely than laymen, though we have to bear in mind that a serious lay consensus about the property rights of churches might not have supported all the inferences that we draw from clerical sources. However that may be, the duty of any king or other lord to protect churches and their property was always, whether from motives of piety or power, likely to turn into controlling them. There does not seem to be any reason, however, to see control and interference as falling on the property side of the boundary between proprietary and governmental rights. To talk of 'proprietary churches' (*Eigenkirchen*) or talk of a 'proprietary church system' is to interpolate ideas of property into early medieval society that are strange to it.

The elements of hierarchy that can be detected here are social and governmental, not—except in the case of more or less unfree peasants—a matter of property rights. The sources do not suggest that nobles and free men thought of their property as having originated in a grant from a king or other lord, except, of course, when one of them had just received a grant of land in addition to what he had inherited from his ancestors. Even then, if the grant was made *in proprietatem*, *in proprium*, or *in alodum*, it was not conditional or contractual except in so far as all political relations were implicitly contractual. Property confiscated for non-payment of taxes or inheritance dues may be taken as having been by implication conditional

---

[24] Brunner, *Deutsche Rechtsgeschichte*, ii. 384–9, 397; Mitteis, *Deutsche Rechtsgeschichte*, 79–82.

on payment, but the kind of properties that historians call alods could be confiscated as well as fiefs. The use of forfeiture as a punishment tells us more about the value of landed property and the crudity of the punishments available than about the contractual nature of 'feudal tenure'. Confirmations of property rights from a new king need not imply that they had ended automatically with the death of the king or were recognized as being less than complete in other ways. Whether they derived from the owner's ancestors or from a past royal grant that had been made for ever, it could be prudent to seek confirmation of them from a new ruler and get written confirmation of it. Free men do not seem to have thought of their property as 'held' rather than 'owned' in the sense implied by Bloch and Berman. When the verb *tenere* is used in the sources it does not seem to imply the kind of limited and subordinate rights that the English word tenant does today. The idea of 'tenure' as distinct from 'ownership' is derived from distinctions drawn by later academic lawyers. It is inappropriate to this period and indeed for comparative study in general. For that reason I shall not use the word tenure as a synonym either for a category of property or for a unit of property.[25] When I use the words hold, holding, or holder in connection with property they will not imply anything about the rights and obligations attached to it. There is a further problem for anglophones about the use of 'holding' as a technical term of feudal law. It is traditional to translate *tenere de* as 'holding of'. This expression, by its very peculiarity, has come to suggest something distinctive and odd about medieval property. It implies the kind of technicality that I maintain is misleading for a period in which the rules of landholding, in so far as they were fixed, cannot safely be deduced from the law that would later be applied by lawyers to the kinds of property that came to be called fiefs. I have therefore decided to use the phrase 'holding from'. Although not much, if at all, less odd, it is at least not a pseudo-technical term.

In addition to their own inherited properties, some nobles and other free men held lands from kings or churches with more restricted rights. Counts and other royal officials might hold parts of the king's estates ex officio, and kings sometimes granted smaller holdings to followers and servants for restricted terms in return for special military or other services. These royal grants, with similar grants by other lords, are generally taken to have constituted a development from the relations of lord and vassal that produced the classic fief, but we really know very little about them. Most of what is known about fiefs and benefices before the twelfth century comes from records that were made in great churches in order to safeguard their prop-

---

[25] On its use for units of property, above, n. 4.

erty. When bishops or abbots made grants of their land to nobles and lesser free men—or when kings did it for them—the conditions varied according to circumstances and the status of the parties, but one point was nearly always made, or should have been if the bishop or abbot was doing his job conscientiously. The fundamental and ultimate rights of the church to the land were not to be impaired. As a means to this end a fixed term was often imposed on the beneficiary's rights. A bishop or abbot might on occasion grant his church's property to a kinsman without fixing a term, but the usual rule was that church property should not be granted for more than a fixed number of lives or a fixed term of years. That did not apply to church property that was held by peasants: the custom of allowing more or less unfree peasants to inherit their land in practice did not pose the same threat as allowing free men to do so, and consequently the rules that were elaborated in canon law generally ignored peasant property.

Beyond these general rules there was, as usual, a good deal of variation. The degree of uniformity imposed by canon law was offset by the working of local custom and the traditions developed in individual monasteries. From the late ninth century at latest some churches made grants to their servants or others they wished to favour not in the form of land but of annual rents: the 'money fief' was not therefore a later development that appeared in the new cash economy after 1100, though it was certainly much used then.[26] What is striking about the general pattern of rules about the benefices or fiefs, as they came to be called, that were held from churches is the way that they reflected the local norms that governed property carrying what were thought of as full rights: property with full rights set the standard. Thus, where full property was often shared between kinsmen, inheritance rights in benefices or fiefs, though restricted, might also be shared. Rites for the transfer of fiefs, though probably including acknowledgements of subordination and services, were likely to involve the same kinds of public handing over of symbolic objects as were made in full grants. Where full property owed military service, then churches were likely to make their tenants, or some of them, fulfil royal demands on their behalf, in which case the tenants would owe much the same obligations as did the owners of full property. Sometimes, however, a church gave small holdings to men who could defend its property and carry out local policing duties, in which case the obligation was different from that on full property. Rules about fiefs or benefices that were granted to people of low status also borrowed from the prevailing norms of peasant property. Inheritance dues on fiefs, for instance, may have first become customary

[26] See index: money fief.

when churches extended them from their unfree to their free tenants. Such dues served the useful purpose of reminding tenants that their rights were limited and temporary. Occasional rulings that bishops and abbots, either in particular cases or in general, did not need to be bound by their predecessors' grants help to account for the belief that all benefices were at first granted for the life of the grantor. Such rulings were intended to preserve the property of God, his saints, and his churches from their negligent custodians. The relation between a layman and his son was quite different from that between a bishop and his successor and the relation of both to their property was different. Rules about church property cannot be applied automatically to lay property.

Yet the application of early medieval rules about church property to lay property is very largely what all the ideas of 'feudal law', and indeed of feudo-vassalic relations in general, depend upon. The academic and professional law of fiefs that was created in twelfth-century Italy owed more to the practices developed over the past centuries for grants to laymen of ecclesiastical land than it did to those of lay lords. This must cast doubt on the modern idea of 'feudal law' as an expression of the norms of lay society in the earlier middle ages. My argument is that a large part of the rules of fiefholding as historians of feudalism understand them seems to derive, not from social norms of the lay nobility in the earlier middle ages, but from the practices that the clergy devised to protect the property of the church.

### 3.4. *A hypothesis about property law after 1100*

Customary law during the early middle ages allowed social, economic, and political change to be reflected in the rights and obligations of property more directly than would be the case when changes would be mediated through professional law. By the twelfth century, however, the dominance of customary law was being undermined. The growth of population and of the economy provoked more disputes over land, more clearances of new land, and a greater land market, while more silver, coined and uncoined, was available to use in buying land.[27] Meanwhile, at the end of the eleventh century, the investiture contest provoked arguments about the difference between office and property and stimulated the development of canon law at just the same time as the academic study of Roman and Lombard law was growing in Italy.[28] How closely these developments were connected with social and economic change, and which caused what, cannot be dis-

[27] For the use of money in land purchases: Spufford, *Money and its Use*, 34–5, 48–9, 98–9, 109–11, 213–15, 246.
[28] On office and property: Hoffmann, 'Ivo von Chartres'.

cussed here, but two other changes that were closely connected both with social and economic change on the one hand and with educational developments on the other had the most obvious and direct effect on property law. They were the coming of more powerful and bureaucratic government and the coming of professional law.

From quite early in the twelfth century any ruler at whatever level who made his government effective was likely to begin to make use of the growing number of literate servants who were available to help him maintain and extend his power, keeping records of his subjects' obligations and arguing the case for increasing them. Since land was the basis of power and wealth many demands fell on property-owners. Those with large estates, who were meanwhile starting to use the new means of increasing their own incomes, thus needed to employ people to argue about the precedents and rights and wrongs of what their rulers demanded. Governments could not ignore customary rights, especially the rights of their more powerful and influential subjects, but the precedents and norms were generally sufficiently vague, and the respect for rulers sufficiently high, for them to be able to secure a good many of the taxes and dues they demanded. Lords could be left to exercise local authority that had become entrenched in custom, provided they allowed appeal to superior authority, but they could be encouraged to secure grants or confirmations of their rights, thus paving the way for the development of theories of the delegation of all authority from above. All this was made easier by the traditional respect for kings and belief in their duty to do justice to all their subjects. As communications improved, both rulers and other lords began to copy each other's more profitable practices. Given the variety of past custom and the difficulty of drawing boundaries between different areas of custom and different categories of property-owners, it was often possible to extend obligations from one area or category to another. One example of this was probably the requirement that the heir to property should perform homage to his lord—however lordship came to be defined—and, sometimes, pay an inheritance tax at the same time. Another is provided by the so-called 'feudal aids' which spread widely from their apparent place of origin in Anjou, though, incidentally, they were more often levied from non-nobles than from people who look like noble fiefholders. While obligations on what had earlier been accepted as full property were raised, its rights (so far as the two can be separated) were not much diminished. In many ways they were made more secure as more regular jurisdictions and courts were established to protect them and as the possibility of appeal to higher authority became more real. That particularly applied to the rights of laymen who had benefices or fiefs on church lands: well-established courts in which judgements were given by laymen were likely to favour the claims of laymen to go on holding lands that had been in their families for several generations. It is no accident, though it was paradoxical, that it was in the twelfth century, when the power and influence of the church was in some ways at its height, that its attempts to prevent the permanent inheritance of its property by its lay tenants finally failed.

Among the literate advisers and officials whom governments and large landowners employed to increase their power and income can soon be discerned men who had a particular expertise in arguing about law and custom and in judging disputes. Whether and how soon one can call any of them professional lawyers depends on one's definition of a professional lawyer, but it is clear that by the end of the thirteenth century a good many cases in higher courts were beginning to be decided by people who had a new kind of legal expertise. Instead of the old unstructured discussions and judgements made by the consensus of senior members of an assembly that was supposed to represent the community of the kingdom or locality, cases were argued by men with a more esoteric knowledge of law and were judged by judges who spent their time judging. The result was greater consistency and uniformity within each kingdom or lordship and more consistent divergencies between them: separate legal systems were appearing, each with its own vocabulary and rules of property law—property law being, of course, one of the most important and profitable subjects for lawyers then, just as tax law is today.

The first more or less professional lawyers had appeared in north Italy by the beginning of the twelfth century as products of the schools of Lombard and Roman law. The problems posed there by grants of ecclesiastical property, compounded by the problems posed by imperial claims to authority that had long passed into other hands, were grist to the mill of both academics and professionals. The result was the book that became known as the *Libri Feudorum* and the commentaries that it soon accumulated. The next clear evidence of a distinct legal profession comes from England, where by the beginning of the thirteenth century the proliferating royal courts were dominated by a small, close-knit group of professional advocates who, by the end of the century, were also staffing the judicial bench. There must have been many other semi-professional lawyers in the country: people with enough training and experience of the complex and esoteric rules that royal courts, royal taxation, and royal legislation produced to be able to advise landowners who could not afford to employ the advocates of the royal courts as everyday advisers but needed some guidance through the maze of property law.[29] In France and

[29] Brand, *Origins*.

Germany the origins and character of the legal profession are harder to detect, partly no doubt because dispersed jurisdiction made for less esoteric law and a more diverse profession than in England, but partly perhaps because less work seems to have been done on the subject. When legal historians in either country think of professional lawyers they seem to think of Roman lawyers. But long before any wholesale 'reception' of Roman-law procedures rulers and great landowners must have needed advisers and advocates with practical knowledge of the handling of property transactions and disputes. The élite among those they employed may have studied Roman law, or at least acquired a smattering of it at university, possibly with a smattering of the law of fiefs alongside, but the substance of the law of property they practised was shaped not by that but by quite different forces. It was shaped by the practical problems of government, litigation, and the transfer and management of property, all carried out against a background of various and often inconvenient custom. Some of the members of the élite of university graduates, like many others who worked in the courts without ever having had a formal academic education, must have spent enough of their time with these problems for us to consider them professional, or at least semi-professional, lawyers and judges. If they were, it was because they acquired training, experience, and employment in legal practice and in judging after they left university, not because they had studied the texts of Roman law or the *Libri Feudorum*.

The differences between legal systems were in many ways less significant than the characteristics of professionalism that they shared and that divided them from the old law of the earlier middle ages.[30] One of the most important characteristics was the use of literacy. Professional law need not always be literate law, but in this case it was. The legal professions of Italy and France started off with strong links to the universities. English lawyers were not normally educated in universities but they were still trained on written documents—the writs used in actions in the royal courts—and worked in a highly bureaucratic and therefore record-keeping system. When people in the middle ages referred to written law they normally meant Roman law, but whatever their view of it, the difference between Roman and non-Roman law was not, in legal practice as distinct from legal education, really a matter of one being a written system and the other unwritten. Charters, deeds, custumals, and the records of governments, courts, and property-owners mattered far more to practising lawyers, even those who prided themselves on their Roman law, than the *Corpus Juris Civilis*, the *Libri Feudorum*, or any glosses or treatises written on either of

---

[30] On the significance of professionalism in law: Luhmann, *Differentiation of Society*, 127–36. On literacy and law: Goody, *Logic of Writing*, 133–66.

them. The texts of canon law, from their nature, were much more important to canon lawyers, but then canon law was largely irrelevant to lawyers who had to argue cases in the secular courts that now adjudicated on most important cases about church property. While non-Roman law used writing, Roman law as actually practised correspondingly had a strongly customary character: a great deal of the actual substance of property law in all systems, as of conveyancing and court procedures, was based on customs worked out over the years. Now, however, so far as law concerned the property of people who could afford lawyers and litigation in higher courts, the customs it followed were not the vague and variable customs of the population at large but the customs of lawyers and the courts they dominated.

Better record-keeping and closer argument produced more explicit rules and, to some extent, greater consistency of rules, though ingenious rationalization of exceptions is just as noticeable. It also brought greater emphasis on particular words, the most important of which, in the context of this book, was 'fief'. By the thirteenth century the lands of nobles and even the lands of great churches were coming to be called fiefs, though it would be some centuries before the new fashion had spread, for instance, to all areas of Germany. In England the word was applied even more widely to all heritable free property. How and why this revolutionary change of terminology took place is not yet clear to me. Partly it was undoubtedly due to the influence of the new kind of lawyers. The first good evidence of the deliberate conversion of alods to fiefs that I have found comes from early twelfth-century Montpellier, where the lord of the town may well have been taking advice from academic lawyers. Academic or professional legal advice may also lie behind the slightly later creation of *fiefs de reprise* or *feudi oblati* elsewhere in France and in Italy and Germany. In all these areas the point seems to have been to secure a measure of political subordination from the new fiefholder, often symbolized by oaths and some kind of ceremony of homage. Those who accepted their new position as fiefholders did so because, one way or another, political conditions gave them no choice: they might, for instance, be negotiating with a lord or city government that threatened them with greater military power. Often, however, they may not have objected because, particularly when they were negotiating with the king of their kingdom, they accepted a measure of subordination, and because fiefs had ceased to seem an inferior type of property. On the contrary they were what nobles held. No diminution of rights of property as such was normally involved in the creation of *fiefs de reprise* except over castles, to which the new fiefholder might have to allow access for the lord, particularly in case of war. The use of the word in England after 1066 is particularly puzzling, given that it does not seem to have been introduced at the conquest as a deliberate ploy to enforce subordination on the powerful and that, when its meaning becomes clear in the twelfth century, it was used quite differently both from the way it had been used in Normandy before 1066 and from the way that it was coming to be used in other parts of France.

Everywhere the difference between the rights and obligations of the new kind of fiefs and those of other property depended more on political circumstances and the status of the owner than on any general distinctions between types of property that can be traced back to the days of pre-professional law. Fiefs were inherited on terms that were sometimes more restricted than those of other property held by people of similar status, but that tended to follow local custom. Inheritance normally required the performance of homage and might be subject to the payment of dues. Failing heirs the fief would go to its lord, however he was identified. Outside England the obligation to military service, so often seen as a key feature of 'feudal tenure', was generally nominal. That, combined with the evidence about the way the various obligations of fiefs originated in each country, is one of the strongest reasons for rejecting the traditional idea that the fiefs of Bloch's 'second feudal age' had evolved out of 'service tenements' held by 'specialized warriors' in the first.[31] Most of the properties that were called fiefs after 1200, and all the larger ones, had not been fiefs or benefices before 1100. What had happened was not a process by which originally precarious 'service tenements' granted by warrior lords to their vassals gradually acquired new rights but one by which new methods of government and new kinds of legal argument imposed more regular obligations on all property, including that which had been thought of as carrying full and unrestricted rights. At the same time a large amount of property—including, outside England and parts of Germany, more or less all of the property of the people who mattered most—was made into a virtually new category: the fief that was thought of as the characteristic property of nobles and, indeed, as restricted in principle to nobles. In so far as it was a new category it was one with many variants, since the obligations imposed on fiefs in different kingdoms or principalities varied widely. The connection between the new obligations and the new name for noble property was not coincidental, since both were produced by the same innovations in government and law, but it was not simple. Some of the obligations of fiefs in the later middle ages were similar to some that had been owed by properties that had been called fiefs or benefices earlier, but that was not why the

---

[31] Bloch, *Feudal Society*, 446; cf. 163–7.

fiefholders owed them. They owed them because governments now imposed them.

One important result of more bureaucratic government and land-management and of the new kind of legal arguments they provoked was that rights of government and rights of property became more clearly distinguishable. That does not mean that the line always came where we might expect it. Rulers could not immediately override the customary rights of those whose right to local governmental powers and jurisdiction had become entrenched in custom, even if they wanted to. For many peasants there continued to be no distinction between rent and taxes: the services and dues they paid to their lord might help him to fulfil the duties that the king imposed on his property, but they paid them to him much as they always had. For most kings petty jurisdictions over peasants could be left to lesser lords with more political profit than financial loss. Wider and higher kinds of jurisdiction were a different matter. Those who exercised it might be made to acknowledge at least that their authority was delegated from above. In 1158 the emperor Frederick I opened his campaign to recover lost imperial rights in Lombardy by declaring, with the advice and support of academic lawyers, that all jurisdiction was derived from the emperor. He might not be able to get back all the jurisdiction and dues that had passed into the hands of counts and cities but he could at least make them acknowledge that they acted as his deputies. In so far as he won an acknowledgement it was, in the end, all he won, but what is striking is how little evidence there is that the principle was questioned. Presumably that was because it fitted traditional, if unformulated, ideas about the rights and duties of kings and seemed not to infringe the customary rights of subjects. While many lords and local communities, both in Italy and elsewhere, had for long exercised local authority without any formal delegation, churches and towns had from time to time secured royal charters by way of title. In thirteenth-century France the gradual extension of the appellate jurisdiction of the king's court bypassed argument about the principle of delegation. In thirteenth-century England, where royal jurisdiction was already very wide, the demand that those who exercised any kind of governmental or quasi-governmental authority should produce royal charters to warrant their titles evoked much grumbling but, again, little argument about the principle.

Conceptualizations of anything like the 'feudal pyramid' or a 'hierarchy of tenure' as they are understood today, so far as they are discernible at all, begin to appear in this period. The social hierarchy had long been taken for granted and, because it was taken for granted, it needed no serious argument: all that was needed was to preach submission. In England the making of Domesday Book was probably responsible for articulating a hierarchy of property rights that became imprinted on the minds of property-holders by the way that governmental demands were channelled through it. The German 'mirror' literature of the thirteenth century (the *Sachsenspiegel*, *Schwabenspiegel*, etc.) is often supposed to have set out a similar hierarchy but, as I shall argue in chapter 9.7, the hierarchy described there was only later interpreted as one of property rights. In France the ramshackle hierarchy of power and government that had emerged from the age of customary law had by the thirteenth century been transformed into a hierarchy of jurisdiction. The lord of the kind of property that was now classified as a fief, as indeed of other property, was the lord who exercised jurisdiction over it. Since so many of the demands of government at every level had long been fulfilled by controls or dues on the property of their subjects there is a sense in which the hierarchy of jurisdiction can also be envisaged as a hierarchy of property, though it was a very untidy one. But property rights were not in reality very significantly distributed through the hierarchy: what lords at its intermediate levels enjoyed were much more like governmental rights. They exercised controls over the property of their subjects and took cuts from it when they could, but the person who held most of the rights of property was the one in actual possession immediately above the peasants—that is, the person who would once have been described as the holder of an alod, *proprietas*, or full property. In fact, conceptualizations of all kinds seem to have remained very rudimentary. I have found no real evidence that anyone, even academics or lawyers, formulated any scheme, or needed any scheme, which coordinated social, political, and tenurial hierarchies or envisaged anything quite like any of the various modern notions of a feudal hierarchy. It does not seem, for instance, that anyone needed to think of communes as vassals or *seigneuries collectives* in order to fit towns into accepted ideas of social order.[32] Nor does anyone, even in England, seem to have gone so far as to argue that all fiefholders by definition derived their rights from royal grants to their ancestors. Readers of the *Libri Feudorum* could have used its brief introductory passage of conjectural history about the origin of benefices to do so, but the result would presumably have cut too radically across traditional ideas: when it was written it had not applied to all noble property in the way it would seem to do when noble property was in principle classified as fiefs.[33] Fiefs, like the earlier properties from which they had descended, were, in traditional language, 'held from' their lords or, in France, 'moved from' them, but that does not appear to have meant to

---

[32] Petit-Dutaillis, *Communes françaises*, 103–23.
[33] Below, chapter 6.8; Lehmann, *Langobardische Lehnrecht*, 84.

people in the middle ages that they had all once belonged to him and that, as a result, their holders' rights were reduced.

While academic law had only indirect effect on the practice and substance of property law, especially outside Italy, it produced a number of rules, distinctions, and arguments that had some political significance at the time and much influence on later ideas about feudalism.[34] As early as the twelfth century academic lawyers were distinguishing rights of government and rights of property that traditional terminology seemed to confuse. The word *dominium* was always a stumbling-block and *proprietas* became another when lords increased their demands on their subjects' properties that had once been *proprietates* but were now called fiefs. According to the *Libri Feudorum* a fief or benefice did not enjoy *proprietas*.[35] The result was argument about whether *dominium* and *proprietas* belonged to the lord or the fiefholder, and the solution was found in dividing *dominium directum* from *dominium utile*. Distinctions were also drawn between different kinds of fief according to the adjectives applied to them in charters, the variations in their obligations, or the status of their owners.[36] The theory of the inalienability of sovereignty received some attention from medieval academics and has therefore received some from intellectual historians, but its possible conflict with the theory of delegation of governmental authority propounded by Frederick Barbarossa does not seem to have been explored either in the middle ages or since.[37] Presumably that was because the theory of delegation itself received so little critical attention. Academic lawyers in late medieval Italy were able to apply the rule to the subjects of cities or princes while more or less ignoring its application to the rulers themselves.

Perhaps most important of all for the development of post-medieval ideas of feudalism, the academics rationalized the confusion of rights and obligations that the combination of varying custom and new law had produced.[38] The traditional values of their society made it natural for them to stress the contractual obligations on both lords and fiefholders or vassals. In particular they rationalized a fiefholder's obligations by appealing to the loyalty and gratitude that seemed to be required by the *Libri Feudorum*'s assumption that fiefs were created by grants from lords—an assumption that made more sense in twelfth-century Italy, where most fiefs were held from churches, than it would either there or anywhere else in the fourteenth century, when they included almost all noble property. That

[34] Stein, *Regulae Juris*, 127–61.
[35] Lehmann, *Langobardische Lehnrecht*, 125, 143 (in both Antiqua and vulgate texts).
[36] See index: *dominium*, fiefs.   [37] e.g. Riesenberg, *Inalienability*.
[38] Cf. Goody, *Logic of Writing*, 166.

historical explanations were not a strong point of legal scholarship is demonstrated by the *Libri Feudorum*'s little bit of conjectural history about the origin of fiefs and the failure of later medieval jurists to develop it much further. By the time that a historical approach came into fashion in the sixteenth century the categories of the academic law of fiefs were so firmly ingrained that it was more natural to concentrate on looking for their origin by developing the conjectural history than to look at early medieval property quite apart from them.

In general what the academics supplied to the law of property were methods of argument and habits of close attention to the words of written texts. How much of this might have come from professional law without the specifically academic input it is hard to know: English law developed rather similar, though not identical, methods and habits without such a direct academic link. The limitation of the academics' approach as a guide to historians was that they approached the subject through the study of texts, and especially through textbooks. When they discussed fiefs they started from the *Libri Feudorum* and made sense of it by using commentaries and other tracts. While the professionals were not much interested in other kinds of property because their clients were not so much concerned with it, the academics were not much interested in it because it did not figure in their basic text. They therefore paid little attention to distinguishing fiefs from other kinds of property: hence the interest in classifying different kinds of fiefs but the lack of any definition of fiefs as a category of property with distinctive rights and obligations.

## 3.5. *Conclusion*

My hypotheses about the development of property law lead to the conclusion that before the twelfth century the law of property, because it was customary law, probably reflected social values fairly well. Yet the standard form of property for nobles and other free men at that time was something much more like the common modern idea of 'freehold property' than the modern idea of 'feudal property'. It certainly did not correspond to Weber's ideal type of the fief as a 'service tenement' that is granted in return for services.[39] From the twelfth century on, property law did not reflect social values and social relations nearly so directly. Rulers and professional lawyers, as part of society, shared many of its values, but their interests and methods of work got in the way of the reflection. Social values were therefore mediated through particular political and legal cultures.

---

[39] Weber, *Theory of Social and Economic Organization*, 351, 373–8.

Yet it was in this period that the noble fief and the feudal pyramid or feudal hierarchy of tenure that came to be considered the keystones of feudalism became established in anything like the form they are supposed to have had. They were the creation of the stronger, more centralized, more bureaucratic, and more effective government that developed after the twelfth century, and of the professional law that went with it, not of the age of customary law before it.

# 4

# GAUL AND THE KINGDOM OF THE FRANKS

## 4.1. *The Merovingian period*

By the time of the Merovingians, ideas and norms about property seem to have been fairly similar all over Gaul. Everywhere the basic form of landed property was what Levy called 'private ownership',[1] and there now seems no reason to suppose that the barbarian invaders of Gaul had recently been converted to this from more primitive and communal ideas. The traditional belief that Franks, Burgundians, and Visigoths progressed at different rates from 'Germanic' clan property towards absolute ownership according to their degree of Romanization rests on little but a priori and outworn theories of social evolution.[2] Roman forms and traditions survived better in the south than the north, but to judge from the law-codes the chief difference between the laws of property in different parts of Gaul, apart from differences in terminology and procedures of litigation, may have been in the rules of inheritance. In practice, even when those who had to resolve disputes were agreed about the appropriate code to follow and knew what it said, they may well have found that it did not cover their case. The varying drift of local custom, subject to all the pressures of power and influence, must have created many more haphazard variations, whether cases were decided by what people at the time may have called Roman law or whether they followed what historians call barbarian law.[3] None of these variations affects the fundamental ideas and norms about the landed property held by nobles and other free persons.

Landed property in sixth- and seventh-century Gaul seems to have been thought of primarily as belonging to free persons who had it by inheritance—that is, as coming to them, as the Franks put it, *de alode* (or *alodo*) *parentum*. Some, or even much, land held in this way may have originated from royal grants that had been forgotten, but it does not seem that people of the time believed that all property had started in this way and we have

[1] Levy, *West Roman Vulgar Law*, 87.
[2] Murray, *Germanic Kinship Structure*, 183–215 *et passim*.
[3] Ibid.; Wood, 'Disputes', 21.

75

no right to impose later myths of that sort on them. Normally a man's or woman's heir would be his or her children or, if there were no children, a varying sequence of close kin. Sometimes heirs seem to have agreed, at least for a while, to hold an estate jointly and divide the income, but the codes made provision for dividing inheritances, and rights were evidently thought of as belonging to individuals, or groups of individuals, rather than to kins as such.[4] Because prospective heirs sometimes felt aggrieved when lands that they had hoped to inherit were given to the church, and said so, and because churches preserved records of disputes about their property, surviving sources may give an impression that property was supposed to be, or had once been, more or less inalienable. That may be misleading. Whether or not the barbarians who invaded Gaul had any system for alienating land before they came under Roman influence, by the time we have evidence they were conveying it by straight sales as well as through dowries, adoptions, and testamentary bequests. There must always have been tension, however, between the rights of a landowner and those of his possible heirs, and this presumably grew as occasions for alienation multiplied. It is possible to think of social, economic, and political reasons why they should have multiplied during the Merovingian period, but those which appear most clearly in documentary records are the spread of Roman testamentary practices and the increasing number of gifts to the church. One formula for charters giving land to churches starts with the statement that Roman law and ancient custom allowed anyone to give property to a church but goes on to suggest that donors might say that they had bought what they gave from their kin with their own money (*rem proprietatis nostrae*,[5] *quem de parente nostro ... propria pecunia comparavimus*).[6] Alienations to ordinary lay people would presumably be even more vulnerable to claims from disappointed heirs, but some people may have argued, and argued successfully, that they could dispose more freely of what they had acquired for themselves than what they had inherited *de alode parentum*. How soon a normative rule about this came to be generally accepted is hard to say: rules under customary law are generally only a basis for negotiation anyway.[7] The fear of trouble from disappointed heirs probably explains why people who proposed to give or leave land away from

[4] *Leges Burg.* 52–4 (xiv); *Pactus Legis Sal.* 222–3 (clix–clx); *Lex Rib.* 101 (c. 50); *Formulae*, 20, 24, 50–1, 78–9, 83–4, 86–8 (And. 46, 55, Marculf, I. 12, II. 6, 12–14, 17); Murray, *Germanic Kinship Structure*, 183–215; James, *Origins of France*, 84–7.
[5] *Nostris* in printed text. [6] *Formulae*, 20 (And. 46).
[7] Moore, *Social Facts*, 38–40. A good many references to property that was acquired along with what was inherited come in gifts of both: *Formulae*, index *sub comparatum*; Geary, *Aristocracy*, 38–78. The purpose of mentioning both may have been simply to explain different titles.

their heirs, or who merely wanted to protect their widows and children from other kinsmen, sometimes got royal authority to carry out their testamentary intentions or at least announced them publicly.[8]

The same general rules seem to have applied both to large and small properties, however differently they may have worked in practice, provided that they belonged to people who were considered free enough to be able to appeal to some kind of public tribunal. The extensive estates which the nobleman Abbo (d. 739) left to his monastery of Novalesa were widely scattered and included many small properties that he seems to have been able to dispose of as freely as his greater estates. Some of Abbo's small holdings had peasant tenants as well as servants to work them, but since they were apparently independent of any larger units that might have imposed a quasi-manorial constraint on control of them, other small holdings belonging to humbler people may have been equally independent, at least in formal terms.[9] Abbo's wealth and power must have given him greater freedom than such people would have enjoyed, but it still seems that the characteristic property of both great and lesser free men was that which came to them *de alode parentum* and was heritable and alienable without permission of any superior. Free men with small holdings might be bullied by the powerful into surrendering their land, but until that happened their rights over it were supposed to be the same as the rights of the great.[10]

The most important stimulus towards new forms of property, involving new divisions of rights, seems to have come from the church. Before 584 Chilperic I complained that all the wealth of his fisc (that is, of his royal estates[11]) had passed to the church. According to Gregory of Tours's tendentious account, Chilperic used to trample on his father's charters and tear up his subjects' wills when they gave land to churches.[12] Any success he had in frustrating individual gifts was like sticking his finger in the dike. One estimate of church property by the mid eighth century puts it as high as a third of the cultivated land of Frankish Gaul.[13] Kings, nobles, and

[8] Paul Fouracre suggested to me that this is the explanation of *Formulae*, 50–1 (Marculf, I. 12–13), which Hallam, *View*, 158–9, 311–14, thought had created hereditary benefices.

[9] His will is in Geary, *Aristocracy*, 38–78.

[10] J. Balon's definition of 'allodium' as 'un grand domaine détenu . . . par l'aristocratie salique' (*Structure*, 465; *Fondements*, 50–72, 125) is unconvincing in view of texts like *Formulae*, 64–5, 77–8 (Marculf, I. 34, II. 6) and conveyances of small holdings without apparent reference to any superior; cf. Murray, *Germanic Kinship Structure*, 183 n.; Müller-Mertens, *Karl der Grosse*, 66–89.

[11] In order to avoid unnecessary technicalities, as well as confusion over the word 'fiscal', I shall generally use expressions like 'royal estates' or 'the king's own lands' rather than fisc (or the customary English term 'the royal demesne', on which see Reynolds, *Kingdoms and Communities*, 219–20).

[12] *Libri Hist.* 320 (VII. 46).

[13] Wallace-Hadrill, *Frankish Church*, 124–38; cf. Herlihy, 'Church Property', 86.

peasants, both rich and poor, gave land to the church in large estates and in small plots, they gave it for ever, and what they gave was supposed by church law, as well as by some of the donors' explicit desires, to be inalienable. In practice that could not always be maintained. There were many complications. To start with, it was not at all clear who was supposed to control and manage the property given to God and his saints. The extent of a bishop's right over monasteries and other churches in his diocese was at first genuinely uncertain. It was not just because of wicked and worldly bishops that lands claimed by monasteries passed out of their control and sometimes into the hands of the bishop's friends and relatives. It was not just because of wicked or negligent kings that land claimed by churches passed into the hands of lay nobles. As ecclesiastical property grew, churches had a genuine need to delegate the management of remote estates to people on the spot who seemed to have the power and influence to protect them. Much thereby slid into the hands of lay nobles in return for small rents that were supposed, so long as they were paid, to symbolize a recognition of the church's rights. As generations succeeded each other the tenants' right inevitably tended to become more entrenched.[14] A church sometimes allowed the tenants of land over which it had superior rights to pass it on to their children or even alienate their rights in it.[15] One answer to the problem posed by distant estates was to exchange them for more convenient ones, since the rules against the alienation of ecclesiastical property did not apply to exchanges. Worthwhile exchanges depended, however, on still having some worthwhile rights to bargain with. Besides, distant estates could still have their uses, while land near by could also be vulnerable to looming pseudo-protectors.

Another answer to both kinds of threat was for churches to make an explicitly short-term grant by way of what became known as *beneficia* or *precaria*—that is, grants made as a favour, supposedly in answer to the prayer of the beneficiary.[16] These were meant not to entail any diminution to the church's rights. Some of the early *precaria* were made to local clergy and were revocable by the bishop or abbot at will, but as they were extended to laymen, and in particular to laymen for whom the king had interceded, they developed a more contractual character.[17] Though the grantee was still forbidden to alienate he tended to gain in security of tenure during the term of his grant and, as life-grants became more

---

[14] Lesne, *Propriété ecclés.* i. 445–50.

[15] *Formulae*, 5 (And. c. 1); Wallace-Hadrill, *Frankish Church*, 138.

[16] Lesne, 'Diverses Acceptions'. The sources have various forms of the word *precaria*. For convenience and consistency I have taken the singular as *precarium*.

[17] Lesne, *Propriété ecclés.* i. 314–32, 450–2.

common, so, willy-nilly, did the usual drift towards inheritance. Some *precaria*-holders owed mere token rents, some owed larger sums, but the entrenching of tenant rights is suggested by the way that default of payment sometimes incurred a penalty rather than outright forfeiture. Although historians, influenced no doubt both by the claims made in ecclesiastical sources and by the traditionally simplistic notion of unitary 'ownership', have tended to see the church's loss of control over precarial lands as a loss of full and unambiguous property rights to unjust usurpers, the position cannot have been as black and white as this suggests. That is not to maintain that churches were never unjustly bullied or cheated out of their rights. It is rather that property rights are rights which are recognized and protected by the law of the relevant society. Although the rights which tenants of churches exercised over their lands did not amount to what clerical scribes called *jus proprietatis*, they were likely to be protected, and not merely because laymen stuck together in secular courts. In the conditions of customary law (including what contemporaries called Roman law), any free person in early medieval Gaul who had occupied—and, better still, whose father or mother had also occupied—land as long as the neighbours could remember, would surely have had at least some claim to be protected in his tenure of it. Any free person who had accepted land as a tenant, and who remained a loyal and dutiful tenant, had some claim to pass on his holding to his children. Irrespective of the terminology of the time, therefore, however vaguely rights may have been categorized, and however little the church liked the situation, the rights of property in *precaria* and benefices were in legal practice divided. This is clear, for instance, in what may have been one of the earliest and most common forms of *precarium*: that in which someone who gave land to a church received it, or part of it, back for his or her lifetime, possibly with some other property.[18] In such a case the church's right to what it had been granted, or to income from it beyond any agreed rent, was thus deferred and the donor's right was correspondingly preserved. In theory the gift was only postponed. It remained a full gift and ideas about the property rights of churches did not need to be revised. In practice things might turn out otherwise: prevailing ideas of prescription and inheritance made it difficult not to concede some kind of validity to claims that tenants based on long occupation, even when they had no documentary title and the original grant had been intended to be short. Early medieval societies recognized security of tenure and inheritance as right just as they recognized the protection of the church's property as right. There was thus right of a kind on both sides: property rights were divided.

[18] e.g. *Benedicti Regula*, 139 (59. 5).

Even if the church had not had to surrender some of its rights over some of its property to lay tenants those rights would not have been absolute. Prohibition of alienation is in itself a derogation from absolute rights. Apart from that, the church does not seem to have been absolutely free of all duties in respect of its property. Chlothar I had to give up his attempt to tax the income of all the churches in the kingdom—which would presumably have amounted to some kind of tax on its property—but Gregory of Tours's horror at this and other attempts to raise taxes suggests that churches may not have been quite secure in their freedom from all taxation.[19] Grants of immunities from dues and services at first applied only to the existing properties of the beneficiary and needed to be extended each time more was acquired. This was remedied by Chlothar II, but immunity still may not have meant that all tenants and dependants of the church were automatically exempt from all military service and judicial dues.[20] Grants of exemption of *ingenui* and *serviles* on church property from the penalty for failure to do service (*herebannum*) suggest that the freedom of tenants of church property from some military obligation, however irregularly imposed, could not be entirely taken for granted.[21] Whether, however, it lay on them as individuals or on the land they occupied seems impossible to tell: very probably the distinction was not clearly made at the time. The idea that churches owed no military service (whether expressly in respect of their property or not) at this time may be influenced by the scarcity of information about Merovingian military obligations in general as well as by the complaints evoked by Carolingian demands.[22]

Lay owners suffered some of the same restrictions on their property rights as churches and some that were different: they were in principle more free to dispose of their property but had to take account of the claims of their potential heirs. The most obvious limitation on all property, apart from any imposed by division of rights with peasants or others who had subordinate holdings, was that it was subject to confiscation by the king. The penalty of forfeiture for disloyalty (*si quis homo regi infidelis exstiterit*) was first stated in a surviving code in the seventh century but it was being applied, apparently according to more or less recognized legal forms, long before. It does not seem to have made any difference officially whether the supposed traitor's land was held by royal grant or by inheritance. Even church land could be lost if a bishop got into trouble.[23] The obligations owed by laymen in respect

---

[19] Gregory of Tours, *Libri Hist.* 136 (IV. 2).
[20] Goffart, 'Old and New in Merovingian Taxation'; Lesne, *Propriété ecclés.* i. 260–7.
[21] *Dip. Regum Merow*, nos. 28, 95; Lesne, *Propriété ecclés.* ii (2), 472, 494.
[22] e.g. Lesne, *Propriété ecclés.* ii. 456.
[23] Fustel de Coulanges, *Les Origines*, 51–4, 60–2; *Dip. Regum Merow.*, no. 8; *Lex Rib.* 101 (c. 50); cf. Geary, *Aristocracy*, 86, 141–2.

of their property are obscure. Franks prided themselves on not paying the kind of land-taxes they regarded as a mark of unfreedom, but military service, attendance at assemblies, and payment of associated dues seem to have been recognized as some kind of general obligations. People may have accepted and fulfilled them—so far as they did—in their capacity as free men rather than as property-holders, but the reality seems more complex than that implies.[24] The obligations of peasants with subordinate holdings were certainly attached to the land they occupied, so that, when they owed them to the king rather than to the landowner, the landowner might suffer both from the service and from any penalties for its non-performance: hence many of the immunities that churches secured. As in many societies of customary law, these uncertainties and anomalies seem not to have been confronted at the time. They were certainly not resolved. Presumably if anyone refused to do military service in a noticeably contumacious way he would be liable to forfeiture for disloyalty, but it is impossible to say that the obligations lay on property as such or that property-holding involved, or did not involve, an implied contract. Either to deduce that it did or to assume that it did not would be to impose our concerns and conceptualizations on sources which do not raise the issue. One other restriction on property rights should be mentioned, however vestigial it was in practice. The presence on estates of peasants with customary rights in their holdings and customary limitations on their dues and services must sometimes have constituted some kind of drag on free exploitation by the owners. Peasants were, of course, essential to the running of the estates and thus to the enjoyment of the benefits of property, but any talk of the supposedly full and untrammelled rights of alods should take them into account.

It has often been said that the Merovingians regarded the kingdom as their property or 'personal possession', sometimes with the implication that they did so because they were too primitive to distinguish government from property, or public rights from private rights, and that the way that the kingdom was repeatedly carved up between them is evidence of this. Sometimes these assertions go with references to Merovingian 'absolutism'.[25] As I argued in chapters 2.2 and 3.2, all this rests on nonsensical assumptions. Later it became accepted that each kingdom normally had only one king, but that need not mean that there was anything more 'primitive' about divided kingdoms. Territorial division is one way of dividing power between rivals and one that is far from uncommon in modern life.

[24] Reuter, 'End of Carolingian Expansion', 397–8; Goffart, 'Old and New in Merovingian Taxation'; Gregory of Tours, *Libri Hist.* 232, 364 (V. 26, VII. 42); Fustel de Coulanges, *Monarchie franque*, 288–303.
[25] Fustel de Coulanges, *Monarchie franque*, 38–40, 122–5; Lavisse, *Hist. de France*, ii (1), 171; Pirenne, *Mohammed and Charlemagne*, 57–8.

As for absolutism, some Merovingian kings, like many other rulers since Ahab and Jezebel (and before), abused their power and seized their subjects' property unjustly on occasion, but the ideas and rules of the time distinguished their own estates (the royal fisc) from the rest of the kingdom. There were rules, whether or not they were always kept, that governed such matters as the confiscation of property and—though these are less clear—taxation and military service.

The kings had officials at the centre, most notably a mayor of the palace (who looks rather like a chief of staff), and counts to look after different areas of the kingdom. Parts of the royal lands seem to have been attached to particular offices and held by the office-holders.[26] Much land that ended up as the hereditary property of counts no doubt started—perhaps in late Roman times—as the official endowment of their counties, but not all such endowments were 'alodialized' by this kind of slow embezzlement. In 688 Theuderic III gave the abbey of Saint Denis an estate which had reverted to the king after being held by three successive mayors of the palace.[27] The Merovingian kings must also have had bodyguards, courtiers, and other miscellaneous servants. They, or some of them, may have been generally known as *antrustiones*, the members of the king's *trustis*, both of which are words of Germanic origin. Another Germanic word, *leudes*, has sometimes been associated by historians with these royal servants or followers but probably applied to a wider category, maybe including all the king's subjects. There has been much argument about the words and about the way that the groups they denote may have been related both to the war-bands of earlier Germanic kings and to the Carolingian *vassi* whose appearance is traditionally taken as signalling the beginning of true feudo-vassalic institutions.[28] The argument is complicated by the scarcity of references to *antrustiones*, *leudes*, and so on, and by the tendency of historians to want to identify words with phenomena, identify each word with a distinct relationship, and then use the result to trace a continuous line of development from barbarian war-bands to the vassals of the later law of fiefs. The best information about *antrustiones* comes from the form of an oath prescribed for them. Someone who became a royal *antrustio* was expected to come to the palace, in arms, and take an oath of *trustis* and fidelity 'in the king's hand' (*in manu nostra*). He then had a higher value (wergeld) put on his life.[29] Whatever ritual this implies it looks as though the relation it created

[26] Gregory of Tours, *Libri Hist.* 196, 198, 340, 390 (V. 3, VII. 22, VIII. 22); Irsigler, *Untersuchung*, 136, 223–4.
[27] *Chartae Latinae*, xiii, no. 570; Claude, 'Untersuchungen', 15–17, 56–70; Bergengruen, *Adel und Grundherrschaft*, 174–7.
[28] Kienast, *Fränkische Vasallität*, 3–73, surveys it and cites many of the sources.
[29] *Formulae*, 55 (Marculf, I. 18).

was sufficiently close and interpersonal to suggest that only some of the king's servants enjoyed it. There were probably degrees of commitment and status within the royal service which it would be rash to connect with particular words that happen to be recorded. The rite of initiation of *antrustiones* may have been called a commendation, though, for what it is worth, neither the word *commendatio* nor *commendare* is used in this particular text. Elsewhere in the formulary and in other texts of the time they are used in connection with the inauguration of relations of protection and service, quite often combined with *in manus*. Commendation must, however, have involved widely different kinds of relations. An abbot who commended himself, his monastery, and its lands into the king's hands and was taken into the king's protection (*in nostro mundeburdo* or *in mundeburdem vel defensionem nostram*) was clearly in a different relation and had different rights and obligations from a poor man who commended himself into the power and protection (*in vestrum mundoburdum*) of another because he could not support himself.[30] Just what significance *in manus* bears must also be doubtful: we cannot assume that it always denoted a physical act. It may have been used figuratively then as it certainly was in other periods. If it did denote a physical act it may not always have been the same act— hands can be used in many ways—nor need the acts have always borne the same significance to contemporaries.[31] It would also be not merely rash but wrong to conclude that only close, interpersonal relations were symbolized by oaths or were politically significant. Counts were supposed to make all their *pagenses*, which presumably means all the free men of their counties, promise and swear fidelity and *leudesamio* (which presumably meant some kind of loyalty or fidelity) to the king.[32]

It may well be that kings made grants of land to some of their followers (whether called *antrustiones* or anything else) on limited terms, apart from what was held by palace officials and counts ex officio. If they did so, perhaps they gave it revocably or for life and perhaps the grantee would then owe more service than he did already, but evidence of all these possibilities seems to be lacking.[33] So does the evidence for similar grants by great nobles to people above peasant status, though they must have had

[30] *Dip. Karol.* i, nos. 2, 72 (752, 772: both, I admit, slightly late for the Merovingians); *Formulae*, 158 (Tours, 43).
[31] Kienast, *Fränkische Vasallität*, 3–11, 45–8, 74, gives references for other commendations, drawing rather different conclusions from mine.
[32] *Formulae*, 68 (Marculf, I. 40): the formulary has *paginses*. On *leudesamio*, e.g. Kienast, *Fränkische Vasallität*, 45–8.
[33] Brunner's suggestion that royal grants might convey restricted rights (*Deutsche Rechtsgeschichte*, i. 294, 308) seems to derive from the use of the word *beneficium* and a desire to trace early origins of 'feudal tenure'. It seems not to have been pursued recently, though see chapter 9.4 for similar arguments about tenth- and eleventh-century German grants.

followers and clients, while it might be supposed that some of their estates were big enough to have given scope for this sort of delegation and patronage. Abbo's will suggests that those whom he mentioned as holding property from him *in benefitio* were at best semi-free, enjoyed their holdings by his favour, and—in his view—had no rights against him or his heirs.[34] The reason Abbo mentioned them was that he was asking the monks of Novalesa to continue his benevolence to them: it is possible that his larger estates had tenants who did not need to be mentioned because their higher status protected them better, but this seems rather unlikely. Abbo's contemporary Count Eberhard also had tenants holding by his favour (*per beneficium nostrum*). He described one of them as his *servus* while others whom he had favoured or benefited were his *vassi* (*quod . . . ad vassos nostros beneficiatum habui*).[35] The word *vassus* occurs in the early sixth-century version of the Salic laws, where it seems to denote a servant of the kind who might today be called a blue-collar worker.[36] Other references, including that in Eberhard's charter, indicate the nature of the service and status of *vassi* less clearly.[37] Perhaps the word could be used for servants or subordinates of various sorts. It may not have had any particular connotations of social or legal status.

It may be that partible inheritance, by constantly splitting noble estates, and gifts to the church, by reducing their total extent, deprived their owners of much need or opportunity to make restricted grants to people above peasant status. At all events the only estates from which we know that nobles and other undeniably free persons held significant amounts of land were those of churches and kings. The social stratification which undoubtedly existed above the level of peasants was not generally reflected in a hierarchy of property rights.

## 4.2. *The Carolingians:* vassi *and benefices*

The Carolingian age is traditionally seen as marking a decisive stage in the development of feudo-vassalic relations. I shall not try to deny that the forms of noble property characteristic of the later middle ages owed a good deal to the Carolingians, but political and social conditions were so different in the ninth century from what obtained in the thirteenth that it seems to me important not to approach ninth-century relations as if they formed some kind of prototype for those of 'classic feudalism'. Rather than using

[34] Geary, *Aristocracy*, 60–8; cf. Lesne, 'Diverses Acceptions'; James, *The Franks*, 219; Wallace-Hadrill, *Long-Haired Kings*, 6–7.

[35] *Regesta Alsatiae*, i, no. 127.     [36] *Pactus Legis Salicae*, 132 (35. 9).

[37] *Leges Alamannorum*, i. 38 (36. 3), ii. 59 (74). For the history of the word: Hollyman, *Développement*, 114–22; Kienast, *Fränkische Vasallität*, 89–93.

later information to fill in the gaps in the evidence, we need to try to dismiss our knowledge of it. It may also be useful to try to separate the information about eighth- and ninth-century changes in property rights and
political loyalties from each other and from wider social change, and to
avoid such ingenious explanations of the whole complex of change as the
introduction of the stirrup.[38] It is always fun for historians to find reasons
for what they have already labelled as supposedly epoch-making developments, but the reasoning is more convincing after one has established what
it is one is explaining. It may, finally, also be useful to suspend judgement
about new ideas as the motor of change, whether they concerned property,
patronage, or social relations. The Carolingian 'vassal benefice', with its
special obligation to military service, was the result of political compromises worked out, as political compromises always are, within the context
of existing custom and values. One compromise was that between the
wealth and privileges of the church and the needs of a new dynasty of
highly ambitious rulers. Another was between the church and all the various people, including bishops as well as laymen, who claimed various kinds
of rights over its property. Both compromises paid regard to current ideas
about the rights of property, but both—like so many compromises—at the
same time created problems that would in time, and in changed political
circumstances, stimulate new arguments and the drawing of new distinctions. There is nothing very original about this argument but it still needs
to be stated here.

The word *vassi*, or sometimes *vassalli*, which was mentioned at the end
of the last section, becomes much more common from the late eighth century, when it seems to have come to be used of the laymen who served
kings and lords both in their armies and for all kinds of general purposes
of defence and government. On his way back from Spain in 778
Charlemagne appointed not only Frankish counts and abbots in all of
Aquitaine but also Frankish *vassi*, 'as they are called' (*necnon alios plurimos
quos vassos vulgo vocant, ex gente Francorum*).[39] This was partly just a
change of terminology: kings and lords had had servants of this kind
before, even if they had not generally been called *vassi*. But it was more
than that. Whatever word was used, it needed to be used a lot because
Charles Martel and the next few generations of his descendants were
clearly good at getting followers and using them. Carolingian *vassi* needed
to be mentioned more often than royal soldiers and administrators had
been before.

It seems very likely that becoming the *vassus*, first of the mayor of the

---

[38] Bullough, 'Europae Pater', 84–90.    [39] *Vita Hludowici imperatoris*, 608.

palace and then of the king or emperor, involved taking an oath, probably with some further ceremony of subjection and commitment such as kneeling and touching hands in some way. Oddly enough, however, the formularies we have do not include anything about it; some of the references to ceremonies that look like what we expect do not explicitly mention *vassi*; and those that do look like special cases. One of these is that of duke Tassilo of Bavaria. In 757 he came, along with the great men of Bavaria, to King Pippin, who was also his uncle, and commended himself in vassalage (*in vasatico, in vassaticum*), in the Frankish manner, by his own hands into the hands of the king, and swore fidelity to Pippin and his sons as a *vassus* ought to do to his lords. In one account this involved innumerable oaths on holy relics, in the other the particular relics are specified to emphasize their holiness.[40] Tassilo's case was very special indeed. His duchy had once been independent but, having been forced into subjection to Pippin, he had rebelled and was now being humbled. The ceremony he performed cannot be taken as paradigmatic for ordinary vassals and he may have been called a *vassus* only on this one occasion in order to stress his humiliation.[41] The only other case where people of high rank were called anything like *vassi* or *vassi dominici* in surviving sources seems to be when a chronicler made Louis the Pious tell his rebellious sons to remember that they were his *vasalli* and affirm their faith to him by oath—which looks as if a similar point was being made as was made about Tassilo.[42] Louis probably saw his sons as mere boys, as Pippin had probably seen his nephew.

Counts and other, grander royal servants must also have taken oaths and may well have gone through a rite like Tassilo's, though with fewer oaths and maybe less ostentatious abasement.[43] They do not, however, seem to have been called *vassi* or *vassalli* and there seems to be no reason to suppose that the rites of their appointment were copied from an already established rite that was peculiar to *vassi* and had been given special force because of the close interpersonal bond it symbolized. The rite undergone by all or any royal servants may have been like that of the earlier *antrustiones* but the relation it symbolized cannot have been the same when or if it was generally extended to *vassi*: members of a bodyguard have a

[40] *Annales Regni Francorum*, 14–15. Odegaard, *Vassi and Fideles*, 24–32, points to the rarity of the expression *in vassaticum/in vasatico*.

[41] As implied e.g. by Ganshof, 'L'Origine', 37–8, and Kienast, *Fränkische Vasallität*, 112–17, 556.

[42] *Ex Vita Walae*, 563; Odegaard, *Vassi and Fideles*, 32–3, 43–6, whom I find convincing on *vassi*. Kienast, one of the few later writers on the subject to discuss Odegaard's arguments, seems to have been less convinced: *Fränkische Vasallität*, 126–8.

[43] Some of those who took the oath at Quierzy in 858 (*Capit.* no. 269) may have been ordinary *vassi*, though most were probably more important, but the circumstances made it another special case: it was not a rite of appointment. See also Odegaard, 'Carolingian Oaths', 292–5.

closer, more personal relation to the person they guard than government employees who, even if they see and touch the king on their first appointment, may see him seldom thereafter. Counts, as counts, apart from any initiation ceremony and whatever the words of their oaths, had closer relations with the king and greater obligations to loyalty and service than mere *vassi*. Given the vast extent of Charlemagne's empire and the large number of *vassi* who seem to have been scattered over it, it is at least arguable that some or most of them may have been appointed by counts or royal *missi* and made their ritual commitment to them as representatives of the king or emperor. How exclusive their commitment was is not absolutely clear. Some had their own land and their own preoccupations. Many must have felt closer to their count than to the king, just as soldiers do to the officers of their own regiments. How far being a royal *vassus* inhibited one's relation with other lords, apart from the count, is unclear. Anything like the same sort of commendation and commitment to two lords, especially if one of them was the king, may well have been thought improper. In 805, on the other hand, it was ordered that no one was to take an oath of fidelity to anyone but the emperor and one other lord (*unicuique proprio seniori*).[44] When plans were made in 806 for dividing the empire rules were made about the rights of any free man to seek a new lord after the death of his first lord, which have been taken to show that only one lord at a time was allowed. The lords in these rules, however, were kings, and relations between them were delicate.[45] Some of the ideas of an originally exclusive commitment that later became diluted and deformed by the rise of 'multiple vassalage' seem to derive from old and romantic ideas about the loyalties of the Germanic war-band and the reasons for the fall of the Carolingian empire. They are not well substantiated by taking items of Carolingian legislation like that of 806 as if they were statements of accepted and permanent norms about the relations between all lords and their followers rather than attempts to deal with particular political situations.[46]

This account may play down too much the importance of ceremony and tradition in cementing the relation of *vassi* to the king. It does so deliberately in an effort to adjust the balance: it is important to note how slight the evidence from the eighth and ninth centuries is and how much the older standard accounts rely on setting it in a framework of ideas about feudo-vassalic institutions that are derived from much later evidence. The tendency is to stress ceremonies and the norms and values they are

---

[44] *Capit.* no. 44 c. 9.                  [45] *Capit.* no. 45 c. 7–10; cf. no. 136 c. 9.
[46] e.g. Ganshof, 'Les Liens', 159; Stutz, *Herrenfall*, 68, on a different aspect of the 806 *divisio*.

supposed to have implied rather than the practicalities, the day-to-day functions, of the Carolingian *vassi* as royal servants. Brunner's account, which probably lies behind many later ones, including accounts written by those who have not read his, consists largely of statements of general principle about the apparently general conditions and values of Carolingian 'vassalage' that rely on a slim selection of evidence, some of it consisting of items of legislation that are very unlikely to have reflected general norms.[47] Another general tendency is to talk about all 'vassals' as if the relations of all lords with their followers were much the same. Though other great men naturally had servants, clients, and followers, and some of these were quite often called *vassi* or *vassalli*, most of the evidence we have relates to royal *vassi*. Royal *vassi* fulfilled different functions from others and the relations of the king or emperor with his servants were rather different from those of other lords with theirs. Apart from anything else, the emperor legislated about the relation of other lords with their *vassalli*, setting out the offences on each side that would justify the other party ending it.[48]

Neither the Carolingian kingdom nor the empire in which it became subsumed was created or held together merely by direct interpersonal bonds.[49] Part of the job of counts, *vassi*, and all other royal servants was to secure the loyalty and obedience of everyone else. Most people who are called the king's *fideles* in surviving sources were naturally relatively important: they generally got into the sources because they were in royal service or at least in contact with the king. But all the king's subjects were supposed to be faithful to him: *infideles* were traitors to the king and kingdom who were punishable. There is no evidence of a neutral group between them and the king's *fideles*.[50] It may be that general oaths of fidelity to the king were discontinued from some time before 789, but there is no real evidence of this beyond the excuse made by traitors in 786 that they had never taken them.[51] From 789, at any rate, all males over twelve years old were supposed to take oaths of fidelity to the king or, later, the emperor. In 802 the oath was to be faithful to the emperor as a man ought to be to his lord (*sicut per drictum debet esse homo domino suo*). The word *dominus* was so widely and variably used that this may not imply (though it is not impossible that it did) that the oath was based on oaths taken to other lords and alluded to the kind of obligation a man might feel to his

---

[47] Brunner, *Deutsche Rechtsgeschichte*, ii. 349–68.

[48] *Capit.* nos. 77 c. 16 (though not expressly mentioning *vassi* or *vassalli*), 104 c. 8.

[49] Nelson, 'Kingship and Empire', 225–34 *et passim*.

[50] Though in other contexts degrees of fidelity could of course be envisaged: *Trad. Freising*, no. 193*b*.

[51] Odegaard, 'Carolingian Oaths', 284 n. I do not find convincing the connection in Poly and Bournazel, *Mutation féodale*, 114–15, with the quashing of unlawful oaths.

local and immediate lord. The wording of the rest of the oath, apart from this phrase, reflected the rather more restricted duties that subjects owed to a king as distinct from those that servants owed to their masters. Oaths to kings, even if they had not always been taken regularly, had been taken long before 802 and their form may already have been traditional.[52] In 854 all Franks in Charles the Bald's kingdom were to swear to be as faithful to Charles as they knew how, as a Frankish man by right ought to be to his king.[53] To judge from the later use of such phrases in England and Italy, oaths of this kind became embedded in a widely diffused tradition.[54] Whatever the origin or implication of their wording, oaths of fidelity that were taken so generally cannot have created a 'personal bond between the subject and the king' or have been meant to do so.[55] In 873 Charles the Bald required immigrants to take an oath of fidelity if they were to have *proprietas* in his kingdom. Earlier on some immigrants had commended themselves to the king—which may have come to much the same thing— before getting confirmation of the lands they had held.[56] What bound subjects to the king was the fact that he was king: that was why they were supposed to be faithful and obedient to him. What first bound both great men and *vassi* to the Carolingians, on the other hand, even before Pippin became king, was surely not so much any particular ceremony or oath but their military success and their generosity. When they secured the power and authority first of kingship and then of empire they seem to have managed to combine their reputation for generosity—sustained and reliable generosity—with a reputation for reasonably just as well as successful government.

Success and generosity needed resources. Just which king or mayor of the palace first used the model of precarial holdings to draw a balance between his own need of men and money and the church's right to its lands, whether he used the model consciously and deliberately, and whether he and his successors are to be seen rather as spoliators of the church or as its reformers and protectors—all these questions are of secondary importance in the context of this book.[57] No ruler who wanted to tap the resources of the Frankish kingdom effectively could afford to ignore the enormous wealth of the church. The system of *precaria* offered

---

[52] *Capit.* no. 34; Odegaard, 'Carolingian Oaths' surveys the arguments and evidence, though his arguments are apparently rejected by Poly and Bournazel, *Mutation féodale*, 115.

[53] *Capit.* no. 261.

[54] See chapters 6.9 and 8.2. Cf. the similes in the Strasbourg oaths: Nithard, *Histoire*, 104, 106.

[55] Ganshof, 'Charlemagne et le serment'.

[56] *Capit.* nos. 25, 33–4, 278 c. 5; *Dip. Karol.* i, no. 179 (and see below).

[57] Though see e.g. Lesne, *Propriété ecclés.* i. 450, ii (1), esp. 270–88, ii (2); Goffart, *Le Mans Forgeries*, 7–11; Wallace-Hadrill, *Frankish Church*, 131–42.

a useful method by which pious kings could make use of supposedly surplus church lands to support soldiers, subject both to the payment of an agreed rent to the church concerned and to the preservation of its title. According to the system which becomes discernible from the 740s the lands of each great church were divided into two, so that part was left at its own disposition. Poorer churches were supposed to be exempt and if a church on whose lands the government created *precaria* for defence purposes subsequently fell into poverty the arrangement was supposed to be terminated.[58] In 779 the standard payments made to a church by anyone occupying its land in this way by the king's command (*de verbo regis*) were—probably—raised; a requirement for grants to be recorded in writing was imposed; and the government promised that the distinction between *precaria verbo regis* and those made by churches *spontanea voluntate* should be preserved.[59] One distinction, incidentally, which was not made was between *precaria* (or *precariae*) and benefices: both words were used to describe both the holdings and the various terms on which they were held.[60] From the king's point of view the object of the system was presumably to provide a livelihood for his *vassi* and to scatter them round the country to support the counts and, in newly conquered territories, to act as occupying forces.

The system set out in all this legislation, like many other schemes that look good at the time, needed a great deal of record-keeping, a great deal of honesty, sympathetic appreciation of the situation and motives that had provoked it, and willingness on the part of everyone to keep it going after the situation had changed.[61] Not surprisingly, all these were not forthcoming. Even if they had been, misunderstandings were bound to arise from the fudging of property rights that was inherent from the start. Although benefices granted by the king officially remained the church's property (*res ecclesiarum*), property rights over them, looked at analytically, were divided *de jure* as well as *de facto*. It was not just that benefices owed services to the king as well as payments to the church to which they officially belonged, but that the king chose the tenants and fixed the terms of the whole transaction. Every benefice of this sort was in some sense a royal benefice: it was a benefit granted by the king's favour. There were, moreover, plenty of ways in which it could get absorbed into royal property.[62] At least some surveys of royal estates included such benefices, while some

[58] *Capit.* no. 11 c. 2.   [59] *Capit.* no. 20 c. 13; Constable, 'Nona et Decima'.
[60] *Capit.* nos. 20 c. 13 (forma Langobardica), 81; Lesne, *Propriété ecclés.* ii (2), 363 n.; Lesne, 'Diverses Acceptions'.
[61] On record-keeping see Martindale, 'Kingdom of Aquitaine', 169–70.
[62] Hincmar, *De Villa Novilliaco*, 1168; *Rec. Charles le Chauve*, no. 427; Lesne, *Propriété ecclés.* ii (2), 185–97.

monastic surveys omitted them.[63] No matter how it was all wrapped up, benefices *verbo regis* were removed from the property of the church and attached to that of the kingdom (*de jure aecclesiae . . . subtracta atque ad publicum nostrum* [i.e. *regis*] *redacta*): in modern terms one could say that they were, at least temporarily, nationalized.[64] When property came to the king, even by mistake, he might treat his own title as lawful. Only he, by his favour, could reverse the error.[65] Furthermore, although a ninth-century keeper of records at Le Mans cathedral tried very hard to prove otherwise, the system set up by Charlemagne and his predecessors did not provide for automatic reversion of church property on the death of the tenant.[66] Restitution involved a royal decision and did not generally involve expropriating the holder of a benefice.[67] Even Charlemagne himself, however, as the terms on which benefices *verbo regis* were granted suggest, may have preferred to avoid direct showdowns with the clergy. During the ninth century ecclesiastical lobbying and ecclesiastical records (whether genuine or falsified) ensured that a fair amount of land was restored, though increasingly at the initiative of the benefice-holder or a local magnate, with only a more or less formal approval from the king.[68]

Meanwhile churches continued to grant land as *precaria* or *in beneficium* (or *per beneficium*, *pro beneficio*, etc.) on their own account. Many of these grants were made to people of very low status who would have few or no rights in the property against their lords. They are not really relevant here, but they need to be remembered as constituting part of contemporary ideas about what a *precarium* or benefice was.[69] Other holders of benefices or *precaria* were the sort of *homines militares* to whom even Archbishop Hincmar conceded a prima-facie right to leave their benefices to their sons, provided they served and defended the church both generally and in the king's service—and especially if they were nephews of the archbishop.[70] Some of the benefices that churches created on their own initiative were intended, as this suggests, to help provide the military service that was owed to the king from church estates. Whatever the position under the Merovingians there is no doubt that under the Carolingians churches normally owed such

[63] *Capit.* no. 80 c. 5–7; *Polyptyque de Saint-Bertin*, 13 (interpreted by Lesne, 'Diverses Acceptions', 14–24); Lesne, 'Les Bénéficiers', 214–16; Verhein, 'Studien II', 376–88.

[64] *Gesta Aldrici*, 31, which appears to be genuine: Goffart, *Le Mans Forgeries*, 281–3.

[65] *Rec. Charles le Chauve*, no. 427 (p. 455).

[66] Goffart, *Le Mans Forgeries*, esp. 9–10, 231–4.

[67] Lesne, *Propriété ecclés.* ii (2), 244–54, 369–75; Nelson, 'Charles the Bald and the Church'; though see *Formulae*, 322 (Form. Imp. 46).

[68] Ganshof, 'Benefice and Vassalage', 161; Lesne, *Propriété ecclés.* ii (2), 320–81; Goffart, *Le Mans Forgeries*, 286; Wallace-Hadrill, *Frankish Church*, 270–4.

[69] Lesne, 'Diverses Acceptions' and 'Les Bénéficiers'; Dubled, 'Notion de propriété'.

[70] Hincmar, *Pro Ecclesiae Defensione*, col. 1050.

service from their own lands, apart from those taken over by the king, and
that they owed various traditional payments which were probably more
regularly taken than they had been earlier, as well as emergency taxes for
defence against the Danes. There seems to be little doubt either that,
although the relation between the size of an estate and what it owed may
not have been regularly computed or enforced, each church's obligations
were at least roughly connected with the extent of its property.[71]

The Carolingians also granted benefices, presumably for the same purposes and on much the same terms, from their own estates, but the evidence of this, as of similar benefices granted by other secular lords, is less
good than it is for those on ecclesiastical land. More work on the sources
about this is needed and it will need to be critical and rigorous. It is no use
assuming that all references to *beneficia* or land held *de beneficio regis* et
cetera concern what can usefully be described as fiefs or what Ganshof
called 'des tenures vassaliques' (translated as 'tenures in vassalage' or 'vassal benefices').[72] Ganshof defined benefices as holdings for life that were
intended to provide maintenance for the tenant, who owed service to his
lord but no money rent,[73] but he saw their character from the eighth century as determined by the 'union of benefice and vassalage'. Some problems of this concept have been discussed in chapter 2. What it meant in the
context of Carolingian history, according to Ganshof, was that from the
eighth century the holding of a benefice normally came to involve becoming a *vassus* of the grantor through commendation to him, so that the terms
on which benefices were held changed during the period to accommodate
or incorporate the obligations and ethos of 'vassalage'.[74] Furthermore,
Ganshof maintained, from 744 the Carolingians made their grants *in beneficium* rather than *in proprietatem*:[75] 'vassal benefices', he thus seems to suggest, had become accepted as a normal and acceptable form of landholding,
if not as the predominant form. Although parts of this argument have been
undermined, the references other historians make to vassals and their

[71] *Capit.* nos. 73 c. 5, 75, 77 c. 9, 280; *Notitia de Servitio*; Verhein, 'Studien II', 378; Lesne,
*Propriété ecclés.* ii (2), 387–503; Lot, 'Les Tributs'; Nelson, *Charles the Bald*, 29–30, 213, 250.
[72] Ganshof, 'Charlemagne et les institutions', 390 (= *Frankish Institutions*, 52) and 'Benefice
and Vassalage', 159.
[73] Ganshof, 'Note sur les origines', 174, and *Frankish Institutions*, 51, citing *Capit.* no. 132,
which refers to services customarily due from benefices without specifying them or mentioning
rent either way; in 'Les Liens', 156, he says that 'le cens qu'il devait payer au maître de la terre,
était minime', though here he is by implication talking about quasi-precarial benefices before
their 'union' with vassalage.
[74] e.g. Ganshof, 'Note sur les origines', 182–3, 187; 'Benefice and Vassalage', 163–5, 170;
*Feudalism*, 40–3. Most of my references to Ganshof's discussions of benefices will be to 'Note sur
les origines' and 'Benefice and Vassalage', which seem to contain the essence of the arguments
which he repeated in *Feudalism* and later articles with references to many of the same sources.
[75] 'Les Liens', 155; 'Note sur les origines', 175 n.; though see 'Note sur la concession'.

benefices, vassalic tenure, *Lehen*, and so on, sometimes accompanied by references to Ganshof and earlier scholars, suggest that the general outline of the interpretation is often accepted even when it is not explicitly stated.[76] The use of such words implies that the characteristic eighth- and ninth-century benefice is taken to be one that was held by someone bound to the grantor by close and personal obligations of service and that this bond of 'vassalage' was the determinant characteristic of the rights and obligations attached to such properties. This may not always be what is intended, but it is important to confront the possible implications in order to disentangle the evidence about benefices and property rights in general from that about relations of service. Disentanglement is essential if one is to avoid assuming what is to be proved.

In a full, careful, but extraordinarily neglected study published as long ago as 1924, Lesne demonstrated that 'le sens juridique' or 'technique' of the word *beneficium* (apart from its many other senses) amounted during the eighth and ninth centuries to nothing more precise than a revocable grant conveying less than full property rights. In addition, moreover, he showed that the word was used for property held ex officio by bishops, abbots, and counts and even for the landed endowments of rural churches. Presumably this was because all these people held office by the king's favour while the counts did so, at least formally, only at his pleasure. The word also continued to have the very broad sense of a benefit or favour.[77] However marginal or anomalous these usages look to us there is no reason to suppose they were less common or obvious at the time or had less effect on general ideas about what a benefice was and what obligations were attached to it. In the light of Lesne's findings many of the references to benefices and holdings *jure beneficiario* that editors of the *Monumenta*, for instance, noted as *Lehen*, or that others have continued to describe as fiefs or vassal benefices, look very dubious.[78] To start with, a good many benefices that are said to have been on royal property seem to have been held by counts. Although some royal estates were not managed directly by the count in whose county they lay, some certainly were, so that it is surely probable that references to lands held by counts in or by the king's benefice relate to lands they held and managed ex officio, which would often include

[76] e.g. Werner, 'Missus', 230. It is noteworthy that, in contrast to Werner's criticisms here of the use of evidence on administration, for anything to do with vassalage and 'les terres tenues en fief' he seems to rely largely on Ganshof, principally 'Les Liens'; he seems not to have read Odegaard, *Vassi*, to which he refers without details.

[77] Lesne, 'Diverses Acceptions'. Ganshof, 'Benefice and Vassalage', 159, similarly warns that it is necessary, 'in examining the texts, to eliminate all those which do not quite clearly and indisputably refer to vassal benefices'.

[78] e.g. Ganshof, 'Benefice and Vassalage', n. 76, where only the references from the capitularies seem to be to benefices held by *vassi*.

church lands within their counties.[79] Some may have been extra properties granted personally to individual counts by royal favour, but it seems unreasonable to assume that that was normally the case.[80] It is misleading to assimilate the benefices of counts to the relatively small estates which were now coming to be assigned by *ad hominem* grants to soldiers who might also act as counts' assistants.

It is equally misleading to assimilate references to churches as being royal benefices to the benefices that were granted to laymen out of church lands.[81] Great churches were often referred to as royal benefices, whether they were held in the normal way by bishops or abbots or were granted by special favour to lay nobles.[82] The benefice or favour here was the grant of the church to its incumbent: it did not affect the church's right to its property. Though dependent on royal protection and correspondingly vulnerable to royal demands, churches officially held their lands with as full rights as were envisageable at the time. Even when a church lent property to the king to serve as benefices for royal servants its title was supposed to be unimpaired. In 858, when Louis the German invaded the western kingdom and summoned its bishops to meet him, Archbishop Hincmar reminded him—and others—that churches were not the sort of benefices and royal property (*non talia sunt beneficia et huiusmodi regis proprietas*) that a king could do what he liked with, and that bishops ought not, like laymen, to commend themselves *in vassalatico* to anyone or take such oaths as were forbidden by canon law. In this context the connection between benefice and vassalage that Hincmar made is explicable without deducing

[79] Metz, *Karolingische Reichsgut*, 171–87, 198–213, 220–7; Lesne, 'Diverses Acceptions', 46–55.

[80] As Lesne pointed out: 'Diverses Acceptions', 49, and see below. This would eliminate or render doubtful, e.g., all four cases cited by Ganshof in *Frankish Institutions*, 52 n. 390, as 'undoubtedly . . . tenures by vassalage' (the first should be *Dip. Karol.* i, no. 117) and, from 'Benefice and Vassalage', 162 n., the cases concerning the Nibelungen (that of 776 should be 796), the case of 807 (cf. Metz, *Karolingische Reichsgut*, 178 on another exchange, though without royal permission), the case of 793, which is also one of the four first mentioned (it was Count Kerold, not Count Helmoin, who held *in beneficio domni regis*). Three or four of the 18 cases of grants *ad proprium* he cites in 'Note sur la concession' seem to be of former count's benefices as against four former 'vassal benefices'. Also likely or possible references to ex officio holdings are *Rec. Pépin I et II*, no. 5 (cf. Martindale, 'Kingdom of Aquitaine', 148); *Formulae*, 291–2 (Form. Imp. no. 6); *Rec. Charles le Chauve*, nos. 24, 46; *Dip. Karol.* iii, Lothar I, no. 129 (cf. Lesne, *Propriété Ecclés.* ii (2), 366); ibid. Lothar II, no. 5; Devic and Vaissete, *Hist. Languedoc*, ii (preuves), col. 306–8 (a viscount rather than a count); *Annales de Saint-Bertin*, 152–3 (869), described by Werner, 'Missus', 230 as fiefs; *Dip. Germ. Karol.* Arnulf, nos. 28, 149 (cf. Metz, *Karolingische Reichsgut*, 203, 213). *Capit.* no. 132 c. 6 is a difficult case and so perhaps is *Rec. Charles le Chauve*, no. 24.

[81] As e.g. Ganshof, 'Benefice and Vassalage', 161; cf. Lesne, 'Diverses Acceptions', 28–44, 47–56. *Rec. Charles le Chauve*, no. 275 may come under this head: cf. Martindale, 'Kingdom of Aquitaine', 148.

[82] Bishops' lands could on occasion be absorbed in a count's ex officio benefice: Lesne, *Propriété ecclés.* ii (1), 85.

either that the two invariably went together or that 'vassal benefices' were
the only or most obvious kind. He did not try to argue that churches ought
not to be considered benefices, and he did not have to argue that they were
exempt from the normal duties of benefices. There were different kinds of
benefices and those held by bishops were one kind. They might be held by
royal favour, they might even be in some measure under royal control, but
the obligations that bishops owed to the king were different from those that
laymen owed.[83] In so far as bishops were royal servants—and Hincmar
took their duty to king and kingdom seriously—they were not the same
sort of servants as royal *vassi*. There is no evidence that Louis would have
disagreed with that or that he was trying to assimilate episcopal benefices
to those of *vassi*, much as he may have wished for the same obedience
from bishops as from *vassi* or counts. He had not, however, summoned the
bishops as lay nobles but because they carried weight as bishops. The frag-
mentary survey of royal and ecclesiastical property in the diocese of Chur,
which is thought to have been made before the Treaty of Verdun, refers to
benefices which belonged to country churches. One at least was held by a
clerk.[84] This one, and probably the others as well, are likely to have been
humbler versions of the same sort of benefices as bishoprics and abbeys:
they consisted of the endowments of their respective churches, and the
duties their holders owed were surely ecclesiastical.[85] When Einhard interceded with a bishop for a *parvum beneficiolum* to be given to a friend of his
who was a priest he is unlikely to have been thinking of a quasi-feudal or
military holding.[86] Other ninth-century references to benefices which look
anomalous from a feudo-vassalic point of view are those which seem to
have been held by peasants, perhaps in much the same way as some of
Abbo's or Eberhard's peasant tenants had held bits of their land *in benefitio* in the previous century. At least some owed rents, which would put
them outside Ganshof's definition of benefices.[87] Again, the connotation of
holding in or by benefice is that it is dependent and carries obligations, not
that the obligations are of a particular kind.

The point of all this is not to score points off previous scholars but to
draw attention to the danger of assuming what is to be proved. If one starts
off by believing that 'vassalage' was becoming the dominant bond of society, that 'vassal benefices' or fiefs became the dominant form of landholding during or soon after the Carolingian age, and that they are to be

[83] *Capit.* no. 297. On the audience of the letter: Nelson, 'Public *Histories*', 283.
[84] *Bündner Urkundenbuch*, 376, 378; Ganshof, 'Zur Entstehungsgeschichte'.
[85] Metz, *Karolingische Reichsgut*, 221; cf. e.g. *Dip. Karol.* i, no. 148.
[86] Einhard, *Epistolae*, no. 30; though see Boutruche, *Seigneurie et féodalité*, i. 213, 384.
[87] Lesne, 'Les Bénéficiers', 73–81; *Dip. Germ. Karol.* Ludwig der Deutsche, no. 52 (at least
partly genuine: Stengel, 'Fuldensia V', 53–63).

detected through the use of variants of the word *beneficium* in the sources of the time, then one will see both vassals and their benefices all over the place and will assume that there was an essential link between them. But seeing them where they may not be present makes it impossible to assess the extent to which the practice of granting land with restricted rights in return for military service spread in reality and the effect that its spread may have had on contemporary attitudes towards property rights in general. My point is not to deny that kings and lay nobles had followers and servants who are often referred to as *vassi* or *vassalli* or that they often granted land to them on more or less restricted terms and in return for services which are likely to have been predominantly military. Although many references to lands as royal benefices are probably either to land held by counts ex officio or to benefices that kings and emperors created on church estates, the relative rarity of unambiguous references to benefices held by *vassi* on royal land can be explained without deducing that such benefices were themselves rare. Royal gifts may have normally been recorded in formal diplomas only when they were made *in proprietatem*. Church lands granted as *precaria* or benefices *verbo regis* were supposed to be recorded in writing as part of the bargain Charlemagne made with the clergy. Any record that might be made of a transaction between laymen would be preserved only if the property later passed to a church. Even so there are quite a few references outside the capitularies (royal ordinances) to benefices on royal lands. In 762, for instance, King Pippin I gave property to Prüm abbey that his father had left him *in alode* and that a vassal of his own had held *per beneficium*.[88] Ganshof found four cases in which Louis the Pious granted full rights to *fideles* or *vassi* who had formerly held *in beneficio* or *beneficiario jure*.[89] In 845 Charles the Bald made a similar grant to one of his faithful men (*fidelis*) and in 876 he gave another an estate *usufructuario et jure beneficiario* for two lives.[90] In 889 one of King Odo's faithful men, to whom the king had formerly granted a benefice, secured the extension of the grant to cover the lives of himself, his wife, and his son, if he should have either, provided that they each served the king faithfully for it.[91]

[88] *Dip. Karol.* i, no. 16.

[89] 'Note sur la concession': I exclude the cases where the only evidence of previous holding in benefice is that the grantor was a vassal or where Ganshof deduces that he was a vassal.

[90] *Rec. Charles le Chauve*, nos. 69 (cf. Nelson, 'Public *Histories*', 288 n.), 411 (cf. Martindale, 'Kingdom of Aquitaine', 148–9, 151). Other references to royal benefices (apart from those of counts, or on church lands, or held by clergy): *Rec. Charles le Chauve*, nos. 91 (cf. Martindale, 163–4), 152–3; Migne, *PL*, 104, col. 1204–5. *Cod. Dip. Nass.* no. 56 may qualify, but Adalbert was a count: Airlie, 'Political Behaviour', 98. The property of Bertinus in *Rec. Pépin I et II*, no. 57 (Martindale, 180) could have reverted to the royal estate without having been granted temporarily as a 'vassal benefice'.

[91] *Rec. Eudes*, no. 3.

Some capitularies, moreover, imply the existence of benefices, probably apart from those of counts, on royal estates in those areas of central Francia in which the *missi* were probably most active.[92] The difference between counts' benefices and those of *vassi* or *vassalli* was clearly marked in 869 when *vasalli dominici* were ordered to survey and list the benefices of counts while counts surveyed and listed those of the *vasalli*.[93] It also seems reasonable to suppose that not all the *vassi* settled in more distant and newly conquered areas for purposes of defence either could have been found holdings on church lands or were given estates on full and permanent terms. Benefices created by lay nobles on their own lands, leaving aside those created on either royal or ecclesiastical land by counts who may have been acting on behalf of the king, are even worse recorded, but even a quite superficial search through some obvious footnotes has produced a few references.[94] More could no doubt be found, both on royal and noble estates.

All the same, it is important to go on remembering the wider use of the word *beneficium* and its derivatives to refer to benefits or favours given and received rather than to define a category of property.[95] According to a diploma of 898 Louis the Pious had granted the church of Narbonne *quedam beneficiola* for ever.[96] Even the phrase *in jure beneficiario* may say less about the terms on which land was held than about the origin of the title to it: it had come by royal favour. This, for instance, might apply to a grant made *in jure beneficiario* and *in hereditate* by Charles the Bald to the successors of Spanish refugees who were said to have originally received their property in Septimania from Charlemagne *in jus beneficiarium*.[97] How different the terms of either grant were from what they would have been if they had been made explicitly *ad proprium* and for ever is unclear: the need for renewal of the first grant and Charles the Bald's stipulations that the grantees should remain faithful to him could be explained by their status

[92] e.g. *Capit.* nos. 33 c. 6, 34 c. 10, 46 c. 6–7, 80 c. 7: on the last, cf. Lesne, 'Diverses Acceptions', 14–19, 49–51. On the *missi*: Werner, 'Missus', 204–9.

[93] *Ann. Saint-Bertin*, 152–3.

[94] *Regesta Alsatiae*, i, no. 127, cited (from Pardessus) by Ganshof, 'Note sur les origines', 175 n.; *Urkundenbuch S. Gallen*, ii. 6–7 (no. 386); Einhard, *Epistolae*, no. 68; Favre, *Eudes*, 242–3 (all cited by Lesne, 'Diverses Acceptions', 20 n.; his other references are all from the tenth century); *Codex Dip. Fuldensis*, no. 83, cited by Metz, *Karolingische Reichsgut*, 219. Pippin I's grant to Prüm mentioned above, cited by Ganshof, 'Note sur les origines', 185, may also qualify if the benefice had been held before he became king.

[95] *Benefacere*, for instance, though given 'feudal' meanings in e.g. Niermeyer, *Lexicon*, was used in one of Charlemagne's letters apparently meaning to do well in battle: *Epist. Karol. Aevi*, ii. 528 (no. 20).

[96] Devic and Vaissete, *Hist. Languedoc*, v. 95–7.

[97] *Rec. Charles le Chauve*, no. 34; cf. nos. 40, 46 and other grants of *aprisiones* discussed below.

as immigrants and the sensitive area in which they were settled. Even alod-holders, after all, as we shall see, might lose their land for infidelity.

The general sense of a favour may explain the well-known grants of benefices to great princes. According to the *Annales Regni Francorum*, Pippin III (later King Pippin I), after invading Bavaria, installed his eight-year-old nephew Tassilo, whose position had been usurped by Pippin's own rebellious brother, as duke of Bavaria *per suum beneficium*.[98] Much of the discussion of this entry has started from the premiss that *beneficium* already had the sense of a defined category of 'feudal' property by this date, and that this is confirmed by Tassilo's commendation of himself to Pippin in vassalage eight years later, which has already been discussed.[99] There are problems of circularity in the argument. It seems more probable that the word *beneficium* was intended to convey Pippin's position of superior-ity and generosity, and to indicate that Tassilo's relation to him was sub-ordinate, rather than to assimilate it to that of soldiers settled on small estates in return for military service. If anything it was more like the rela-tion to the king of bishops and counts who held their offices, and their appurtenant estates, by his favour. Tassilo's age, however, the family con-nection, and the fact that Bavaria was only marginally within the Merovingian kingdom all make it different from that relationship too. What happened in 749, like what happened in 757, was a matter of poli-tics, not of property law. Property law in any case was not clear enough to provide a form of words that would have seemed to contemporaries to wrap up a transaction like this in a recognizably neat and legal package. In 826 a claimant to the kingship of Denmark, Harald Klak, was baptized and, according to one account, surrendered himself and his kingdom—which in the event he failed to secure—to Louis the Pious. In another version Louis granted him the county of Rüstringen in Frisia.[100] Neither account uses the word *beneficium*, though there is no reason why it should not have been suitable for the grant of a county, and no reason either why its use should have made any difference to what happened or how contemporaries viewed the event. In various accounts of subsequent cessions of Frisian counties or territory in 841 and 850 the word was sometimes used and sometimes not. In each case the terms of the grant are unstated. It is unlikely either that anything like a recognized set of conditions could have provided a model for the arrangement or that the arrangement helped to create such a model.[101]

[98] *Ann. Reg. Franc.* 8.
[99] The arguments are surveyed by Odegaard, *Vassi and Fideles*, 24–32, 90–6; cf. McKitterick, *Frankish Kingdoms*, 33, 65–6.
[100] Ermold, *Poème*, 188–90; *Ann. Reg. Franc.* 169–70. For Harald Klak: Jones, *Vikings*, 104–5.
[101] *Ann. Saint-Bertin*, 39, 59, 168, 184–5, 188; *Ann. Fuldenses*, 39–40.

It is, however, worth seeing if it is possible to disentangle from the welter of varying usages something like a set of rights and obligations appropriate to one of the humbler kinds of benefice—that is, the kind of benefice that looks as if it was created to provide a holding for the kind of man who was often described as a *vassus* so that he could be relied on for effective military service. While doing so, of course, one needs to bear in mind that there were other kinds of humble benefices that sometimes get into the records and from which no military service and perhaps no services at all may have been required: small holdings given to monastic servants, a lay lord's old nurse, and so on. To start with the creation and grant of a benefice: there seems to be no unambiguous evidence about the formalities that were necessary during this period. The commendation to the grantor which is sometimes mentioned in connection with a grant may, like the commendations discussed in connection with the Merovingian period, not always refer to anything one could call a ceremony.[102] Commendation explicitly 'into the hands' (*in manus*) of the grantor sounds rather more like a rite, but in so far as references to commendations of either kind concern immigrants or people caught up in Carolingian conflicts which necessitated the making of a new political commitment, they cannot be taken as implying that those who were already subjects had to commend themselves in order to take up a benefice.[103] Just as I have suggested that kings or emperors may not have taken oaths in person from all their *vassi* on appointment, so it seems to me improbable that they can have taken oaths or gone through any kind of ceremony from all the petty *vassi* who were given benefices all over the empire at the moment they were given their land. Counts or *missi* may have sometimes put *vassi* into possession of their benefices on the king's lands and perhaps on church lands too, though perhaps those who received church lands *verbo regis* had to be installed by a representative of the church as well.[104] The ceremony of installation may have included an oath but the evidence is not clear: the oaths that we know counts took from *vassi* (as from others) do not seem to be connected to the grant of benefices.[105] Whether or not the grant of a benefice involved a ceremony, there does not appear to be any evidence that the holding of a benefice from one lord normally excluded, or was meant to exclude, holding one from another. In the arrangements for partitioning the empire it was agreed that no one should hold benefices— which in the context presumably means royal benefices—in more than one

---

[102] See chapter 2.2.

[103] Einhard, *Epist.* nos. 25, 27–8 (on which cf. the different interpretation of Nelson, *Charles the Bald*, 59); *Dip. Germ. Karol.* Ludwig der Deutsche, no. 113. See next section.

[104] *Dip. Germ. Karol.* Ludwig der Deutsche, no. 113.          [105] *Capit.* nos. 25 c. 4, 34.

kingdom, but that does not imply a general rule concerning all benefices of all lords in more normal circumstances.[106] Since the holders of benefices *verbo regis* had direct obligations both to the king and to the church whose land they held, the creation of such benefices from the start inevitably involved a kind of multiple lordship. So long as royal government was effective this potential source of conflicting loyalties, like others felt by anyone who had a lord apart from the king, may not have been very troubling: many benefice-holders may never have been worried by it.

As for the services owed in return for a benefice, it seems very likely, as is generally believed, that all or most royal benefices, whether on ecclesiastical or royal lands, were primarily designed to provide reliable military service at minimum cost. That would explain why *vassi* were given benefices not only in central Francia but in distant and newly conquered regions.[107] According to orders issued in 807, when regulations were made about the amount of military service owed by free men according to their property, all benefice-holders without exception had to join the army. This probably referred only to those with royal benefices (whether on church or royal land), though it is impossible to be sure. In 808 the military service of all who held benefices from anyone was put on the same footing, along with that of independent property-holders. Everyone then was supposed to serve in proportion to the size of his holdings reckoned in manses.[108] Some benefices were large enough for their holders to be responsible for producing several soldiers, for some had men under them who were 'housed' (*homines casatos*) and were also expected to serve.[109] This may imply that the original benefice-holder granted out subordinate benefices on the lines of what historians call 'subinfeudation', but it need not.[110] It may be that some *homines casati* were already settled on the land when he received it. Aeckard, who followed his father in a royal benefice in the Wetterau (Hesse), which consisted of a chief manse (*mansus dominicatus*) and fourteen other manses, would have been responsible for producing at least two soldiers besides himself. The other two, however, could have been men whom we might classify as peasants. Rather than receiving their manses as 'vassal benefices' by 'subinfeudation' they may have held them by effectively hereditary right before a benefice had been granted over their

---

[106] *Capit.* nos. 45 c. 9, 136 c. 9, 194 c. 5; cf. Ganshof, 'Benefice and Vassalage', 174; 'Note sur les origines', 159.

[107] e.g. Italy (chapter 6.3); *Capit.* no. 148 c. 4.

[108] *Capit.* nos. 48, 50 c. 1–5. Cf. Reuter, 'End of Carolingian Expansion', 399–401. On manses, among much else: Goffart, 'From Roman Taxation'.

[109] *Capit.* nos. 74 c. 7, 80 c. 5.

[110] There is also no need to suppose 'subinfeudation' behind the men of counts in *Capit.* no. 50 c. 4, who could be either royal benefice-holders or those who held *de proprio suo* and came under the count's command.

heads to Aeckard's father. In 839 the emperor gave Aeckard full and perpetual rights, with freedom of disposition, over the estate. Its military
obligations should then have remained the same in principle as they had
been before, even if Aeckard felt less pressure to fulfil them.[111] Benefice-
holders with Germanic names in the diocese of Chur may well have been
brought in and settled there for military and political purposes.[112] Their
formal military obligations were presumably no different from those of
their neighbours who held similar amounts of land, but,
having been given their land expressly so that they should serve and on
condition that they did, they were presumably supposed to be more
reliable.

Some of those who held benefices created by churches *spontanea voluntate*, like those who held them from nobles, also presumably helped their
lord fulfil his own military obligations and served under his command.[113]
Those who held enough served in person, those who did not clubbed
together. Most royal benefices designed to provide service presumably
came into the first category. It is easy to imagine what a lot of anomalies
and opportunities for sea-lawyering the whole system of military service,
including that from benefices, could have involved if it had been strictly
put into practice, but it may well have worked in a rough and ready way to
produce a rather better army than could have been mustered without
benefices, at least in the short run. In the long run the sons or grandsons
of *vassi* who had been settled on smallish benefices, like some of those in
the diocese of Chur, may, like the *agrarii milites* of twelfth-century
England, have soon ceased to be of much more use than their peasant
neighbours, especially for long-distance operations.

Whether *vassi* who were given benefices were supposed to perform more
judicial and administrative duties, helping counts and so forth, than they
would have owed otherwise, is not clear.[114] The phrase 'aid and counsel'
(*auxilium et consilium*), which is often associated with feudo-vassalic obligations, came into use in the ninth century but it seems to have been associated with bishops and lay magnates rather than *vassi*.[115] *Vassi* had to help
and perhaps advise counts but few would have had the standing to advise
the king. Those who were granted benefices *verbo regis* may have normally
expected not to pay rent, but since those who held church land were supposed to pay rents to the church concerned and some peasants whose holdings were described as benefices owed rents and even labour services, it is

---

[111] *Hessisches UB: Zweite Abt.* i. 13–14 (no. 27).          [112] *Bündner UB*, 375–96.
[113] *Capit.* nos. 50, 73 c. 7–8, 74, 75, 77 c. 9, 16.
[114] *Capit.* nos. 25 c. 4, 48 c. 3, 61 c. 5, 73 c. 8, 148 c. 4.
[115] Devisse, 'Essai: *consilium et auxilium*'.

difficult to believe that any general rule against the payment of rent by benefice-holders can have obtained.[116]

That benefices of all sorts were regarded as in principle temporary and revocable is probable. As yet, before the original and wider sense of the word was forgotten, the point of referring to any holding as a benefice was presumably to indicate that it was held by favour: by the same token the grantor or his heir may often have intended a reminder that it was enjoyed at and during his pleasure. Except in the case of benefices *verbo regis* on church land, that need not have meant that the owner of the land would invariably want to prevent the tenant from passing it on to his son or that the owner's heir would normally take back what his predecessor had granted. Arguments that 'vassal benefices' were at first restricted to the life of grantor and grantee because vassalage itself was originally a commitment between two individuals are unconvincing. Arguments about *Herrenfall*, the word used to denote a supposed rule that benefices were lost on the death of the grantor, are particularly weak.[117] They rely on evidence about the loss, or possible loss, of benefices held from kings or churches, both of which were in different ways special cases. No general rules about vassalage and 'vassal benefices' granted by any lord can be deduced from such cases. There is, in fact, no reason why there should have been any general rule in the first place. So far as the succession of the benefice-holder is concerned, a good many benefices were probably always inherited in practice. It would accord with prevailing ideas of what was right to allow a loyal and competent son to succeed to his father's holding. For a king with hundreds of benefices to deal with, or even a count acting on the king's behalf, it would be administratively practical to do so. The way that some benefices created *verbo regis* on church land were effectively inherited, for instance, suggests that inheritance may have been frequent from the start and was not the result of weakening royal control.[118] The inheritance of counties was another matter, but the office of count was quite different from the benefice of an ordinary soldier, even if it was also, for good reason, called a royal benefice. If those who received benefices, or their successors, sometimes got confirmations of their titles from their lords, or their lords' successors, that would not, in the conditions of early medieval law, mean that their rights in the mean time had been invalid. It was just a sensible precaution for anyone whose property was formally dependent upon the

---

[116] Lesne, 'Les Bénéficiers', 73–81; Constable, 'Nona et Decima'; *Capit.* nos. 20 c. 13, 140 c. 4, 280.

[117] e.g. Brunner, *Deutsche Rechtsgeschichte*, ii. 341–2, 345; Stutz, *Herrenfall* (and Roth, *Geschichte des Beneficialwesens*, 416–18, 429–33, and *Feudalität*, 180–3, which seem to provide Stutz's chief evidence); Ganshof, *Feudalism*, 41–2.

[118] e.g. the case of Aeckard, cited above.

continued favour of the grantor.[119] Even those who held *ad proprium* sometimes found confirmations useful.[120] Benefices may, however, have tended
to be inherited according to different rules from other property: as the
making of grants for specified lives suggests, kings and other lords may
have preferred to have each benefice held by a single tenant who would be
responsible for the service rather than leaving it to be divided or squabbled
over by possible heirs.[121] More work might establish the strength of the
preference or at least the extent to which any preference that can be
detected in surviving sources was enforced.

Properties granted as benefices, then, were often—perhaps generally,
and probably from the start—inherited, but inherited, as they were held,
precariously, and were probably never intended to be freely alienable.
Precariousness itself, however, was relative, from the start and not just
because kings lost control. Benefices were confiscatable but, ostensibly,
only for good cause.[122] There is no reason to see the promises of due
process of law which kings made to their men in general as concessions
which changed the conditions of benefice-holding.[123] Kings and other
lords were not supposed to act arbitrarily. Of course in practice they might,
and it would have been difficult for an ordinary *vassus* to withstand either
counts or great churches with royal—and possibly divine—authority
behind them. In spite of that, any free man who held a benefice in the ninth
century, like those who had held *precaria* from the church in earlier centuries, had certain rights in it: ejection from what he had held peaceably
and dutifully for some time, particularly if his father had held it peaceably
and dutifully before him, would constitute a prima-facie case for protection by a court. Confiscations for failure to perform service, for instance,
could presumably have been contested by arguments about the adequacy
of summons, the amount of service due, and so forth. The difficulty that
churches had in evicting sitting tenants illustrates the point.[124] There is,
however, no evidence that benefice-holders in dispute with their lords had
more right to judgement by their peers than anyone else: all judgements
were supposed to be made by some sort of consensus of the members of

[119] The confirmation of this kind that Ganshof cited as evidence of the prevalence of
*Herrenfall* (i.e. the automatic lapse of a benefice on the death of its lord) was that of a tenant 'by
*aprisio*', which he argues was analogous to tenure by benefice (for which see below), but he said
that he saw no reason to doubt that *Herrenfall* applied also to benefices 'in the strict sense of the
word': 'Benefice and Vassalage', 163.

[120] e.g. Ganshof, 'Note sur la concession', 597 (no. XVII).

[121] *Urkundenbuch S. Gallen*, no. 386; *Rec. Charles le Chauve*, no. 34; *Rec. Eudes*, no. 3.

[122] *Capit.* nos. 20 c. 9, 77 c. 20, 254 c. 3; *Trad. Freising*, no. 257 (though this may well be a
'peasant' rather than 'vassal' benefice).

[123] As argued by Dhondt, *Études*, 19–21.

[124] Lesne, *Propriété ecclés.* ii (2), 244–54, 369–75.

the judging assembly, whether it was a county assembly or merely that of a lordship. Free men who held benefices were in an anomalous position: those who held benefices from churches may have had to plead their cases, at least in the first instance, in the church's own court, which dealt in general with the less free, rather than in the county. On the face of it, therefore, they had less protection than the holders of alods, however small, who could take their cases direct to the public courts of their counties. Those who held benefices from the count could presumably argue with him in his court and might hope for support from their fellows, but there do not seem to have been any special rules about this. Again, it is hard to envisage that benefice-holders were better protected than alod-holders in the way that traditional theories about vassalage and the judgement of peers suggest.

In so far as the previous paragraphs have set out the conditions on which the general run of military or quasi-military benefices were held in the ninth century they look rather ill-defined and not all that different from the conditions of other kinds of property. The formal precariousness of such holdings, which was their most pronounced characteristic, was shared with other kinds of benefice, whether those held by great men as the appurtenances of their offices or those held by peasants which were too small to owe military service—as well, of course, as with peasant holdings that were not called benefices. In real life, however, as distinct from textbooks, the recognition of a general category does not depend on its exact definition. Starting, it seems, from the model of *precaria* on church land, the custom of granting land to free men, for military services and on formally revocable and temporary terms, must have become widely known through benefices *verbo regis*. It may be in this way that it spread to lay estates. One result of the expansion of this kind of benefice-holding may have been to make it more respectable for nobles and free men to hold land on restricted terms. Another may have been to create a general notion of what a benefice entailed and what rights and duties were attached to it, but that is less likely: too much still depended on the size of the benefice and the status of its holder for any very clear idea to emerge. Whether the expansion of benefice-holding under the Carolingians involved anything that it is useful to call the 'union' of benefice and vassal is very doubtful.[125] Not all *vassi* seem to have been given benefices, and the proportion who got them is unknowable. Some benefices were held by people who are not called *vassi* in the surviving sources or who, even if they are, seem to be quite different kinds of people, with different obligations, from the royal *vassi* who have so often been taken as the paradigm for 'feudal tenants'. There is no

---

[125] Ganshof seems to have developed the idea (e.g. 'Note sur les origines') from Mitteis (*Lehnrecht*, 518–19), who apparently took it from Brunner, *Deutsche Rechtsgeschichte*, 367.

evidence that *vassus* now came to mean benefice-holder: it only makes investigation more difficult if one confuses the two categories. There is, moreover, no evidence at all that benefices replaced land held *in proprium* (or *in proprietate*, etc.) as the normal holdings of nobles or free men.

## 4.3. *Full property under the Carolingians*

The use of the word alod seems to have broadened in this period. A piece of property held with the normal full rights could be described as an alod, and the word could now cover both inherited and acquired land, although, as a reference to *alodes de hereditate et de conquisitu* shows, the distinction between the two was sometimes worth making, perhaps because a rule that acquisitions could be disposed of more freely than inherited land was accepted.[126] Grants of land *in proprium* sometimes specified that they were to be freely disposable.[127] After acquired property had been inherited once it must have been liable to become absorbed in the rest of the inheritance so that heirs would resent being deprived of it. The resentments of heirs who felt defrauded by gifts to churches provoked legislation in their favour early in the ninth century. In 818–19 it was laid down that property given to any ecclesiastical person without the consent of any free persons who might thereby be disinherited was to go back to the disinherited. Another piece of legislation from about the same time, however, reiterated the right of free men to give their property to churches. If they did it publicly and properly their heirs could not object. One could even give one's part of a shared inheritance and get the count to make a division. The whole subject was obviously highly contentious: both heirs and churches might make claims that the norms of the time would recognize as valid. It looks as though churches therefore began to devise a new method of averting trouble. Laplanche, who pointed to the significance of this legislation many years ago, found the first records of consent by kinspeople of the donors of land to churches very soon afterwards.[128] The long-term results of the way that churches protected themselves from the new law and then adapted that method to cope with new problems in the following centuries will be discussed in the next chapter.

Most of the transfers of alods that we know about were made to churches, but it looks as if by now, if not earlier, the first requirement for any valid transfer of land to anyone was (apart from the consent of

[126] *Capit.* nos. 242, 270 c. 4.
[127] *Trad. Freising*, no. 166a; *Rec. Pépin I et II*, no. 38; *Formulae*, 305–6, 320 (Form. Imp. nos. 27, 44); *Rec. Charles le Chauve*, nos. 5, 10.
[128] *Capit.* nos. 138 c. 7, 139 c. 6; Laplanche, *Réserve*, 54–68.

potential heirs) a public ceremony, probably including the transfer of a symbolic object but perhaps also, even in a transaction between laymen, a charter or charters.[129] However good the title to it, infidelity to the king could—and sometimes did—result in the loss of inherited alodial land.[130] Though successive arrangements for partition of the empire said that any-one should be able to keep his inheritance (as distinct from his benefices) in any kingdom, confiscations during the reigns of Louis the Pious and his successors suggest that that afforded little protection to great men caught up in the quarrels of the royal family.[131] In troubled times alods may not have been much safer than benefices.

Alods owed more defined and probably heavier services under the Carolingians than they had earlier: the Carolingians did not increase their control over the landed resources of their realms merely through creating benefices. Military service was now more clearly owed in respect of prop-erty than it had been earlier. Alods, like benefices, were assessed by the number of manses they comprised. In 808 anyone with four manses had to serve whether the manses were his own or held in benefice.[132] In real emer-gencies everyone (*omnis populus*) might be called out for the defence of the country in what was called *lantweri*.[133] Some service at local courts seems to have been at least notionally incumbent on all free men, while royal *vassi*, whether or not they held benefices, were supposed to do more, particularly when counts called on them.[134] It has been held that churches and benefice-holders alone had to pay the taxes raised by Charles the Bald to pay off the Danes and that alodial lands were exempt.[135] That may be right, but the only records we have are those made by aggrieved clerics who were not concerned with the burdens that fell on lay landowners. In the same way it may be wrong to assume that the various traditional payments and dues that we know of from ecclesiastical sources were paid only from church property, though they may have been. Even if these were normally passed on to peasant tenants the landowner might presumably have to shoulder some responsibility for seeing that they were paid.[136]

All the same, alods—land held *in proprium* and for ever—were what was

---

[129] McKitterick, *Carolingians and the Written Word*, 62–8, 91–4, 97–8, 118–20.

[130] *Dip. Karol.* i, nos. 180–1, 208.

[131] *Capit.* nos. 45 c. 8–11, 136 c. 9, 194 c. 5–7, 242 c. 7, 274 c. 3; *Dip. Germ. Karol.* Ludwig der Deutsche, no. 113; *Rec. Charles le Chauve*, no. 428; Hincmar, *De Villa Novilliaco*, col. 1168; Airlie, 'Political Behaviour', 140. Promises of due process in deprivation of honours (e.g. *Capit.* no. 254 c. 3) probably cover independent property too (cf. *Capit.* 205 c. 6: Nelson, 'Public Histories', 278 n.).

[132] *Capit.* nos. 48, 50.          [133] Ibid. no. 204.

[134] Ibid. nos. 48, 50, 61 c. 5, 73–4, 273 c. 27.          [135] Lot, 'Les Tributs'.

[136] Nelson, *Charles the Bald*, 213, 250; McKitterick, *Frankish Kingdoms*, 190; Lesne, *Propriété Ecclés.* ii (2), 404–27.

most wanted. Ganshof's suggestion that royal grants *in proprietatem* became exceptional and grants *in beneficium* the rule has not been borne out by the subsequent publication of charters and studies.[137] Many grants of benefices were no doubt made without being recorded in surviving documents, but on the other hand much of the land that is recorded as royal benefices—and which in the end became lost to the king—was not in any case 'granted' at all: it was held by counts ex officio, while some that was on occasion counted as part of the king's land was held by bishops or abbots and was therefore royal property only in a rather special and limited sense. The balance is difficult to draw, but there seems little doubt that kings and those to whom they made grants still thought in terms of full and perpetual rights as what a generous king ought to give to his loyal servants by way of reward. Benefices remained a second-best. Whether people at the time consciously envisaged benefices turning into alods through the passage of time, as well as through a subsequent more complete gift, the way in which they were by various means transmuted into alods suggests that the ninth century cannot really be characterized as having what Metz, for instance, called a 'feudal attitude to property'.[138] It is impossible to guess at the relative proportions of benefices and alodial lands, but Herlihy's survey of land transactions in continental western Europe between the eighth and twelfth centuries produced a 'vast majority' in which 'the overlord is not mentioned, as his permission was apparently not sought for the transaction'.[139] It seems likely that a good many of such cases were of land which either had no 'overlord' because it was held alodially and *in proprium* or had effectively become so even if it had once been held with more restricted rights.

Leaving statistics aside, however, some hint at what were considered normal rights of property may be deduced from the terms laid down for newly cleared land. Clearances in the Carolingian empire were not made in a desert-island situation in which people could do exactly what they wanted or thought fair without reference to superior authority. Anyone who found it prudent to get a charter to validate his title would have to accept provisions that the king or lord would be prepared to grant. Nevertheless the terms set out for a new holding might be likely to reflect some kind of consensus about what would be right, unhampered by the

---

[137] See Tessier's analysis in *Rec. Charles le Chauve*, iii. 200–5; Dhondt, *Études*, 259–76; Martindale, 'Kingdom of Aquitaine'. Ganshof may have somewhat modified his position on the importance of grants in full property and the time when they were superseded: cf. 'Note sur les origines', 175 n., 'Les Liens', 155; 'Note sur la concession'.

[138] 'Die lehnrechtliche Denkweise des 9. Jahrhunderts': Metz, *Zur Erforschung*, 81.

[139] Herlihy, 'Church Property', n. 27, presumably using 'overlord' to mean the immediate lord.

vested interests and conflicting claims that were likely to encumber old
areas of settlement. The series of documents concerning lands occupied by
Spanish refugees in the county of Narbonne and elsewhere in Septimania
as *aprisiones* are therefore useful in suggesting the property rights and
arrangements that were considered normal.[140] It is probably wrong to see
the word *aprisio* as the name of a category of property with distinctive
rights and obligations: it sometimes meant simply a clearance, like the
German *bivanc* or the Italian *preisa* (or the later English word assart), but
it seems to have been accepted that someone who cleared and cultivated
land had some kind of right by the fact of his clearance. As one man
claimed in 852: 'It is clearly true that I hold these properties, but not
unjustly, because I took them out of the waste as a clearance (*quia de eremo
eas tracxi in aprisione*).'[141] According to a royal letter of 812 some of the
uncultivated land that Spanish settlers had acquired seems to have been
royal property (*fiscum nostrum*).[142] What this implies either about royal
rights over wasteland in general or about the condition of royal land in the
area is unclear. What seems clear is that the Spaniards, as immigrants, were
liable to oppression and hostility from their neighbours. At least some of
them therefore—like some Saxons in the north—got royal charters to
secure their holdings.

The first surviving charter is dated 795. It says that the Spaniard, John,
who had fought well against the infidels in Spain before settling at
Fontjoncouse (Aude), had commended himself to Charlemagne when he
came to ask for a formal grant of the land that he and his men had cleared
and cultivated. This reference to commendation may be one reason why
*aprisiones* have sometimes been assimilated more or less closely to
benefices,[143] but in this case the commitment looks like one to be a faithful subject rather than what historians generally call a vassal.[144] The rights
enjoyed by John and his successors, along with the other Spaniards who
also came to the area and cleared land there, look more like those of full

---

[140] The documents listed here with their dates in brackets (distinguishing those of the same
year as a and b) will be referred to in the following notes simply by those dates (with a or b where
necessary): *Dip. Karol.* i, nos. 179 (795), 217 (812); Devic and Vaissete, *Hist. Languedoc*, ii
(preuves), col. 97–100 (815a); col. 100–1 (815b); col. 109–11 (816); col. 185–7 (834); col. 287–8
(852); col. 306–8 (858); ibid. v, col. 92–3 (897); col. 95–7 (898); col. 137–40 (918); *Rec. Charles le
Chauve*, nos. 40 (844a), 43 (844b), 46 (844c), 94 (847), 120 (849); *Rec. Louis II etc.* no. 54 (881);
*Rec. Eudes*, no. 1 (889); *Rec. Charles le Simple*, no. 27 (899); 'Cart. de Fontjoncouse', nos. 8
(1106×21), 9 (1108). They are discussed by, among others, Imbart de la Tour, 'Les Colonies',
Dupont, 'L'Aprision', Müller-Mertens, *Karl der Grosse*, 61–5.
[141] 852. Cf. Marca, *Marca Hispanica*, app. col. 769. For references to *bivanc*, suggesting some
similarities: *Dip. Karol.* i, no. 213; *Codex Dip. Fuldensis*, no. 471; *Dip. Germ. Karol.* Ludwig der
Deutsche, no. 109; for *preisa*: *Reg. Farfa*, no. 311.
[142] 812.                                              [143] e.g. Ganshof, 'Benefice and Vassalage', 152, 163.
[144] 795, 815a, b.

and permanent property held *ad proprium* than of benefices. That was how
Charles the Bald saw them. In 844 he referred to *aprisiones* in the county
of Béziers as made by permission of Charlemagne and Louis the Pious and
possessed *quasi proprietario jure*. In 847 he granted three of his faithful men
the *res nostri proprietatis* they and their fathers had held *per aprisionem*, as
their predecessors had held them, *ad proprium* and *ad proprietatem*.[145]
According to John's original charter, later confirmations and amplifications
of it, and similar charters to others, the Spaniards owed no rents, dues, or
services beyond what other free men owed. They could pass on their land
to their descendants or, if they lacked descendants, alienate it.[146] John himself, and no doubt others of similar status, gave houses and lands to some
who had come with him and were commended to him and had him as their
lord (*beneficiavit illis . . . et ipsi homines ad tunc sui commenditi erant et illum
habebant patronum*[147]), though objections were raised when some of the
more powerful of the Spanish tried to take over the holdings of others who
saw themselves as having made their own *aprisiones*.[148] Nevertheless they
were left to deal with most of their affairs among themselves, coming under
the count's jurisdiction only for more serious crimes, though they would
be under his command in their military service.[149] This seems to be the
nearest thing to a lay 'immunity' that can be found in Carolingian sources
and the circumstances were obviously rather special, not least because
these useful immigrants had evidently complained about being harried by
the local count. The charters specify that the lands the Spaniards held *per
aprisionem* were not part of the count's benefice nor had their holders been
beneficed by him, though they could commend themselves to counts or
royal *vassi* if they wished and would then hold any lands they thus acquired
by whatever agreements they would make.[150] It is pretty clear that all these
details came to be set down, not because the later grants were intended to
be more permanent or more generous than the earlier ones, but because the
immigrants faced troubles with their neighbours and especially with
counts, viscounts, and other local authorities, and turned to the king to sort
them out.[151] As the century wore on these troubles got worse and royal
power became less effective. By its end kings Carloman and Odo had
allowed the count's rights to pass to the church of Narbonne.[152] In 918 an
attempt was made to reassert the count's rights to military services and
dues from certain men of the abbot of Montolieu (Aude) *sicut alii Spanii
debent facere de illorum aprisione*, but the church produced documents

---

[145] 844a, 847; cf. 849 and 899.                    [146] 795, 815a, b, 844c.
[147] The printed text has *patronem*.                [148] 834, 816, 844c.
[149] 815a.                                           [150] 816, 834.
[151] Dupont, 'L'Aprision', 206–11, thinks that 844c marks a change of policy.
[152] 852, 858, 881, 897, 898.

showing the lands concerned to be alods of the church and the count's representative failed to produce any to refute them.[153] In the early twelfth century John's successor commended himself to the archbishop as his lord, admitted that Fontjoncouse belonged to the archbishop, and promised not to exclude him from it. The decline from full property rights was complete, while the survival of the charters is, incidentally, explained. But it was not at all what had been intended in the ninth century.

The kind of benefice that was granted to royal *vassi*—that is, revocable holdings granted in return for service of a predominantly military nature— does not, therefore, seem to have become the dominant form of landholding by nobles and free men before 888 either in reality or in contemporary perception. In particular there does not seem to be any evidence to suggest that great nobles held this kind of benefice or formed their ideas and expectations about property by analogy from it. It is therefore misleading to refer to great men generically as, for instance, *Lehnsträger*.[154] Great men rose further through royal favour, but most of them were great men in the first place because they had great estates *in proprium*. Assimilating the property of Carolingian lords to that of nobles under the later law of fiefs by referring to them as *les grands féodataires*, *Lehnsträger*, *Lehnsherren* or similar words in other languages is the result of old habits, notably the habit of telescoping centuries of medieval history which has been inherited from the earliest post-medieval writers on the law of fiefs, who knew much less about the middle ages than is known now. It may also derive from the use of ecclesiastical records on which we have to rely for lack of any others: nobles may appear in them as holders of benefices or *precaria*—which, of course, sometimes derived from gifts they or their ancestors had made to the church from which they now received their former land back on more or less restricted terms. Most importantly, perhaps, it seems to reflect the misconception that Lesne pointed out and that has already been frequently mentioned here: the misconception, that is, that the word *beneficium* can normally be assumed to refer to something in the nature of a 'vassal benefice'. Great men often held lands by royal favour or benefice. They held bishoprics and abbeys, for instance, and other estates that kings might give them temporarily or for life, but all of these are likely to have been held on distinctly different terms from anything held by the ordinary

---

[153] 918. Dupont, 'L'Aprision', 391, suggests that the argument on behalf of the count tried to substitute the notion of benefice for that of *aprisio* so as to make the military services into mounted services, but it was the church's side that introduced the notion of benefice and there is no evidence to show that the services demanded were significantly greater than those owed by *aprisio*-holders earlier.

[154] e.g. Classen, 'Verträge von Verdun und von Coulaines', 7: an article which I found in other respects extremely helpful.

*vassi*—terms that would be determined by high politics and their own high status rather than by the considerations that shaped the kind of benefice that was granted to people of lower status.

## 4.4. *Counts and the problem of the end of the empire*

Most of the lands held by great men that are referred to in the sources as benefices were those that formed the endowments of the office of count. It is misleading to refer to these lands as fiefs or *Lehen* just as it is misleading to call the counts themselves vassals. Although one can see why the counties that some great men accumulated in the ninth century came to be seen as the origin of the great fiefs of later centuries they were not fiefs yet. Counts did not exercise their authority over their own property in the way which is considered typical of 'classic feudalism'. Like the holder of any kind of benefice at the time, a Carolingian count enjoyed some of the rights or incidents of property over the estates he held and managed for the king, but so do people who occupy land ex officio in many societies. It can hardly be a defining mark of feudalism in what Ganshof called its narrow sense. Ganshof suggested that a significant step towards feudalism in that narrow sense came with the assimilation of the count's office (his *honor*[155]) to his benefice. This happened, he thought, because from the time of Charlemagne counts were bound in vassalage to the king, which was the reason why their ex officio estates came to be called benefices. Counts therefore, he suggested, felt the same desire to pass on their benefices as other vassals did, while the similarity between the ceremonies of investing counts with counties and vassals with benefices induced a confusion between the office and its appurtenant land.[156] This seems to put too much emphasis on words, to which Ganshof tended to attribute primary or central meanings derived from later law. At the same time it ignores the absence of evidence that the words *vassi* or *vassalli* were actually applied at the time to counts.[157] It also puts too much emphasis on ceremonies of which, as I have already argued, there is only slight and casual evidence. The argument that counts were subjected to new 'vassalic' obligations seems weak. As I have already suggested, it is hard to see that, if they had

[155] *Honor*, like most of the words given 'technical meanings' in the historiography of feudalism, seems to have had a vaguer meaning, at least in the early middle ages, than he assigns to it: Lesne, 'Diverses Acceptions', 47–8; Niermeyer, 'Remarques', 254–5; Nelson, 'Public *Histories*', 278 n. An earlier interpretation made the *honor* cover ex officio lands and restricted *beneficium* to *ad hominem* grants: e.g. Levillain, 'Les Nibelungen', 344: Levillain's findings need revision if Lesne's argument about words is accepted.
[156] *Feudalism*, 52–6.
[157] Odegaard, *Vassi and Fideles*, 1–50, and above, at nn. 39–48. Though cf. chapters 6.4 and 9.3 for the different usage in Italy and, later, in Germany.

been, it would have attached them more closely to the king than they were attached by their office. Charlemagne bound his counts to obedience by the forms of patronage and punishment that were traditional in his society. He succeeded because of his success in war and—it seems—by heroic efforts at supervision. Even so there was constant danger that counts would plunder the royal lands under their charge or absorb them into their alodial property—a danger that was much more likely to come from counts, and would be much more dangerous if it did, than from *vassi* with their relatively tiny benefices.[158] The embezzlement of royal property, which was almost as dangerous to royal power as the inheritance of counties, may have gone a fair way before inheritance became established. A county with little or no royal property was a county that brought in less to the king and was harder for him to control.[159] As conflicts between different parts of the empire and attacks from outside multiplied during the ninth century kings found it more difficult to supervise their counts and more tempting to buy their support with grants of royal estates. However it was that kings lost their estates, so far as they lost them to counts, whether by embezzlement or grant, it surely did not happen by comital estates being turned into something like the benefices of *vassi*.[160] It came because they were assimilated to alods.

Nor did counties become hereditary by following a general trend towards inheritance that had started with lesser benefices. The count's benefice was quite different. Carolingian emperors and kings who as a matter of course left the holders of small benefices to pass on their holdings equally of course paid more attention to counties. Some counts were left in post for long periods and might be followed when they died by kinsmen, but counties mattered too much for that to be taken for granted in anything like the same way.[161] If one looks at the Capitulary of Quierzy (877), not in a search for the origin of the eventually heritable titles and lands of counts but in the circumstances of its promulgation, it does not seem to be a royal surrender to a new principle of inheritance. It makes provision for the offices and families of counts and others in Charles the Bald's kingdoms who might die during the king's absence in Italy: no one should feel aggrieved if, when he returned, the king changed the arrangements made in his absence and gave a county to someone else.[162] Royal authority in many parts of the empire was, however, by this time in trouble and counts

---

[158] *Capit.* nos. 33 c. 6, 46 c. 6–7.
[159] Dhondt, *Études*, 21–5, 236–53; Martindale, 'Kingdom of Aquitaine'.
[160] Ganshof, *Feudalism*, 52–4.
[161] Werner, 'Missus'; Airlie, 'Political Behaviour', esp. 194–219; Nelson, *Charles the Bald*, 50–8.
[162] *Capit.* no. 281 c. 9.

may have been less well supervised than they had been. Inheritance of office, like the embezzlement of official lands, could be both a consequence and a cause of declining royal power, but it does not seem helpful to confuse the two. There does not seem to be any evidence that the submergence of the office of count into the count's ex officio land was a significant factor in either. The ways that kings struggled to keep control of counties, even when their lands were diminished, the varying degrees of their success in different parts of the empire, and the way that some counts went on thinking of themselves as in some way royal officers—all these suggest that royal office as such continued to have some significance apart from the land attached to it.[163] A county took a long time to become a piece of property like the royal lands that, by grants or without grants, so many counts and others absorbed into their alodial holdings.

It is impossible to attribute the dissolution of the Carolingian fisc or the disintegration of the Carolingian empire to new forms of lordship, new forms of property, or new ideas about property. It is certainly possible to connect the rise of the Carolingians with new bonds of loyalty in so far as Charles Martel and his successors clearly achieved unprecedented success in marshalling their subjects to fight for them and run their government. But it is not clear that the relation between the king and either his counts or those who were now called his *vassi* was new in the sense that it drew on new ideas or values. What was new was the ambition and success that made it work. Once the Carolingian kingdom was established relations must have changed through the multiplication of *vassi* and their duties, but that was more a result of events than of new ideas. A new—or, rather, newly exploited—form of property, the benefice *verbo regis*, can also be connected with the rise of the Carolingians, but that too was not quite a cause of their success. They could not have got away with using church property so extensively if they had not had considerable authority already. Power over *vassi*, benefices, and benefice-holders was not enough either at the beginning or at any later stage of their rule. The Carolingians at their height took dues and services from all property and exercised authority over all property-holders. When they ran into trouble they did not do so because of the peculiar characteristics of the bond between lord and man or because one sort of property replaced another. It was not peculiar to the middle ages that, in a time of conflict and trouble, a distant central government should be less able to secure obedience and loyalty than the commanders on the spot. Invoking the peculiarities of vassalage and commendation to explain the inability of the later Carolingians to control their kingdoms is otiose. It

---

[163] Werner, 'Missus'; Nelson, *Charles the Bald*, 258–60.

is easy enough without that to understand how they lost control over their officials and their kingdoms as a whole and thus over property-holders within it. As a result a lot of property changed hands, while property law changed in so far as the obligations of property-holders were either no longer enforced or were enforced by local lords—counts or churches or anyone else—instead of the king. The evidence that this resulted from significantly new ideas about political loyalties or about the normal rights of property is, however, hard to come by. It was a matter of politics rather than of political theory or land law.

# 5

# THE KINGDOM OF FRANCE, 900–1100

## 5.1. *The problems*

THE area considered in this chapter is more or less that contained in what came to be known as the kingdom of France. After a brief period when its kings secured part of the middle kingdom, the boundaries of the western kingdom seem to have remained much the same from the treaty of Verdun until the thirteenth century. I shall occasionally refer to areas outside the kingdom, like the areas east of the Rhône that now form part of France or parts of the Low Countries that lay just within the empire. Inconsistent as this may be, I do it partly because pieces of evidence from those areas sometimes provide particularly tempting illustrations of conditions that I suspect were also found within the kingdom and partly because I am aware that by focusing on the kingdoms of France and Germany I am squeezing out the borderlands between them. Partly too I have put in some references here because French historiography has, quite understandably, tended to work within the boundaries of modern France. As a result, information about these areas has contributed to the picture of feudo-vassalic institutions associated with France.

Discussing the whole kingdom at once, wherever one draws its boundaries, may seem hopelessly foolhardy and superficial. Generalization about property rights in the kingdom of the Franks before 888 is hazardous enough: any uniformities that one deduces from royal legislation and royal charters probably mask a great deal of local variation. After 888 generalizing about the western part of the empire becomes even harder, since local customs were even more likely to diverge when central control weakened. Some historians have claimed that the very idea of the western kingdom as a whole kingdom fell into abeyance, so that the kingdom of the Franks came to be thought of as covering only those parts of the north that were under direct royal control. It has more recently been recognized, however, that this implies a crude view of the use of words and names. It is true that the words *Francus* (translatable either as Frank or Frenchman) and *Francia* were most often used in connection with the relatively small area to which royal activity and influence became restricted and that lords in other areas who were in practice virtually independent, with their followers, were often identified by the names of their regions or lordships. That need not, however, imply that the kingdom, if and when people thought about it, was always thought to be restricted to the area directly ruled by the king. In some contexts it clearly was not. While Franks, Burgundians, and Aquitanians were often regarded as separate peoples they were also, at least in some contexts, seen as belonging to the one kingdom.[1]

However that may be, the argument to be propounded here is that important changes in rules of property did not take place merely because ancient and inherent cultural differences between different areas provoked different developments in each. They were also caused by political changes that started from experiences common to the whole western kingdom, as well as to some areas beyond its borders. Though different areas did indeed have different traditions and went through different political experiences during the tenth and eleventh centuries, all started from some degree of subjection to Carolingian government and jurisdiction, and all were affected in their different ways by its decay. Moreover, although a fine accumulation of regional studies has drawn attention to variations of social structure and legal development within the kingdom, it would be wrong to conclude that the regions they describe always formed coherent units of custom. It is seldom easy to establish what was general and fixed custom in any single region before the thirteenth century. Customary law had not yet been codified within provinces, and the political units that moulded its development were not fixed. In any case the coverage here will not be anything like complete: published works of the sort that this book relies on for guidance to the sources are not available for all regions, and it has to cover too much for proper attention to variations.

As for the sources themselves, they pose their own problems. With the decline of royal authority they become almost entirely restricted, not merely to records that were preserved by great churches, but to those that were actually made by them in the first place. Apart from chronicles, saints' lives, miracle stories, and so on, all of which may contain occasional information about property relations, we have to rely very largely on cartularies that were compiled in cathedrals and monasteries to record the rights held or claimed by the churches themselves. Cartularies are full of information about property law but it is not always easy to interpret. To start with it is all *ex parte*. Records of disputes put the case of the church concerned. Even the documents that record—or purport to record—gifts to it were often drawn up by its own scribes. Some were written, years after

---

[1] Schneidmüller, *Nomen Patriae*; Brown, 'Franks', 32–53.

the supposed transaction, by the scribe who compiled the cartulary. Cartularies may also be a misleading guide to the terminology and norms of property law in a region: the customs they record and the words they use may be those favoured in a particular religious house rather than those of the lay community around it. The most important of all the drawbacks of cartularies as a source for the history of political, social, and property relations among the laity derives from the difference between ecclesiastical and secular views of property. Almost all the documents they contain concern church property and relations between clerical lords and lay tenants.[2] Few historians since the seventeenth century seem to have worried about the extent to which it is valid to make deductions about the relations between a king or lay noble and his followers from evidence about those between a bishop or abbot and the tenants of his church's lands.[3]

What is striking as one approaches the subject of free and noble property in the kingdom of France between about 900 and 1100 is that the greatest danger of teleology does not come from nationalist categories— that is, from assuming that the area we think of as France was always the same and was different from other areas—but from the categories of feudo-vassalic relations themselves. Discussion of the rights and obligations of property in the period has often been cast in the form of a search for the origins of a supposedly classic feudalism. Any search for origins is almost bound to involve a teleological concentration on anything that seems to lead to what is seen as the full development of the phenomenon. Although in some areas, notably Flanders and parts of the south, Carolingian ideas of public authority seem to have survived better than they did elsewhere, it is none the less argued that the political order which would emerge in the twelfth and thirteenth centuries was everywhere, even in those areas, shaped by the interpersonal relations of vassalage and fiefholding.[4] Thus relations between kings and counts from the tenth century on are seen predominantly, if not exclusively, in terms of what historians call vassalage. The power that the feudal system—and here 'system' is the precise word required—has exercised over the minds of deeply learned historians is exemplified in the old controversy whether counts were the king's *fidèles ou vassaux*. Lot noted in passing the rarity of the words *vassi* or *vassalli* in his

[2] Among rare exceptions see especially '*Conventum*', discussed in the next section. For grants from lay people to lay people see below, n. 181. Few editors of cartularies seem to have listed charters granted by laymen to laymen.

[3] Though see Duby, *Société mâconnaise*, 13–14.

[4] e.g. Poly and Bournazel, *Mutation*, 57–81, 97–9, 298–310; Lemarignier, *Gouvernement royal*, 170–6; Richard, *Saint Louis*, 51, though cf. 62; Magnou-Nortier, *Foi et fidélité*. Barthélemy's doubts about *la mutation* do not apparently extend to *féodalisme* itself, nor his doubts about the distinction between alods and *tenures* to the category of *tenure* (on which see index: *tenere*): Barthélemy, 'Mutation'.

sources but explained it away without embarrassment. More important, both he and Dumas were too sure of the reality of fiefs and vassalage as the basis of values and relations in the tenth and eleventh centuries to need to worry much about the scarcity or weakness of evidence that his idea of vassalage corresponded to the ideas of the period he was studying. Even Flach, though he made shrewd points about Lot's retrospective use of later evidence and the idea that feudal theory had preceded feudal practice, did not succeed in shifting debate out of the categories that had been erected on the basis of sixteenth-century study of the academic law of fiefs.[5] Some of the old assumptions about the dominance of feudo-vassalic values still underlie most discussions of relations between kings and the great nobles whom Lot called 'les grands vassaux'. Just as non-recognition of royal authority is often taken as evidence that individual counts were not royal vassals, or were breaking their vassalic oaths, so the recognition of royal authority by counts—even if only to the extent of witnessing a royal charter or two—is seen as evidence that they were royal vassals, while their vassalage is taken as implying that they held their lands and office in a quasi-feudal or proto-feudal subordination.[6] Relations between counts or other magnates and lesser landowners are interpreted in much the same way: those who seem to be a great man's followers or subordinates are often described as his vassals, whether or not the word is used in the sources. If he seems to have had some kind of control or influence over them and their alienation of land, that is taken to imply that they held their lands as fiefs, whether or not that word is used or any obligations are specified.[7] The recovery of government is thus seen as a function of the increasingly close connection between vassalage and fiefholding and of the stabilization of the rights and obligations of lords and vassals.

Some of those who discuss fiefs and vassals after 900 seem to accept that the 'union of benefice and vassalage' was achieved in the ninth century. Poly and Bournazel, for instance, talk of it as already old by the tenth century, though restricted to 'des groupes sociaux relativement peu nombreux', Devailly seems to assume it in Berry, and Bur sees it as established in Champagne from before 1000.[8] Duby's influential work on the

[5] Lot, Fidèles ou vassaux?, 249 et passim; Dumas, 'Encore la question', 213–14, 355–62, 371; Flach, Origines, iv. 10–13, and e.g. i. 245–6, iii. 55, 75–6, 79, 115–16, iv. 47, 521; cf. Guilhiermoz, Essai sur l'origine, 128–30, 130, 142, 331–45.

[6] e.g. Bur, Champagne, 87–9, 209–22, 405; Devailly, Berry, 164; Duby, Société mâconnaise, 91; Guillot, Anjou, i. 1–20, 124; Lemarignier, Gouvernement royal, 32–3, 59–65; Poly, Provence, 160–1.

[7] e.g. Bur, Champagne, 405; Devailly, Berry, 161–8; Duby, Société mâconnaise, 97–8, 125, 149–58; Fossier, Picardie, 547; Guillot, Anjou, i. 17–19, 28–30; Lemarignier, Gouvernement royal, 173–6; Poly, Provence, 160–71, 127–54; Tabuteau, Transfers, 63–5, 95, 99; Warlop, Flemish Nobility, 33–9; but cf. Fournier, Auvergne, 284; Giordanengo, Droit féodal, 223.

[8] Bur, Champagne, 404; Devailly, Berry, e.g. 133–4, 221; Poly and Bournazel, Mutation, 105.

Mâconnais, on the other hand, put the decisive moment of union there around 1030, though he thought that it did not affect relations between king and counts until Louis VII and Philip Augustus strengthened their personal bonds with great nobles in the area by making them turn some of their alods into fiefs.[9] Duby's argument may assume either that Ganshof was wrong (at least so far as concerned the Mâconnais) in placing the union in the Carolingian age or that the union had broken down along with the rest of the Carolingian order by 1000. Those who see the union as already established, on the other hand, may think that it had been achieved when Ganshof thought and had survived subsequent troubles. Perhaps the uncertainty is to be explained by a break in the interests of historians between Carolingian and later history.

Differences in dating the supposed union of vassalage and fief are less important here than the virtual unanimity in using the categories of classic feudalism and in seeing the link between vassal and fief as the key to future development. This begs a lot of questions that need to be considered directly. The first problem concerns the categories themselves. It is not just or even primarily a question of terminology, though terminological confusion is vastly confounded by the historiographical tradition of refer-ring to property as a fief, irrespective of the words used in the sources, whether because its holder is referred to as a vassal, or because historians think he was what is now called a vassal, or simply because that is how his-torians normally describe land held by medieval people who they think were above peasant status. Analysis of the use of individual words and their derivation, thought-provoking and helpful as it may be as a guide to the sources, does not, however, provide the complete answer to questions about the rules of property. The relation between words and phenomena is too uncertain to make it helpful to lay too much stress on words, let alone on their derivation, which often seems to affect current usage very little.[10] Abstract nouns like *feo, fevum, feudum, beneficium,* or *casamentum* cannot be assumed to have had consistent meanings outside their contexts. Even if one context suggests some content for a word, that content cannot be assumed to be inherent in the word itself in such a way as to be transferred to other contexts and other cases. Contexts, unfortunately, are often unhelpful in this period, since it has left us few of the kind of normative records which the more effective governments of both the ninth and thir-teenth centuries produced. Most of the chronicles and charters on which

[9] Duby, *Société mâconnaise*, 151, 406, 408, 414.
[10] Above, chapters 1.2 and 3.2. Cf. e.g. Hollyman, *Développement du vocabulaire*; Bur, *Champagne*, 393-5; Magnou, 'Note sur le sens du mot *fevum*'; Poly 'Vocabulaire'; Poly and Bournazel, *Mutation*, 117-29.

we have to rely are non-committal about the nature of political relations and the obligations that were expected to attach to landowning in general. Charters quite often say nothing about the rights and obligations of the pieces of property that are being conveyed. Scribes may have used apparently classificatory nouns to describe pieces of property without being concerned to distinguish anything we might call different and definable categories of property. Even if they were interested in distinctions, the words used in records compiled within different monasteries against a background of customary law and kept by the monasteries for their own use could not have had the technical senses they might acquire in later ages of professional law. Expressions like *in feodo* or *ad medium plantum*,[11] for instance, are unlikely to have implied the same rights and obligations in each case, irrespective of the scribe, the area, or the status of those concerned in the contract. Nouns like *feodum* or *beneficium*, even if different scribes would have agreed about the meanings they attached to them, need not have been used so as to indicate the particular rights and obligations attached to the properties concerned.

While there is no reason to assume an association of particular words with particular categories of property, so that the use of different words would imply correspondingly different rights and obligations, it seems equally misleading, on the other hand, to assume that, for instance, the three words *beneficium*, *casamentum*, and *feodum* were normally synonymous and that all can be assimilated to what historians think of as fiefs. Words expressly said in one context to mean the same thing (*beneficium quod vulgo dicitur feodum*[12]) may have been used in quite different ways by other people at other dates or places, or by the same people when they were thinking about distinguishing different aspects of property. *Casamentum* seems to have been used quite often in the eleventh century in much the same context as *feudum* or *feodum*, but that does not mean that one can assume that any property referred to as a *casamentum* had all the attributes later associated with fiefs any more than one can make a similar assumption about references to *feva*, *feuda*, properties held *in feodo*, et cetera. As for benefices, they must surely be seen against their Carolingian background. The division of historiographical interest between Carolingian and later history is presumably to blame for a tendency to discuss them in this period without reference either to the earlier use of the word to describe the land that a count held ex officio, or to the impact that benefices *verbo regis* must have had on expectations about what a benefice might entail. It is hard to believe that people in the Mâconnais in 1100 would generally

[11] Poly, *Provence*, 154.    [12] *Actes intéressant la Belgique*, no. 6 (1087).

have assumed that land held in benefice owed no service and, in particular, no military service.[13] The breakdown of Carolingian power can surely not be assumed, without argument, to have wiped out all the associations and expectations created by Carolingian use of church lands.

It is not just the reification of nouns that poses problems. Adjectives and phrases derived from nouns also need caution, and so do verbs. Two verbs may be mentioned here by way of illustration of the difficulties of interpretation. The first is *concedere*, which, according to Lot, in the tenth century had 'la signification très précise de "donner une terre en fief"'.[14] The only evidence he cited in support of this firm statement was Flodoard's use of the word in the mid tenth century for Charles the Simple's concession of Normandy to Rollo, which Lot was arguing had been that of a fief. Lemarignier, who followed Lot's interpretation, added that Flodoard used *concedere* consistently in this sense.[15] He too offered no further discussion or citations, but a far from thorough look through Flodoard's *Annales* and his History of Reims lends some support to his view.[16] *Concedere* does not seem to have been one of Flodoard's favourite words. He uses *conferre*, *dare*, and *reddere* much more. When he uses *concedere* it generally seems to be for grants which are limited in one way or another: when it is used for a king's appointment of a bishop it may be that Flodoard saw a limitation in the king's capacity as much as the bishop's right. When Flodoard used *concedere* for the grant to the Normans he may therefore have done so because he wanted to play it down. But it cannot be justified to argue from his use of the word half a century or so later that the original grant had itself been significantly limited, let alone that it had been deliberately limited so as to conform to the conditions later associated with fiefs. Charles the Simple's own charters, which were not in print when Lot was writing, occasionally use *concedere* and cognate nouns in connection with perpetual grants.[17]

*Concedere* is not a key term in most arguments. *Tenere* is more important, since later lawyers and legal historians would make the words tenure and tenement into technical terms. But, as I have already argued, there does not seem to be any reason to assume that 'holding' was always distinct from 'owning' or 'having'.[18] In the Merovingian formularies *tenere* seems to be juridically neutral, as do *habere* and *possidere*. Hollyman pointed out that when churches and laymen were given land to have, to hold, and to

---

[13] Duby, *Société mâconnaise*, 152 n.      [14] Lot, *Fidèles ou vassaux?*, 180.

[15] Lemarignier, *Recherches sur l'hommage en marche*, 80.

[16] Flodoard, *Annales* and *Hist.*

[17] *Rec. Charles le Simple*, nos. 6, 14, 23, 27, and index: *concessio*. Cf. *Rec. Charles le Chauve*, index: *concedere*.

[18] Du Cange, *Glossarium*, viii. 57. See chapter 3.3.

possess, the phrase was probably borrowed complete from the *Digest*.[19] It is highly unlikely that the three words expressed three different meanings that contemporaries would have distinguished consistently.[20] *Tenere* seems to have come into frequent use in eleventh-century documents and seems often to be the word chosen to combine with *de* in order to indicate the church or person who retained superior rights over property. The stages by which this happened need further investigation: the assumption that *tenere de* is the correct technical term may have filtered examples of *habere de* from historical view.[21] In the mean time the chief point to notice is that it is rash to assume that *tenere* implies restricted or dependent rights.[22] Two charters of Saint-Julien, Tours, dated 1059 and 1063, record how Duke William of Normandy confirmed to the abbey some property that Adam, the duke's vassal (*vassallus*), had given to them as he held it from William quit and free (*quiete et libere ut eam tenuerat*). Adam seems, in fact, to have originally had full rights in it.[23] At the time of his first gift, however, he had been disinherited by William and it was not until after negotiations between the abbey and the duke that he was again received back in peace and the gift could be secured. William then made his own grant of the property, not only as Adam had held it from him (*sicut Adam meus vassallus de me tenuit*), but as he himself held it (*sicut ipsa die in manu mea tenebam . . . sicut ego teneo*). Whatever the status of Adam's original rights, *tenere* as applied to those of the duke is surely not indicative of restriction or subordination. An account of the early history of Saint-Flour (Cantal), written either early in the twelfth century or shortly before, tells how Amblard de Brezons and his wife, who had the vicariate and a large fief (*feudum*) at the place, decided, around the 1020s, to refound the monastery there. An earlier foundation had been granted to Cluny late in the tenth century but the lord of Nonette had seized its lands and settled (*cassaverat*) many knights, including Amblard, on them. Amblard needed this lord's agreement, since the lord *held* in alod what Amblard *had* in fief (*qui hoc quod ego in feudo habebam in alodio tenebat*).[24] If this scribe saw any signif-

---

[19] *Formulae*, index: *tenere*; Hollyman, *Développement du vocabulaire*, 55–6.

[20] Niermeyer, *Lexicon*, 1018 (*tenere*, senses 3, 5).

[21] Hollyman, *Développement du vocabulaire*, 44–5, has one example; cf. 55–6 for *habere* used with *feudum*.

[22] Didier, *Droit des fiefs de Hainaut*, 111–12, points this out.

[23] *Rec. ducs de Normandie*, nos. 142, 156, esp. (for its status as full property) p. 341 (*Trado autem . . . ipsum alodum perpetualiter ad possidendum ex concessione Adam* (sic) *de Sancto Briccio vassalli mei qui eam* (sic) *prius tenuit*), and cf. ibid. no. 46; Tabuteau, *Transfers*, 95–112, esp. 102–3; and below.

[24] Fournier, *Auvergne*, 571–3.

icant difference between *tenere* and *habere* it was what later lawyers and historians of feudalism would consider the wrong one.[25]

Obviously words cannot be ignored: they are the substance of our evidence. This chapter, like those that follow, will have to focus on words like alod and fief but starts from the premiss that such words (or rather the Latin approximations to them that we find in the sources) did not have fixed or technical meanings, at any rate before the thirteenth century. Another premiss will be that relations and obligations associated with property should be envisaged as post-Carolingian rather than as proto-feudal: they are more likely to have been conditioned by what had gone before than by what was to come. The previous chapter concluded that Carolingian rules about property did not break down because old ideas about alods as the norm of property had been superseded by the rise of vassalage or because the 'union of benefice and vassalage' had made the 'vassal benefice' into the dominant or normative form of property. The hypothesis propounded here on the basis of this second premiss is that, with the weakening of royal power and jurisdiction, some of the old distinctions between types of property became blurred. Whoever controlled or tried to control any area is likely to have tried both to extort obedience and services of some kind from landowners within it and, at least on occasion, to influence or control the inheritance or transfer of their rights. Whether such *de facto* activities produced changes of custom *de jure* would presumably depend on the length of time during which they went on as well as on the number of relatively large landholders in the area and their willingness or ability to stand together in defence of what they saw as their rights or ancient custom. New distinctions, new ideas and norms, developed only as new political conditions became settled enough to produce something that seemed like custom. A third premiss is that those who managed the property of great churches were likely to have rather different preoccupations from those of lay lords and were constrained by rather different rules and requirements in dealing with their property. This means, as Duby pointed out forty years ago,[26] that we need to be cautious in deducing norms that governed lay property from records about church property. It is ironic that arguments about feudal tenure that have so often stressed the bond of lord and vassal and the developing ethos of a warrior aristocracy should have been based almost exclusively on sources that include very few grants from lay lords to lay followers.

---

[25] For a contrast between *tenura vel jus* and a holding *ad medietatem*, which was said to have *nullam tenuram nullam proprietatem nullumque jus*: Verriest, *Régime seigneurial*, 103–5.
[26] *Société mâconnaise*, 13–14.

## 5.2. *Government and political relations*

As the kings of the western Franks gradually lost control of large parts of
their kingdom, some areas fell under the control of counts or other local
rulers, while some parts were virtually without any government at all
except over peasants, many of whom had long been more or less completely under the jurisdiction of their lords rather than that of the count
and his deputies. Both situations threatened law and order in general and
property rights in particular, but in different ways for different kinds of
rights and different kinds of property-holders. When and where government was preserved or restored it was often both unstable and weak, limited alike by rivalries and by the need to leave all but the most bulliable
people to settle their own disputes for themselves. It is easy enough, reading chronicles and cartularies in the light of the traditional history of feudalism, to see why the tenth and eleventh centuries have been called a
period of feudal anarchy. How universal and fierce the disorders of the
tenth and eleventh centuries were, and how widely and flagrantly the
rights of property were flouted, is, however, very hard to say. A society as
unequal and authoritarian as that of France—like that of most of western
Europe at the time—could not survive the increasingly obvious weakness
of its supreme authority without increasingly frequent and serious
breaches of law and order. On the other hand, it was a society which had
always relied heavily on local co-operation and consensus for much of its
policing. Ecclesiastical sources almost certainly make the situation look
worse than it was, not least because their writers were so obsessed with
what they saw as the plunder of church property. Some straight plunder-
ing certainly took place, but part of what chronicles and cartularies present as such might make more sense for historians if it were seen as the
result of a conflict of values and interests. On the one hand stood monks
and clergy who were determined to preserve the property of God and the
saints and on the other were laymen who thought in terms of family rights
and inheritance. Both sets of values were valid in the terms of their own
time. One reason why churches suffered so much in the tenth century was
that they had hitherto relied so much on the king for protection. Once that
was gone the scales were weighted against church property. Not that the
Carolingians had always leant on its side, but the clergy had learnt to live
with the plunderings of kings. Now that churches could no longer rely on
protection—however self-interested—from a powerful king, and often
found the protection of counts just as dubious and expensive, they had to
develop other strategies. The cartularies suggest that they put up a pretty
good fight by trying to get influential people on their side, securing con-

sent to gifts from heirs and lords, and generally exploiting what they had as efficiently as possible.

While the breakdown of central government made the old norms harder to enforce, France did not fall into a total moral vacuum in which the rules of property or of political obligations became irrelevant. Alods and benefices continued to be granted and disputed, while complaints about lawless behaviour imply the norms that were—allegedly—being broken. The evidence of disputes does not suggest that ideas about custom and right, including the rights of property, changed significantly. The accepted norms just became harder to enforce. There was even less likelihood than there had been of getting an authoritative—let alone written—statement of the law, while most people in most parts of the kingdom had no real possibility of appealing to the king as a last resort. Where disputes, rather than being settled by the sword, came before a court or assembly, their settlement was therefore less rule-based and more a matter of inevitably vague and disputable custom and of personal status. Status had always mattered but now there was little to gainsay it.

In the 1020s Hugh of Lusignan compiled—or had compiled—a catalogue of complaints against Duke (or Count) William V of Aquitaine that still reflect some of the traditional norms.[27] Hugh recognized comital authority up to a point and his references to benefices, fiscs, and *placita* suggest that his recognition was based, however shakily, on Carolingian structures, while his determination to get what had been held by his father and uncle reflects even older values. His self-justifications imply that custom allowed recourse to self-help and war sooner than it would have done two hundred years before or two hundred years later. At either of those times legal procedures offered a better alternative than they did in his day, but even in his day it was still advisable to claim to be acting in self-defence and under provocation. Provocation could include being prevented from getting what one's kinsmen had held, even if they had had only subordinate rights in it, but even if one was provoked one needed to maintain as much show of honesty, reasonableness, and loyalty as possible. Hugh probably held some property independently of what he had from William,[28] but he did not accuse the count of trying to take from him anything he held with full property rights. He accepted, whether willingly or not, that rights in the fortresses he held in some way from the count or under his authority, or from the bishop with the count's agreement, were divided. At Gençay (Vienne), he agreed, *una pars sit mea et alia tua*, and he would sur-

[27] '*Conventum*'. It is discussed by Poly and Bournazel, *Mutation*, 137-42, who cite earlier works.
[28] e.g. perhaps Confolens (Charente) and Lusignan (Vienne): '*Conventum*', 545.

render the fortress to the count when required.[29] He also seems to have recognized an obligation to military service, though there is no reason to suppose that its extent was exactly worked out. In so far as all this suggests a change of values and rules from Carolingian times it may be primarily because political circumstances had made some rules irrelevant. The disputes between Hugh and his count were not of the sort in which property could have been classified into categories according to its rights and obligations, so that Hugh's fortresses could be assigned to one or another category accordingly.

As in the case of so many relations of the period that historians have long described in terms of vassalage, it is hard to fit this one into them and it does not seem either scholarly or rational to do so. Hugh did not refer to himself as the count's *vassus* or *vassallus* and it is not clear whether he would have been considered one in Carolingian terms. The *vassi* who held *fevos* in the fortress of Vivonne look slightly more like the kind of *vassi* who held benefices in return for military service in the ninth century. The *regales vassi* who, according to Odo of Cluny, were being taken over by ambitious marquises or counts in the early tenth century could have been very like them—if Odo, writing later on, got them right.[30] There are other occasional references to *vassi* in documentary sources that suggest that the old general sense of servant or follower survived throughout the eleventh century, but the nature of their service, whether military or governmental, and thus the basis of their relation with their lords, must have changed since the ninth century.[31] In the vernacular Hugh may have been referred to as a vassal: he was a noble and a fighter and that, with no particular connotations of relation to a superior, is what the word seems to have meant later on in, for instance, the Song of Roland.[32] Dudo of Saint-Quentin may have had that sense in mind when he made Charles the Simple's counsellors refer to Rollo (before his treaty with the king) as a reliable and easy vassal of sagacious mind (*sagaci mente vasallus constans et lenis*). Whatever Dudo meant by the word, it seems to be the only occasion when its application to one of those whom Lot called 'les grands vassaux' has been noted.[33]

Though historians persist in using the word vassal themselves it seems to be generally agreed that by the eleventh century it had become rare in the sources they use.[34] Of course the disuse of a particular word need not

[29] 'Conventum', 546–7; cf. 543 (Vivonne).
[30] Ibid. 543; Odo, Vita sancti Geraldi, 653, 660–1.
[31] e.g. Rec. ducs de Normandie, no. 142; Cart. Saint-Aubin, no. 667.
[32] See chapter 2.2.   [33] Dudo, De Moribus, 166.
[34] Guilhiermoz, Essai sur l'origine, 130, 142, 339; Lot, Fidèles ou vassaux?, 249; Dumas, 'Encore la question', 214, 361; Duby, Société mâconnaise, 150, 192; Bur, Champagne, 396; Giordanengo, Droit féodal, 101; Poly, Provence, 139–41, has one case that does not seem to fit the feudo-vassalic mould.

mean that the relation it had stood for had disappeared. Historians who note the rarity of *vassus* or *vassallus* suggest that *fidelis* and, increasingly, *miles*, were used instead and meant much the same. But there seems to be even less reason to suppose that either of these two words normally denoted a partner in the dyadic, affective, interpersonal relation traditionally characterized as vassalage than there is to suppose that *vassus* did so.[35] In some contexts *fideles* or *milites* may have stood in that relation to their lords, or something like it, and felt the kind of loyalty to him, while he felt the kind of responsibility to them, that ideas of feudo-vassalic bonds prescribe, but some *fideles* may have been either subjects or subordinates in a wider sense and some may have been little more than loyal friends. People described as *milites* need not have been in the service of anyone, whether temporarily or permanently. As for the witnesses to the charters of counts or other powerful men, who are sometimes taken to be their 'vassals', they could have been present in great men's courts for other reasons than that implies. That is not to say that there were no relations like those implied by the use of the word vassal. In the conditions obtaining in the kingdom of France during the tenth and eleventh centuries, when the institutions of government were at best fluid and enforcement was weak, nobles often had to rely on interpersonal bonds and mutual oaths to protect themselves against each other and to bind their soldiers in loyalty. But we do not know that their relations with their followers were always or even generally initiated by a ceremony like the homage of later law, or that they involved the same rules as had either been applied to benefice-holding under the Carolingians or would later be applied to fiefholding by those whom lawyers would call vassals. Relations between nobles did not exist in a vacuum apart from other relations.[36] It is hard to see how they could have when the status of people and of their property was so variable and ill-defined.

Whether loyalty or fidelity implied relations of subordination or not depended on circumstances and the status and power of the parties. When Fulbert of Chartres wrote to the same count of Aquitaine as was embroiled with Hugh of Lusignan about the obligations to a lord of those who had sworn fidelity to him (and, more briefly, about the reciprocal obligations of the lord) he may have been thinking primarily of people like Hugh, and perhaps even of Hugh himself, and he may also have been thinking of the knights or soldiers (*milites*) who held his own benefices. These were the kind of people who created most trouble.[37] But that does not mean that he

---

[35] For the following argument see also chapter 2.

[36] For a classic statement of a vacuum theory: Halphen, 'La Place de la royauté'.

[37] Fulbert, *Letters and Poems*, nos. 51 (also discussed in chapter 2 at nn. 10, 20) and 9. Cf. Ivo of Chartres, *Epistolae*, col. 214.

saw their obligation to loyalty and obedience in totally different terms from
that of all Christian people or was thinking only of them. As a bishop he
was bound to maintain that all subjects should keep their oaths, maintain
the peace, and obey the powers that be. He would also teach that oaths—
if lawful—should be kept.

By the eleventh century southern lords who were otherwise more or less
independent of each other or anyone else are recorded as using mutual
oaths to secure their treaties. Sometimes the oaths and treaties involved a
measure of subordination of one party to the other, but sometimes not.[38]
Soldiers who transferred themselves to another captain might be required
to take an oath to him, while kings and counts constantly tried to make
their alliances stick by mutual oaths and promises, some of them involving
gestures or ceremonies reminiscent of the later rite of homage and
fidelity.[39] Whether oaths or ceremonies implied the kind of obligations or
subordination of one to the other that were later associated with homage
probably depended on the relative status and military clout of the parties
and the nature of any previous disputes between them. What Duby calls
the first recorded rite of entry into vassalage from the Mâconnais may have
been designed simply to ensure that Walter of Berzé stopped being a nuisance to Cluny and attacking its property.[40] Fulk IV of Anjou certainly did
not intend to make himself the vassal—in any sense—of the abbot of Holy
Trinity, Vendôme, when he swore faith to him, putting his hands in the
abbot's hands, as secular custom required (*sicut mos secularis exigit*). He was
simply making peace and promising not to bully the abbey any more.[41]
Trying to fit the oaths and ceremonies of this period into the later lawyers'
categories of homage and fidelity does not make sense. Trying to explain
anomalies by invoking further categories like *hommage en marche* or 'servile
homage' only exacerbates the anachronism. Similar anachronisms are
involved in assumptions that people who are said to have committed or
commended themselves to another thereby 'entered vassalage' or that the
'commendation' of land made it into a fief.[42]

Members of the military élite must often have formed close relations

[38] Cheyette, 'The "Sale" of Carcassonne'; Magnou-Nortier, 'Fidélité et féodalité'.
[39] Richer, *Histoire*, 16, 34, 104, 122, 168, 268 and many other examples (see Van Luyn, 'Milites').
[40] Duby, *Société mâconnaise*, 149; *Rec. Cluny*, no. 3324.
[41] *Cart. Trinité Vendôme*, no. 175. Cf. Devic and Vaissete, *Languedoc*, v, col. 499, which is difficult to interpret.
[42] Odo, *Vita Geraldi*, col. 660, 667 may use *commendare* in something not unlike the senses traditionally given to it. But *Rec. Cluny*, no. 3324, referred to above, may be much less definite. For the 'commendation' of land that looks like an outright gift, e.g. *Cart. Trinité Vendôme*, no. 97, but cf. Guillot, *Anjou*, 298 (at n. 107). For other uses of 'commend' and its derivatives: Duparc, 'Commendise'.

with each other and with their commanders. According to the hagiographer of Count Burchard of Vendôme a knight called Ermenfrid, who had hitherto been subject (*subditus*) only to the king of France, submitted himself into Burchard's hands and power before fighting alongside him, because it was not the custom for a Frank to embark on battle without the presence or orders of his own lord.[43] If this was a universally recognized custom it must have been often breached, but the usual assumption that feudo-vassalic norms were universally accepted but constantly broken raises more problems than it solves. Some soldiers suffered from conflicts of loyalty but remained loyal to one side or another despite their suffering. Some may have done so because of their oaths or because they were given fiefs, but some who served merely for keep or wages may have been just as loyal. We are simply not told why most *milites* fought for their generals or what bound them in their service. What we are not entitled to do is to deduce from the lack of records of secular government that France was a moral and political vacuum in which there was no idea of the public interest, that the only bond between lords and men was that of 'vassalage', and that this universally recognized bond was nevertheless constantly being broken. If relations were fluid that may have been not only because of the difficulties, rather than the immorality, of the age, but because they were more complex than the feudal model implies. At the time when the knight Ermenfrid fought for Count Burchard he may already have been what a feudally-minded historian would call a *fidelis* of Count Burchard, though a more literal translation would make him only loyal or faithful to him.[44] He also held a benefice from Burchard as well as property of his own. These relations may have been consequences of the ceremony on the field of battle but they may have predated it.

Oaths were meanwhile also used for more general and governmental purposes. The custom of taking general oaths of fidelity on the Carolingian model is well recorded in the south and it may have been more common elsewhere than is sometimes suggested. Dudo of Saint-Quentin refers to general oaths in moments of crisis in Normandy.[45] This may reflect Norse rather than northern French practice,[46] but it does not seem unlikely that counts or other lords who claimed some kind of governing authority would have tried to require their subjects—and particularly those of higher status, who mattered most and were hardest to control—to take some kind of loyalty oath or go through some other ceremony to mark their subjection.

---

[43] Eudes, *Vie de Bouchard*, 19.
[44] Ermenfrid was *potentiis et divitiis seculi valde sublimis venerandoque comiti fidelis*: ibid. 17.
[45] Magnou-Nortier, 'Fidélité et féodalité'; Dudo, *De Moribus*, 226, 247.
[46] Searle, *Predatory Kinship*, 61–90.

While the mere reference to *fideles* or to rebels returning to fidelity after a revolt need not imply the taking of oaths, lack of record is not, in the circumstances, good evidence that they did not.[47] In the twelfth century Wace told how, after Duke William defeated the rebels in 1047, they gave him hostages to keep the peace, did fealty and homage, and swore to obey him as their lord and to demolish recent fortifications.[48] The point of such oaths and ceremonies was to acknowledge and symbolize political subjection. They need not have affected property rights and there was no reason why they should. The various oaths (generally classified as oaths of fealty or fidelity) by which southern counts, viscounts, and bishops tried to secure control over castellans did not apparently always affect the castellans' rights to alienate their fortresses and pass them on to their heirs, though an heir might be under pressure to renew his father's oath. It was apparently only from the twelfth century that such oaths were sometimes supplemented by the formal conversion of their alods into fiefs, and even then the implications for their rights and obligations varied.[49]

During the eleventh century an increasing amount of evidence suggests that things were beginning to settle down and that a new order was becoming established. The governments that emerge into view differed, however, from Carolingian government in important ways. The first and most obvious difference was in the size of the territories they ruled. Much of the kingdom had by then been parcelled out, though with many inconsistencies, much untidiness, and many uncertain boundaries, into areas under the kind of jurisdiction that later became known as the ban. The lords of these smaller areas within the castellanies were gradually extending their jurisdiction over free landholders within the borders they were trying to establish. Government at this level had to depend more on control of property than Carolingian government had done. Lords with the ban relied in the first place on their control of peasants and their holdings and the extraction of dues and services from them. When they extended their power over alodholders they did so by imposing rather similar controls, dues, and services on them. The development of banal lordship and its extension over free landowners is one sign of pressure on all property. Lists of dues and customs, whether owed to churches, counts, or other lords, are another, while grants of customary dues point the same way.[50] Dues

---

[47] Poly, *Provence*, 161, and Giordanengo, *Le Droit féodal*, 13, both assume that *fideles* or people in fidelity must have taken oaths.

[48] Wace, *Roman de Rou*, ii. 43 (ll. 4195–4200). Roger Middleton kindly helped me with this passage.

[49] Magnou-Nortier, 'Fidélité et féodalité', 127–8.

[50] e.g. *Cart. Trinité Vendôme*, no. 2; Haskins, *Norman Institutions*, 281–4; *Carts. Bas-Poitou*, pp. 90, 346–8; *Cart. Saint-Corneille*, no. 39.

worth granting were worth having. The subject's burden was the lord's profit.

At the level of castellanies or banal lordships, therefore, rights of government and rights of property were much less easy to distinguish than had been the case under Carolingian rule. Above that level there was in some areas very little governmental superstructure before the twelfth century. In others, where counts or dukes established or maintained their authority, they needed to tap the wealth of their greater subjects, but, lacking the legitimacy of kingship, they had to build up loyalty, obligation, and fear on the foundation of what might at first be little more than alliance or voluntary submission. In practice the early Capetians do not seem to have had much more authority than did counts. It looks as though all these higher rulers kept their demands for services from their greater lay subjects fairly vague for quite a long time while leaning more heavily on the lesser and, sometimes, on churches. When William the Conqueror founded Saint-Étienne, Caen, he forbade the monks to cut down trees in the woods he gave them and reserved his hunting rights there. It is not impossible that earlier counts of Normandy had already started to control, or try to control, hunting on the property of all their subjects, but they are more likely to have started with the property of churches and peasants than with that of their hunting friends.[51] Restraint in making demands on the powerful seems to apply to military service as much as anything else: between 900 and 1100 (and indeed for the best part of two centuries thereafter) it does not appear to have been a formal or fixed obligation on noble property. Nobles might feel an obligation to fight for king or lord, and rulers like William of Normandy made it difficult for them to refuse to do so, but there is no evidence that French nobles in general held their lands on the formal condition that they should serve in their lords' armies, let alone that they should provide any specified amount of service. Some rulers, as we shall see, like churches, are known to have made grants of land on restricted terms to their followers and servants in return for military or other service, and all may have done so, but no king or count, let alone anyone lower down the scale of government, had the vast and far-flung estates that had at once required delegated management and given scope for patronage under the Carolingians. What rulers at any level had to do was to make their subjects pay dues and accept controls on the land they already held—acknowledge, in effect, that their property was held under government. When they needed armies, they could then supplement their household troops with paid soldiers and could make those with full

[51] *Actes de Guillaume le conquérant*, no. 4; *Rec. ducs de Normandie*, no. 64; cf. Petit-Dutaillis, *Studies*, ii. 166–7.

property rights serve and contribute too. With more stability it might be more possible and profitable to assume that heirs to what had originally been subordinate property would be loyal, allow them to inherit, and perhaps get them to pay dues for the privilege. By that time they looked so like other heirs that it might even be possible to get the others to pay dues as well. As, when, and where government became more established and effective, rulers in any case needed to make land grants to servants less often. Instead, servants could be left to recoup themselves from the dues they collected and could be assigned annual sums from the growing revenues of property and government.[52] Charters meanwhile more often promise to guarantee titles, apparently in court, and more often refer to past arguments as well as, or instead of, past use of force. By this stage the authority of the more powerful rulers, like the dukes of Normandy or the counts of Flanders, would presumably have become distinguishable to anyone who might have thought about it as governmental rather than proprietary. Even so, the nature of their government and the dues and services they received made the distinction less clear than it had been in the high days of the Carolingian empire.

Eleventh-century rulers had much less in the way of an institutional structure through which to watch over their property and adjudicate that of their subjects than the Carolingians had inherited and developed. For obvious reasons that applied most decidedly at the level of those nobles who had since the ninth century become effectively independent of enforced authority. Hugh of Lusignan did not apparently appeal to any specific tribunal or demand any particular kind of judgement in his disputes with the count of Aquitaine. At about the same time as he was complaining about the count, Count Richard II of Normandy tried to mediate between Count Odo II of Blois and King Robert but, it seems, abandoned the attempt when Robert made difficulties about allowing Odo to be judged by Richard's (and presumably Odo's) peers.[53] Since there is no evidence that Odo and Richard regarded themselves, or were regarded, as vassals of the king in the sense of the later law of fiefs, or that 'peers' had the particular connotation that they would acquire in that law, Richard was probably demanding a hearing before other counts, who would be their social and political equals and might be expected to sympathize with a fellow-count against the king. The same may apply to the stipulation in the treaty between Henry I of England and the count of Flanders in 1101 that

---

[52] e.g. *Actes des comtes de Flandre*, no. 50; *Cart. gén. de Paris*, no. 199, discussed below; Bournazel, *Gouvernement capétien*, 105–6: the distinctions drawn by Baldwin, *Philip Augustus*, 538 (n. 73) seem to me unreal. On 'money-fiefs', below, at nn. 184–6, 212–14.

[53] Fulbert of Chartres, *Letters*, no. 86; cf. Halphen, 'Lettre'.

the count would not fail to fight for Henry according to the treaty, unless
the king of France judged that he should not by the judgement of his peers
who ought to judge him.[54] Lower down the social and political scale, in
counties and lesser lordships, the old norms of collective judgement survived, at least as norms. Those who dominated the process—when the lord
or his official allowed them to do so—were probably the men of greater
wealth and status, who were likely to be the holders of full property, rather
than those whose holdings might be called fiefs or benefices.[55] When peers
are mentioned they are often the fellows, associates, or apparent social
equals of individuals engaged in some transaction. When the count of
Flanders ordered in 1111 that nobles and knights who were accused of
breaking the peace had to clear themselves by the oaths of twelve of their
peers, it may have been partly because it would be too easy for them to get
dependants to swear what they told them. *Villani* and others who were
accused, however, also had to swear with the same number of their equals
(*cum totidem aequalibus suis*).[56] The idea that the 'judgement of peers' originated in courts of vassals finds no support in the evidence from France
in the tenth and eleventh century: there is, in fact, no evidence that separate courts were held for vassals, whether defined as fiefholders or not, in
this period.[57] In 1100, in fact, courts as such were still fairly irregular and
rudimentary above the level of those through which lords ruled their peasants and the lesser landowners under their ban. In some areas settlements
between nobles could only be made by arbitration. In Normandy, on the
other hand, the duke's court had something like effective supervision or
jurisdiction over everyone, including churches, well before the end of the
eleventh century. All this, however, is speculative, since it is not until well
on in the twelfth that we begin to catch more than occasional glimpses of
governments at work or more than occasional echoes of disputes.

## 5.3. *Benefices and the lands of counts and churches*

The word benefice continued to be used in the multifarious and often
ambiguous senses that had long attached to it. Some or all of the *beneficia*
that, in the early tenth century, Gerald of Aurillac was slow to give but,
having given, was slow to withdraw, and that he tried to prevent other

[54] *Diplomatic Documents*, no. 1.

[55] Reynolds, *Kingdoms and Communities*, 23–34, though undue attention is there paid to the
groups of peers in north France. Feuchère, 'Pairs', argues backwards from later evidence and
even in the thirteenth century has little evidence of fixed panels. His evidence for connecting
those who owed watch duties with later peers who judged seems weak.

[56] *Actes des comtes de Flandre*, no. 49.

[57] Neither Ganshof, *Recherches* and 'Transformations', nor Feuchère, 'Pairs', could find any
in their respective areas.

lords from withdrawing from their vassals, may have been landholdings.[58] Some, however, could have been employment in return for wages or keep, protection against others, or favourable terms for holding subordinate land, rather than the land itself. The late eleventh- and early twelfth-century Saint-Aubin cartulary uses *beneficium* for the spiritual benefits granted to donors in return for land.[59] The word also continued to be used, as it had been earlier, for the endowments of lesser churches and the rights of parish clergy in them.[60] In this kind of context it is misleading to assimilate benefices to fiefs, so as to make the word into a symptom of the 'feudalization' of the church.[61]

When the word benefice was used for landed property it was sometimes applied, as it had been in the ninth century, to the lands that counts had originally held ex officio and the ecclesiastical property that they had under their care.[62] The lands of counts and viscounts were still, in the eleventh century and beyond, sometimes called their benefices or honours, or even fiscs or fiscal (i.e. royal) lands.[63] In 1030 the king was able to take a mildly firm line with a count who held benefices from Saint-Germain-des-Prés.[64] By then, however, many people farther away from Paris must have forgotten the old contexts in which these words had once been used, so that new contexts gave them new connotations.[65] In the 1020s Odo II of Blois accused Robert the Pious of saying that Odo was unworthy to hold any benefice from him and of condemning Odo without judgement. That was all the more unfair, Odo said—or Bishop Fulbert said for him—since the benefice that the king apparently wanted to confiscate was, according to Odo, not royal property (*de tuo fisco*) but what had come to Odo by inheritance from his ancestors by the king's grace.[66] The inheritance he referred to was that of his kinsman, Count Stephen of Meaux and Troyes, who had died without immediate heirs. According to Ralph Glaber, it should by

[58] Odo, *Vita Geraldi*, 651, 653; cf. Dudo, *De Moribus*, 279 (Count Theobald's promise: *Hucusque rei gratia quasi pro beneficio tibi serviens militabo*).

[59] e.g. *Cart. Saint-Aubin*, nos. 114, 121, 170–1.

[60] A distinction made in Hainaut between *feodum* and *beneficium* in 1129 might fit here: Didier, *Droit des fiefs*, 6 n.

[61] Fournier, *Auvergne*, indexes under *féodalité* the benefice referred to at 535 n., which consisted of rights held by a clerk in a church; cf. Bur, *Champagne*, 394.

[62] *RHGF*, ix. 665; Devic and Vaissete, *Languedoc*, v, col. 240–50; Arbois, *Champagne*, i. 453 (seen by Bur, *Champagne*, 399, as an early reference to the grant of a fief); *Vita Bertulfi*, 638.

[63] Hugh of Lusignan's scribe's use of *beneficia, benefitium*, and *fiscum* suggests the memory of old usages: '*Conventum*'.

[64] Tardif, *Monuments*, no. 260.

[65] Benefices: *Chartes de Saint-Maixent*, 26–7; *Rec. Cluny*, nos. 680, 688, 774, and Duby, *Société mâconnaise*, 91; Arbois, *Ducs de Champagne*, i. 453; *Cartulaire de Béziers*, no. 49; Guillaume de Jumièges, *Gesta*, 101; 'Cartulaire de Saint-Maur', 369–70; *Gallia Christ. Nov.* no. 386. Fiscs: Poly, *Provence*, 97–9; 'Ex gestis Ambasiensium Dominorum', 241.

[66] Fulbert, *Letters and Poems*, no. 86.

right (*jure*) have gone back to the king, but Odo, to judge from his letter, did not regard it as part of the royal estate: in so far as he saw it as a royal benefice that may have been because he needed royal grace or favour (in effect a royal alliance) to secure it.[67] He may not have regarded his original counties of Blois, Tours, and Chartres as benefices in any sense that implied that his own rights over them were limited by continued dependence on royal favour. While it seems fair to deduce that by the eleventh century, if not before, most counts thought of their counties, like the lands within them that were under their more direct control, as theirs by inheritance, that would not prevent them from sometimes seeing recent gifts as the kind of benefice or favour for which they still felt an obligation to the giver. In 1096 Count Stephen of Blois recognized that of the four abbeys he had *a patribus meis quasi sub jure regali dimissas* there was one that he had *in benefitio* from the duke of Burgundy. The duke's predecessor had given it to Stephen's father about forty years before in return for help against the count of Nevers.[68] Whether the word in this case implies anything one could call a legal restriction on Stephen's property rights is, however, unclear.

Although counts increasingly regarded both their offices and the lands attached to them as their own, the property of counts does not seem to have been generally referred to as their alods. In the far south it may have been. In 1085 Count Peter of Mauguio (Hérault) gave to Gregory VII and his successors *per allodium* himself and all his property (*omnem honorem meum*), including both his county and the bishopric of Maguelone, as he and his predecessors had held them *in allodium*. What the grant was meant to involve at the time or what it involved later is hard to say. Peter promised that he and his successors would hold the county by the hand of the popes and would pay them an ounce of gold a year. Urban II considered that the agreement had made the counts of Mauguio into *Romani pontificis milites*. Since Peter also promised to allow free elections to the see of Maguelone, he may have envisaged the relation as concerned with religious obedience rather than a permanent surrender of rights over secular property.[69] At any rate his twelfth-century successors do not seem to have been trammelled in their grants to the lords of Montpellier by any remembrance of papal 'overlordship'.[70] In 1125 and 1146 settlements of their frequent disputes referred to the count's rights in his county as if they were complete.[71] In

---

[67] Rodulfus Glaber, *Hist.* 104 (III. 2); Bur, *Champagne*, 157–8; Dunbabin, *France*, 192. All this assumes that the traditional association of the letter with Stephen's inheritance is correct.
[68] *Rec. Cluny*, no. 3717; Bur, *Champagne*, 202.
[69] *Gallia Christ.* vi, instr. col. 349–51; cf. *Liber Instrumentorum*, introd. pp. iii–v, nos. 40–1.
[70] *Liber Instrumentorum*, nos. 57–93.
[71] *De honore vero comitali in quo comes habet proprietatem*: ibid., nos. 61, 74.

1215 Innocent III would grant the county, which, he said, was known to belong *ad jus sive proprietatem Romanae ecclesiae*, but that was in different political and religious circumstances, when lawyers were creating a new sort of property law out of the old words and relations.[72] However that may be, by the late eleventh century the lands of counts in the far south may have often been called alods rather than benefices.[73] For the lands counts granted out to their subordinates or soldiers *beneficium* may have been replaced by *fevus*.[74]

More often, however, the lands of counts were simply said to be theirs, without any reference to conditions or title: in so far as counts became effectively independent of superior authority they did not have to define and defend their titles to property in court. Juridical status was irrelevant. On occasion title still mattered, as it did to Dudo of Saint-Quentin. Writing early in the eleventh century, Dudo was adamant that when Charles the Simple gave the land beyond the Epte to Rollo the Norseman he gave it *in alodo et in fundo*.[75] The origin of the count (or duke) of Normandy's position was sufficiently well known and sufficiently anomalous for Dudo to want to make it look legitimate—presumably according to the norms of his own day.[76] The point he was making in using the phrase he did was probably that the grant had been permanent and unconditional.[77] He may well have been substantially right. Whether or not in 911 (or thereabouts) Charles hoped to be able to revoke his concession later, neither he nor his successors had been able to do so.[78] Given the way that the word benefice could be used of counts' lands and offices in the eleventh century with so little, if any, apparent connotation of dependency, Dudo could almost have used it, but *in alodo et in fundo* was better. In fact the grant included more rights than the usual royal concession of an alod, which was not normally envisaged as embodying the kind of political control conveyed by the grant of a county.

The supporters of the king either in 911 or in Dudo's time might well have objected to his formulation if they had known of it, but any suggestion that they would have seen Charles's concession as what later lawyers or historians would have called a grant *en fief* must be misleading:[79] few of the conditions later associated with such grants can be assumed to have

[72] *Gallia Christ.* vi, instr. col. 367.          [73] Cf. Poly, *Provence*, 97.
[74] Magnou, 'Note'; Cheyette, 'The "Sale" of Carcassonne'; Devic and Vaissete, *Hist. Languedoc*, v, col. 548–9, 551–4. The use of *fevus* is discussed later in this chapter (5.5).
[75] Dudo, *De Moribus*, 168–9 (c. 28).
[76] On Dudo: Searle, *Predatory Kinship*, esp. 61–7.
[77] Yver, 'Premières Institutions', 313–16.
[78] Cf. the recognition of Richard I's hereditary right by Louis IV: Dudo, *De Moribus*, 226 (c. 71).
[79] e.g. Lemarignier, *L'Hommage en marche*, 80 (on the use of *concedere*, see above at nn. 14–15).

attached to them in the early eleventh century, let alone in the tenth.[80] That Rollo underwent a ceremony of formal submission that may have resembled what later became known as the ceremony of homage, and that this made him in some sense the king's man; that he may well have promised some kind of military assistance to the king;[81] and that he and his descendants sometimes fought under or alongside later kings—all this does not make the grant 'feudal', nor would it be illuminating to compromise by describing it as 'proto-feudal'. What the so-called homage and later relations imply is that the territory ceded to Rollo was probably generally envisaged, by Normans as well as by kings, as still forming part of the kingdom.[82] If early eleventh-century rulers of Normandy allied with their kings, or recognized their authority, more than many other counts did at the time, that was not because of the terms on which Rollo had originally received his counties, which were surely less exigent than those of counts whose titles went further back, but because the political geography of northern France made alliances intermittently useful to both sides.[83] In the context of tenth-century politics Louis IV's invasion of Normandy during the minority of Richard I can be understood, not as the exercise of a recognized right of wardship, but as an attempt to assert royal authority at a time of Norman weakness. In the context of tenth-century law it could have been justified as the action of a king in defence of the rights of a minor subject, whether seen as an alodholder or a count, rather than as a lord's exercise of wardship as later lawyers might define it.

The same applies to the apparent intervention of Henry I in the tangled disputes between the counts of Anjou and Vendôme. Fulk Nerra (d. 1040), count of Anjou, married the daughter of a count of Vendôme and subsequently managed to secure the inheritance of Vendôme for the daughter of the marriage. As a result, he and his equally ambitious son, Geoffrey Martel, were then able, allegedly with the consent of King Henry, to take over control of the estates of Fulk's grandson, Burchard, count of Vendôme, who was a minor. There is no need to postulate either a pre-existing, regular, and recognized hierarchy of property or formal rules of wardship in order to explain either Henry or Geoffrey's interest in the inheritance or the description of Geoffrey as the lord from whom the young count held his honour. Nor need the 'law of the deserter and rebel' that was invoked to justify Geoffrey's confiscation of his resentful and rebellious nephew's inheritance presuppose any rules peculiar to benefices

[80] See section 5 of this chapter.
[81] Though Richer's evidence, cited by Lemarignier, *L'Hommage en marche*, 80, is not good: his information is obviously garbled.
[82] Though see Dudo, *De Moribus*, 250, and Searle, *Predatory Kinship*, 67.
[83] Bates, *Normandy*, 5–6, 8, 14–15.

or fiefs. According to the writer of the cartulary of Holy Trinity, Vendôme, who seems to have felt sympathy for both sides at different stages of the story, the king had indeed given young Burchard's honour to Geoffrey under an agreement that Burchard and his mother should hold it from Geoffrey. Subsequently Geoffrey bought out his sister's rights. That may have been what gave him enough control to treat Burchard's attempt at independence as unlawful rebellion. This sort of situation created precedents that would later be rationalized to create the idea of a regular hierarchy of property, but to interpret them as if those ideas already existed is to ignore the implications of the grievances and quarrels that the cautiously worded cartulary account reveals.[84]

Dudo used the traditional language of property law to justify the title of the counts of Normandy. Other counts who apparently obtained their titles and land with less formality no doubt thought up justifications for themselves, more or less disingenuously, in terms of what they thought was reasonable custom. It seems difficult to find hard evidence from the tenth and eleventh centuries that, when the old idea that comital land was royal land that counts held ex officio lapsed, it was replaced by a perception of it as being held from the king in any sense that would imply less than the accepted full rights of property. It is certainly not generally said in the sources to be held from him. When historians have supposed that counts already held their property as what are now called fiefs it has been because they have worked backwards from twelfth- or thirteenth-century relations; because they have deduced a fief from the use of the word benefice, which is supposed to be always synonymous with fief; because they assume that counts who were referred to as the king's *fideles*, attended the royal court, however rarely, or ever took an oath to the king, must have been his vassals and therefore held their lands as fiefs from him; or because they have deduced fiefs from occasional royal consents—or supposed royal consents—to comital donations to churches.[85] But none of these reasons is convincing. When counts attended the king's court, subscribed his charters, or fought under or beside him, that need not mean that they recognized themselves to be the king's men or to hold their lands from him in any other sense than that in which everyone in a kingdom was the king's subject and every free alodholder held, or owned, his property under the king.[86] When Count Herbert of Vermandois defected from King Ralph in

<hr />

[84] *Cart. Trinité de Vendôme*, no. 6; cf. Guillot, *Anjou*, 23, 26–31. For varying views on hierarchy, but all presuming the validity of feudo-vassalic principles: Lemarignier, *Gouvernement*, 172; Duby, *Société mâconnaise*, 158–65, 422–4; Bur, *Champagne*, 218.

[85] Above, n. 6.

[86] *Gallia Christ.* viii, instr. col. 297, and x, instr. col. 360, for instance, surely do not show that Fulk Nerra was Robert the Pious's 'vassal for Anjou': Lemarignier, *Gouvernement*, 60.

931 and *sese committit* to Henry the Fowler, that may have involved a ceremony that would later be called homage, but there is no evidence that,
either in practice or in contemporary theory, it affected his title to his lands
in either the eastern or western kingdom.[87]

Nor does it appear that when, a little later, various great men either did
or did not declare themselves for Louis IV and took oaths to him, that was
thought to have any bearing on their rights in their property. Civil war
could, of course, endanger property and power in practice, but that is what
civil war does, irrespective of the particular system of property law. In the
course of the tenth century, though no doubt at different times in different areas according to differing local circumstances, counts seem to have
felt less and less need to seek permission from the king to give away what
would once have been seen as royal land. In the eleventh century they occasionally did so, but so irregularly that it seems unconvincing to postulate a
dependent property relation and a consequent rule that grants needed the
assent and confirmation of the king in order to explain these cases. It is
more economical to explain them by political circumstances, as, for
instance, when the land donated, or the church to which it was given, lay
in or near an area where the king had power or influence.[88] Around the
middle of the eleventh century Geoffrey Martel confirmed the gift to
Saint-Maur-sur-Loire (Maine-et-Loire) of properties in his own honour
or benefice and those of the count of Poitou and the viscount of Thouars.
The count and viscount both gave their consent but it is fairly obvious that
no one thought to ask the king.[89] Although in other contexts the word
benefice continued to denote land held with definitely restricted rights, in
the context of this charter neither it nor honour seems to have had any connotations of dependency. They were simply traditional words for a count's
or viscount's lands, which could apparently include both the territory
under his control and his property in a more direct sense.[90] When two successive counts of Poitou ceded to two successive counts of Anjou lands *pro
beneficio* in northern Poitou that had been in dispute between them, the
same impression is conveyed of old words losing their old connotations in
new circumstances. Here the expression may have been a face-saver for the
counts of Poitou, since the counts of Anjou do not seem to have treated

[87] Flodoard, *Annales*, 15; cf. Flach, *Origines*, iv. 521, and Bur, *Champagne*, 91, 405.

[88] e.g. *Rec. ducs de Normandie*, no. 3; Arbois, *Ducs de Champagne*, i. 484–5; *Rec. Philippe I*, nos.
9, 21, 103.

[89] 'Cartulaire de Saint-Maur', 369–70; cf. below, at n. 177, and Guillot, *Anjou*, ii. 98–9. Royal
consent is not recorded in any of the grants cited in n. 65, including that in Arbois, *Ducs de
Champagne*: Bur, *Champagne*, 399, says that King Lothar subscribed the charter but it appears
to be merely dated by his regnal year.

[90] For possibly full property not belonging to a count but also called a benefice (*de meo proprio
beneficio*): *Cart. des abbayes de Saint Pierre*, no. 12.

the territories concerned in any way that suggests submission or obligation.[91]

My conclusion so far as the property of counts is concerned is that the
word benefice, when it was used either of counts' offices or their lands in
the tenth and eleventh centuries, should not be taken as a synonym of fief
in the sense that would later be given to the word either by medieval academic lawyers or by modern historians of feudalism. It is less unreal to
compare tenth- and eleventh-century counties either with Carolingian
counties or with the alods of their own time than to assimilate them to the
fiefs or alods of traditional feudal history, but the contrasts are as illuminating as the similarities. As late as 1100 references to counts' benefices
may sometimes have evoked the relations that explain the Carolingian origins of the expression, but the relations between king and counts had
changed since then, both in practice and in principle. Counts' offices and
lands were in some ways assimilated to their hereditary alodial property
but though Dudo and the scribe of Peter of Mauguio's charter used the
word alod for them it was not a very appropriate one either. Counts stood
in a different relation to the king from that in which alodholders in their
counties stood to them. Political and legal conditions made the juridical
status of counts' offices and lands different from what it had been earlier
or would be later, but they were not conditions in which anyone needed or
wanted to analyse it for our benefit. In so far as tenth- and eleventh-
century counts saw themselves under an obligation to the king and connected their obligation with the laws and customs by which they may have
thought that they held their lands and offices, it was probably because the
troubles which nearly submerged the French monarchy did not wash away
all the prestige attached to the title of king. References to Flanders or
Normandy as *regna*[92] were backhanded acknowledgements of the prestige
of kingship: their rulers were kinglike in their authority—rather more
kinglike than the king of France was at the time.

Churches and their lands were sometimes referred to in the tenth and
eleventh centuries as royal benefices or as part of counts' benefices in the
old Carolingian manner.[93] The survival of old traditions, however distorted, about the connection between counts and churches may be implied
in the joint decision of count and bishop about the fortress of Vivonne
(Vienne) about 1025, though that may have been just a matter of local politics.[94] It looks clearer in a story told around 1100 at Grenoble, just outside

[91] Bachrach, 'Feudal Politics', and works he cites on pp. 112–13.

[92] Werner, 'Kingdom and Principality', n. 22.

[93] *RHGF*, ix. 665; Arbois, *Ducs de Champagne*, i. 484–5; cf. Lesne, 'Diverses Acceptions',
45–6, 51–5.                                                                [94] '*Conventum*', 543.

the eastern boundary of France in the kingdom of Burgundy. According to the cartulary of Grenoble cathedral, Bishop Isarnus, who had been bishop of Grenoble in the later tenth century, was called count, for in those days the bishop held his whole bishopric (except what he chose to give away) in peace, as an alod, without any challenge from any forebears of the late eleventh-century counts, who had not been there then.[95] According to this—obviously *ex parte*—account, Guigo the Old later assumed the title of count and seized lands from Isarnus's successor around the middle of the eleventh century. The cartulary's explanation of what had happened still assumes that proper relations between count's land and bishop's land should have followed what look like Carolingian lines. As Giordanengo has pointed out, the story does not fit the traditional feudal interpretation that was later imposed on it.[96] In the kingdom of France some bishops acquired comital rights, while all probably suffered depredations, as did Isarnus's successors.[97] It is hard to know how far counts who took over church lands in these centuries were consciously using or abusing their old authority and how far, like other nobles who did the same, they were simply using their local power.

Despite occasional echoes of the old system, however, churches were not generally envisaged as holding their land either from the king or from counts. They held them absolutely and for ever, like alods or inheritances, as indeed they had officially done even when their lands formed part of comital benefices. That did not necessarily exclude restraints and obligations on their property, but no services that they owed were seen as derogating from the permanent, secure, and unconditional nature that church property was supposed to enjoy. How long counts went on trying to get military service from churches is unknowable, but by the eleventh century any general and formal obligations seem to have lapsed. Philip I is recorded as making a demand for military service from the abbot of Saint-Médard and another from the bishop of Chartres. In each case the basis of the obligation looks vague and in each case it was resisted.[98] Even in Normandy, where references to tenure in alms in the eleventh century suggest that the new privilege supposedly implied in the phrase could have been a response to the relatively high level of obligations by then imposed on everyone in the duchy, there is no evidence that churches owed formal quotas of service before the conquest of England.[99]

[95] *Cartulaires de Grenoble*, 93.
[96] Giordanengo, *Le Droit féodal*, 19–22, 94.
[97] Guyotjeannin, *Episcopus et comes*, 3–56.
[98] Hariulf, *Vita Arnulfi*, col. 1389; Ivo, *Epistolae*, col. 40–1.
[99] Tabuteau, *Transfers*, 37, 106–7, 292 (n. 230); cf. *Actes des comtes de Flandre*, no. 13, and Martin, *Histoire de la coutume de Paris*, i. 219.

Church property seems not to have been normally envisaged as held from anyone.[100] Contemporary sources do not suggest that the mere giving of land to a church made the donor the lord of either church or land in such a way as to retain any rights in the property he or she gave.[101] One exception comes from 1092, when Philip I specified that the church of Saint-Melon, Pontoise, which he was giving to the archbishop of Rouen, was to be held from him both *in fedium* and for ever. The context suggests that here, as in at least some of the cases in which lay alods were said to be held from someone, the implied relation was one of politics rather than of property rights.[102] Philip's charter went on to explain that what the archbishop held within the royal fief (*de fedio meo*) was to be held from him and owe service to him, while what formed part of the archbishopric was to be held from the duke of Normandy.[103] Philip's fief here was clearly the area under his political control.[104] His difficult relations with the dukes of Normandy made it essential to spell out the political implications of a concession to their most eminent subject. It would be over a century before churches were incorporated into anything that was envisaged at all like a general hierarchy of property. When that happened it may have been because the way monks and clerics managed church property had stimulated laymen to start thinking about property in hierarchical terms. The efforts that churches made to keep track of what they had granted to laymen, whether they called it benefices, fiefs, or anything else, must have familiarized many free and noble laymen with the idea of land 'held from' a church, however much they tried to forget about it. The multiplication of parish churches offered new property to grant, while the complexity and divisibility of tithes and church offerings lent themselves to an elaboration of layers of rights which perhaps came easily to those who were accustomed to think in terms of an ecclesiastical hierarchy. That kind of hierarchy may have been as much or more in the minds of those who recorded the consent of bishops to the grant of lesser churches and their lands, or the holding of such churches from them, as the feudal hierarchy which

[100] Saint-Evroul stood in the fief of Bocquencé and the lord of Bocquencé made gifts to it, but Orderic did not think of him as lord of the church or of what he gave: Orderic Vitalis, *Hist. Eccl.* ii. 80–4.

[101] Rights retained for life under an agreement (*precarium*, benefice) were a different matter and implied the church's superior rights.

[102] For alods: below, at nn. 176–9.

[103] *Si vero est de archiepiscopatu de comite Normannorum teneat cujus est archiepiscopus*: *Rec. Philippe I*, no. 127. Whether *de archiepiscopatu* means within the diocese (or province) or part of the archbishopric's endowment does not much affect my argument. Other exceptions: Tabuteau, *Transfers*, 37; *Cart. Saint-Vincent du Mans*, no. 807; *Cart. Saint-Aubin*, no. 325; *Dipl. Belgica*, i, no. 168 (for which see below, at n. 240). There must be others, though some at least would not need distinctively feudal interpretations.

[104] See below, at n. 204.

jumps into the minds of historians.[105] Meanwhile the consents to gifts that churches got from the lay lords of donors must have stimulated the lords to positive thinking about their rights over the property of their subjects. Perhaps we should think less of the church and its property being 'feudalized' than of property rights being 'ecclesiasticized'.

The word benefice also continued to be used as it had been earlier for land that counts and churches granted to others, whether laymen or clergy, sometimes for several lives but with the intention of keeping it within the endowment of the county or church. Preserving the precise status of their endowments may have become less important to counts once they were no longer responsible to the king for their comital lands, but it remained vital to churches. Rents and services for such lands are not very often mentioned. When they are it generally looks as though the tenants were fairly humble.[106] That may not be an accident of the sources: churches sometimes granted benefices to more important people in return for the grant of an alod or for general promises or hopes of protection, rather than for formal service, but they would expect heavier and more precise payments or services from the less influential and powerful. There was, however, presumably nothing to stop a church asking for more specific service from a noble if it wanted.[107] The real problem was, as it had always been, to keep a lien on any property that was granted for more than one life.[108] If there was a trend to inheritance of benefices during the tenth and eleventh centuries it was because, in the absence of effective royal protection, churches found it harder to enforce their reversionary rights: the drive towards *de facto* inheritance and the tendency of custom and lay public opinion to transform it into a right were not in themselves new.[109]

As in the past, church grants were sometimes called *precaria* or *praestaria*, but the different words do not seem to imply different rights and obligations—in other words different categories of property.[110] The same applies to *feodum* and its variants when they came to be used of similar grants.[111] William the Conqueror seems to have been in a position to hand out something rather like a Carolingian benefice *verbo regis* from the land of Mont-Saint-Michel, though the document that regulated the dues and

---

[105] Bur, *Champagne*, 394–5; Guillot, *Anjou*, 458; Olivier-Martin, *Histoire du droit français*, 185.
[106] Van Luyn, 'Milites', 38; *Chartes de Saint-Maixent*, no. 14; Poly, *Provence*, 90 n.; *Cartulaire d'Apt*, no. 26.
[107] *Chron. de Saint-Pierre de Bèze*, 306–7.
[108] *Rec. Cluny*, no. 2118; *Hist. Tornacenses*, 337–9; Guillot, *Anjou*, 298 at n. 107.
[109] Duby, *Société mâconnaise*, 55 n., 63–4, 151–2. See section 5 of this chapter.
[110] *Cartulaire d'Apt*, no. 26; *Cartulaire de Saint-André*, no. 35; Bur, *Champagne*, 183 n.
[111] *Hist. Tornacenses*, 338–9; Guillot, *Anjou*, 298; *Actes intéressant la Belgique*, no. 6; *Cart. Montiéramey*, no. 18.

services owed to the abbey refers to the property as held *in fedo*, not *in beneficio*.[112] There is no need to suppose a deliberate imitation of the old system: the obligations are quite different from those prescribed in Carolingian capitularies. Rights of inheritance are not referred to in this instance, presumably because, unlike the services, they had not been at issue: the abbey was probably prepared to let its tenant, William Paynel, pass on the property, provided that its ultimate and reversionary right was protected, just as had often happened with benefices *verbo regis*. Disputes about inheritance may have erupted later, as they so often had with the earlier royal benefices on church land. Meanwhile the old *precaria* or *beneficia* that left donors to the church a life interest in what they had given away continued in use, whether those words were used or not. In 1061 Waleran, a *miles* of King Philip I, who had granted part of his inherited property (*de rebus sue proprietatis . . . omne hoc quod . . . pater suus ibi in proprio jure tenuerat*) to Beauvais cathedral, was nevertheless still holding it *in beneficio* of the cathedral.[113]

Though the absence of lay records makes it impossible to do more than guess at the source of innovations, ecclesiastical determination to keep tabs on church property may have formed precedents for some of the dues that later came to be considered characteristic of noble fiefs. Historians tend to draw a rather firm line between succession dues taken from peasants (*mainmorte*: heriot in English) and those taken from free or noble fiefholders (*rachat*, etc.:[114] relief), but the customary derivation of the latter directly from the customs of the war-band has the flavour of the conjectural history practised by nineteenth-century evolutionary anthropologists. There is some slight evidence to suggest that the survival or memory of old traditions could have lain behind succession dues in England, but *rachats* in France may have had a more immediate precedent in those demanded by churches from their tenants.[115] Such payments may have been primarily intended as symbols and reminders of the limited rights of inheritance on which churches insisted, and were probably paid chiefly by peasants. Perhaps they came to be extended to other tenants, and copied by other lords, as and when that became practicable.[116] Whether or not these dues really originated on church lands, others of course did not, like those based on old comital dues or the emergency aids for ransom, knighting, and marriage, which must have been first taken by secular lords. Not long after the

[112] Haskins, *Norman Institutions*, 21–2; cf. Tabuteau, *Transfers*, 56–7.

[113] *Rec. Philippe I*, no. 9; Guyotjeannin, *Episocopus et comes*, 95, sees this as one of the first references to a fief held of the bishop.

[114] Terminology varied: e.g. Giordanengo, *Droit féodal*, 12.

[115] Petot, 'L'Origine de la mainmorte servile'. See index: succession dues.

[116] *Cart. Beaulieu*, no. 50; Tabuteau, *Transfers*, 56–7, 59–61; cf. Poly, *Provence*, 90 n.

first evidence of these lay aids, however, there is evidence that some
bishops and other clergy had devised reasons of their own (going to Rome,
burning of the cathedral, purchase of land) for similar demands: which side
copied which is therefore hard to tell.[117] The most important management
tool of all that the great churches passed on to lay lords and lay governments was record-keeping. The impression that churches made their
greatest recoveries of property at about the time when cartularies began to
multiply may, if it is correct, not be accidental.[118] Ironically, the recoveries may also have provoked the lay backlash that made it impossible for
churches to maintain their hard line on inheritance into the twelfth century, but that was also a product of developments in government that were
by then already under way.

## 5.4. *Other full property: alods and inheritances*

In some parts of the kingdom, including parts of the supposedly more feudalized north and west, historians now seem to agree that alods survived in
quite large numbers at least into the twelfth century.[119] Perhaps their
number—or rather the number of properties held with full rights, whatever it was called—is still underestimated. The areas where later medieval
lawyers presumed property to be alodial unless it were proved not to be
were much more widely distributed than one might suppose from some
modern discussions of feudalism.[120] The whole argument has been focused
too much on words. Before the twelfth century lay property seldom got
into surviving records unless it passed to the church. If one starts from the
assumption that everything given to churches that was not explicitly
described as an alod must have been a fief then one is likely to go seriously
astray. Land held with the fullest rights available to laymen had never been
invariably described in every donation as alodial. Words like *proprietas*,
*proprium*, and *hereditas* had long been acceptable equivalents and they still
were, both in Normandy at one end of the kingdom and outside its borders
in Provence at the other.[121] In the 1030s a Norman donor gave *totam hereditatem suam quam communi voce alodum dicimus*.[122] Others who alienated
inheritances may not have bothered to mention common usage, especially

---

[117] Stephenson, 'Origin and Nature', 62. See below, at nn. 153–4.
[118] Duby, *Société mâconnaise*, 9–10, 245–6; Poly, *Provence*, 365; Tabuteau, *Transfers*, 9.
[119] Bouchard, 'Origins of French Nobility'; Fossier, *Enfance*, 956–61; Herlihy, 'Church Property'; Boutruche, *Une société provinciale*, 2–30; Bur, *Champagne*, 395; Chédeville, *Chartres*, 291; Fossier, *Picardie*, 636; Fournier, *Auvergne*, 284; Poly, *Provence*, 132–4.
[120] Chénon, *Alleux*, 111–79.
[121] Above, chapter 4.1, 3; Tabuteau, *Transfers*, 96–9; Poly, *Provence*, 76.
[122] *Rec. ducs de Normandie*, no. 93; Tabuteau, *Transfers*, 100–1, 108. For *proprium* as particularly common in the Gâtinais of Poitou: Beech, *Rural Society*, 86.

if and when it was no longer all that common. The sources that I have consulted suggest to me that terminology changed during the post-Carolingian centuries and that the word alod came to be less used, except in the south, for the land of people of higher status.[123] This change of terminology did not automatically mean that the properties concerned lost rights or gained obligations. In other words, rights of property that people at the time thought of as complete did not change merely because surviving documents do not happen to include a particular word. It may not be too rash to guess that any land which a donor calls his or her inheritance, possibly with reference to consent by kinspeople to the donation but without reference to any limitations on the terms by which the property was held or to its obligations to a previous grantor, could equally well have been described as an alod or was held on terms which would once have been associated with alods.

One of the chief reasons for identifying property of unspecified status as feudal rather than alodial seems to be that the consent of a lord was recorded when it was given to a church.[124] But seigniorial consent was sometimes given to the grant of estates which are expressly called alods. In Normandy during the 1040s Jumièges abbey made a sizeable payment to Roger of Montgomery for his consent to the grant to the abbey of an alod under his lordship or government (*in mea ditione*), while Count William of Normandy and other lesser counts subscribed Roger's charter.[125] Several other charters from the time of Richard II of Normandy onwards record the count or duke's consent to the grant of alods.[126] Others which do not explicitly refer to alodial properties may nevertheless concern them. In 1025 Richard gave Jumièges a general confirmation of lands granted by his subjects (*fideles*), *vel de suis beneficiis que nostris sunt juris vel de paternis hereditatibus*. Paternal inheritances at this date sound like what historians call alods (or, more often, allods).[127] In 1055, when the abbot of Marmoutier (Indre-et-Loire) was worried about the security of a gift of property to which no one but the donor's brother appears to have had a likely claim (though it may have been insecure because of its situation in

---

[123] Cf. Musset, 'Reflexions'; for the south, above, at nn. 68–73. Usage there needs fuller investigation, distinguishing the use of *beneficium* from *fevus* etc.

[124] Beech, *Rural Society*, 86; Fossier, *Picardie*, 546; Lewis, *Southern French Society*, 157; White, *Custom, Kinship, and Gifts*, 133 and nn. 222–6; Tabuteau, *Transfers*, 179–87, though cf. 102–3. Some of the works cited above in n. 7 take this line as well as deducing fiefs from supposed vassals: e.g. Duby, *Société mâconnaise*, 153, 158.

[125] *Rec. ducs de Normandie*, no. 113.

[126] Ibid. nos. 36, 45–6, 93, 156 (on this case, above at nn. 23–4). *Gallia Christ.* xi, instr. col. 226. *Rec. ducs de Normandie*, no. 94 and *Actes de Guillame le conquérant*, no. 6 may also be confirmations (below, at n. 151).

[127] *Rec. ducs de Normandie*, no. 36; cf. Tabuteau, *Transfers*, 104. For the choice of spelling, see chapter 3 n. 1.

the Vexin), he decided that the best course was to get a confirmation from 'William, prince and duke of the Normans, and, to say plainly what you might otherwise discover with difficulty, king of all his land'.[128] One sees his point. Despite periods of rebellion, the counts or dukes were by now maintaining an increasingly close control over Normandy and that meant maintaining control over landowners.[129] Normandy was in some ways unusual, but the Norman cases of comital consent to the alienation of alods may be exceptional in their explicit terminology, and in having been noticed, rather than in substance. In 1093 the count of Flanders gave his consent when the founders of the abbey of Ham (Somme) gave the abbey alodial property and granted general permission for *milites* or men to give it their possessions in his county.[130] Eleventh-century counts of Anjou, Dammartin, Mâcon, Maine, Poitou, and Valenciennes—and no doubt others—all seem to have given consent to gifts of what look otherwise like independent properties—that is, properties in which the donors' kins had rights of some sort in the way that they would have had in alods.[131] Some eleventh-century royal grants add immunity or confirmation to grants by others of what may be similar kinds of property.[132]

These cases are too few to prove anything except the danger of making easy assumptions about the status of eleventh-century property and the need to look critically at the implications of consents to grants. Pending more thorough searches with this in mind, the small cluster of cases in Normandy and Anjou are significant in so far as they come from what are often thought of as feudalized areas with relatively little alodial property.[133] They were also, however, like Flanders, areas under relatively strong comital control. In Anjou, as in Normandy, it is surely likely that eleventh-century counts were asked to give their consent to gifts not—or not only—because they were lords or overlords in the sense of the later law of fiefs but because they were regarded as the effective rulers of their coun-

[128] *Rec. ducs de Normandie*, no. 137. Cf. Le Cacheux, 'Une charte de Jumièges' for alodial property said to be held by inheritance but also by gift of Duke William.
[129] For scepticism on their earlier power: Searle, *Predatory Kinship*.
[130] *Actes des comtes de Flandre*, nos. 13, 17; cf. nos. 44, 73.
[131] 'Cart. Saint-Maur', 369–70; *Cart. Saint-Aubin*, nos. 35, 68, 114, 160; *Rec. Philippe I*, no. 11; *Rec. Cluny*, no. 3475 (Duby, *Société mâconnaise*, 158, considers this property a fief, but it is surely part of the count's fief: see below, at nn. 145–7 and 198–203); *Cart. des abbayes de Saint-Pierre*, no. 12; *Actes intéressant la Belgique*, no. 6. For other possible Anjou cases see White, *Custom, Kinship, and Gifts*, n. 11 on p. 254: among 15 examples (concerning 14 properties) of confirmation or consent by lords to Saint-Aubin gifts listed here 3 refer only to the count's consent, 1 to consent by the count and a lesser lord, 8 (7 properties) only to lesser lords, and 3 do not appear to refer to consent by any lord. I have not followed up the references to the gifts to the other abbeys.
[132] *Rec. Philippe I*, nos. 9, 11.
[133] White, *Custom, Kinship, and Gifts*, 133; Tabuteau, *Transfers*, 95–112 *et passim* sees Norman 'ownership' largely replaced by 'tenure' during the eleventh century.

ties.[134] The same may well apply to some castellans or other lords who established control over smaller areas. Some consents given by these lords, as by counts, may have been thought necessary because the property had once been given to its present donor or his predecessor by the lord or his predecessor, but this should not be assumed in every case.[135] Nor is it plausible to postulate as the only alternative a previous *reprise* (the surrender of an alod to a lord who regrants it to its former owner as a fief): that seems altogether too elaborate and formal to have been common in the circumstances of the time.[136]

It is not that a clear rule about the free alienability of alods was changed to a clear rule against it.[137] The rule—though the word norm would be more appropriate in tenth- and eleventh-century conditions—was always a tricky one to apply. There had always been tension between the right of the owner to alienate and the right of his potential heirs to inherit. The pressure to secure consents and get them properly recorded came at first as much or more from the beneficiary's desire for security as from the donor's fear of breaking rules. In the ninth century royal threats to revoke any gifts to churches that defrauded heirs of their rights had, it seems, led some churches to require and record the consent of potential heirs.[138] By the tenth and eleventh centuries it looks as though it was becoming accepted (if it had not been earlier) that lands that people acquired on their own account were more freely alienable than those they inherited. The norm may have owed something to customs derived from Roman law, especially in the south.[139] Meanwhile, as the recording of consents by donors' wives and families multiplied in the tenth century, royal confiscation became less of a danger but self-help by powerful and uncontrolled laymen who could plausibly claim an interest in donated properties was a very real one.[140] A precaution first taken in one circumstance was found even more useful and

[134] White, *Custom, Kinship, and Gifts*, 222–7. *Cart. Saint-Aubin*, no. 721 and *Cart. Trinité Vendôme*, nos. 96–7, 130 (about the same case, on which cf. Guillot, *Anjou*, i. 335–8, ii. 118–19) are very suggestive and so is the general permission allegedly given by Fulk Nerra: Guillot, *Anjou*, i. 368 n., though the terms here are unclear: I suggest inserting, or understanding, *suos* before *vicos et castella*. If, as Guillot suggests, the distinction is between lands held from the count ('en sa mouvance') and the rest of the county ('l'ensemble de ses États') the request for confirmation of a gift *de casamento comitis* would not be as anomalous as the cartulary seems to suggest.
[135] *Cart. Marmoutier/Vendômois*, nos. 4–8, 12; 'Cart. Saint-Maur', 369–70 (viscount of Thouars); *Cart. Saint-Vincent de Mâcon*, no. 21; *Rec. Cluny*, nos. 3067, 3577, 3640–2; *Cart. Molesme*, ii. 217–18; *Cart. Saint-Aubin*, nos. 114, 721; *Actes de Guillaume le conquérant*, no. 6. Consents continued to use similar phrases in the twelfth century: below, 5.5.
[136] The evidence about *fiefs de reprise* is discussed at the end of this chapter.
[137] For its implied continuance, e.g. *Cart. Molesme*, no. 694.    [138] Chapter 4.3.
[139] Fournier, *Auvergne*, 536 n. 7 is a very clear example; cf. *Cart. lyonnais*, no. 10, especially the *terram quam ego emi . . . in alodio*, which does not go to his brother.
[140] Laplanche, *La Réserve coutumière*, 66–76.

appropriate in another. As churches became more numerous, richer, and better organized, so they elaborated their records and, as part of that process, their recording of consents. It looks as though during the eleventh century many great monasteries decided that it was prudent to secure consent, not only from a donor's kinsmen who might have claims to inherit, but from anyone who had the kind of authority and power that would enable him either to protect or to disturb the church's hold on its property. This could mean getting consent from several people for each gift, whether they were counts or other local lords who for one reason or another might be able to make trouble. By the late tenth century Cluny was already securing the consent of relatively insignificant men to grants of the inheritances of people referred to as their *fideles*. That may say more about the structure of power in Burgundy and the efficiency of the abbey's administration than about any such reduction of the grantors' property rights as might have resulted from a formal submission or 'commendation' of themselves and their lands.[141] Even if there were evidence of commendation or oaths of fidelity, that, as I have argued, need not have involved a transfer of property rights.[142]

A case from Anjou may provide a useful illustration of the problem of interpreting consents. Between 1006 and 1028 Guy, the treasurer of Angers cathedral, gave the church of Saint-Martin at Le Lion d'Angers (Maine-et-Loire) to the abbey of Saint-Aubin at Angers, with the consent of his wife and sons and by the authority of count Fulk of Anjou and the bishop of Angers. Two successive lords of Craon (Mayenne), *ad quorum casamentum pertinebat*, also consented. When Guy became a monk at Saint-Aubin his eldest son succeeded to the paternal inheritance and maintained and enlarged his father's gift. All this, at least, is what was recorded in the cartulary of Saint-Aubin at the very end of the century. Monastic memory may then have exaggerated the formalities of consent to the original donation, however, for Guy's younger son, who in turn succeeded by hereditary right to the paternal honour, withheld the property. Not until the 1050s did he allow the abbey to buy him out for £130, whereupon he surrendered all rights to the property on behalf of himself and his heirs and successors. This second transaction was once again authorized by the count and the bishop and by yet another lord of Craon, *ad cujus casamentum pertinebat locus ille*, and who got £30 for his rights or claims, whatever they were.[143]

---

[141] Duby, *Société mâconnaise*, 126 and n. 63. His interpretation follows tradition: Chénon, *Alleux*, 28.

[142] On commendations, see chapter 2.2.

[143] *Cart. Saint-Aubin*, no. 160; cf. Guillot, *Anjou*, i. 335–8, ii. 128.

Similar cases occur in dozens of eleventh-century cartularies: donors and their heirs might so easily be in a position to resume occupation of property they had granted—or were alleged to have granted—to a church. The particular context in which I wish to use this particular case, however, is that of the relation between the donors and those, apart from their kin, who gave consent to the gift. I have already suggested that the count of Anjou's consent could have been given as effective ruler rather than as the lord who had granted a fief. The bishop may be here partly because he was a figure of general authority in the area and partly because he might be supposed to have authority over a church, especially one that belonged to the treasurer of his cathedral.[144] At all events I do not feel any necessity to elaborate arguments that the bishop's consent need not imply a link of feudal lordship as that is usually understood.

The real problem concerns the lords of Craon.[145] Perhaps Guy's property was what historians call a fief and had originated in a grant from a lord of Craon—perhaps a grant that had explicitly reserved superior rights. But perhaps not. Although phrases like *ad quorum casamentum pertinebat* or *de cuius feudo erat* seem to be commonly taken as meaning that the donated property was a *casamentum* or fief, that must be a mistranslation. The Saint-Aubin charter, like the others which use such phrases, does not refer to Guy's property as a *casamentum* but as belonging to the *casamentum* of the lords of Craon. Although Le Lion d'Angers is not so close to Craon as to make it obvious that the lords of Craon would have had some general control or jurisdiction over it, it is not that far off. They could have loomed over landowners and their properties at Le Lion, or merely over this family and its property, in other ways than by formally granting them fiefs. If the property at Le Lion had been granted by the lords of Craon on deliberately restricted terms one might have expected them to have asserted their rights against Saint-Aubin on their own account. Instead it was the donor's heir, not any lord, who felt defrauded and who caused trouble for the church. Given that we know that the consent of rulers or other powerful men—lords in a very general sense—was sometimes given for the alienation of alods, there does not seem to be any reason to suppose that the right that Guy and his heirs enjoyed in what was called their inheritance was not of much the same kind as it would have been if the inheritance had been called an alod. That is to say, their rights were probably what contemporaries thought of as complete property rights, formally undivided with any superior, although subject, *de facto* or *de jure*, to those with mili-

---

[144] Cf. *Rec. Philippe I*, no. 9; *Rec. Cluny*, no. 3717.
[145] For their relations with the count: *Cart. Saint-Aubin*, no. 721; *Cart. Trinité Vendôme*, nos. 96–7, 130; Guillot, *Anjou*, i. 335–8, ii. 118–19.

tary or political power in the area. The restriction of rights by governmental or quasi-governmental power looks at least as likely as that associated with what historians call fiefs. Governmental or quasi-governmental
approval of donations could be used by churches to bring pressure to bear
on donors who changed their minds, and on their heirs, so that this sort of
consent was almost as useful in practice to churches as was the consent of
the lord of property held on formally restricted terms.

As the consent of lords—however defined and whatever the nature of
their authority—was more and more often demanded, so custom would
make it seem necessary, though the frequency with which lords gave
general permissions for gifts may simultaneously have undermined the
custom. A royal charter of 1136 gave a layman an alod with full rights of
free disposition in terms very like those of Carolingian grants,[146] but the
scarcity of grants by kings to laymen between 888 and the twelfth century
makes it impossible to know if that represented a continuous tradition.
Even if it did, kings may not have observed the rules in practice, while
other lords need not have followed royal forms at all. Practice probably varied according to the status and influence of the owner who wanted to alienate. Any lord might think twice about allowing the kind of smallholders
who were most likely to owe significant dues and services to give their
holdings to the church. For more important people consent was more
likely to be a formality, unless, for instance, their land was in a politically
sensitive location or the ruler patronized a rival church. Where the land
market was relatively active—and probably becoming more so—many
alienations probably went ahead without consent. Consents to alienations
to other laymen were anyway less likely to be recorded than were those to
churches. The records of some alienations suggest some of the power politics that made nonsense of any rules, whether feudo-vassalic or not. By the
eleventh century comital authority in the Mâconnais had disintegrated so
far that a count of Mâcon was impelled to give some lands (referred to as
*condaminae*) that he claimed as part of his wife's inheritance to a man who
seemed to be powerful in the area at the time, in order to secure the rest of
her estate (*honor*). The *condaminae* finished up with the monks of Cluny,
who claimed to have been given them by the countess's brother Wigo, who
had held them *jure paterno*, but before the abbey could secure them it had
to negotiate with another lord who was described as *capud et dominus omnis
istius honoris*.[147] The count's need to conciliate or negotiate with others
about property, and then the abbey's need to do likewise, can be better

---

[146] Tardif, *Monuments*, no. 420.
[147] *Rec. Cluny*, no. 3577, dated by Bruel *c.*1080, by Duby *c.*1030 (*Société mâconnaise*, 151 n.)
or *c.*1040 (ibid. 158 n.).

explained by *Realpolitik*, conducted against the background of old ideas about property rights, than by postulating any formal division of rights over the property as between lord and tenant. Wigo and his predecessors had probably regarded the property as entirely theirs. It was his death without sons and the consequent dispute over his inheritance that threw the title to his land into doubt.

To the historian seigniorial consent to the alienation of alods blurs the distinction between fief and alod. For contemporaries the blurring may have worked rather differently. People at the time were not thinking of a straight contrast of fief and alod. Fiefs, as we shall see, did not yet represent a coherent category of property. No one at the time was probably doing much in the way of classification, but it may not be too unrealistic to envisage property in the tenth century as falling into three main classes: full and free property, whether described as alods, inheritances, *proprietates*, or anything else; property that was granted with subordinate and restricted rights to free commoners or nobles; and property that had subordinate and restricted rights because it was held by unfree peasants. As time went on the first class seems likely to have become divided, so that rights in the smaller alods of less rich and powerful people became rather less full and free and therefore more like those in the other two classes. People of high status were often outside any effective jurisdiction, but if they took their property disputes to a local ruler or sought arbitration from their neighbours, rather than settling them by force, they could appeal with fair confidence to general norms about their right to inherit or alienate their property and about its exemption from burdens. The terms they used to describe their property might not matter much, because their wealth and status would a priori suggest that they had rights which other people of high status also enjoyed and might combine to protect. Peasant alodholders who resisted claims on their property, on the other hand, could not rely on their own status: their best hope would be to rely on the status of their land. The word alod may therefore have mattered more to them. By 1100 a good many alodholders of intermediate status may have fallen under the ban of local lords so that their property became part of a separate discourse from those about the land of great men. Their alods, being subject to the jurisdiction of other alodholders, were, if not necessarily and immediately less secure, none the less robbed of some of their old status.

Tenth- and eleventh-century charters say very little about the services and dues that were owed from inheritances or alods. Given the nature of the records, this need not mean that none were owed. Rulers of the whole Frankish kingdom had been able to respect and protect alods to a large extent because they could lean more heavily on church lands and their own great estates for a good part of the men and money they needed. Even then, however, alods had owed military service, court service, and probably some dues and emergency taxes to the king, or to the count as his representative.[148] In the tenth century many counts, or would-be counts, probably tried to maintain or increase the old obligations on their own account, but with records gone and rules forgotten the system broke down in some areas and was distorted in others. New rulers, or would-be rulers, lacked the old legitimacy, so they had to work hard to get accepted, especially by those who had the wealth and power to provide the military support every ruler needed and the status to attend his court and speak up either in helpful support or in dangerous opposition. While different lords met with different degrees of success, and while varying conflicts and compromises diverted custom along varying courses, the difference between the services owed by greater and lesser alods was likely to be accentuated.

The distinction between great and small, between those who held the ban and those who came under it, seems to apply to money payments and other dues, which seem to have been paid chiefly, or only, by the relatively humble. Some customary dues, like *albergum* and *fodrum*, survived from the days when they had been officially taken by counts. Any landowner with peasant tenants had probably always passed on his obligation to them. Now, while the owners of small alods without tenants might still be having to pay the old dues, or something like them, to those who had succeeded, by fair means or foul, to comital rights, larger landowners may well have kept for themselves whatever their peasant tenants had once paid to counts.[149] New rulers at whatever level no doubt thought up new dues from time to time and imposed them on those who were least able to resist, who might include such alodholders as came under their ban. This may account for some of the 'customs' that were paid to counts and other lords in the eleventh century.[150] When William the Conqueror made what look like grants of alodholders, complete with their alods, to churches, he may have been confirming what the alodholders had given earlier and adding the customary dues they owed to him.[151] When lords in Maine forbade their men to give all their holdings to the Le Mans churches lest their services should be lost, or when the churches made arrangements to see that this did not happen, the properties concerned may have included holdings that, whatever they were called, would have been thought of as carrying

---

[148] Chapter 4.3.

[149] Duby, *Société mâconnaise*, 79–80; Poly, *Provence*, 124–5.

[150] Lemarignier, 'Dislocation'; Duby, *Société mâconnaise*, 55 n.; Guillot, *Anjou*, i. 371–2; Tabuteau, *Transfers*, 37–8, 71, 91; *Cart. Trinité Vendôme*, no. 2; *Rec. ducs de Normandie*, no. 151; *Gallia Christ.* xi, instr. col. 226.

[151] *Rec. ducs de Normandie*, no. 94; *Actes de Guillame le conquérant*, no. 6.

full rights.[152] The so-called 'feudal aids' to pay for the lord's emergency expenses for knighting, ransom, marriage, and so on, also seem to have originated in dues levied on properties that may have been of this kind. The earliest evidence of such aids seems to come from the later eleventh century, in charters of Mont-Saint-Michel and Saint-Vincent, Le Mans.[153] It looks as though a custom that originated in west France later spread from there as lords saw its advantages.[154] Cases like these illustrate the way that the old categories were becoming blurred and altered. In the 1080s a Norman inheritance that had been adjudged to its owner by a right judgement so that he held it *in suo dominio ut proprium hereditatem* nevertheless owed rent to someone described as its chief lord and was indeed said to be held from him.[155] It may not have been unique or even unusual. The vulnerability of relatively small landowners to pressure, both from lords of the ban and others, no doubt helps to explain how some alods would in the age of professional law come to be reclassified as *censives*— inherited peasant properties that owed rent to a lord and were considered to be something less than alods.[156]

The evidence about military service is particularly difficult. References to an obligation to provide it, and even merely to men serving in armies with no allusion to their obligation to serve, are often taken as evidence of fiefs. But no tenth- or eleventh-century lord who wanted to raise an army for more than home-guard service could have relied only on those who held formally dependent property. Rulers of any standing must have needed to call on their richer and more powerful subjects and neighbours, who were, of course, those most likely to have held the kind of inherited property that was sometimes called alodial. Calling on them may have been all they could do: it looks as though, right through the eleventh century, rulers or would-be rulers relied less on fixed rules than on persuasion, backed by promises or threats, when they wanted military support from their nobles. In the troubled years of the early tenth century, according to Odo of Cluny, great men usurped control of royal vassals (*regales vassos insolentia marchionum sibi subjugavit*). Duke William I of Aquitaine tried to

---

[152] *Cart. Saint-Vincent du Mans*, nos. 175, 212, 537, 807; *Cart. des abbayes de Saint-Pierre*, nos. 12, 15. The likelihood of alodial status varies among these. Properties described as *beneficia* seem to me more likely to have had restricted rights than those described as *feva* or *casamenta*: see below, 5.5.

[153] Haskins, *Norman Institutions*, 21–2; *Cart. Saint-Vincent du Mans*, nos. 751, 807.

[154] For the later development of the aids, see index: aids.

[155] Tabuteau, *Transfers*, 328 (n. 125); cf. *Rec. ducs de Normandie*, no. 113.

[156] Chénon, *Alleux*, 43; Fossier, *Enfance*, 956–61; Perrin, *Seigneurie rurale*, 667; Boutruche, *Société provinciale*, 21–8, 110; id. *Seigneurie et féodalité*, 705–6; Duby, *Société mâconnaise*, 248, 389. Cf. the interesting thesis of Génicot, *Économie rurale*, i. 69–88, and, on the classification, Richardot, 'A propos des personnes'.

attract Gerald of Aurillac from the service of the king (*a regia militia*) into his own. He failed, but he got Gerald's nephew instead.[157] A hundred years later Duke (or Count) William V seems to have got only intermittent service from Hugh of Lusignan, even though Hugh, while he presumably had some full property of his own, also held some fortresses from the count.[158] Even in Normandy, despite much search and argument, historians have failed to find precedents for the kind of fixed quotas of service that were imposed on England after the conquest. There, however, as in Anjou and Flanders, for instance, it is hard to believe that counts did not get pretty effective service without formal rules or quotas.[159] The greatest and best-documented offensive army that was raised in eleventh-century France does not seem to have been raised from those with formally dependent property.[160] William the Conqueror apparently issued a general summons to his subjects in Normandy and supplemented that by a recruiting drive in other parts of France.

In areas where comital power was less well established a lot may have depended on contracts between individuals. Over the border of the kingdom in Provence, William Gaucelin and his wife in 1047 gave their faithful man Bernard part of their inheritance in the county of Antibes for ever, *ad proprium alodem*, to do with it what he chose. The gift was made in return for Bernard's love, affection, and goodwill, on account of his service and fidelity, and for the assistance that he gave them and would choose to give them (*pro amore et dulcedine et benevolentie tue et propter servicium et fidelitatem et per adjutorium quod nobis facis et in antea cupis facere*).[161] To see this as creating a kind of conditional alod or to suppose that it assured service and fidelity in future seems unrealistic. Bernard was to buy, or had bought, a horse and hauberk that William must have hoped would make his service the more valuable, but William promised a penalty of £3 gold if he or his heirs tried to revoke the gift. Leaving force aside and relying on the terms of the charter, William cannot have had much chance of securing service if or when his beautiful relationship with Bernard came to an end.

The need to furnish garrisons for the fortifications that appeared all over the country from the late tenth century on must have intensified demands for regular military service. There does not seem to be any evidence that alodholders were automatically exempt from it. Some at least of those who owed garrison service at Vendôme in the 1020s (before the town was taken

---

[157] Odo, *Vita Geraldi*, col. 660–1 (I. 32).   [158] '*Conventum*'; above, at nn. 27–9.
[159] Tabuteau, 'Feudal Military Obligations' and *Transfers*, 67–8, 93–4, 110; Bates, *Normandy*, 168–9, 258–9; Guillot, *Anjou*, i. 379–91.
[160] Van Houtts, 'Ship List'.   [161] Poly, *Provence*, 138 n., with discussion.

over by the counts of Anjou) had estates that suggest relatively high status. At least one of them was alodial and others may have been.[162] Some of the knights who lived in and around fortresses in the Mâconnais may have had a formal obligation to guard them. If they did, it need not have been because they had what were then thought of as restricted property rights.[163] In Anjou and Normandy local lords demanded garrison service from church tenants:[164] they are surely even more likely to have demanded it from lesser landowners who did not have churches to complain on their behalf. Some lords in eleventh-century Maine got military service of some kind (though not necessarily very much) from people who may have otherwise had more or less full rights in their land.[165] Some got unspecified services which may have been partly or entirely military,[166] but lesser landowners, whatever their rights, were more likely to have their military obligations, of whatever kind, precisely specified than were more influential people. Most of the military or quasi-military obligations mentioned in the charters seem to be of a home-guard kind rather than anything distinctively noble. A reference to the *aribannum* in Poitou in the 1020s points to an obligation that probably, like other customary dues and services deriving from old public duties, lay on all peasant and near-peasant landholders, whatever the status of their land.[167] The duty of lending a horse to one's lord each year, which is also found here and in other parts of western France, and which has traditionally been taken to represent a residual military duty of noble character, was probably not in origin noble at all. Horses were used to carry messages as well as soldiers, and those who had to lend a riding horse or pack-horse (*runcinus*, *summarius*) are most likely to have been the free but not noble landowners who were quite likely to hold property of more or less alodial character.[168] When churches acquired land subject to these military or carrying services they might have to make special arrangements to get the services remitted, even though their own titles were assumed otherwise to be at least as good as those of lay alodholders. Altogether it is probably as misleading to draw a hard line of status between military service and other obligations as it is to connect military service with any particular category of property.

[162] *Cart. Trinité Vendôme*, no. 2.          [163] Duby, *Société mâconnaise*, 157–8, 161–2.
[164] *Cart. Saint-Aubin*, no. 220; Orderic Vitalis, *Hist. Eccl.* ii. 80–2.
[165] *Cart. Saint-Vincent du Mans*, 175, 337, 439.          [166] Ibid. 212, 807.
[167] *Chartes de Saint Maixent*, no. 86; cf. *Carts. du Bas-Poitou*, 347, and references given by Prou, 'De la nature du service', Dillay, 'Service', Garaud, *Châtelains*, 97–9, 117–20. For another area, e.g. *Rec. Philippe I*, no. 153. General peasant obligations to some kind of military service can also be deduced from later charters of liberties exempting local communities from them.
[168] *Cart. Saint-Vincent du Mans*, 537; *Cart. Saint-Aubin*, nos. 303, 667. Beaumanoir saw it as a burden on a poor *gentil homme* (*Coutumes*, § 793–800), but see chapter 7 for changes in categories by then. The value of the service and type of horse are relevant: Guilhiermoz, *Noblesse*, 185 n. 35, 194 n. 54; Dillay, 'Service'.

For many landowners the duty of attending courts, like the obligation to military service, may well have lapsed in the tenth century or soon after, as and where the courts ceased to function. Where nobles remained outside any effective jurisdiction, however, some of them may have found it politic to attend the court of a local magnate or even of several local magnates, and with time their attendance would be likely to create a customary obligation. A stronger obligation lay on those lesser alodholders who were brought under jurisdiction of banal lords or castellans, who presumably profited from some relics of the old obligations of vicarial courts, however obscure and unjust the stages by which they had established their authority.[169] Those who attended courts may have been spoken of as doing so in order to offer 'aid and counsel'. This phrase had originated in the ninth century and had probably spread since then through being used in church charters.[170] It is most likely to occur in ecclesiastical grants of property that specify the obligations of the grantee, but those whose aid and counsel would be most desired by any ruler or lord would be those of higher status, who, in all but the smallest lordships, would be holders of full property. What this meagre selection of evidence and conjecture comes down to is that alodholders in the tenth and eleventh centuries might or might not owe military and other services. Whether they did or not, and how formal their obligation was, had less to do with any general rights or obligations attached to alods than with the structure of local politics, the development of local custom, the personal status of the alodholder, and his relation to those who held power in the locality.

It was probably normal for conveyances to be made at courts or assemblies, so as to secure maximum publicity. When full and free property was transferred the ceremony may more often have involved the transfer of a symbolic object than the performance of any act that symbolized subjection. When rulers gave land they would no doubt often demand such an act, and probably an oath of fidelity too, but that need not have automatically limited the rights conveyed or extended the obligations on the property until a rule was made that it should do so.[171] When land was restored after confiscation or conflict, an oath or other act of submission would be particularly necessary and diminished rights might be part of the price of reconciliation, but to see the second as the consequence of the first is overstrained and anachronistic.[172]

Confiscation, of course, always remained a possibility, however good one's title, as it had always been, though now the confiscator was likely to

---

[169] Poly and Bournazel, *Mutation féodale*, 87–103.                    [170] Chapter 4, at n. 115.
[171] For varying ceremonies in Normandy, most of them at the transfer of apparently full rights: Tabuteau, *Transfers*, 119–40.
[172] Orderic Vitalis, *Hist. Eccl.* iv. 88, 154.

be a local lord rather than the king. Chronicles and charters are full of allegations of straight seizures, some by enemies, but some by those who were in effect rulers. Presumably the confiscation of free inheritances, whether they were called alods or anything else, would, except in conditions of total disorder, need more justification than the confiscation of land held with less complete rights, but although alods or inheritances were thought of as complete property, forfeiture was never apparently ruled out as always unjustifiable.[173] Apart from outright confiscation, the lord's right to take over property on failure of heirs (escheat[174]) is normally seen as distinctively feudal and therefore as implying that a property was a fief. In this age of vague categories and variable custom lords seem to have taken over, or tried to take over, property that lacked heirs but had hitherto carried full rights. Louis VI seems to have tried it on twice in the 1120s.[175]

Most landowners in tenth- and eleventh-century France, even those who were outside and above any formal jurisdiction, are likely to have been subject at one time or another to some kind of lordship or domination, whether we call it government, patronage, protection, or oppression. That being so, it is unconvincing to explain such relations as having normally arisen out of either the grant of property on restricted terms or of the kind of personal submission that is called commendation and is sometimes supposed to have entailed a restriction of property rights. The combination of power politics and customary law will explain equally well the seigniorial consents to gifts of inheritances to the church, the variety of vague or not so vague obligations that landowners owed, and a whole range of other vicissitudes that inherited property underwent. The realities of politics or the memory of a recent grant, or both, may also explain occasional references to alods as 'held from' lords. Two brothers-in-law of Count Richard II of Normandy held their alods from him, and a vassal of his grandson William is said to have held an alod from him.[176] Around the middle of the eleventh century a charter of Count Geoffrey Martel of Anjou records his consent to gifts made to Saint-Maur-sur-Loire by two of his *fideles* and friends and the wife of one of them *ex rebus vel beneficio quod de nobis aliisque senioribus tenere videntur*. Part of the property was *ex honore et beneficio* of Geoffrey himself. Another part belonged both to the honour of the count of Poitou and the benefice of the viscount of Thouars, so the charter records their consents too.[177] The words *ex rebus vel beneficio* suggest

[173] Musset, 'Huit essais', 51–5; Painter, 'Lords of Lusignan', 29; *Cart. Saint-Aubin*, nos. 113, 721.
[174] Though the various Latin forms of escheat could be used in other senses: Niermeyer, *Lexicon*, 387 (*excadentia, excaduta*).
[175] Chapter 7.5.           [176] *Rec. ducs de Normandie*, nos. 46, 142.
[177] 'Cart. Saint-Maur', 369–70.

that the status of the properties was various or doubtful, while the donors were said to 'appear to hold them from us and other lords'. The past history and present status of much land must have been uncertain, but inheritances or alods could apparently be 'held from' some superior without thereby losing their traditional rights. The Norman inheritance mentioned earlier as paying rent in the 1080s to the lord from whom it was held may perhaps not have been an alod, but it does not look like a fief of the classic sort either, since it had been adjudged to its owner, not in the court of the lord from whom it was held, who was said to be its chief lord after (*post*) Count Roger of Montgomery, but in Roger's own court.[178] Relations between property-holders and those referred to as their lords did not always—if ever—fit the categories of later lawyers' law.[179]

The conditions of property-holding changed much between 888 and 1100 but the changes were piecemeal and patchy, depending on the way that political structures developed in different areas and the different rights or obligations that became entrenched in custom. Some of the changes had terminological consequences. Irrespective of terminology, however, the rights and obligations attached to property inherited by nobles or free men were different in 1100 from what they had been two centuries before, because government had changed and custom had been adapted accordingly. What proportion of nobles and free men in different parts of the kingdom by then held their land with what they thought of as full rights is unknowable, but there does not seem to be hard evidence to support the belief that the proportion had become much smaller in any part of the kingdom than it had been in 900 or 1000. Duby suggested that lords in the Mâconnais had stopped granting alods by 1030.[180] Since, however, virtually all his material came from cartularies of churches, which were prohibited from alienating their property for good, and since grants by laymen to laymen are rare until after 1100, evidence either to support or refute his hypothesis, whether for Burgundy or elsewhere, is hard to come by.[181] One or two pieces nevertheless suggest that it would not work for other areas. Count Geoffrey Martel of Anjou seems to have sold one property outright and, though he later confiscated it, he then granted it to his previous purchaser's tenant free and quit and apparently for ever. Later

[178] Tabuteau, *Transfers*, 328 (n. 125). For varying senses of *capitalis dominus*, see index: *caput*.
[179] Luchaire, *Actes de Louis VII*, 394–5 (no. 309). [180] Duby, *Société mâconnaise*, 151.
[181] I have searched, fairly cursorily, *Rec. de Philippe I*; *Cart. gén. de Paris*; Tardif, *Monuments*; Luchaire, *Louis VI*; Luchaire, *Louis VII*; *Liber Instrumentorum*; Guillot, *Anjou*, ii; *Rec. de Henri II*; *Actes des comtes de Flandre*; *Actes des comtes de Namur; Rec. des comtes de Pontieu; Actes intéressant la Belgique; Rec. des ducs de Normandie*. Professor Emily Tabuteau tells me that there are no Norman grants to laymen between 1066 and 1100. A search of cartularies would of course yield more lay charters and allusions to past lay grants.

in the century Fulk Réchin made at least one grant which looks as if it included full property rights, while both he and Geoffrey made judgements about alods that suggest no animus against them.[182] In 1112 Louis VI turned a benefice granted by his father into property to be held for ever by hereditary right, and in 1136 he made another perpetual grant with free disposition in entirely traditional terms except that he safeguarded the life interest of the beneficiary's wife.[183]

So far as I can see, most nobles, whether or not their property is referred to in the sources as alods, still held it in 1100, as alodholders had held theirs in 900 or indeed in 700, not by virtue of a grant that anyone remembered but by inheritance. The only evidence that by 1100 nobles held the bulk of their estates as fiefs seems to be the description of areas under their control as their fiefs or *casamenta*. In the next section of this chapter I shall argue that this does not normally seem to imply either restriction of their property rights or increase in their obligations to a superior. If that is correct then their lands, apart from any granted to them by churches, were presumably held with full rights. What that meant, I suggest, is that, whatever words were used, nobles and free men thought of their inheritances simply as *theirs*. In so far as they recognized obligations as incumbent on their property, they thought of them as obligations of an honourable sort, which should not be increased without their consent and which did not imply any diminution of their own rights. They may well even, however unrealistically, have thought of any services they owed as a personal obligation, irrespective of their property. Second, the owners of inheritances or alods assumed, maintained, or hoped, with the inconsistency that is common to humans, both that their property was fully heritable and that they could dispose of it, if necessary with the consent of their kin and their ruler—the first being rather more difficult to get than the second. Third, they assumed, maintained, or hoped that it could not be taken from them without judgement.

## 5.5. *Fiefs*

The words *feo* or *feu* and *fevum* or *fevus*, from which the *feudum* or *feodum* of the later lawyers seem to derive, have been found in charters of St Gall in the late eighth century, in those of the bishop of Lucca in the ninth century, and with increasing frequency in Burgundy and the southern part of

[182] *Cart. Saint-Aubin*, nos. 113, 381 (though the editor refers to this as an enfeoffment); Guillot, *Anjou*, ii. 130 (C 182), 219 (C 352).
[183] *Cart. gén. de Paris*, no. 161; Tardif, *Monuments*, no. 420: these cases are discussed in chapter 7.2.

the kingdom of the West Franks during the tenth.[184] In St Gall charters of 786 and 792 the *feo* or *feus* is an annual rent, while in Burgundy around 900 the various forms of the word are said to have had the sense of gift, reward, or payment, often apparently in money or kind. A prohibition of 899 against any grant *per fevum* of land that was being given to the bishopric of Maguelone (Hérault), however, clearly envisages the reward in the form of land.[185] As references multiply during the tenth and eleventh centuries, first in the south and then further north as well, an increasing number of them are to landed property. Among these a good many relate to subordinate and therefore apparently less complete property, including what looks like the property of peasants.[186] Many churches seem to have gone over to using one of these words for what they would once have called benefices or *precaria*.[187] In some charters, however, one of them is used to denote superior property or the area under the control or government of a superior,[188] in some it is ambiguous,[189] and in some it seems to be used both for subordinate and superior rights.[190] Perhaps these usages were connected: references to a subordinate property which was to be held *in feudum, in feudo*, et cetera may have evoked the sense of being in the fief (or gift, or obedience) of the lord under whose authority it lay. In parts of the south, where some of the earliest uses have been found, the nouns *feu* or *feo* (or adjectives derived from them) seem to be used of subordinate properties on comital estates.[191] That may perhaps help to explain how *fiscus* (the old word for royal property) was sometimes used in widely separated areas of the kingdom as an apparent synonym for fief.[192] It may also explain why the viscounts of Carcassonne had, according to charters of 1068, held their

[184] Lucca: chapter 6.4. St Gall and Burgundy: Schneider, *Annales du Midi*, 80 (1968), 480–1, and *Urkundenbuch S. Gallen*, nos. 105, 133; Poly and Bournazel, *Mutation féodale*, 120–9; Poly, 'Vocabulaire'.

[185] *Cart. Maguelone*, no. 3; cf. *Cart. Conques*, no. 262 (916).

[186] *Cart. Béziers*, nos. 36, 49; *Cart. Conques*, nos. 3, 57, 237; Poly, *Provence*, 146 n.; *Cart. Trinité Vendôme*, no. 65; Fournier, *Auvergne*, 175 n., 571 n.; *Cart. Marseille*, no. 167; 'Cart. Fontjoncouse', no. 7; *Rec. Cluny*, nos. 2912, 2994, 3400, 3642; Tabuteau, *Transfers*, 325 (n. 392), 346 (n. 158), 364 (n. 1); *Cart. Molesme*, nos. 65, 694; *Cart. Saint-Vincent de Mâcon*, no. 21; *Gallia Christ.* xi, instr. col. 129; *Rec. Philippe I*, no. 127; *Cart. Saint-Aubin*, no. 220; *Cart. Vierzon*, no. 91; 'Conventum', 543 (*fevos vassalorum*), 547 (Hugh's *fevum* which the count was to give to Hugh as security, presumably ranked as restricted and subordinate property).

[187] *Cart. Conques*, no. 262; Guillot, *Anjou*, i. 298; *Cart. Marseille*, no. 423; Haskins, *Norman Institutions*, 21–2; Poly, *Provence*, 288–90. But see the distinction made in Hainaut in 1129: Didier, *Droit des fiefs*, 6 n.

[188] Devic and Vaissete, *Hist. Languedoc*, v, no. 100; *Cartulaire de Saint André*, no. 35*; *Rec. Philippe I*, no. 11; above, at nn. 143–5.

[189] Tabuteau, *Transfers*, 301 (n. 114); *Cart. Saint-Aubin*, no. 667.

[190] *Cart. Béziers*, no. 43; *Rec. Philippe I*, no. 103; *Actes de Guillaume le conquérant*, no. 6; *Rec. Cluny*, no. 3627.

[191] Poly and Bournazel, *Mutation féodale*, 124–6; Magnou, 'Note'.

[192] Niermeyer, *Lexicon*, 436: fiscus, senses 6–9.

lordships or *honor*, perhaps including Carcassonne itself, as *fevos* through or by (*per*) the counts of Toulouse.[193] The viscounts' *fevi* may have been envisaged as the offices and lands they supposedly derived from the relation of viscount to count. All *general* explanations of usage are, however, likely to be fallacious: there were plenty of reasons why landowners and scribes should have used old words in new ways and new words in varying ways. We have far too little evidence to make guesses about reasons worth while. My concern is not in any case with the derivation of words or explanation of their use but with the rights and obligations that words, taken in context, may reveal—or conceal.

Sometimes a fief[194] was explicitly contrasted with what was held as an alod or in alms, in which case it seems to imply fewer rights or more obligations, but that does not mean that such properties could be expected always or often to have the same or similar rights and obligations, or that these would have been in every respect different from those of alods.[195] In the later eleventh century one document in the cartulary of Saint-Vincent, Le Mans, contrasted a fief with a *censiva*, while another may contrast the duties of a fiefholder with those of a *colibertus*.[196] These cases foreshadow later distinctions, but many in other cartularies do not. Variable usage did not end with the eleventh century.[197]

In the eleventh century, as also in the twelfth, the phrases that refer to a fief or *casamentum* as that of someone with superior rights over property that is being given to a church are most often used to explain the interest of a lord who is giving consent to the grant, though they occasionally occur in other contexts.[198] I have already argued that some—perhaps many—of the properties granted subject to such consent were themselves held with what were thought of as full rights, so that the rights over them of the lord

[193] Devic and Vaissete, *Hist. Languedoc*, v. 548–9, 551–4, discussed by Cheyette, 'The "Sale" of Carcassonne'.

[194] For simplicity I shall generally use this word rather than one of its Latin forms for the rest of this section.

[195] *Cart. Conques*, no. 57; *Cart. Molesme*, no. 694; Tabuteau, *Transfers*, 37, 346 (n. 158). *Cart. Saint-Aubin*, no. 667 (written in the twelfth century) refers to what looks like full property given 1082–1106 as *supradictum fevum*.

[196] *Cart. Saint-Vincent du Mans*, nos. 307, 807 (and cf. 751).                    [197] Chapter 7.2.

[198] Fiefs: *Cart. des abbayes de Saint-Pierre*, no. 13; *Cart. Marmoutier/Vendômois*, no. 12; *Rec. Philippe I*, nos. 50, 103, 127; *Actes de Guillaume le conquérant*, no. 6; Orderic Vitalis, *Hist. Eccl.* ii. 82; *Cart. Saint-Vincent du Mans*, nos. 137, 351; Ivo of Chartres, *Epistolae*, col. 171; *Actes des comtes de Flandre*, no. 71; *Cart. Saint-Aubin*, no. 114; Loisel, *Mémoires de Beauvais*, 267; *Rec. Saint-Nicaise*, 16; Longnon, *Documents de Champagne*, i. 466; Luchaire, *Louis VII*, 371–2, 386, 398 (nos. 150, 268, 330); Arbois, 'Document'; *Rec. Cluny*, no. 4244. *Casamenta*: Fulbert, *Letters and Poems*, no. 9; 'Cart. Saint-Maur', 369–70; *Cart. Marmoutier/Vendômois*, no. 4; *Cart. Saint-Vincent du Mans*, nos. 212, 260, 807; *Cart. Molesme*, ii. 217–18; *Cart. Paray*, no. 152. For *caput* used in a similar way: *Rec. Cluny*, nos. 3577, 3067, 3640–2. The interest of the lord in the property given in *Cart. Saint-Aubin*, no. 667, is explained both as *de cujus casamento erat* and *de cujus mariagio erat*.

to whose fief or *casamentum* they belonged were of a political or governmental rather than a proprietary nature. In such cases there is seldom any
hint that the fief or *casamentum* was itself dependent on anyone else. There
are exceptions, as in the dispute over the church of Le Lion d'Angers, discussed above, where the *casamentum* of the lords of Craon, to which Le
Lion belonged, was in some way subject to the counts of Anjou.[199] In
another dispute, which concerned the church of Craon itself, Craon was
referred to as an honour that Count Geoffrey Martel maintained was part
of his paternal fief (*de fevo suo paterno*), so that its lord should not have
given its church away without his consent.[200] Tendentious as part of
Geoffrey's argument was, he does not seem to have denied that the lords
of Craon had the rights of property normally associated with an inheritance
or alod, while the fact that he had in the mean time confiscated their inheritance need not mean it either. There is as little reason to suppose that
Craon, whether described as a *casamentum* or an *honor*, was a fief held from
the counts of Anjou, in the sense that historians of feudalism normally
envisage this, as there is to suppose that Le Lion d'Angers was a fief held
from the lords of Craon.[201] As for Geoffrey Martel's allusion to his own
paternal fief, this, like other eleventh-century references to the fiefs, *casamenta*, or benefices of counts, seems even less likely to imply restricted
rights of property.[202] When Count William of Poitou gave a *fevum* from his
own *fevum* to Bishop Jordan of Limoges and at the same time made it into
an alod, it is very improbable that he asked, or should have asked, permission from the king or anyone else.[203]

Twelfth-century references to the king's fief, in similar terms and contexts, should make it impossible to argue that even at that comparatively
late date the word always had connotations of dependency.[204] On the other
hand, I have to admit that the count of Flanders's anxiety that the obligations he undertook to the king of England in their treaty of 1101 should not
cause him to forfeit his fief to the king of France seems at first sight to call
for interpretations along the lines of classic feudalism.[205] It could be said
that it implies that the count, despite his virtual independence, recognized
what is often called a 'theoretical' feudal obligation. The problem here is
to know whether any theory that anyone at the time might have held (and

---

[199] Above, at nn. 143–5. See also e.g. *Cart Saint-Vincent du Mans*, no. 751.

[200] *Cart. Saint-Aubin*, no. 721; *Cart. Trinité Vendôme*, no. 96. Cf. 'Cart. Saint-Maur', 369–70.

[201] For other references to *casamenta*, e.g. Fulbert, *Letters and Poems*, no. 9; *Cart. Molesme*, no. 233.

[202] See section 3 of this chapter.                    [203] *Cart. Saint-Étienne Limoges*, 55–6.

[204] Luchaire, *Actes de Louis VII*, 363–4 (nos. 82, 85), 371 (no. 147), 408 (no. 396), 431 (no. 559), 448 (no. 652), 451 (no. 674); *RHGF*, xvi. 832. For one from 1092, above at nn. 102–3.

[205] *Diplomatic Documents*, no. 1.

we have precious little evidence of any) need be seen as distinctively feudal. I would rather postulate that the obligation—which might better be
called vague or doubtful than theoretical—was to the king as king, not as
lord of a fief. The word fief may have been used in the Anglo-Flemish
treaty because it was by now used of noble properties in England and the
document was drawn up for the king of England: it is hard to believe that
its use implies that the count of Flanders was thought of as enjoying fewer
rights in his county than those of a normal inheritance or alod.[206] An alodholder's failure to answer a call to war, like rebellion, might incur a penalty
that could extend to an attempt at forfeiture. The danger was rather remote
for Count Robert, but if treaties were to be formally recorded in writing it
maybe made sense to provide for it.[207]

Perhaps one of the advantages of the word fief, for those who weighed
it carefully against others, was that it was so unspecific: I am tempted to
guess that in some contexts it was little more than a convenient word for
property that, for one reason or another, did not look quite like an alod or
inheritance of the traditional sort. It might thus cover both properties that
carried fewer rights than a normal alod or inheritance and the governmental or quasi-governmental rights that counts and other lords had established or were trying to establish over free men and their properties. Both
Geoffrey Martel's paternal fief and, later, Louis VII's fief look like the
areas under their respective political control, whereas William of Poitou's
*fevum* looks more like his immediate property. Other mentions of counts'
fiefs in the eleventh century could mean either.[208] Rights in churches and
mills were another form of property that did not fit into the normal picture
of an alod. Neither form of property was one that springs to mind as the
typical nexus between lord and vassal, but both were occasionally called
fiefs. Both were financially profitable and produced income that could be
easily divided, so that complex networks or layers of rights were sometimes
formed in them, between kinsmen as well as between lords and vassals as
historians normally envisage them.[209] That in itself may have made it
harder to absorb such items of property into inherited alods. Although
property rights could be transferred without the use of any word that we

---

[206] Cf. Galbert of Bruges, *Histoire*, 152–3, and below, chapter 7.5.

[207] He also worried that if he did not do homage to the emperor he might not be able to have
the *feodum quod ab eo tenere per antecessoriam debeo*: Lambert, bishop of Ardres, *Epistolae*, 196.
But cf. the count of Namur's title and freedom of disposition in 1163: *Actes des comtes de Namur*,
no. 15, and the alods of the count of Vermandois acquired by the count of Flanders in 1167:
Gislebert of Mons, *Chronique*, 88.

[208] Cf. a (relatively rare) reference to an archbishop's *fevum*: *Cart. de Saint-André*, no. 35*.

[209] *Cart. des abbayes de Saint-Pierre*, nos. 12, 13; *Cart. Marmoutier/Vendômois*, no. 1; *Rec.
Cluny*, no. 2994; *Cart. Conques*, no. 3; *Cart. de Saint-André*, no. 205; *Cart. Montiéramey*, no. 39;
Bur, *Champagne*, 395; Devailly, *Berry*, 245–8.

might interpret as classificatory, the word fief could perhaps sometimes be useful, whether it was meant to be totally non-committal or whether it was meant to imply that the rights conveyed were less than alodial.[210]

Bearing in mind all the dangers of teleological interpretations, I suggest nevertheless that by the end of the eleventh century the totally non-committal use of the word had been outweighed by its more frequent use with connotations of dependency or subordination. That is to say that I suspect that, despite the way that charters still referred to counts' fiefs and the king's fief, many people would have assumed that landed property described as a fief was held with less than the rights associated with alods or inheritances: it was 'held from' a lord who enjoyed not merely the rights of government over it but also some of the rights of property. Some of these he would hold at the expense of the fiefholder, some they would both hold. Meanwhile, however, although charters, since they deal almost exclusively with landed property, inevitably give the impression that *feoda* or *feuda* normally consisted of land, the word continued to be used for wages or other rewards paid in money or kind.[211] The *beneficium quod vulgo dicitur feodum* of 1087, which is often cited in discussions of the evolution of feudal property, was an annual livery of grain, money, and chickens to *milites* who are not said to have any land at all.[212] As this reminds us, there was nothing new about a 'money-fief', nor does there seem to be any reason to consider it a secondary development, though the grant of regular sums of money presumably became more frequent as lords began to exploit their rights more systematically and as coin became more abundant.[213] The use of the word fief for land may also have contributed to a semantic shift, when it was used for monetary rewards, from single payments to more permanent and regular wages.[214]

None of this need be confusing if we can wrench our minds away from the idea that words have core meanings that we ought to be able to deduce from all their uses, that this particular word (or group of words) had a core meaning to do with restricted rights and extra obligations, and that the writers of charters normally used it in order to define the rights and obligations of properties that the charters conveyed. Eleventh-century scribes— and there is no reason to suppose that they were different in this respect

---

[210] *Cart. Conques*, no. 3 (especially the *phevum presbyterale*: the priest's rights were presumably meant to be limited); ibid., no. 57; *Actes de Guillaume le conquérant*, no. 6; *Gallia Christ.* x, instr. col. 129; *Cart. Molesme*, ii. 217–18.

[211] Niermeyer, *Lexicon*, 415 (sense 2), 417 (sense 14).

[212] *Actes intéressant la Belgique*, no. 6.

[213] On coin: Spufford, *Money and its Use*, 60–1, 85–6, 98–103, 247–8.

[214] Niermeyer, *Lexicon*, *beneficium*, senses 2, 31; *feodum*, senses 2, 14. For a different view: Lyon, *From Fief to Indenture*.

from their contemporaries—do not seem to have ascribed to the nouns used for property the symbolic power that historians of feudalism find in them. Long tradition had given *alodis* connotations of permanence and freedom, but property could none the less enjoy those attributes without the word being used. To suppose that estates were not called fiefs at first because of a concern for linguistic purity, that scribes sometimes carefully avoided using the word, or that, when it was used, it symbolized a new category of property is unnecessary and unreal.[215]

The fief of so-called classic feudalism is a hereditary property held by someone above peasant rank with fewer rights and more obligations than those of an alod. Most historians of feudo-vassalic relations suggest that fiefs of this sort had become established by 1100, if not earlier, as the holdings of the people they describe as vassals. This interpretation is reflected in the way that many medieval historians use the word vassal to describe a fiefholder, and in the more or less explicit glossing of 'vassal' as the free or noble follower of a lord who performs only such free and noble duties as giving aid, counsel, and military service.[216] Duby's work on the Mâconnais, although nearly forty years old, still offers the fullest explanation of how fiefholding, as generally understood, arose, at least in that area. Nothing seems to have been published since that offers a hypothesis and evidence that are anywhere near as rich and precise and therefore as worth testing. About 1030, according to this classic account, rivalry for vassals between lords in the Mâconnais led them to give up either granting alods or assuming control over their vassals' alods by the commendation of the vassals. Instead they granted benefices to their followers, but benefices that became transformed into fiefs (a word that became current at about the same time) when the new land-nexus superseded the old personal relation between lord and vassal. Whereas benefices had not hitherto owed significant services, the new holdings owed military service, aid, and counsel, often of an unspecific nature, but did not normally owe money rents.[217] As fiefholding spread, vassals came to hold from more than one lord, so that the purely personal bond of lord and man was weakened, while the vassal gained security of tenure provided he performed his services, vague as they may have been until the twelfth century. He also gained the rights to leave his lord and land, to alienate it with his lord's consent, and to object to its alienation by his lord. Most important of all, from about 1075 fiefs became fully heritable.[218] This trend towards inheritance during the eleventh century seems to be generally accepted.[219]

[215] Bloch, *Feudal Society*, i. 166; Guillot, *Anjou*, i. 49 n.    [216] Above, 5.1.
[217] On rent, cf. Duby, *Société mâconnaise*, 55 n., 152, 157.
[218] Duby, *Société mâconnaise*, 150–8.
[219] Bloch, *Feudal Society*, 190, 196–7; Poly and Bournazel, *Mutation féodale*, 132–3; Poly,

The first point to consider is the suggestion that at some point lords came to replace full grants of property to their followers by restricted grants to those who were already bound to them by bonds of personal fidelity. I have already cast doubt on the evidence that lords stopped making full grants.[220] There are other difficulties. One is that, as Duby pointed out, the evidence he uses to detect changes in relations between lords, those whom historians call their vassals, and their property, like much that is used by other scholars for other areas, relates to church property.[221] It therefore refers only in passing to relations between lay lords and their lay followers, subjects, and tenants. Another concerns the definition and identification of vassals so that statements about them are not circular. A third is that of demonstrating a change from homage or commendation as the reason for a grant to homage as the result of one.[222] Homage is not often mentioned at this date, and nor are oaths or other ceremonies at the transfer of property. It is difficult to believe that all the various kinds of property that were described as fiefs could have been granted with the same kind of ceremony—and a different kind of ceremony from that accompanying other sorts of grant. Ceremonies at the grant of subordinate properties may have been intended to imply subjection more than were ceremonies conveying full properties, but the relative social standing and political power of the parties may have affected it as much as anything else.[223] The subject needs fuller investigation, avoiding both the circular arguments of calling anything homage that looks like the later ceremony, or of deducing fiefs from homage or homage from fiefs, and any assumption that ceremonies between clergy and laymen necessarily reflect ceremonies and relations between lay lords and their followers. One point about the bond between lord and man which must be made here, however, is that there does not seem to be any reason to believe that there had ever been a general rule against holding benefices, or other dependent properties, from more than one lord. If individual lords in the tenth century objected to their followers holding benefices from someone else—and it needs to be demonstrated in individual cases that they did—the Carolingian evidence suggests that that was probably because political divisions made multiple links embarrassing and dangerous, not because

*Provence*, 145–9; Giordanengo, 'Vocabulaire et formulaires', 86 n.; Magnou-Nortier, 'Fidélité et féodalité', 132; Richardot, 'Fief roturier', 332; Tabuteau, *Transfers*, 63–4, 100, 325–6 (nn. 146, 149), 325–6 (n. 392).

[220] Above, at nn. 180–3.   [221] Duby, *Société mâconnaise*, 13–14.
[222] Ibid. 152.
[223] For varying ceremonies, though mostly involving ecclesiastical, not lay, lords, e.g. *Gallia Christ.* xiii, instr. col. 227 and Magnou-Nortier, 'Fidélité et féodalité'; *Cart. Trinité Vendôme*, no. 65; Tabuteau, *Transfers*, 119–40; Duby, *Société mâconnaise*, 149 n., 153 n.

multiple links were themselves either the cause or result of political disintegration.[224]

Given that we know that some people who held alods owed services of various kinds, including military service and court service, which probably varied between regions according to political conditions and custom, and given that all information about services before the twelfth century is so scanty, it is hard to establish what services, if any, were particularly characteristic of those subordinate properties that were described at the time as fiefs. They probably varied from place to place, as well as according to the status and relations of the parties. The late eleventh-century contrast of a fief and *censiva* in the Le Mans cartulary suggests that fiefs did not owe money rents, but some properties elsewhere that were called fiefs did owe them. If most examples of rents come from farther south, that may be only an accident of the survival of sources—or of what has been noticed in them. The few Maine cases may be no more typical of northern fiefs (or properties, however described, that were held on restricted terms by free men) than are the few examples of rent in the south typical of southern fiefs.[225] The Maine cases may, however, be significant as an example of the way that more systematic exploitation and better record-keeping were beginning to provoke disputes that led to new distinctions.[226]

The connection between fiefs and military service at this period is both extremely obscure and central to arguments about feudo-vassalic institutions. It is obscure because the charters say so little about services of any kind and because other records of services are still rare. It is central because in later centuries military obligations came to be closely associated in ideology—though not significantly in practice—with nobility and with fiefs, and because this association has so often been seen ever since as a survival from earlier times. I have already argued that the military obligations of nobles between 900 and 1100 depended on their political situation rather than on any limitation on their property rights as then understood: whether or not they had to serve in the armies of their rulers or other powerful neighbours, most nobles held most of their property with what were thought of as full rights, not as either what they called fiefs or with the range of obligations that would later be considered typical of fiefs. All the same, counts and churches did not stop needing the soldiers they had

---

[224] See chapter 4.2. The argument about Hugh of Lusignan's proposed simultaneous tenure of fortresses from William of Aquitaine and Fulk of Anjou was conditioned by his particular agreement with Fulk and William's fear of quarrelling with Fulk: '*Conventum*', 546, cf. 542.

[225] *Cart. Saint-Vincent du Mans*, nos. 118, 307, 751, 807; cf. Poly, *Provence*, 90 n.; *Chartes de Saint-Maixent*, no. 14; *RHGF*, ix. 665; Haskins, *Norman Institutions*, 21–2; Monboisse, *L'Ordre féodal*, 134.

[226] See the examples cited by Dillay, 'Le "service" '.

secured in the ninth century by granting benefices just because the services of these soldiers were no longer required by the king. Even if there were more cost-effective ways of raising offensive armies, the grant of land with restricted rights and firm obligations still had its uses. It had them perhaps most of all for great churches, which needed men for defence and policing and would not want to maintain them as household retinues. Besides, the grant of benefices by churches to laymen was by now traditional and expected. Calling this kind of benefice a fief or *casamentum* would not automatically change the rights or obligations attached to it. The problem is to know if and when more grants with military obligations and restricted rights began to be made, and if and when the obligations and rights were changed. Above all the problem is to know about grants made by lay lords.

Some properties held by Saint-Vincent, Le Mans, in the late eleventh century had owed military service to their lords before their owners granted them to the abbey. Taken with the contrast that the abbey's cartulary sometimes makes between fief and *censiva* and with its references to what are traditionally known as 'feudal aids', that may make them look like fiefs.[227] Some of them may, however, be as well, or better, classified as full or alodial property, especially when one bears in mind that evidence for military service from full property in the west of France is also relatively good—or relatively less bad.[228] Both there and elsewhere, references to *milites* or *caballarii* and, especially, to *milites fevati* or *milites casati* have sometimes been used to fill in the gaps in evidence. Men referred to as *milites* need not, however, have held land, whether as fiefs or alods, or owed service for what they did hold. *Milites fevati* or *milites casati* seem to be referred to more rarely in the eleventh century than modern usage suggests,[229] while *casati* and *fevati* who are not called *milites* may be peasants with merely subsidiary military obligations; their *casamenta* or *fevi* may have been definable only as something less than alods. *Milites* on church estates, moreover, who are inevitably more likely to occur in the records than those on lay property, may not have been required to do much military service of a very high-level or professional kind.[230] What they did was

[227] *Cart. Saint-Vincent du Mans*, nos. 337, 439, 751, 807. I have not seen the MSS also referred to by Flach, *Origines*, ii. 553, 555.                                    [228] Above, 5.4.

[229] *Rec. Philippe I*, no. 50; Niermeyer, *Lexicon*, 111–12, 151–2; Van Luyn, 'Milites', does not mention either, nor (judging from their indexes) do the eleventh-century sources used by Bur, *Champagne*, Devailly, *Berry*, Duby, *Société mâconnaise*, Guillot, *Anjou*, Tabuteau, *Transfers*, or Fossier, 'Chevalerie', though cf. Fossier, *Picardie*, 549 n. Lambert's *Annales Cam.* does not use the expression *miles casatus* as suggested by Duby, *Hommes*, 276, and Poly and Bournazel, *Mutation féodale*, 168. *Caballarii* with fiefs (Niermeyer, 111–12; *Cart. Saint-Aubin*, no. 220) need not have been soldiers: Niermeyer, ibid.

[230] *Chron. de Bèze*, 306–8; Ivo, *Epistolae*, no. 28; cf. Fulbert, *Letters*, nos. 9, 10; *Cart. Saint-Trond*, no. 21; Dillay, 'Le "service"'.

important to churches in troubled times, since grants of land may often have been the best way for those who did not fight themselves to get defenders, but it is unlikely to have been as important to lay lords who had less land available to grant out and more possibilities of raising forces in other ways. None of those who owed garrison service at Vendôme in the 1020s is said to have held a fief. The only reason to suppose that any of them did may be that some are said to have 'held' their land and that the viscount's land, for which he owed his share, was called a benefice. That, however, seems to have been a traditional word for the land of viscounts, as of counts, and 'holding', as I have already argued, is not significant.[231]

Where lay lords may have tried most seriously to connect military obligation with restricted rights of property was in the actual command of fortresses. Alodholders might be required to serve in garrisons from time to time, but no count or other lord who built more fortresses than he could himself look after was likely to have intended to hand them all over to castellans as full alods or inheritances. At first, however, the difference between castles held as what historians call fiefs and those held by custodians with fewer property rights was, it seems, unclear enough to be open to different interpretations later on.[232] The difficulty that historians have had in assigning individual fortresses to one class or the other may arise less from the loss of records than from the anachronism of the categories. Military commanders may not always have had the time or facilities to record the arrangements that they made as well as great churches did—not that church records were invariably effective in precluding future dispute. Even if full and explicit conditions were imposed, they are unlikely to have fitted into the mutually exclusive categories of fief and custody that would eventually be worked out in different conditions a century or more later. The custodian of a castle would—or should—have regarded himself as responsible to his lord for its safety at the same time as he enjoyed some of the rights of property in it and hoped to hand on both responsibilities and rights to his son or sons. His rights would presumably have been weaker, and his obligations greater, than those of a castellan who built his own fortress on his own alod but took an oath of fidelity to a local magnate. In any dispute, however, the difference of principle between the two situations might be diminished by appeals to similar norms of loyalty and rights of inheritance, supported by wishful remembering on one side or both. Though we would have a very different idea about the relations between

---

[231] *Cart. Trinité Vendôme*, no. 2, which Guillot, *Anjou*, i. 49 n., and Dunbabin, *France*, for instance, interpret differently. For garrison service, above, at nn. 162–5.

[232] 'Ex gestis Ambasiensium Dominorum', 241 (Bur, *Champagne*, 306, makes Chaumont a fief); Guillaume de Jumièges, *Gesta*, 101; Guillot, *Anjou*, i. 317–52; Poly, *Provence*, 150–6; Génicot, 'Trois thèses', 451; Yver, 'Châteaux forts'. Cf. *Consuetudines Feudorum*, 88.

Hugh of Lusignan and the count (or duke) of Aquitaine in the 1020s if we had the count's side of the story, we might still not be sure who had originally built all the fortresses about which they quarrelled, whose lands the fortresses stood on, or the terms on which they had changed hands since.[233]

The security of tenure and rights of alienation attached to properties described as fiefs are difficult to establish, as they are for other property, first because it is often difficult to know the status of property that was being granted to churches with seigniorial consent; second, because customary law tended to turn regular practices into normative customs; and third, because historians of feudalism have so often taken *ex parte* statements on individual cases as normative without considering whether they represented either common or accepted practice at the time. What has already been said about consent to the alienation of full property suggests that the recording of consent to the alienation of fiefs, whether by the lord or the tenant, may not always imply a general rule.[234] The transfer of subordinate property was presumably more likely to require consent than was that of properties held with fuller rights. When lords gave away property over the heads of fiefholders, on the other hand, some fiefholders could evidently make enough nuisance of themselves for churches to want to record their witness or consent to their lords' gifts.[235] Meanwhile holders of property with less than alodial rights and more than alodial obligations presumably always had less security against confiscation than did alodholders. In view of all that is known about customary law, however, that is unlikely to mean that they were supposed to be without any right to judgement. The traditional belief that fiefholders had to attend their lords' courts and could only make their protests or claims there, at least in the first instance, may not imply any great disability at this date. The churches, castellans, or other nobles from whom free people were most likely to hold property on restricted terms would often be the holders of the chief or only court for the area anyway. A fiefholder's duty of attendance would not necessarily be very different from that of his neighbours who held their land with full rights but were under the lord's jurisdiction. When confiscation threatened or new services were demanded, the social status of the owner, rather than

[233] 'Conventum'.
[234] In Tardif, *Monuments*, no. 247 the count's and bishop's general permission seems intended to make unnecessary that lords from whom fiefs were held.
[235] Duby, *Société mâconnaise*, 154 n.; Tabuteau, *Transfers*, 187–8, 364 (n. 1); *Rec. ducs de Normandie*, no. 95. Cf. Galbert, *Histoire*, 132 (though it seems anachronistic to borrow the term *abrègement du fief* from later law to describe what was complained of here: Ganshof, 'Droit urbain', 407 n., 413–14).

the formal status of his land, might, subject to power politics, be the crucial determinant of any judgement that could be obtained.

Of all the changes in dependent landholding that have been connected with the increased use of the word fief in the eleventh century the most important concerns heritability. The idea that the eleventh century saw a trend towards inheritance goes back to the twelfth-century Lombard *Libri Feudorum*, where it looks like pure conjectural myth designed to explain the present.[236] Most of the sixteenth-century French scholars from whom ideas of feudalism derive were so anxious to reject the authority of Roman law that one might expect later historians of French feudalism to have rejected the Lombard law and the contribution of the emperor Conrad II's legislation of 1037 to the heritability of fiefs along with it. Montesquieu indeed maintained that fiefs in France were already hereditary before Conrad—as Montesquieu thought—made them so in Germany.[237] By the nineteenth century, however, such concerns had faded and the study of feudalism had become intermittently eclectic. Guilhiermoz, for instance, used Conrad's law as a milestone on the road from the life benefices on church lands granted by the Carolingians to the full inheritance of fiefs found in later medieval sources.[238] Twentieth-century historians know the road well enough to be able to ignore the milestone. They also seem to ignore the way that the road starts from a misunderstanding or ignorance of the Merovingian and Carolingian evidence and that its course depends on taking ecclesiastical sources as evidence of generally accepted norms. The whole idea of a trend through time, rather than a constant tension throughout the age of pre-professional law, needs more critical thought. Although we have to rely on ecclesiastical sources we must keep reminding ourselves that lay property was governed by values and norms which were deeply rooted in lay society. Ever since the sixth century the notion of alodial property, or the alod, had set the standard as the right and normal form of property. It was what free men and women expected to inherit from their parents and pass on to their children or other close kin, subject only to the kind of duties that a free man should owe freely to his king and neighbours. At least since the eighth century kings and great lords had made grants of land or office (benefices) to some of their servants for life or during pleasure, and it seems probable that they and lesser landowners would always have made the occasional life-grant to dependent relatives or servants. Some may have extended such grants to provide for the widows or even, on occasion, the children of the dependant, but laymen are less likely to have had regular recourse to grants for several lives than were

[236] Below, chapter 6. 8.          [237] Montesquieu, *De l'esprit des lois*, book 31, c. 29.
[238] Guilhiermoz, *Essai*, 197–200.

churches. Familiar as such grants are in our sources, they look as if they were designed as compromises between the canon law against alienation on the one side and lay expectations of inheritance on the other.

Kings and other lay lords worked under different constraints. Any king worth his salt would want to ensure that the lands attached to important offices were held strictly ex officio and would not be inherited without special permission, but even Charlemagne seems to have been ready to allow ordinary benefices to pass from father to son more or less automatically. During the tenth and eleventh centuries lay lords probably followed much the same policy as the Carolingian kings, though in a less systematic way. Having neither the resources nor the need to give benefices to soldiers or servants on a Carolingian scale, they may have been more anxious to ration their grants to life-tenures, but they cannot always have found it easy to resist the claims of sons and widows. The disintegration of royal estates and comital powers in many areas during the tenth and early eleventh centuries shows how difficult it could be for lords to keep control of dependent properties, whatever they were called. Whenever a subordinate property remained for two or more generations in the hands of a family that enjoyed the rank normally associated with full property rights, it would be liable to slide out of seigniorial control and become a full inheritance or alod.[239] When that happened it was not just by wrongful usurpation: any free person who occupied land that one of his or her parents or close kin had occupied peacefully had a claim which deserved to be protected by law and custom, subject to being weighed against the claim of anyone else—including, of course, that of a lord who might claim superior rights.

Like Carolingian kings before them, lords might be fairly relaxed about allowing *de facto* inheritance—which the passage of time would make more or less *de jure*—to loyal subjects to whom they had granted church lands. When Bishop Harduin of Noyon-Tournai got into trouble with the king around 1027, he took refuge with the count of Flanders and in return offered the count twelve churches (*altaria*) which were to revert to the bishop after three generations. This was not very different from what might have happened under the old system of benefices *verbo regis*, except that the benefices would probably not have consisted of churches: few of the churches concerned probably existed a hundred years earlier anyway. What happened afterwards ought not to have happened under the old system, though something like it well might have: as a twelfth-century chron-

---

[239] e.g. *Rec. Cluny*, nos. 2777, 2845, cited by Duby, *Société mâconnaise*, 155 n. 27: the rights and wrongs of the cases are, of course, unknown. *Cart. de Paray*, no. 38, shows an apparently vestigial distinction surviving.

icler put it, the count granted the twelve churches to his nobles *in benefi-cium* and they distributed them *in feodum* to the *milites* who served them. It then, naturally, became very difficult for later bishops to recover the property.[240] Lords were more likely to be wary of allowing inheritance of the castles and fortified settlements that became so vital to control of the countryside in troubled times. Whatever the past history of a fortress—and that might well be a matter of dispute—a powerful count might claim that it was his, to be passed on to its occupier's heirs only with his permission, while the occupier would take his stand on ancestral rights. Whatever the rights and wrongs of Hugh of Lusignan's grievances in the early eleventh century, one thing that shines through his grumbles is his belief that what his father or uncle had held should have come to him. The count of Aquitaine seems to have gone a part of the way to meet that claim.[241] Their dispute would surely have been different if either had had decent records. Lay lords may have issued more charters than have survived, but at least until the late eleventh century few of them in France seem to have main-tained the kind of administration that was likely to produce many docu-ments or preserved what it produced very efficiently. Records, however, were not everything: whether or not they kept them, counts of Flanders, Normandy, and Anjou who were capable of maintaining political con-trol over alodholders were presumably able to do as well or better with fiefholders, even if they sometimes let them pass on their fiefs to their sons.[242]

Records, moreover, could be double-edged. The making of a charter must have invited commitment one way or the other. To make a grant only for the life of the recipient would fly in the face of normal expectations. On the other hand as soon as rights of inheritance were set out on parchment they must have become more definite. Unless they were restricted to two or three lives, which laymen found repugnant and churches often found futile, their definition in a charter would have combined with the obliga-tions that more powerful rulers were imposing on all property to blur the boundary between property that was formally dependent and property that was thought of as complete. This is what seems to have happened in the twelfth century, when grants of property are recorded as being made explicitly both in fief and in inheritance for ever. I shall return to these grants in chapter 7. For the time being the point I need to make is that I

---

[240] *Hist. Torn.* 337–9; *Dipl. Belgica*, i, no. 168; cf. Warlop, *Flemish Nobility*, i. 85. I take *altaria* here to imply fairly wide rights over the churches as well as the receipt of their revenues.

[241] '*Conventum*', on Chizé, Civray, Gençay (esp. 547–8), Vivonne.

[242] Guillot, *Anjou*, i. 319 n.; *Cart. Trinité Vendôme*, nos. 66–7 (cited by Bloch, *Feudal Society*, 196). *Actes des comtes de Flandre*, nos. 73, 76, 105, 110 are suggestive for the early twelfth cen-tury.

have not found hard evidence of similar grants before 1100. Perhaps others undertaking closer work on smaller areas could find some. My hypothesis is that they were rare. While Emily Tabuteau's meticulous survey of property transactions in eleventh-century Normandy revealed no explicit references to permanent inheritance of fiefs, she drew attention to the phrase *in feodum et hereditatem* as an apparent innovation of the twelfth century.[243] In the mean time, if we are to think in terms of a trend towards inheritance of fiefs granted by lay lords, it might be more accurate to see it as a trend from vague and undefined rights in subordinate properties (often described as fiefs) towards recorded and therefore more precise rights, rather than one from no inheritance to inheritance of all or most fiefs as if they formed a single category of property.

Those who managed the property of great churches could not be impervious to lay values. Bishops were often generous to their kinsmen. Conscientious abbots could not always deny all rights to a loyal tenant's loyal heirs, if only because such rights were deeply embedded in the society from which even monks could never be entirely insulated.[244] Canon law, however, prohibited the permanent alienation of church land, and, while bishops might sometimes treat the law rather casually, monks were likely to build up a corporate loyalty to their houses that would encourage them to observe it. Hence the compromise solution of limiting dependent holdings (except those of peasants, which could be more summarily controlled) to the life of the grantee or at most one or two lives more. Cartularies provide evidence of church land that had been—in the view of the church—wrongly passed on to heirs, presumably after grants for single lives. There may be rather fewer explicit references to property retained after grants for several lives had expired, but this cannot have been unusual.[245] Grants for several lives, like other compromises, satisfied neither side, for they meant having to try to evict families after they had got thoroughly settled. Local lay opinion, which mattered in the settlement of disputes, would be almost bound to be hostile. Even in the late eleventh century and the early twelfth, when religious enthusiasm was bringing in what superficially looks like a rich harvest of restitutions, restitution generally took the form of a new gift that might have to be paid for. It would be rash to deduce from the *ex parte* statements of cartularies that all those

---

[243] Tabuteau, *Transfers*, 305 (n. 146). Neither Niermeyer nor Du Cange draws attention to the association of *feodum* etc. and *hereditas*. Indexes to French charters do not generally seem to include an entry for *hereditas*.

[244] *Cart. Béziers*, no. 43; *Cart. Saint-André*, no. 206.

[245] My impression of the proportion of different kinds of reference comes largely from secondary works, some of which are more concerned with gifts to churches than with grants by them, and few of which happen to be concerned with the distinctions I am drawing.

who, the charters say, had repented of their wrongful detention of church property really conceded that they had had no right to lands that had been in their families for generations.[246]

Duby used charters of Cluny, Paray, and the cathedral of Mâcon in support of his argument that fiefs in the Mâconnais changed from life tenancies to hereditary tenancies during the eleventh century. They do not, however, seem to me to show a very clear trend, whether for lay or ecclesiastical property.[247] What they show is the disparity of views between laity and clergy about inheritance of property held from churches. Some churches and some laymen made grants for single lives;[248] some property held from laymen may have been inherited, rightly or wrongly;[249] some that was held from churches, or claimed by them, had been passed on by the tenants to relatives, though in some cases this could have been under grants for a limited number of lives;[250] in other cases, right up to 1100, the churches regarded the inheritance as wrongful.[251] Only two of the documents cited could possibly be evidence of ecclesiastical acceptance of unlimited inheritance: the first because it states no term to the grant, and the second on the ground that the heirs mentioned may have been going to inherit Cluny's *salvamentum*.[252]

Just because the eleventh-century trend towards the inheritance of fiefs has been so unquestioningly accepted, therefore, it remains highly questionable as regards fiefs on church estates as well as on lay estates. If the evidence that the churches of the Mâconnais had fully accepted their lay tenants' automatic rights of permanent inheritance by 1100 is not fully established, if they were at best still slightly grudging about it, then one would like to know when and why they really made the decision to abandon the struggle they had carried on so stubbornly for centuries, and when and why churches in other areas did so too. In England, efforts to enforce canon law against the alienation of church property helped provoke the murder of an archbishop, but both there and in France one gets the impression that

---

[246] e.g. *Cart. de Richerenches*, no. 187; Giordanengo, *Droit féodal*, 43 n.; cf. Weinberger, 'Precarial Grants'.

[247] The following notes refer to all the documents cited in *Société mâconnaise*, 152 n. 15 and 155 nn. 27–8 (except for C 3062 and C 3334 which do not seem to bear on the particular issue), using the same abbreviations and with Duby's dates in parentheses.

[248] Churches: C 2118 (*c.*1030), C 2950 (*c.*1040), C 2729 (1020), C 3161 (*c.*1050), C 2912 (1036). Lay grants for life are referred to in C 3627 (1087), C 3750 (*c.*1100), P 111 (*c.*1050), and possibly M 471 (997–1015).

[249] C 3278 (1049–1109 or *c.*1050), C 2845 (1023), and cf. C 2777. The property in P 38 may not have been dependent.

[250] C 3503 (1076), C 3221 (*c.*1080), C 3400 (1064)

[251] C 3278 (1049–1109 or *c.*1050), C 2845 (1023), C 3472 (1074), M 563 (1100), M 26 (1074–96).

[252] C 3503 (1076), C 2124 (*c.*1030). For *salvamentum*: Duby, *Société mâconnaise*, 175, 344; Bur, *Champagne*, 360–5.

for most bishops and churches the problem may have become easier when the new canon law of the twelfth century went over from blanket condemnations of all alienation of ecclesiastical property to emphasis on the need for proper consent.[253] That, however, is only a very small part of the answer. Some churches did not apparently use the latitude allowed them to make many permanent grants, except of the small properties held by peasants. These had always been accepted as in effect permanent, because the rights attached to them were so comfortably restricted and so easily controlled. Some churches may, at least for a while, have kept in hand the estates they had recovered or preserved, while others went over to leases for terms of years rather than for lives.[254] All this needs to be investigated further and to be related to the apparently gradual dying down of disputes about inheritance. My provisional hypothesis is that by the twelfth century churches were confronted by better-organized lay governments and jurisdictions, which made it increasingly difficult for them to resist the constant pressure from lay tenants for permanent inheritance. The result for church property was surely less a change of law—since it was the customary law of lay society that was at issue—than a change of policy in estate management. As such it has to lie outside the scope of my present enquiry.

One point about inheritance that lies within my scope must be mentioned. It is sometimes said that lords normally required that fiefs should pass to single heirs rather than being divided or shared as alods so often were. Given the vagueness and variability of all rules before the thirteenth century, however, it is probably a mistake to look for differences in the eleventh century between the rules for subordinate properties in general and the rules for full property in general. Churches that had specified the lives in their grants would presumably (if those in charge kept awake) try to limit inheritance to those named in the original grant, while lords who wanted military service might try to specify single inheritance by a competent male. Since alods and fiefs existed in the same society, however, it seems likely that the inheritance of fiefs tended to follow much the same social norms under customary law as did the inheritance of alods.[255]

Before 1000 the references to fiefs are too various and too gnomic to suggest that any definable category of property with consistent rules and obligations lies behind them. In the eleventh century, as references multiply and as some become more informative, the word fief seems to have been

---

[253] Cheney, 'Inalienability' and 'Litigation'; *Corpus Iuris Canonici*, i, cols. 682, 687 (C XII, Q. 1, 16; Q. II, 12); Le Bras, *Institutions ecclésiastiques*, 259–60.

[254] Schmitz, *L'Ordre de Saint Benoît*, v. 9–20; Valous, *Le Temporel*, 85–9; Bur, 'Aux origines du fermage'. Fee-farms: *Rec. Henri II*, no. 264, though cf. no. 492.

[255] Bur, *Champagne*, 470–5; Guillotel, 'Dévolution'; Ourliac, *Études*, 199–205. See index: inheritance rules.

becoming the obvious one to use of any property in which nobles and free men had partial and subordinate rights. Although in some contexts the word had quite other connotations there does not seem to be any evidence that contemporaries were either worried or confused. Few people then would have had cause to put the different uses together and worry about them, and it is hard to see how, if they had, it would have affected political and legal realities. What is important to recognize is that there is no strong reason to suppose that when a subordinate property was described as a fief it represented a new or distinct category of property. No hard evidence seems to have been produced to suggest a wave of a new sort of grants by lords to their military followers that created a new sort of obligation to service and loyalty. That need not mean that there was none, but the change needs to be demonstrated. The 'union' of benefice or fief with vassalage or homage remains as hard to pin down in the eleventh century as in the ninth—harder, in fact, since, in the absence of records of royal legislation, we are even more dependent on documents that deal with ecclesiastical property. Since as yet there was no way that rules about properties granted by different lords in different parts of the kingdom could have been codified, the property they granted, whether described as fiefs or not, naturally carried different rights and obligations. Much time, much legal argument, and much bad history would be needed before anything remotely like a consistent system, and thus a coherent 'concept of the fief', would be created. Before that, given the political fragmentation of the kingdom and the working of customary law, the rules about all kinds of property varied widely. Those about subordinate properties above the peasant level are likely to have varied most of all, since lords would be relatively free to make over property to their followers on terms that suited both sides. Churches would tend to develop their own traditions, but many of these would not be normative for lay lords. Some lay lords and some churches may have made some grants in inheritance, some may have made demands for military service, or exemptions from all service, without binding others to do the same. Some lords were tougher than others about confiscations or enforcing the terms of their grants, and some would be tougher with some tenants than others. Where custom became fixed it presumably worked within the estates or political units of the time, which did not always correspond with the provinces for which codes of customs were later compiled, let alone with the regions that historians study. Altogether it seems meaningless to discuss fiefs before the twelfth century either as if everything that was not described as an alod can be assumed to have been a fief, or as if everything that was called a fief (or a benefice) carried the same rights and obligations. The first alternative projects a careless use of later categories into a period in which they had not been worked out; the second confuses word and phenomenon.

It is almost certainly wrong to say that fiefs began to replace alods during this period. Partly that is because the evidence does not suggest that nobles and free men normally held their lands in fief by 1100. Partly it is because the categories were so fluid and unclear. It is often said that one way—even the chief way—that rulers and lords extended their power in the eleventh century was by turning their subjects' alods into fiefs. Examples of what later lawyers would call *fiefs de reprise* (fiefs granted in return for the surrender of full alodial rights) are, however, hard to come by before the twelfth century. Chénon suggested that many alods were converted into fiefs from the tenth century to the thirteenth, but the only evidence he gave of such a transaction that was supposed to have taken place before 1100 came from a story told after 1200:[256] an heiress who surrendered her alod to the bishop of Thérouanne (Pas-de-Calais), supposedly some time in the eleventh century, did so, she said, because she had heard that many nobles had found security that way.[257] Other references to the conversion of alods into fiefs before 1100 do not seem to be much better substantiated.[258] Gerald of Aurillac (d. 909) handed over a small and isolated estate which he could apparently not protect into the keeping of someone else (*ad custodiendam commendasset*), which presumably meant that he gave up some or all of his rights in it. There is, however, no evidence of the obligations in either direction that were incurred by this 'commendation', that homage was done, or that the property was regarded as held in fief either by Gerald or from Gerald—whatever that might have meant either to him or his biographer.[259] Some references are to grants of life benefices by churches in return for gifts of alods, which were not meant to create a permanent relationship.[260] Similarly, when someone who had maintained that his land was not part of a church estate had to accept defeat, that might turn what had hitherto been independent property into what was called a fief. It did so, however, against a different background from that which seems to be implied in the descriptions of the classic *fief de reprise*.[261] This kind of settlement of disputes between churches and laymen may have constituted one more way in which the management of

---

[256] Chénon, *Alleux*, 43–6.

[257] Lambert of Ardres, *Hist.* 607–8; for the date: Warlop, *Flemish Nobility*, i. 37.

[258] e.g. Mitteis, *Lehnrecht*, 505, who refers to Chénon; Ganshof, *Feudalism*, 121 ('undoubtedly very common between the ninth and twelfth centuries'); Bloch, *Feudal Society*, 197; Poly and Bournazel, *Mutation féodale*, 131–2, 138 (the reference to Bonnassie seems valid for Catalonia rather than Septimania); Poly, *Provence*, 138.      [259] Odo, *Vita Geraldi*, col. 667.

[260] *Rec. Cluny*, no. 2118, cited by Poly and Bournazel, *Mutation féodale*, 132; *Chron. de Bèze*, 413, cited by Richard, *Ducs de Bourgogne*, 106, to whom Poly and Bournazel also refer.

[261] e.g. *Chartes de Saint-Maixent*, nos. 123–4, 235.

ecclesiastical property suggested useful possibilities to lay lords.[262] Perhaps French lords were already converting their subjects' alods to fiefs before 1100. Nevertheless, although the scarcity of charters issued by laymen to laymen makes it impossible to be sure that they were not, it is suggestive that a thorough study of all recorded transfers of property in Normandy has not produced any evidence that the dukes made any formal conversion of alods to fiefs.[263] Except when they were dealing with castles which they could argue were held by special delegation from themselves, even counts of Anjou and Normandy needed some justification to make direct attacks on the rights of free men in their inherited property. If they had justification in an individual case they might as well confiscate the property outright rather than convert it into a fief. Getting a significant proportion of their subjects to accept formally reduced rights would surely have caused enough comment to have been recorded. What rulers at all levels seem to have done in the eleventh century, when they could, was to enforce obligations on all their subjects, including alodholders. The effect at this stage was to blur distinctions still more than they had become blurred in the tenth century rather than to accentuate and use them.

## 5.6. *Conclusion*

By the twelfth century disputes were beginning to stimulate the drawing of distinctions, while increasing professionalism in record-keeping and legal argument was beginning to make the distinctions more consistent. Particular rights and obligations therefore began to be associated with different words, but it was a slow process. As yet, before the process had really got going, full inheritances, whether or not called alods, set the standard of rights and obligations for property held by people above peasant level, as well as for the more prosperous peasants. That being so, one would expect that the rights and obligations of less complete property would reflect in a glass darkly the rights and obligations of alods. By and large it looks as if they did, but they need to be investigated much more closely without being squashed into the categories of later professional and academic law. In the mean time, before considering how government and law developed in France after 1100 and how, as a result, the words fief and vassal came to be used in the senses that historians of feudalism attribute to them, it will be useful to look at the way they had come to be used in Italy. It was from there that at least some of the new usages were introduced to France as part of the apparatus of the new kind of expert law that seems to have developed first in Italy.

[262] Above, at nn. 114–18.          [263] Tabuteau, *Transfers*.

# 6

# ITALY

## 6.1. *The problems*

MANY of the problems of non-Marxist feudalism in Italy are similar to
those of French feudalism that were sketched at the beginning of the last
chapter, in particular the problems created by the imposition of categories
created by later historians. The historiography of Italian feudalism, however, includes its own paradoxes. Although the whole idea of feudalism
originated from a north Italian book, the first post-medieval French
scholars who used the *Libri Feudorum* to elucidate French history were so
anxious to play down any dependence of France on Roman law or
Lombard precedent, and their successors had their eyes so firmly fixed on
the north, that Italy came to seem as marginal to feudalism as feudalism did
to the history of Italy. Carlo Sigonio (d. 1588) derived the origin of fiefs
from the time of King Authari (584–90),[1] but, after French historians had
effectively postponed their appearance in France to the Carolingians, it
must have seemed reasonable to attribute their introduction into Italy to
Charlemagne. By the nineteenth century feudalism had become closely
connected with an agricultural stage of human evolution, while medieval
Italy was seen as the land of urban continuity and the rebirth of civic culture. Italian feudalism had to be squashed in chronologically between the
Romans (or even the Carolingians) and the age of the communes. C. G.
Mor's *L'Età feudale* started in 887 and ended in 1024, paradoxically missing both the introduction of Carolingian benefices *verbo regis* at one end
and the ordinance of Conrad II that is generally taken to have formed the
basic text of the *Libri Feudorum* at the other.[2]

More recently historians of medieval Italy have turned their attention to
the countryside. The most obvious result has been some distinguished
work using feudalism primarily in its Marxist sense. Meanwhile, however,
some Italian and French historians of Italy have become interested in
studying feudo-vassalic relations there.[3] The tension here between the

[1] *Opera Omnia*, ii, col. 33–4, n. 55.
[2] Cf. more recently, Sestan, 'Problemi', 87–8, 119–20.
[3] Wickham, *Mountains and City*, pp. xiii–xxxiii and Dean, *Land and Power*, 1–10, survey
recent works.

desire to use the construct and the need to admit that it does not always fit local conditions is sometimes acute. While feudalism in its non-Marxist sense has generally been seen as a foreign import into Italy, whether brought by Franks, Normans, or Germans, it is also seen to have taken a distinctively Italian form. Oaths of fidelity and immunity (i.e., in Italian usage, rights of jurisdiction, however acquired) seem to loom larger in most discussions of what Italian historians characterize as feudal institutions or relationships than they generally do in France or England.[4] I shall argue that this is explicable in terms of legal and political developments in the twelfth century and later rather than of earlier social and political norms. In the twelfth century the new profession of academically trained lawyers began to work out rules and arguments about the property of the kind of people who could afford to consult them, using the texts that seemed to them relevant and the precedents formed largely from the management of church land and disputes about it. If we start, not from a model of feudalism that has been constructed from what sixteenth-century and later historians understood of the texts compiled by these lawyers and their successors, but from the rights and obligations of Italian property in the earlier middle ages so far as they are discernible in the sources of the time, some of the paradoxes of Italian feudalism disappear or become irrelevant. Removing paradoxes is not the same as solving problems. It is notoriously difficult to generalize about Italy and this chapter, like the previous one, is too restricted in its use of the sources and its coverage of widely varying regions and periods to do more than make suggestions about possible solutions to the problems posed by such material as I have seen. As usual, I have found most of the primary sources I cite through references in secondary works, and the secondary works I have read are heavily biased towards the north, especially Lombardy. I have entirely ignored Sardinia and deal with Sicily and the south only between the Norman invasion and the thirteenth century. I hope, however, that my arguments and evidence are sufficient to suggest the inadequacies of the models of feudalism with which students of medieval Italy have worked, the inadequate knowledge of Italian politics and academic law that produced those models in the first place, and a possible alternative line of argument for others to test.

## 6.2. Before 774: the Lombard kingdom

Whatever ideas about property the Lombards brought with them when they invaded Italy, and whatever ideas the Romans they found there had about it, the prevailing norms in the following centuries look not very

[4] Tabacco, 'Fief et seigneurie'; Conti, *Formazione*, 191; Fasoli, 'Città e feudalità', 366–7, but also Rippe, '*Feudum sine fidelitate*'.

different from those prevalent in contemporary Gaul. The Roman law followed by those, whether inside or outside the Lombard kingdom, who thought of themselves as Romans was not that of the classical jurists, or of Justinian, let alone the simple set of rules about absolute property with which feudal custom has traditionally been contrasted. It was what Levy called—rather unfortunately in terms of the English implications of the word—the 'vulgar law', that is, a customary law in which the terminology and distinctions of classical Roman law had become blurred.[5] From the time of the first Lombard laws in the seventh century and the first surviving charters and records of disputes rather later, it seems probable that nobles and free men who thought of themselves as Lombards and those who thought of themselves as Romans had much the same ideas about the rights that they and their like ought to have over the land that was considered to be theirs.[6]

Throughout the middle ages, from the time when evidence first becomes available, landed property in Italy was quite often shared by members of *consorzerie* who were often kinsmen, though, as alienation became easier and relationships became more complex and distant, not invariably so. This may have derived partly from ancient Lombard tradition. King Rothari envisaged brothers living together and sharing their father's property after his death. He also, however, provided for them to divide their inheritance if they wished, and allowed one who acquired property in royal service to keep it for himself. Although children could be disinherited only for serious crimes, so long as their father lived they were his heirs, not joint owners with him.[7] Shared property of this kind is, in any case, like similarly shared property in Gaul, not the same as the 'communal property' or 'clan property' that historians used to associate with the Germanic barbarians. Individual people of free status were apparently thought of as owners, whether they held their property jointly or not, and whether their property was called their *proprietas*, their *proprium*, or simply their *res*. Whether their rights in it were characterized as *dominium*, *possessio*, or anything else, they were adjudicated in courts or assemblies that apparently tried to apply the norms that they derived from locally accepted custom, adjusted presumably in accordance with what was known of legislation by the king, the emperor, or any other locally accepted authority.[8]

The right of current owners to dispose of their property was restricted

[5] Levy, *West Roman Vulgar Law*; Classen, 'Fortleben'.
[6] Leicht, *Diritto privato*, iii. 102–3, 193–4; Wickham, *Early Medieval Italy*, 69–70.
[7] *Leges Langobardorum*, 39–46 (Rothari 153–75, esp. 167–8).
[8] Wickham, 'Land Disputes'.

by the rights of their heirs, but, while alienation must have been difficult
and rare, it cannot have been unknown in the seventh century, or Rothari
would not have had to restrict and regulate it.[9] It became more common in
the eighth century. Liutprand, though also legislating to protect heirs,
especially daughters, against alienations, decreed in 713 that any sick
Lombard might give away property, apparently without limit, for the good
of his soul.[10] During the eighth century churches seem to have acquired a
lot of new property, but how much of this was the result of gifts that would
have been absolutely impossible before 713 is another question. Churches
did not extend their holdings only through gifts and bequests. Records of
sales between laymen suggest that there was some small land market. It
may have been growing, but with the seventh-century evidence so sparse,
and earlier evidence outside the laws virtually non-existent, it is impossible to make any real estimate of change.[11] It is, moreover, hard to imagine
that churches, whether Arian or Catholic, could have got along before 713
without gifts. At least one or two gifts just before then seem to have been
made by people who look like Lombards.[12] Meanwhile the situation among
those following Roman law, inside or outside the kingdom, was not necessarily all that different. Classical Roman law had made varied provision for
conveyances of property, while gifts to churches had continued to be
allowed under the vulgar law even when the land market became less
active, but just because heirs or potential heirs lived according to what was
called Roman law they would not all be piously unselfish. Comparisons
with France and elsewhere suggest that under early medieval law gifts to
the church would always be easier for those without children or close kin.
Perhaps Liutprand was not so much creating entirely new possibilities as
confirming a right that some had already claimed. Perhaps he had reasons
for needing to adjust the always uneasy balance between the demands of
the clergy and the norms of lay inheritance. Later on the law of property
would be significantly affected by the adjustments that kings and emperors would make to the balance in circumstances where we can make better
guesses at their reasons.

The rights of property-owners were also limited by the possibility of
confiscation. Some crimes incurred forfeiture of property to the king,
though in the case of others part or all of what was lost went to heirs or
other close kin.[13] Apart from what was confiscated, property that was left

---

[9] *Leges Langobardorum*, 44–6, 61, 63 (Rothari 168–75, 227–9, 233–5).
[10] Ibid. 100–2, 105, 130 (Liutprand 6 and cf. 1–5, 7, 14, 65, 73).
[11] Sales are referred to in *Cod. Dip. Longobardo*, nos. 23, 26, 36–7.
[12] *Cod. Dip. Longobardo*, nos. 14, 16 are suggestive, but cf. Wickham, 'Economic and Social
Institutions', 17–25, and *Early Medieval Italy*, 43, 109.
[13] *Leges Langobardorum*, 18, 42, 98, 181–2 (Rothari 1, 3–4, 163; Grimoald 5; Notitia 5).

entirely without heirs also apparently went to the king, though this may not have happened often since the process of *thinx* allowed anyone who feared to die without heirs to adopt one. Once heirless property had gone to the king it stopped there: no other claims on it were allowed, even, presumably, from a lord whom the deceased had served and whose property he might have held on subordinate and restricted terms.[14] When illegitimate children shared in an inheritance then other close kin took a cut, and if there were none then the king got their share.[15] Only in exceptional circumstances did anyone but the king have the right to take over property that lacked heirs. If a duke or other free man gave land to someone who then decided (with royal permission) to leave the kingdom, taking his heirs with him, then the donation reverted to the donor or his heirs. A freedman (*libertus*) who became *fulcfree* could leave his property to his children or dispose of it beforehand like other free men, except for what he had got from his *benefactor* or *patronus*. That went back to the patron, as did the rest of a freedman's property if he had no heirs.[16] What was acquired in the service of a duke or other lord also went back to the donor: it is possible that, since not all in service were freedmen, this applied to what the freeborn acquired from their service too, but in context it clearly applies to the *libertus*. Donations to the free, like those to people who afterwards emigrated, were presumably assumed to be permanent, apart, of course, from grants made by churches, to which I shall return shortly. The particularity of the freedman's circumstances makes it implausible to see this set of rules about their property as implying the existence of benefices 'in the technical sense' and foreshadowing the growth of something like fiefs held by free men.[17]

As for obligations, Roman land taxes went on being demanded by Byzantine exarchs in the areas they controlled but were not apparently maintained generally by Lombard kings, though some may have survived here and there along with other dues that the kings continued to take and that did not fall so directly on property.[18] Military service seems to have been accepted as a general obligation on free men (*arimanni, exercitales*), who were apparently assumed to be property-owners, rather as it was among the Franks. By the eighth century the amount owed was adjusted to the size of estate.[19] Some of the lesser *exercitales* no doubt felt their

[14] Ibid. 59 (Rothari 223): although this appears in the middle of a section on the unfree it appears to apply to the free. For the lord's claim, ibid. 60 (Rothari 225) and below.

[15] Ibid. 41 (Rothari 158–60).

[16] Ibid. 46, 60 (Rothari 177, 225). The reversion of the *benefactor*'s gift is subject to the condition, *si eas* [sc. *res*] *non oblegavit in libertatem*, which I do not understand.

[17] Cf. Sestan, 'Problemi', 37.    [18] Wickham, *Early Medieval Italy*, 75.

[19] *Leges Langobardorum*, 194 (Aistulf 2); cf. 128, 138, 197 (Liutprand 62, 83; Aistulf 7); *Cod. Dip. Longobardo*, no. 114; Tabacco, *Struggle*, 96–8.

primary loyalty to their duke or other local noble, but that does not mean
that they held their land from him or owed their service to him in any
formal sense. The maintenance of roads and bridges (and, one may guess,
fortifications) was apparently a general obligation which probably fell in
the first instance on property-holders, though their peasant tenants would
have felt the brunt of it.[20] Such obligations suggest that the sense of public property and the public good was not extinguished in the Lombard
kingdom: when royal land was referred to as public land that was presumably because the king was responsible for the kingdom and its welfare.[21]

Most of those who held land with restricted rights were peasants, who
concern us here only in so far as one must notice that custom made their
rights, weak as they were, a drag on the property rights of their lords, and
in so far as the boundary between free and unfree was as yet very vague.
The prohibitions against buying land from *servi* and *aldiones* illustrate the
uncertainties at the border as well as the burdens below it.[22] Nearly all
grants of land mention or assume that peasants, most of whom presumably
ranked as more or less unfree, lived on it. Presumably, like many peasants
elsewhere, they held their land, with its obligations, in effect hereditarily
and for ever, subject to custom and their lord's jurisdiction. Free men
might also hold subordinate property, but they could take claims about it
to public assemblies and public judgement. Most of our information about
subordinate property concerns what was held from churches, and most
comes from after the Carolingian conquest, but there is just enough from
before it to suggest that some practices recorded in the ninth century were
older. In 681 two powerful local nobles secured a grant, apparently without term, of property belonging to the church of Aquileia. The church
doubtless hoped to retain what Roman lawyers would have called
*dominium*.[23] The transaction was recorded in duplicate documents referred
to as *libelli* or *livelli*. Later on, grants to people of high status in some
(though not all) areas that followed what they called Roman law might
instead have been called *enfiteusi*.

Words like *libellus* (or *livellus*), *enfiteusis* (in any of its spellings), *conduc-
tio*, *locatio*, *precaria*, *praestaria*, and *beneficium* (though this last was as yet
less common here than in the north) suggest the survival or revival of different legal traditions in different regions and different monasteries. The
different words do not, however, seem to represent consistent and contrasting sets of rights and obligations.[24] Grants made *livellario nomine* to

[20] *Capit.* nos. 91 c. 4, 93 c. 7.                    [21] *Leges Langobardorum*, 128 (Liutprand 78).
[22] Ibid. 63, 128, 181–2 (Rothari 233–5, Liutprand 78, Notitia 5).
[23] Leicht, *Diritto privato*, iii. 189.
[24] Leicht, 'Livellario nomine'; Wickham, *Early Medieval Italy*, 141, and *Mountains and City*,
48–9. Feenstra, 'L'Emphytéose', Toubert, *Structures*, 518–19, and Grossi, 'Problematica strut-

powerful nobles would probably require little or nothing by way of rent or service, while those to peasants would impose heavy obligations and perhaps even labour services, though presumably anyone receiving a *livellus* would rank as effectively free since he or she could make a mutually binding contract. Here, as in Gaul, those who granted land to churches might reserve the usufruct for life, while grants made by churches of land they already owned might, by the eighth and ninth centuries and perhaps before, be for one, two, or three lives or for any unspecified term. In the tenth century Farfa abbey (Lazio) favoured twenty-nine-year grants.[25] Whatever the length of time they envisaged, whatever the terminology of their grants, churches intended—or should have intended, if they had conscientious bishops or abbots—to maintain their ultimate rights and reversionary interest. In the ninth century two bishops of Lucca regained control of estates by claiming that they were not being properly looked after under the terms of their *livelli*, which specified, as many did, that the property should be improved.[26] The obligation *ad meliorandum* had originally belonged only in certain categories of Roman grants but had become embedded, apparently as common form, in many that were made by churches, however the document was described.[27] In this instance it served to secure the return of estates that probably seemed in danger of moving out of church control altogether. As in France and elsewhere, the crux was that lay norms of inheritance conflicted with the obligations of bishops and abbots to preserve the endowments of their churches. Even the formality of notarial drafting, together with the standard use of duplicate deeds at a period when subordinate property in the north might be granted without deeds at all, could not protect Italian churches from the troubles that also beset churches in less literate parts of Europe.

The Lombard royal estates seem to have been managed by royal officials, chiefly those called *gastaldi*. The kings did not apparently give away much but when they did it was apparently with full and permanent rights, though that did not prevent Aistulf from revoking his predecessor's gifts.[28] There is no evidence that kings made grants of land for life to free men. The laws suggest that the lands that gastalds looked after were not envisaged as theirs, except perhaps in a purely ex officio sense. If they made unauthorized grants or allowed unfree people on royal land to alienate their holdings that was a crime. If it was committed knowingly their own

turale' find more significant distinctions than I do. For an eleventh-century view: Toubert, *Structures*, 533–4.

[25] Leicht, 'Livellario nomine', 132–46; *Cod. Dip. Long.*, no. 124; Toubert, *Structures*, 521–7.
[26] *Placiti*, nos. 57, 71.                     [27] Cf. Grossi, 'Problematica strutturale'.
[28] Wickham, *Early Medieval Italy*, 41, 133; *Leges Langobardorum*, 194 (Aistulf 1); for property acquired from the king by serving him: *Reg. Farfa*, no. 1224.

property was forfeit (*inpublicare faciat*).[29] The woods or pastures of *arimanni* that are later found in private ownership look more like usurped common lands than usurped royal property.[30] While kings got away without either giving away much land or granting it to free men on restricted terms, nobles on the whole may not have had much opportunity or need to do either. Leaving aside the southern duchies, which effectively left the kingdom pretty soon, large estates seem to have been fewer and less large than those of Frankish nobles. The powerful men against whose misdoings Aistulf, for instance, legislated were presumably richer than most, but more of their power and influence must have come from royal favour and service and less from enormous estates than seems to have been the case in Gaul.[31] Like the king, royal officials and other nobles had their followers (*gasindii*), though, whereas the king's gasinds might be great nobles themselves, those of the nobles would be lesser nobles or free men and even, on occasion, *liberti*.[32] A free man might enter the service of the follower (*fidelis*) of a royal gasind so that layers of patronage were formed, as one might expect in this kind of society, but there is no evidence that they entailed any reduction of the client's official rights over his property or his duty to king and kingdom.[33] If service entailed the taking of an oath it is not recorded in the laws. Liutprand alluded to an oath that he implied was taken to the king by all free men, but whether this was a regular practice or a figurative way of talking of their obligation to loyalty is unclear.[34] There is also no evidence that the conveyance of land involved any oath or ceremony of subjection from the recipient. A case of 762 implies that a transfer between laymen was expected to be made by charter, as well as requiring the public ceremony of *thinx* and a countergift or *launechild*. The transfer of a symbolic object from the donor to the recipient of property may have been customary, but the references to it I have seen all came after the Frankish conquest. For those without documents, thirty years' quiet possession gave title except to what had been public (that is, royal) land, which required twice as long.[35]

[29] Tabacco, 'Dai possessori', 222–5; *Leges Langobardorum*, 126–7, 181–2 (Liutprand 59, Notitia 5).
[30] *Reg. Farfa*, nos. 290–2; Tabacco, 'I Liberi' (1964), 17.
[31] Wickham, *Early Medieval Italy*, 133–4.
[32] Leicht, 'Gasindii' gives references, but there does not seem to be any reason to deduce from Rothari 225 (as he does in 'Il feudo', 83) that gasinds were normally freedmen.
[33] *Leges Langobardorum*, 191 (Ratchis 11).
[34] Ibid. 181–2 (Notitia 5); Tabacco, 'Dai possessori', 222–5.
[35] *Cod. Dip. Long.*, no. 163; *Leges Langobardorum*, 134–6 (Liutprand 73, 78); Leicht, *Diritto privato*, iii. 102–3, 193–4; Classen, 'Fortleben', 23.

## 6.3. *Political relations and government from 774 to the twelfth century*

There does not seem to have been any general expropriation at the time of Charlemagne's conquest, but some Lombard nobles forfeited their land as a result of resistance or subsequent rebellion.[36] More importantly, Charlemagne extended to Italy his policy of settling his *vassi* on lands borrowed from churches for the purpose. That, together with changes in the rights and obligations of full property, will be discussed further in later sections of this chapter. The point to be made here is that there is very little evidence that the introduction of the words *vassus* or *vassallus* (or *bassus*, *bassallus*, *guasso*, etc.[37]) implied any very significant change of ideas. The words themselves certainly seem to have come in with the Franks. Charlemagne's ordinances referred to vassals and to lords having men *in vassatico* where Lombards would have referred to gasinds and men *in gasindio*, but the new word did not entirely and at once replace the old. As Lombards ceased to be defeated and distrusted enemies the two vocabularies and traditions presumably became merged.[38] While kings, churches, and other lords seem to have granted land to their followers on restricted terms more often than they had done earlier, and some of the followers were called *vassi*, there is no reason to believe that all *vassi* or *vassalli* held such land.[39] Vassals were quite often referred to in north Italy and Tuscany between 900 and 1100, generally when they were present at disputes or the granting of charters. A few can be identified as landowners or holders of benefices in the sense of offices, but most get into the sources simply because they were present in assemblies as vassals—that is, as the servants or followers of the emperor or some lesser lord. Whether or not they held land and how they held it is generally unknown.[40] It seems improbable that the courts or assemblies of vassals referred to in the late eleventh century and the early twelfth consisted only of those who held fiefs or benefices. Apart from all the people who might attend a court concerned with local law and order, a bishop's court, even if called a *curia vassallorum*, would

[36] *Dip. Karol.* i, nos. 112, 214.

[37] Budriesi Trombetti, 'Prime ricerche', 282 n., 283–338.

[38] *Capit.* nos. 20 c. 9, 90 c. 11, 13, 93 c. 6, 94 c. 4–6, 13, 216 c. 4; *Placiti*, e.g. no. 64; Leicht, 'Gasindii'.

[39] Though land could be granted *in bassalitico*: Benedetto, *Chronicon*, 167–8. When vassals were granted land on less than full terms it might, however, be *a livello* not in benefice: Bordone, 'Società e potere', 426–7. The surrender of King Berengar in 952 (Regino, *Chronicon*, 166) may suggest the association of vassalage and benefice, but cf. that of Tassilo (index: Tassilo). Regino in any case illustrates German rather than Italian usage. For vassals in general and their status: Budriesi Trombetti, 'Prime ricerche', 278–349, esp. 338–9.

[40] Budriesi Trombetti, 'Prime ricerche', 282–35. Cf. Rippe, 'L'Évêque de Padoue', 414, 418–22.

include a good many clergy, clients, and servants who did not hold episcopal land.[41] In other words, it looks as though in Italy, until the twelfth-
century academics got hold of it, the word may have kept something like
its ninth-century sense. Here, however, it was sometimes applied to people
of higher status than seems to have been usual among the Franks and could
even be applied to clerics: the abbot of Corbie presided over a plea as the
emperor's *vassus* and *missus* in 812.[42] He was a benefice-holder in so far as
his church might have been called a royal benefice, but that would have
been a quite different use of the word benefice from that implied in its use
for 'vassal benefices'.[43]

The Carolingians seem to have intended to maintain the full rights and
jurisdiction of their predecessors to military service and attendance at local
courts, though the emperors themselves may have started rather soon to
undermine their control by granting immunity from comital jurisdiction to
great churches. By 813 free men were getting out of their public duties
through fraudulent grants to churches. Soon after that the abbey of Monte
Amiata in Tuscany was making some of those—presumably free men—to
whom it granted *livelli* agree to attend its courts.[44] This looks like a first
stage in establishing more or less exclusive jurisdiction over the church's
tenants and taking over the royal dues and services they owed. For a ninth-
century king, however, it was more important to secure military service
than to worry about attendance at local courts. Throughout the century
kings strove to enforce the military obligations of those with full property
rights—even on occasion trying to get those with only movables to serve
too—as well as of benefice-holders. In the 890s King Lambert was concerned to emphasize that the obligation was owed to him, not to the
counts.[45] The troubles of Bishop Ratherius of Verona in the tenth century
and the ordinance of Conrad II in the eleventh alike suggest the importance
that the German emperors still attached to military service.[46] The fact that
these two episodes concerned service from benefices held from churches
and counts does not mean that people with independent property were
exempt. Royal efforts to secure dues like *fodrum*, which were paid by free
men or *arimanni* with their own property, suggest otherwise. The trouble
for the king or emperor was that from the tenth century the dues and services of *arimanni*, like their loyalty, went rather to counts than to him.

As late as 883 it was still possible for a king, Charles the Fat, to dismiss
a count, Guy of Spoleto.[47] It turned out to have been a rash thing to do but

[41] Rippe, 'Commune urbaine.'                    [42] *Placiti*, no. 25; Lesne, 'Diverses Acceptions'.
[43] See chapter 4.2.
[44] *Capit.* no. 93 c. 5; Leicht, 'Livellario nomine', nos. 4, 6, 10, 11.
[45] *Capit.* nos. 74, 165, 203, 218, 224–5.    [46] See next two sections.
[47] *Annales Fuldenses*, 100.

that does not mean that it was considered to be *ultra vires*. In 898 Lambert of Spoleto, as king and emperor, forbade counts to give *arimanni* in benefice to their own men. *Arimanni* were free men, but what had been happening was presumably that some count or counts had transferred their services—in other words, had diverted to the count's subordinates or clients obligations that were owed to him as a representative of the king. The rest of Lambert's ordinance suggests that, as well as protecting royal rights against abuse by counts and their subordinates, he was responding to complaints from his and their subjects.[48] It may have been good policy to do so. Meanwhile, the charters of his rival, Berengar I, suggest that at least some royal property in Berengar's part of the kingdom, although managed by counts, remained sufficiently under royal control for him to give it away, even if he may have done so often with the consent of the count concerned or at his instance.[49] The rivalries of kings, however, inevitably undermined royal control over counties, and this, despite the apparent power of Otto I and his successors, was exacerbated under kings who spent most of their time north of the Alps. As time passed and counties remained in the same families for generations, dismissal became less and less practicable, while the distinction between a count's hereditary lands and those he held in virtue of his office became blurred. It did not, however, entirely disappear. Even in the eleventh century counts still found it worth while to get full and outright grants of royal property in their counties. The distinction may have been largely notional, and often ignored in practice, but it was still recognized even in the twelfth century.[50]

At the same time comital rights and jurisdictions themselves became fragmented. Berengar I seems to have been the first king to grant exemption from comital jurisdiction to laymen, but, quite apart from formal grants, the division of inheritances and local power politics had by the twelfth century replaced many of the old counties by a network of new lordships. Their lords, who were often called counts, claimed at least some of the traditional comital dues and jurisdictions. By then many such claims could be validated in the usual way by the accumulation of custom behind them.[51] In some areas the result was so complicated that it could not be mapped on the ground at all.[52] That does not mean that all territorial

[48] *Capit.* no. 225. On the rights of *arimanni*, below, n. 109.
[49] *Dip. Berengario I*, e.g. nos. 15, 19, 25, 54, 93, 104, 107, 114.
[50] *Dip. Otto III*, no. 421; *Dip. Konrad II*, no. 101; *Dip. Konrad III*, no. 51.
[51] *Dip. Berengario I*, nos. 32, 76, 94, 137. Much has been written on the subject briefly surveyed in the following sentences: see e.g. Tabacco, 'L'allodialità', 'La costituzione', and *Struggle*, 153–63; Wickham, *Mountains and City*, pp. xx–xxii.
[52] e.g. *Libro Verde*, no. 110; Manaresi, *Atti di Milano*, nos. 5, 8, 25, 27, 38; Patruccio, 'Più antiche carte', 86–8, 96–8.

authority had disappeared: dues and petty jurisdiction over individuals were more fragmented in some areas than was effective power. By 1100 the confusion was beginning to be tidied up as local lords worked out boundaries between their jurisdictions and as the great cities began to establish control over the neighbouring countryside. These changes have sometimes been represented as the re-establishment of public power after the anarchic age of private and feudal power. Other historians have argued that in Italy a sense of the public welfare and public government never disappeared. That is surely correct, but the implied contrast with the archetypal feudalism of north France is misleading. Jurisdiction in France during the tenth and eleventh centuries did not coincide neatly with property boundaries any more than it did in Italy: in both cases lordships that secured the general criminal and other jurisdiction that came to be recognized as the ban or *districtus* did so by extending control over people who had once been independent property-holders living only under royal and comital jurisdiction. In neither country can feudo-vassalic links be shown to have preceded and shaped the jurisdictions established in the twelfth century. The distinction between private and public is also unreal. It is true that the language and forms of the old *res publica* were preserved in Italy as they were not in France, especially by urban notaries and élites. But the contrast may be more a matter of form than of substance, and even more a matter of historiographical tradition. Though the north lacked the great civic and legal inheritance that Italy enjoyed, ideas of public good, expressed through custom and collective judgement, survived there through the supposed 'feudal anarchy' of the tenth and eleventh centuries.

By the twelfth century any German king who wanted to come to Italy, be crowned emperor, and receive the dues and services to which he felt he was entitled, would find himself bargaining for fidelity and alliances rather than asserting a recognized authority. The oaths taken—or supposed to be taken—to Henry IV in 1077 may suggest that things had not by then deteriorated so far but, given the troubles Henry was facing, they may give an impression of routine that was already unreal. Already the rise of the great cities and their assumption of dues and services, first from their citizens and then from people in the countryside around, was probably undermining the traditional authority of both emperor and counts.

## 6.4. *Benefices and fiefs, 774–1037*

When Charlemagne settled his *vassi* on the lands of Italian churches he seems, perhaps in deference to Italian custom, to have allowed the churches affected to take rather more by way of money rent from their unwelcome tenants than was usual elsewhere.[53] The system of benefices *verbo regis* must have been particularly useful when an army of occupation was needed, but it became rooted in custom here, as it did in France. Traces of the division between the land a church retained for its own use and what was used for royal benefices can be found two centuries later.[54] Perhaps royal estates were also used to provide benefices more readily here than in the north, where Frankish kings may well have felt more proprietary about their estates and used them in person more often.

The word benefice was, of course, used in a variety of senses in Italy as it was elsewhere.[55] Sometimes, as in the Frankish kingdom, it denoted the offices of gastalds and of the counts who were now put over them. As in the north this does not mean that the royal or church lands that counts and gastalds managed for the king were now 'feudalized' so that king or church formally sacrificed any rights in them. In 811 Farfa abbey claimed properties from a gastald who held them, he said, because another gastald had given them to him *in beneficium pro publica causa* so that he held them *in beneficio . . . a parte publico domini regis*.[56] A count's benefice was his office and the lands that went with it. When counties came to be inherited and counts became effectively undismissable that was the effect of a shift in the balance of power between king and count that became fixed in custom, not of any formal change in their relations that can be connected with the use of the word benefice.[57]

Bishoprics and abbeys, as well as suffering the grant of benefices *verbo regis*, granted land for their own purposes, presumably much as they had done before. Sometimes they gave it *in beneficio, nomine beneficii, beneficiali ordine*. Around the middle of the ninth century the word *feus* or *feum* appears in Italian sources, when lands belonging to the see of Lucca were said to be held *in feo* and *per feum*. The form *fegum* seems to have been common in the eleventh century, and was generally superseded by *feudum* only towards and after its end.[58] As in contemporary France all these words, which we translate as fief, were often used in a non-committal way, as, for instance, in specifying that land being conveyed lay next to someone else's fief.[59] In such cases the fiefs often look like properties with

---

[53] Brancoli Busdraghi, 'Formazione', 53; *Capit.* nos. 20 c. 14; 74 c. 7; 210 c. 10.

[54] *Placiti*, nos. 104, 126; *Dip. Otto III*, no. 303; Nobili, 'Vassalli'.

[55] Chapter 4.2.

[56] *Placiti*, no. 24: according to the Farfa account no one could say how the first gastald had acquired the properties, so perhaps they were not part of what should have been assigned for benefices.

[57] See previous section.            [58] Budriesi Trombetti, 'Prime ricerche', 378–89.

[59] Most of the eleventh-century Farfa references seem to be of this nature: Toubert, *Structures*, 1105; cf. Hoffmann, 'Kirchenstaat', 32–3. Usage in the lands conquered by the Normans is discussed later in this chapter (6.10).

restricted rights rather because they belonged to peasants than because they were the result of honourable, contractual, or military grants. Eleventh-century documents sometimes use *beneficium* and *feudum* or *fegum* as implied or explicit synonyms, but the range of their use was not the same:[60] benefice had a far wider range of uses, including lands or offices held from the emperor, which do not seem to have been called fiefs before the twelfth century. Since the habit of giving permission for the grant of full property did not spread to Italy, except where the Normans introduced it, the particular use of the word fief for the lordships of French counts and others, including the king, when they gave such permission is not found here. Another word that should be noted at this stage is *investitura*, which seems sometimes to have been used to denote a type of holding with some kind of restricted rights rather than, or as well as, the ceremony by which rights were transferred.[61]

In 1964 Piero Brancoli Busdraghi argued that grants in benefice (or in fief) were at first normally made without written documents, that before 1037 they did not convey the kind of rights that later professional lawyers would call *jura in re*, and that, unlike *livelli* or *enfiteusi*, they were originally made primarily to secure military service.[62] I shall now argue that these contentions cannot be sustained. They relied on the use of what seem to me anachronistic legal concepts and ignored evidence that does not fit. Before doing so, however, I should like to make clear that the learning and cogency of the argument and the evidence produced in support of it have greatly stimulated me in my effort to propound a different set of hypotheses that seem to fit the evidence better.

I start with the question of written records. It is true that benefices and fiefs were different from *livelli* and *enfiteusi* in so far as the latter were essentially written forms of conveyance while the former may sometimes or often have been granted without written record—that is, presumably, simply by investiture.[63] That was particularly likely to be the case when the word benefice was applied to properties held by peasants below or near the border of freedom, while some people above that level who claimed benefices did so without producing documentary evidence.[64] On the other

---

[60] Budriesi Trombetti, 'Prime ricerche', 382–4; *Reg. Farfa*, no. 1154.

[61] In the twelfth century Obertus de Orto thought that this was its proper use: Lehmann, *Langobardische Lehnrecht*, 115–16. Perhaps this influenced his son: Anselminus de Orto, *Super contractibus*, 17–20. Cf. Cammarosano, *Le Campagne*, 104.

[62] Brancoli Busdraghi, 'Formazione', esp. 53–95.

[63] It is tempting to wonder whether in some cases, like the 1000 Farfa case mentioned below (or Budriesi Trombetti, 'Prime ricerche', 369, 372–3, 380, 382, 386), *per fegum* or *per faegum* might indicate a type of investiture analogous to *per fustem* or *per baculum*; cf. Du Cange, *Glossarium*, iii. 186–7? But this would not cover all uses.

[64] e.g. *Placiti*, nos. 64, 104.

hand, Charlemagne himself had ordered that benefices *verbo regis* should be recorded, and it would be surprising if churches that already recorded grants of other kinds did not sometimes record both what they had been forced to concede and what they now conceded on their own account using this particular word. Sometimes they did. In 1000 the pope granted land and rights *juri et nomine beneficii* for three lives, subject to a rent and rather unspecific military obligations. The requirement that the property should not be alienated may mean less that the grantee could not transfer his rights in it than that it was to remain the property of the Roman church.[65] In 1026 the bishop of Arezzo gave property to his cathedral architect *beneficiali ordine* for ever, but without power to alienate.[66] A case that exemplifies many of the uncertainties about categories took place in 1000, when the abbot of Farfa brought a plea before Count Teduin, claiming various lands that the count himself was apparently holding. Teduin denied that he claimed most of them by charter or document or in any other way (*neque per cartulam neque per breve neque per ullam inventam rationem*) except *per fegum*, by grant of a previous abbot, though he said that he held a church and attached property *per libellum* from named clergy. 'My lord,' he said to the abbot, 'let me hold the land from you, if you please, in the same way as I held it from your predecessors.' The judgement of those present was that the count should hold the land from the abbot: 'If you please, lord abbot,' they said, 'give him the property as a fief (*ad fegum*)', and the abbot took a rod (*baculum*) in his hand and gave it to him in fief (*et tradidit illi in fegum*).[67] Here the implication is that the alleged earlier grant *per fegum* had been made without written record and perhaps that the new grant was made by the public investiture rather than by a new record, but Farfa did in fact make its own record, in which the story is told, even if it did not give a copy to Teduin. The abbey was still distinguishing grants *per fegum* from those made in writing in the early twelfth century but it would be rash to deduce a general rule from that.[68] In the conditions of the time it was inevitable that practice would vary and that terminology and the conditions of grants would vary too.

Some of the evidence that has been cited, whether by Brancoli Busdraghi or others, to show that benefices (or fiefs) were precarious and carried no enforceable rights, no *jus in re*, over the properties granted relates to the benefices of counts or clergy, which are irrelevant to titles to other benefices.[69] Much of it is also tendentious, since it comes from

[65] 'Doc. Terracinesi', no. 1; Toubert, *Structures*, 1098–1102.
[66] *Doc. Arezzo*, no. 125.     [67] *Placiti*, ii, no. 257.
[68] *Reg. Farfa*, nos. 989, 1322; *Liber Largitorius Pharphensis*, nos. 1277, 1420.
[69] e.g. Brancoli Busdraghi, 'Formazione', 66.

churches and is designed to justify their claims. More cases were probably decided in favour of benefice-holders than surviving records suggest, for there was a real conflict of norms as well as of interests. Whether a church granted its land by *livellus* or as a benefice—in so far as the two were consistently distinguished—it would deny that its tenants had any rights after the expiry of any term that had been fixed in the original grant.[70] Many laymen would probably have disagreed: for them a family that had been settled on property for two or more generations would prima facie have a prescriptive right to it. In these circumstances it seems inappropriate to draw distinctions between the relative rights of *livelli* and benefices and to talk in terms of categories like *jus in re*. Grants by churches made *in beneficio*, *per fegum*, or by some similar phrase do not look consistently different in what they conveyed from those made in traditional forms like *livelli* and *enfiteusi*.[71] Grants made without documentation were harder to argue about, but that did not necessarily mean either that they conveyed different rights and obligations or that laymen considered them less valid. Often the crucial question was probably the status of the parties. Peasants may not always have gained in security from having their duties and dues recorded in *livelli*: local custom and the judgement of their neighbours, if allowed to prevail, may often have served them better than a record made by an ecclesiastical landlord. On the other hand people of noble or at least free status, who could appeal to the judgement of their neighbours in assemblies held before a lay court, might find documentary evidence useful—provided, of course, that the document said the right thing.

Laymen who made grants that they intended to be temporary and partial presumably made them without documentary record more often than churches did, but the evidence of benefices, fiefs, or other restricted forms of property granted by laymen apart from kings is so slight before the twelfth century that almost everything one can say about them is a matter of guesswork.[72] The most likely guess is that lay grants were even more difficult to fit into the categories created by later professional lawyers than were those made by churches. In the first half of the twelfth century the

[70] Some grants failed to mention a term, but permanent alienations, though they occurred, look contrary to the spirit of canon law. *Reg. Sublacense*, no. 139 was perhaps allowable as made to another church, though whether it would then have been seen as conveying *proprietas* (as Leicht, 'Livellario nomine', 103) is unknowable.

[71] Leicht, 'Livellario nomine' and 'Il feudo', 78 n.; Wickham, *Mountains and City*, 97–8; cf. *Cod. Dip. Bobbio*, no. 107; Gerbert, *Briefsammlung*, no. 6; *Placiti*, no. 257; *Doc. Arezzo*, no. 125. The distinctive qualities Toubert ascribes to fiefs (*Structures*, 1161–72; cf. 877) seem to be based largely on evidence from after 1100.

[72] The text of *Reg. Mantovano*, no. 46, purportedly of 1011 and cited by Budriesi Trombetti, 'Prime ricerche', 381, as the first example of the form *feudum* and for its mention of *feudum perpetuum et honorificum*, was written in the thirteenth century and is described by its editor as spurious.

cathedral chapter of Verona was locked in intermittent conflict with the counts of Sambonifacio over the possession of Cerea (Veneto). The estate had been granted in 1038 by three of the church's clergy, *libellario nomine* and at an annual rent, to someone who then transferred it to Marquis Boniface of Tuscany. Boniface's successor, Godfrey of Lotharingia, granted it to one of the Sambonifacio family, but in the great papal–imperial conflict of the late eleventh century the Sambonifacio, with Verona, took the opposite side from Godfrey's daughter, the Countess Matilda. In the 1140s some witnesses thought that Matilda had taken back Cerea at one stage, while others apparently thought that the Sambonifacio had held it throughout. It does not seem necessary to invoke any specifically feudo-vassalic norms to explain these conflicts and uncertainties: Cerea was a place worth controlling. By 1146–7, when professional lawyers were involved, it was disputed whether either family had held in fief, in benefice, *jure conductionis* (or *conditionis*), or even *colonario jure*.[73] It seems highly probable that the eleventh-century grantors and grantees would have found it very difficult to say—except that no marquis or count would have thought he held anything *colonario jure*.

As for the argument that benefices and fiefs were essentially wages for military service, that is true if we look only at those benefices that were created on church or royal land in order to fulfil royal requirements for service and look at them from the point of view of the grantors. It does not mean that that is how property granted in benefice was regarded by its holders or by the local assemblies that shaped customary law. After a benefice had remained with one family for several generations, and after the erosion of royal power had allowed the original obligations to be forgotten, it would seem to its holder, and probably to his lay neighbours, to be much more than his wages. For them it was his inheritance. Counts might go on demanding the old royal services or demand dues instead, but the fluidity of local politics made their demands less regular and less obviously legitimate. The link between property and service must, in these circumstances, have been undermined by time. Besides, many fiefs and benefices that were granted by churches—and these are the ones we know most about—may not have been granted for military service at all. Count Teduin may have owed some kind of service to Farfa for the fief he claimed—and retained—in 1000, but if he did it was not mentioned in the plea. Probably the most the abbey hoped to get from him was some kind of general protection and favour. The chapter of Verona could hope for

---

[73] Ughelli, *Italia Sacra*, v, cols. 754–5, 788–9; Ficker, *Forschungen*, iv, nos. 97, 116; Simeoni, 'Origini', 110–29, and 'Per la genealogia', 311–23. The case and documents are surveyed by Cavallari, 'Il Conte di Verona', 218–25, 234–7, 255–8 and Schioppa, 'Le Rôle'.

something of the same sort from the counts of Sambonifacio and hardly even that from the more remote Canossa family. When Boniface of Tuscany granted Cerea to Hubert of Sambonifacio he presumably hoped for military and political support but there is no evidence that he made any formal or specific requirement of service. Lesser people with fiefs or benefices on church lands generally owed more specific and more demeaning services, but there was no hard and fast line between rents and labour services from people of low status and military service from nobles. Some people owed both and might do so, it seems, whatever the name they or their lords applied to the original grant—if it was remembered.

The crucial problems that fiefs and benefices posed in the ninth, tenth, and eleventh centuries concerned their security and heritability. Kings and emperors adopted various lines on both issues. When Louis II in 865 ordered that none of his *fideles* was to be deprived of his benefice without legal sanction he may have had those who held church land in the forefront of his mind. Perhaps too he was also protecting holders of royal land against counts or even promising protection against himself. A year later, however, he ordered that his vassals who failed to serve duly in his campaign to Benevento were to lose both their own property (*proprium*) and their benefices.[74] In the tenth century control over royal land passed from absentee kings to present and hereditary counts, but churches and clergy could still be vulnerable to royal, as well as comital, pressure. In 968 an assembly under the presidency of a count acting in the name of the emperor condemned Bishop Ratherius of Verona for confiscating benefices: although the benefices concerned had been held by canons of his cathedral they seem to have owed military service to the king. At least part of the reason for Ratherius's condemnation may have been that his transfer of the property to purely ecclesiastical purposes reduced the service he could provide.[75] In 982, when Gerbert became abbot of Bobbio, he was not only appalled at the amount of the abbey's property that had been granted out, whether as *precaria* or benefices or by *livelli*, but had to meet demands from the empress to grant more. The difference between the various types of grants seems to have been relatively unimportant. Would the abbey be able to get back the land it granted? What would it retain if he met all the requests?[76] It was Gerbert who drafted Otto III's ordinance of 998 which ordered that every grant of church land, whether by *libellus* or *enfiteusis*,

[74] *Capit.* nos. 216 c. 4, 218 c. 4.

[75] *Ratherii Vita*, col. 134; Ratherius, *Briefe*, 142–3; Weigle, 'Ratherius', 13, 21–6. Weigle's work is fundamental. Although his tendency to assimilate all benefices to *Lehen* is sometimes misleading, it seems that the canons had been doing military service and that these were in effect benefices *verbo regis*.

[76] Gerbert, *Briefsammlung*, no. 6; Nobili, 'Vassalli'.

was to last only for the life of the bishop or abbot who made it and was not to bind his successor. Gerbert seems here to take it for granted that churches would make their grants in writing, but that did not affect the right to be conveyed. Any grant, whether made in writing or by custom, was to be quashed if it did not promote the welfare of the church.[77] It is unlikely that this ordinance was either widely known or generally obeyed: Gerbert himself, as pope, made a grant for three lives in 1000 that was presumably intended to outlast his pontificate.[78]

## 6.5. *Benefices and fiefs, 1037 to the early twelfth century*

Seen against the background of previous legislation and the shifting uncertainties of customary law in a fragmented kingdom, Conrad II's ordinance of 1037 might be expected to have had as little lasting effect as earlier royal decrees. His purpose in issuing it seems to have been opportunistic. Archbishop Aribert II of Milan had recently supplied him with useful forces in Burgundy, but now the archbishop had become unreliable and Milan was in uproar. Conrad needed to settle the troubles of a strategically important city and, to judge from the content of the ordinance, he also wanted to secure the service that he had hitherto received from the archbishop and those who held benefices from him. The disputes and disorders in Milan seem to have been complex, and a non-specialist's difficulty in understanding them is increased by a long tradition of interpretation in the light of feudal categories and certainties that are hard to find in the sources. The position seems to have been that both tithes and a good deal of the archiepiscopal lands had been held since 983 (if not before) in benefice by *milites* of the city, including both the leading men known as *capitanei* and those of somewhat lower status called *valvassores*. These presumably formed the backbone of the forces that Aribert had sent to Burgundy. The archbishop was a tough politician and a tough defender of the rights of his church. It looks as though he had been trying to recover some of its property, for the confiscation of a vavassor's benefice seems to have been one of the causes of the revolt of 1034 or 1035.[79] In 1037, when Conrad came to Milan and summoned a council to deal with the subsequent troubles, Aribert refused to answer a claim to one of his estates that was brought by a *transmontanus*—who could well have been someone with whom Conrad was particularly likely to sympathize.[80] The wealth of interpretation that

---

[77] *Constitutiones*, i, no. 23.                              [78] 'Doc. Terracinesi', no. 1.

[79] Brancoli Busdraghi, 'Formazione', 95, suggests that the confiscation was made by a *potens*, i.e. a *capitano*, but that is not what Arnulf, *Gesta*, 14, says.

[80] Arnulf, *Gesta*, 14–15; Landulph, *Mediol. Hist.* 58, 64; Wipo, *Opera*, 34–5; cf. Violante, *Società*, 135–65; Bognetti, 'Gli Arcivescovi'.

has been lavished ever since the twelfth century on the decree that Conrad now issued is such that it is necessary to set out its terms in full. It was intended, he said, to reconcile lords and knights (*seniores, milites*) so that they could devote themselves to his service and that of their lords.[81]

1. No knight, whether of bishops, abbots, abbesses, marquises, counts, or anyone else, who held a benefice on royal or church land (that is, presumably, no knight who held a benefice by the grant of a marquis or count on royal land, by the grant of the relevant bishop, abbot, or abbess on church land, or by anyone else on either sort of land) was to lose it unless formally and properly convicted of an offence according to the law (*constitucionem*) of Conrad's predecessors and the judgement of the accused's peers. This applied both to Conrad's own greater *vasvasores* and to their knights, or, alternatively (depending how one reads it), to those who held either from his greater vavassors or their knights.[82]

2. If, in the case of an accusation against a greater vavassor, the accused said that the judgement had been unjust or malicious, or if the peers failed in judgement towards their lord, then the accused should retain his benefice until he and his peers could come with the lord to the emperor, in whose presence the matter would be decided. Whichever side decided to appeal to the emperor should give the other six weeks' notice.

3. Cases concerning lesser men were to be decided before their lords or an imperial official (*missus*).

4. When any knight, greater or less, died, his son or his son's son should have his benefice, subject to the customary gift of arms by greater vavassors to their lords. Failing a son or grandson, a legitimate brother who shared the same father could inherit, provided that he was made a knight and satisfied the lord if he had offended against him.[83]

5. No lord was to make an exchange, *precaria*, or *libellus* of any benefice held by his knights without their consent.

6. No one was to evict anyone unjustly from property (*bona*) held by full rights (*proprietario jure*), *per precepta*, by lawful *libellus*, or by *precaria*.

7. The emperor would take the *fodrum* as his predecessors had done but would no longer demand what they had not taken.

There is much that is difficult to interpret in all this. That is not surprising when one remembers that even professionally drafted modern legislation does not always avoid ambiguities that are revealed only when disputes arise. Conrad was dealing with a particular crisis, his ordinance

[81] *Dip. Konrad II*, no. 244.

[82] . . . ut nullus miles episcoporum abbatum abbatissarum aut marchionum vel comitum vel omnium, qui benefitium de nostris publicis bonis aut de ecclesiarum prediis tenet nunc aut tenuerit vel hactenus iniuste perdidit, tam de nostris maioribus vasvasoribus quam et eorum militibus sine certa et convicta culpa suum beneficium perdat, . . .

[83] This rather obscure condition seems to apply only to a brother. Perhaps it related to a particular case at issue in 1037?

contained no interpretation clauses to explain the words he used, and the next century would see large changes in society, politics, and legal argument. It is therefore vital to try to look at the 1037 ordinance in its contemporary setting rather than through the interpretations lavished on it by professional and academic lawyers in the twelfth century and later who assumed that it was designed to deal with their problems in the way that they needed.[84]

Although my clause 1 includes crown lands, with which church lands had customarily been closely connected, it starts with the clergy. The list of types of grant in clause 5 reinforces the impression that the ordinance was primarily concerned with the tenants of church land. Later lawyers would be surprised that it did not deal with the rights of counts, but if Conrad was primarily concerned with church land—and, indeed, with the tenants of the archbishop of Milan—the issue would not arise. All churches held their land for ever. If he or any counts thought about their rights in their offices and the lands annexed to them, it was not the time to open that can of worms. Conrad's priority was to settle the troubles of Milan and conciliate those who might serve in his armies—and who had presumably been aggrieved by the assertion of royal rights to *fodrum*, which may have been in abeyance for some time before his expeditions to Italy. His ordinance was concerned with the rights of people called vavassors. At Milan the word seems generally to have been used to denote a status, namely that just below the *capitanei*, but here vavassors seem to include those whom the Milanese called *capitanei*.[85] Some vavassors held land granted to them by *capitanei* but their lower status may not always have corresponded to a lower position in a hierarchy of property. Some 'lesser vavassors' may have been among those referred to in clause 1 as knights of 'greater vavassors', but some may have held their benefices directly from counts or churches. The impression that the words *capitaneus* and vavassor denoted positions in a feudal hierarchy was derived from the writings of later academic lawyers after the words had ceased to be used in Italian cities for status groups.[86] In the ordinance, however, any ambiguities about status or position in the hierarchy of property were irrelevant, since its object was, it seems, to guarantee security to everyone who held church land and to everyone below the counts who held crown land. It was evidently taken for granted that they all owed military service and were of the status that Conrad and other influential people thought deserved protection.

Among those with whom the ordinance was concerned, the difference

---

[84] Cf. Mitteis, *Lehnrecht*, 399, for a different approach.
[85] Keller, 'Soziale und politische Verfassung'.          [86] Below, 6.8.

between greater and lesser that is made in my clauses 2 and 3 looks as likely, or more likely, to be one of status or size of holding, as of position in a 'hierarchy of tenure'. Richer and more influential people could appeal to the emperor but people of lower status with smaller holdings needed to have their affairs settled locally. On a strict construction the protection of a tenant pending appeal applies only to the greater, but that would have been rather a pointless and improbable restriction, given the general tenor of the ordinance: the lesser vavassors were probably meant to remain in possession pending their local appeals. Both groups had the right to be judged in the first instance by their peers. This was not in principle a new right. All judgements were supposed to be made collectively and the neighbours or equals of any accused ought to have expected, and been expected, to take part. Some of the earliest charters of liberties that granted rights or confirmed customs to local communities contain promises that members of the communities, who look lower in status than the people that Conrad was concerned with or those that historians think of as fiefholders, would be tried for crimes or evicted from their property only by custom and a local trial. Some charters made it clear that this meant being judged only by members of that community.[87] What Conrad did was what the grantors of such charters did: he confirmed the right to be tried by one's equals. In this context one's equals may have seemed to be those who held benefices on similar terms from the same lord, so that Conrad's decree in effect gave exclusive competence to particular members of what might otherwise have been a more general local assembly. His promise about the *fodrum* is also reminiscent of other charters of liberties. As for inheritance, it is sometimes said that the Milanese *capitanei* already had full hereditary rights in their benefices and that Conrad extended the right to those whom the Milanese called vavassors. Clauses 1 and 4 seem, however, to be conferring equal rights on all. It may well be that the kind of people who would be called *capitanei* had been better able to defend their rights against the archbishop (or any other church from whom they held) than were those with lower status and smaller benefices. That does not mean that Aribert and all other bishops or abbots would have willingly conceded their claims. The inheritance of benefices on church lands had long been a disputed issue: Conrad was simply coming down on the opposite side from Otto III.

The intention of clause 5 has been debated.[88] It is probably directed less against a lord who alienated over his tenant's head, thus presenting the tenant with a new lord, than against one who forced a tenant to exchange his

[87] Reynolds, *Kingdoms and Communities*, 23–34; Daviso, 'Carta di Tenda', 142; *Cod. Dip. Cajetanus*, no. 213; *Dip. Hein. IV*, no. 336. See index: peers.
[88] Brancoli Busdraghi, 'Formazione', 97–100.

benefice or constructively deprived him of it by granting the use of the land to someone else. The archbishop of Milan would have been more likely to do this than to alienate the property of his see outright. Taken together, clauses 5 and 6 reinforce the suspicion that the distinction between benefices or fiefs on the one hand and *libelli* or other subordinate grants on the other was unclear. Clause 6 even assimilates these forms of property to what was held *proprietatis jure* in so far as all were protected against arbitrary confiscation: though it does not explicitly mention holdings in benefice, the whole ordinance implies that they must be included here too. No one involved in the legislation would have thought that clause 6 meant giving equal protection to horny-handed and unmilitary peasants who might hold under *libelli*: clauses 4 and 5 are both about knights—those who were supposed to fulfil the archbishop's military obligations to the emperor and had been causing trouble in Milan. Nor would the clergy have admitted that a custom like the gift of arms in clause 4 implied that every greater vavassor (whether a *capitaneus* or not) had an unequivocal right to permanent inheritance. Inheritance might, for instance, be allowed for only a few generations, as it was when churches made grants for several lives. The gift of arms may have survived from barbarian custom, but churches that supplied their knights with arms may have done so for more practical and less archaic reasons. Since succession dues above the peasant level seem to be seldom referred to in Italy, the custom mentioned here may have been purely local—or, perhaps, was introduced by royal servants familiar with succession dues taken from *ministeriales* in Germany.[89] Oddly enough, despite its presence in an ordinance which was later taken to be the foundation of the law of fiefs, it did not apparently survive to be discussed in the *Libri Feudorum*.[90]

Though Conrad's decree did not achieve his own immediate purpose it was not a dead letter. In 1046 the bishop of Cremona said that he gave a benefice with hereditary rights as the glorious emperor lord Conrad had ordained at the siege of Milan for all kinds of vavassors both great and small who served their lords. The record incidentally added that that was the ancient custom of the bishop's predecessors anyway.[91] Oaths to be taken in Italy to Henry IV in 1077 distinguished the justice that was to be done about benefices according to the right judgement of peers (*rectum*

---

[89] Chapter 9, at n. 153.

[90] Though see e.g. Muratori, *Antiquitates*, i, col. 633–4; Manaresi, *Atti di Milano*, no. 76; *Statuti della provincia romana*, 18, c. 6. Succession of a daughter might require a payment (Lehmann, *Consuetudines: Antiqua*, 21 (VI. 14)) and that of a more distant heir might mean that the lord took a year's income: Bonaini, *Statuti inediti*, ii. 967; *Statuti di Bologna*, ii. 58.

[91] *Placiti*, no. 366: the grammar is uncertain, as so often in Italian pleas of this date, but this seems to be the sense.

*judicium parium*) from matters that pertained to law, which were to be decided by the right judgement of judges.[92] This need not mean that those who were judged by judges always had a rougher deal but it does suggest that a distinctive procedure for cases involving benefices had become accepted as normal. On the other hand it is hard to be sure that the distinction was regularly observed all over the kingdom or that benefice-holders regularly secured the rights Conrad had granted them. Cases in which churches claimed property from laymen seem sometimes to have gone in favour of the churches because laymen failed to appear: some of these cases may have concerned the kind of grants that, whatever they had been called, might have been thought to come within the 1037 ruling. If any of the cases in which the property of churches was put under protection pending litigation came within it then that looks like an infringement of clause 2.[93] If any of these cases did indeed concern benefices then it looks as though such cases were not always heard in the lord's court. Many nevertheless must have been, if only because the counts and bishops from whom many benefices were held would be likely to have courts which would be the obvious places to start proceedings. Counts' or bishops' courts would not be 'feudal courts' in the sense of being attended only by tenants of benefices or fiefs.[94] What should have happened after 1037 was presumably that only the other benefice-holders among those present would judge cases that might involve eviction from benefices. The oaths of 1077 suggest that this was remembered and accepted in principle. Whether it always happened is another matter. It must also be doubtful that the arrangements for appeals laid down in 1037 were regularly followed. By the twelfth century both lords and tenants seem to have gone to city courts at Milan and Pisa, perhaps sometimes in the first instance, and the same may have happened elsewhere.[95]

When property remained with the holders of benefices or fiefs for generations it was not necessarily because of the new law: at Cremona the bishop thought that his predecessors had long granted hereditary benefices. The reason that Cerea remained with the Canossa and Sambonifacio families was more their respective powers than any mere law. In changed circumstances the chapter of Verona finally got the property back in 1146.[96] Both sides in a dispute may sometimes have accepted a compromise that ignored the terms of the ordinance, however it was

[92] *Constitutiones*, i, no. 68.    [93] *Placiti*, iii, e.g. nos. 344, 350, 351; 370 and 392.
[94] Above, at nn. 40–1.
[95] Manaresi, *Atti di Milano*, nos. 1, 18; Bonaini, *Statuti*, ii. 961, 962, 964.
[96] Ughelli, *Italia Sacra*, v, cols. 754–5, 781–3, 788–91; Ficker, *Forschungen*, iv, nos. 97, 116; *Dip. Lothar III*, Plac. Richenza no. 4; Simeoni, 'Origini' and 'Per la genealogia'.

interpreted.[97] If some churches were taking greater pains to specify conditions and keep records, that was not because of Conrad's law, which bypasses the issue of written records: churches everywhere were keeping better records. Some churches, moreover, went on making grants for three lives, which one would think made nonsense of the 1037 rulings.

In Italy, as in other countries, the most important qualification for secure property rights was social status. The countess Matilda ordered that property she gave to S. Andrea, Mantua, was not to be alienated by *enfiteusis*, *livellus*, benefice, or otherwise. It was to be granted only by *livellus* to persons of inferior condition for rent.[98] Peasants could be allowed effectively hereditary rights because, with a bit of pressure and care, their obligations could be increased or, if that failed, they could be evicted more easily than those who could appeal to public opinion beyond their lord's court. Peasant tenants were profitable—indeed were essential to the working of estates—in a way that tenants of higher status were liable not to be. Conrad's law affected the way that distinctions of status were drawn in several ways. First, in conferring rights on some people, or confirming their rights, it invited attention, sooner than it might otherwise have been given, to the need to draw a line through a grey area between those considered suitable to be protected and those not.[99] Some—perhaps many—properties that were called fiefs or benefices had such an unambiguously unmilitary and menial character that their tenants could not have hoped to bring them within the scope of the 1037 ordinance, if they had heard of it. Some that look as if they should have come within its scope may have been excluded, and not only because their lords were too powerful. It was also because of a peculiarity of Italy within the west European scene. By the end of the eleventh century a new kind of law and a new kind of lawyer were beginning to appear there. The new lawyers studied documents and drew distinctions from them. One of the documents they studied was the ordinance of 1037. It was probably the text of that ordinance which led them to lay an emphasis on the military character of benefices in general that made little sense either in their own time or, if they had known it, in Conrad's. I shall return to the new law and the new distinctions later. The important point here is that, although in the tenth and eleventh centuries fighting was regarded as an occupation for nobles, and although nobles were also those whose fiefs or benefices were most likely to be protected, it is not at all clear that by 1037 most of them admitted that they owed

[97] *Reg. Farfa*, no. 1302.
[98] *Reg. Mantovano*, no. 92; cf. Tiraboschi, *Nonantola*, ii, no. 185.
[99] See chapter 9 at nn. 182, 208–15 for the different way in which such attention may have been attracted to the same need in Germany.

military service to the king or emperor for every (or any) benefice that they held from churches, let alone that they actually performed it. Archbishop Aribert's services to Conrad II were exceptional. Few of those who held benefices from other churches and who secured permanent hereditary rights in them may have served in imperial or royal armies.

As custom developed, those who secured protection sometimes got more than the ordinance of 1037 had granted. It had excluded daughters from any rights but, though local custom and opinion seem to have varied, they were often given some rights, even in Milan, where, if anywhere, the terms of the ordinance ought to have been remembered. This looks like the result of pressure to apply to benefices what was accepted as normal custom in the inheritance of full property.[100] It suggests that while the details and original purpose of the decree might be forgotten its general thrust was effective in so far as it strengthened rights that already had some validity under customary law. As time passed new cases raised new problems. Conrad and his advisers might have agreed with some of the rulings and new distinctions that resulted if they had thought about them but might have disagreed with others.

One subject that Conrad's ordinance did not mention must have caused a mounting number of disputes in the following century. That was the right to alienate a benefice or fief, whether it had been granted by a church or lay lord. Twelfth-century treatises on the rights of fiefs or benefices show that rules about this varied: in parts of Lombardy, including Milan, fiefholders were allowed to alienate freely.[101] In the eleventh century and earlier custom had probably varied not only from place to place but from case to case, with fewer detailed conditions than the treatises invoked.[102] Greater certainty came in 1136. Lothar III then legislated with much the same purpose as Conrad had done a century before, that is, to secure military service, but this time imperial needs worked against those who held benefices or fiefs. To judge from the preamble of the new ordinance, Lothar was confronted in Italy by lords—presumably for the most part counts and churches—who blamed their production of what seemed to him inadequate forces on alienations by their benefice-holders. He therefore forbade any sale of a benefice or part of one that would reduce its use-

---

[100] Budriesi Trombetti, 'Prime ricerche', 372–3; *Cod. Dip. Cremonae*, i, p. 100, no. 36; for the opinions in the early treatises: Lehmann, *Consuetudines Feudorum*, 8, 13, 16–17, 21, 35 (I. 1, IV. 1, VI. 4, 14, IX. 4); Anschütz, *Lombarda-Commentare*, 85. For opinions on full property: *Liber Papiensis*, 319–22.

[101] Below, at n. 178.

[102] e.g. *Reg. Farfa*, no. 829; Budriesi Trombetti, 'Prime ricerche', 372–3 (Milan); Conti, *Formazione*, 191; Ficker, *Forschungen*, iv, no. 102. Alienations had obviously taken place without the lord being able to prevent them, e.g. when Boniface of Tuscany acquired Cerea.

fulness to the empire or its lord.[103] The ordinance, like Conrad's, used the word benefice, and by implication referred only to those owing royal service, but, like his, it was interpreted as applying more generally.[104]

## 6.6. *Full property from 774 to the twelfth century*

The standard for property held by free people was not set in the ninth, tenth, and eleventh centuries by benefices and fiefs. The normal way that people above the humbler kind of peasant expected to hold their property was in the traditional form of *proprietas* or *proprium*. The Frankish word alod was used occasionally in contemporary sources, though less often than in the writings of historians who use it automatically as the appropriate counterpart to benefice or fief.[105] King Berengar I's printed charters include seventeen grants of property to laymen for ever, using some such phrase as *jure proprietatis* and specifying freedom of alienation.[106] At least one grantee received property that had formerly been held by his father, perhaps in benefice from the local count, while two received lands forfeited by those who had been *in nostra infidelitate*, rather than having formed parts of the royal estates proper that had formerly been attached to counties. The traitors had presumably held their lands with full rights, though that had not protected them from confiscation.[107] Grants with similar rights were made by Berengar's rivals, with one of Rudolf of Burgundy's charters commenting that law and justice gave each man such rights (i.e. presumably of free disposition) over his own property (*de suis propriis*).[108] King Lambert forbade counts to give *arimanni* in benefice to their own men. The point was not to prevent 'subinfeudation': *arimanni* seem to have been meant to have full rights in their land, but, just for that reason, they were supposed to be directly under comital authority. Some of them may well have appealed to the king to keep them there.[109]

By the eleventh century there must have been little that emperors could give away, except when they gave counts full title to what they already held ex officio, but such grants as are recorded seem to have been made in much

[103] *Dip. Lothar III*, no. 105.

[104] Manaresi, *Atti di Milano*, no. 18; Lehmann, *Langobardische Lehnrecht*, 125.

[105] *Capit.* nos. 203 c. 8, 218 c. 4 (where *honores* are clearly full property, as they are in no. 74 c. 1, though in no. 225 they are units of comital jurisdiction).

[106] *Dip. Berengario I*, nos. 6, 8, 9, 14, 15, 19, 25, 32, 54, 56, 91, 93, 104, 107, 114, 127, 140.

[107] Ibid. nos. 91, 127, 140.

[108] *Dip. Lodovico III*, nos. 12, 14, 16, 18; *Dip. Rodolfo II*, no. 10.

[109] Above, at n. 48. The full property rights of the *arimanni* are suggested by *Capit.* no. 225 c. 4 (contrasting their houses with *domos rei publicae*; cf. no. 216 c. 5), 5, and possibly 6. For the suggestion of 'subinfeudation': Tabacco, 'I Liberi' (1964), 62–5.

the same terms.[110] Henry IV apparently gave some Italian land *in benefi-cium*, but he also made formal grants that seem to embody full rights. Two of his charters expressed the rights of disposition in terms which may have been intended to be more restrictive, but they still seem to convey some-thing more like traditional full property than what historians would call a fief.[111] The property of counts, of course, formed a special case, in so far as part of it was officially held as a royal benefice, ex officio.[112] It would, however, represent the reality of the counts' situation better to say that their benefices became absorbed in their alods or *propria* than to refer to the whole complex of their property as fiefs.[113] The grants in fief that twelfth-century emperors made to counts reflected a quite different legal and constitutional situation from that implied by the old view of counts' benefices.

Property enjoying what were thought of as full rights was supposed to be conveyed, as it had been before the Carolingian conquest, by a public ceremony and a formal document. The investiture of benefices or fiefs by a gesture or transfer of a rod or other symbolic object was probably derived from the ceremony used for conveying full rights. In 898 King Lambert legislated to prevent fraudulent conveyances made in order to avoid service partly, it seems, in order to protect the right of *arimanni* to have their con-veyances recorded.[114] However much lesser freeholders may have been bullied, their rights of alienation did not come to be restricted as they often were in France.[115] Italian churches do not seem to have adopted the cus-tom of getting consent from counts or other local lords to gifts that were made to them by the owners of full property. The clauses granting consent from someone under whose lordship the donated land lay seem to find no place in Italian charters of the tenth and eleventh centuries, except in the south, where they obviously result from the introduction of Norman cus-tom.[116] Since the custom of giving consent seems in France to have led to a need to get it, the absence of the custom from Italy helps to explain the continuing freedom of alienation that Italian freeholders enjoyed. The real obstacle to alienation for them must have come from their kin, not from the local count or other lord. The lordship of villages or parts of villages or fortifications was sometimes shared between groups of lesser nobles in such a way as to make it difficult for any of them to dispose of his or her

[110] *Dip. Otto III*, nos. 50, 70, 154, 213, 223, 293, 299, 312, 379–81, 382, 408, 410, 421; *Dip. Konrad II*, nos. 67, 77.
[111] *Reg. Farfa*, no. 1302; *Dip. Hein. IV*, nos. 135, 183, 288–9.
[112] For the continuing formal recognition of the distinction, above, n. 50.
[113] Tabacco, 'Allodialità'. German historians of Italy generally refer to counts' lands as *Lehen*.
[114] *Capit.* no. 225; cf. no. 224.     [115] See chapter 5.4–5 (or index: alienation).
[116] See below in this chapter (6.10).

rights. In these circumstances one might have expected the distinction between what was inherited and what was acquired to be significant, but those who conveyed property in this period do not seem to have appealed to it as they did in France. By 1231 slightly different rules for the inheritance of acquired property from what had already been inherited were associated in the kingdom of Sicily with Frankish custom:[117] rash as it may be to assume that this represented an ancient difference of custom, or to generalize from it to the rest of Italy, it suggests that Lombard law had not developed the distinctive rules for acquisitions that are sometimes thought, on the basis of French law, to have been a general medieval phenomenon.

As King Berengar's grants of confiscated property imply, all property continued of course to be subject to forfeiture for crime. As under the Lombard kings, forfeited property went to the criminal's heirs in some circumstances and to the king in others.[118] The practice, not least in deciding whether there were other heirs, no doubt varied according to political circumstances. The king—or anyone else in charge—might also claim property, even when there was no crime, on failure of heirs. As under the Lombards, this need not imply that heirless property had been held with less than the normal full rights.[119] There is no great point in wondering about Henry V's claim to succeed to the countess Matilda's lands by inheritance any more than there would be in wondering whether his seizure of what German historians call her *Reichslehen* might have been justified as a 'feudal escheat'. Whatever the legal position—which is deeply obscure, given the agreement they seem to have made in 1111 as well as her previous grant to the papacy—this was clearly an act of political expediency that could be justified in almost any system of property law with almost equal implausibility.[120]

Full property continued under the Carolingians to carry the normal obligations of military service and attendance at public courts. How long these survived after the atrophy of royal power is uncertain but it seems likely that, as in France, counts probably maintained their rights over lesser landowners better than they did over the greater—many of whom, in any case, came to claim comital rights themselves. As in France, one consequence of the fragmentation of local authority was probably to make the lesser freeholders or *arimanni* more vulnerable to extortion of new or higher dues than they had been when they had more chance of appealing to royal authority. All the same, the obligation of landowners to pay dues,

---

[117] *Konst. Fried. II*, 282 (III. 27).                         [118] *Constitutiones*, i, no. 32.

[119] Muratori, *Antiquitates*, v, col. 615–16; Budriesi Trombetti, 'Prime ricerche', 384.

[120] Overmann, *Gräfin Mathilde*, 43–4. For the suggestion that the 1111 agreement made Henry her heir, see Simeoni's comments in Donizo, *Vita*, 97–8 n.

whether in respect of old military obligations or not, does not in itself mean that they held their land with what were then thought of as less than the full rights appropriate to their station.

## 6.7. *The eleventh-century papacy: fiefs and oaths of fidelity*

It has often been said that eleventh-century popes, under the influence of the feudal norms of the secular world, made grants of fiefs and took oaths of fidelity from secular rulers. This is partly true but only partly: a good deal of the argument relies on the interpolation of the later concept of the fief, with its supposedly ancient and customary rules, into sources that do not mention fiefs at all. Often this is done by assuming that the taking of an oath of fidelity implies the grant of a fief or something that approximates to what historians think of as a fief. My argument so far, however, suggests that if an eleventh-century bishop or abbot—and therefore also, surely, a pope—granted a fief he was not imitating lay practices but following ecclesiastical traditions of managing church property. As for oaths of fidelity, the assumption—for it seems to be more of an assumption than an argument—that they imply fiefs ignores much earlier evidence. Kings in Italy had long made a wide range of their subjects swear to be faithful. In the tenth century Bishop Atto of Vercelli referred to oaths to the king taken by the bishop's own knights. In 1077 the oaths to Henry IV, while they do not specifically mention fidelity, imply a general obligation that must have involved something of the sort.[121] It is, in any case, bizarre to suggest that the concept of faith or fidelity was one that the church needed to borrow from lay society at any level. The idea of getting laymen or clergy to swear to respect the rights of St Peter and be obedient to his vicar could perfectly well have occurred to the eleventh-century popes on their own. When it came to secular relations, popes had always had to rely on respect and fidelity rather than armies, and as a result they may well have used oaths more often than we know.[122]

The Normans of south Italy are often seen as the first and most obvious example of a new papal policy of creating fiefs. Robert Guiscard is said to have been made a papal vassal and been granted his lands as a papal fief in 1059.[123] The oath he took then, however, does not refer to either a fief or

[121] Atto, *Epistolae*, col. 103; *Constitutiones*, i, no. 68.

[122] Some of the early oaths of fidelity from southern France noted by Magnou-Nortier, 'Fidélité et féodalité', were made to bishops; cf. *Liber Instrumentorum*, nos. 41–2, 46–7. The distinction she draws in *Foi et fidélité*, 12, between faith and fidelity seems to me overstrained for this period: above, chapter 2.2.

[123] e.g. Jordan, 'Eindringen'; Hoffmann, 'Langobarden, Normannen, Päpste'. Zerbi, 'Il termine "fidelitas"', and Tirelli, 'Osservazioni', take more nuanced lines but still assume the existence of feudo-vassalic rules at this period.

a vassal.[124] On the other hand, Geoffrey Malaterra, writing at the very end of the century, did use the word fief in connection with the treaty made between Robert's brother Humphrey and Pope Leo IX in 1053. According to Geoffrey, Leo gave Humphrey all he had conquered, and might conquer further south (and thus away from papal territory), as a hereditary fief (*terram . . . haereditali feudo sibi et haeredibus suis possidendam*).[125] It is hard to be sure what meaning Geoffrey attached to the phrase he used, but he was probably thinking of the kind of terms on which grants of church property were normally made to nobles—though, writing when he did, he must have had to keep in a separate part of his mind the disputes that they so often caused. Unsubstantiated as the story is, it is testimony to the carefree attitude of historians to the evidence of fiefholding that, as the one eleventh-century reference to Norman lands as papal fiefs, it should not have received more attention. In 1080, when Robert Guiscard took another oath to the papacy, Gregory VII was said to have invested him with the land that Nicholas II and Alexander II (but not Leo IX) had granted him. 'Investiture' need not have implied a fief, and Robert, for what it is worth, referred to the lands granted to him as *proprio sub dominio meo*.[126] There was, after all, no reason why he should have accepted as a papal fief what he had conquered for himself. As Amatus of Montecassino made him tell the emperor, he had won his land by the help of God, St Peter, and St Paul, and was willing to submit to the pope as their vicar. If the emperor wanted to give him something, he would acknowledge that, but that was it.[127] Papal recognition was valuable for legitimacy and it could be advantageous to Robert to submit to some kind of papal lordship, especially against the emperor, just as it could seem useful to the prince of Capua to submit to papal lordship against Robert himself, but that need not involve accepting that one's conquests were really church property and held from the church. The negotiations of 1059 and the investitures or grants of 1080, 1128, and 1130 do not seem to have implied any more subjection than was implied in maintaining faith, keeping the peace, respecting church property, and paying traditional papal dues.[128]

However familiar Robert Guiscard, for instance, was with oaths exchanged between laymen, the oath he swore to Pope Nicholas II in 1059 need not have been modelled on any pre-existing and standard feudo-vassalic oath, even if we suppose that such a thing existed. It seems to suit the particular circumstances of their relations too well for that. The same

---

[124] *Rec. ducs normands d'Italie*, no. 6.      [125] Gaufredus Malaterra, *De Rebus*, 15.
[126] Gregory VII, *Register*, 514–17.      [127] Amato di Montecassino, *Storia*, 321.
[128] None of the sources for what Caspar (*Roger II*, 501) called the *Belehnung* of 1128 seems to imply the grant of a fief. For the document of 1130: Hoffmann, 'Langobarden', 173–6.

goes for the oaths of the princes of Benevento and Capua in 1073. When Robert took his second oath in 1080 papal record-keeping enabled some of the terms of the 1059 oath to be used again. One sentence from his oaths also appeared in the oaths taken by the archbishop of Aquileia in 1079 and the emperor in 1111.[129] Other parts of their oaths differed according to circumstances. The archbishop undertook, along with more recognizably ecclesiastical obligations, to provide military assistance to the church of Rome. That, together with a reference to counsel, seems to be the reason why his oath has been described as rich in feudal terminology, but to infer anything like fiefholding from an obligation to military service is quite unjustified. It was a time when the pope might well need the archbishop's help, but not one in which there was any close correlation between military service and fiefholding.[130] The reference to counsel fits the stereotype of the supposedly feudal obligation to counsel and aid still less: even if an obligation to give counsel had been owed only by fiefholders or vassals (however understood), the *consilium* mentioned in all these oaths is not that which was to be given by the oath-taker to his lord.[131] The same doubts apply to the feudo-vassalic character of the oath that had been imposed on the king of Croatia and Dalmatia in 1076 when a papal legate invested him with his kingdom—and, according to the traditional interpretation, thus made it a papal fief. On that occasion the religious aspect of the relationship was emphasized by the king's promise to see that church dues were paid and that the clergy lived chastely and well, to protect widows and orphans, to abolish the slave trade, and so on.[132]

In 1077 Gregory claimed that Corsica belonged *ex debito vel juris proprietate* to the Roman church, and that those who had hitherto held it with violence had failed in service, fidelity, subjection, and obedience to St Peter. This could be interpreted to mean that he thought that the island was a papal fief, but again it does not need to be.[133] Whatever idea of the law of property Gregory had or thought relevant, service, fidelity, subjection, and obedience were not exclusively secular obligations or owed only by those who held lordships or properties that were called fiefs. It is very hard to know what was meant by the grants of their honours to the Roman church by the counts of Provence and Mauguio in 1081 and 1085 respectively, but once again neither the word fief nor the word benefice was used in the records we have and the successors of both grantors appear to have

[129] Gregory VII, *Register*, 30–1, 35–6, 428–9; *Constitutiones*, i, no. 87.
[130] Zerbi, 'Il termine "fidelitas"', 133; for military service owed to the pope by *oppidani* as well as *milites* within the territory he ruled, see e.g. Deusdedit, cited by Jordan, 'Eindringen', 47.
[131] See index: aid and counsel.
[132] *Liber Censuum*, no. 72.      [133] Gregory VII, *Register*, 574–6.

held their counties with undiminished rights.[134] Another mysterious transaction was that by which the Countess Matilda of Tuscany maintained in
1102 that she had given all her property to the Roman church by the hand
of Gregory VII. According to what she said in 1102, she had originally
wanted a charter to be made but, if it had been, it was no longer in existence or at hand.[135] Since, so far as we know, Matilda continued to have full
control of her lordships throughout her life they may have been granted
back to her for her lifetime, by benefice or *precaria*, in the way that property given to churches so often was. Perhaps no formal regrant was made,
but it might be less anachronistic to envisage something of that sort than
to see her gift as creating what later Italian lawyers and historians would
call a *feudo oblato* (the equivalent of the French *fief de reprise*). Meanwhile,
of course, popes could deal with lords in the territories they tried to control around Rome in the normal ways that ecclesiastical lords did, such as
getting them to surrender property to the church of Rome in return for a
grant of its use for three lives.[136] Altogether, there seems to be less evidence that popes granted land as fiefs—whatever was meant by the word—
than that other prelates did. Any grants they did make should surely be set
in the context of what evidence we have of other fiefs at the time, not of
later feudal theory.

References to homage are equally unlikely to have implied anything distinctively feudo-vassalic. In 1130 Roger II of Sicily agreed that he and his
successors would do homage and fidelity to the pope and his successors and
in 1139 this became liege homage and fidelity.[137] So far as words are concerned, however, the first reference to *homagium* that seems to have been
noticed in Italy occurs in a late ninth-century document about services
owed to a church under a *livellus*. So far as the phenomena of rituals of submission are concerned, Italian peasants sometimes swore fidelity *per
manus*.[138] It is therefore difficult to make homage look in origin either
exclusively feudo-vassalic or particularly secular. In 1079–90 a complaint
seems to have been sent to Gregory VII about affairs in the bishopric of
Penna (Abruzzi).[139] Ganshof drew attention to this as an early reference to
homage, which he thought of as a significant sign of feudo-vassalic relations, because the document states that the bishop of Penna had received

---

[134] Ibid. 589–91; *Gallia Christ.* vi, instr. col. 349–50. For the Mauguio gift see chapter 5 at
nn. 69–72.

[135] *Constitutiones*, i, no. 444; Overmann, *Gräfin Mathilde*, 143–4, 241–2.

[136] *Liber Censuum*, no. 97. Cf. Jordan, 'Eindringen'.

[137] Hoffmann, 'Langobarden', 173–8. Hoffmann's discussion of the obscure clauses *si . . .
remanserit* is extremely interesting, but its relevance to my argument depends on the assumption
that rules about *Herrenfall* and *Mannfall* were already standardized and accepted.

[138] Fasoli, 'Castelli e signorie rurali', 57 n.; Brancoli Busdraghi, 'Formazione', 272.

[139] *Libellus querulus*, 1462–7.

those who had wrongly held the lands of his see into the fidelity of holy church *per hominium et sacramentum*.[140] The document also, however, records how an earlier pope had replaced the then bishop, who had committed homicide, by another and had summoned the sinner: 'Come into our presence and do homage to this our brother [presumably the new bishop] in the presence of all.'[141] The deposed bishop was, it seems, to continue to hold the lands of his former see until he could recover what had been lost through his misdeeds or negligence. It is therefore legitimate to interpret his homage, as Ganshof did, as analogous to that done by the tenant of subordinate property, but it could also be seen as the sign of a more general submission or subjection. Homage, like fidelity, fitted as well into ecclesiastical as secular ideas of subordination.

The oaths of fidelity that popes received in the eleventh and early twelfth centuries may well have helped to form custom for academic feudal lawyers to adapt and follow, but there seems to be no evidence that they followed what was then established feudal custom. This is important when one considers what is traditionally known as the Investiture Contest. In 1095 the Council of Clermont ordered that no ecclesiastic was to accept office or ecclesiastical property (*ecclesiae honorem*) from lay hands and that no bishop or priest should do liege fidelity with his hands to a king or other layman (*regi vel alicuius laico in manibus ligiam fidelitatem faciat*).[142] The point was surely not to prohibit any particular ceremony because it was distinctively lay, let alone 'feudal'.[143] It was that churches should not be in the gift or control of the laity and that the allegiance—in the broadest twentieth-century sense of the word—of the clergy was not to be owed to the powers of this world. The fact that liege fidelity *in manibus* seems, by the standards of traditional ideas of feudo-vassalic rules, to confuse fidelity and homage, compounding the confusion by making the fidelity 'liege', should warn us that these distinctions did not exist until they were hammered out in argument. When the word *hominium* was introduced into the argument about clerical investiture in England in 1107 it probably did not mean anything different from the *ligia fidelitas* of 1095. The Investiture Contest afforded an early occasion for drawing of distinctions. It was only centuries later that the varying distinctions that were made in different arguments would be squashed together to create what was intended to be a coherent set of categories.

[140] Ganshof, 'Note sur l'apparition', 31.
[141] *Veni ante nostram praesentiam et coram omni multitudine huic nostro confratro hominium fac.*
[142] Mansi, *Collectio*, xx, col. 817 (c. 15, 17).
[143] See Ivo of Chartres's comment about the irrelevance of forms *sive fiat manu, sive fiat nutu, sive lingua, sive virga*: *Libelli de Lite*, 645, and also ibid. 501, and the material collected by Classen, 'Wormser Konkordat'.

## 6.8. *The beginning of academic law*

The essential requirement for any subject of academic study in the middle ages was a text—preferably one of high authority and complexity—to be lectured on, expounded, and discussed. By the late eleventh century those who studied Roman law had the full text of Justinian's *Corpus*, including the Digest, while for those who started from Lombard law the laws issued by Lombard, Carolingian, and German kings of Italy had been collected together and rearranged under topics in a way that was bound to stimulate dicussion.[144] As a result glosses, commentaries, and new treatises began to accumulate around both bodies of law. So far as surviving sources tell, it was the Lombardists who first became interested in current problems of property law. It may, however, be misleading to distinguish the two schools too sharply: Lombard lawyers knew some Roman law, while, even if the Romanists did not produce any early treatises on the problems of benefices and fiefs, they must have thought about them. Irnerius would have met them in the courts he attended as a judge, and he made a few allusions to *feuda* or the rights of *feudatarii* in his glosses on Roman law or in remarks reported by others.[145] However that may be, the earliest works on the subject that survive seem to have come from the Lombard lawyers of Pavia. That was the conclusion of Carl Lehmann, whose work on the early manuscripts of what became known as the *Libri Feudorum*, completed almost a century ago, has not been superseded. In fact it has been very little used. Until recently no one since his time seems to have done much more than dip into the *Libri* for particular points. Now that interest in it has revived among a few scholars they seem, so far as I know, not to have concentrated on the earliest texts that it contains. Since Lehmann's work relied on that of Laspeyres sixty years before that, it is no criticism of either of them, or of those who are now working on the later stages of the compilation, to suggest that further work on the earliest stages might now be rewarding.[146]

Lehmann showed that the compilation that he called the Antiqua was made, probably in Milan, but possibly in Pavia or Bologna, around the middle of the twelfth century. The letters of the Milanese judge Obertus

[144] Weimar, 'Legistische Literatur', 132–4, 165–6.

[145] Spagnesi, *Wernerius*, 124–32 and nos. 2, 3, 5; Pescatore, 'Stellungnahme'; Meijers, *Études*, iii. 261–77; Brancoli Busdraghi, 'Formazione', 433–4: I have not been able to see the work by Rota referred to there.

[146] Lehmann, *Consuetudines* and *Langobardische Lehnrecht*; Laspeyres, *Ueber die Entstehung*. Weimar, 'Legistische Literatur', 165–6 makes some emendations; see also Classen, *Studium*, 36–7, 48–68; Giordanengo, *Droit féodal*, 123–5. For work on the later stages: Weimar, 'Handschriften'; Montorzi, *Diritto feudale*.

de Orto formed the latest part of it, though Lehmann did not think that Obertus actually made the compilation himself.[147] The earlier parts of the Antiqua, before Obertus, had, Lehmann thought, originated as five separate very short treatises written between the last years of the eleventh century and 1136—hence the apparently rambling repetitiousness that may be the first impression a reader receives from the *Libri*. Very tentatively, since I have not worked on the manuscripts, I suggest that there may have been six of these mini-treatises (or extracts from treatises), rather than five, and that the earliest may not have been written until rather later than Lehmann thought, just possibly not before 1125.[148] I also suggest, however, that my amendments, even if they are right, are not very significant. However one divides and dates the Antiqua, what we have are five or six little tracts, or bits of tracts, all written within a few decades of 1100. Ariprandus's *Summula* and commentary on the *Lombarda*, which deal with some of the same problems, may not be much later.[149] That means that we have either six or seven tracts, all written within a couple of generations at most. Others may well have been written that did not survive, while some of the miscellaneous bits and pieces that were added to later recensions of the *Libri* may be derived from the same period.[150] The problems they deal with—security of tenure, the rules of inheritance, rights of alienation—were not new but they were now being discussed in a new way. It was evidently a way that interested a fair number of people. Although Lehmann preferred the title *Consuetudines Feudorum* to *Libri Feudorum* for the whole book, because it was what the older manuscripts and earlier printed versions used, neither the early tracts nor those that were added later are really statements of custom. One may deduce custom by looking between the lines of the early tracts for what their writers took for granted, but they themselves were less interested in accepted custom than in problems. Their writings are discussions in which authoritative texts were used to formulate rules and make distinctions about the problems of practical law

[147] Lehmann, *Consuetudines: Antiqua*, 1–7; cf. Weimar, 'Legistische Literatur', 166; Classen, *Studium*, 59.

[148] The treatise Lehmann called 1e may also be a composite work. For arguments about the dates and relationships of the treatises, see the Appendix at the end of this book. In the rest of this section I shall use the form of citation used there, i.e. referring to the individual treatises by Lehmann's numeration and to matter in them simply by title and section number (e.g. I. 1) of the Antiqua text in Lehmann, *Consuetudines: Antiqua* or by the abbreviated title *Ant.* and a page number.

[149] Anschütz, *Lombarda-Commentare*. See Appendix.

[150] e.g. Lehmann, *Langobardische Lehnrecht*, 183 (*LF* II. 56), on which see below, at n. 181. Brancoli Busdraghi, 'Formazione', 235 n. 16, suggested that Ardizone's capit. extraord. c. 27 (*Langobardische Lehnrecht*, 192–3) might be an early Summula; cf. Lehmann, *Langobardische Lehnrecht*, 192 n. See also e.g. his capit. extraord. c. 21 (and *LF* II. 52. II–III).

posed by grants of property over which the grantors wished to retain some control. They were academic discussions, even if their authors were dealing with real problems of current law that defied easy categorization and therefore wrote in a style that one modern legal historian has characterized as 'arid empiricism'.[151]

None of these earliest treatises forms what one could call a finished work of literature. In that respect, as in others, the letters of Obertus de Orto mark a new stage.[152] Obertus was a judge and consul at Milan in the middle of the century, served as an imperial *missus*, and was one of the Milanese panel that gave an opinion on the Cerea case in 1146. His letters, which must have been written around the middle of the century, are literary productions in the genre of instructive letters.[153] It was he who first derived *feudum* from *fidelitas* or *fides* and *beneficium*, following Seneca, from *benevolentia*.[154] He seems to have had considerably more knowledge of Roman law than did the earlier treatises, and to have enjoyed displaying it, with hypothetical cases about Titius and Sempronius and so on. Not that Obertus was overawed by Roman law: as Classen has pointed out, he lifted a remark from the Codex about the authority of custom and neatly reversed its sense so as to leave Roman law with merely auxiliary authority.[155] Obertus's work is not only more sophisticated than the earlier treatises in its literary form. It is also more sharply focused on precise problems and hypothetical cases. Even when he is discussing the same subjects as the earlier treatises what he says is less closely related to any of them than they were to each other. Two other works from around the middle of the century that were not incorporated into the Antiqua need to be considered along with those that were.[156] If Anselminus de Orto's treatise on different kinds of contracts for land was written, as appears probable, by the son to whom Obertus addressed his educational letters, it may come from a little later than the father's work.[157] The statement of Pisan custom on fiefs was drawn up in 1160 but may incorporate older material. Although it was a statement of custom or practice to be followed rather than an academic treatise, it probably drew on academic works: part of the wording of the

---

[151] Brancoli Busdraghi, 'Formazione', 434.

[152] I have followed Lehmann in taking Obertus's work to include Antiqua X and all of Antiqua tit. VIII except VIII. 16.

[153] For the date, see Appendix. On Obertus's career: Classen, *Studium*, 50–68.

[154] *Ant.* 26: VIII. 8; 36: X. 1.

[155] *Ant.* 24; Classen, *Studium*, 62 n.; Schioppa, 'Le Rôle', 359–65. The need for three summonses (VIII. 29), without any reference to the alternative of a peremptory summons, may be traditional, rather than (or as well as) Roman: cf. below, at n. 227, and chapter 9, at n. 227.

[156] In addition to the more doubtful cases mentioned in n. 150.

[157] Anselminus, *Super contractibus*. See Appendix and Weimar, 'Handschriften', 40 n.

causes of forfeiture, for instance, is very close to that of the treatise Lehmann called 1a.[158]

Lehmann regarded the ordinance of 1037 as the starting-point or foundation of the *Libri*.[159] It is easy to see why. The treatise that comes first in the *Libri* (Lehmann's 1a) starts with an explanation of the way fiefs were granted that seems to derive from an attempt to make sense of Conrad's decree. Archbishops, bishops, abbots, abbesses, and *praepositi* are said to be able to give fiefs (that is, fiefs that would be protected by law), if that was their ancient custom, and so can marquises and counts, who were formerly called *capitanei*. Those who receive fiefs from any of these, namely those who are properly called vavassors of the king but are now called *capitanei*, can also give fiefs that will be protected. Those who receive these fiefs are called lesser vavassors. There, however, for the writer of 1a, and it seems for others, the *jus feudi*—the rights of security and inheritance protected by the rules laid down for fiefs and adjudicated by the fiefholder's peers—stopped. What the lesser vavassors granted to those whom 1b, in a very similar passage, called the smallest (*minimi*) would not be protected.[160] This is not actually very close to what the 1037 ordinance had said and still less close to what it seems to have intended. The trouble was that Conrad's ordinance, which the writers must have met in the collections of Lombard laws in the *Liber Papiensis* or the *Lombarda*, raised more problems for them than it solved.[161] At one end of the social hierarchy it omitted to protect counts, at the other it gave no guidance on drawing a line under those whom it did protect, and in the middle it seemed to imply a correlation between status or size of holding and position in a hierarchy of grants.[162] Interpolating the *capitanei* and supposing that the meaning of the word had changed may seem to us an unnecessarily complicated solution but it presumably resulted from arguments about which we can only guess. Making the name of each group correspond to a grade in the hierarchy of grants made the various orders of status look as neat as medieval academics liked. The exposition in 1a is closely paralleled in the next tract (1b) and reflected in 1c, while 1d seems to be a slightly garbled and rearranged version of the 1037 text, interspersed with additions and attributed to a King Lothar who may have been picked up from the heading of another entry in the part of the *Lombarda* in which Conrad's ordinance was entered.[163] Ariprandus's

---

[158] Bonaini, *Statuti*, ii. 967.

[159] *Langobardische Lehnrecht*, 77; *Consuetudines: Antiqua*, 2.

[160] I. 1, 4; III; VI. 4.          [161] *Liber Papiensis*, 583, 635.

[162] For suggestions of status as the real criterion: e.g. 1d (VI. 7: *ex ordine militum*), and *plebeji* in the definitions inserted into Obertus's letter: VIII. 16.

[163] VI. 7 and *Ant.* 18 n. 3; *Liber Papiensis*, 635, 636. The relevant parts of the *Lombarda* (i.e. III. 8–11) are more fully (if less accurately) seen in *Codex Legum Antiquarium*.

*Summula*, which never got into the *Libri Feudorum* with the other tracts, started as a commentary on *Lombarda* III, tit. 8, which included Conrad's ordinance. At least part of his little text follows the 1037 text closely.

Yet, in spite of all this, and in spite of other ways in which I shall argue that the 1037 law influenced the tracts just as it had already influenced the development of customary law, it may have been less important than Lehmann's remark implies. Much as these academic lawyers revered the texts they studied, they brought to them information and problems about fiefs and benefices that could not be found in them. These problems were the real starting-point and they were old in 1037. What was new was that they were now being confronted by scholars who tried to solve them through the study of texts. The ordinance was one of their texts. It was relevant for some of the problems that interested the scholars, but they met it in the context of the Lombard laws as a whole, with their glosses and commentaries. For some problems, like the rules of inheritance, other parts of the laws were more use. In some ways, to judge from the tangle that discussions of counts, *capitanei*, and greater and lesser vavassors got into, Conrad's decree was more of a stumbling-block than a starting-point. Not that that made it useless or unimportant: however much the writers of our tracts drew their problems from contemporary society and however difficult they found some of their texts, they were academics and they obviously found the difficulties and arguments stimulating. Academic law would not have got very far without hard texts and hard cases.

The problems that primarily concerned the writers of the early treatises had to do with the inheritance and secure tenure of fiefs or benefices—both words being used interchangeably. The only indication of the old use of *beneficium* for a count's benefice is that 1b thought that the fiefs (as he calls them) of counties, marquisates, and other high offices (*aliarum dignitatum*) should not be heritable, though inheritance in them was now usurped, while 1c said that the heirs of marquises, dukes, and counts should not succeed unless invested by the emperor.[164] 1a, however, clearly included marquises, dukes, and counts among all those who enjoyed the rights of fiefs (or benefices) that by implication included heritability. Opinions on the necessity for heirs to seek investiture varied. Some writers discussed investiture only in connection with new fiefs or when, for instance, an heiress's husband or son was allowed to hold her fief.[165] That may reflect earlier custom by which heirs in practice, at least on occasion, succeeded without reinvestiture.[166] 1d and Ariprandus, however, thought that investiture was necessary both when there was a new lord and when there

---

[164] V. 3; VI. 1; IX. 1.       [165] I. 5–7; IV. 1; VI. 4; IX. 4.
[166] Simeoni, 'Per la genealogia', 322, 323.

was a new tenant. 1d required it within a year and a month, while Ariprandus allowed the same delay to a knight but thought a *privatus* should have only a year and a day.[167] It is not clear from Obertus's first letter whether he thought investiture necessary on each succession.[168] In his other letter he said that investiture within a year and a day was needed by many courts, though not at Milan, on succession both of lord and tenant.[169]

None of the writers seems to have been much interested in people whom they excluded from the rights of the sort of fiefs they were discussing, and so they barely allude to the rights of inheritance such lowly fiefholders enjoyed.[170] What mattered were the rules of inheritance that applied to those with protected fiefs, and here the dependence on Lombard laws about full property is very clear. The joint succession of brothers seems to be taken for granted. 1b would only allow single succession if the father specifically ordained it. 1a and 1b evoke Rothari's law about the grades of kin, though 1a says that nowadays inheritance went even beyond what had then been allowed.[171] For fiefholders the normal rules were limited in some ways, such as the succession of daughters, or of brothers or their descendants when the fief had been granted to one of them rather than to their father. These limitations could, however, be lifted by the terms of the grant or by agreement with the lord.[172] 1a contrasted the exclusion of daughters from the inheritance of fiefs with their rights under ordinary law and explained it by their inability to prosecute the feud, which evokes Liutprand's legislation about full property. Ariprandus, who also mentions the feud, combines this reason with women's inability to perform service, but he seems to be the only one to do so.[173] 1d allows a daughter to inherit if there is no son, but only if the lord allows and she pays him for the privilege.[174] The later idea of single male inheritance as a norm of feudal tenure that is supposed to have resulted from the origin of fiefs in grants made in return for military service thus receives little support from these texts. In taking the line they did they both reflected the norms that had been applied to the inheritance of free property in Italy before their own time and foreshadowed those that would later govern the inheritance of noble fiefs there.

---

[167] *Ant.* 20 (VI. 11); Anschütz, *Lombarda-Commentare*, 195, 196. Cf. Lehmann, *Langobardische Lehnrecht*, 177 (*LF* II. 52; III).

[168] Cf. *Ant.* 24 (VIII. 2: fiefs as acquired by investiture or succession) and 25 (VIII. 5: investiture of old and new fiefs).

[169] *Ant.* 36–7.                                          [170] Though see 1e (VII. 7).

[171] I. 2, 3; IV. 1; V. 2.

[172] I. 2; VI. 4, 8; VIII. 17, 24, 25; IX. 3 (with an appeal to Ratchis's law).

[173] Anschütz, *Lombarda-Commentare*, 195. Obertus does not apparently do so, despite his remarks about service at X. 1, 6.

[174] VI. 14.

The difference between the rules for full property and those for fiefs and benefices was that, in cases in which custom tended to regard the right to inherit full property as less strong, the lords of fiefs were given a prima facie right to take them on failure of heirs. This makes the fiefholder's right look rather like that of a peasant, except for two important differences. First, the terms on which fiefs were granted often prevented the prima facie right from being exercised, and second, the fiefholder was protected against the lord's arbitrary action by the judgement of peers and appeal to an outside court.

Security of tenure for fiefs involved rules about their confiscation. 1a and 1b, in their struggles to make sense of what they thought Conrad II had said, maintain that the smallest vavassors (whom they envisage as holding from the lesser vavassors) could be evicted, but not if they served on an imperial expedition to Rome—the sort of exception that illustrates the difficulty in drawing straight lines through the muddle of custom.[175] If any of these unprivileged fiefholders had paid his lord anything for the fief, moreover, the lord had to repay the price in order to evict him.[176] That may imply that the people of low status and small fiefs who were normally excluded from the privileged class of fiefholders that interested lawyers were more likely to have bought their holdings than were the privileged. This seems quite likely: the higher the status of anyone receiving church land—or other land—on restricted terms before 1100, the more likely they were to get it by favour or force rather than for a cash payment. But it is a question of likelihood, not of rule: rules like that depend on the kind of distinctions between categories that were only now being created by academic lawyers. The point here was presumably that, when eviction was permitted, equity required repayment. 1a and 1b also say that those who held fiefs as gastalds or custodians could be evicted at the end of a year, 1a adding a reservation if the fief had been granted for a fixed term.[177] As in France and elsewhere lords and lawyers were evidently beginning to want to distinguish between what had been granted heritably and what had, in the lord's view, merely been put in the custody of a subordinate or servant. All these concessions to those not officially covered by the protection offered to the fiefholders who really interested the lawyers support the contention that the ordinance of 1037 had not created entirely new rights. Those excluded from it—however the line was drawn—were not supposed to be entirely subject to their lord's whim.

[175] I. 1; III.
[176] I. 4; III. Cf. 1c (VI. 4 § 1; IX. 4; *non* in VI. 4 § 1 must be a mistake: cf. the corresponding passage in IX. 4 and the variant readings to VI. 4 § 1, note z). *Dip. Lothar III*, p. 229 reports a relevant case of 1136.
[177] I. 4; V. 1.

All the writers except Ariprandus, even those who do not list other offences, mention unauthorized alienation of a fief as a possible reason for confiscation. Some say that any alienation needed consent, others allowed half the fief or less to be alienated without. Some said that if part was alienated without consent and the fiefholder died without heirs then the alienated portion would revert to the lord along with the rest. Milan and other places were, however, said to allow free alienation, though that did not prevent Obertus from approving of Lothar III's prohibition of it. Pisans were allowed to give fiefs to other Pisans without seigniorial consent.[178] In discussing alienation and Lothar's ordinance, Obertus refers to fraudulent conveyances *per libellum*. The earlier writers had not noted any distinction between grants in fief and *per libellum*, but it looks as though, after alienation was forbidden in 1136, *libelli* were used as a method of evading the law. Evidently the manœuvre had already been thought up by the time that Obertus was writing.[179] The fraudulence of grants *per libellum* might be taken to suggest something like the distinction between subinfeudation and complete alienation by substitution as legal historians understand it: Obertus asks rhetorically if anyone could doubt that a sale made for ever *libellario nomine* for a rent of a few pence is not a fraudulent alienation. But the distinction is not quite the same and does not imply the same background of assumptions. If subinfeudation had been regarded in the way that historians of feudalism would expect, then emperors, rather than forbidding alienation and then being frustrated by fraudulent *libelli*, could have simply insisted that any donor or vendor should reserve services. Presumably the reason no one thought of that was that fiefs and benefices so seldom owed fixed services: the demands of the emperor, even the demands of counts, were too occasional to be fixed in custom. They had for long represented something different from the normal and accepted obligations that people would expect to take on with property that they acquired. The discussions of other permissible reasons for forfeiture are not very informative about services. Failure to serve is the only reason specified by Ariprandus and is mentioned by 1c and Obertus, but in Obertus at least it looks a little theoretical.[180] The other tracts that list reasons include among them desertion of one's lord or failure to help him in

<hr/>

[178] II § 2; V. 3; VI. 6, 11; VII. 7; IX. 5; Anselminus de Orto, *Super contractibus*, 19 (for *investitura*, see above at n. 60), Bonaini, *Statuti*, ii. 963 (is there a distinction here between selling and giving?). Ariprandus's omission of the subject presumably relates to its omission from the 1037 ordinance, which he is following closely here: he mentions alienation by the lord. For Lothar's ordinance, above, at nn. 103–4.

[179] VIII. 15 and cf. the distinctions drawn by Anselminus de Orto, *Super contractibus*, 14, 17, 19. 1b had said *Quod dictum est alienare, intelligas de libello*: V. 3.

[180] VI. 10; X. 2 § 6; Anschütz, *Lombarda-Commentare*, 195.

battle, but neither of these implies any fixed or regular obligation to fight for him in the first place.

Three of the early treatises (or four if one divides 1c), along with Obertus and the Pisa customs, give lists of other offences besides alienation that deserved forfeiture. Ariprandus, though not giving a list, refers to one he had apparently seen.[181] Conrad's ordinance, with its reference to forfeiture after conviction of an offence, may have prompted the writers to think about offences that would justify confiscation.[182] The lists vary, but failure to serve and/or desertion of the lord in battle, revealing his secrets or not warning him of danger, seducing his wife, daughter, or other female relatives or affines, attacking him or his castle, or killing his brother or son turn up in several. 1c, incidentally, seems to reflect the reality of Italian lordship by referring to lords in the plural. What is striking about these lists is that they so obviously envisage fiefs as held from laymen. That seems at first sight to refute my argument that much of the law of fiefs that developed from now on was based more on past disputes over church land than on past customs about lay property. The argument is not, however, that free men never held fiefs or other dependent properties from lay lords, only that such fiefs did not apparently contribute much to the later law of fiefs. Some of the arguments in the treatises related equally to land held of lay and ecclesiastical lords, but many would be particularly relevant to church land: it was churches that worried most about permanent lay inheritance of their lands, and two tracts allowed the successor of an abbot or bishop to revoke grants made by his predecessor more easily than could the heir of a layman.[183] If, on the other hand, one were to think of offences meriting confiscation then one might well think of those against a secular lord or at least find more interesting arguments about them. Counts, who might worry less about a subordinate's permanent inheritance, provided he and his heirs were loyal, than would bishops or abbots, might worry more about threats to their own local control through acts of hostility or betrayal. By the early twelfth century lay lords—not only counts but the kind of people who could be envisaged as the greater or lesser vavassors of 1037— were probably beginning to organize their own property and extend their control over the property of their subjects by the use of rules and methods that look rather like those already developed by churches. Whether or not powerful nobles themselves were yet expecting to argue in court with their

[181] II; VI. 5 and IX. 5; VI. 11; X (cf. also VIII. 29); Bonaini, *Statuti*, ii. 967–8; Anschütz, *Lombarda-Commentare*, 195. The similar content of Lehmann, *Langobardische Lehnrecht*, 183 (*LF* II. 56), printed as *Constitutiones*, i, no. 55 as a doubtful ordinance of Henry III, suggests that it may just possibly have come from about the same time as the early treatises, when lists like this were being compiled and discussed, though *Constitutiones*, i, no. 56 looks less likely to be so early.
[182] See the gloss to it in *Liber Papiensis*, 584.                   [183] I. 5; II. 6; IV. 2.

subordinates rather than use force against them, the new lawyers were thinking about their disputes in the new legal terms.

The lists in the treatises look as if they reflected traditional values. Any Lombard gasind or, later, any *vassus* who deserted his lord in battle, committed adultery with his wife, or attacked his house would presumably have been thought to deserve some fairly fierce punishment. That does not mean that the lists as they stand embodied ancient custom. Unwritten custom does not automatically produce lists and, much as medieval academics liked textual authority, the Lombard laws provided only a few examples of offences for which property could be confiscated.[184] The self-contained character of the lists in the tracts, together with the similarities and differences between them, suggests that they were the product of discussion within the school or schools from which the tracts emerged—a discussion conducted between people who naturally shared the values of the society to which they belonged but were now applying them in a new way. It is tempting to wonder whether the disturbances and conflicts of the time, just when secular lords may have been beginning to extend their control over their followers' property and make it more formal, may have provided useful instances of offences that would merit confiscation. One good example could have been the alleged behaviour of the followers of the Countess Matilda. They were said to have transferred themselves to Count Albert of Sambonifacio after her death (and probably after Henry V's too) and then seized the castle of Canossa from him and held it and his wife by force. It was the kind of story that, however small its core of truth, would have been widely told and have lost nothing in the telling. Whatever it was that really happened, however, probably happened after 1125, which is a bit late for the earliest treatises that mention adultery with a lord's wife or an attack on his castle.[185] Perhaps there were other cases, or perhaps the lawyers just worked out their lists for themselves.

All the treatises that discuss procedures talk of peers, presumably deriving the word from the 1037 decree. For 1a, 1b, and Ariprandus, the peers are *pares curtis*, suggesting that they functioned in a local court that may well have dealt with other matters too. For 1e and Obertus they are peers of the lord's house. The relation between judgement by peers and other

---

[184] *Leges Langobardorum*, 18 (Rothari 1, 3–7, 10, 13). Carolingian legislation had lists of offences by lords that may have been stimulating: *Capit.* no. 104 c. 8 (c. 7 was in the *Liber Papiensis*) and cf. no. 26 c. 12, 13; no. 77 c. 16, and also c. 20 for confiscation of a benefice from one who fails to respond to a summons from a lord (not the king) for help against an enemy. *Liber Papiensis*, 348, has the verb *concubitare* (*cucubitare, cucurbitare*) used by 1a, 1c, and 1d in connection with offences against the lord's wife. I am assuming that *LF* II. 56 was part of the discussion rather than providing a precedent (above, n. 180).

[185] Further details of the case are given in the Appendix, with references. Matilda's followers are also discussed in Fasoli, 'Note sulla feudalità'.

methods of proof is not entirely clear: 1a speaks of decisions *per pares curtis vel breve testatum*, while others refer to oaths and oath-helpers or witnesses.[186] Various problems, like the lack of peers or witnesses, or their refusal to testify, are confronted by some writers, while Obertus discusses, among other matters, systems of choosing peers and whether, if a bishop rejected a vassal who declared he had been invested by the bishop's predecessor, the vassals in the bishop's court could judge. Obertus thought that that kind of case would be better heard by an outside judge. Although 1c and 1d followed Conrad's law in mentioning appeal to the emperor or his officials, by the time of Obertus cases involving fiefs were coming before city courts at Milan and, it seems, at Pisa and Padua too.[187] However the judgement of peers worked in practice, it was an important contribution of Conrad II's ordinance to the law of fiefs—not because it created collective judgement but because it preserved it at least into the beginning of the age of professional law.

This survey barely scratches the surface of the material in the Antiqua. Its texts deserve much closer study. In particular they need to be studied in the light of what can be discerned in other sources about actual practice at the time they were being written or before. Only thus can their intellectual creativity be appreciated. Their authors were not simply reporting current practice, let alone traditional custom. They were working at problems and expressing opinions. But while they are an uncertain guide to current practice and a very poor guide to past custom, they are extremely suggestive about the origin of various doctrines and assumptions of later professional law. These texts became part of the textbook on which any lawyer who attended a university for long enough would be trained. It was now that the terminology of the law of fiefs became set in the form in which seventeenth-century historians would meet it and pass it on to their successors. 1c (VI. 1–6) and 1d refer to benefices, 1b and 1e refer to fiefs, and 1a, 1c (IX), Ariprandus, and Obertus use both words interchangeably. 1a sometimes uses the word *fidelis* for the tenant of a fief but sometimes *vasallus*. 1b, 1c, and 1d speak of *fidelis, miles, tenens feudum, investitus,* or *clientulus*. For 1e, Ariprandus, and Obertus, the tenant was always a vassal. For lawyers from now on, vassals meant fiefholders. The 'union of vassal and benefice (or fief)' was now accomplished, not by social or political change but by academic usage.[188] Vavassors, incidentally, come into the *Libri Feudorum* only in passages that are trying to make sense of Conrad's law or

[186] I. 4–7; V. 1; VI. 7–14; VII. 22–4 (in VII. 22 the court seems to be a count's); VIII. 3–4, 22–3, 26–7; Anschütz, *Lombarda-Commentare*, 195.

[187] Manaresi, *Atti di Milano*, e.g. nos. 1, 18; Bonaini, *Statuti*, ii. 961, 962, 964; Ficker, *Forschungen*, iv, no. 108, is a case of 1138 very like that posed by Obertus.

[188] On this concept, see index: union.

are derived from others that try to do so. One of these was the section on definitions that was interpolated into Obertus's first letter in the last stages of the compilation of the Antiqua. Here vavassors were firmly identified as those who of old held fiefs from *capitanei*.[189] Since this definition survived in the *Libri* long after the word had slipped out of use for a status group, historians who approached the middle ages through the *Libri* naturally took it to be an essentially feudal word. The fact that *capitanei* sounded so like those who came to be described as holding *in capite* in England (though not, I think, elsewhere) helped to mask a misunderstanding that can be traced back to the intelligent efforts of early twelfth-century lawyers to understand a text from nearly a hundred years before.[190] Only a few of the early writers seem, however, to have been bothered with this particular problem. Others who referred to the 1037 ordinance were not interested in the problems of greater and lesser vavassors.

As this suggests, one of the kinds of difference that one can detect between the tracts is that their authors were interested in different subjects. This needs further and closer investigation. In spite of their different interests an important result of their cumulative work was to shape the incoherent mass of custom about subordinate property into new categories. The most important of these was the category of what one might call protected fiefs: that is, the only fiefs that, in the opinion of the lawyers, were true fiefs and enjoyed the rights of inheritance and security that were guaranteed by the judgement of peers. Outside lawbooks the word fief would for long continue to be used much more widely and it would often be difficult to decide which individual properties should be protected by the *jus feudi* and why. The new category was a jurist's category and can only be understood as such. Given the assumptions of medieval society about rights and social status, given the purpose and text of Conrad II's law and the way it had passed into customary law by the time the first treatises were written, it is easy to see how these academics, who shared those assumptions and were familiar with custom, began to associate fiefs—proper fiefs protected by the *jus feudi*—with nobles and military values, though not with precise military obligations. 1e (a late part of the Antiqua, according to Lehmann) justified a debtor's right to reclaim land pledged in fief by saying that a fief was not to be sought for the sake of money but for love and honour of the lord.[191] As a rationalization it was no worse than many other learned rationalizations of customary rules, but it would have made little sense of most grants of fiefs or benefices a hundred or two hundred years before.

---

[189] VIII. 16.     [190] See index: *caput*.     [191] VII. 6.

The later stages by which the *Libri Feudorum* were formed may be dealt with more briefly. Whoever put the Antiqua together may have been working rather mechanically. Whether the early treatises were originally complete as they stood or whether they were abstracted from larger works, their original authors had been tackling genuine intellectual problems. The intellectual quality, or indeed the purpose, in the way that the early mini-treatises were combined and attached, with all their consequent repetitions and contradictions, to Obertus's letters, is less apparent. Perhaps, however, that is unjust. A possible explanation of the way such extraordinarily short treatises were put together could be that the compiler started with Obertus's letters and then added some extracts from other works (or lecture notes) that offered a variety of views on topics that puzzled or interested him. However that may be, once the compilation was made it seems to have acted like a magnet to new material. Frederick I's ordinances of 1154 and 1158 (to be discussed below) were probably added to the existing texts quite quickly. The most important event after that in the history of the *Libri*, which enabled them to exert their enormous influence on medieval historiography, was their incorporation into Roman law. Pilius (d. after 1220) was the first lawyer from the school of Bologna who is known to have read and used the Antiqua. He apparently met it when he moved to Modena, where he wrote his *Summa Feudorum*, probably around the turn of the century.[192] That need not mean that he was the first Bologna lawyer to think about fiefs or become acquainted with the work that Lombardists had been doing on them. When, for instance, men like Obertus de Orto's son Anselmus (or Anselminus) went to study at Bologna or when leaders of both academic traditions met at Roncaglia, some Romanists may surely have been open-minded enough to notice that there were good arguments to be made about fiefs.[193] Pilius and his successors evidently appreciated that good arguments had already been made. From now on the earlier texts became increasingly authoritative, to be discussed and expounded while ever more distinctions were drawn and structures of reasoning erected above and around them.

Just as Roman lawyers could take on the law of fiefs with no apparent sense of incongruity, so they could also incorporate useful material from canon law. It was about now that the letter of Bishop Fulbert of Chartres about the obligations of fidelity was copied from Gratian's Decretum into the *Libri*, and soon after that the 'new form of fidelity' was added.[194] The

---

[192] Meijers, *Études*, iii. 261–77; Rota, 'L'Apparato di Pillio', 8–25.

[193] Note also the arguments about Cerea: Schioppa, 'Le Rôle', 359–63.

[194] Lehmann, *Langobardische Lehnrecht*, 120–3; Giordanengo, '*Epistola Philiberti*', 815–27; Weimar, 'Legistische Literatur', 165–7.

oath of fidelity inserted here is short and spare and was perhaps not based on any earlier text, but the explanation or expanded version that follows is more interesting. The best way to find its source might be to search through the surviving texts of earlier oaths. At first they had probably varied a good deal, but it looks as if they became more standardized wherever written records were preserved. Most of our evidence concerns oaths taken to ecclesiastical lords and preserved in their records.[195] Perhaps the 'new form of fidelity' in the *Libri*, like Fulbert's letter, was as likely to have come from such a source as from secular records. Contacts between lawyers went in both directions. After the law of fiefs had become connected with Roman law in the schools, canon lawyers might learn about them together. Innocent III's letters about the quarrels between Philip Augustus and John in 1203 do not seem to allude to the academic law of fiefs, but when he wrote to England in 1215 his references to vassals and the judgement of peers suggest that he or an adviser may have known something about it. Perhaps he had even met some of the texts that became part of the *Libri Feudorum*.[196] The title *De Feudis* in Gregory IX's Decretals of 1234 contains two of Innocent III's letters that deal with problems of church property in the traditional way, reminding us of the original link between those problems and the law of fiefs. Not long after, the corresponding title in Hostiensis's *Summa* on the Decretals draws heavily on the *Libri Feudorum*, and ranges widely into problems about purely secular property.[197]

The final additions to the *Libri* were made within the first half of the thirteenth century, including most notably the *Extravagantes* of Jacobus de Ardizone, while at the same time the Antiqua treatise attributed to Hugh of Gambolo (1c) was dropped. This produced the 'vulgate' form of the *Libri*, which was soon after tacked on to the texts of Roman law as the tenth section of the Novellae or Authenticum. From now on it would be glossed and discussed along with the rest of the *Corpus*, while Roman lawyers who commented on current politics in terms of legal rights and obligations would tend to slip into the vocabulary of fiefs and vassals even when they chose most of their citations from the Codex or Digest.[198]

Much of the modern image of non-Marxist feudalism, together with the

[195] For examples of Italian oaths see references to this chapter in the index: fidelity, oaths; Muratori, *Antiquitates*, i. 633–4; Otto and Rahewin, *Gesta*, 191. *Liber Instrumentorum*, a notable example of a lay record from Montpellier, contains a large number of eleventh- and twelfth-century oaths. Cf. Magnou-Nortier, 'Fidélité et féodalité'.

[196] Innocent III, *Selected Letters*, nos. 82–3.

[197] *Corpus Iuris Canonici*, ii. 526 (III. 20); Hostiensis, *Summa Aurea*, ff. 153–155 (recte 156). Cf. the additional remarks noted by Acher, 'Notes', 130.

[198] e.g. Azo, quoted by Kienast, *Deutschland und Frankreich*, 684; John Bassianus, quoted Meijers, *Études*, iii. 261. On these later stages and the glosses: Weimar, 'Handschriften', and Montorzi, *Diritto feudale*.

difficulty of reconciling it with the evidence of medieval property law as practised, becomes more comprehensible when the content and compilation of the *Libri Feudorum* are considered in the context of their time and distinguished from later interpretations. I have already suggested that the opening passage of the whole book, with its worries about counts, *capitanei*, and vavassors, may have conveyed the impression that Conrad II's ordinance was more important than I suspect it was. Immediately after this passage comes another that also still exerts a baleful influence over medieval history. According to 1a, lords in earliest times had the power to confiscate fiefs at will. Afterwards they began to grant them for life, but a fief did not yet pass to its holder's sons by right. It was for the lord to confirm it to those he chose. Now, however, things had become stabilized so that all enjoyed the right. When Conrad set out for Rome (*proficisceretur Romam*) he was asked by his *fideles* in his service to extend the right to brothers and nephews on the father's side if the benefice-holder died without a legitimate heir.[199] There does not seem to be any sound reason to look for a core of truth in this piece of conjectural history. That the part before Conrad was pure conjecture seems obvious, and even the part about him looks like a reconstruction from a text of his ordinance—and probably one that lacked its date at the siege of Milan.[200] Conrad had made his expedition to Rome for coronation ten years before he granted the ordinance and does not appear to have gone there again in 1037–8.[201] The ordinance was surely issued at the demand, not of members of his army (at least his 1037 army), but of the local rebels against Archbishop Aribert whose service in future he hoped to assure. The ingenious explanation devised by the author of 1a can only be made to fit earlier evidence, which we have but he did not, by cutting the earlier evidence to fit it. None of the other writers of the Antiqua seems to have been interested in this kind of explanation, while the vulgate text merely elaborated 1a's myth of origin by inserting annual tenancies as a second stage, before life tenures. It was not until the *Libri* came to be used to explain the course of medieval history that the passage would really come into its own.

There is, however, a good deal of the later image of feudalism that is not in either the Antiqua or the whole vulgate text. Although the few historians who refer to it sometimes say or imply that the *Libri* contain a definition of fiefs, there is nothing in the text that could be considered a definition of them as a category of property with distinctive rights and obligations. There is no attempt to distinguish fiefs from alods, which are mentioned only four times in the whole book, with no discussion of their

[199] *Ant.* I. 2.    [200] As did that in *Liber Papiensis*, 583–4.    [201] Wipo, *Opera*, 36, 54–7.

229

character.[202] In the absence of any concern with the difference between fief and alod, it is perhaps natural—though, in view of the practices that we shall see developing at the time when the text of the *Libri* was developing, it is surprising—that there is no mention of the conversion of alods to fiefs (*feudi oblati, fiefs de reprise*). Nor is the boundary between privileged and protected fiefs and others explored systematically. It is sketched here and there, where the writers had their attention drawn to particular problems, but none of the later contributors to the book did anything to resolve the implied uncertainty of some of the earliest between drawing it according to the position of the grantor in a hierarchy of grants, according to the size of the holding, or according to the social status of the tenant. Nor did any of the writers of the *Libri* take as one of the marks of their sort of fief its possession of exceptional jurisdiction. A lord had to offer his fiefholding tenants the judgement of their peers, but that appears more as a duty than a right: the fiefholder himself had no more jurisdiction over tenants who did not hold fiefs than did the owners of other property. A lord might or might not have *districtus*: some fiefs could be under the *districtus* of the lord from whom they were held.[203] The link between fief and 'immunity' had not yet appeared in Italian law or, if it had, had not yet been noticed by the academics, though by the reign of Frederick I the words *immunis* and *immunitas* were occasionally used in grants to towns and individual laymen—another instance of the influence of practices developed in connection with ecclesiastical property.[204] Nor as yet had lawyers started to work out any theory of the division of property rights between lord and vassal: *dominium divisum* was still to be invented. There is nothing in the *Libri* about 'feudal aids' or, apart from the brief allusion in Conrad's ordinance, about anything that looks like a 'feudal relief'. Lastly, none of the texts in it uses either the word homage or the word *vasallagium*, which William Durandus, writing late in the thirteenth century, thought was the word used in Italy for what in France was called *homagium*.[205]

---

[202] Lehmann, *Langobardische Lehnrecht*, index: *allodium*. The character of the distinctions to which later academics were given is illustrated by the *Feudorum Typus* at the beginning of the 1574 glossed text reprinted by Montorzi, *Diritto feudale*, 108.

[203] *Ant.* II. The only other reference to *districtus* in Lehmann's index is to Frederick I's prohibition of the sale of imperial jurisdiction: Lehmann, *Langobardische Lehnrecht*, 179.

[204] *Dip. Frid. I*, nos. 104, 438, 737, 853, 869, 946.

[205] See chapter 7, at n. 119. Some cases where homage was referred to in Italy during the twelfth century are mentioned in the next section. For usage in the kingdom of Sicily in the first half of the thirteenth: *Konst. Fried. II*, ii. 226 (II. 36); Loud, 'Monarchy', 312.

## 6.9. *Politics and the new law in the twelfth century*

The early stages by which the new schools of law began to influence the practice of law are obscure. By the eleventh century judges and notaries already formed something rather like a legal profession in the larger Italian cities. They must have been open to influence from the schools just as the schools were open to influence from civic practice and experience. The ruling élites of the Lombard and Tuscan cities were thus well placed to put to practical use ideas that they probably picked up from their bishops and local abbots. In 1095 the bishop of Asti invested the consuls of Asti, on behalf of all the citizens, with the fortified place of Annone *in beneficio* and apparently for ever (*de hinc in antea*). In 1097 the Countess Matilda invested two men of Cremona *nomine benefitii*, on behalf of the church and commune of Cremona, with the whole county (i.e. the comital rights) of the *Insula Fulcheri*.[206]

Cities soon granted land in benefice or fief as well as receiving it. The rights that had been secured to benefices by Conrad II's ordinance had been confirmed in custom, and were now being shaped in learned discussion, in such a way as to make them almost as good and as honourable as those of full property—perhaps even better. Fiefs, unlike most other forms of property, were beginning to have rules that were beginning to be generally recognized in circles that had access to legal advice. A fief of the kind that was subject to these rules, unlike other forms of property in which the grantor retained superior rights, and, indeed, unlike ordinary full property, could only be held by someone of at least moderately high status. It was therefore not merely as respectable as full property but may have been beginning to acquire a certain élite status. More practically, it was hereditary and offered the possibility of fixing the rules of inheritance in advance; it did not normally involve any obligations beyond a general promise of peace and goodwill, though others could be added by agreement at the outset; and it was protected against arbitrary confiscation. All this must have made the grant of fiefs an ideal method for a city that wanted to make terms with local nobles in order to extend its control over the countryside. What the nobles got out of it would depend on the terms made, but they often had to make terms of some kind. In 1118 seven citizens of Cremona, on behalf of the people, invested certain knights *per feudum* with the estate of Soncino. Sons were to succeed fathers according to the custom of fiefs (*secundum usum feudi*[207]) and, in default of sons, daughters could succeed if

---

[206] *Codex Astensis*, no. 635; *Cod. Dip. Cremonae*, i. 92–3 (no. 203).
[207] For *usus feudi* apparently meaning the custom or law of fiefs in general rather than of a particular fief: below, at n. 223.

they married men who would live at Soncino and serve the fief. Failing daughters, other possibilities were set out with much the same care to provide for eventualities in accordance with customary norms as is manifest in the Antiqua. Whether or not any of the influential Cremonese or their advisers had studied law in the schools, they evidently had similar ideas and preoccupations to those who had. The knights of Soncino were to take an oath to the commune which mentioned the procedure to be followed if any of them should commit a crime deserving forfeiture. While, like other oaths of the period, it was drafted to suit the particular circumstances, it was in effect an oath of fidelity. The knights swore to fight (*ostem . . . fatiemus*) along with the people of Cremona or with part of them if reliably notified. Each of the knights said that he would be faithful to the commune, like a vassal to his lord.[208]

Since this last phrase echoes that used in Carolingian oaths to kings and emperors, it probably need not imply that Cremona was turning what had earlier been an interpersonal noble relationship to collective use.[209] Both in receiving and granting fiefs (or benefices) and in getting oaths of fidelity, moreover, cities were probably following precedents set by churches, not nobles. A bishop's court might meet in his city and leading citizens might well be among his vassals (whether that meant fiefholders or servants and followers). When towns required those who held fiefs to behave like vassals to their lords they were probably thinking of the obligations of episcopal or abbatial clients or servants. When they said that they were to behave like a lord's *fideles* they may have meant the same or have been drawing an analogy with non-noble tenants. The earliest document on which I have happened in which the grantee of land is to serve like a vassal is a Milanese deed of 1079.[210] Two brothers who received church property (already held in benefice, apparently at second hand) agreed, as part of careful rules about inheritance, that so long as their heirs held it one of them would do fidelity and serve as a vassal ought to serve his lord according to the custom of Milan. In 1089 someone, who may have been above peasant status but was not described as a noble or knight, received land in Tuscany from Passignano abbey at an annual rent with the obligation to be helpful to the abbot and his successors in good faith like a good *fidelis* to his lord.[211]

To get those who held strategic property and power near by to surrender it to the city and receive it back in fief, making a promise of fidelity at the same time, may have seemed an obvious extension of a city's use of

---

[208] *Cod. Dip. Cremonae*, i. 100 (no. 36).                    [209] Chapter 4, at n. 54.

[210] Budriesi Trombetti, 'Prime ricerche', 372–3.

[211] Conti, *Formazione*, 191. The grammar of the sentence is rocky, as so often in eleventh-century Italian documents, but this seems to be the meaning.

benefices or fiefs. The first deliberate and unambiguous example of this—
the creation of a *feudo oblato*—that I have met in Lombardy comes from
1126.[212] There may have been earlier cases. Across the Alps in
Montpellier, where a law school is known to have been in existence a little
later, the lord of Montpellier had used that method of securing the submission of local lords as early as 1112.[213] The Italian transaction of 1126
was negotiated by Piacenza. Half of a fortified place (*castrum*), with its
appurtenances, was to be held *per feodum et beneficium* and would pass to
both male and female descendants of the grantee.[214] In 1132 a group of
joint owners gave their alod (using that word) in another *castrum* to
Piacenza and also included in the transaction half of yet another *castrum*
that they held in benefice from Bobbio abbey. This they could not give outright but only *libellario nomine*, to be held from them by the commune at
an annual rent. While the only obligation on the new fiefholders that was
mentioned in the 1126 record was to defend the commune's title to its new
property, those who turned their property into fiefs in 1132 swore to be
faithful to the commune and to help to defend it. They also undertook to
pay an annual money rent for what they now held *per feodum et beneficium*
and not to alienate it in such a way as to injure the city. All their men who
lived in the places conveyed to the city were to take an oath to it of the kind
taken by the men of the city's *capitanei*.[215] From 1141 on, various *castra* or
parts of *castra* around Genoa were surrendered to the city and regranted in
fief. Other lords made treaties with Genoa that did not involve actual
grants in fief but look as if they came to much the same thing.[216] From now
on the practice of securing grants of full property (sometimes called alods)
and granting them back in fief is known to have been adopted by a number of cities, including Arezzo in Tuscany. The documents I have seen use
the word fief, not benefice.[217] Presumably in each of these cases what the
fiefholders got for surrendering their original rights was peace with the city
on the best terms they could get.

In 1157 the papacy took up the system for three *castra* in the territory
over which it was trying to establish or maintain control. In one of these
negotiations it was agreed that the pope and his successors would be
allowed to confiscate the fief only by the judgement of good peers who

---

[212] This is the first noted by Brancoli Busdraghi, 'Formazione', 465.
[213] See chapter 7, at n. 7. [214] *Reg. Magnum di Piacenza*, no. 53.
[215] Ibid. no. 49: the grant of the fief is not expressly recorded but is implied in the promise to
hold *per feodum et beneficium*. The grammar is at times surprisingly poor for the date, which may
suggest minimal academic participation.
[216] *Cod. Dip. Genova*, nos. 111–12, 147–50.
[217] *Reg. Magnum di Piacenza*, nos. 61–2; *Libro Verde d'Asti*, nos. 36, 165, 177, 180–1; *Carte
capit. Asti*, no. 30; *Doc. Arezzo*, no. 357; *Reg. Chart. Pist.* no. 42; *Rigestum Albe*, no. 119; probably *Cod. Dip. Padovano*, no. 710.

would not be enemies of the fiefholder. In the other two the new fiefholders were to do homage and fidelity.[218] In the following year the pope made a treaty with Orvieto that did not allude to fiefs or the law of fiefs but required the consuls to do liege homage to him and the people to do fidelity according to the custom of the pope's other cities.[219] In this case there does not seem to be any reason to suppose an implied fief, for neither homage nor fidelity was restricted to fiefs. But though an obligation to fidelity did not always imply a fief, the grant of a fief was, it seems, coming as a matter of course to involve the swearing of fidelity. In circumstances where that seemed unsuitable the fact might therefore be noted: procedures and records were becoming sufficiently regular for exceptions to be exceptions rather than variations. They imply rules.

The first example that has been noted of the grant of a fief that expressly exempted the grantee from doing fidelity comes from 1131, when a lawyer invested the prior of S. Cipriano, Venice, with the rights and dues he might receive, by right of a benefice he held from the bishop of Padua, from lands that had come to the priory (*quarum proprietas seu dominium in prefatum monasterium devenerat*). The prior was to hold this fief for ever without doing fidelity or owing any service except by prayer.[220] Obertus, who thought that in principle no investiture should be made without fidelity, allowed exceptions to be made if specifically agreed. Fiefs without fidelity were known at Pisa by 1160.[221] Obertus himself is excellent evidence of the conjunction of learned law with the practice of the courts. It may well have been he who advised on Frederick Barbarossa's legislation in 1154 that attempted to prevent evasion of the law on alienation of fiefs by making grants *nomine libelli*.[222] Practice, however, did not always call for the kind of arguments that Obertus deployed in his learned letters. He was included in the panel of Milanese judges who were consulted in 1146, along with judges from Brescia, about the Cerea case. Both groups decided that the countess Matilda could not be shown to have held Cerea as a fief, so that none of the new learning about the custom of fiefs (*feudi usus*) was applicable. That left the case to be decided according to the laws (*secundum leges*), which gave scope to use some Roman learning instead.[223]

That Frederick Barbarossa should have been said both to have promoted the transition of Italy from a feudal to a bureaucratic state and to

[218] *Liber Censuum*, nos. 101–5, 107.
[219] Ibid. no. 106: *beneficium* is here used to mean a gift. Cf. nos. 91, 94–5, 120 for other methods of extending control without granting fiefs.
[220] *Cod. Dip. Padovano*, no. 226; Rippe, 'Feudum sine fidelitate'.
[221] Lehmann, *Consuetudines: Antiqua*, 26, 37; Bonaini, *Statuti*, ii. 965.
[222] Above, at n. 179. For his presence at Roncaglia: Otto and Rahewin, *Gesta*, 118–19.
[223] Ughelli, *Italia Sacra*, v. 788–9; Classen, *Studium*, 55–6; Schioppa, 'Le Rôle', 159–63.

have tried to turn it into a feudal kingdom like France, with a range of other possibilities to choose from, is testimony to the varying understandings of feudalism.[224] If all relationships between emperors and their subjects were feudal then of course Frederick's were, but while his requirements of oaths of fidelity from his Italian subjects were feudal in that very broad sense, it is not at all clear that they were expressions of feudo-vassalic values and bonds or implied the creation of fiefs.[225] Some of his grants of fiefs, like his ordinances about fiefs in 1154 and 1158, were, however, concerned with feudal law, not as a part of traditional customary law, but in the particular sense of the new, academic law of fiefs.[226] The study of the new, learned law of fiefs was not yet fully integrated with that of Roman law as it would be a hundred years later, and the four masters of Bologna who advised the emperor about the royal rights or dues (*regalia*) in 1158 may not have known as much about it as did those of Pavia or Milan, though they may have picked up something while they were at Roncaglia. All the same, whoever drafted Frederick's legislation about fiefs in 1154 and 1158—or parts of it—was clearly thinking in its terms. The learned lawyers who advised on the method of summoning the Milanese were, however, clearly thinking in Roman-law terms.[227] It seems probable that neither the emperor nor the beneficiaries of his charters always had the same kind of legal advisers at hand, or always took the advice of those they had. In trying to understand why some grants were made *in feodum* and some were not, and what *in feodum* meant, we have to bear in mind that some of them were probably made according to older ideas of customary law and used words accordingly.

Frederick's object was to recover what he saw as his rights in Italy. He hoped to make counts acknowledge that their counties were in some sense imperial benefices; to secure the military service that he thought they, the great churches, and all their respective benefice-holders should have owed; and to receive all the dues that counts and others—including the rulers of the shockingly independent cities—should have been collecting on his behalf, especially the *fodrum*. On his first visit in 1154 he was presumably met with the same sort of excuse about alienated benefices that had met Lothar in 1136, for he reissued Lothar's prohibition of alienation by those

[224] Ficker, *Forschungen*, ii, § 324, and cf. Koeppler, 'Frederick Barbarossa', 583, and Appelt, 'Friedrich Barbarossa', 71; Tabacco, *Struggle*, 216, and 'La costituzione'. For other important discussions: Brancoli Busdraghi, 'Formazione', 462–500; Haverkamp, *Herrschaftsformen*. Frederick's relations with the pope and the trouble over the word *beneficium* are discussed in chapter 9.6.
[225] As seems to be assumed by Haverkamp, *Herrschaftsformen*.
[226] Cf. ibid. 325; Appelt, 'Friedrich Barbarossa'.
[227] Otto and Rahewin, *Gesta*, 204 (III. 29). Cf. above, at n. 155.

beneficed with fiefs—a word that had not appeared in either Conrad II's or Lothar III's laws. The closing of the loophole of fraudulent grants by *libellus* is a sure sign that he had taken local professional advice—possibly from Obertus, who is known to have been present at Roncaglia. The requirement that every fiefholder (*infeudatus*) should seek investiture from his lord within a year and a day—presumably either of his own inheritance or that of his lord—may also have come from Obertus.[228] Frederick's own preoccupations are indicated by the last clause of the new ordinance: anyone either in Italy or Germany who failed to comply with a summons to an imperial expedition to Rome would forfeit to his lord any fief that he had from a bishop or other lord. It seems that there was no question here of confiscating the property of counts, let alone bishops: what Frederick wanted was to forestall their excuses. In this context fiefs were properties held from counts and bishops that owed service to the emperor.

Four years later, on his second visit, the emperor issued another ordinance to the same effect, adding several new clauses, some of which again suggest the involvement of professional or academic lawyers.[229] Duchies, marquisates, and counties were not to be divided, and, if any other fief were divided, provision had to be made for all who had part of it to do fidelity. It may be pressing the language too far to infer from 'any other fief' (*aliud autem feudum*) that duchies, marquisates, and counties were coming to be envisaged as fiefs, but in 1159 one count at least thought that the rule against alienation covered his estates as well as lesser fiefs.[230] Another clause seems to undermine the judgement of peers, though here again that may be inferring a non-existent intention: whereas peers sworn in by the lord were to decide a dispute between lord and vassal (a word that suggests the new law), a dispute between two vassals was, it seems, to be decided by the lord. The legislation as a whole suggests that even professional lawyers could not always be clear about the categories they used: their categories were still unformed and in flux. We may guess that for lawyers and their clients fiefs were more or less noble or honourable properties, with particular privileges as well as some particular, if often vague, obligations, but we have to remember that other people were still using the words fief and benefice in still wider and more uncertain ways.

Prohibitions of alienation or division of benefices or fiefs (whatever the words meant), even threats to confiscate them, were not answers to Frederick's problems. The whole system of comital benefices as royal offices, and of lesser benefices as sources of military service to the emperor, was moribund if not dead. Some of the early Antiqua writers may have

---

[228] *Dip. Frid. I*, no. 91; though there are references to it before Obertus: above at nn. 167-9.
[229] Ibid. no. 242.         [230] Ibid. no. 257.

thought that duchies, marquisates, and counties ought not to have been inherited by right, but it was not politically possible for the emperor to dismiss counts or even, as Otto of Freising unrealistically hoped, suspend them from office while he was in the country.[231] It would have been impossible to disentangle what counts held in benefice from what had originally been their own full property: in 1152 Frederick confirmed a charter of Conrad III that had itself confirmed to Count Guy of Biandrate what he held as his own *proprietario jure* and what he held as benefices *beneficiario jure*, but Guy himself may not have known which was which. Few later charters refer to counts' benefices at all.[232] The emperor made more practical use of legal advice by getting a list of royal rights and dues in Italy— not that that in the end necessarily got him the dues, but, combined with a declaration that all jurisdiction was derived from the emperor, it gave him something to bargain with.[233]

One might have expected that when Frederick granted or confirmed the *districtus* or other regalia to those who offered political or military support he would from now on have taken a leaf out of the cities' and lawyers' books and made his grants in fief. In fact, so far as his surviving charters show, he did so occasionally but not regularly. Perhaps the decision whether a grant would be made in fief or not, like other more detailed provisions contained in charters, was taken in the first instance by the beneficiaries: whether or not the charters granted all their recipients asked for, they may have been, at least in part, cast in the terms they suggested. To receive property or jurisdiction in fief, as some counts and other favoured individuals did, might be better than receiving it simply for ever: it might make special terms about inheritance and so on easier to arrange, and, given the way that lawyers were using Conrad's orders about the judgement of peers, a grant in fief would give as good a chance of fair judgement as one could hope for.[234] The old phrases detailing the freedom of disposition of full property seem to have been given up by now, so that rights of alienation may not have been much affected in practice either way. Having the grant not merely *in feodum* but *in rectum feodum* or *in rationabile feudum* presumably meant no difference of substance but may have emphasized that it was made under the new law of fiefs.[235] As for cities, one might be tempted to guess that Genoa and Pisa asked for their privileges to be

[231] Otto and Rahewin, *Gesta*, 117–18.
[232] *Dip. Frid. I*, no. 36 and cf. 20, 32, 99, 110, 347. The benefice in no. 142 was held from a bishop, not the emperor.
[233] Ibid. nos. 237–8; Otto Morena, *Hist.* 58–61; Otto and Rahewin, *Gesta*, 236–41.
[234] e.g. *Dip. Frid. I*, no. 700.
[235] Ibid. nos. 290, 316a (ii. 493–4), 339, 368 (and 531), 463, 466, 558, 635, 699, 897, 939. But cf. nos. 395, 433–4, 452, 457, 462.

granted in fief because both cities were accustomed to using the word in their treaties with neighbouring nobles, were it not that other cities that created *feudi oblati* on their own account did not get their charters in these terms. Perhaps opinions varied: a good deal of the learning about what lawyers called fiefs (such as about the causes of confiscation or the judgement of peers) would as yet have been hard to apply to cities or other collective fiefholders.[236]

There remain plenty of puzzles, as for instance about the German who received property *per rectum feodum* according to German custom or the nobles who received one grant in fief and another not.[237] Perhaps the advantages to the recipient one way or the other were marginal and grants were made in fief simply because professional lawyers familiar with the new law were involved in the negotiations. Perhaps sometimes a grant was assumed to be in fief without saying so—though whether both sides, or their successors, would have agreed about what they assumed is much more doubtful. One would imagine that grants that were made hereditarily or for ever but not explicitly in fief were subject to normal customary law, but custom itself cannot have been exempt from influence from the new law any more than it was from politics. Whatever the terms of grants or of general legislation, they could be amended by royal favour: exemptions were granted from the rules against alienations, while some subjects carefully asked for special authorization to do what the law allowed.[238] Some charters included promises that the beneficiary, whether an individual, a church, or a city, would remain under direct royal control, but the desire for what the editors of Frederick's charters call *Reichsunmittelbarkeit* need not imply that they were thinking of a specifically feudal kind of hierarchy.[239] In any large organization and under any legal system it may be an advantage to be directly under the boss rather than under one of his minions.

From the point of view of the emperor or his advisers, a grant in fief may have implied a useful acknowledgement of subjection but an oath of fidelity or an annual rent might do as well. Even making someone think they needed a grant or confirmation meant something, especially when a charter confirming the beneficiary's property implied that all that he or his ancestors had held had come to them by royal generosity. Charters granting jurisdiction also took on a new colour after the declaration at Roncaglia in 1158 that all jurisdiction derived from the prince and after the prohibi-

---

[236] *Dip. Frid. I*, nos. 356, 367, 477, and *Constitutiones*, i, no. 337; for other towns: *Dip. Frid. I*, nos. 120, 259 (but this grant was at pleasure), 369, 372, 410, 455, 524, 530, 640, 653.

[237] *Dip. Frid. I*, nos. 522; 271, 290, 458, 466–7.

[238] Ibid. nos. 264, 271–2, 455–6, 640, 848; *Hist. Pat. Mon. Chart.* ii, no. 108.

[239] *Dip. Frid. I*, nos. 337, 434, 465, 736. See chapter 9, at nn. 129, 261–4.

tion, issued at the same time, on selling any *districtio* or jurisdiction when one sold the alod to which it had been attached.[240] There is no evidence that grants in fief as such implied any particular service, let alone military service. Frederick had to get what service he could in Italy primarily by negotiation, which meant granting favours but not necessarily granting them in fief.[241] It is true that Pisa and Genoa made commitments to military service in 1162 in return for their charters of privileges in fief, but the commitments were for a particular campaign, not because they were corporate fiefholders. Meanwhile many people were required to take oaths of fidelity who could by no stretch of the imagination be seen as fiefholders either in the sense used by twelfth-century lawyers or in that of historians. The practice of requiring all citizens between the ages of fifteen and seventy to swear fidelity to the emperor at regular intervals had been developing for many years before it was enshrined in the Treaty of Constance in 1183. In the treaty the different kinds of oath are made clear: royal vassals (*vassalli nostri*) were to do fidelity as vassals, and all others were to do it as citizens. How many people held fiefs directly from the king in Lombardy by now is doubtful, but there were some, and they formed a traditional category that presumably needed to be mentioned for that reason.[242] Since 1158, meanwhile, all oaths of fidelity to anyone else had been supposed to reserve fidelity to the emperor explicitly.[243]

However one evaluates Frederick I's Italian policy and its rather moderate success, and however difficult it is to see just how much either traditional customary law or the new professional law contributed to it, there is no doubt that his reign had a significant impact on the development of the new law. There was much occasion for the taking of professional advice both by the emperor and by the nobles and cities who had to negotiate with him. The way that the emperor, the pope, and the cities used grants in fief confirmed the association of fiefs with people of high status and thus their privileged character. Consequently, although not all noble property was yet thought of as held in fief, there may well have been a tendency to assume that it was or might be. Fiefs were sometimes described as honourable, just, right, lawful, conditional, or gentlemanly (*gentile*):[244] such a description looked better even though it presumably did not alter the rights and obligations involved. All this must have emphasized the contractual nature of fiefholding and may have contributed to a

[240] Ibid. nos. 47, 114, 134, 238, 241, 339, 462, 699.
[241] e.g. ibid. no. 524.                          [242] Ibid. no. 848; cf. no. 712.
[243] Ibid. no. 242. Fidelity in cities (none of which apparently held their privileges in fief): ibid. nos. 362, 369, 372, 455.
[244] Ibid. nos. 226, 290, 368, 466, 699, 872, 897, 939; *Cod. Dip. Cremonae*, i. 125, 178–9 (nos. 193, 485); *Doc. Vercelli*, no. 10.

misunderstanding of fiefs and fiefholding that arose as soon as historians started to study the middle ages through the literature of the law of fiefs. Lawyers who wrote about that law were, naturally, concerned only with the relations of lords with their more or less noble fiefholders, but early modern historians who did not realize that all medieval rulers had been supposed to rule all their subjects, and not just their noble subjects, justly and with their consent, assumed that the contractual-seeming relationships they found in the law of fiefs must have been peculiar to nobles and therefore to vassalage and fiefs. Meanwhile, one principle of great importance both for the future of feudal theory and of more general political theory had been established at Roncaglia in 1158: namely, that all jurisdiction and governmental authority was exercised by delegation from the emperor.[245] From there, given the link between noble property and rights of jurisdiction, and given the way that Frederick sometimes confirmed and protected existing properties and rights as if they all derived from previous royal grants, it is easy enough to see how noble property, like noble jurisdiction, would come to be thought of as entirely derived from ancient royal grants. The idea of property that was held in fief as having originated in royal grants may also be inferred from the opinion of the canonist Huguccio (d. 1210) that the *regalia* of churches were held, not as *proprietas*, but in fief.[246]

## 6.10. *The Norman south*

Before the Norman invasion the rights and obligations of property in the south may not have been very different from what they were further north. The most important difference, apart from some influence of the Byzantine system of themes on military service, was probably the absence—so far as the evidence apparently shows—of anything like the Carolingian benefices *verbo regis*.[247] The use of the word *bassi* in 886 suggests influence from the kingdom of Italy, but it may have been no more than linguistic and is very unlikely to have implied anything about property rights.[248] The Normans undoubtedly brought some of their own ideas and practices with them, although, since nobles did not normally hold land in fief in Normandy and the later ideas about feudal tenure had not yet been worked out, they could hardly have brought anything like what historians call the concepts of vassalage and the fief.[249]

Information about grants made by the leading Normans to their follow-

[245] *Dip. Frid. I*, no. 238.
[246] Quoted by Fried, 'Regalienbegriff', 459. For church property as fiefs, below, at n. 302.
[247] On themes: Tirelli, 'Osservazioni', 987 (I have not been able to see the works of Cassandro to which he refers).
[248] Taviani, 'Pouvoir et solidarités', 600.                      [249] See chapter 5.3, 5.

ers has to be gleaned from casual references in contemporary or near-con-
temporary histories or chronicles, though a few charters to churches have
implications for the rights of lay grantors or their subjects. Although historians traditionally refer to Norman lordships as fiefs from the eleventh
century on, none of the sources suggests that Robert Guiscard and the
other princes thought of their own lands as fiefs, whether held from the
pope or anyone else, or that either they or the more important of their
followers thought of the grants they made to them in a similar way—
whatever they understood by whatever form of the word fief they may have
known or used.[250] It seems more probable that the lands and lordships that
the more important Normans secured, whether by conquest or grant or a
combination of the two, were generally assumed to be the kind of hereditary full property that nobles normally held at home in Normandy.[251] Fiefs
are referred to in eleventh-century sources, but not as what look like great
noble estates or lordships.[252] In 1068 one of the knights of the city of
Aversa, Aldoin, who described himself as a Frank, gave to a local church a
small piece of land that he said he had *causa fegus beneficii* from the princes
of Capua, as was the custom of Franks in the area (*sicut mos Francorum est
in his regionibus*). Another Frank, who was in Aldoin's service (*armigerus
ipsius domno Aldoino*), gave another piece, evidently by agreement with
Aldoin. A few years later the same church acquired another bit of land
from yet another Frank who had it *per fegum beneficii*, as was the custom—
though not this time explicitly of the Franks—in those parts (*sicut consue-
tudo in his Ligurie partibus*).[253] The form of the word *fegus* might suggest
that it had come in from northern Italy independently of the Normans, but
arguments about Latin forms are made very uncertain by uncertainty
about which vernacular the scribes were translating from and how far
north French and north Italian—or south Italian—vernacular forms differed.[254] The reference to Frankish custom need not imply that the rights
and obligations of property described as fiefs were just the same as they
might have been in Normandy: what appeared to be Frankish custom in

[250] For relations with the pope, above (6.7).

[251] Gaufredus, *De Rebus*, 18–19, 22–4, 38–9, 59, 90–1, 100; Amato, *Storia*, 200–1, 273, 293,
321; Gattola, *Ad hist.* 164–5; *Tabularium Cas.* nos. 241, 251; Alessandro di Telese, *De Rebus*,
105–7. For full property in Normandy, chapter 5.4.

[252] Cahen, *Régime féodal*, 47 n. lists some examples; a few others are e.g. Gattola, *Ad hist.* 222;
*Tabularium Cas.* nos. 282, 329–30; Alessandro di Telese, *De Rebus*, 97. I have not deliberately
searched for references.

[253] *Cod. Dip. Aversa*: S. Biagio, nos. 43, 53. The case endings quoted are as in the printed text.
There are other references to benefices, mostly in quite unspecific senses: e.g. Gaufredus, *De
Rebus*, 36, 37, 39, 76; *Carte latine*, no. 1. Amato, *Storia*, 273, refers to a grant as *en benefice*, but
the lateness and translation of the text make it difficult to interpret.

[254] The form *fevum* (or *fevus*) occurs in the early twelfth century: *Regii Neap. Arch. Mon.* nos.
511, 521.

south Italy was what Franks there (presumably Normans) did. They may
have adapted their customs and categories to new needs and conditions.

Contemporary use of the word fief in Normandy, as in the rest of France
and indeed in the kingdom of Italy, suggests that the fiefs that people like
Aldoin acquired were granted to them on terms that, although perhaps
restricted, were not restricted in any uniform way. They may have covered
estates ranging from small holdings given to fairly simple soldiers to whole
fortresses entrusted to the commanders of garrisons.[255] The donor may
often have thought that he was giving whatever he gave—especially if it
was a fortress—into the custody of his man, with inheritance as a mere
possibility dependent on good service and success in holding it against
enemies. The grantee may have taken a different view. Either way, as time
passed and things settled down, the fief might turn into full property without anyone thinking much about it: perhaps that in itself extended the local
connotations of the word fief. As early as 1068 and 1073 the donors of the
two Aversa charters were able to give away full and permanent rights without apparently getting permission from their lords (except in so far as
Aldoin's *armiger* got Aldoin's). There is no evidence that the church to
which they made their gifts held what it received from them as fiefs or on
terms that correspond to historians' ideas about feudal tenure: here as elsewhere churches at this date normally held their land with the fullest possible rights. The rights attached to properties that were called fiefs at the
time no doubt varied for many reasons, including the status of the parties.
A charter granted in 1087 to Cava abbey (Campania) by Duke Roger Borsa
mentions the duke's *feudatarii* and those who held his fiefs, however they
held them (*tenentes pheuda nostra, qualiter ea tenent*).[256] As for the *vassali*
either of the duke or the abbey, who are also mentioned in the same charter, they may not have held any lands from their lords at all.

References to fiefs multiply in the twelfth century, though some of them
are very unspecific. In the mid-twelfth-century royal survey of military
service, the *Catalogus Baronum*, fiefs are properties with particular and
specified military obligations that distinguished them from what were
called patrimonies or inheritances—although, of course, fiefs were also
inherited.[257] Later in the century fiefs that had been entered in the
*Catalogus* were sometimes called quaternated (i.e. registered) fiefs. That
was because properties that carried quite different rights and obligations
were also sometimes called fiefs: this included some peasant properties,

---

[255] For fortresses: Gaufredus, *De Rebus*, 19, 59, 76; Noyé, 'Féodalité'.

[256] *Rec. ducs normands*, no. 59.

[257] Jamison, 'Additional Work', esp. 9 n., 14 n.; *Cat. Bar.*, esp. p. xv, and for *hereditagium
feudi*, e.g. nos. 506, 508. Cf. Cuozzo, 'Milites', 134.

which are very unlikely to have owed the military services of quaternated fiefs, and others, whether held from churches or lay lords, that probably did not owe them either. The use of the word was spreading: the *Catalogus* used it for noble property that would once not have been called fiefs, and by the thirteenth century it could even be applied to church property. The first example I have noted anywhere in Italy comes from the kingdom in 1208, when Frederick II gave property to a church *in perpetuum feudum*.[258] Clearly the word fief did not yet denote a category of property with distinctive rights and obligations. One's fief could by now mean nothing more specific than one's property: fiefs held from the king, great fiefs, or quaternated fiefs were particular kinds of fiefs that by their nature occur most frequently in royal records. From the government's point of view the most important distinction may sometimes have been between quaternated fiefs and everything else, but sometimes it was between quaternated fiefs held directly from the king and those held from others. Sometimes it was between quaternated fiefs that consisted of great lordships with extensive jurisdiction and small fiefs held by people over whom the king would not bother to claim exclusive jurisdiction. This distinction presumably lies behind that drawn by later lawyers between fiefs held in barony and those held as simple fiefs (*in feudo plano*), though it must have created much legal argument over individual cases.[259] It took professional lawyers to make such distinctions, and they could not make them without squashing the variety of custom into categories that could not have been thought of in the eleventh century and that remained full of anomalies. The use of *vassalli* to mean tenants in the Constitutions of Melfi suggests that the academic law of fiefs had reached the south by 1231, perhaps in the form of the *Libri Feudorum*.[260] The use of *vassallagium* in a Beneventan charter of 1225 as an apparent synonym for *hominium* implies that the new academic law was being combined with local custom.[261] The new law presumably promoted the idea of fiefs as characteristically noble, even while the word continued to be used more widely here as it was, in despite of the lawyers, everywhere.

Just as the Normans are unlikely to have brought with them any clear 'concept of the fief', so they are unlikely to have brought any clear idea of a feudal hierarchy of property or of subinfeudation as something distinct

---

[258] *Carte latine*, no. 87.

[259] Ughelli, *Italia Sacra*, i. 1125–7; *Carte latine*, nos. 134–5, 138, 147–8, 155, 161–2; *Konst. Fried. II*, e.g. 68, 70–2, 132, 252, 272, 280 (I. 44, 47, 87; III. 5, 21, 27); *Acta imp. ined.* i, no. 818.

[260] I have not searched *Konst. Fried. II* for textual borrowings. Dilcher, *Sizilische Gesetzgebung*, collects many parallels (listed pp. 878–9), but the few I have looked up show similarities in the substance rather than suggesting use of the text.

[261] Loud, 'Monarchy', 312; cf. e.g. *Konst. Fried. II*, ii. 226.

from other transfers of rights. All large estates, whether lay or ecclesiastical, had people living on them who held their own property with greater or lesser rights and obligations according to custom and status. Over some of these people a lord's right might be merely a matter of government or jurisdiction, over others he might have some rights that we would classify as proprietary. The Norman conquerors must often have overridden the rights of their new subjects or tenants, but that does not mean that rights as such were not recognized: even peasants had *hereditates*, and lay lords, like churches, might have to bargain with them, recognizing and even extending those rights on occasion.[262] What would later be called subinfeudation (on the assumption that the estates of great lords already formed a top layer of fiefs) must have started very soon: Aldoin of Aversa had his land by 1065. Many Normans presumably got their property by some sort of grant from their leaders or lords, but not all: if Orderic Vitalis had said only that William of Échauffour held his land under (*sub*) the count of Loritello we might assume that he was another case of early 'subinfeudation', but Orderic also tells us that he acquired it through his marriage with a Lombard noblewoman. A descendant appears in the *Catalogus Baronum* holding fiefs under the count in the usual way.[263] The *Catalogus*, seen through the spectacles of later feudal theory, certainly gives an impression of a hierarchy of property rather like that of Domesday Book.[264] As with Domesday, however, the conceptualization may have been the result of the record rather than its premiss. It is clear in the *Catalogus*, as it is in Domesday, that holding (*tenere*) did not imply a subordinate and restricted form of property: people were said to hold their patrimonies and heritages, and they are not always said to hold their fiefs from anyone.[265] Unlike Domesday, the *Catalogus* is not a register of titles but only of military obligations.[266] In some places it shows several layers of military obligation and of property, but the layers of property were recorded only because of the obligations. At the top of the hierarchy, the units are more governmental than proprietary,[267] while at the bottom are people who can have been little more than peasants.

The rights and obligations of property, whatever the words used to denote its units and however it was conceptualized, were undoubtedly

[262] *Tabularium Cas.* no. 213; *Carte latine*, no. 2.
[263] Orderic, *Hist. Eccl.* ii. 126; *Cat. Bar.* nos. 362–3, 380.
[264] See chapter 8.4; the English *Carte Baronum* of 1166, with which the parallel is closer than with Domesday, is also discussed there.
[265] Cuozzo, *Commentario*, sometimes inserts *de rege in capite* where it does not occur in the text: e.g. nos. 402, 404–6, 409*.
[266] See e.g. the entries about church properties mentioned in Jamison, 'Additional Work', 19–20.
[267] Jamison, 'Additional Work', 20, and 'Admin. of Molise', 543, 547.

altered by the Norman invasion. Although the invaders seem to have been
perfectly willing to acknowledge the authority of Lombard laws on occasion, they probably introduced some of their own customs simply because
they took them for granted.[268] One example of this was the custom by
which lords in tenth- and eleventh-century France gave consent to gifts
that were made to churches by people under their authority, even if the
donors had what were thought of as full property rights. This became quite
common under the Normans although it seems to have been rare in the rest
of Italy.[269] Monte Cassino included free rights of alienation in a charter it
granted to its men in Traietto (now Minturno in Lazio) in 1061, but as
tenants of church land they otherwise presumably had less than full
rights.[270] To judge from the Aversa charters that have already been mentioned, Normans did not always ask for seigniorial consent to their grants,
but, as in France, the custom tended to create a norm that required it.[271]
The so-called feudal aids were also surely introduced from Normandy,
perhaps before 1100, for they were known in Normandy by then, but they
seem to be first attested rather later. Another Norman introduction by the
thirteenth century, if not before, may have been a difference between the
rules of inheritance to acquired and inherited property.[272] The words alod,
vavassor, baron, and essoin may be others. The first three, however, did
not denote anything very new, even if vavassors may have been people of
lower status here than they were in Lombardy. An alod was presumably
property with the rights locally accepted as full and complete. As for
'essoin', which may have denoted a new and Norman item of legal procedure, it is not so directly concerned with property law.[273]

Other changes probably derived less from the invaders' different ideas
or customs than from the conditions of conquest. When Norman soldiers
were first given fortresses or lesser properties they were presumably
expected to help to defend them and extend their lords' conquests. If
things went well their obligations would become more or less fixed in custom, but the form in which their successors' service was recorded in the
mid twelfth century cannot have been pre-ordained from the start. Taxes,
dues, and services owed by Lombard nobles or peasants, or by Normans
who took over property from them, probably went on being demanded and

---

[268] On Lombard laws: Ménager, 'Législation', 446.         [269] Above, at nn. 115–17.
[270] *Tabularium Cas.* no. 213; cf. *Rec. ducs normands*, no. 59.
[271] Gattola, *Ad hist.* 222; *Tabularium Cas.* no. 329; Jamison, 'Norman Administration', 473–4.
[272] *Konst. Fried. II*, 272, 282 (III. 20, 27); cf. Jamison, 'Norman Admin.', 473–4. On the aids,
chapter 5 at n. 153.
[273] Alod: *Tabularium Cas.* no. 281. Vavassor: Cahen, *Régime féodal*, 30, 51 n., 54; *Cat. Bar.*
no. 839. Baron: Jamison, 'Additional Work', 14 n., 21. Essoins: Gattola, *Ad hist.* 222; *Regii Neap.
Arch. Mon.* no. 531.

paid according to the best terms each side could obtain, modified by bullying, evasion, or misunderstanding. Oath-taking may have become a more
important bond of society in the early days of the conquest because, with
no king or other leader wielding traditional authority, the invaders were
driven to make terms with each other by mutual oaths, just as they sometimes tried to secure the submission of their Lombard subjects by making
them take oaths.[274] All such oaths can reasonably be described as oaths of
fidelity so long as that does not imply a standard form: some that are
recorded were clearly designed to fit the circumstances in which the parties found themselves.[275] In 1087 Duke Roger gave the abbot of Cava
(Campania) permission to take oaths of fidelity and homage (*juramentum et
homagium fidelitatis*) from his vassals as the duke did from his.[276] Fidelity,
homage, and vassals need not here, any more than anywhere else, have
implied fiefholding or noble status. There is other evidence that lordship
or patronage was not invariably attached to landholding.[277] Meanwhile, in
spite of oaths, conflict brought accusations of treachery and consequent
forfeitures that could be as well, or as ill, justified under Lombard as
Frankish law, on whatever terms the forfeited property was held.[278]

The features of the twelfth-century kingdom of Sicily that are generally
considered most distinctively feudal were the product of a systematic organization of its government that cannot have been extended to the mainland
much before 1130. The most striking evidence of the new bureaucracy is
the *Catalogus Baronum*, which is thought to have been made and revised in
the 1150s and 1160s. The military obligations of fiefholders that it
recorded were presumably then considered to be established in custom,
but, given the political vicissitudes of the mainland before 1128, the custom cannot in many cases have been very old. In some it was probably no
older than Roger II's own reign and an earlier royal survey to which some
entries seem to allude.[279] At least some of the services owed by churches
are likely to have been imposed recently by the creation of something like
the Carolingian benefices *verbo regis*.[280] Whatever had been the rule before
the *Catalogus*, military service after it was apparently owed to the king

[274] Gaufredus, *De Rebus*, 18–19, 22, 37–8.
[275] Gattola, *Ad hist.* 222; *Tabularium Cas.* no. 282; *Regii Neap. Arch. Mon.* no. 531.
[276] *Rec. ducs normands*, no. 59.
[277] *Tabularium Cas.* no. 282 mentions a promise of help about land held from others; the relationship with Roger de Miglia in the 1117 document mentioned in Muratori, *Rerum Ital. Scrip.*
ii (1), 316–17, may not have been connected with land.
[278] Gaufredus, *De Rebus*, 59, 76; Gattola, *Ad hist.* 222; *Tab. Cas.* no. 251. For Lombard law:
Gattola, *Ad hist.* 164–5; and cf. *Chart. Conversano*, no. 53 with Alessandro di Telese, *De Rebus*,
97, 99–100.
[279] *Cat. Bar.* pp. xv–xx; Jamison, 'Norman Admin.', 244–63, 338–41.
[280] *Chron. Casaur.* 891–2; Jamison, 'Norman Admin.', 468–70, and 'Additional Work', 18–21;
Loud, *Church and Society*, 153–4.

alone, and the additional service said in it to be 'offered', whether from fiefs or other property, was no doubt intended to be the thin edge of a royal wedge of heavier obligations. Some kinds of taxes (*adiutoria*, *aduamenta*, *collecta*) were being paid to the king occasionally before the end of the twelfth century and more regularly in the thirteenth. In 1238 *addohamenta* were paid on fiefs and *collecta* on patrimonies, but everyone except the poor and the collectors was supposed to pay one or the other. Frederick II's constitutions attributed to King William an ordinance regulating the emergency aids taken by lords. Lay lords could take them for knighting a son and the marriage of a daughter or sister, but for ransom or the purchase of land only in connection with royal service. Prelates of churches could take them for consecration and attending a papal council, but for other expenses only when they were incurred on royal service. As in France, these aids were apparently taken by nobles from their subjects in general, though whether that included their noble subjects is unknown. There is apparently no evidence that the king took them from nobles.[281]

Anyone who held property directly from the king was subject to particular demands and restrictions. On the face of it the category fits the feudal model of 'tenants in chief', but it was apparently defined in terms of the *Catalogus*, where, as I have argued, the hierarchy is one of jurisdiction and service rather than of property and certainly did not result from an original hierarchy of grants.[282] It looks as if from a fiscal point of view the government was most interested in the great fiefs of counts and barons, but it also regulated baronial jurisdiction and interfered in the affairs of those who came under it in a way that makes nonsense of feudal theory.[283] By 1231 an inheritance due (called, as in England, a relief) was owed to the king by those who held from him and to them by those who held fiefs from them—subject to royal regulation.[284] The barons' rights to reliefs are as likely to have been copied from those the king had over them as vice versa, though they could equally have extended their demands on their free subjects from those they made on the unfree. Either way there is no evidence at all that reliefs here derived from any ancient feudo-vassalic bond—though, of course, that is not to say that they definitely did not. By 1231 the king also claimed some sort of rights over the wardship of minor heirs and even required barons to ask permission for their own marriages, while

---

[281] Jamison, 'Admin. of Molise', 547, 558–9; 9–13, 28–30; *Acta imp. ined.* i, no. 812; *Konst. Fried. II*, 272 (III. 21–2). See index: aids.

[282] On the meaning of *in capite* in the *Catalogus*: Jamison, 'Additional Work', 15 n. See index: *caput*.

[283] *Konst. Fried. II*, 68, 70–2 (I. 44, 47); Jamison, 'Additional Work', 18, and 'Admin. of Molise'.

[284] *Konst. Fried. II*, 278 (III. 25).

as early as 1160 great discontent had been caused by the control William I
exercised over the marriage of his barons' daughters in their fathers' lifetimes.[285] There were also controls on alienation: at first they may have been
only on the alienation of *regalia*—that is, the royal dues and rights of jurisdiction that counts and barons exercised—but Frederick II required permission to be sought for any alienation or exchange of fiefs and *res
feudales*.[286] The idea of rights of jurisdiction and local government as
*regalia* evokes Frederick I's legislation, though whether it was a case of
influence, and in which direction, or of parallel developments needs more
investigation. At all events there seems to be no evidence of any myth that
derived rights of property from grants of land by the first Norman conquerors. Frederick II may have taken the simpler view that all fiefs held in
barony—perhaps all property rights in the kingdom—were held in effect
by his own grant.[287]

The twelfth- and thirteenth-century kings of Sicily maintained and
extended their authority by some means that would come to be classified
as feudal. Most of their most apparently feudal powers were, however,
developed after 1130 with the assistance of bureaucrats and, by the thirteenth century if not before, of professional lawyers. The similarities with
England are obvious and well known. It is tempting to wonder how much
mutual influence there may have been, for instance through the movement
of government servants between the two countries.[288] There were, however, more differences than have always been noticed by historians who
have thought in terms of universal feudal customs. Despite similarities
between the surveys that produced the *Catalogus* and the English *carte
baronum* of 1166, the 'feudal hierarchy' in the kingdom of Sicily looks, if
anything, more like the hierarchy of jurisdiction that developed in France
than like the English hierarchy of property rights. In each case, however,
the hierarchy seems not to have reflected older ideas or past grants of land
but to have been produced by legal and governmental developments of the
twelfth and thirteenth centuries—if the English twelfth century can be
taken to have started in 1086. In Sicily, as in France, the so-called 'feudal
aids' were not taken by the king or other lords from nobles because of any
traditional feudo-vassalic bond: they were taken by lords, including
ecclesiastical lords, from their subjects in general and possibly only their

[285] *Konst. Fried. II*, 274, 278–80 (III. 23, 26); Ugo Falcando, *Liber*, 78.
[286] *Konst. Fried. II*, 252 (III. 4, 5); *Carte latine*, nos. 161–2.
[287] *Acta imp. ined.* i, no. 818: the rest of the sentence about those *qui feuda tenent in baronia ex
concessione nostra in Marsia et comitatu Albe* suggests that not all of them were recipients of new
grants.
[288] Jamison, 'Sicilian Norman Kingdom', 249; Richard fitz Nigel, *Dialogus*, 18, 35–6.

non-noble subjects.[289] What was most alike and most distinctive about the
kingdoms of Sicily and England was nothing to do with feudo-vassalic relations. It was the early development of bureaucracy and the power of the
state. In 1178 a royal judge decided that someone was not a man of the king
because his property was not held *de feudo*, he did not hold it *in feudo de
curia*, and did not do service to the king for it.[290] If we were to suppose that
*homo* was a 'technical term' of feudal law and was always used in the same
sense, that would drive a coach and horses through my argument, but the
point that was being made was presumably that the property was not a fief
in the sense used in royal records—a quaternated fief. In other contexts
contemporaries would surely have thought of all the free men of the kingdom—and everyone else—as the king's men and *fideles*. The king of Sicily
exercised his extensive powers over them and their property not because
they were his vassals but because they were his subjects.

## 6.11. *Professional law and government*

The effect of the development of academic and professional law in the
twelfth century was to produce a separate set of rules about the kind of
property that lawyers called fiefs: that is, property held by people of sufficient status to be able to claim the advantages offered by the interpretation
of the law of fiefs in the *Libri Feudorum*—and, presumably, to be able to
employ lawyers. At first only some property held by such people counted
as fiefs, for many nobles and free men must still have held their lands and
jurisdictions in the traditional manner, as their own full property, whether
called alods or not. The number of estates that counted as fiefs became
restricted in some ways and extended in others. By 1216 Milan had secured
an oath from the archbishop and abbots not to create new fiefs.[291] In 1221
Modena turned all property within ten miles of the city into alods or *propria* and provided for those who had held fiefs to redeem their lords' rights.
This followed disputes between the commune and the clergy about *livelli*
and *precaria* (whatever that meant by this time) and looks like a general
defence of the property rights of citizens against ecclesiastical restrictions.[292] Some cities also worried about fiefs held from secular lords,
but this was primarily because of the divisive effect of the networks of

[289] *Konst. Fried. II*, 272 (III. 20–1); Jamison, 'Norman Admin.', 473–4, and 'Admin. of
Molise', 31–2.
[290] Cuozzo, 'Milites e testes', 134.
[291] *Liber Cons. Mediol.* 120 (XXIV. 7): this seems to be making a different point from
Lehmann, *Consuetudines: Antiqua*, 12 (II. 7) to which the editors refer.
[292] *Stat. Mutine*, pp. cxv–cxvi, 332–41.

patronage that lords created by making citizens into their vassals, whether that involved giving them fiefs or not. At Ferrara it seems that, even as late as 1287, vassal did not necessarily mean fiefholder.[293] On the other hand, the later middle ages saw an increase in the number of noble properties that were called fiefs, partly because city-states continued the twelfth-century policy of extending control over the *contado* by getting nobles to convert their alods into *feudi oblati*, and partly perhaps as this process, combined with similar grants by the emperor and pope, and with the implications of the usage of the *Libri Feudorum*, made the word fief seem the right one for any noble property. Wherever professional lawyers were influential, fiefs thus came to be thought of as noble properties with the rights and jurisdictions (especially *districtus*) that nobles were expected to enjoy over their rural property.[294]

Lawyers did not control the use of language by others, particularly in rural areas where they were thinner on the ground. Some peasant properties continued to be called fiefs, while in some contexts a *feudum* could be a salary.[295] In one village in Roman territory the word vassals was used in 1273 to include all the inhabitants, even *massarii*. In another in 1277 the 'noble vassals' were noble to the extent that they owed military service on horseback, but they could only keep their horses with subsidies from the lord and the use of a meadow that was set aside for them. They can hardly have maintained a life-style that would have made them look noble in a wider world, and were probably unaware of the privileges that the academic law of fiefs might have bestowed upon them.[296] A lord in this area could still create what were in effect *feudi oblati* in 1297 for quite ordinary people with apparently quite small holdings as a way of extending his property.[297] What—among much else—is not clear is the extent to which properties that professional lawyers would have recognized as fiefs were held from or under the great fiefs that were their primary concern. Baldus, for instance, writing in the late fourteenth century, referred to what would now be called subinfeudation but his references look rather theoretical.[298] There seems to be little evidence of 'subinfeudation' to people above peas-

[293] Fasoli, 'Ricerche', 250, 276–7; Dean, *Land and Power*, 116 n.
[294] Chittolini, 'Infeudazioni'; Dean, *Land and Power*, 74–8, though note the reconversion of fiefs to alods, 87.
[295] Redon, 'Seigneurs et communautés', 175 (c. 5), 177 (c. 31), 182–5 (c. 3); Dean, *Land and Power*, 74–5, 99–102.
[296] *Statuti della prov. romana*, 5–12 (esp. c. 2), 365–72; cf. the *milites* in ibid. 18.
[297] Caetani, *Documenti*, 103–8.
[298] Baldus, *In usus feudorum*, e.g. f. 7v referring to practices *hodie*. Sometimes, however, e.g. f. 92, he is commenting on earlier texts.

ant level at Ferrara, and perhaps there was not much at Milan or elsewhere in the north either.[299]

The existence of separate sets of rules for the fiefs that were recognized as such under the lawyer's law of fiefs and for other property—apart of course from the rules for rented properties and such peasant holdings as fell below the level of alods—did not mean that there were two separate legal systems with separate lawyers and separate courts. Since the law of fiefs was taught along with Roman law, the same professionals were presumably capable of dealing with both. The question of courts is more complicated. Those who write about 'feudal jurisdiction' in medieval Italy from the thirteenth century on are concerned not so much with rights of jurisdiction *over* fiefholders, along with the judgement of peers, but with the right of jurisdiction held *by* fiefholders over all their subjects or tenants, whether the subjects or tenants held fiefs or not.[300] Before the twelfth century people who had then been reckoned as fiefholders would have been less likely to have the kind of jurisdiction that came to be classified as *districtus* than were the owners of full property. That changed when the word fief came to be applied to the property of nobles who were likely to have rights of jurisdiction. City governments tended to be jealous of independent jurisdictions in the country round about, restricting their independence by providing a right of appeal to city courts and general supervision.[301] Where fiefs were allowed to survive, or were newly granted or created as *feudi oblati* by later medieval lords of cities, on the other hand, they normally carried with them *districtus* and, according to the newer legal formulation, *merum et mixtum imperium* over their inhabitants. Some lords held their jurisdictions in fief even while they were allowed to keep as full property or alods the lands over which they exercised it. By the fifteenth century fief and jurisdiction had come to be effectively synonymous in Lombardy, which helps to explain why estates belonging to churches that had exercised jurisdiction over them long before the new categories had been thought of came to be classified as fiefs. Those who created the special category of *feuda pontificia* for church lands were being tidy-minded and probably did not realize that the very idea of the church holding its property in fief would have been inconceivable before the twelfth century.[302]

---

[299] Budriesi Trombetti, *Vassalli e feudi*; Dean, *Land and Power*, 63. Chittolini does not refer to it.

[300] e.g. Chittolini, 'Infeudazioni'.

[301] Fasoli, 'Ricerche', 251; Budriesi Trombetti, *Vassalli e feudi*, 88 n.; Chittolini, 'Infeudazioni', 65–9.

[302] Bueno da Mesquita, 'Ludovico Sforza'; Chittolini, 'Infeudazioni', 38–58, 66–9; cf. Baldus, *In usus*, f. 5v.

What was originally distinctive about 'feudal jurisdiction' was what was exercised not by fiefholders but over them. Conrad II's ordinance had protected fiefholders by assuring them of the judgement of their peers. In so far as the lords of fiefs were at first most likely to be counts or bishops this did not necessarily mean a separate court for disputes about fiefs. Lords with *districtus* may still have heard cases about fiefs in their normal courts, but, if they did so, they should have allowed fiefholders to be judged separately by other fiefholders—the vassals, as they were now called. We know that the principle of the judgement of peers in cases about fiefs was still recognized by twelfth-century academics and that such cases were still judged accordingly in some courts, but that may be because as yet professional judges and lawyers had not got such a tight grip on the courts as their successors achieved.[303] After the middle of the thirteenth century little seems to be heard of the judgement of peers except in academic writings. Some rural communities that secured charters of liberties included people who were called vassals or whose lands were called fiefs, but none of the charters I have seen mentions the judgement of peers.[304] Presumably the rapid restriction of the protection afforded by the 1037 ordinance to the more or less noble would have excluded these rustic vassals and fiefholders before they knew of it, so that the judgement of peers did not become a matter of popular demand.

It is at first sight more surprising that it did not survive better in citystates, where professional lawyers, who should have known about it from the *Libri Feudorum*, abounded, and where at least some fiefholders were nobles who could afford to employ them. Perhaps the nobility was often too divided to be able to make use of a procedure that depended on consensus. In the Milan customs of 1216 and the Bologna statutes of 1288 the peers of courts seem to be thought of more as witnesses or summoners to investiture than as defenders of a fiefholder who faced eviction.[305] Later, under the *signoria*, there were no regular meetings of estates or parliaments to maintain the solidarity of noble fiefholders against the princes. One place where both the phrase and a form of judgement by peers seem to have survived slightly longer in practice was the kingdom of Sicily. Charles II of Anjou acknowledged that counts, barons, and other holders of fiefs who were accused or brought suits in the royal court ought to be judged by their peers.[306] According to Andrew de Isernia, royal judges decided all cases

[303] Classen, *Studium*, 89–90.

[304] *Statuti della prov. romana*; Toubert, 'Statuts' does not mention it. Chris Wickham kindly tells me that he does not think it appears in those he knows.

[305] *Liber Cons. Mediol.* 119, 123 (XXIV. 7, XXV. 9); *Statuti di Bologna*, 57–8: a vassal here could bring his case before the peers but he could also bring it before the *judex potestatis*.

[306] Pertile, *Storia del diritto*, vi (1), 136–7; cf. 96–100, 226–7.

except those which might involve the confiscation of a quaternated fief. These, but only these, were subject to the judgement of peers.[307] Baronial solidarity during the troubles of the thirteenth century may have helped to preserve this vestige of collective judgement. Elsewhere in Italy, strongly as collective activity developed in the cities, it had become increasingly divorced from legal procedures. Presumably, when professional judges and lawyers ousted older forms of collective judgement from the courts, the judgement of a fiefholder's peers disappeared too.

The way that the rights and obligations of properties called fiefs developed in the later middle ages was determined by the noble character attributed to the fiefs that were recognized as such by the lawyers. Rulers, whether communes or princes, allowed their noble fiefholders special liberties and privileges in return for oaths of fidelity, some kind of military support or at least absence of opposition, and the acceptance of some controls. From the thirteenth century fiefholders—or vassals, as they were now often known—might be required not merely to seek investiture on their own succession and that of their lord, but to turn up regularly and register their fiefs. Far from being a survival of an old feudo-vassalic custom, this was a bureaucratic innovation designed to emphasize a new subordination according to the new law of fiefs.[308] Oaths of fidelity had become entrenched in Italian noble politics, and thus in fiefholding, during the twelfth century. With Obertus's etymology of *feudum* and *fidelitas* reinforced by the insertion of Fulbert's letter and the 'new form of fidelity' into the *Libri Feudorum*, they were equally entrenched in academic law. It is not surprising that scholars who based their ideas of medieval law and society on academic writings about the law of fiefs should have seen fiefs, fidelity, and homage as essentially connected. But, though the lawbooks did not mention it, since it was irrelevant to their concerns, oaths continued to be taken from peasants and others whose property, whatever it was called locally, would not have been classified as fiefs by lawyers, but who were expected to be loyal and obedient *fideles*. If the wording of oaths taken from citizens or peasants followed those in the learned texts, that was because lords employed professional lawyers, not because the idea of taking oaths had been borrowed from some ancient feudo-vassalic practice.[309] When the oaths administered to fiefholders were elaborated or the holding of fiefs from other lords was forbidden, that was because the people who held fiefs were politically dangerous. When the rules of

---

[307] Andreas de Isernia, *In usus feudorum*, ff. 110–111v; cf. ff. 82, 112, 115, 282–3.

[308] Budriesi Trombetti, *Vassalli e feudi*, 57–93; Dean, *Land and Power*, 121–4.

[309] *Statuti prov. romana*, 15, 103, 113–14, 129; Redon, 'Seigneurs et communautés', 195–6; Caetani, *Documenti*, 75–6; Dean, *Land and Power*, 16.

succession to fiefs were restricted it may have been for similar reasons of policy: an advantage of fiefs was that their grant made it possible to alter the normal rules of inheritance either by enlarging or restricting the range of heirs. Some fiefs could be granted to be held at will, without inheritance.[310]

The military obligations of noble fiefs, except those granted to mercenary captains as a way of anchoring them to one state, were, it seems, pretty notional. Nobles might have a military ethos, and their rulers might hope that this included a sense of obligation to loyalty and service, but they had no formal or fixed military duties. In practice the important military obligation was often that which lay on all citizens. Later, under the *signoria*, the employment of mercenaries made fiefs and vassals still more irrelevant to the recruitment of armies, except as inducements and rewards for mercenaries. The extent to which fiefholders were exempt from general taxes or were separately taxed presumably varied according to political circumstances.[311] In Ferrara in 1287, when fiefs were still held from a number of different lords, rather than predominantly from the Este lords of the city, vassals who were citizens did not have to give *collecta* to their lords unless they chose.[312] Succession dues seem to have been paid chiefly by the relatively humble and may derive rather from old peasant obligations than from those of nobles.[313] As for 'feudal aids', they seem, as in France or the kingdom of Sicily, to have been connected to fiefs only in so far as fiefs became the characteristic property of nobles with rights of jurisdiction that enabled them to take such dues from their own tenants and subjects. Since references to the aids seem to be relatively late and the purposes for which they were given look similar, lords may well have copied them from French or Sicilian precedents.[314]

Some restrictions on fiefs were also imposed on other property. From the thirteenth century some cities forbade their citizens to sell property to outsiders and sometimes, if non-citizens paid higher taxes, to acquire it from them. This presumably covered all categories of property. When the transfer of land to churches was prohibited or restricted it also seems to have applied to all kinds of property. Where the alienation of fiefs was more strictly controlled it might be because useful fines could be raised from that

---

[310] Budriesi Trombetti, *Vassalli e feudi*, 87 n.; Dean, *Land and Power*, 16, 51–8, 119, 124, 129–33; Chittolini, 'Infeudazioni', 67.

[311] Bueno da Mesquita, 'Ludovico'; Dean, *Land and Power*, 77–97, 129–33.

[312] Budriesi Trombetti, *Vassalli e feudi*, 87 n.

[313] Manaresi, *Atti di Milano*, no. 76; *Statuti di Bologna*, 58. See index: succession dues.

[314] *Statuti prov. romana*, 5–12 (c. 13–14); Budriesi Trombetti, *Vassalli e feudi*, 89 n.; Dean, *Land and Power*, 116. The *adiutorium nuptiarum sponsalium* owed by *rustici* to S. Alessandro, Bergamo, in 1130 (Manaresi, *Atti di Milano*, no. 3) was of a different nature, since it must have been paid on their own marriages not on an occasion when the lord had exceptional expenses.

kind of property. It could be justified by reference to the texts of the law of fiefs but it cannot, in view of what we know of earlier history, be explained as a survival of ancient feudo-vassalic bonds. Controls on the relatively small properties that were still sometimes called fiefs look more akin to those on peasant property, while those on great noble fiefs were obviously designed, if not merely as excuses for licences or fines, to prevent them from falling into hostile hands. Planning controls on city building and the laws that some cities imposed on the use of agricultural land were applied to all property, including both fiefs and supposedly full property.[315] Lastly, of course, all property remained confiscatable. If the law developed on the basis of Conrad II's ordinance had been applied fiefs might have been better protected than other property, but, as we have seen, the judgement of peers seems to have been forgotten. Fiefs might be seized by their lords for lack of heirs, while other properties would presumably go to the government (which might be the same as the lord of the fiefs), but whether a noble fief was confiscated was a matter of politics, to be justified by government lawyers, rather than of ordinary law.[316]

While rulers and their lawyers elaborated rules about all property, including the fiefs they used to reward and control their most influential and dangerous subjects, the academic lawyers elaborated their theories and arguments about the rules. The problem of explaining whether *dominium* or *proprietas* belonged to the lord or the vassal was resolved—more or less—by distinguishing between *dominium directum* and *dominium utile*.[317] Phrases like *feudum francum*, *feudum rectum*, or *feudum nobile*, which seem to have originated as empty compliments, began to be given distinctive meanings, though, as this generally meant saying that they owed no services, and most of the fiefs that interested lawyers owed few or none anyway, it may not have made much difference in practice.[318] More importantly, the doctrine that all jurisdictions and governmental authority were delegated from above, which had been set out by Frederick I in 1158 and perhaps independently by the kings of Sicily, was elaborated.[319] The muddle of jurisdictions that had evolved over centuries was tidied up into *districtus* and *merum et mixtum imperium* and all were stated to be derived from grants, though the argument was now used to enhance the authority of the rulers of city-states rather than that of the emperor.[320]

[315] Pertile, *Storia del diritto*, iv. 371–7, 384–95; Bocchi, 'Regulation'.
[316] Redon, 'Seigneurs et communautés', 630; Dean, *Land and Power*, 119.
[317] Feenstra, 'Origines du dominium utile'; Willoweit, 'Dominium'.
[318] Dean, *Land and Power*, 124–5; cf. *Stat. Mutine*, 333, 337–8; Baldus, *In usus*, ff. 4, 5v, 92.
[319] Above at nn. 245, 286–7.
[320] Baldus, *In usus*, f. 4; Chittolini, 'Infeudazioni', 69–70, though Frederick's legislation and the arguments of medieval lawyers make it impossible to agree with his n. 143 (on p. 98) that it is anachronistic to see this doctrine as medieval.

Although academic lawyers admitted that the law of fiefs followed custom and therefore varied from place to place as Roman law did not,[321] their
university education in Roman law encouraged a broad eclecticism, so that
north Italians cited cases about kings, barons, and knights through their
reading of—say—John de Blanot, William Durandus the elder, or Andrew
de Isernia.[322] Combined with their tendency to carry on debates that had
started in the earliest texts of the *Libri Feudorum*, this makes it difficult,
without knowledge both of the earlier texts and of the variations of practice through time and place, to know when someone like Baldus is talking
about real practice in the duchy of Milan and when he is simply con-
structing a good academic argument. One thing is fairly clear: though values and norms common to medieval Europe undoubtedly underlay much
of the professional law of fiefs, they cannot be deduced directly from the
rules and practices that occur in the lawbooks or from the justifications that
the writers adduced for them. Many rules were the product of the new law
and the new government, while the justifications, however historical in
form, were rationalizations that do not seem to make much sense of the evidence we have of earlier rules and practices. Baldus thought that early
twelfth-century statements of ancient Lombard law represented the rigour
of feudal custom. He also repeated the myth, first stated in treatise 1a of
the Antiqua and slightly elaborated in the vulgate *Libri*, about the origin of
fiefs and their gradual progress towards inheritance and security.[323] The
scene was set for the legal historians of the sixteenth and seventeenth centuries to study the middle ages through the history of fiefs and for the eighteenth century to turn it into the history of feudalism.

## 6.12. *Conclusion*

Because the traditional model of non-Marxist feudalism was constructed
on the basis of the academic law about fiefs that developed first of all in
twelfth-century Italy, some of the evidence of so-called feudo-vassalic
institutions from twelfth-century and later medieval Italy fits it quite well.
Just as notable, however, are the parts of the model that do not fit. These
include all the assertions or suggestions that fiefs were the archetypal form
of noble property before the twelfth century, that they derived from grants
of land made by early medieval rulers in return for military service, and
that their rights and obligations were a reflection of general social norms.
Italy provides in some ways better evidence than any other part of Europe

---

[321] Lehmann, *Langobardische Lehnrecht*, 115 (*Ant.* VIII. 1), 165, 203; Baldus, *In usus*, ff. 2v, 41.
[322] See the list of authorities in Baldus, *In usus*, f. 2v as well as his citations throughout.
[323] Ibid. ff. 9, 10v.

that late medieval fiefs were a creation of the academic and professional law and of the new bureaucratic government that developed together from the twelfth century. In so far as the new law started from older practices, as it undoubtedly did, they were not, so far as we know, practices developed by noble warrior lords and their followers but by the clergy, partly under royal pressure, for the administration of church lands. Some similar practices were applied on royal and, more obscurely, on noble estates, but they were probably less well developed and offered fewer precedents for the lawyers to work from. If one needs to find an intermediate link between earlier church practices and those developed—rather patchily—by Frederick Barbarossa it is probably to be found in the ways that city governments dealt with local nobles, not in the way that nobles dealt with their own followers or tenants.

The estates that came to be called fiefs by professional lawyers in the twelfth century and later came to have rather different rights and obligations both from the earlier kind of fiefs that had been held from churches and from the full property that had characteristically been held by nobles. That was because the rights and obligations of all property were changing with changes in government and law. When nobles had their property turned into fiefs in the twelfth century their property rights as such were normally almost, if not entirely, unaffected: what they acknowledged was a merely political subjection. Later their rights might, according to political circumstances, become more circumscribed. At the same time, however, their political subordination was mitigated by their extensive rights of jurisdiction. Historians of Italian feudalism often emphasize oaths of fidelity—sometimes taking them as evidence of actual fiefholding—and 'feudal jurisdiction' or 'immunity'. These were indeed characteristic of the political and legal arrangements about noble land that were developed from the twelfth century. Earlier, customary law about free or noble property must have differed in many ways from place to place and time to time. It also seems to have differed (except in the Norman south) from the customs that obtained in France in two ways that have not, I think, been noticed: namely in the maintenance of formal freedom of alienation and in the absence of any distinction between acquired and inherited property. But the most distinctive characteristics of the law that came to govern Italian fiefs were produced not by customary law or by any peculiarity of Italian noble society. The feudal law of Italy was an academic and professional law that was being developed in the cities of north Italy even before the end of the eleventh century. It was an early and notable part of what is called the twelfth-century renaissance and one that has not received its due attention.

# 7

# THE KINGDOM OF FRANCE, 1100–1300

## 7.1. *The transition to professional law and government*

THE evidence that I have examined for the terminology of property in twelfth-century France is at first confusing. On the one hand the growth of evidence confirms the suspicion expressed at the end of chapter 5 that, as rulers and landlords became more demanding and more effective, the distinction between full and subordinate property became in some ways blurred. On the other hand, there is also evidence that during the twelfth century rulers began to exploit a distinction between what the records explicitly call alods and fiefs. By the thirteenth century it is clear that this was not the same distinction as that drawn in the ninth century between alods and benefices. What we seem to have is a new terminology that gradually resulted in the construction of new categories. By the thirteenth century the word alod was restricted in many areas, chiefly if not exclusively, to the property of the relatively humble, while the property of people of high status, which would once have been considered alodial, was described as fiefs. Fiefholders were beginning to be occasionally called vassals, though this was still rare and probably indicates the influence of lawyers with some knowledge of the academic law of fiefs. Exceptions and anomalies were many and various, not least because the actual rights and obligations of property were seldom changed when the words changed. Rationalization of past custom into rules so as to create categories of even approximate coherence and consistency was a slow business which would be the work of professional and academic lawyers over centuries.

In the twelfth century, though it is too early to talk about a legal profession in France, it looks as though government at almost every level, including the government of larger estates, was beginning to use men who were at least semi-professionals in the job of making records and arguing from them. Grants of liberties and customs show that some of the subjects of governments were learning to argue back and play the system for themselves. The difficulty for rulers was that the universal acceptance of the premisses of customary law made it impossible to ignore custom, particularly when it had already been argued about and, 'since what is uncertain

258

cannot well be preserved',[1] recorded. Each time that Philip Augustus and his successors extended their control over another part of the kingdom, they and their servants had to work within a different set of variations in terminology and practice. As time went by more royal and higher seigniorial servants came to the job after acquiring the rudiments of an academic education in Roman law, which stimulated them to intelligent rationalization, fitting as much as they could of the terminology and conditions they found into a few categories, creating hybrid categories (*franc-fief, franc vilenage*, etc.) to cover the most anomalous bits, and sometimes introducing a few terms from Roman law or the *Libri Feudorum* to lend tone to the result.[2] In this process the difference between the supposedly Roman law of the south and the supposedly customary law of the north was probably much less important than later professional wrangles and historical traditions have claimed.[3] There does not seem to be much reason to suppose that the administrators and lawyers used by thirteenth-century kings of France and their northern nobles were any less competent and resourceful (and sometimes unscrupulous) than the lawyers of the south. The particular legal system any of them used was less important than the way in which they used it so as to turn old and customary notions about property into something more systematic and more advantageous to their employers or clients. Since rulers and their advisers, both in north and south, lived within a world in which the justification of present law was either present consensus or past custom, or, preferably, both, they naturally tried to secure consensus by appealing to ancient custom. Whatever success their appeals to history had with their contemporaries, modern historians should be more critical. What we know about the rules of property before the age of professional law makes it impossible to see the category of the fief, as it came to be understood in late medieval France, as having emerged directly from social relationships between lords and vassals in the earlier middle ages. It may still be too teleological to envisage fiefs as a distinct and coherent category of property before 1300, but in so far as it would become one later it was because of legal arguments that had been provoked by the way that government developed in the twelfth and thirteenth centuries.

---

[1] ... *quia quod incertum est bene non potest custodiri*: Lafaille, *Annales*, preuves, 4.
[2] Richardot, 'Franc-fiefs', 'Fief roturier', and 'A propos des personnes'; Vidal, '*Feudum honoratum*'; Feenstra, 'L'Emphytéose', 1308–11; Giordanengo, *Droit féodal*, 106–22, 145.
[3] Ourliac, 'L'Esprit du droit méridional' and 'Législation'; cf. Petot, 'Droit commun'.

## 7.2. *Words and concepts: the twelfth century*

The first hard evidence I have found for a secular lord's deliberate conversion of his subjects' alods into fiefs held from him comes from the far south
of the kingdom. That is not surprising, once we have got beyond traditional stereotypes about the heartland of feudalism in the north. What
these conversions—the creation of what came to be called *fiefs de reprise*—
needed was a clear concept of both alods and fiefs. In the south the word
alod seems to have continued to be used of noble properties while it went
out of use in the north. The word fief and its derivatives seem meanwhile
to have retained more unambiguous connotations of subordination. If, as is
not impossible, the idea of *fiefs de reprise* originated in south France, it may
have been partly because common usage thus made the contrast more
obvious. However that may be, the idea may have occurred not so much to
southern nobles themselves but to their legal advisers. This hypothesis,
which must be tentative in view of the chance survival and finding of evidence, is suggested by the fact that the first deliberate creation of *fiefs de
reprise* that I have found took place at Montpellier.

Montpellier is known to have been an early centre of the teaching
of Roman law. There were notaries and other professional or semi-
professional lawyers there by the 1130s, and Placentinus taught Roman law
there later in the century.[4] Classen thought that there might have been
students from Provence in Pisa in the 1120s, and it is not impossible that
by then students from Montpellier or thereabouts, only a little further
west, had studied in Lombardy or that Lombard lawyers had got as far as
Montpellier.[5] If so—and, again, this is all conjecture—influence may not
all have gone in one direction. The first *feudo oblato* that seems to be
recorded in Lombardy dates from 1126 and the first to use the word alod
from 1132.[6] The first *fiefs de reprise*, explicitly converting the alods of four
neighbouring castellans to fiefs, are recorded at Montpellier in 1112–14.
They look very like the result of a deliberate policy.[7] In Lombardy the
interpretation of Conrad II's ordinance had produced the idea of a fief as
permanently heritable property, with few or no obligations beyond those
of full property and with perhaps even greater security.[8] The idea of per-
suading nobles to accept this kind of honourable property instead of their
alods—the word alod being probably more familiar in south France than
in Lombardy—may have originated at Montpellier. Lawyers in south

---

[4] Gouron, 'Les Étapes' and 'Autour de Placentin'.
[5] Classen, *Studium*, 39–40; Baumel, *Histoire*, 101–4, 142–4, 175–83.
[6] Chapter 6.9.           [7] *Liber Instrumentorum*, nos. 402, 404–5, 432–4, 436–8, 507–23.
[8] Chapter 6.5–6.

France who had studied Lombard or Roman law texts may even have
extended their studies to the texts of the Frankish law that at least some
people in the area may still have thought of as their own.[9] If they did they
would have met alods there as well as in current usage.

Irrespective of all this speculation, the remarkable cartulary that was
made for William VIII (d. 1202), the last independent lord of Montpellier
before his lordship passed to the king of Aragon, shows that for almost a
century he and his ancestors had made a practice of getting the lords of
fortresses round about to surrender their alodial rights in them, often for a
sizeable price, and take them back as fiefs, to be held for ever.[10] It is not
immediately obvious how much more this involved than the older southern practice of getting oaths of fidelity from castellans.[11] The terms of the
grants were various and show that a mere statement that property was to
be held in fief did not automatically define its obligations. Conditions
needed to be specified. In some charters the immediate heirs were more
narrowly defined than in others;[12] some fortresses were to be surrendered
to the lord on demand while others were not.[13] The texts of the oaths taken
by the holders of many of these castles are preserved, sometimes with a
note that homage was done as well, though it is hard to know how much
that would have increased the obligations of the oath. Becoming someone's
man, which is what historians gloss as homage (and which had already been
sometimes denoted by the words *hominium* or *homagium*), seems as yet to
have involved very various relationships.[14] Some castellans took oaths
without apparently having to convert their alods into fiefs: in 1196 one of
these did homage to William VIII of Montpellier and swore to surrender
his castle on demand.[15] Homage, it seems, still did not always and
unequivocally entail fiefholding. In 1201 William got another castellan,
who had acquired his castellany by marriage, to acknowledge that he, his
wife, and their daughter held it *ad feudum honoratum* from William. The

[9] Though consciousness of this may have declined since William I of Montpellier referred to
*lex mea salica* (i.e. his Frankish law) in 985: *Liber Instrumentorum*, no. 70; cf. Poly and Bournazel,
*Mutation féodale*, 331–3.

[10] *Liber Instrumentorum, passim.* For the earliest cases, above, n. 7. In the 1130s and 1140s the
phrase *ad feudum et ad totas* (or *totos* or *omnes*) *honores* was used (ibid. nos. 104, 235, 309, 531). It
was also used in the cartulary's texts of the same period in connection with the lord of
Montpellier's tenure of comital rights (nos. 66–7, 71, 72) and of his tenure of Tortosa, although
it was not in the count of Barceiona's charter for this (nos. 95, 152). The *Liber Instrumentorum*
deserves much fuller and more careful use than I have been able to give it.

[11] Chapter 5, at n. 49. The example of the counts of Barcelona may have been influential,
though apparently their purchases and regrants of castles did not yet normally use the word fief
for the new holding: Bonnassie, *Catalogne*, 687–706, 746–68; Bisson, 'Feudalism', 156. Cf.
Giordanengo, 'Vocabulaire et formulaires'.

[12] e.g. *Liber Instrumentorum*, nos. 538, 556, 566.

[13] e.g. ibid. nos. 416, 519, 533, 538, 566.

[14] See index: homage.

[15] *Liber Instrumentorum*, no. 460.

predecessors of this castellan had regularly taken oaths to the lords of Montpellier but none seems to have made any formal surrender, nor did William apparently pay anything for the agreement of 1201. The new and honourable fiefholder did homage and agreed to surrender his castle on demand, though it was also agreed that he held his *dominium, dominationem, et senorivum* as well as his father-in-law had ever had and held it.[16] It looks as though, as the lords of Montpellier extended their military and political authority, the castellans around had come to accept that subjection, however its conditions might vary, might mean accepting that one's property was a fief rather than an alod. The analogies with the use of *feudi oblati* by north Italian cities in the same period are striking. It is tempting to guess that lawyers trained in the schools had a hand in the scheme. Meanwhile, of course, whatever was intended, those who now became fiefholders, like those who simply took oaths, were not always obedient and submissive.[17]

How the lords of Montpellier acquired and extended their own rights in their lordship is obscure but less complicated and difficult to understand if one does not start by imposing all the rules of the later law of fiefs on the skimpy data. In 985 the count of neighbouring Mauguio had made over property at Montpellier to William I, apparently with full rights, *sicut lex mea* (i.e. William's) *salica commorat*.[18] At various times in the twelfth century the count of Mauguio granted and confirmed various comital rights over roads and minting to the lord of Montpellier *ad feudum* and received homage for them, but that did not apparently affect the character of the rest of the lord's right in his lordship. What, if anything, the fief that the lords of Montpellier held from the count in 1121 and 1146 consisted of beyond these rights is unclear.[19] In 1164 William VII and the count swore mutual oaths of fidelity to each other, but without apparently doing homage in either direction, in much the same form that was used when such oaths implied subordination.[20] In 1171 a would-be count of Mauguio made a bid for support by granting his predecessor's rights in two castellanies *in perpetuum jure certi feudi* to one of William VI's sons in return for nothing more than homage and *albergum* (an obligation to provide billets or a payment instead) for ten knights a year.[21] In 1190 William VIII acknowledged that he held from the count of Toulouse and Mauguio *ad feudum francum et honoratum*, not only the comital rights that he already

---

[16] *Liber Instrumentorum*, no. 336; cf. 448. Cf. Vidal, '*Feudum honoratum*'.
[17] e.g. *Liber Instrumentorum*, nos. 122, 402–21.
[18] Ibid. no. 70. Baumel, *Histoire*, 41–3, despite his respect for feudalist doctrine, seems to me to make good sense of this.
[19] *Liber Instrumentorum*, nos. 57–91, 94–5; Baumel, *Histoire*, 96–7, 109–21.
[20] *Liber Instrumentorum*, no. 79.                              [21] Ibid. no. 86; cf. no. 93.

held from him, but also several dependent castellanies in which William's forebears had acquired full alodial rights decades earlier. He did homage but did not have to agree to surrender the castles.[22] Four years later, when the count gave up his claim to another castle which William's great-grandfather had acquired in 1112, the agreement took the form of the count's grant of it to William *in feudum*, with provisions for its surrender on each succession on either side as well as once a year and, if required, in war.[23] Obviously all these transactions took careful negotiation. Phrases like *ad feudum honoratum* or *ad feudum francum et honoratum* were not used because fiefs carried a standard package of obligations and restrictions of rights which were thereby mitigated or waived. As in Italy at the same period, they were probably used because the word fief implied an acceptance of superior authority that could more easily be accepted by those who had hitherto been totally independent if it were wrapped up with ideas of honour and freedom.[24]

Meanwhile the lords of Montpellier had frequent quarrels with the bishops of Maguelone, who had property and rights in Montpellier as well as lordship over the suburb of Montpelliéret, where the lords of the town proper also had property. Complicated disputes between the bishop and William V were settled about 1090, when, *inter alia*, the bishop allowed William to keep the whole *fevum* his predecessors had held while William surrendered any claim in the churches of Montpellier and Montpelliéret and in property of the church of Maguelone that he had apparently seized or tried to seize.[25] What William's fief consisted of is unclear. In 1140 William VI acknowledged that he held property *ad feudum* from the church of Maguelone and had done homage for it. His homage also apparently covered the town, but that may mean simply that the good behaviour he promised covered it all.[26] On the other hand the bishop may have claimed more: in 1156 he got a royal charter or charters in which he claimed the lordship of Montpellier as a fief of his church, but, apart from the fact that William might not have agreed, it is not clear that the bishop meant that the whole town was church property.[27]

---

[22] Ibid. no. 87; cf. no. 89.     [23] Ibid. no. 88.

[24] Cf. chapter 6, at n. 233.     [25] *Liber Instrumentorum*, nos. 40-1; Baumel, *Histoire*, 76-81.

[26] *Liber Instrumentorum*, nos. 43, 55.

[27] *Layettes*, i, nos. 141, 143. The documents cited by Lewis ('Seigneurial Administration') from *Liber Instrumentorum* do not seem to me to support his contention that the bishop was 'overlord' of the 'section of Montpellier' that he says was all the lords of Montpellier held. Only the oath of 1140 seems to mention homage, while the two documents that he says showed appeals going from the lord of Montpellier's court to that of the bishop concern respectively a testament and a marriage. The relations of the lords of Montpellier with the papacy seem to have even less feudo-vassalic implications than did those of the counts of Mauguio, for which see chapter 5, at nn. 68-71.

Political and property relations within the lordship of Montpellier are complicated for us by the fact that Montpellier was by now a flourishing town. The rules of urban property are commonly seen as having developed outside the traditional framework of feudal land tenure. It may, however, be more realistic to envisage them as having developed along one line from the original norm of full or alodial rights while rural property developed along another. By the twelfth century the word alod may have been going out of use, or have already gone out of use, in the town of Montpellier, as it did in other towns.[28] It is occasionally used in the cartulary for property within the lordship, but *honor* was also used, whether as a synonym for alod or, perhaps, to denote properties of uncertain status. Some properties were conveyed without either word being used.[29] In 1113 William V declared that, according to custom going back to his grandfather's day, no burgess of the town could give, sell, or pledge property (*suum honorem*), including by way of marriage settlement, to a knight, church, or clerk (*militi vel sancto vel clerico*).[30] Though allusions to this custom continued to be made through the century, the custumal made at the end of the century does not refer to it, but simply sets out the rules of inheritance and says that the men (*homines*) of Montpellier could dispose of property freely, though purchasers had to pay a due (*consilium*; also called *laudimium*) to the lord.[31] At least some of those who owned property that looks like that described in the custumal owed regular rents in money or kind, including *albergum*, though, probably in consequence of a lively property market, some dues as well as some rents were owed by one subject of the lord to another.[32] Properties that William VIII acquired in 1200 and 1202 were described as free alods in the cartulary, but when the texts of the two charters use the phrases *pro libero alodio* and *pro libero et absoluto alodio* the emphasis is rather on the completeness of what he got than on what the vendors had had.[33] There were other rentpayers on the lord's own estate (*condamina*). There were also people whom the cartulary refers to as *feudales* or *feudatarii* or as holding *ad feodum* or *nomine feudi* from the lord or from someone else. Where this last group fitted in I do not know, but some were knights or soldiers (*milites*) whose primary obligations were presumably military. Some of them if not all, however, also owed *consilium* and some

---

[28] References to the *allodiation* of property in Flemish towns, for instance, seem to be using the word because it is familiar to historians rather than because it is in the documents: e.g. Ganshof, 'Le Droit urbain', 400–1.

[29] *Liber Instrumentorum*, nos. 172–4, 180–1, 225, 235, 465 (note the heading). For the use of *honor* for property apparently carrying full rights: ibid., e.g. nos. 92, 95, 100–1, 104, 225, 313, 478, 556.

[30] Ibid. no. 127.          [31] Ibid. no. 244; cf. e.g. nos. 174, 225; *Layettes*, i, no. 721 (4, 11, 14).

[32] *Liber Instrumentorum*, nos. 172–4, 179, 181, 249–60.          [33] Ibid. nos. 307, 570.

kind of annual payments. A slightly later and fuller version of the customs of Montpellier says that all the men of the town owed some kind of military service (*hosta et cavalgata*).[34] It seems likely that the rights and obligations of holders of the various types of property within the lordship (apart from that of humbler and less free peasants) were more similar to each other than any of them were to the rights and obligations of the noble alodholders and fiefholders outside with whom the lord negotiated on a more equal footing.

The apparently careful drafting of many of the charters in the cartulary, as well as its whole compilation and arrangement, shows that the lords of Montpellier had some exceptional servants. I have hazarded the guess that the advice they gave profited from contacts with Lombard lawyers. But that does not imply that the lawyers of Montpellier adopted all the doctrines that were developed in Italy as the law of fiefs was elaborated or that they had read any of the early texts that went into the *Libri Feudorum*. The documents in the cartulary do not, for instance, seem to favour the word vassal. Over the border of the kingdom in Dauphiné, where rather similar uses of oaths of fidelity and *fiefs de reprise* have been found in the twelfth century, the influence of the *Libri* has not been found before the 1220s.[35] But, however they were trained, lawyers were well enough known in Montpellier to be distrusted by the time when the customs of the lordship were written into the cartulary: litigants were not supposed to employ trained lawyers (*legiste*) in the court of Montpellier.[36] Clearly that did not stop the lord using them on his conveyancing,[37] but even the most skilful and academically minded lawyers could not create tidy categories at a stroke out of the confusion of the terminology, notions, and phenomena presented to them by custom. If anything, by superimposing new words and new hybrid categories, they made it all more complicated.

I have found twelfth-century evidence of some episodes in the north that look like the creation of *fiefs de reprise*. As in Montpellier the word used in these transactions was fief (or in one case *casamentum*) rather than benefice. According to Gislebert of Mons, writing nearly thirty years later, the count of Flanders in 1167 used the conversion of an alod into a fief to be held from himself as a means of extending his power in Vermandois,

---

[34] Ibid. nos. 104 (p. 221: rights over *firmancias et placita militum*); 177, 247; *Layettes*, i, no. 721 (88); Baumel, *Histoire*, 227–8.
[35] Giordanengo, *Droit féodal*, 79, 111, 189, 192, 198–200; on Provence: Giordanengo, 'Vocabulaire romanisant'.
[36] *Liber Instrumentorum*, no. 244; *Layettes*, i, no. 721 (8).
[37] Gouron, 'Autour de Placentin', 341–5. *Liber Instrumentorum*, no. 476 (1191) refers to gifts *inter vivos*, and no. 570 (1202) to *res corporales et incorporales, actiones, peticiones, persecutiones in rem, personales vel mixtas*. For similar developments just outside the kingdom: Giordanengo, *Droit féodal*, esp. 112–22; Poly, *Provence*, 151 n. 119.

and in 1185 a castellan in the area, who had long held his castle from the count, transferred it to the king and received it back in fief.[38] The acknowledgement of a modicum of political subordination, rather than any decrease in rights of property or any significant increase in specific obligations, was presumably the issue here, as it was in Montpellier and Italy. The same probably applies in 1172, when Louis VII, after one of his forays into Burgundy, gave back to the count of Mâcon *in casamentum* three fortresses that he had taken from him and that the count had presumably held with full rights before this.[39] A year later Raymond of Toulouse is said to have become the man of Henry II and his sons for Toulouse, which he was to hold from them *in feudo et hereditate*, though, as this phrase comes in an English chronicle and echoes English usage, it should not be taken too literally as a statement of what the count thought happened.[40] On the other hand another English chronicler, Ralph of Diss, did not use that phrase but did use the word alod, which was rare in England, when he recorded a change in status that he obviously considered significant: in 1181 the count of Sancerre, who sided with the count of Flanders against King Philip, lowered the royal dignity by subjecting his fortress of Saint-Brisson (Loiret) to the lordship or rule (*dominationi*) of the count and doing homage to him for it. Saint-Brisson had been held of old *allodii jure* and the transaction thus reduced it from liberty to shameful servitude. Ralph did not spell out servitude as fiefholding, but he may have meant that.[41] It would be nice to know if any of these cases could be traced to influences either direct from Italy or from Montpellier or anywhere else in the south where similar practices may have already been adopted.

Any such influences as there may have been were neither pervasive nor consistent. The word fief was sometimes being used in ways that look new, but sometimes it was used in much the same varied or indefinite ways as it had been used in the eleventh century, while few cases of either old or new usage fit neatly into the framework either of the *Libri Feudorum* or of the feudo-vassalic structure that historians have built on it. According to a charter of 1123 Philip I had granted Stephen the marshal two-thirds of the tolls on bread at Paris *in feodo*. Now Louis VI gave them to Stephen *in jure perpetuo et in feodo et ut ligio homini nostro*, and, as Stephen had already given half the tolls to his son-in-law, Louis now made the son-in-law's right perpetual too. Like Stephen, the son-in-law was to hold his share

---

[38] Gislebert of Mons, *Chronique*, 88, 180.

[39] *Cart. Saint-Vincent de Mâcon*, no. 631; Duby, *Société mâconnaise*, 414.

[40] *Chron. of Henry II and Ric. I*, i. 36; *Oxford Dict. Med. Latin*, 920 (5e). Cf. Benjamin, 'A Forty Years War'.

[41] Ralph Diceto, *Opera*, ii. 9; for Saint-Brisson: Suger, *Vie de Louis VI*, 272.

directly from the king *in feodo et in ligietate hominii*.[42] The combination of *feodum* with *jus perpetuum* seems to be new. On a traditional interpretation it would simply exemplify the completion of the well-known trend towards the full heritability of fiefs, but there is no reason to suppose that either Louis or Stephen, or both of them, thought that all properties called fiefs ought to be inherited, and that Philip's charter had therefore been somehow defective or anomalous. At least as late as the reign of Philip Augustus royal grants in fief were sometimes made for life.[43] Contrasts were sometimes made, as they had been in the eleventh century, between alods and fiefs, but the evidence does not suggest that these two words were consistently used to define what were generally recognized as the two main categories of property. Other contrasts could be drawn. In 1129 a fief was contrasted with a benefice: the context leaves it unclear whether being a benefice meant that it had fewer obligations or that it formed part of a church's endowment—or something quite different from either.[44] Charters dealing with large lordships could also contrast land held in fief from land held in domain.[45] In such cases what was held in fief seems simply to have been what was under the rule of the owner of the lordship, as distinct from his immediate property within it: the rights and conditions of this subordinate property were probably not at issue. A royal charter of 1168 used the word fief in four ways: it confirmed a grant by one Baucendus of property *tam in terris quam in nemoribus quam in feodis*, which altogether constituted a fief, commonly called a knight's fief, which was held from the fief of someone else (*de cujus feodo Baucendus totum tenebat ipsum feodum qui vulgo feodus militum dicitur*).[46]

Throughout the century the kings of France continued to make grants of land to laymen (as well, of course, as to churches) carrying what appear to be full rights of the traditional sort, with no mention of holding in fief.[47] They also confirmed transactions and adjudicated in disputes about apparently full property without always seizing the chance of declaring it to be anything less.[48] The count of Ponthieu, also in the area of supposedly classic feudalism, sometimes did the same, while all the grants of Norman

---

[42] *Cart. gén. de Paris*, no. 199; cf. Tabuteau, *Transfers*, 305 (n. 146).

[43] *Rec. Philippe Auguste*, nos. 769, 950, 1280.          [44] Didier, *Droits de fiefs*, 6 n.

[45] Tardif, *Monuments*, no. 667 (the earliest example I have happened to notice, though the contrast is implied much earlier, e.g. Tabuteau, *Transfers*, n. 1 on p. 364); *Rec. Philippe Auguste*, nos. 399, 517, 519, 621, 1360; Lot and Fawtier, *Histoire des institutions*, ii. 105. But in *Cart. Château-du-Loir*, no. 150, the *feodum et dominium* conveyed seem to be the same thing.

[46] Tardif, *Monuments*, no. 609. Part of the property had been acquired, part was inherited.

[47] *Cart. gén. de Paris*, no. 161; Tardif, *Monuments*, no. 420; cf. Milo de Bray's *honor*, held *jure hereditario*, translated (Suger, *Vie de Louis VI*, 126–7) as *son fief*; Luchaire, *Actes de Louis VII*, p. 374 (no. 164); *Rec. Philippe Auguste*, nos. 106, 134, 166, 402, 1655, 1767.

[48] *Hist. gloriosi regis Ludovici*, 164–5; *Rec. de Montmartre*, 93; Duchesne, *Hist. Francorum Scriptores*, 584–5; *Rec. Philippe Auguste*, nos. 55, 398, 581, 645, 799, 895.

property made by Henry II which are in print appear to carry the normal full rights.[49] Normans with property in England would have been accustomed to having it described as fiefs and the word may therefore have sometimes been applied to full property in Normandy too, but here the connotations of political subordination that made it useful in Montpellier or Italy or occasionally elsewhere in the north cannot have been important. The property-holding subjects of the dukes of Normandy, though sometimes rebellious, were already well accustomed to being under government. What fief means in the great list of *feoda Campanie* made for the count of Champagne in 1172 is hard to say, but it is very improbable that predecessors of all of the two thousand or so people listed, or even most of them, had been granted lands from predecessors of the count, had held it under him with less than the usual full rights, or had had their lands formally converted into fiefs. Whether or not those listed in 1172 would all have accepted the word fief as applied to their lands, they probably thought that they had the same rights in them as their ancestors had enjoyed.[50]

By and large, what is new seems in the north to come less from any direct influence from the academic law of Italy than from the way that lords everywhere were beginning to extend their power and authority through more professional government and estate management, including the more systematic collection of dues and holding of courts, better record-keeping, and the extension of jurisdiction over more people and more solid blocks of territory. None of this seems to have relied primarily, if at all, on property relations of a merely feudo-vassalic kind. The word vassal, meanwhile, continued to be used very rarely in documentary sources and chronicles, while its use in vernacular literature did not generally have the feudo-vassalic sense that the editors of literary texts seem compelled to suggest was primary.[51] As in Montpellier, homage does not always imply fiefholding. In 1112 the beneficiary of a grant from Louis VI of property that was to be held *hereditario jure . . . in perpetuum* nevertheless did homage for it.[52] Galbert of Bruges's description of people doing fealty and homage to the new count of Flanders in 1127 has often been cited as exemplifying the ceremony of 'entry into vassalage', but Galbert seems to be describing the recognition of a new ruler by his subjects. Those who held *feoda* and *officia* from the count did homage, but so did many others, including many

---

[49] *Rec. comtes de Pontieu*, nos. 80, 83, 100, 160, 167: no. 139 combines *in feodum et homagium* with perpetual and hereditary right (cf. Philip Augustus's grants, below); *Rec. Henri II*, nos. 40, 94–5, 328, 398, 492, 547, 606, 709, 723.

[50] Longnon, *Documents*, i. 1–74; cf. Evergates, *Feudal Society*, 61–74, 234 (n. 4).

[51] Chapter 2 n. 19. For the rarity of 'vassal' in twelfth-century royal documents: Luchaire, *Actes de Louis VII*, p. 380 n.

[52] *Cart. gén de Paris*, no. 161.

citizens of Bruges who are very unlikely to have held their lands in fief. Immediately after the last count's murder, according to Galbert, the lord of Ypres, who wanted to make himself count, captured merchants visiting the fair there, wherever they came from, and made them give security, swear fidelity, and even, it seems, do homage to him.[53] On that occasion *hominium* did not even imply being a permanent resident and subject. Throughout the century the significance of oaths and ceremonies seems to have depended on circumstances and the status of the parties, and so did the meaning of words like *homagium, hominium, dominus ligius* or *homo ligius*, and *commendare*.[54] There was as yet no standard text or court to privilege any particular use.

A good many of those listed as apparently owing some sort of duty or dues to the count of Champagne in 1172 are described as *ligii* or *ligei*. *Ligius* has been taken to mean that 'liege homage' had been done.[55] It may well be that everyone in the list had performed a rite of homage and some had done a special, 'liege homage', but procedures and records were probably less carefully distinguished, standardized, and regular than they would become in the thirteenth century. Homage itself is mentioned much more rarely than it would be in the later Champagne lists.[56] Whether or not all those listed in 1172 had gone through a recognized ceremony or taken an oath, and whatever the rights and obligations attached to their property, the reason why they were entered in the count's records is surely that he or his officials must have reckoned that all the people here were in one way or another his men.[57] So, of course, were many other people, but those listed were presumably the ones who owed enough, or whose status was high enough, to make it worth listing them individually, whatever the precise nature of their bond with the count and whatever words were used to describe it. The people holding mills or parts of mills, for instance, may be there because of the financial, rather than the military, value of their obligations and are less likely than, for instance, the owners of the 'great fiefs' at the end of the list to have been in close relations with the count. Like

[53] Galbert, *Histoire*, 35 (accepting the reading suggested by Thomas, 'Notes'), 83, 87, 89–90. Cf. e.g. Ganshof, *Feudalism*, 71 (a good example how translations introduce the word vassal); Le Goff, 'Rituel symbolique', 358–60.

[54] Duparc, 'Commendise' and 'Libres et hommes liges'; for 'liege' relations cf. Gislebert of Mons, *Chronique*, e.g. 10–12, 250–3, and for the differences of interpretation late in the thirteenth century cf. William Durandus, *Speculum Juris*, pts. 3 and 4, 307.

[55] e.g. Evergates, *Feudal Society*, 66.

[56] Though see Longnon, *Documents*, i, nos. 1, 488–90, 770.

[57] Though only a few are so described. I noted Longnon, *Documents*, i, nos. 1954, 1956–8, 1974, 1989, 1991. People owing custody but not called *ligius*: ibid., e.g. nos. 109–14, 116, 124, 127–30. Neither owing custody nor called *ligius*: nos. 150–1, 153–9, 161–9. The intermixture of categories at these points (among others) makes the difference look more than accidental, but it is hard to be sure what it means.

ecclesiastical lords, and probably like many other counts and lesser lay lords whose records have not survived, the count of Champagne probably wanted to have records of obligations of all sorts, including any obligations owed to other lords by people in what he thought of as their patch, so that they could exert their authority more effectively and withstand rivals.[58]

The previous two centuries must have obscured the sense that everyone in the kingdom might be considered the king's subjects or men, but Abbot Suger, for instance, probably thought they were. He may have thought that all great men owed homage to the king, though if, as seems probable, many took up their inheritances without doing it, he must have realized it. The area within which the king was accustomed to give orders and get them obeyed was limited—regrettably so in Suger's eyes—so that lords outside it might object to his interference with their customary rights, but there is no evidence that they had any ideas of feudal hierarchy that would have inhibited the king from dealing directly with their subjects. Theories of that sort would only later be worked out by lawyers and constitutional theorists to provide arguments to suit the circumstances of their own times and the interests of their clients. Suger's statements about the delicate relation between the king's rights in the Vexin and those of Saint-Denis have often been seen as exemplifying feudo-vassalic structures, but other interpretations fit the evidence less anachronistically. According to Suger, the Vexin was *proprium feodum* of Saint-Denis. In his life of Louis VI he says that Louis acknowledged that he held it from the church and took its standard from the altar as if from his lord. Later Suger wrote that Louis would have done homage (*hominium*) for the county if he had not been king.[59] It has been suggested that abbot and king had in fact done a deal over the Vexin that conveniently obscured the shaky nature of both their titles.[60] That looks credible but, even if there had been nothing to hide, the past history of homage suggests that Suger was not concerned with whether Louis was or was not a 'vassal'—a word that, incidentally, Suger did not use. What he was anxious to stress was the completeness of Saint-Denis's rights, while at the same time avoiding any suggestion that the king was in a position of subordination. Louis VII held land in the lordships of other subjects without apparently making any fuss about it, and presumably without doing homage.[61]

In 1185 Philip Augustus refused to do homage to the bishop of Amiens for the county of Amiens, which he had just acquired. The reason for his

---

[58] Cf. Archives Nationales, LL 1157 (a Saint-Denis cartulary), ff. 240–2, of which Dr Lindy Grant kindly showed me a photocopy and which records a list of garrison services and other dues owed to a tenant of the abbey.

[59] Suger, *Vie de Louis VI*, 220, and *Œuvres*, 161–2.                    [60] Barroux, 'L'Abbé Suger'.

[61] Luchaire, *Actes de Louis VII*, p. 386 (no. 268); id., *Institutions*, ii. 327.

refusal, according to his charter, was that the king should not do homage to anyone. In a similar charter of 1192 Philip admitted that his predecessors were known to have done homage for the fief of Hesdin, but in 1213 he declared that they had not been accustomed to do it to anyone.[62] All this accords well enough with the evidence that kings of France were beginning to claim the dignity and standing that kings were expected to have, without bringing in theories of vassalage and feudal hierarchy to explain it. When Suger referred to the fidelity that was owed to the kingdom and crown he was more probably thinking of a duty owed from the whole kingdom than merely from either those whom historians call his vassals or from what they call the royal domain.[63] Louis VII and Philip Augustus both on occasion took churches under their protection and promised that they should remain always either with the kings of France or with the crown of the kingdom and not be granted to anyone else. The charters suggest that they were acting as kings of their kingdom, who promised not to delegate this part of their responsibilities, not as mere lords or overlords.[64]

The dealings of twelfth-century kings with counts and great lords, and the dealings of great lords with each other, do not suggest either that counties were normally regarded as fiefs (whatever that meant) or, despite the few apparent *fiefs de reprise* that have been mentioned, that kings had a consistent policy of converting them into fiefs. When Suger told how the duke of Aquitaine admitted to Louis VI that the count of Auvergne had Auvergne from him, as he himself had it from Louis, he did not refer either to Auvergne or to Aquitaine as a fief. The mere reference to them as 'had' or 'held' from the king made Suger's point well enough, and past use of the phrase suggests that it need not have implied that either duchy or county was held with less than the normal full rights and minimal obligations of noble property.[65] In 1143 the count of Blois did homage to the duke of Burgundy and admitted that he held various properties, including the whole county of Troyes, *de feodo ducis*, but the word fief is used here, as it had often been used in the past, to describe the superior, not the subordinate, property, while homage, as I have argued, need not have meant that either party held anything less than the traditional complete rights in their

---

[62] *Rec. Philippe Auguste*, nos. 139, 445, 1309; cf. no. 1813. For Alphonse of Poitiers's refusal to do homage, presumably on grounds of dignity: Wood, *French Apanages*, 73–4, but cf. 78.

[63] Suger, *Œuvres*, 267; Reynolds, *Kingdoms and Communities*, 279–80.

[64] *Layettes*, i, no. 143; Luchaire, *Actes de Louis VII*, pp. 438–9 (no. 611); *Rec. Philippe Auguste*, no. 22. Promises not to alienate royal lordships that the king was developing jointly with a church were prompted by a different situation: the church would want to be assured that the agreement would not be jeopardized by a change of partner: e.g. *Rec. Philippe Auguste*, nos. 71, 117, 188–9, 205.

[65] Suger, *Vie de Louis VI*, 240. See index: *tenere*.

property.[66] About 1163, the count of Toulouse, desperate for help against Henry II, told Louis VII that he surrendered his land into the king's hands and that he and all his property were the king's, but his rhetoric did not involve talking about fiefs.[67] In practice relations between king and counts were still in many cases more like those between independent powers than Suger would have admitted. As a result of peace negotiations in 1185 after a brief war between Philip Augustus and the count of Flanders the county of Amiens was transferred from the count's lordship to that of the king. In consequence, Robert of Boves, as count of Amiens, did homage to the king—apparently for the first time. This pleased him because it meant he was no longer the man of the count of Flanders, whom he hated.[68]

The most immediate and persistent problems the kings of France faced in securing a measure of authority over their counts came from Normandy and the lordships that Henry of Anjou added to his grandfather's inheritance. Lemarignier declared that Suger lost no opportunity of recalling that Normandy was a fief. He cited two instances as evidence. In the first Suger made an ambassador tell Henry I that the liberality of the king of France had bestowed Normandy on him *tanquam proprium feodum*.[69] The words he used evoke his description of the Vexin as *proprium feodum* of Saint-Denis: perhaps they reflect a habit of thinking in the terms used for church lands, but what he wanted to imply here, as when he wrote about the duke of Aquitaine and the count of Auvergne without referring to fiefs, was surely political subjection. Lemarignier's other case is less convincing: when Louis enlarged William Atheling's fief (*feodum ejus augmentavit*) he seems to be using the word in a context in which it may refer, as it sometimes did, to a unit of property without reference to its status.[70] By the end of the century other writers occasionally referred to the Norman inheritance as held in fief. Gislebert of Mons says that Henry II, as a result of his marriage, had Normandy, Aquitaine, Brittany, and Anjou *in feodo* from the king of France.[71] Guillaume le Breton in his verse *Philippidos* also described Henry's lands as held from the king of France *nomine . . . feodi*.[72] By then, however, things were changing.

There are plenty of references to the performance of homage to the king

[66] Longnon, *Documents de Champagne*, i. 466; Bur, *Champagne*, 404. Bur's connection of this with a link established in 1058 applies only to St-Germain: ibid. 202, 291. For earlier usage: chapter 5, at nn. 143–6, 198–203.
[67] *RHGF*, xvi. 69 (no. 219).
[68] Gislebert of Mons, *Chronique*, 183–5. Cf. a similar transfer and consequent homage in 1104: Orderic Vitalis, *Hist. Eccl.* vi. 58.
[69] Lemarignier, *Hommage en marche*, 94; Suger, *Vie de Louis VI*, 106. To judge from his comments on the rickety bridge, was Suger the ambassador who actually delivered this speech?
[70] Suger, *Vie de Louis VI*, 112.          [71] Gislebert of Mons, *Chronique*, 83.
[72] Guillaume le Breton, *Philippidos*, 93–4.

of France by the dukes of Normandy and their Angevin successors.
Because of the likelihood that each of them would cause trouble to the king,
and because successive wars built up the custom of doing homage each
time peace was made, they were probably required to do homage more
regularly than, as yet, other great men probably were. Chroniclers who tell
how the kings of England had to do homage to the kings of France, however, refer to Normandy or their other French lands as fiefs much less
often than do modern historians. This applies even when they specify, for
instance, that the homage was done for Normandy or that the king of
France granted Normandy to be held from him.[73] Nor does the word fief
seem to be used when Henry II received homage from the count of
Brittany or made his sons do homage.[74] Of course the failure of one chronicler to use a particular word does not prove anything about the legal
status of property any more than does its occasional use by another, but its
absence from official charters is suggestive. While the editors of Philip II's
charters say that Philip 'investit Richard . . . des fiefs qu'il tenait de la
couronne de France', the treaty they print seems to accept that Richard
was already duke of Normandy, does not call Normandy a fief, and deals
merely with mutual surrenders of disputed lands and so forth. Both the
French and English chroniclers they cite seem equally unconcerned with
anything like feudo-vassalic rules.[75] The two kings made another treaty
soon after Richard's accession in order to safeguard their lands while they
both went on crusade. They then agreed that anyone in either's lands who
made war would, if he failed to heed lighter penalties, be disinherited. The
fiefs (*feudi*) thus confiscated would become the property (*proprietas*) of the
lord from whom they were held (*a quo feodi movebunt*).[76] In terms of later
legal theory the fiefs should already have been the *proprietas* of those in
whose *mouvance* they were, but at least some of them were in fact probably the traditional kind of inheritances with full rights of property.[77] Later
treaties between Philip and Richard contain references to fiefs, but some
are to the king's fief in the sense of the area under his government. Others
are either to properties that people held of one or other king, or to

---

[73] *Chron. de Sens*, 148; Orderic Vitalis, *Hist. Eccl.* vi. 180; Symeon of Durham, *Opera*, ii. 258;
Florence of Worcester, *Chron.* ii. 72–3; *Hist. gloriosi regis Ludovici*, 161; *Chron. Henry II and Ric.
I*, i. 191–4, 306, but cf. ii. 70; Robert of Torigny, *Chron.* 132, 162, 180, 208, but cf. 240; Roger
of Howden, *Chron.* i. 177, 215, ii. 6; Gervase of Canterbury, *Hist. Works*, i. 112, 435, 450; Ralph
Diceto, *Opera*, i. 291, ii. 58; John of Salisbury, *Letters*, ii. 562–4, 636–8.
[74] William of Newburgh, *Hist.* 114; Robert of Torigny, *Chron.* 197–8; *Rec. Henri II*, nos.
468–9, 488.
[75] *Rec. Philippe Auguste*, no. 262, and sources cited there.
[76] Ralph Diceto, *Opera*, ii. 74 (the variation in spelling between *feudi* and *feodi* is in British
Library MS Cott. Claudius E 3, fo. 128 as in the printed text).
[77] For *mouvances*, below, at n. 144.

lordships that Richard held outside the agreed limits of his duchies and counties.[78] In many cases like this the word may be used in its sense of a unit of property with no very precise—if any—connotation of a category with distinctive rights and obligations.[79] When Eleanor of Aquitaine did homage in 1199 it was, according to one of Philip's biographers, for the county of Poitou which belonged to her by hereditary right.[80] This is the traditional language of full property.

Given the previous accessions of dukes of Normandy, Philip's alleged grumble that John should have come and asked for his inheritance and done homage for it rather than seizing it without permission, while understandable in the circumstances, does not look well grounded in precedent.[81] It may have been something of a victory for Philip that in the treaty of Le Goulet John acknowledged that he would hold all his fiefs as his father and brother had held them from the king of France, *et sicut feoda debent*.[82] When it came to their actual confiscation, however, John's French lands do not seem to be referred to as fiefs, even by French writers, nor was their seizure justified on grounds peculiar to fiefs. Innocent III used the word and its derivatives when writing to both kings in 1203, but he was either referring to people and property belonging to the fief of the king of France or disclaiming any jurisdiction in the law of fiefs, by which he may have meant jurisdiction over secular property in general.[83] Later letters he wrote to England suggest knowledge of the academic law of fiefs.[84] It was that law which explains the only contemporary reference I have found to the king of England as a vassal of the king of France: the Roman lawyer Azo (d. 1220) used an earlier stage of the famous dispute between the two kings to answer the question whether a king could transfer his vassal to another who was the inferior or equal of the vassal (*utrum dominus rex possit vasallum suum alii minori vel pari ipsius vasallo delegare*).[85] Neither king, in any case, seems to have made use in their dispute of lawyers who knew about this kind of law. Even in the charges against John that Philip and his son presented to the pope in 1216, packed as they were with what Petit-Dutaillis called falsehoods and contradictions, fiefs were referred to only

[78] *Rec. Philippe Auguste*, nos. 357, 361, 376, 517; cf. *Chron. Henry II and Ric. I*, i. 192, ii. 50; Robert of Torigny's interpolation in Guillaume de Jumièges, *Gesta*, 338–9 (on which: Hollister, 'Normandy', 231).

[79] Cf. e.g. *Rec. Philippe Auguste*, no. 723; *Layettes*, i, no. 647.          [80] Rigord, *Gesta*, 146.

[81] Roger of Howden, *Chron.* iv. 95. Richard had done homage before his investiture at Rouen, but that was because he had done it in his father's lifetime: *Chron. Henry II and Ric. I*, ii. 50, 73.

[82] There is no infinitive after *debent*: *Rec. Philippe Auguste*, no. 633; *Layettes*, i, no. 578.

[83] Innocent III, *Selected Letters*, no. 20; *RHGF* xix. 440–3. Cf. *Rec. Philippe Auguste*, nos. 899–900.

[84] See index: Innocent III.

[85] Azo, *Quaestiones*, 86; cf. Lehmann, *Consuetudines Feudorum: Antiqua*, 23, 29; Lehmann, *Langobardische Lehnrecht*, 181 (= *Dip. Frid. I*, no. 242).

when the king of England was said to have many lands *in feodo regis Francie*. The fief here is that of the king of France, not the king of England: the word has the same sense of a superior property or lordship, not a sub-ordinate one, as it had had in Innocent's reference to the fief of the king of France in 1203 and in many earlier French charters.[86] The arguments put forward in 1216 about the law of inheritance and about a custom of the kingdom of France by which a murderer's property was forfeit seem to be applied to property in general. Despite Suger, despite Guillaume le Breton, despite the other occasional references to fiefs, and despite what-ever Innocent may have thought, it is hard to believe that Philip and Louis seriously maintained, or other Frenchmen seriously thought, that dukes of Normandy and counts of Anjou held their duchy and county with fewer rights than were normally attached to the property of counts.

That kind of property—or part of it—might once have been called alo-dial, but the word does not seem to have been used of the Norman and Angevin lordships in the twelfth century, any more than it was of other great lordships. For us to argue whether Gascony or any other part of the Angevin dominions was or was not alodial by this date is therefore unreal: legal categories do not exist in the air when no one is using them. The kings of England never seem to have denied that their lands across the Channel were part of the kingdom of France or that—presumably as a result of this—they owed homage to the king of France.[87] The implications of this for the Angevins became more dangerous and distasteful when Philip Augustus began to exploit the reserves of authority latent in the title of king and combined them with the developing ideas and practice of government so as to turn nominal authority into something like effective jurisdiction. Once under jurisdiction the Angevin rights, like the rights of other French counts, became matters of property which were vulnerable to adjudication and consequently to confiscation. That is what happened to John's rights in 1202. It could have happened even if they had still been envisaged as alods according to Carolingian law. The importance of this *cause célèbre* in my argument is not only that it illustrates the uncertain cat-egories of the time for us. It must also, by its notoriety, have done a good deal to publicize new issues and form new customs. Many nobles, with their advisers and administrators, may, hearing about it, have been led to

---

[86] Roger Wendover, *Flores Hist.* ii. 183–90; Bémont, *De Johanne*, 65–8; on this episode: Petit-Dutaillis, *Déshéritement*, 102, though cf. Louis VIII's letter of 1224: *RHGF*, xix. 760. For earlier usage, chapter 5.5.

[87] Apart from the homages, see e.g. Duchesne, *Hist. Franc. Scriptores*, iv. 731. Whether Gascony was included in homages before 1204 seems unknowable (Chaplais, 'Traité de Paris'), but the only evidence that it was perceived in the early thirteenth century to be outside the king-dom or an alod (which would not be the same thing) is that Philip and Louis did not invade it.

associate the doing of homage with a firmer political subordination than they might have done otherwise. During the thirteenth century they also came to associate it with fiefholding.

## 7.3. Words and concepts: the thirteenth century

Although the idea of holding property in fief was not yet being applied deliberately and systematically to counties and duchies, Philip II's later charters suggest that the royal government was beginning to use it when dealing with lesser people or with the lesser properties of great men. From 1186 surviving royal charters making perpetual grants to laymen sometimes, though not always, said that the property, whether land or rents, even if it was to be held either explicitly in inheritance or by implication for ever, or—still more emphatically—as freely as the king had held it, was to be held *in feodum et hominagium ligium*.[88] Similar phrases were used in grants of rents by the counts of Ponthieu and Flanders in 1195 and 1200 respectively.[89] The rent in the Ponthieu charter was to be held by hereditary right (*jure hereditario*) as well as *in feodum et homagium*. In the many grants of land and rights in Normandy that the king made in the years after 1203 the phrase *in feodum et hominagium ligium* became more or less standard, varied by *in feodum et hominagium, in hommagium ligium, in feodum ligium*, et cetera (*in feodum* on its own is rare).[90] In some cases, both concerning Normandy and elsewhere, any such phrase is, for no obvious reason, entirely omitted. Some charters also fail to say that the land is to be held from the king, but as that phrase had not in the past been peculiar to fiefs, its omission is not very significant.

The point of saying that property was to be held *in feodum et hominagium ligium*, if it had a deliberate purpose, was not, it seems, that a charter which used the phrase would automatically convey fewer rights or more obligations than one which, by not doing so, might be assumed to convey the full traditional rights of an alod or inheritance. Most of the Norman charters say that the lands conveyed were to be held according to Norman custom and were to owe the accustomed services. Presumably one point of using the phrase in grants of property in Normandy was to stress the new obedience to the king owed by everyone in the newly conquered duchy. This essentially political purpose rather than any reduction in property rights may have applied elsewhere. In 1218 and 1220 Philip made exchanges of property in which what he gave was to be held *in feodum et*

---

[88] *Rec. Philippe Auguste*, nos. 198, 397, 470, 519, 548, 551, 556, 560, 608, 669, 714, 722, 755, 762, 764, etc.

[89] *Rec. comtes de Pontieu*, no. 139; *Oorkonden der Graven van Vlaanderen*, no. 143.

[90] *Rec. Philippe Auguste*, ii–iv *passim*.

*hominagium ligium* and what he received had belonged to his opposite number (who was also his subject) by hereditary right (*quod* [or *que*] *ipsum jure hereditario contingebat*). In the second case the land that the king granted was to be held in the same way and with the same liberty that he had held it.[91] The same general purpose of securing an acknowledgement of political subordination may explain many of the more numerous conversions of alods into fiefs by other lords that can be found from now on, often though not only in areas where academic Roman law is most likely to have brought knowledge of the law of fiefs with it. Like the earlier *fiefs de reprise* that have been mentioned, these sometimes concerned fortresses and sometimes made use of compromise categories like *feuda franca*.[92]

It remains difficult to be sure about the amount of deliberate policy, let alone the amount and nature of professional law, that lay behind the terminology of Philip Augustus's charters. Perhaps knowledge of English practice, whether transmitted through Normandy or otherwise, was influential: even the greatest men in England were said to hold their land in fief and did homage for it—though it may be rash to assume that all of those to whom Philip granted land in homage 'did homage' to him for it. If the English precedent was noted it must have seemed attractive. On several occasions, usually when dealing with an inheritance which was (or could be made to look) doubtful, Philip Augustus's charters refer to properties as fiefs, or held *in feodo*, that would probably not have been so described earlier.[93] Other charters, however, that record other hard financial or territorial bargains that he drove, or homages that he secured, do not use the word. The variation is reminiscent of Frederick I's Italian charters:[94] perhaps the explanation in each case lies in the varying demands of recipients as well as in the varying advice available, though Philip's administration was better placed to build up consistent practice. Whatever importance any individual case may have had as a precedent, and however much they all helped to create new categories and attitudes, however, the use of the word fief may not at the time have been the vital factor:[95] at this date all those

---

[91] Ibid. nos. 1535, 1627. Cf. nos. 1023, 1195.

[92] David, *Patrimoine foncier*, 79–80, 113–14, 307–11 and *Cart. lyonnais*, e.g. nos. 168, 365, 448; *Ordonnances*, i. 697; Monboisse, *L'Ordre féodal*, 100–1; Giordanengo, *Droit féodal*, 79, 189, 192, 198–200; *Rec. d'actes relatifs à Guyenne*, nos. 35, 197, 266, 301, 617, 689; Brussel, *Nouvel examen*, 386–7 n.; *Layettes*, v, no. 431; *Les Olim*, i. 571–3 (xvi); Boutruche, *Société provinciale*, 127–35, 246–7; Chénon, *Alleux*, 45–6. On the apparent rarity of *fiefs de reprise* in the area of Paris custom: Martin, *Histoire de la coutume de Paris*, 220.

[93] *Rec. Philippe Auguste*, nos. 399, 580, 723, 1418–19, 1421; cf. Gislebert of Mons, *Chronique*, 275.

[94] Chapter 6.9.

[95] *Rec. Philippe Auguste*, nos. 398–9, 581, 621, 678, 1045, 1133, 1227, 1259, 1268, 1313–14, 1321, 1360.

who received charters cannot have understood it—or its absence—in the same way. Perhaps the reason why Philip's later grants were not more often made *in feodum et hominagium ligium* was that so many were of rents or small and humble properties that may have seemed politically insignificant. The people who received them were not those who most needed to be reminded of their duties of obedience.

Whatever the policy, or the degree of deliberate intention, that lay behind the increasing number of surviving grants of property that were made both in fief and for ever, and however difficult it is to disentangle cause and effect, they surely contributed to the trend by which, during the thirteenth century, fief became the characteristic word in much of the kingdom for the property of people who enjoyed what may roughly be called noble status. This was an important change in terminology, which would have been noticed sooner if historians had not so often referred to all the properties that nobles (or those they consider nobles) had held in preceding centuries as fiefs irrespective of the words used in the sources. The change may have been facilitated by the way that the word fief had long been used, not only for subordinate property, but for superior properties or units of government, and sometimes for units of property apparently irrespective of their rights and obligations.[96] In the north the long disuse of the word alod for lordships which, not being under any effective jurisdiction, had not needed to be labelled or classified at all, may also have favoured the adoption of a new label. On the other hand practice there may by the thirteenth century have been influenced by that of the south, where the change seems to have been promoted by recognition of the difference between fiefs and alods. The influence of academic and professional law on the use of oaths of fidelity combined with the creation of *fiefs de reprise*, which seems so clear at Montpellier from the early twelfth century, can be found elsewhere in the south by the early thirteenth.[97]

As the power and prestige of the monarchy increased, homage and attendance at the king's court seemed a natural manifestation of loyalty, solidarity, and indeed of high status. Since homage so often went together with fiefholding in royal charters, many great men may have slipped into thinking of their lands as fiefs without noticing what was happening. Lesser lords presumably accepted the same label and a corresponding position under their counts in much the same way. Doing homage and holding in fief meant an acknowledgement of subordination, but it was an hon-

[96] See chapter 5.5. Some grants *in augmentum feodi sui* are probably best put in the third, unspecific category: e.g. *Rec. Philippe Auguste*, nos. 501, 577, 588, 714 (to a bishop), 721–2, 1686, though not 1363. No. 735 may contain a scribal error.
[97] Giordanengo, *Droit féodal*, esp. 111–22, '*Epistola Philiberti*', 837–40, 'Vocabulaire romanisant', and 'Vocabulaire et formulaires'.

ourable kind of subordination, distinct from that of peasants, and may not
at first have seemed to imply much, if any, more subjection or obligation
than seemed customary and right. The great lords who in 1209 joined with
the king in legislating about homage, service, and dues owed from divided
*feodalia tenementa* probably did not think their ordinance applied to their
own estates, but that may have been less because they would never have
thought of their property as fiefs (whatever that meant to them) than
because it probably did not occur to them that it might: rules so often seem
to be made for others, and especially inferior others. Just what properties
they intended the ordinance to apply to is, at this date, almost anyone's
guess, beyond the virtual certainty that they would have been those of free
men or nobles.[98] In 1224 Louis VIII referred to his own fiefs of Poitou as
having been confiscated, along with other fiefs within the kingdom of
France (*de quibus et aliis feodis de regno Francorum moventibus*), from John
of England.[99] Joinville used the word *fiez* to refer to counties that the count
of Champagne sold to the king, though here the word seems to be used in
the sense it had when land held by someone in domain (i.e. directly) was
contrasted with land held in fief (i.e. by others above peasant level under
his lordship).[100]

The change of usage is exemplified in Beaumanoir. For him, writing in
the Beauvaisis during the 1280s, the principal determinant of the status of
property was—or ought to have been—the status of its owner. He regarded
all lordships in the kingdom, as well as in the Beauvaisis, right up to counties or baronies held directly from the king, as held in fief or in *arrière-
fief*.[101] Gentlemen (*gentius hom*) normally held their property as fiefs,
which were distinguished from other inheritances (*eritages*), which
Beaumanoir called *vilenages*, by not paying any rent and by slightly different rules about inheritance, succession dues, wardship of minors, and so
on.[102] Since there were, he said, no alods in the Beauvaisis, it is tempting
to guess that some of the *vilenages*, as well as many of the fiefs, would once
have ranked as alods: it is not impossible that some *vilenage*-holders
thought they still did. There were, however, plenty of rough edges to the
distinctions Beaumanoir struggled to make. He was noticeably fussed
about the misfits that occurred when gentlemen acquired *vilenages* or, even

---

[98] *Rec. Philippe Auguste*, no. 1083; cf. nos. 1353, 1600. For varying guesses at the motives
behind the ordinance: Mitteis, *Lehnrecht und Staatsgewalt*, 665; Petot, 'L'Ordonnance de 1209'.
In view of those who joined in making the ordinance I find it hard to believe that it was intended
to apply only to the 'royal domain' (as e.g. Metman, 'Inféodations'). It was apparently kept no
better in areas under direct royal jurisdiction than elsewhere: Ourliac, 'Législation', 474–5.

[99] *RHGF*, xix. 760.                              [100] Joinville, *Histoire*, 32.

[101] Beaumanoir, *Coutumes de Beauvaisis*, § 322. The idea of a hierarchy of property is discussed below.

[102] Ibid. § 386, 462–97, 505–50, 672, 703.

worse, when an *homme de poosté* (a man under power or jurisdiction: a commoner) acquired a *franc fief*—which here means any fief, not a specially superior or honourable one.[103] At the other end of the kingdom from the Beauvaisis, the Customs of Toulouse, which were compiled just about when Beaumanoir was writing, included a section on fiefs. The fiefs it deals with seem to be properties outside the city, some of them rent-paying, which were presumably acquired by townsmen, often no doubt as safe investments, but came under the authority of external lords.[104] These Customs, compiled by and for presumably non-noble townsmen, are not evidence that fiefs in the south were normally any less noble than fiefs in the north. There were probably gentlemen in the south who deplored social climbers just as much as Beaumanoir did. The royal legislation that penalized the acquisition of fiefs by non-nobles applied in both areas and suggests that the phenomenon was common enough to be worth taxing.[105]

Beaumanoir's problems about fitting social status to categories of property did not arise because status was becoming important for the first time. It had always been important, but now, like everything else, it was becoming more defined. The link between gentlemen or nobles and fiefs was not a memory of a real past but a piece of thirteenth-century (and later) ideology. Nor were Beaumanoir's problems caused just by the difficulty of making simple rules about status and property rights, though this may have become harder as the land market grew and as property and dues were more systematically exploited and recorded. All this made anomalies more frequent and more noticeable, but what really created the problem was the recognition of it as a problem—the new zeal for systematic statement and argument which made variations into anomalies.[106] Not everyone was up to the intellectual challenge posed by classification: the Norman *Summa de Legibus* made holding in parage into a category comparable to holding by homage, burgage, or alms.[107] But classification was bound to be difficult when it was applied to the muddle of past custom.[108]

Perhaps the most striking example of the change in the status of fiefs is that churches were now sometimes said to hold their property in fief. In 1259 the abbey of Eysses (Lot-et-Garonne) held Eysses *in feodum* from the count of Toulouse, and in 1267 the prior (*prepositus*) of Évaux (Creuse) claimed that he held his property in Évaux *in feodum et homagium ligium* from the bishop of Limoges.[109] The academic lawyer John de Blanot, probably writing early in the third quarter of the century, seems to have

[103] Beaumanoir, *Coutumes de Beauvaisis*, § 1496–1507.
[104] *Coutumes de Toulouse*, 132–42, 247.
[105] Below, at nn. 213–14.      [106] Cf. *Établissements de Saint Louis*, ii. 252–3.
[107] *Coutumiers de Normandie*, iii. 2.      [108] e.g. 'Comptes et enquêtes', 43.
[109] Tholin and Fallières, 'Hommages', 43; *Les Olim*, i. 699–700 (ix).

assumed that, since the bishop of Mâcon did homage to the king for the county of Mâcon, the church therefore held the county from the king *in feudum* just as the count held it from the church.[110] Nevertheless there are some hints that the new terminology had to be made palatable to some churchmen. One bishop in Languedoc was recorded in 1271 as holding *in feudum honorabile* while the Templars held *in feudum liberum*.[111] Laymen could also be reluctant or uncertain about the new terminology. When nobles in the Agenais had to take oaths to Alphonse of Poitiers as count of Toulouse in 1259 most acknowledged that they held their lands in fief from him, and did homage to his commissioner accordingly. Some land, however, was said to be held from him without reference to its status, some was said to be held from him freely (*francaliter*), and some was apparently held at once freely and in fief. Homage could be owed either way.[112] Holding freely here seems to indicate not so much a category of property as a claim to a relative absence of obligation. Like free or honourable fiefs claimed by churches, it may also imply a certain resistance to the idea of describing as a fief the lands one has inherited and enjoyed as one's full ancestral property.

The increase in the monarchy's power and prestige seems to have provoked few direct and outright rebellions, but, combined with the increasing demands and more systematic administration of lesser lords and with changes in the terminology and methods of the law, it evidently provoked legal arguments both in theory and in practice. More of the practical disputes will be considered later, when I discuss the obligations of property. As for theoretical problems, they could be addressed more directly and effectively by those who had been trained in the new academic law of fiefs than they were in works like that of Beaumanoir. Hints at the spread of the new law to France come in the use of the word vassal and of forms of oaths of fidelity derived from the academic texts. Both seem as yet to have been restricted to the south. Whereas Beaumanoir and other works of northern customary law like the *Établissements de Saint Louis* do not seem to use the word vassal at all, it appears occasionally in documents (some recording the creation of *fiefs de reprises*) from areas where the academic law of fiefs may have been introduced along with Roman law.[113] A more impressive

---

[110] Acher, 'Notes sur le droit savant', 152, 162–4, 168. For John's treatise and its date: Meijers, *Études*, iii. 170 and n.

[111] Lafaille, *Annales*, 11, 23–4; cf. Bisson, *Assemblies*, 319–21.

[112] Tholin and Fallières, 'Hommages', e.g. 13–14 (nos. 4, 5), 24 (no. 17), 30–1 (nos. 30–1), 54–5 (no. 2); the records of *c.*1271 and *c.*1279, being briefer, are less explicit: Tholin and Fallières, 'Prise de possession'; *Livre d'Agenais*; cf. Lafaille, *Annales*, 1–51.

[113] *Cart. lyonnais*, no. 365; *Layettes*, iii, nos. 3040, 4208; *Correspondance admin.* no. 546; Giordanengo, *Droit féodal*, esp. 111–22, '*Epistola Philiberti*', 837–40, and 'Vocabulaire et formulaires'.

example of the new legal learning occurs in the work of John de Blanot, who has already been mentioned in connection with the extension of the word fief to church property. John brought his training in Roman law to bear on French customs about homage (*de homagiis sive hominitiis*), assimilating the learning of Roman law and the *Libri Feudorum* to French terms and conditions pretty effectively. Although the rite of homage is not mentioned in the *Libri*, oaths of fidelity are.[114] John clearly saw no significant difference between them—though, incidentally, he mentioned that the rite varied by custom in different places and, like Glanvill and Bracton in England, referred to the mutual obligations it created.[115] At one point he recognized that not all inheritances were fiefs and that it was possible to do homage (*homagium*) without making one's property a fief.

The most famous problem of homage that John discussed was whether the man of my man is my man, and whether a man should help the baron to whom he has sworn fidelity, even in a war against the king. In the specific case of a war between the king and the duke of Burgundy, which should the duke's man fight for?[116] The whole discussion, with its talk of barons and men rather than of vassals (though he refers to vassals elsewhere[117]), is testimony to John's knowledge and concern about the real world of France outside the *Libri Feudorum*, but that does not mean that his conclusion, that the man of my man is not my man, represented accepted custom. As he pointed out, some people said that all the men in the kingdom were the king's men, while he himself conceded that, even if all were not in the king's power by right of homage, all were in it by right of the natural jurisdiction that the king had in his kingdom. The king had the right to call on them for the public welfare even if, when the king and the duke were in conflict, John thought that the first duty of the duke's men was to him.

John's example was taken from a real confrontation during Louis IX's minority, but the conflict of loyalties that it addressed must have become of almost exclusively academic interest by the time he was writing—except for people in Gascony. There his conclusion might have been generally approved. In the rest of the kingdom it would have got anyone who appealed to it into trouble. In any case, if custom had been established and obvious when he was writing, John would not have discussed it. The questions he discussed were open ones—at least to academics—and were only now coming to be discussed systematically.[118] A little later another

---

[114] Lehmann, *Langobardische Lehnrecht*, index.  [115] Acher, 'Notes', 149.
[116] Ibid. 156–62.  [117] Ibid. 175–7.
[118] Cf. *Établissements de Saint Louis*, ii. 75–7. A twelfth-century agreement: *RHGF*, xvi. 15–16. See also chapter 9, at n. 260.

academic lawyer, William Durandus, bishop of Mende (d. 1296), demonstrated the confusion of words and concepts that confronted those who tried to reduce customary law to tidy categories. Like John, William used *homagium* to denote a ceremony but also, perhaps, for the relation it created. 'What in Italy or elsewhere', he wrote, 'is called vassalage (*vasallagium*), in France is called homage. We [the French or southern French?] colloquially call provincial noble fiefholders vassals [or: call provincial nobles fiefholding vassals?]; commoners [or fiefholding commoners?] we colloquially call our men.'[119] There seems to be an inconsistency or contradiction here, at least in my translation, but if it is also in William's text, as I think it is, that only emphasizes the problems.

Two classic examples of uncertainty about the meaning of being someone's man and the loyalties and duties it might imply come from Joinville's Life of St Louis. In 1248 Joinville refused to take the oath of faith and loyalty (*foy et loiautei*) to the king's children that Louis wanted his barons to take in case he did not return from his crusade. The reason he gave was that he was not Louis's man (*je n'estoie pas ses hom*). He nevertheless accompanied the king on crusade and served him faithfully. The moment at which he considered that he had become Louis's man probably came in 1252 when the king retained him formally in his service for an annual sum to be paid to Joinville and his heirs *in feodum et homagium ligium*. Joinville then did liege homage to the king against all men, saving his fidelity to the counts of Champagne and Bar.[120] Doing homage was probably the vital point. The fact that Joinville's salary was to be held in fief may also have been important, but perhaps only in so far as homage and fief seemed to go together. Either way, the past history of fiefholding makes it clear that Joinville's 'money fief' was not a way of assimilating new methods of rewarding service to the ways that nobles had anciently held land and to ancient bonds between them and their lords. The new association of homage with noble and honourable fiefholding may also lie behind Joinville's report of Louis's justification of the concessions he made to Henry III of England in the treaty of Paris. Louis said that Henry had not hitherto been his man but had now entered into his homage (*houmaige*). The problematical status of Gascony (which will be discussed shortly) makes this case more difficult, but, whether Aquitaine was reckoned to be a fief or not, Louis may have meant that Henry's performance of homage restored the old formal relation, which had not, as I have argued, at the

---

[119] *Quod autem in Italia, vel alibi vocatur vasallagium, in Francia homagium appellatur. Nos autem provinciales nobiles feudatarios, vasallos: plebeios vero, nostros homines vulgariter appellamus*: William Durandus, *Speculum Juris*, pts. 3 and 4, 307. The punctuation is that of the 1668 edition. Cf. *Konst. Friedrichs II*, ii. 226 (II. 36).

[120] Joinville, *Histoire*, 41-2, 48, 178, 243-4; *Documents historiques*, i. 620.

time been thought of in terms of fiefholding.[121] At a time when so many legal categories were still unclear the most important point may have been that Henry had now in effect admitted that in Aquitaine he was Louis's subject. According to Joinville Louis worked for peace among his subjects (*sousgis*) and especially among neighbouring rich men and the princes of the kingdom (*les riches homes voisins et les princes dou royaume*).[122] Before Joinville himself had been what he called Louis's man he had presumably considered himself his king's subject and had certainly felt a pretty strong loyalty and duty towards him.

Against the background of the increasing status attached to properties known as fiefs, it is easy to see why references to alods in surviving sources seem to have become rare by the thirteenth century.[123] At the lowest level, seigniorial pressure had by then probably eroded the rights of many small alods under the jurisdiction of the ban and turned them into what were already, in some areas, classified separately as *censives*. Those that survived had presumably done so because lords had been able to get the control and dues they wanted without worrying about terminology, or because alod-holders, whether or not they lost out over control and dues, had managed to stick to their label. In Gascony some non-noble free men cherished the title of alod, while others of apparently similar condition simply called their lands free (*habent terras suas . . . francas et liberas*). Yet other *homines francales* recorded their lands as held *in feodum inmediate* from the king-duke.[124] Perhaps they, with other peasants who might once have ranked as alodholders, saw the vital contrast not as between alod and *censive*, with alods as the better choice, but as between alod and fief, with fiefs as better. Fiefs were what gentlemen held, so they wanted their lands to be fiefs, and in this case they apparently met no objections.

Higher up the social and governmental scale, claims to hold alods seem to have become ever rarer as time went on. Some people of noble, or near-noble, status held what were called alods in Gascony in 1274 but many had fiefs, while a number were at around this time having their alods converted to fiefs.[125] The most characteristic Gascon alodholders were probably the humble lesser men (*homines minores*) who were proud to be free but made no claim to hold fiefs like the nobles.[126] As for the terms on which Gascony

[121] Joinville, *Histoire*, 245.      [122] Ibid.
[123] Chénon, *Alleux*, 111–200, surveys regional variation in the 'presumption of alodiality' in the later custumals.
[124] Boutruche, *Société provinciale*, 123–4; *Rec. d'actes relatifs à Guyenne*, nos. 247–50, 537, cf. 695. Bémont (ibid. 328–9) preferred to call some of these lands *censives*. Cf. Richardot, 'Fief roturier', 322 n., for *terra libera de omnibus dominationibus*, rather than an alod.
[125] *Rec. d'actes relatifs à Guyenne*, e.g. nos. 1, 91–107, 177 (and 577). For *fiefs de reprise*: nos. 35, 197, 266, 301, 617, 689. For alods above peasant status, e.g. nos. 237, 252, 632.
[126] Boutruche, *Société provinciale*, 31–8, 123–4.

itself was held, it was not apparently until near the end of the century that the kings of England seem to have contended that the duchy had been, or ought to be, an alod.[127] To us, as to later lawyers, the advantages of such an argument may seem obvious. The growth of royal power and jurisdiction that made homage and fiefholding seem increasingly natural to loyal subjects of the king of France must have made them increasingly repugnant to a king of England with lands in France. That the alternative was to hold one's duchy as an alod may not, however, have been as obvious then as it became later. In 1259 the treaty of Paris did not say in so many words that Henry was to hold his lands in fief or as a fief. What it said was that he and his heirs were to do liege homage to Louis and his heirs for what Louis would give to him and his heirs in fief and in domain, and also for Bordeaux, Bayonne, Gascony, and all the land that Henry held on that side of the Channel in the kingdom of France in fief and in domain and for the islands, if there were any, that he held which belonged to the kingdom of France.[128] 'In fief and in domain' here serves presumably to distinguish the properties or lordships of others under Henry's rule from what he held directly.[129]

The comment by Louis that Joinville recorded (that Henry was now Louis's man as he had not been before), combined with the probability that by now the performance of homage by a noble implied fiefholding, probably means that despite the non-committal language of the treaty, Henry's French lands were now thought of as fiefs in the new sense of the word. Some French chroniclers thought that the treaty actually said that the king of England would hold his lands from the king of France *in feodum*, presumably because they now took it for granted that that was how counts and dukes normally held their counties and duchies.[130] But, while Louis may have thought that he was converting Gascony from an alod to a fief, he is quite likely to have assumed that it always had been one and thought that what he was doing was restoring a legal relation that had lapsed. In making Henry his man he was simply restoring him and his land to the position his predecessors had held within the kingdom. Presumably that was worth while, though his generosity in the political and military situation of the time remains as puzzling now as it was to Joinville. Perhaps Louis acted out of Christian charity, perhaps out of far-sighted cunning,

---

[127] Chaplais, 'Traité de Paris' and 'Duché-Pairie de Guyenne'.

[128] *E de ce que il dorra a nos e a nos hoirs en fiez e en demaines nos e noz hoirs li ferons homage lige e a ses hoirs rois de France, e ausi de Bordiaus, de Baione, de Gascoingne e de tote la terre que nos tenons deca la mer Dangleterre el roiaume de France en fiez e en demaines e des illes, saucune en i a que nos teignons qui soient du roiaume de France: Diplomatic Documents*, no. 302; cf. ibid. no. 305 (Louis's charter) and *Layettes*, iii, no. 4554.

[129] Above, at n. 45 and chapter 8, at n. 138.     [130] *RHGF*, xx. 412; xxiii. 16.

perhaps out of the usual human muddle of motives. However that may be, if he had thought he was changing the legal status of the land from what it had been before 1204, rather than simply bringing it within the ambit of the law once more, one might have expected the treaty to be more explicit, along the lines of other documents that converted alods into fiefs. Given the past history of the Angevin lands, the different usage in England, and the current use of the word alod, interpretations at the time may well have varied.

The first date that has been suggested for any evidence of an English argument that Gascony had been an alod before 1259 seems to be 1286. If that date is correct it was then proposed, presumably by some adviser of Edward I, that Gascony had been an alod before 1259 and that, since the French had not fulfilled their obligations under the treaty, it still was. Early in the fourteenth century it was said that the argument had been put forward in the arbitrations before Boniface VIII around the turn of the century. If it was, neither the pope nor the French apparently took it up. Although it appears in various memoranda apparently copied at various times,[131] the actual treaties, like the drafts and the records of direct negotiations, seem to ignore it. Instead they concentrate on issues of custom and jurisdiction, of the fulfilment of past treaties, and of the customary liberties of Gascony, which could all have applied as well to one sort of property as the other.[132] Presumably the argument about alodiality was suggested by someone who had noticed the conversion of alods into fiefs both within Gascony and elsewhere. Since such transactions seem often— so far as they are recorded, which is not very often—to have been made in order to symbolize political subordination, it may have seemed a bright idea to use alodial tenure to symbolize autonomy at this higher level. Like other bright ideas it apparently turned out rather hard to exploit.

The English articles that were said to have been presented to the pope in 1298 and 1302 begin with a claim that before the treaty of Paris Gascony had not been *de feudo regis Francie, set de allodio regis Anglie*. They go on to develop an argument that burgeons with citations to the *Libri Feudorum* along with a few to the Digest.[133] The first article serves as a marker in the

---

[131] Chaplais, 'English Arguments', 211–12 (PRO, C 47/27/5/19); Dupuy, *Histoire du différend*, preuves pp. 21–3; *Eng. Med. Dip. Practice*, no. 237; 'Journal des conférences', 243, 247; Bock, 'Documents', 91. It is not clear why PRO, C 47/27/5/18, 19 are dated 1286. Other copies (C 47/28/1/38–9) are dated in the PRO list to *?c.*1329. C 47/28/1/39, which bears a note *Vacat ex causa secretius exprimenda*, also includes after *la dite terre ne movent pas du roialme de France* the words *mais de l'empire*: cf. Chaplais, 'English Arguments', 205 n.

[132] Chaplais, 'Duché-Pairie'; *Eng. Med. Dip. Practice*, nos. 149, 237; *War of Saint-Sardos*. Reference to the liberty or liberties of Gascony (e.g. Cuttino, 'Another Memorandum Book', 96) need not presuppose alodiality, though it may allude to it.

[133] *Eng. Med. Dip. Practice*, no. 237, where the references are identified. The use of *vassallus*

development of feudal terminology: whereas, as I have argued, in the old days of pre-professional law any property *de feudo regis Francie* would have been understood as being under royal authority rather than as being itself a fief in the classic sense,[134] the lawyer who drew up the articles assumed that the phrase denoted a fief held from the king of France. The expression *de allodio regis Anglie*, on the other hand, clearly—if inconsistently—meant an alod belonging to (rather than held from) the king of England.[135] The article went on to concede that the treaty had required the king of England to do fidelity for Gascony and then admitted cagily that he was said to have done it. Like John de Blanot, the author takes homage and fidelity to be synonymous, for he argues that if such homage had indeed been done, that would not mean that either *dominium* or *proprietas* could have been transferred. A fief could not be created by bare words, nor would fidelity make the land *feudalis* or transfer *dominium directum*. Although all this could be made to apply to the transfer or demotion of an alod, the line of argument here and in the next four articles is directed much more to fiefs than to anything to do with alods. In this it follows the glossators, who had developed ideas about different sorts of *dominium* in order to explain the rights of fiefholders and distinguish them from the rights of their lords, whose lands in this context, incidentally, are not generally classified either as fiefs or anything else.[136] University-trained lawyers, who were accustomed to combining the *Libri Feudorum* with genuine Roman law and to adapting Roman law to fiefs, could do little with the *Libri*'s sparse and uninformative allusions to alods.[137]

Equally, given the humble character of most Gascon alodholders, the king of England's administrators in the duchy may not have taken kindly to the idea of the king-duke as one of them. Nor would anyone engaged in Gascon government have supposed that alodholders were automatically free of services or superior jurisdiction, which was what the king of England wanted to be.[138] From all angles it was probably easier and more profitable to develop arguments about sovereignty (*superioritas*, *sovereinete*, etc.). The word may make them look more modern to us, but, though they may have been first propounded slightly later than the alod argument, they

also reflects the *Libri*, as may the spelling of *feudum* (though that was traditional in parts of southern France). Another memorandum, PRO, SC 1/48/170, referring to *le tenaunt*, suggests a background of English law.

[134] Chapter 5, at nn. 143–5, 198–203.
[135] Cf. Brussel, *Nouvel examen*, 389 n. (from 1220).
[136] Feenstra, 'Origines du dominium utile', esp. 84, 92 n.; Giordanengo, 'Vocabulaire et formulaires', 97–9.
[137] Lehmann, *Langobardische Lehnrecht*, 150, 179, 200, 202; cf. the 5¼ line chapter *De Franc Alleu* in Jacques d'Ableiges, *Grand Coutumier*, 325.
[138] Boutruche, *Société provinciale*, 116 n., 119, 156–7, 169–70, 239–45.

were developed faster. The medieval idea of sovereignty (as distinct from any of the various modern ones) followed readily enough from contemporary ideas about jurisdiction and government and fitted well enough into contemporary ideas about kingdoms.[139] The idea of the noble alod as a defence against royal power, on the other hand, was as yet little but a gleam in a lawyer's eye. The fact that it used old words and adapted old concepts does not mean that it had had a continuous history. By the time it had been adapted, under the stress of war and law, so as to connect alodiality with sovereignty and with being explicitly outside the kingdom, it made fair nonsense of the old categories. That is not surprising, for it was not a survival from Carolingian custom but the creation of professional lawyers, making the best case they could and working in quite different conditions with a very imperfect knowledge of the relevant history. By the time that the viscount of Béarn claimed, not merely to be sovereign, but also to hold alodially, few of his subjects had alods: perhaps that was just as well. The difference between the conditions of his alod and theirs might have been embarrassing.[140]

## 7.4. *Words and concepts: the feudal hierarchy*

During this period we begin to get indications that people envisaged something like what historians call a feudal hierarchy or hierarchy of tenure within France. Looked at without the spectacles of later feudal theories, however, the indications are slight and late. The most obvious form of hierarchy in lay society, which may have been in the back of people's minds even if they did not articulate it, was the social hierarchy. One of Philip II's registers, for instance, seems to be thinking of that kind of hierarchy when it arranges its lists under the headings of counts and dukes, barons, castellans, and vavassors.[141] It would, however, be wrong to assume that this represented a hierarchy of property or tenure. As the *Livres de Jostice et de Plet* later pointed out, dukes, counts, viscounts, and barons could hold their land from each other.[142]

As I argued in chapter 5, the evidence I have surveyed suggests that from the eleventh century people who held land with what were thought of as full rights but were under the power or authority of some kind of lord

---

[139] Chaplais, 'Souveraineté'; Reynolds, *Kingdoms and Communities*, 256–61, 319–24.

[140] Tucoo-Chala, *Vicomté de Béarn*, conflates the arguments for sovereignty and alodiality, but that for sovereignty appears to have been put forward first: see esp. 7–14, 81–5, 106–29, 160–6 (and cf. Vale, *Angevin Legacy*, 16, 59–61). For the alods of subjects: Tucoo-Chala, *Gaston Fébus*, 169 n.

[141] Baldwin, *Government*, 262 and n. 11. For vavassors, see index: vavassors.

[142] *Livres de Jostice et de Plet*, 67.

were sometimes said to hold their land from him.[143] From the late eleventh century, if not before, the expression 'to move from' (*movere de*) was also used, apparently in much the same way, to indicate a subordination that was sometimes merely political rather than involving any derogation from rights of property as such. By the thirteenth century, when the word fief was applied to much property held with full rights, both fiefs and alods were regularly said to be held from (or move from) someone else.[144] A subject with the normal full rights of property could thus also be referred to as a tenant.[145] Some subjects or tenants, of course, had reduced rights. Peasants did so, and so did those who held land, especially from churches, on terms entailing subordinate and limited rights. Above those levels, however, the hierarchy implied in 'holding from' someone, or having property that 'moved from' them, looks more like a hierarchy of government, which corresponded roughly to the social hierarchy, than it looks like a hierarchy of property rights. The changes in words, concepts, and phenomena in previous centuries show that this hierarchy had not been created by the grant of property from lords to men. Much property, including fiefs, seems to have been conveyed by putting the new owner in the same place as the old, rather than by making a new layer of property rights. Property that was granted, whether to a church or to laymen, probably continued to be thought of as held from the donor only for two reasons. The first was that the donor deliberately reserved rents from it, as might happen, for instance, when townsmen used land as a safe investment.[146] The second, and, I suggest, more common, was that the donor and his successors exercised authority and power in the area in which the property lay and wanted to continue to do so, whatever the rights he conveyed.

The way that the pattern of 'holding from' reflected political authority is exemplified in references to church property. It does not seem to be merely because records multiply that the property of great churches begins to be referred to in the twelfth century as held from the king or from counts, while from the thirteenth it is also said to be held in fief. Whether bishops or great churches held from counts, or counts from bishops and

---

[143] Chapter 5, at nn. 176–9.

[144] *Novum Glossarium*: M, col. 878–9; Poly and Bournazel, 'Couronne et mouvance', 220. For a selection of other examples: alods held from (*ab*): *Rec. Philippe Auguste*, no. 197; *Layettes*, v, no. 431; Boutruche, *Société provinciale*, 242; held *sub dominio et districtu*: *Rec. d'actes relatifs à Guyenne*, no. 237. Unclassified property moving from: *Cart. Trinité Vendôme*, no. 340 (1092); *Rec. Philippe Auguste*, nos. 621, 647; fiefs moving from: *RHGF*, xix. 760; *Les Olim*, i. 418–19, 424–5; services (*corvede*) moving from: *Rec. Philippe Auguste*, no. 890; rent moving from: *Les Olim*, i. 491. A lordship and a fief had *per*: Giordanengo, *Droit féodal*, 31, 32 n.

[145] Matthew Paris, *Chronica Majora*, ii. 658. This may reflect English usage rather than what Philip said, but I suspect that he could have used the word.

[146] e.g. *Coutumes de Toulouse*, 132–42, 247; Richardot, 'Fief roturier'.

churches, was a matter of local politics and of the relations of jurisdiction that were now being constructed out of political relationships. It might sometimes be the result of recent and remembered grants, but often it was not. When Louis VII confirmed a purchase made by the abbey of Montmartre he said that his parents had founded and loved the abbey, but his charter does not worry about such points of feudal principle as whether either the whole monastic estate, or this new acquisition, was or was not held from him. Nor does it state that any of these transactions made him its lord.[147] Of course he was its lord—though not apparently the immediate lord of the new property—but that was because the monastery lay in the area that was under his political authority, not because of any particular donation. Churches did not lose rights in their property when it was described as held from counts or kings. In so far as more effective lay government and jurisdiction promoted the security of property in general, their rights were made more secure. In so far as their property acquired more obligations it was because, as we shall see, governments, and especially the king's government, were increasing the obligations on all property.

Areas of political control and government became units of jurisdiction as courts began to establish their authority and more systematic administration began to produce firm boundaries between the units. As discontented litigants appealed from one lord's court to another, the hierarchy of political authority and power—the hierarchy of 'holding from'—became a hierarchy of jurisdiction. Evolving as it did from the power politics of the tenth and eleventh centuries, it was a ramshackle hierarchy. By the thirteenth century phrases like 'high and low justice' were being bandied about but they did not arrive complete with definitions.[148] Rules had to be worked out. Some were made to suit hard cases and produced more problems later on. The earliest judgements of the king's court that are preserved in *Les Olim* include quite a few in which the jurisdiction of lower courts was at issue: in all the circumstances there may well have often been genuine uncertainties, as well as debating points, about the jurisdiction of courts over particular areas, particular cases, or particular people.[149]

Beaumanoir seems to have envisaged three main layers of jurisdiction. The first comprised that of those who held fiefs in the county of Clermont. All of them, he says, had high and low justice in their fiefs, and so did

---

[147] *Rec. Montmartre*, 93.
[148] e.g. *Les Olim*, i. 19 (xv); 919 (lxxxviii); *Établissements de Saint Louis*, ii. 36–7, 50, 59–63, 67–9, 206–9, 439.
[149] *Les Olim*, i. 417–19 (ii–v), 424–9 (xi–xii, xiv–xvii, xix), 431 (xxvi); cf. ibid. 5–6 (xiv), 8–9 (xii, xiv, xvii, xix), 19–22 (xv, xx), 29 (vii–viii).

churches which had long held *eritages francs*.[150] Both categories raise problems: the churches because of the obvious difficulty of deciding which were old enough and free enough, and the fiefholders because Beaumanoir points out elsewhere that sometimes high and low justice were divided. Perhaps he meant to attribute full rights only to those holding directly from the count. In practice, moreover, as he says, all these jurisdictions were very confused territorially.[151] Above this rather uneven level Beaumanoir seems to envisage only two layers of jurisdiction: appeals in the Beauvaisis went first to the count of Clermont, as a tenant in barony, and then to the king.[152] The *Établissements de Saint Louis* and the *Livres de Jostice et de Plet* give rather different pictures, as well they might, considering the way that the judicial system had grown.[153] The profits of government and jurisdiction stimulated the conceptualization and recording of layers of hierarchy. The royal legislation of 1275 that imposed controls on gifts to the church envisaged three or more layers of lords who might claim the penalties for infringement. A case of 1270 suggests that there could be more.[154] Some of the layers may have been created by fairly recent sales or gifts: with more systematic jurisdiction and imposition of dues, and with more legal advice on conveyancing, those with claims to jurisdiction and dues were more likely to reserve their rights over those to whom they conveyed lesser lordships and jurisdictions. How much, and how regularly, the units of jurisdiction, once established, were altered by minor changes of property and lordship is uncertain. John de Blanot was not sure about the extent of a lord's jurisdiction over his liegemen's other fiefs and over the fiefs of his non-liegemen.[155]

What gave the hierarchy its shape, even in the early stages of its formation in the twelfth century, was the position of the king at its head—not as a lord over vassals or as the grantor of fiefs, but as *king*—the quintessential type of prince or ruler in medieval ideas, the supreme ruler of the natural and given unit of society that was constituted by a kingdom and its people.[156] I know of no text from France before 1300 that refers to the king in purely feudo-vassalic terms, as a lord who held authority only over those who held their land from him because he or his predecessors had granted it to them or their predecessors. Calling the subjects of his kingdom his vassals is a modern habit that derives from the usage of late medieval lawyers who were interested only in those they considered fiefholders, not

[150] Beaumanoir, *Coutumes*, § 295, 1641.                    [151] Ibid. § 1653.
[152] Ibid. § 294–5.
[153] *Établissements de Saint Louis*, ii. 36–7, 206–8; *Livres de Jostice et de Plet*, 66–7, 83.
[154] *Ordonnances*, i. 304 (c. 7); *Les Olim*, i. 851. See below at n. 213.
[155] Acher, 'Notes', 174–5.                    [156] Reynolds, *Kingdoms and Communities*, 256–61, 319–23.

in the nature of political relations between king and subjects.[157] Before 1200 royal authority had for long been effectively restricted to a small area, but that was not because any theory of the time that we know of permitted kings no authority over the men of their men. Suger liked to portray counts and dukes as holding their land by royal favour and, at least in the later years of his life, came to think that the king should not do homage for what he held from Saint-Denis.[158] Holding church property had not in the past normally implied being in any general and political sense under church lordship, but more systematic government and jurisdiction were producing more systematic ideas. By the time of the *Livres de Jostice et de Plet*, Philip Augustus's objection to doing homage to anyone else for any land he held had been turned into a maxim not merely that the king should not do homage, but that he ought not to hold from another.[159] This may have been wishful thinking on the part of subject lords, for by 1303, and perhaps before, the king's acquisition of land in subordinate lordships was becoming a grievance to his subjects.[160] In the context of royal promises not to keep such acquisitions in his own hand it is unlikely that the objection came from general feudal principles against a king's holding of land from his subjects. That would have worried him more than them. Any general principle of *Leihezwang* (a supposed obligation on a king or other lord to grant out again any fiefs that came to him by confiscation or for lack of heirs) is equally ruled out by the way that the king of France had earlier taken over so many lordships.[161] What may have worried people by 1303, and certainly worried the Champenois and Burgundians by 1314, was surely the extra foothold in other jurisdictions that extra royal property gave to royal officials.

In the extension of royal justice, as in so much else, the reign of Philip Augustus marks a stage. Before it, royal jurisdiction, like other jurisdictions in different parts of the kingdom, was little more than notional. Nevertheless the notion mattered: even Henry II of England paid lip-service to it, and once Philip was in charge the royal court began to function with more effect.[162] The confiscation of the Angevin inheritance, the manipulation of the inheritances of Vermandois and Champagne, the protests of the barons of France against ecclesiastical jurisdiction—all these and much more must have raised the prestige of the king's court. From the 1250s its records show it in action. Some appeals came even from Gascony,

---

[157] See e.g. Boulet-Sautel, 'Droit romain', 500 n.
[158] Above, at nn. 59–64.                         [159] *Livres de Jostice et de Plet*, 67.
[160] *Ordonnances*, i. 357–8 (8–9), 558 (4), 572–3 (33–4), 574 (3), 578 (3), 697 (5).
[161] Though there was a *Leihezwang* within a year and a day for properties in Champagne in the late thirteenth century (Evergates, *Feudal Society*, 38).
[162] Duchesne, *Hist. Franc. Scriptores*, iv. 731; Baldwin, *Government*, 37–44, 137–9.

though at first they were referred back.[163] Most, of course, came from near at hand and from counties under direct royal authority, while many issues were sent back to be decided by local custom in local courts, but that was a matter of course according to medieval custom and law. Ideas, however vague, of a law common to the kingdom were beginning to grow.[164] The 'custom of France' often meant the local custom of the Île-de-France, but it could mean something more.[165] Beaumanoir's exaggeration of the wide range of appeals and of royal legislative authority is itself significant of the way that things looked in the late thirteenth century. Historians comment more often on his view of holders in barony as sovereigns than on his remark that, if he did not explain that he used *souvrain* to mean a count or duke, his readers might think that he meant the king.[166] Royal legislation was often ineffective, but that was common in medieval conditions. Ineffectiveness does not seem to have been the consequence of any idea of a hierarchy of rights that allowed the king to legislate only for the area under his direct authority. Some royal legislation was ineffective within the area under direct royal authority as well as elsewhere, while the legislation about alienations in mortmain and non-noble fiefs had some effect even in Gascony.

By 1303 royal jurisdiction was expanding locally as well as by way of appeal. Royal officials in different parts of the kingdom were summoning before local royal courts people who thought they were under other jurisdictions. Philip IV's reform ordinance suggests that he needed to pacify the discontented.[167] A great many clauses of the complaints laid before Louis X in 1314–15 were designed to protect lower jurisdictions against royal encroachment.[168] To see the discontented through the spectacles of 1789 as selfish nobles protecting their feudal rights is anachronistic. The jurisdictions that they wanted to preserve were held by nobles, but they were feudal neither in the Marxist sense of being exercised exclusively or mainly over peasants nor in the feudo-vassalic sense of being exercised exclusively or mainly over fiefs. Nor do the grievances presented to Louis X suggest that royal jurisdiction was resisted on the grounds of a feudo-vassalic principle that the man of my man is not my man. It was resisted because it was being extended at a time when local jurisdictions had become established in custom—and when the king was desperate to get men and money for his

---

[163] *Rôles gascons: supplément au tome premier*, pp. cxiii–cxviii.
[164] Petot, 'Droit commun'.
[165] Roger Wendover, *Flores*, ii. 186–8; Wood, *French Apanages*, 41; cf. *Les Olim*, i. 422–4, 572–3; also *curia gallicana*: Baldwin, *Government*, 139.
[166] Beaumanoir, *Coutumes*, § 1043.
[167] *Ordonnances*, i. 358 (8–9); Chaplais, 'Souveraineté'; Benton, 'Philip the Fair'.
[168] *Ordonnances*, i. 551–80.

wars. Seigniorial jurisdictions, however confused, overlapping, and conflicting, represented local custom and were, it seems, preferred by their
subjects for everyday use (with the possibility of an appeal beyond them)
as well as cherished by their lords. People wanted to be tried in their own
castellanies according to their own local customs and by their own neighbours and peers. Since the documents of 1314–15 are concerned with royal
and not seigniorial oppression it would be wrong to deduce from them that
everything in seigniorial gardens was lovely, but equally it is quite possible
that the traditional right of judgement by one's peers was threatened more
at this period by royal officials and lawyers than by the traditional local
courts.[169]

The social hierarchy was a permanent, if malleable, fact, and by the thirteenth century the hierarchy of government and jurisdiction had become
another. It was also a fact that jurisdiction and property were linked,
though in rather an untidy and inexact way. How contemporaries conceptualized these facts is much more mysterious. By now the hierarchy within
the new monastic orders, as well as the hierarchy of the whole church,
must have made the idea of layers of authority much more widely familiar
than it had been before the twelfth century. Yet none of this means that
people thought in terms quite like the modern medievalist's feudal hierarchy of tenure. In Normandy, as in England, fiefholders may have come
near to doing so because of the way that their properties were listed and
that services and dues were taken from them according to the lists: hence
the later belief that Norman vavassors were defined in terms of their position in the hierarchy.[170] Elsewhere, though the facts were not so very different, they were different in ways that probably made notions of them
slightly different. People who took part in local government and law, as a
fair number of those who ranked as fiefholders in the thirteenth century
would have done, must have begun to get an idea of the layers of jurisdiction immediately above them. Even more people were liable to face
demands for dues and taxes from more than one lord, which would have
given them an unpleasant consciousness of the layers of authority above
them. Linking these layers with social status and with property may have
been natural for people who were used to thinking of the layers in terms of
one person 'holding from' another.

There is a sense, therefore, in which it is probably appropriate to talk of
a hierarchy of property as a thirteenth-century concept, even though parts
of it may have been clearer in the minds of lawyers than of laymen. We also

[169] *Ordonnances*, i. 366–7 (60–2), 552 (11), 558–9 (1–2, 8, 11), 562–3 (2–4), 566 (17); Benton,
'Philip the Fair', 285, 290–2, 297–9.
[170] Chapter 2, at nn. 21–2.

have evidence that at least some people had myths of the origin of their properties in grants by Frankish kings, though we need to note that it was not only titles to fiefs that could be traced to a distant king Charles. Titles to alods could too, so that in so far as people may have thought of the hierarchy as having originated from grants—and the evidence of this sort that we have hardly demonstrates that any such idea was generally held—it was not strictly a hierarchy of fiefs.[171] The hierarchy that people envisaged was therefore only a rough approximation to that which later lawyers and historians would elaborate. We have no reason to suppose that its roughness means that people before 1300 were making a poor shot at the later formulations. Once one starts thinking in such teleological terms it is only too easy to ignore evidence that does not fit. One such untidy piece of evidence is the use of back/front rather than up/down terminology. The word *retrobannus* appears in 1133 (though it may of course have been older), *retrofevale*, *retrofeodum*, and *retroacapitum* later in the century.[172] The idea of a society arranged in vertical layers was not the only one around.

## 7.5. *The rights and obligations of property*

Terminology is one thing and the notions or concepts that one can try to detect behind it are another. Actual rights and obligations are something else again. When property came to be labelled and classified in new ways during this period the rights and obligations attached to it by custom could not be altered overnight. They were none the less gradually reshaped, often with the help of a good deal of bad history. Beaumanoir's incidental remark that alods were free of dues to anyone stands near the beginning of the myth of alods as absolute property.[173] Where the weakness of comital power or the remoteness of royal power had allowed nobles to remain independent of superior jurisdiction, and where the idea of their property as alodial had survived or was revived, then it was indeed effectively absolute. That of their subjects was not. Where peasant alods survived and were described as free of obligations that was probably because they were being contrasted with *censives*. The only extra duty imposed on one Gascon alod that was turned into a fief in 1281 was to do homage and give each new king-duke a pair of white gloves. The duties of the new fiefholder would otherwise continue to be the same as those he had done before and as other

---

[171] Boutruche, *Société provinciale*, 123–4.
[172] Navel, 'L'Enquête de 1133', 14–15; Niermeyer, *Lexicon*, 918; Du Cange, *Glossarium*, v. 747–9.
[173] Beaumanoir, *Coutumes*, § 688.

alodholders in the area did.[174] Obligations and rights in other parts of France were no doubt different in detail, but the variations and complexities might appear as great as they do in Gascony if we had more information as detailed as that revealed by the returns to the enquiry of 1274. The subject is enormous. I shall discuss here only those changes to customary rights and obligations that seem to me particularly significant for my subject.

To start with inheritance: the tendency for the succession of fiefs to favour the eldest son and discourage division, in contrast to the normal (or relatively normal) equality and division of other property, becomes discernible in the better records of this period, though it was never complete and consistent.[175] When Hostiensis remarked that the French used primogeniture he must have been comparing their customs (or what he thought were their customs) with those of Italian and German fiefs, not with other kinds of property, with which he would not have been concerned.[176] People of high status may have begun to favour primogeniture before their property was generally known as fiefs. If so that would make any connection between it and the supposedly aboriginal military functions of fiefs even less convincing. Finding reasons why rules might have been made is, in any case, not the same as finding evidence of the rules themselves. It is hard to find evidence of the consistent application of any of the supposed rules of feudal inheritance in this period, while the earliest apparently normative statements of them often look more like maxims uttered in argument than rules of law. Philip II's grants *in feodum et hommagium ligium* tended to limit inheritance to the children of the beneficiary and his present wife, and sometimes to sons or even a single son, but the practice looks too variable to reflect either firm policy or firm custom.[177] In any case it would presumably have affected only one generation without further dispute—dispute which, in the case of small estates, would probably not be recorded or form a precedent to be followed elsewhere.[178]

Where succession to fiefs came by custom to be more restricted than succession to alods, the lord's right to seize fiefs that lacked heirs (what later feudal lawyers called escheat[179]) would presumably be more valuable.

---

[174] *Rec. d'actes relatifs à Guyenne*, no. 689; cf. nos. 177, 197, 266, 301, 617.

[175] e.g. Beaumanoir, *Coutumes*, § 461–7, 1477–8; Martin, *Coutume de Paris*, 222–3, 235–63; Giordanengo, *Droit féodal*, 207–10. There were many shared fiefs in the Agenais in 1259: Tholin and Fallières, 'Hommages'.

[176] Acher, 'Notes', 130, citing remarks in a MS of his *Summa* not in printed editions. Cf. Jacques de Révigny's allusion to primogeniture as English rather than French: *Œuvres*, 88.

[177] *Rec. Philippe Auguste*, especially from about no. 750 on.

[178] For a recorded dispute: Wood, *French Apanages*, 38–9.

[179] The word was sometimes used in other senses: Niermeyer, *Lexicon*, 387 (*excadentia*, *excaduta*).

Some alods, however, also went to the ruler on failure of heirs: in thirteenth-century Gascony, whereas an intestate and heirless fiefholder's property went to his lord, an alodholder's went to the duke.[180] Before so many properties carrying full rights had become known as fiefs those that lacked heirs had sometimes been taken by lords. Around 1129 Louis VI seized the property of a benefactor of the abbey of Morigny (Seine-et-Oise) who died without heirs, apparently on the ground that he had come from the royal household (*quoniam de familia eius ortus*), although there is no reason to believe that he had held the property as less than a traditional full inheritance. Louis was persuaded to restore what the abbey claimed to have been given by the dead man.[181] Whether laymen would have considered his seizure lawful it is hard to tell, but he was not very successful in his attempt to impose a new count on Flanders when Charles the Good died without heirs. There, as in the county of Boulogne in 1173, the men of the county felt that they ought to choose the successor to an heirless count, and their wishes could not safely be ignored.[182] Deciding whether property at this level was really heirless and choosing an heir was politically sensitive. Even Philip Augustus manipulated vulnerable inheritances rather than seizing them. Presumably better records and the increasing formality of law made the so-called escheat of valuable lordships harder thereafter.

Inheritance, however, was more and more likely to need formal acknowledgement by the heir's lord. I have already suggested that even before noble properties came to be classified as fiefs lords or rulers were beginning to require their more important subjects to recognize their authority by doing homage. By the early thirteenth century heirs of property in Champagne were not merely having to do homage but were supposed to be able to identify their fief and say whether it was liege or not, while in at least parts of the south the oaths they took were beginning to follow forms taken from the *Libri Feudorum* or other learned texts.[183] From then on lords with competent record-keepers and legal advisers could make the systematic taking of homages and 'recognitions of fiefs' profitable, whether for political or financial purposes.[184] Although the scarcity of earlier records makes it impossible to be sure, the previous history of free property makes this look much more like a development of the new government and law than a survival of ancient custom from the time when fiefs had not been fully heritable.

I have suggested that the first time that people above peasant status paid

---

[180] Boutruche, *Société provinciale*, 243.     [181] *Chronique de Morigny*, 47, 48–9.
[182] Galbert of Bruges, *Histoire*, 81–4, 151–3; Gislebert of Mons, *Chronique*, 90–1.
[183] Longnon, *Documents*, i. 75–, e.g. no. 2888; Giordanengo, '*Epistola Philiberti*', 837–47, and *Droit féodal*, 145.
[184] e.g. Peyvel, 'Structures féodales'.

succession duties (reliefs, *rachats*, *acapta*, *placita*, etc.[185]) it was on land they held from churches.[186] Such dues seem to have spread to a good many areas and a good many properties by the thirteenth century, when their incidence was becoming fossilized by written records. That incidence does not fit traditional feudal interpretations very neatly. In 1127–8 the count of Flanders granted the Templars all reliefs from the lands of deceased persons in his land of Flanders, while the castellan of Saint-Omer gave them the payment *quod reliquum dici solet*, which he ought to receive by custom of the land from any *feodatus* belonging to his castellany or his fief. In 1160 the count remitted to the abbey of Saint-Winoc (Nord) a due (*emptionem que vulgo dicitur cop*) that it had been accustomed to pay to him and his predecessors on the death of the abbot.[187] It seems at least as likely that these customs were evidence of the early development of government in the country as that they were a survival from the relations of lords and vassals in that mythical age when noble property was held as fiefs but 'the heritability of fiefs had not yet become an established custom'.[188] In Ponthieu the count reserved his right relief (*rectum relevaminum*) from a property that he granted in 1179 *jure hereditario* and free of all other dues.[189] The royal ordinance of 1209 about divided inheritances assumes that *rachat* was due from *feodalia tenementa*. Whatever that phrase meant in the early thirteenth century, the incidence of inheritance dues varied according to local custom.[190] In Beaumanoir's time most fiefs in the Beauvaisis paid *rachat* only when they passed to collaterals, but in some of its lordships all fiefs owed them. Beaumanoir does not mention succession dues on *vilenages*, but wardship rights over the two sorts of property were not all that different.[191] In Gascony alods seem to have normally been exempt in 1274 from the *sporla*, *acaptum*, or *acaptamentum* normally paid from fiefs to the king-duke, but at least one abbey owed it on the land it held *in allodium liberum*.[192] The *sporla*, however, was not a succession duty of the normal kind, since it seems often, if not invariably, to have been paid, not on the change of property-holder, but on the accession of a new duke. Whether the more ordinary kind of succession due was owed to other lords does not appear. *Sporla* is mentioned here only because historians have linked it to dues paid at succession of the property-owner by considering both kinds

[185] Distinctions of meanings between the different names are more likely to have been drawn by later lawyers and historians than by contemporaries: see e.g. Richardot, 'Fief roturier', 519 n.
[186] Chapter 5, at nn. 114–16.   [187] *Chron. Bergues-Saint-Winoc*, 118–19.
[188] As suggested by Ganshof, *Feudalism*, 137.
[189] *Rec. comtes de Pontieu*, nos. 100, 132, 356. For aids, below.
[190] *Rec. Philippe Auguste*, no. 1083; cf. *Ordonnances*, i. 55–6.
[191] Beaumanoir, *Coutumes*, § 471, 506–50; cf. Jacques d'Ableiges, *Grand Coutumier*, 311.
[192] *Rec. d'actes relatifs à Guyenne*, nos. 100, 197, 216, 301, 537; cf. pp. 340–1. Cf. Tholin and Fallières, 'Hommages', e.g. 20–2, 45–7; *Livre d'Agenais*, 10–17.

ering both kinds of payment as relics of a time when the link between lord and man ended at the death of either, and by using the paired German words *Herrenfall* and *Mannfall* to describe them.[193] The Hospitallers of Toulouse are recorded as imposing dues, apparently in the late twelfth and early thirteenth centuries, both on the death of their tenants and on the death of the prior.[194] Presumably this was simply their policy as landlords, which they may have been more free to apply than were lay lords who had to deal with many properties under their jurisdiction without any recorded grant behind them. Neither these Toulouse dues, nor the Gascon *sporla*, nor the more usual kind of succession dues seem very likely to have been survivals of an archaic relationship.

A further obstacle to seeing French inheritance dues in distinctively feudo-vassalic terms concerns those that should, under later theories of feudalism, have been paid to the king by counts and dukes, as well as by the humbler subjects who were under direct royal authority. Ganshof represented the hundred marks that Louis VI allegedly took from Flanders after the election of William Clito as a relief that was due because reliefs survived everywhere as a relic of the time when fiefs had not been fully heritable.[195] But Flanders was surely not a fief in Ganshof's sense in the early twelfth century.[196] Galbert of Bruges's account makes the payment look more like Louis's price for supporting William's bid for the county. It also makes the citizens of Bruges concede that a count's heir would owe the king arms (*armatura*) for lands he held *in feodum* from the king, but it is clear that this meant possible extra lands, not the county itself. This gratuitous statement, as Pirenne called it, was made for the needs of argument. It is interesting as suggesting ideas about fiefs that were around at the time—and perhaps the citizens' acceptance of succession dues as normal in Flanders—but there is no reason to suppose that even this limited relief had normally, if ever, been paid.[197] Apart from that, the first evidence of anything like succession dues payable by great lords to the king comes, significantly, from the reign of Philip Augustus. He took large sums, or valuable estates, from a number of great lords and ladies, but, significantly, they were all people about whose inheritance he could make difficulties.[198] That Philip did not get a relief from Richard I but got one from his brother John illustrates his opportunism.[199] Gislebert of Mons maintained that the

[193] Ganshof, *Feudalism*, 139; cf. Brunner, *Deutsche Rechtsgeschichte*, ii. 341–2; Mitteis, *Lehnrecht*, 137, 590.

[194] Richardot, 'Fief roturier', 518–19.       [195] Ganshof, *Feudalism*, 136–9.

[196] Chapter 5.3, and at nn. 205–7.       [197] Galbert of Bruges, *Histoire*, 151–3.

[198] Baldwin, *Government*, 277–9.

[199] Baldwin, *Government*, 278, represents payments made by Richard as a relief, but cf. *Chron. Henry II and Richard I*, 73–4.

relief paid by the count of Flanders and Hainaut was owed by law in France, but maybe that was because Gislebert thought the count's submission to paying it needed excuse.[200] Payments from great counts and dukes on their inheritance, although occasionally made after Philip's reign, apparently did not, in the event, become customary.[201] Political reality was against them: by the time that feudal theory had been developed to justify them, custom had ruled them out.

Freedom of disposition was another grey area. The right to alienate had been regularly specified in Carolingian grants of alods to laymen, but it was much more rarely mentioned in royal charters after 1100, even if they granted property for ever and did not specify that it was to be held in fief.[202] The right must have been eroded in the mean time by the blurring and changing of the old categories and by the custom of getting consent to gifts to the church. It was also, of course, limited in practice by the rights of heirs.[203] By the twelfth century, charters and the occasional record of customs reveal a variety of restraints on the disposal of properties that might once have been called alods and would for the most part from the thirteenth century be called fiefs. Sometimes, for instance, alienation to certain classes of person or institution (most often the clergy or churches) was prohibited or needed special permission. Sometimes the lord was given a right of pre-emption. It would be wrong to deduce general rules, let alone archaic feudal principles, behind the variations. Charters may embody at most the policy of one ruler or landlord, while the custom laid down in supposedly normative texts may not have been either ancient when the record was made or consistently applied thereafter. To judge from the way that Louis IX's brother, Alphonse of Poitiers, and later kings chased up past alienations which might have been made without the consent of lower lords, some lords did not apply any rules firmly or consistently. Any rules that there were may not have paid attention to the distinction between what legal historians call subinfeudation and substitution. Some charters show lords taking part in the transaction themselves, so that one could say that the alienation took the form of what we call substitution: that is, it put the new owner in the same relation to his lord as the previous one had enjoyed. A considerable proportion of charters before the thirteenth century, however, do not say that the property conveyed was to be held from anyone. As the land market grew, as services were more

---

[200] Gislebert of Mons, *Chronique*, 275.

[201] *RHGF*, xxi. 255. Works on fourteenth-century or later finance and administration do not seem to mention them.

[202] Exceptions: Tardif, *Monuments*, no. 420; *Rec. Philippe Auguste*, nos. 263, 402, 1112, 1372; Richardot, 'Fief roturier', 335 n. (from 1327).

[203] Laplanche, *Réserve coutumière*, 134, 137–44, 192–3, 198; Ourliac, *Études*, 199–226.

systematically extracted, and as charters were more precisely drafted, the distinction between subinfeudation and substitution becomes visible to us, but it would be some time before lawyers worked out terminology and rules.[204]

Lords who tried to control alienations could do so most effectively where they had reasonably effective jurisdiction.[205] In 1206 the monks of Saint-Ouen, Rouen, got the king to cancel a sale of property *de quorum feodo* that had been made without their consent, but they had to pay more than the original purchaser to get it for themselves.[206] Where jurisdiction was effective a wide range of properties might be affected. In Montpellier, although alods were in principle freely disposable, a due known as *consilium* or *laudimium* was nevertheless owed by their purchasers, while special consultation and permission were needed for alienations to churches, clergy, or knights.[207] Even where custom continued to insist on alodial liberties, government officials sometimes ignored it. In 1202 the count of Flanders gave one of his subjects explicit permission to alienate an alod, evidently because the local bailiff had made difficulties.[208] Louis IX ordered his bailiffs in Languedoc to stop taking dues on the sale of alods, but dues were being taken in Périgord in 1315.[209] The 1274 Gascon returns suggest that dues were not normally paid to the king-duke on the sale of either fiefs or alods, or were too rare or insignificant to mention, but one *prévôt* said that alodholders alienating their lands had to do so through him and that he received a *venda* for his trouble.[210] Dues taken by officials, however wrongly, became customary if they went unchallenged for long enough. Nevertheless, the continued and officially endorsed claim of alods to freedom (or greater freedom) of disposition is noteworthy in view of the way that by 1300 so many former alods had lost the freedom in losing their name. It is tempting to suggest that snobbery had a price, but that would be unfair. Most properties classified in the thirteenth century as fiefs had for long been in a grey area of non-classification: we cannot say that their owners deliberately chose status rather than freedom of disposition.

Before 1100 it had not been unknown for lords to be paid for their consent to gifts of property—even full property—to the church.[211] It was probably in this period, however, that more of them began to exploit the

---

[204] Richardot, 'Fief roturier', 344. The rules in the ordinance of 1209 (*Rec. Philippe Auguste*, no. 1083) obviously had little effect on general practice. See above, at n. 146.

[205] Cf. Sautel, 'Note sur le droit', 691–2.　　　　[206] *Rec. Philippe Auguste*, no. 943.

[207] *Liber Instrumentorum*, nos. 127, 244; also 112, 139, 167–8, 172–3, 234, 465.

[208] *Oorkonden*, no. 203.　　　　[209] *Ordonnances*, i. 65 (c. 23), 554 (c. 4).

[210] *Rec. d'actes relatifs à Guyenne*, no. 680; I deduce that *vende* were rare, not from a thorough search, but from Bémont's omission of them from his glossary. Cf. Boutruche, *Société provinciale*, 122, 242.

[211] Chapter 5 at n. 143.

possibility systematically. Alphonse of Poitiers made significant profits out
of it, having enquiries made into past alienations and imposing penalties on
them. He met with some objections from subordinate lords for overriding
their rights and on occasion had to concede that he would not step in if they
exercised proper controls, but it does not look as if there were any established rules, beyond custom, about which lord had the authority.
Alphonse's own alienations were, it seems, made without permission from
the king, but after his death his policy of controlling what in French
became known as *amortissement* (in England gifts in mortmain) was taken
over, along with some of his officials, by his nephew, Philip III.[212] In 1270
the count of Blois denied, in effect, that churches needed royal consent to
acquire properties held under him (that is, apparently, in a castellany
belonging to him). He was, he said, so great a man that he could deal with
such matters himself: the three or four layers of lordship between him and
the land at issue did not apparently worry him.[213] In 1275 a royal ordinance
set out a tariff of penalties by which the past alienation both of alods and
of fiefs held from other lords was penalized less heavily than that of fiefs
and *censives* held directly from the king, but they were still penalized.[214]
The royal government was, it seems, like that of Alphonse before it,
slightly hampered by having to respect the rights of those lower down in
the hierarchy of jurisdiction, but it was not totally inhibited by them.[215]
Although lords may have imposed controls of their own where they could,
fiefs in this context were not primarily properties whose owners enjoyed a
special, originally affective, relation to their lords and were therefore especially subject to control by those lords. So long as the memory of alodial
liberties survived, fiefs in the context of royal policy were simply properties that were not alods (though many of them would once have been) and
were therefore easier for the government to tax, irrespective of what lords
lower down the hierarchy might do. The difference between the two kinds
of property was more the product of the new sort of government, legal
argument, and legal records, than of ancient values and customs.

The same ordinance of 1275 imposed a fine on non-nobles who acquired
fiefs, including those held under other lords.[216] This too followed precedents set by Alphonse,[217] and by other lords before him, and, since those
qualified to serve suitably were apparently exempt, seems to have been
originally intended to secure military service. In view of the past history of

[212] Guébin, 'Amortissements'; *Les Olim*, i. 831, 884.                    [213] *Les Olim*, i. 851.
[214] *Ordonnances*, i. 303–4, 323–4, 553–7, 561–7, 746, 798; ii. 22.
[215] *Les Olim*, ii. 108. Some effort was even made to apply the ordinance in Gascony: Chaplais, 'Souveraineté', 455–9.
[216] *Ordonnances*, i. 304 (c. 7).
[217] *Correspondance admin.* nos. 941, 1213, 1271, 1276, 1321; *Enquêtes admin.*, 304.

military obligation and the vagueness of the concept of nobility, it is difficult to envisage it as deriving from any very old tradition. By 1315 its fiscal purpose had become dominant and was arousing discontent in several
parts of the kingdom.[218] The prohibition and the fines were important
enough for royal servants and other favoured people to seek exemption
and, by prompting some to secure formal ennoblement, played a significant, though not decisive, part in starting the process which created the
juridically defined nobility of the Ancien Régime.[219]

The right to build fortifications on one's property came into question as
lords extended their controls over their lordships more systematically. For
later feudal lawyers and historians castles were quintessentially feudal
property, but the chapter devoted to them by the eighteenth-century jurist
Nicolas Brussel shows how difficult it was to deduce rules about fortifica-
tion that did not do violence either to his sources or to his ideas about feudal society.[220] In the twelfth-century cases Brussel cited he deduced
*mouvances* from disputes, but this involved reading a good deal of the law
of fiefs as he understood it into twelfth-century sources: he had both to
assume unrecorded subinfeudations and to explain how lords retained
authority over subinfeudated castles. In Champagne, he said, fortresses
could not be built even on alods without consent of the count, but the cases
he cited from 1209 and 1284 show that alodholders seem to have thought
that they could build them. In 1209 the noble concerned put a temporary
stop to his building on one alod and made another alod into a liege fief of
the countess in order to be able to fortify a house there that would be under
her authority and would be surrendered to her if she required. In 1284 it
appeared that royal officials had stopped a less important alodholder from
fortifying a house. He pointed out that there were already several fortified
houses on his alod which were held in fief from the count. This suggests a
complication of categories, which probably turned out to be totally irrelevant anyway, since the count soon afterwards became king as Philip the
Fair. The house no doubt remained for the time being unfortified. The
rules about alods and fiefs, jurability and rendability, *grande force* and *petite
force* in what Brussel thought of as feudal law were not in reality grounded
in an archaic bond between lords and the vassals to whom they had granted

---

[218] *Ordonnances*, 554 (c. 2), 572 (c. 32), 574 (c. 1); cf. Chaplais, 'Souveraineté', 455–9. There
is, however, no note of the legislation in *Coutumes de Toulouse* (above, at nn. 104–5).

[219] e.g. *Archives historiques de Poitou*, xiii, nos. 209, 272, 313; Rogozinski, 'Ennoblement';
Barthélemy, 'Lettres d'anoblissement', 198–207. Other motives, apart from straight status, could
relate to jurisdiction (being under royal jurisdiction might suit a royal official): *Les Olim*, i. 108,
761–2, ii. 191–2; *Actes du Parlement*, nos. 464, 2192, 2212, 6973, 7497; also perhaps hunting: *Actes
du Parlement*, i. 401 (no. 590).

[220] Brussel, *Nouvel examen*, 378–90.

fiefs, but were worked out through individual cases by more or less professional lawyers.

The general belief that attendance at courts was a characteristic obligation of fiefholders and that this was linked with their right to judgement by their peers is only half true: all courts were supposed to be composed of at least a representative selection of those over whom jurisdiction was exercised, and it was they who were supposed to do the judging.[221] Fiefholders did not have the right to judgement by peers because of their fiefs, but they were now more likely to preserve it because their higher status made them harder to browbeat. It also made their attendance in court more desirable and more likely to be recorded: judgements made by people of higher status had proportionately more authority. Within the fief of any lord (using the word fief in one of its older but still current senses) the suitors and judges who would be most needed in any court would be those whose property was by the thirteenth century likely to be described as fiefs. They would be likely to take the lead in dealing with all subjects as well as with disputes about their own property. By the end of the thirteenth century separate courts for fiefholders were apparently being held in Flanders to deal with matters concerning fiefs, but this seems to be an innovation.[222]

As for security against confiscation, my argument about the confiscation of Normandy has already suggested that no property was totally secure in the early thirteenth century, any more than it is at any time or in any other society. Nevertheless, as rules became more formal and fixed, outright confiscation of all property above peasant level probably became harder. In particular, when appeals to the king's court became more a matter of course, it became harder for any lord except the king to confiscate property without being challenged. In so far as fiefs were more vulnerable than alods—and it is not clear that in general they were—it might be because noble property tended to be classified as fiefs and nobles were the sort of people most likely to get into the sort of political trouble that could entail confiscation. In the case of the more ordinary sort of crimes that entailed forfeiture, alods were, however, not necessarily any better protected than fiefs: in Gascony the only difference was that alods were forfeit to the king-duke whereas fiefs went to their lord.[223] One way in which fiefs might, on the other hand, have been better protected than other property would have been if their confiscation had, as later ideas of feudalism maintain, been uniquely subject to the judgement of peers. There may have been some truth in this in the thirteenth century, though not for the reasons tradi-

---

[221] Above, chapter 2.3.
[222] All Ganshof's references to separate courts in *Recherches* seem to be late.
[223] Boutruche, *Société provinciale*, 156–7, 243.

tionally alleged. Although some references to the judgement of peers in the twelfth century and the early thirteenth look as though they reflect the old norms of collective judgement for all, with the peers of the accused or of the litigants taking a prominent part, others suggest that the word peers was coming to be applied more narrowly to élites who may have been the leading or exclusive judges in courts. There may have been regular panels of such peers in some places, but the evidence of them that has hitherto been cited seems to be weak in the thirteenth century and even weaker before then.[224] In the twelfth century any such élites above the peasant level are very unlikely to have held their land with anything less than what were thought of as full rights.[225]

In the thirteenth century, however, when noble property came to be classified as fiefs, fiefholders were those who were best placed to withstand the erosion of collective judgement by the growing authority of professional judges and lawyers. Beaumanoir reserved judgement by peers to fiefholders, and implied that they had it because they were, or ought to be, gentlemen.[226] Others spoke of barons, or dukes, counts, and barons, as having the right to judgement by their peers.[227] Perhaps the use of the phrase 'judgement of peers' with reference to people of high status reflects the influence of learned law, but if so, new ideas had not entirely ousted old ones: Beaumanoir thought that when bailiffs judged cases that did not concern fiefholders they should nevertheless take counsel with the wisest— presumably of the whole assembly.[228] The 'peers of France' illustrate both the importance of social status, rather than ancient feudal custom, in the way that judgement of peers worked in thirteenth-century France and also its weakness to withstand the advance of professional law. The small group of great nobles who became known as the peers of France was a social and political élite within the larger group of those who would come to be seen as the direct tenants of the king—those who in English terms eventually came to be called tenants in chief.[229] At intervals throughout the thirteenth century and into the early years of the fourteenth the peers of France tried

---

[224] *Diplomatic Documents*, no. 1; *Rec. Henri II*, no. 234; Luchaire, *Actes de Louis VII*, no. 419; Gislebert de Mons, *Chronique*, 185; Bémont, *De Johanne*, 65–7. See chapter 5, at n. 57.

[225] Ganshof, *Recherches*, 72–3, identified the men·of higher status who took the lead in witnessing and judging with fiefholders, and also suggested (85–7 *et passim*) that feudal and non-feudal cases were judged in separate tribunals. Both arguments rested on applying the categories of the later academic law of fiefs to sources that, as he admitted, did not make the distinctions clear.

[226] Beaumanoir, *Coutumes*, § 1507; cf. § 23–6. In *Kingdoms and Communities*, 54, I wrongly translated *homme di fief* as 'men of the fee' [i.e. fief]. They are clearly fiefholders.

[227] *Établissements de Saint Louis*, ii. 124–5; *Livres de Justice et de Plet*, 68.

[228] Beaumanoir, *Coutumes*, § 23, 35–6, 45. The other men of the count who are to be judged by those who are their peers (§ 45) may not be fiefholders. Cf. *Coutumiers de Normandie*, i. 34 (IX. 9); *Ordonnances*, i. 559 (c. 11), 566 (c. 17).

[229] Chapter 8, at nn. 164–9.

to claim exclusive rights to judge each other, but all they won was the right to be judged only in the king's court—and even that was, at least for a while, shared by other counts and barons.[230] It was a hollow victory, for the king's court was inevitably the court in France that was bound to be the most dominated by professional lawyers. Academic lawyers might enjoy discussing the judgement of peers, but professional lawyers were not likely to tolerate it. Jacques d'Ableiges mentioned the peers as the most noble men of France and as entitled to plead only in the Parlement, but he said nothing about them judging each other.[231] When the sixteenth-century lawyers took up the topic of the judgement of peers they argued much about the origin of the peers of France and found some of the thirteenth-century cases about them, but what they had to say about the principle of the judgement of peers seems to have come not from practice but from academic literature on the law of fiefs.[232]

Military service in this period fits the feudal model no better than it had done earlier. Historians have traditionally tended to exaggerate the noble and therefore feudo-vassalic character of armies by deducing formal obligations from lists of those present at musters. Significant obligations continued, however, to rest on commoners, whether from town or country, and whether they fulfilled them by fighting, by payment in money, or by providing transport and supplies. In so far as fiefholders were particularly in request that was because the properties that were called fiefs by the thirteenth century were, by and large, those of nobles, which meant, by and large, those whose wealth, ethos, and training would make them most useful in an army—and most likely to be mentioned by chroniclers as present in it. If their ethos and training did not bring them to the field, their wealth might provide a compensating payment to the lord or king who had summoned them. In the twelfth century, however, the obligation on nobles was on the whole probably vaguer, because less quantified and less enforced, than that on many commoners. When counts of Flanders made contracts to supply forces to kings of England they stipulated that in case of war between England and France they would serve the king of France with as few men as they could.[233] In the event, despite frequent Anglo-French wars, they do not appear to have been greatly embarrassed. The rather partial turn-out to support the king against the threatened imperial invasion

---

[230] Lot, 'Quelques mots'; Sautel-Boulet, 'Rôle juridictionnel'; *Établissements de Saint Louis*, ii. 124–5; *Livres de Jostice et de Plet*, 68.

[231] Jacques d'Ableiges, *Grand Coutumier*, 479–81.

[232] Loyseau, *Œuvres: Livre des seigneuries*, 25, 33, and *Livres des offices*, 102; Pithou, *Opera*, 490–500, 504–5; Haillan, *Histoire*, 162–3, 229–32, 330, 700. Cf. Jackson, 'Peers of France'.

[233] *Diplomatic Documents*, no. 1; *Rec. Henri II*, no. 234. On the service involved: Brown, 'Military Service', 31–3.

of 1124 may have been an expression of a rather patchy solidarity of the kingdom. My argument so far implies that it cannot have been the performance of a traditional feudo-vassalic duty.[234] In the twelfth century demands from counts and other lords on their subjects may have been more precise and harder to evade than demands from the king on them, but most fixed quotas that individual landowners owed to lords may still have been those for garrison duty, like those so painstakingly recorded for the count of Champagne in 1172.[235] A good many people in the Champagne list did not, however, apparently have to serve in garrisons. Since the totals at the end of the list refer to them all as *milites*, it is not impossible that they all owed other military service, but if they did the uncertain status of many of their properties makes it look rather unlike a feudo-vassalic obligation.[236] The heavy obligations imposed by Henry II of England on the count of Toulouse in 1173 were obviously a special case explicable in terms of power politics and were presumably not long, if ever, enforced, though they exemplify the trend of the times in their allegedly precise formulation.[237]

Normandy looks exceptional. Fixed quotas of service seem to have been imposed there after the conquest of England. As in England, service was owed through the hierarchy of lordship. Since there is no record of any objections to the initial imposition of quotas the system was probably more an example of the new precision of demands and record-keeping than of any immediately perceptible increase in obligations. Some of the properties that owed service to the bishop of Bayeux in 1133 must have been part of the church's patrimony, but some may have been held with full rights, subject only to the bishop's banal or other jurisdiction. Many people whose lands were described in 1172 as fiefs owing quotas of service in the English manner had probably ranked as full (or alodial) property in the eleventh century. The references to the service—small but quantified—said to be owed in 1133 from the Bayeux estates to the king of France are mysterious.[238] None is mentioned in the returns from the rest of the duchy in 1172.[239] Perhaps they reflect memories of service in the Auvergne in 1126.[240] At all events it is hard to envisage many times in the twelfth

[234] Suger, *Vie de Louis VI*, 218–30.
[235] Longnon, *Documents*, i. 1–74 (and above, nn. 57–8); cf. Gislebert of Mons, *Chronique*, 74; Baldwin, *Government*, 294–5.
[236] As Evergates, *Feudal Society*, 63. For only two castellanies is it explicitly said (Longnon, *Documents*, nos. 1285, 1685) that in case of war all the men of the castellany had to turn up. Perhaps this applied to other castellanies too.
[237] *Chron. Henry II and Richard I*, i. 36; Benjamin, 'Forty Years War', 275–6.
[238] Navel, 'L'Enquête de 1133'.      [239] *Red Book*, 624–45; Boussard, 'L'Enquête de 1172'.
[240] Suger, *Vie de Louis VI*, 236; cf. Hollister, 'Normandy, France and the Anglo-Norman *Regnum*', 231.

century when Normans would have served in French armies except when
they were in revolt against their duke, which would presumably make their
legal obligations irrelevant.

In the thirteenth century the making of lists and recording of customs,
as well as the greater exactitude of charters, brought a greater precision to
military obligations outside Normandy. Landowners in the Agenais had to
state their duties when they did homage in 1259. Though there are a few
ambiguous cases, those who claimed to hold freely rather than in fief there
seem to have been free of military service. Most fiefholders owed only one
knight, and one or two owed merely a footsoldier or less.[241] In the Gascon
returns of 1274 most, though not all, fiefholders said that they owed service, generally of one or two knights, but some alodholders also owed personal armed service to the king-duke (or sometimes to his *prévôt*), while
some people said they owed military service as far as lesser men could and
should.[242] It is difficult to envisage how well defined and consistently
enforced all these small obligations would have been before records like
this were made and kept, but it is characteristic that it is these small obligations, not those of great nobles, that are recorded and quantified at all. By
Beaumanoir's time all fiefs in the Beauvaisis were supposed to produce a
horse (*ronci de service*) for the lord to use for forty days once in the lifetime
of each fiefholder. This has traditionally been regarded as the relic of a
feudo-vassalic obligation to combatant service, and Beaumanoir may himself have thought of it rather like that.[243] There are two objections, apart
from that which arises from the change in the use of the word fief. The first
is that Beaumanoir distinguishes this service from the military service to
which the king or lords holding in barony (which for Beaumanoir meant
the count of Clermont[244]) had a right whenever they needed it. Beaumanoir
does not say if that was owed only from fiefs, but the Beauvaisis would
have been exceptional if it was. The second is that eleventh-century precedents for the provision of horses of this kind do not look either noble or
vassalic.[245]

One effect of record and quantification was probably to promote argument, but some arguments had clearly preceded the records we have. In
1226 the count of Champagne is said to have claimed that he ought by the
custom of Gaul (*de consuetudine Gallicana*) to be allowed to go home after

[241] Tholin and Fallières, 'Hommages'.
[242] Boutruche, *Société provinciale*, 123–4; *Rec. d'actes relatifs à Guyenne*, nos. 179, 189, 247,
252, 537, 579.
[243] Beaumanoir, *Coutumes*, § 793–800; cf. Hubrecht: ibid. iii. 118.
[244] Beaumanoir, *Coutumes*, § 296, 322, 1467, 1469, 1471; *pace* Hubrecht: ibid. iii. 6.
[245] See chapter 5, at n. 168, and index: horse service.

forty days at the siege of Avignon.[246] The Agenais knight who, in 1259, maintained that he served, armed and horsed, when the count was present in person and for only nine days, had probably had a set-to with one of the count's deputies before that date, while the inhabitants of Saint-Livrade who claimed that their two knights should serve for forty days according to the custom of the Agenais may have been remembering an occasion when they had been made to serve longer.[247] By about the same time as the Agenais lists were made, the academic lawyer John de Blanot, probably still teaching in Bologna but soon to enter the service of the duke of Burgundy, had found good points for argument about length of service and payment of expenses, about the obligation to follow the king on crusade or, by extension, to serve anywhere far away, and about how a woman fiefholder (*vassalla*) should fulfil her obligations.[248]

During the thirteenth century the demands of the monarchy gradually shaped a new system of military service. In 1197 Philip Augustus, in summoning the dean and chapter of Reims to send their men at arms to him, warned them not to be surprised if new and unheard-of reasons made him seek unaccustomed help from them.[249] He and his son seem on other occasions to have leant on bishops for their personal attendance in armies as well as for the service owed from their property:[250] perhaps it was fiscally profitable to do so as well as making for good propaganda. Philip preserved the Norman system when he took over the duchy, but though he (and others) made a few grants outside Normandy subject to the service of one or two knights, possibly following Anglo-Norman models, he did not extend the Anglo-Norman system outside the duchy. The lists of Norman obligations were copied out and other lists of bishops and lay nobles in other parts of France were compiled, but the only details of military obligations outside Normandy that were noted in the lists seem to have been the non-noble services owed from urban and rural communities under royal jurisdiction and from the lands of royal churches. This was surely not because the new lists were defective 'feudal lists'. It was because military service was presumably only one concern of those who wrote the registers, and because the military obligations of nobles in the kingdom of France had not customarily been quantified hitherto. The lists in Philip's registers also suggest that, while counts and dukes were responsible for bringing contingents from their counties, the king was not particularly concerned

---

[246] Roger Wendover, *Flores*, ii. 312–13. Dr Claire Dutton suggests to me the influence on later practice of the legates' ruling in the Albigensian crusade. Cf. also *Capit.* nos. 192, 273.

[247] Tholin and Fallières, 'Hommages', 57 (7), 'Prise de possession', 77.

[248] Acher, 'Notes', 158–9.       [249] *Rec. Philippe Auguste*, no. 566.

[250] Ibid. no. 1257; *RHGF*, xxiii. 637 (no. 133).

with obligations in respect of individual holdings organized through a hier-archy of property in the Anglo-Norman manner.[251]

It was probably the conditions of conquest as much as any very distinc-tive northern custom that led Simon de Montfort to impose particular obligations on the northern French knights to whom he gave lands in Toulouse in 1212, but these obligations may not, in all the circumstances, have been remembered for very long.[252] Significant change came to Languedoc, as to the rest of the kingdom, because of demands made by royal officials. It was easiest for the king to raise an army in areas where he had direct jurisdiction and officials on the ground to organize the levy, rather than where local government was in the hands of counts and other lords. If that did not produce enough men the next obvious move was to appeal to counts and other great men to bring contingents from their coun-ties or lordships, but as royal administration developed, royal officials began to go into such areas to see that royal demands were fulfilled.[253] In 1247 the king's own brother complained that knights who held in fief from him had been summoned by the royal seneschal.[254] The bishop of Lodève (Hérault) complained in 1255 that the seneschal was summoning his men to *cavalcata*, so that they no longer followed the bishop in his *cavalcata*. This looks like an escort or messenger service rather than real army ser-vice, but the categories were, as usual, variable and blurred: summons to *cavalcata* may have served as the thin end of a wedge.[255] In 1272 other Languedoc bishops complained that they and their men had never had to do military service (*exercitum seu cavalgatam*) for the king before. In the same year the bishop of Mâcon also complained, and so did various local communities in northern France.[256] The pressures were building up. Fuller records show Philip IV quite clearly issuing his demands for mili-tary service not just to those who might be reckoned his immediate tenants but to his subjects (*subditi*). Nobles still mattered most because they had most to give. As the king's needs grew the obligations of nobles, as of all other subjects, were quantified as never before, not on the basis of the category into which their property was classified but according to their wealth, while royal ordinances laying down the rules were enforced by royal officials.

---

[251] Baldwin, *Government*, 171–3, 279–303; Strayer, *Administration of Normandy*, 56–68; *RHGF*, xxiii. 605–734; *Rec. Philippe Auguste*, no. 1807.

[252] Devic and Vaissete, *Hist. Languedoc*, viii, col. 629–30.

[253] *Ordonnances*, i. 345, 350–1, 370, 391–2, 546, xi. 428–30; Langlois, *Philippe III*, 363, 411; *Archives hist. de Poitou*, xiii, nos. 192, 195, 197–9.

[254] Devic and Vaissete, *Hist. Languedoc*, viii, col. 1193.

[255] *Layettes*, iii, no. 4208. Cf. Niermeyer, *Lexicon*, 112.

[256] Devic and Vaissete, *Hist. Languedoc*, x, col. 111–15; *Les Olim*, i. 886–8.

From the start there was liable to be opposition from those who found the royal demands excessive and—what came to the same thing—against custom. Some of these were towns or villages whose charters, they claimed, exempted them from service.[257] Some were churches which wanted their tenants exempted on similar grounds. Right through, other great men probably shared Alphonse of Poitiers's objection to the entry of royal officials into their patches to make demands direct on their subjects. When the subjects of lords below the king raised objections, they did not apparently argue about *mouvances*, that is, about the chain of land-tenure which, according to later feudal theory, ought to have linked each of them to the king. They objected generally as groups within counties or other traditional areas of government and jurisdiction who claimed not to have previously been subjected to the kind of demands now being made on them by the king.[258] When Philip IV's wars and taxes raised exasperation to a point where his successor had to make concessions, several of Louis X's charters agreed that he would no longer summon those who were not his immediate subjects. So far as one can deduce the motives behind the complaints, it looks as though people were thinking in terms of layers of government or jurisdiction, rather than in terms of layers of property rights created, or thought of as created, by past grants of land.[259] The charter to Normandy looks rather different, but that is because customary obligations in Normandy had since the twelfth century run through a recognized and recorded hierarchy.[260] Despite Louis's concessions he still reserved his right to call out everyone in the kingdom in case of emergency. The idea of the kingdom as the supreme lay community was not new, and nor was the idea of a general and public duty of defence, which had underlain both the various obligations to counts and other local rulers of alodholders and other peasants and the vaguer obligations of nobles. Philip IV would have met opposition even sooner if these ideas had not been around. What was new was not merely that it was now the king, not a count or other lord, who was making demands. Much more seriously, it was the scale of the demands he made and the new way that they were quantified and organized. Trying not to tread on the toes of those who had subordinate jurisdictions was a way of trying to avert trouble from them. Trouble when it came was not caused by those who clung to some feudo-vassalic ideal of noble service owed through a hierarchy of property, of which there is little

---

[257] *Les Olim*, i. 886–8, 901, ii. 249.

[258] Cf. (outside the kingdom) Giordanengo, *Droit féodal*, 162–3.

[259] *Actes du Parlement*, i. 399 (no. 569); Devic and Vaissete, *Hist. Languedoc*, x, col. 192–4, 235, 235–8; *Ordonnances*, i. 559 (7), 568 (2), 580 (11). For the distinction between hierarchies of jurisdiction and property, see previous section.

[260] *Ordonnances*, i. 551 (3–4).

contemporary evidence, but from those who objected to frequent service of a kind that their predecessors had not had to do.

By the thirteenth century few fiefs or other free properties, whether called alods or not, probably owed regular rents.[261] Since the medieval view was that people of higher status ought on principle to be free of heavy or regular obligations, the freedom of fiefs from rent was foreshadowed as soon as they came to be thought of as noble property.[262] For much the same reason, combined with the weakness of authority over many of them, nobles in 1100 were also likely to be effectively exempt from taxes. That includes what are misleadingly called the three or four 'feudal aids', that is taxes taken to meet the lord's needs in the emergencies caused by the knighting of his eldest son, the marriage of his eldest daughter, his own ransom, and his crusade. In France, outside Normandy, these seem to have been taken primarily if not exclusively from commoners rather than from nobles or, in thirteenth-century terms, fiefholders. The same applies to the parallel emergency aids sometimes taken by bishops to help pay for such expenses as those incurred at their consecrations, journeys to Rome, holding of councils, or repairs to cathedrals.[263] This may make all such emergency aids seem irrelevant here, but they illustrate three points that are important to my argument. The first of these is the way that feudal assumptions have led historians to ignore the evidence about how the 'feudal aids' actually worked.[264]

The second is the way that, with better communications and more consistent administration, customs became disseminated more widely but were at the same time varied and modified. The three, four, or sometimes five aids became more common partly because lords or their advisers heard about them and thought them a good idea, while retaining the option of raising money from their subjects in the event of such a generally recognized emergency as war. The specified list could, however, be attractive to

---

[261] Exceptions or possible exceptions: *Rec. comtes de Pontieu*, no. 356 (a token rent); *Rec. Philippe Auguste*, nos. 516, 938; Tholin and Fallières, 'Prise de possession', 56 (5); *Rec. d'actes relatifs à Guyenne*, nos. 247, 680 (but some of these are collective rents). Most of the rents from *feva* or *feuda* around Toulouse that Richardot ('Fief roturier') found were owed in the early thirteenth century or before.

[262] Beaumanoir, *Coutumes*, § 467, 688; Boutruche, *Société provinciale*, 123–4.

[263] Stephenson, 'Aids', and 'Origin and Nature', 62, 90–5; Bloch, *Feudal Society*, 223 n. For their apparent origin in west France, chapter 5, at nn. 153–4. *Cart. Saint-Vincent du Mans*, nos. 751, 807 use the word *fevum* in an older sense.

[264] But not all historians: e.g. Stephenson, 'Aids', and 'Origin and Nature', 62, 90, 93–5 (though he did not confront the problem posed by combining his material with his presuppositions about feudalism: see 'Aids', 3 n. 5, 'Origin and Nature', 95, *Mediaeval Feudalism*, 30 and cf. 22, 27, 33–4); Monboisse, *L'Ordre féodal*, 134; Brown, 'Customary Aids', 192 n.; Giordanengo, *Droit féodal*, 64, 163, 205.

subjects too, because they could use it to demand a compromise or concession by which the lord would agree to take aids in only these specified cases.[265] The very limitation of knighthood aids to one son and marriage aids to one marriage of one daughter suggests unrecorded arguments in the background.[266] The list of customary aids was, however, never uniform.[267] Even Alphonse of Poitiers, who started off by taking an aid for his own knighting and soon after took another for a war, and who maintained that the four aids mentioned above formed a general and well-known custom of France, conceded that a fifth (for a lord's purchase of property) was known only in some places.[268] Sometimes an aid for a lord's crusade was conceded only on condition that it was not made a precedent,[269] while in some areas the whole idea of a list of permitted aids may have remained unknown.[270] There were also variations in the way the aids were assessed and levied. The earliest recorded aids seem to have been imposed on individual property-owners at a fixed rate, perhaps because their property rights were sufficiently complete to exempt them from other dues. Later aids seem often to have been negotiated with whole towns or villages. Sometimes the local community then organized the assessment and collection of the aid.[271] Where nobles traditionally stood outside the local community, not enjoying its privileges or contributing to its expenses, they would presumably expect to be exempt from the aids, though that might cause argument.[272] In so far as there was any relation between fiefholding and liability to aids, therefore, it was more likely to be a negative than a positive one, but there does not seem to be any contemporary evidence that the aids were on principle restricted to any category of property: within the local collectivities people with more complete property (whether or not envisaged as alods or fiefs) were likely to be responsible for negotiation,

[265] *Cart. Saint-Aubin*, no. 118; 'Chartes de Saint-Étienne de Nevers', 86–9; Brussel, *Nouvel examen*, 414 n.; Giordanengo, *Droit féodal*, 205.

[266] Earlier cases are less precise: Haskins, *Norman Institutions*, 21–2; *Cart. Saint-Vincent du Mans*, cf. nos. 807 and 751.

[267] Navel, 'L'Enquête de 1133', 19–20; *Coutumiers de Normandie*, 39–40; *Rec. comtes de Pontieu*, no. 132; *Rec. Philippe Auguste*, no. 1189; *Les Olim*, i. 732; Du Cange, *Glossarium*, i. 511–12; Stephenson, 'Aids', 13 n., 14 n.; Giordanengo, *Droit féodal*, 164 n., 204; Kehr, *Steuer*, 136–7.

[268] *Correspondance admin.* no. 746.

[269] *Rec. Philippe Auguste*, no. 237; Brussel, *Nouvel examen*, 414 n.

[270] They are not mentioned in Beaumanoir, *Coutumes*, Tholin and Fallières, 'Prise de possession', or *Rec. d'actes relatifs à Guyenne*, and may have been patchy in Alphonse's lands: *Enquêtes admin.* 138–9 (18); *Correspondance admin.* nos. 546, 1793, though the claims in Devic and Vaissete, *Hist. Languedoc*, x. 192–4 may be false.

[271] In addition to documents already cited: *Correspondance admin.* no. 1968; Stephenson, 'Aids'; cf. Reynolds, *Kingdoms and Communities*, 151, 178–9, 244.

[272] *Les Olim*, i. 458–9, 575, 805, 810–11.

assessment, and collection, but there is no reason to suppose that assessments were determined by categories of property.[273]

The third way that the so-called 'feudal aids' are relevant to my subject is that they illustrate the development of the hierarchy of jurisdiction. At first they seem to have been raised by any local lord who was in a position to impose and collect them. As the administrations of counts and kings became more professional and more ambitious they tried to get in on the act. Alphonse of Poitiers collected aids of all sorts through his own officials. Where subordinate lords within his counties also collected aids his demands naturally irritated both them and those who thus had to pay two sets of aids. Alphonse found it advisable therefore to secure the consent of subject lords, but it looks as though the norms to which he had to defer were very general ones about consultation, consent, and custom. There were as yet no precisely formulated rules about just who could take aids and from whom, and certainly none deriving from any feudo-vassalic principles. It was simpler for Alphonse to take aids from his immediate subjects than from the subjects of barons, knights, prelates, and churches within his counties, but it was men and subjects (*subditi*) he taxed (sometimes by way of a hearth-tax), not 'vassals' in the sense in which that word is now used.[274] Except in Normandy, therefore, where nomenclature and the hierarchy of obligations developed differently, the 'feudal aids' were feudal only because they existed within a society considered 'feudal' for wider reasons or because they were taken by—rather than from—fiefholders. The idea that they were originally imposed on vassals and were derived from feudo-vassalic relations seems to be quite modern.[275] Perhaps it came partly from analogies with England and partly from thirteenth-century references to custom that made the aids look older than in most cases they were: as ideas of feudalism developed it came to be assumed that what was old had rested on the archaic bond of lord and vassal.

Royal taxes, apart from those levied on commoners or churches directly under royal authority, seem to have started with aids for the support of the kingdom of Jerusalem.[276] In 1166 Louis VII imposed a tax of a penny in the pound on everyone in the kingdom for five years and Henry II copied

---

[273] Though the word *tallia* already had implications of unfreedom, it and *auxilium* (or their French equivalents) only gradually came to be consistently differentiated: e.g. *Cart. Saint-Aubin*, no. 118; *Rec. Philippe Auguste*, no. 1189.

[274] *Correspondance admin.* nos. 1793, 1962, 1964-5, 1968, 1974-5.

[275] e.g. Petit-Dutaillis, *Communes*, 110; Lemarignier, *La France médiévale*, 134-5. I could not discern it in Brussel, *Nouvel examen*, 414, 898, or Vuitry, *Études*, 384-404.

[276] Whether Louis VII taxed the laity in general for his crusade remains doubtful: Robert of Torigny's lamentations may have been aroused by taxes on tenants of church lands (*Chron.* 154), while Ralph Diceto (*Opera*, i. 256-7) was writing rather late.

it in his territories, doubling the rate for the first year.[277] Henry's tax seems to have been assessed on rents as well as movables, so that it fell on property, apparently irrespective of its rights and obligations or the status of its owner. How widely Louis's order was obeyed must be doubted: if other counts did not impose it on their own account, as Henry did, it may have remained a dead letter in areas where Louis had no officials to collect it. Rules were made about the Saladin Tithe of 1188 that allowed lords taking the cross to have their subjects' payments,[278] while in 1221 Philip Augustus left the countess of Champagne to collect a twentieth for the Albigensian crusade, deducting her expenses and paying over the rest to him.[279] Louis IX is known to have raised money from local collectivities under his direct jurisdiction for his crusades, for his ransom, for various campaigns, and even for making peace with the English—which was, admittedly, an expensive peace. He may also have been the first French king to take aids for the knighting of his eldest son and the marriage of his eldest daughter.[280]

The impression that Louis IX's taxes were imposed only on towns in what is generally called the royal domain may be misleading, at least to those accustomed to the British (as opposed to American) English use of the word town: the *ville* (Latin) or *villes* (French) of contemporary sources were not all urban, though the taxes of relatively large, rich, and autonomous settlements were more likely to get into the sparse surviving records, because of the problems raised both by their charters and by membership of their communities.[281] Fiefholders were presumably exempt from collectively raised taxes to the same extent and for the same reasons as they were from collective aids raised by other lords. If royal officials made separate demands for aids on fiefholders with peasant tenants, then, unless the assessment was regulated like those of 1166 and 1188, and unless the regulations were effectively enforced, the fiefholders presumably passed the burden on to their tenants. Those with adequate local jurisdiction could try to go further and pass it on to subjects with supposedly full property rights. The position outside the areas under more or less direct royal jurisdiction is obscure. It seems likely that Louis left his brother and other counts to raise the appropriate taxes in their counties. If he did, the

---

[277] Gervase of Canterbury, *Hist. Works*, i. 198; Robert of Torigny, *Chron.* 227.

[278] *Rec. Philippe Auguste*, no. 229: I deduce that the lords of c. 2 are those taking the cross; c. 1 imposes the tenth on rents as well as movables.

[279] *Rec. Philippe Auguste*, no. 1708. The twentieth presumably came from her property and that of her subjects: *de vicesimo parte reddituum vestrorum*.

[280] *Les Olim*, i. 458–9, 747, 848–9. For possible earlier cases and for Louis VIII's Albigensian aid: Stephenson, 'Aids', 4 n., 28.

[281] *Les Olim*, i. 458–9, 575, 805, 810–11, 848–9, 832; ii. 249. The four places named, e.g., in *Les Olim*, i. 832 are clearly not urban; cf. *Ordonnances*, i. 291–3; *Correspondance admin.* no. 1368.

precedents of the first crusading taxes, as well as the evidence of
Alphonse's own aids, suggest that this was more a matter of political prudence and administrative practicality than of any ancient tradition that the
king could tax only those who held their land directly from him.

Under Philip III and Philip IV knighting the kings's son and marrying
his daughter were still useful excuses for taxes, but wars were more frequent than family celebrations.[282] Philip III made those who did not serve
in his campaign of 1272 pay according to their status rather than either the
status of their property or the amount of their wealth.[283] With the reign of
Philip IV, as both taxes and surviving records multiply, it is clear that the
king's demands for money, as for armies, came to be made on his subjects
as such, rather than on his immediate tenants, and were assessed on their
wealth.[284] Rules were gradually worked out and refined. The general principle seems to have been that those who served in the army would not have
to pay. In 1296 the exemption covered all nobles, including ladies and
clergy, and all noble property (*feodum nobile*), because it was burdened with
service, whatever the status of its owner, but by 1302 status was being virtually ignored and only those who actually served in the army were likely
to be exempt.[285] In 1303 even those who had already paid were to be
asked—though not required—to join the army if they were able-bodied.[286]
All this was made possible by the expansion of the royal administration: to
judge from the complaints of his subjects the king now had a network of
increasingly efficient and professional servants in many parts of the kingdom. It was thus possible to make some attempt to raise taxes in areas
where earlier kings had had to leave counts or local lords and their servants
to do the job for him—or for themselves. Naturally this innovation aroused
resentment from both lords and subjects, and on occasion royal officials
had to be told to desist or proceed only with the consent of the lords.[287]
The trouble was that, if nobles were left to raise money from their men,
they might well not hand over all of it. They might even refuse to pay on
their own account while still taxing their subjects.[288]

As with military service, the feudal theory with which historians often
link thirteenth-century attitudes to royal taxation is stated more clearly by
them than by contemporaries.[289] Contemporaries seem, especially at first,

---

[282] Brown, *Customary Aids*, 56–213.                    [283] Vuitry, *Études*, 382 n.
[284] *Ordonnances*, i. 345, 369–72, 391–2, 546; xii. 333–4; *Archives hist. de Poitou*, xiii, nos. 194,
196, 198; Funck-Brentano, *Philippe le Bel*, 461; Strayer and Taylor, *Studies*, 43–88.
[285] *Ordonnances*, i. 350–1, 351 n.; xii. 333–4.          [286] Strayer and Taylor, *Studies*, 64.
[287] *Ordonnances*, i. 351; xii. 333–4; Devic and Vaissete, *Hist. Languedoc*, x. 192–4, 248; cf.
Wood, *French Apanages*, 138–40.
[288] *Ordonnances*, i. 351, 371; Funck-Brentano, *Philippe le Bel*, 461.
[289] e.g. Strayer and Taylor, *Studies*, 77; Bisson, *Assemblies*, 22, 271, 276.

to have resented royal demands simply because they were new and burdensome. The general ideas about rights and obligations that lie behind
both the demands of kings and the resistance of subjects seem to be, first,
that lords—that is, people in authority, of whom the king was the supreme
type—had the right to call on their subjects for extra support and help in
an emergency. Second, while subjects had a duty to help, free men should
not be made to do so without their consent.[290] There is no evidence that
this principle applied only to nobles or fiefholders. People of lower status
were easier to bully, but they were still supposed to be consulted. In individual lordships more detailed rules about emergency taxes may have been
worked out and become customary even before 1100, but it was only as the
thirteenth century advanced that general taxes became common enough
for general rules to be applied. It was also now that systematic arguments
were constructed, studied, and copied.

The first stage in the development of rules took the form of the local
agreements about which emergencies would justify special aids. They
worked both ways, and in the end may have limited taxation as much as
they extended it. Moreover, although some agreements in particular places
conceded that the specified aids could be taken without express consent,
there is no evidence that this was generally accepted in France, as it was in
England after 1215. Alphonse of Poitiers still had to worry about consent
from the payers as well as from their lords. The next stage becomes visible
under Philip IV, when the government began to stress the generally
accepted obligation to help one's ruler in emergencies and developed new
arguments about it. That too worked both ways. When an emergency that
justified a tax ended, so did the excuse for the tax.[291] Once again, consent
was a better justification than any clever argument. Nothing was so important as consent, and, above all, the consent of the people of high status who
had authority over the rest and spoke for them. In late thirteenth-century
terms this meant noble fiefholders (as well, of course, as the higher clergy),
but there is no evidence that anyone in France worried about categories of
property or position in a hierarchy of property. For many practical reasons
the monarchy developed the custom of consulting about taxes locally,
rather than in one central assembly, but the local groups and assemblies
were not constituted precisely according to hierarchies of property. Nor
did they relate to theories about political estates except in so far as theories
of estates were later worked out to suit the methods of consultation that
had gradually become customary.

The predominantly, though not exclusively, noble groups that

[290] Reynolds, *Kingdoms and Communities*, 302–19.     [291] Brown, *'Cessante Causa'*.

produced lists of grievances in 1314–15 clearly thought that they spoke for everyone.[292] They had little to say about taxes, which suggests that the general principles of royal taxation were accepted, however grudgingly. The Normans wanted taxes to be taken only according to custom, including the recorded customs concerning Norman military obligations. The Anglo-Norman military system had made the hierarchy of property a practical reality in Normandy, and, because proportionate money payments if service was not performed had long been part of the system, this affected grievances about taxation there too.[293] The only other suggestion of resistance to royal taxation from people below those whom we might describe as tenants in chief was that the Champenois wanted royal officials to leave lords to raise taxes from their men. It is made clear that 'men' here did not mean only fiefholders, but whether the complainers thought that the king had no right to receive taxes from the subjects of his subjects is unclear.[294] When Philip VI agreed in 1334 to take an aid for knighting his son only from his domain and his subjects who were under his direct jurisdiction, the concession was forced on him by the political realities of the time. However his concession might be interpreted in future, I find it hard to see it as having been made in obedience to ancient principles about feudal tenure and feudal hierarchy.

One last example of a possible obligation on fiefholders may be mentioned, if only to illustrate the hold that ideas of feudalism have over modern scholars. It has been said that count Henry I of Champagne imposed on his subjects the duty of residing on their fiefs so that their services could be properly performed.[295] The evidence for this is a document dated 1165 announcing that the count's court had considered the case of Hugh de Possesse, who had left his inheritance (not described as a fief) in the count's care when he went overseas. Hugh had in the event married in Calabria and settled there. Two other men claimed the inheritance. The count, after taking counsel with his barons, had sent to warn Hugh that if he did not return within a year and a day the count might invest the two claimants with his property, though Hugh's rights might nevertheless be reserved in case he came back. The count reserved his right to a *redemptio*. Apart from the fact that there is no reason to see the property as held with anything less than the traditional full rights, there is no evidence here of any general rule about residence or any concern about services. Arbois drew an analogy with the kingdom of Jerusalem that was surely false: the

[292] Reynolds, *Kingdoms and Communities*, 302–19.
[293] *Ordonnances*, i. 551–2 (2, 5); Strayer, *Administration of Normandy*, 58–68.
[294] *Ordonnances*, i. 566 (c. 19), 579 (c. 11–16).
[295] Bur, *Champagne*, 402, following Arbois, 'Document sur l'obligation'.

needs of defence and the shortage of manpower that prompted the legislation there to which he drew attention—and which William of Tyre
explained as exceptional—had no parallel in Champagne. This was a case
about preserving the rights of the absent and not giving away their land
without a hearing.

This survey, sketchy and incomplete as it is, suggests that the lion's
share of the rights and obligations of property, so far as they can be
analysed today, belonged to the lowest level of fiefholders, not to their
lords. It does not support the idea that 'feudal tenure' meant a distribution
of property rights through the so-called hierarchy of tenure so that the
fiefholder at the bottom had a significantly restricted share of them. In
other words most of the rights of property, as distinct from rights of jurisdiction or government, belonged to those whom lawyers trained in the new
academic law were beginning to call the holders of *dominium utile*, rather
than to the holders of *dominium directum*. In the eighteenth century Pothier
called the two respectively a *domaine de propriété* and a *domaine de supéri-
orité*.[296] Much had changed between 1300 and 1776, but the relation
between the shares in rights of property did not change that much.
Pothier's cautious guess at the history behind the shares was, however,
wrong: the changes in terminology and everything else which I have traced
so far make it impossible to see the rights and obligations of thirteenth-
century fiefs as having derived from grants by Frankish kings to their warriors that had gradually become hereditary.[297]

Lords had the right to security, that is, protection for whatever rights
they had, but the other rights they enjoyed look more like rights of government than rights of property. They probably had the right to take over
property on failure of heirs and could confiscate it for offences that lawyers
would specify with increasing precision. They could get certain specified
and occasional dues, with possibly a small token rent. They normally had
the right to some military and court services. These were often unspecified, but that did not benefit a lord, since they were not supposed to be
raised beyond their past level without consent of the fiefholder—or any
other free property-holder. Some lords restricted or taxed alienations, and
many probably claimed the right to impose a tax (aid) in emergencies.
Beyond these rights what a lord had was jurisdiction, which should
certainly be classified as an attribute of government, rather than a right of
property. By 1315 many lords felt that their jurisdiction was under threat
from the interference of royal officials and from appeals to the king. If it
had not been for the Hundred Years War perhaps the anarchy of feudal

---

[296] Pothier, *Œuvres*, 102.      [297] Ibid. 494.

jurisdiction, as the eighteenth century saw it, might have been eliminated or much reduced before feudalism had been invented.

## 7.6. *Conclusion*

It is sometimes said that the later Capetians re-established the authority of the French monarchy by using and taming the feudalism that had enfeebled their predecessors. It might be better to say that the later Capetians created the system that historians would later characterize as French feudalism. The structure of political relations and of the rights and obligations of property that can be detected in thirteenth-century French sources was the work of Philip Augustus and his successors. Obviously they started from what they found, but what they found does not seem to have included either a set of rights and obligations, or a set of ideas about rights and obligations, that look distinctively feudo-vassalic. Nor did the political order that emerged under them fit the feudo-vassalic model, as usually sketched, at all neatly. Military obligations, irrespective of their origins, did not fit it, and nor did obligations to aids or reliefs. It cannot seriously be maintained, moreover, that what bound the great nobles of the kingdom to the later Capetian kings was the dyadic, affective, interpersonal bond of feudo-vassalic feudalism. The relation between Joinville and Louis IX might at first sight seem to follow that pattern, but Joinville did not apparently hold his land from Louis and, in any case, he enjoyed a much closer relation with Louis than did most other nobles. What had enabled the kings of France to extend their authority and effective power over so much of their kingdom as they had done by 1300 was professional government and professional law.

Professional government and professional law did not develop in a vacuum of political ideas and values. The values on which thirteenth-century French government was built were, however, I suggest, not those of feudo-vassalic feudalism, which would only be articulated later, but ideas, values, and practices of which we have much more evidence, however indirect, in twelfth-century and earlier sources. Ideas about kings and kingdoms were particularly important, and help to explain why Philip Augustus and his successors met with so little opposition when they began to assert the authority that was expected of kings in general but had become unfamiliar in France. Other important ideas that are reflected in the recorded practice of government and law concern custom, jurisdiction, and law. It has become usual to stress the use of the word *consuetudines* in eleventh-century documents to mean dues owed to lords, but the idea of custom was much wider and more pervasive. It was at once one of the most helpful and most unhelpful ideas that rulers had to cope with. Custom was the basis of all law, including the law of property. It impeded the introduction of new obligations on property, but at the same time it was so malleable that, in the hands of competent lawyers, preferably equipped with better records than the king's subjects would have, it could serve his ends as much as it frustrated them.

The substance of the law practised in the king's courts in the thirteenth century, though it looks increasingly professional, seems to have owed little to the new academic law of fiefs that was taught in Italian universities and, increasingly, in some universities in France.[298] Knowledge of the new law was, however, coming in and its reception was facilitated by several factors. The first was the general similarity between the customs and conditions within which it had emerged in north Italy and those in France, including most notably the methods that great churches had developed for controlling their property and the problems that these had created. In France, as in Italy, the word fief was already in use by 1100 to indicate (among other things) property with restricted rights, so that the terminology of the *Libri Feudorum* must have seemed reasonably compatible with that of France, provided that, like John de Blanot, one could assimilate oaths of fidelity with homage. The use of the words homage and fief to indicate political subjection developed in France at about the same time as the use of fidelity and fief developed in Lombardy. After 1300 knowledge of the academic law seems to have become more common and began to get into records as well as legal literature. How much impact on practice is implied by the kind of knowledge that is suggested, for instance, in the references in Jacques d'Ableiges's *Grand Coutumier* to vassals or to the difference between *la seigneurie directe* and *la prouffitable*, is a question that lies outside the scope of this book.[299] Peter Jacobi, writing probably in Montpellier early in the fourteenth century, maintained that none of the customs written in the *Libri Feudorum*, from beginning to end, had any validity in the whole of the kingdom of France, but that does not mean that the ideas in the *Libri* did not influence practice.[300] The question needs to be investigated.[301]

In the mean time, it seems to be clear that when the academic lawyers and historians of the sixteenth century started to investigate medieval law

[298] Fournier, *Histoire de la science du droit*, 100, 183, 291–2, 511, 659, found evidence in fourteenth-century statutes for the teaching of the *Libri Feudorum* in only a few universities but there is no reason to suppose it was not known elsewhere.
[299] Jacques d'Ableiges, *Grand Coutumier*, 234, 288, 295, 297, 305; the allusion to the custom of fiefs (ibid. 301) on alienation could be to the *Libri Feudorum*, but the *coutumes de fiefs* of c. 27 as a whole seem to be local.
[300] Parieu, 'Étude', 438.
[301] As I understand it has been by Dr Magnus Ryan in a Cambridge thesis that was submitted too late for me to see it.

they started from the academic literature on the law of fiefs. Even when they followed Peter Jacobi in denying its authority in France they found its terminology reflected in the records of late medieval French law. That confirmed their belief that, whatever the exact rules about them, fiefs and vassals were what medieval history was about. Since the *Libri Feudorum* used benefice as a synonym for fief, it was natural to connect the fiefs and vassals of the late medieval literature with the benefices and vassals that the historians soon found in Charlemagne's capitularies. The capitularies also told them about alods, and so did fifteenth-century disputes that show how the lawyers of the viscount of Béarn, for instance, had by then begun to exploit the supposed difference between fiefs and alods. If feudal law did not fit into the dualism between customary law and Roman law that concerned academic lawyers throughout the Ancien Régime, that perhaps only illustrated its pervasive influence.[302]

Even if they had not been hampered by an entirely understandable but erroneous belief that noble property had originated in grants of benefices or fiefs made by Frankish kings to their followers, seventeenth-century jurists and historians who wanted to make sense of medieval law found another impediment in their way. Nowhere in their sources could they have found a helpful discussion of the difference between the customary law of the earlier middle ages and the so-called customary law of the late middle ages. Much of the material that Loisel used to demonstrate what he saw as the principles underlying the customary laws of France came from genuine medieval sources, including the recorded provincial customs, but the customs he studied were the product of at least semi-professional law. In being recorded, often by lawyers or government servants, they had lost the fluid character of earlier customary law, but they had not acquired the rule-based character that Loisel's training led him to look for. What he found in the customs were maxims, not principles or rules of law, and they were maxims produced in conditions of law and government quite different from those before the twelfth century.[303] The written customs of the later middle ages reflected a kind of law that was just beginning to emerge in the thirteenth century and was fundamentally different from the pre-professional, customary law of the period when fiefs and feudal law are supposed to have originated. We cannot understand the way that the law of property developed in France before 1300, and the way that it was affected by society, economy, and politics, and then affected them in return, if we look at it through the feudal spectacles that were manufactured in the seventeenth and eighteenth centuries.

[302] Gaudemet, 'Les Tendances', though he does not mention feudal law.
[303] Loisel, *Institutes*; Reulos, *Étude*.

# 8

# ENGLAND

## 8.1. *The problems*

EVER since Sir Henry Spelman used the words of French feudists, backed by what was in the circumstances an impressive amount of genuine medieval evidence, to explain 'the original, growth, propagation and condition of feuds and tenures by knight-service, in England',[1] ideas about feudalism in England have been derived from ideas of feudalism in France and yet, paradoxically, have been different from them in several ways. Deep-rooted traditions of linguistic and pseudo-racial nationalism have fostered the belief that feudalism came to England from France as a result of the Norman Conquest, yet attention here has always been focused on military service and the rights of kings over those who held their land directly from them, both of which, as I have argued, seem hard to find in anything like comparable form in France. One reason why the paradox has not attracted more critical thought is that these phenomena were very early on incorporated into the general model of non-Marxist feudalism, so that those who started from the model and were primarily—or only—interested in England naturally took them for granted, just as those who were primarily interested in France took for granted the contrasting situation there. The model has obscured the evidence for historians both sides of the Channel. Another reason is that since the twelfth century the peculiar development of English law has discouraged English lawyers and legal historians from looking at all closely at other countries.

Comparison is, in any case, made more difficult by the distinctive terminology that, largely as a result of the separate legal development, is taken for granted in English medieval history. Part of it originates from medieval usage and comes straight from the English common law, but a good deal of the traditional terminology of English feudalism is later and some of it has been developed by historians rather than lawyers. The impediment to understanding and comparison posed by the use of a separate vocabulary for only one of the countries which are to be compared is not trivial. As part of my effort to compare the rules of property in different countries I

[1] Spelman, *Reliquiae*, 1.

323

ought to use the form fief, rather than fee, throughout this chapter, but tradition has overcome me: it does not seem possible to talk of 'knights' fiefs', 'fief-farms', or 'fief simple'. I have, however, generally used 'fief' when it stands alone, however odd this may sometimes look to historians of English law. I have also bowed to tradition in using the word tenant more freely than I have in other chapters, because that is what property-owners were called in England. As I have already pointed out and will do again in this chapter, it had no implications of reduced rights.[2] I have generally referred to the people historians call tenants in chief as the king's tenants or the king's tenants in chief or the king's direct tenants. 'Tenants in chief' to mean exclusively a king's tenants, like many other supposedly technical terms of feudalism, seems to be a creation of medievalists rather than of the middle ages.[3] Perhaps my terminology may help jolt my readers into thinking how far and why the phenomena behind the words were different from those of fiefs elsewhere.

One obvious way to make comparison easier might be to arrange this chapter to match those on France, but the different nature of some of the evidence and of much of the historical discussion seems to make that impractical: I have to start with the English evidence and the English discussions in order to show how I think the discussion has been distorted by reliance on the model. I must hope that occasional cross-references in the notes will enable my readers to consider some comparisons for themselves—and to make them with Italy and Germany as well as with France. While doing so, they should also bear in mind that this chapter deals with what became the kingdom of England. Wales and Scotland are considered only in so far as the claims of kings of England to lordship over them involved—or did not involve—seeing them as fiefs.

## 8.2. *Before the mid tenth century*

Discussions of property rights in England before 1066 have tended to focus less on the difference between alodial and feudal tenure than on that between bookland, folkland, and 'loanland' (*lænelandum, lænlonde*). Starting from these words, however, makes it almost impossible to see how far they reflect differences in the rights and obligations of property from those in other countries. Since, moreover, it is quite clear that the political, economic, and legal conditions governing property above the peasant level changed between the seventh and eleventh centuries, it seems probable that, in so far as the same words were used throughout the period, their

---

[2] See index: *tenere*.     [3] Below, at nn. 164–9.

connotations are likely to have changed too. That certainly happened with the word bookland, which is attested from the first third of the eighth century to the twelfth, though less often than modern commentaries sometimes suggest.[4] Folkland, on the other hand, is mentioned in only five places in surviving sources, all but one between the mid ninth and early tenth century. In these instances it may include all land except bookland—presumably including 'loanland' and also peasant land, for which other words might be used on other occasions. In the fifth reference, a poem which cannot be precisely dated, it seems to mean something like 'a country'.[5] The idea that the word represented anything that could be called a definable category of property has depended on assuming that some such constant and consistent category existed and then interpolating the word into centuries and contexts where it is not found.[6] Altogether, it seems more profitable to start from what we know about customs governing property than from the supposed vernacular vocabulary.

It has been suggested that before the conversion of the English to Christianity in the seventh century nobles who held land did so only at the pleasure of the king in whose kingdom it lay.[7] Although we know very little about any English kingdoms before the conversion, it seems implausible that the customs of their inhabitants differed so much from those of the other Germanic-speaking barbarians of north-western Europe, and from those of the other inhabitants of Britain, as to have included no traditional rights of inheritance.[8] It is true that the instability of the early English kingdoms must have entailed frequent confiscations and redistributions, while their smallness would have made it harder for nobles to keep their

---

[4] Venezky and Healey, *Microfiche Concordance: bocland, boclanda, boclande, boclond*, and cf. *bocrihtes*. The earliest occurrence of the word appears to be in Sawyer, *Anglo-Saxon Charters*, no. 1622 (805×832), on which see Brooks, *Early History*, 139. The word is not used in the charter referred to in *Eng. Hist. Documents*, i, no. 88 as 'a most important document for understanding the meaning of "bookland"': Sawyer, *Anglo-Saxon Charters*, no. 298. For simplicity I shall cite all charters listed in Sawyer, *Anglo-Saxon Charters* by the numbers there given to them.

[5] Venezky and Healey, *Microfiche Concordance: folcland, folclande, folclondes*. For another possible reference (as *terrulas sui propriae publicae juris*) see Vollrath-Reichelt, *Königsgedanke*, 216. Unlike 'bookland', folkland is not apparently used in any glosses to explain a Latin word. Vollrath-Reichelt's suggestion (ibid. 192–225) that folkland was royal domain which the king could not alienate without consent could be right for the contexts of the charters she discusses, but on other aspects of her argument see Brooks, 'Anglo-Saxon Charters', 221–2. Where 'bookland and folkland' are referred to as a pair they could mean 'bookland and all other land'; cf. other unspecific words like *erfe, agenland*. The *Concordance* suggests that folkright (*folcriht, folcryht, folcryhte*) also had a fairly wide range of meanings: cf. *folclaga, folclage*.

[6] e.g. John, *Orbis Britanniae*, 74–5, 117–22.

[7] John, *Land Tenure*, 64–79, and *Orbis Britanniae*, 64–8; though Abels's suggestion (*Lordship*, 32) that a noble's land was 'fiscal land' is hard to understand: would this mean that before grants to churches the whole kingdom was 'fiscal land'?

[8] Wormald, *Bede and the Conversion*, 21–2. For the identity of those now called Anglo-Saxons and their relations with others: Reynolds, 'What do we Mean by Anglo-Saxon?'

heads down in distant areas than it was for Frankish, Saxon, or Lombard nobles in the same period. In spite of that, nobles were probably thought to have had a right in principle to pass on their holdings, provided they were loyal subjects of their kings, and may sometimes have done so. There are several suggestions of an assumption of inheritance, and when Bede complained that, under the pretext of founding monasteries, nobles were getting lands ascribed to them by royal edicts in hereditary right, he need not have meant that hereditary right was in itself new.[9] Any periods of local stability would accumulate precedents to strengthen the claims of heirs. Nor need we assume that only those considered noble had hereditary or other rights in their land that their society thought valid. What we know of Frankish and other property in this period suggests that it is wrong to react against old myths of free and equal Anglo-Saxons by positing a gulf between nobles who had rights and servile peasants who had none. The sources show us a very unequal society. Peasants, apart from those who were actually slaves, no doubt had relatively few rights and more menial obligations than nobles, but the free man (*frigman*) or the churl (*ceorl, cierlisca mon*) of the early laws must surely have had quite good rights, though they probably owed rather different obligations from nobles.[10] In such small kingdoms many peasants may have owed their dues and services directly to their kings, but some may have owed them to nobles whom the king set over them or who had inherited their local position. Whether we call noble landowners governors or landlords at this stage is our choice: presumably they received some or all of the tribute from the land and functioned in some sense as local governors. Whether either nobles or those commoners who had land of their own could alienate it is unknowable: there may have been few occasions to do so and therefore few opportunities for rules to develop.[11]

From very soon after the conversion of England began in the seventh century, royal gifts of land to the church began to be recorded in charters known in the vernacular as *landbec* or simply *bec* (singular: *landboc, boc*), so that, although the word bookland occurs less often in the charters than modern commentaries suggest, land conveyed in this way came to be called bookland or booklands.[12] There has been a good deal of argument about

[9] Bede, *Hist. Eccl.* i. 413–14 (Epist. ad Ecgbertum, c. 12); cf. 375–6 (Hist. Abbatum, c. 11); Eddius Stephanus, *Life of Wilfrid*, 140 (c. 65).

[10] e.g. Liebermann, *Gesetze*, i. 3–4, 106, 112, 118 (though on the last of these see next note); Aston, 'Origins of the Manor'; Stafford, *East Midlands*, 29–34.

[11] Ine 63, 67 (Liebermann, *Gesetze*, i. 118) may already have been affected by post-conversion changes.

[12] Venezky and Healey, *Concordance*, as above, n. 4. The suggestions of Rumble, 'Old English *Boc-Land*', about the significance of the place-name Buckland are not affected by my doubts about bookland 'as a legal term'.

what the first of these charters conveyed—whether they were grants of 'immunity' (which presumably in this context meant something like rights of government) or 'simply of land'.[13] Some of it seems to pay insufficient attention to the fact that rights in land are seldom simple or to the possibility that kingdoms in seventh-century England were closer than were those of the Franks or Lombards to the condition of society, not uncommon in agricultural societies of simple technology, in which rent and taxes, rights of property and rights of government, are not distinguished.[14] Land granted to churches presumably had peasants on it who owed something— rent or taxes?—but who themselves had much the same rights of property, protected by the same custom, as peasants elsewhere.

The word bookland must at first have implied somewhat different rights and obligations from those of lay nobles. Church property was granted not merely with the traditional hope or expectation of inheritance but for ever, while bishops and monks did not perform the military services demanded of lay nobles. That need not have exempted people living on church lands, who would presumably be mainly peasants, from traditional obligations to serve in armies or provide support for those who did, until the churches got formal immunities, as some did fairly soon.[15] Practice may have varied between kingdoms and between the estates of different churches, but the problem posed by church estates may well have stimulated the general drawing of distinctions between rights of government and rights of property. The freedom to alienate noted in some early charters to individual bishops, abbots, and abbesses was presumably intended to allow them to be succeeded in their offices and the attached property by non-kinsmen within their communities rather than by the kinsmen who would otherwise have hoped to inherit their land. It was also essential when kings gave lands to laymen who wanted to endow monasteries.[16] Some of these grants may have been royal confirmations rather than royal gifts: in other societies it is not unknown for nobles to attribute their pious benefactions to their rulers. It flatters the ruler and secures his authority and protection.[17] We need not assume that it was absolutely impossible for anyone but a king to give land to a church. However that may be, charters that explicitly include freedom of bequest survive from the second quarter of the eighth century, by which time we know that lay nobles were cleverly securing the benefits of *jus*

---

[13] Surveyed by Wormald, *Bede and the Conversion*, 20–1.   [14] See chapter 3.2.

[15] Wormald, *Bede and the Conversion*, 20–1. For the debate on the privileges of early bookland: John, *Land Tenure*, 64–79, and *Orbis Britanniae*, 64–8; Brooks, 'Development of Military Obligations'; Wormald, 'Age of Bede and Aethelbald', 95–8; Abels, *Lordship*, 43–57.

[16] Sheehan, *Will in Medieval England*, 86–97. Wormald, *Bede and the Conversion*, 27–8 lists works on the early charters.

[17] Panikkar, 'Historical Overview', 27.

*ecclesiasticum* for themselves by the mere pretence of founding monasteries.[18] The pretence soon became unnecessary. By the end of the century
kings were making grants to laymen in the same terms as to churches, that
is, specifying permanent rights of inheritance and free rights of disposition,
even when no future transfer to the church was apparently envisaged.[19] In
779 King Offa of Mercia granted his faithful servant (*minister*) Dudda three
*cassati* for ever *in jus ecclesiasticae liberalitatis*, with permission to leave it to
any of his kin that he chose, and a promise that if any of them committed
a crime this particular land would not be forfeit.[20] The word bookland thus
came to be applied to some lay property. Not, however, to all: whatever the
balance between royal control and noble claims to inheritance before the
conversion, nobles in the following centuries held property that, whether
or not it had originated in some possibly long-forgotten royal grant, was
inherited without being bookland.

Bookland cannot always have carried the same rights and obligations. Its
chief advantage may have been that, even while it granted its holder *ece
erfe*, or land *in sempiternam hereditatem*, or *in hereditatem propriam*, it rather
contradictorily allowed him to disappoint his heirs. The rules of inheritance were probably not unlike those of the Franks, with most land held by
individuals rather than families, and claims to inherit coming from close
kin.[21] Consequently, there was the same tension between the rights of a
current owner and the expectations of his heirs. Whether acquired property was more freely disposable than what was inherited is hard to say.
What seems to be the only evidence of it is late and dubious:[22] it may be
that the development of custom about bookland made it unnecessary to
develop special rules about acquisitions, at least at the social level at which
bookland was held. As in other countries, alienations must often have been
subject to negotiation within families. A charter or landbook that gave current owners unilateral power, backed by royal authority, to ignore the
expectations of their nearest and dearest enabled them to bypass difficult
arguments. But the terms of charters varied. Dudda's allowed him to
choose among his heirs, not to ignore them all. King Alfred the Great of
Wessex ordered that restrictions imposed by past owners of bookland on
its alienation should be enforced. Whether they generally were is another
matter. Alfred himself wanted his bookland kept in the male line, but his
own will exemplifies the difficulty of controlling events after one's death

---

[18] Bede, *Hist. Eccl.* i. 415.     [19] Abels, *Lordship*, 47; Stenton, *Latin Charters*, 59–61.
[20] Sawyer, *Anglo-Saxon Charters*, no. 114.     [21] Loyn, 'Kinship'.
[22] *Leges Henrici*, § 70. 21; cf. Wormald, *Bede and the Conversion*, 22. For the rule elsewhere,
see index: alienation of acquisitions.

even if one is a king.[23] A prudent testator leaving either bookland or other acquired land away from his family, or from the most obvious heir within it, might still think it wise to ask for royal approval.[24] In the later ninth century a noble, the ealdorman Alfred, did just that and at the same time sought permission to bequeath his *erfe* and his folkland, which perhaps in this context both meant the same, that is, the rest of his inheritance.[25] Whatever the terms of charters, many alienations must have been subject to family negotiation, social values, and political pressures, just as they were in the Frankish kingdoms, although royal grants that included freedom of disposition there did not create a separate category of property with a separate name.

Doubts about freedom of disposition as a defining characteristic of bookland are intensified by consideration of church property. The church provided the first model of bookland, but some donors said that churches were not to alienate their gifts and at least one church council in England, as well as many abroad, forbade it.[26] Churches might need to grant lands to nobles for all kinds of reasons, but the property of God and his saints was not supposed to be permanently alienated. In England therefore, as elsewhere, churches often made their grants for one or more lives.[27] We have relatively little evidence of English grants, except those of the bishop of Worcester, but what documents in Old English sometimes call a *laen* (and historians writing in English sometimes call a lease) was very similar to the benefices or *precaria* granted by churches elsewhere.[28] As elsewhere, kings begged church land for themselves and their followers, some donors were allowed to retain a life interest in their donations, and solemn agreements to protect the church's reversionary interest were sometimes forgotten or ignored.[29] In England, as elsewhere, allowing families to hold church property for two or three generations made its ultimate resumption more difficult. By the late ninth century, if not before, land was also granted by kings and lay lords by way of *laen*, that is, on subordinate and

---

[23] Liebermann, *Gesetze*, i. 74 (Alfred c. 41); Sawyer, *Anglo-Saxon Charters*, nos. 509, 1507.

[24] Cf. Sawyer, *Anglo-Saxon Charters*, no. 155: Offa said that his *minister* should not give away land given by his lord (though this had been King Egbert) without his permission.

[25] Sawyer, *Anglo-Saxon Charters*, no. 1508. But in 946 no. 1504 uses *yrfe* to cover *laenland*.

[26] Brooks, *Early History*, 159.

[27] e.g. Sawyer, *Anglo-Saxon Charters*, nos. 1260–1, 1297–1374; Lennard, *Rural England*, 159–70.

[28] Maitland, *Domesday Book and Beyond*, 300–10. *Beneficium* and *praestare* occur occasionally, e.g. Sawyer, *Anglo-Saxon Charters*, nos. 1274, 1368.

[29] Sawyer, *Anglo-Saxon Charters*, nos. 215; 356 and 1797; 693, 1077–8, 1274, 1297–374; 1420, 1444, 1456, 1458; Fleming, 'Monastic Lands'; Nelson, 'King across the Sea'; *Hemingi Chart.* 253–4, 257–60, 264–5. For life interests of donors: Lennard, *Rural England*, 161–2.

temporary terms, though there may have been relatively little need or opportunity for that in the small kingdoms of the time.[30]

Meanwhile, royal authority was developing. What seems to be the earliest reference to folkland occurs in a note on a peculiarly complex and difficult charter of 858 by which King Aethelberht (III of Kent; later also of Wessex) exchanged some land with his faithful *minister* Wulflaf and adjusted the obligations on both estates. According to the note the land that the king got was thus made into *folclande*, which may in this instance mean land owing obligations from which bookland was normally exempt—though bookland is not explicitly mentioned in the charter.[31] Any such exemptions were, however, by now offset by the reservation on all land of three obligations—to military service, bridge-building, and fortress-building.[32] Increased royal authority meant increasing royal demands. It also meant increasing royal responsibility. When kings granted exemptions and privileges they were supposed to do so with formality and consultation.[33] The charters that allowed kings to turn royal estates into bookland so as to leave them to those they chose look like a consequence of distinctions, provoked by increasing royal responsibilities, between the king's personal capacity and property and what belonged to him ex officio.[34] One advantage of bookland, apart from any privileges, remained the book or charter itself, especially if it had names of authority on it. It is difficult to be sure that later references to landbooks are always to royal charters but, if they are, it seems that even royal charters did not always constitute incontrovertible evidence.[35] Their content might be mulled over and one might still have to muster people to support one's oath to the validity of the charters one produced.[36] Nor could even royal charters guarantee subjects against forfeiture. After King Alfred had confiscated a traitor's inheritance his son

[30] Alfred, *Soliloquies*, 48; Lennard, *Rural England*, 142–75; cf. the *læn* in Sawyer, *Anglo-Saxon Charters*, no. 1445, though the particular circumstances here make it impossible to deduce any general rules (e.g. about forfeiture) from it.
[31] Sawyer, *Anglo-Saxon Charters*, no. 328. I find Vollrath-Reichelt, *Königsgedanke*, 65–8, 192–225 unpersuasive: cf. Brooks, 'Anglo-Saxon Charters', 222.
[32] Brooks, 'Development of Military Obligations'.
[33] Sawyer, *Anglo-Saxon Charters*, nos. 168, 298, 328, 335, 715, 1438.
[34] Ibid., nos. 298, 715, 717; possibly also no. 1258. The conversion to folkland in no. 328 presumably recognizes the same responsibility. Cf. Liebermann, *Gesetze*, i. 458–9 on the king's wergeld.
[35] Sawyer, *Anglo-Saxon Charters*, nos. 1445 (even if the key *boc* here was royal, rather than a private charter strengthened by some kind of royal subscription, it was evidence of a transaction between subjects, not of a royal grant), 1460 (*boc* giving free disposition, made at royal command but about a transaction between subjects); *Liber Eliensis*, 99, 101 (*cyrographa*). *Chron. Abingdon*, i. 475 is late and seems to overstate the force of charters. Wills could be called *yrfebec*: Bosworth and Toller, *Ango-Saxon Dictionary*, 598, and one (Sawyer, *Anglo-Saxon Charters*, no. 1536) was called a *freolsboc*. No. 1444 uses *bociunnæ* for a life-grant.
[36] Wormald, 'Charters, Law and the Settlement of Disputes'.

ordered that any old charters (*antiqui libri*) concerning it that anyone might have should be cancelled.[37]

By about 900 there seem to have been three main categories of property, excluding that of the less free peasants. First there was the hereditary property of nobles and free men, with obligations that varied according to local custom and, probably, status; second, property, often called bookland, that was held by charters granting special privileges, often including some freedom of disposition at least for the first grantee and freedom from obligations beyond the three general obligations; third, property that nobles held on restricted rights, generally from a church or king. Allowing for local differences of politics and custom, the first category looks like Frankish alods, while the third is very like Frankish benefices. Any attempt to assimilate these English categories to the alods and fiefs of classic feudal law would, however, be even more misleading than it is for the Frankish alods and benefices of this period. The development of bookland as a separate category seems, not surprisingly, to have affected ideas about property that was defined by not being bookland. Ideas about property did not, in any case, develop in a void. To start with they were presumably affected by economic and social change. For freedom of disposition to have become as desirable as it seems to have been, a land market must have been developing anyway. Political change was also a dominant force in changing the obligations and rights of property in England as it was elsewhere.

The laws make it clear that kings in England, even before they seem to have done much governing, were, like kings elsewhere, more than nobles who happened to have a special title. Like other kings they legislated about nobles and their followers. Ine of Wessex prohibited any noble whose follower, whether free or unfree, committed a crime from receiving any of the financial penalty: the noble should have kept him under better control.[38] As the English kingdoms became more settled, the smaller were squeezed out, and the government of the survivors became more demanding and formal, relations between kings, nobles, and other subjects must have become more varied and complex. The story of the fight to the death between the loyal followers of Cyneheard and Cynewulf shows that the values of the war-band were still cherished, but cherished values do not always represent the realities of everyday life and government.[39] The use of the word *hlaford* (lord) for a king does not mean, any more than does *dominus* in Latin texts here or elsewhere, that kings were in effect 'feudal lords' and their nobles merely their vassals—their 'men' in a feudo-vassalic sense—rather than their subjects. Kings and lay nobles, bishops and abbots, were

---

[37] Sawyer, *Anglo-Saxon Charters*, no. 362.    [38] Liebermann, *Gesetze*, i. 110–12 (Ine 50).
[39] *Two Saxon Chronicles*, 47–9 (as 755).

all *hlafordas*; all of them had authority, but their relations with those over whom they had it were surely different. The followings of nobles could be dangerous or fatal to kings, as Cyneheard's was to Cynewulf, but provided they were kept in order they were presumably useful in armies and in the service of those nobles who served kings as *praefecti* or *ealdormen* governing shires. In the late ninth century Alfred ordained death and forfeiture of all property for anyone who plotted against the life of his own lord as well as for anyone who plotted against that of the king.[40] Under his descendants new changes were brought to both political and property relations by the formation of the new kingdom of England in which nobles, their followers, and all landowners had to live with a powerful and exigent central government.

## 8.3. *From the mid tenth century to 1066*

Just before the middle of the tenth century all the subjects of King Edmund were supposed to swear to be faithful to him as a man ought to be to his lord (*sicut homo debet esse fidelis domino suo*). Given the wide use of *dominus* and the echo of Frankish oaths to kings and emperors, the phrase need not imply that obligations to kings were less well recognized than those to lesser lords, though they were probably less obvious to most people in everyday life.[41] Frankish influence may also be seen in other aspects of government and in the occasional use of forms of the word vassal in the late ninth century and the tenth, apparently for the same sort of lay servants or followers as it denoted across the Channel.[42] It has been suggested that when the Old English Chronicle speaks of people submitting or bowing (infinitive: *bugan*) to a new king it 'must refer to the ceremony of homage' as a feudo-vassalic ceremony rather than one that embodied wider ideas of government.[43] This seems highly implausible. Apart from the difficulty of finding the classic feudo-vassalic ceremony of homage anywhere at this date, the relevant uses of *bugan* (a word of very various uses and meanings) seem to indicate submission rather than any particular ceremony. The submission might be to God, a king, or even a hostile army, but only one recorded example from the chronicle, the charters, or the laws seems to be even remotely feudo-vassalic.[44] It comes in a

[40] Liebermann, *Gesetze*, i. 50 (Alfred 4. 1–2).

[41] Ibid. 190 (III Edmund 1); Campbell, 'Observations', 46–7. For similar phrases, see chapter 4 at n. 53 and also chapter 6 at nn. 208–9.

[42] Asser, *Life of King Alfred*, 41, 44; Sawyer, *Anglo-Saxon Charters*, nos. 478, 559, 666, 755 (references from Maitland, *Domesday Book and Beyond*, 293). See chapter 4.2.

[43] John, *Orbis Britanniae*, 140–1.

[44] Bosworth and Toller, *Anglo-Saxon Dictionary*, 133; Venezky and Healey, *Concordance*: *beag, beah, bugan, bugon*.

writ in which Edward the Confessor gave permission for one Alfrich to
*bugan* to the abbots of Bury St Edmunds and Ely. Alfrich, however, is
known to have bequeathed land to Bury, so that his case fits the model only
if one ignores the difference between ecclesiastical and lay lords. Perhaps
he gave property to both abbeys and retained the usual kind of life benefice
from each.[45] By 1066, although there was still ample scope for the relations
of patronage that one would expect in this kind of society and although
lords exercised authority in local government, the royal government (whoever controlled it) was by the standards of the eleventh century heavily
centralized and very powerful. Though few of its records survive it is difficult to believe that taxation and control of the coinage, for instance, could
have been managed without lists that would justify calling it, like
Carolingian government, at least a borderline or nascent example of what
Max Weber called bureaucratic government.

By the later tenth century it looks as though the distinction between
bookland and other hereditary property of nobles and free men was becoming blurred. King Eadred's will seems to be the last to say whether land
bequeathed was bookland and Edgar was the last king recorded as turning
land into bookland.[46] Thereafter the word may have come to indicate
rather the status of its owner than any specific grant or privilege. As the
kingdom grew, kings may have used charters both to make grants to their
followers who acquired land in newly conquered territory and to confirm
the title of their new subjects. Charters to the latter may not have conferred
new privileges. Without entering into all the problems that surround the
number, nature, and issue of royal charters, it may be possible to agree that
it is improbable that all thegns (that is, in some contexts, people of more
or less noble status), even all those who were called king's thegns, acquired
charters, let alone that all of them preserved their charters. If Bishop
Aethelwold got royal charters to confirm his acquisitions for his abbey at
Ely his *Libellus* did not bother to mention it, any more than it bothered to
use the word bookland.[47] Bookland was, by and large, the land of thegns,
though a thegn's land could alternatively be defined by its extent: anyone
who had five hides of land, with a fortified house and other suitable appurtenances, was likely to be a thegn.[48] Nobles or thegns, in the sense of the
word that denoted status, were likely to have some rights of jurisdiction, at

[45] Harmer, *Anglo-Saxon Writs*, nos. 21-2.
[46] Sawyer, *Anglo-Saxon Charters*, nos. 715, 727, 1515.
[47] *Liber Eliensis*, 75-117; Kennedy, 'Disputes', 186.
[48] Liebermann, *Gesetze*, i. 196, 294, 444, 456 (II Edgar 2, I Cnut 11, *Rectitudines, Gethynctho*);
cf. the various categories in Robertson, *Anglo-Saxon Charters*, no. 84, and the lack of any in e.g.
Sawyer, *Anglo-Saxon Charters*, nos. 1460, 1462. Another use of the word thegn is discussed
below.

least over peasants with holdings on their estates, and perhaps over others, though whether the lands of those others would count as part of the lord's bookland it is hard to say.[49] Domesday Book's information about the situation just before the Norman Conquest, combined with the various eleventh-century classifications, suggests that it was as difficult to put people and their property into tidy categories then as it is in all but the smallest and simplest societies.[50] Tenth- and eleventh-century homilies use the word *bocland* and its variants to mean apparently nothing more specific than one's own land.[51] When King Aethelred ordered at one stage that penalties (*wita* and *bote*) from people with bookland were to go to the king and at another that only the king could have soke over a king's thegn, he was presumably claiming rights over everyone who mattered.[52] Similarly when Cnut ordered that all bookland forfeited by an outlaw should go to the king he presumably meant to get all estates that mattered.[53] If it is right that bookland and other free or noble property had become indistinguishable by 1000, one reason may have been that both kinds of property were subject to the same social norms and political pressures. That, however, is very tentative: an explanation for something that may not have happened is not evidence that it did.

Domesday Book suggests that the rights and obligations of property on the eve of the Norman Conquest were—not surprisingly—very different from those of 700. The free disposition that had originally been conferred by royal charters was now enjoyed not only by nobles but by fairly ordinary-looking commoners. Perhaps the humble were in some cases more free than the great: they might be bullied by the great, but the great were bullied by the king.[54] Bishop Aethelwold's purchases of many small parcels of land for his monasteries, like other purchases which are referred to in tenth- and eleventh-century wills and charters, occasionally ran into trouble from the kinsmen of vendors, but they suggest that freedom of disposition was assumed to be normal by people who surely did not all have royal landbooks.[55] Though Domesday Book's concern with the freedom of

---

[49] e.g. Abels, *Lordship*, 123–4; Roffe, 'From Thegnage to Barony' and 'Domesday Book', 335; Williams, 'How Land was Held', 37–8.

[50] Barrow, *Kingdom of the Scots*, 13, 16–19, 27; Stafford, *East Midlands*, 156–7. Some thegns with *bocriht* owed more than the three burdens: Liebermann, *Gesetze*, i. 444 (*Rectitudines*). Some of the classification for heriots in II Cnut 71 (Liebermann, *Gesetze*, 356–7) looks *ad hoc*. III Aethelred talks of senior (*yldestan*) thegns in 3.1, good thegns in 4, and king's thegns in 11, which suggests vague and varied gradations (Liebermann, 228, 230).

[51] Venezky and Healey, *Concordance*: bocland, bocalanda, boclande, boclond.

[52] Liebermann, *Gesetze*, i. 218, 230 (I Aeth. 1. 14, III Aeth. 11).

[53] Ibid. 316, 364 (II Cnut 13, 77), though cf. *Domesday Book*, i. 280c.

[54] e.g. Sawyer, *Anglo-Saxon Charters*, nos. 1484, 1497, 1504, 1535; Stafford, *Unification and Conquest*, 159–61.

[55] *Liber Eliensis*, 75–117; claims from kin (both after sales and wills): ibid. 87, 94, 97, 101, 104.

alienation enjoyed by those who had held land in 1066, or the lack of it, is with freedom from seigniorial rather than family constraint, its frequent notes about whether people of apparently non-noble status were free to alienate or not would hardly have been made if families had regularly exercised an acknowledged right to stop them.[56] The conclusion must be that there was greater freedom of disposition in England at this period than there was in most of France—perhaps in practice more even than there was in parts of Italy, considering the apparently greater amount of shared property there. Perhaps, subject to the same caution as was expressed at the end of the last paragraph, one reason was political. Tenth- and eleventh-century English kings, like earlier Frankish kings, had enough power and resources not to need to control alienation. It was the fragmentation of power in France that left local lords dependent on trying to control the property of their free subjects in some of the same ways as landowners everywhere controlled that of peasants.

Whether or not charters of some kind were absolutely necessary for the conveyance of bookland in what I suggest was its new and wider sense, is uncertain. Presumably the clergy would be especially likely to want written records, but, though Bishop Aethelwold sometimes mentions documentary evidence of his purchases, he seems to have been more often concerned to record how he had acquired land and by what witness. Perhaps he kept the original charters apart from his narrative account and they got lost while his *Libellus* survived.[57] Nevertheless it looks as though the most important validation of any transfer was that it was made before local witnesses. A royal gift to a church could be symbolized by placing a representative object on the altar and afterwards recorded in a formal charter, but by the eleventh century it seems that neither these procedures nor the publicity of a royal declaration before royal councillors was enough. Surviving writs suggest that Edward the Confessor also announced his gifts to the officials and men of the shire in which the property lay.[58] A meeting of the smaller local government area known as a hundred or of several hundreds seems to have been sufficient for smaller transactions: what mattered was that all transfers were made formally and in public (*coram testimonio populi*).[59]

Obligations to the king, which were considerable, seem to have rested on landowners in general. Military service, or payment instead of it, seems to have been owed in principle by all landowners, probably more or less in

[56] *Pace* Stephenson, 'Commendation', 181 and Milsom, 'Introduction', pp. xxxii, xlv.

[57] *Liber Eliensis*, 75–117.

[58] Harmer, *Anglo-Saxon Writs*, 35–8, 45–54, nos. 26, 28–30, 55, 68; Chaplais, 'Anglo-Saxon Chancery', 170–2, 175.

[59] *Liber Eliensis*, 108, 116.

proportion to their holdings, subject to privilege, bargaining, and local custom.[60] Though lords—probably those with the jurisdictions known as sokes—had some responsibility for their men, the service, at least in Berkshire and Worcestershire, was none the less owed to the king and apparently organized by shires, while penalties for non-performance went to him too.[61] The tax that historians generally call the geld or danegeld seems also to have been levied on all land. In the eleventh century non-payment is known to have incurred confiscation—once again to the king, though third parties prepared to make good the unpaid geld could take over the property.[62] Foreshadowings of the 'feudal incidents' of relief, wardship, and marriage that would later loom so large in the relations of English kings with their subjects can be seen both in heriots (dues payable on death) payable to the king and in early eleventh-century laws about the rights and remarriage of widows.[63] The payment of heriots in horses and arms may suggest that they had originated in an archaic custom by which a lord received a gift from his dead follower's arms and goods, but, even if they had, kings in the tenth century (if not before) had translated the traditional gift into a regular tariff of inheritance dues—a tariff that went up in the eleventh century.[64] Though the laws make the tariff one of status, by 1066 in at least some counties it was related to the size of estates.[65] As for liability to confiscation, responsible opinion in late tenth-century Huntingdonshire was that there was no land there so free that it could not be forfeit.[66]

If a hierarchy of tenure or property is taken to mean a division of property rights and obligations between two or more layers of people, then it may be misleading to think of all or even most pre-conquest property above the peasant level as normally forming one.[67] English society was very unequal, but not all unequal relations affected property rights, let alone property rights arranged in a hierarchy. *Medemran thegnas* were presumably so called because they were middling in status and wealth rather than because they were normally in the middle of a hierarchy of property.[68]

[60] Gillingham, 'Introduction of Knight Service', 61–4. For bargaining by towns: Reynolds, 'Towns in Domesday Book', 306–7.
[61] *Domesday Book*, i. 56c, 172a, 375c–d.
[62] Lawson, 'Collection of Danegeld'; Green, 'Last Century'.
[63] Liebermann, *Gesetze*, i. 242, 254, 356–8 (V Aethelred 21; VI Aethelred 26; II Cnut 70–4); Stafford, *Unification and Conquest*, 148, 160, 165–6, 175, 178.
[64] Brooks, 'Arms, Status and Warfare'. For heriots as designed to secure inheritance: Sawyer, *Anglo-Saxon Charters*, nos. 939 (cf. 1501), 1484, 1486, 1536; cf. *Liber Eliensis*, 100–1, 117.
[65] *Domesday Book*, i. 280c, 298d (other heriots or reliefs: i. 1b, 252a, 262c, 336d, ii. 119a).
[66] *Liber Eliensis*, 98–9.                      [67] See chapter 3.4.
[68] *Domesday Book Studies*, 158; cf. Liebermann, *Gesetze*, i. 358–9 (II Cnut 71. 2), Maitland, *Domesday Book and Beyond*, 165–6.

Land held by nobles or free men from churches formed a two-tier hierarchy—or three-tier, if one includes peasant holdings. So, presumably, did that held ex officio or for life from the king. There must have been much more of this after the kingdom of Wessex expanded to become the kingdom of England so that the royal estates became larger and more widely scattered. Domesday Book suggests that royal land was generally managed by the sheriff of the shire (county) in which it lay. It may often have been the earl or the sheriff who settled the people called the king's thegns on the king's land. Their holdings were generally too small to make these thegns look like those who characteristically held five hides of land. Like the word *miles*, or like the modern word officer, *thegn* thus seems to have been used to denote both a person of high status and the holder of an office or job of relatively low status. These humbler thegns of the king with holdings on what remained in principle royal land may have formed a nucleus of reliable military service and owed other general services, like tax collection, in support of the sheriff, rather like the Carolingian *vassi*. What rights they had in their holdings is uncertain. Some could sell them, and all or most may have had a reasonable chance of passing them on to their sons, provided that they were loyal and reasonably competent. In the event loyalty and military service in 1066 would have doomed most of them. Some of those who held 'thegnlands' on church estates may have had rather similar duties. As in other countries, however, the priorities of churches differed from those of kings or other lay lords, so that it would be misleading to deduce the terms on which the king granted out his lands from those on which churches did so. The greater nobles of the enlarged kingdom of the late tenth and early eleventh century must also have had a correspondingly greater need to delegate the management of their estates than their predecessors had done. Some probably did so on similar terms to the king's, but Domesday Book is less informative about them. While some of the people who held their land under (*sub*) or from (*de*) an earl or anyone else may have been in a comparable position to the thegns on royal estates or—subject to the usual caveats—on church land, it is not clear that all were. There is, as I shall argue, even less reason to believe that someone who was said to be the man of an earl or anyone else was in a similar position.[69] The important point that I wish to make is that I have not found evidence that heritable grants from kings or lay lords normally created what were perceived as permanent layers of rights.

The hierarchy of government was by now at least partially distinct from any hierarchy of property. Earls—or some of them—got a share of heriots

[69] As is suggested e.g. by Sawyer, '1066–1086'; Fleming, *Kings and Lords*, 71 n. makes two men 'hold land from' their lords when Domesday does not say that they did.

and other royal income from their shires and they had much opportunity for influence and patronage, but none of that gave them a formal share in the property rights of people within their earldoms. The units of jurisdiction known as sokes survived the reorganization of local government that followed the enlargement of the kingdom, so that they formed an anomalous relic from the time when government and property were indistinguishable. Whether soke lords had a significant share in the property rights of their free subjects is, however, unclear. While jurisdiction over the property of many free men seems now to have lain in the county, subject to royal intervention, soke lords may still have retained jurisdiction over property within their sokes and received some or all of the fines incurred by their subjects in county or other courts.[70] Military service may have been organized through sokes, though that involves generalizing from the customs of Worcestershire, where most sokes belonged to churches and were therefore characterized by a distinctive proprietary relation.[71] Some soke lords took heriots and no doubt a variety of other dues.[72] Nevertheless, despite these obligations, some, though not all, of the property of sokemen or free men under soke (presumably meaning much the same, though local usage may have varied), and *a fortiori* of any thegns who may have been under soke, carried pretty full rights.[73] Even if property under soke was never called bookland (and we cannot be sure that it never was), some of it was freely alienable and some of its owners could choose patrons outside the soke. The variations that had derived from centuries of varying local customs and from the varying status of both soke lords and their subjects must have been further enriched by individual bargains and judgements. The churches to which some of the biggest as well as the best-recorded sokes belonged no doubt followed different policies with differing consistency. As the *Rectitudines Singularum Personarum* put it, *landlaga syn mistlice*: the laws and customs of lands are multiple and various.[74] To call people under soke tenants and to see sokes as part of a 'tenurial hierarchy' is to darken counsel.

So it is to see commendation as tenurial. *Commendare, commendatio*, et cetera were words of many meanings.[75] The sense that is at issue in Domesday Book seems generally to be that which denotes a relation of

[70] *Domesday Book*, i. 1b, 172a, c, 280c; cf. Kennedy, 'Disputes'.
[71] Abels, *Lordship*, 121–31; *Domesday Book*, i. 173b.
[72] *Domesday Book*, i. 1b; cf. Sawyer, *Anglo-Saxon Charters*, no. 1519, in which the archbishop was perhaps Ketel's soke lord.
[73] Thegns apparently under soke: Barrow, *Kingdom of Scots*, 17 and n. 43 (esp. *Inquisitio Eliensis*, 67, 74, 93).
[74] Liebermann, *Gesetze*, i. 452 (*Rectitudines* 21). Cf. Dodwell, 'East Anglian Commendation'. On the *Rectitudines* and its date: Harvey, 'Rectitudines'.
[75] *Oxford Dictionary of Med. Latin*, 391–2. See chapter 2.2, esp. at n. 42.

patronage or protection, which also seems to be indicated in other ways, such as saying that someone was the man of another.[76] One of the objects for which people sought patrons was certainly the protection of their land. A patron might hope to secure rights over property he protected and some patrons bargained to get them, but Domesday does not suggest that commendation, or having someone as his man, automatically gave him any.[77] Many clients probably gravitated to their lord's banner in war, especially if they were not committed to a soke contingent, but that does not make it helpful to call them tenants, let alone subtenants, of their patrons. Some people were recorded as having held land under (*sub*) or from (*de*) their patrons, but, on the analogy of similar phrases in France, that need not mean that their property rights were reduced.[78] The right to choose a protector for one's property, which seems to be implied in remarks that someone could 'leave with his land' or 'go with his land where he wanted', seems often to have gone with the right to alienate it, but it must be wrong to describe them roundly as 'identical in meaning'.[79] The reason that the two were sometimes interchangeable in Domesday and its related texts may be that both were used in 1086 to illustrate a similar and significant level of status and rights, so that they came to much the same thing for the purposes of the enquiry. Sometimes the Domesday information about both commendation and soke seems to be part of a general desire to explain what rights a church or other lord of a soke or manor had enjoyed over relatively free property, and what they or their successors could therefore now claim.[80] In a good many cases, however, it looks as though commendation needed to be mentioned only because new lords who had come to make their fortunes in England had taken a conveniently broad view of the rights of the predecessors from whom they were supposed to have derived their titles. County and hundred juries made some attempt to record the resulting usurpations.[81] Predecessors who had had only the soke or only the commendation had not, it seems, had as much as the current lords were claiming. Lumping the lands of sokemen and people under commendation in with those held from churches and those we may suspect were held on

---

[76] Though *Domesday Book*, i. 377b uses *commendare* for a short-term grant of land.

[77] *Domesday Book*, i. 50c (Ailwin held *sub Wigoto pro tuitione*), 137d (*ad Wigotum se vertit pro protectione*); Maitland, *Domesday Book and Beyond*, 71–4. Relationships of this kind are suggested in *Liber Eliensis*, 106; Sawyer, *Anglo-Saxon Charters*, nos. 1447, 1462, and (much earlier) 1187.

[78] Maitland, *Domesday Book and Beyond*, 72–3, 154–5. Chapter 5, at nn. 19–25, 176–9.

[79] Round, *Feudal England*, 22. Both were mentioned in *Domesday Book*, i. 199c.

[80] e.g. *Domesday Book*, i. 62d, 66–8, 72b, 127–8d, 129b–d, 133b, 142b–d, 163b, 164d–165a, 172b–c, 174b, 179c, 180c–d (cf. 173b), 190d–191d, 196d–197a, 199d; ii. 310b–311, 313, 367b.

[81] e.g. *Domesday Book*, i. 44d, 57b, 129a, 137d (cf. Round, 'Introd. to Herts. Domesday', 267–9), 199c, 211d, 225d; ii. 6a, 40b, 71b–72a, 148b, 172a–b, 187b, 287a, 313b, and cases cited by Sawyer, '1066–1086', 78–80.

restricted terms from kings or lay lords, obscure as this last category is, calling them all equally part of their lords' estates, and seeing them all as held in a similar 'tenurial hierarchy' can only increase the obscurities of pre-conquest property.

Domesday Book allows us to see more different types of lordship apparently coexisting separately than can be seen in most sources of this date. Feudally minded historians could interpret this by saying that the union of fief and vassalage had not yet occurred in England, but introducing a model that does not seem to fit the evidence anywhere else very well seems less useful than examining the evidence here more closely. The different forms that lordship seems to have taken did not each correspond with a different word. The Old English word *manrædene* may have been translated both as *commendatio* and *hominium* or *hominatio*, but *hominatio* could relate to rights over sokemen. None of the words invariably or even generally had feudo-vassalic connotations at this date—or, indeed, later.[82] In Domesday most of the people described as the men of others, as commended to them, as holding land from them, or as under their soke, look at best on the borderline between peasant and noble, so that rights over them look feudal rather in a more or less Marxist sense than a feudo-vassalic one. Their subjection may well have been symbolized by an oath—perhaps what would have been called a 'hold oath'[83]—or other ceremony but that does not mean that their relation with their lords was the same as that of a noble warrior with his king or other lord. When great men did *manrædene* to kings, *bugan* to them, took *hold athas* to them, or when nobles did any of these things to each other (though we have little evidence of that), it clearly involved a quite different relation from that of a lord—especially a bishop or abbot—with his peasant tenants, clients, or subjects. The crucial determinants of each relation were surely the status of the parties and local custom, not particular words or ceremonies, though ceremonies would of course be affected by custom. The rights that patrons had over their clients must have varied greatly: most of our references to them are not normative and we should not treat them as if they were. Most of the references to pre-conquest heriots, wardship and marriage rights, or escheats that have been taken to prefigure post-conquest feudal relations concern the rights of either churches or the king, not other lay lords.[84] As in other countries,

---

[82] Stenton, 'St. Benet'; *Domesay Book*, i. 225d. See index: commendation, homage. For different uses of *manrædene*: Venezky and Healey, *Concordance: mannrædene, manræden, manrædene, manrædenne, manred*.

[83] *Hyldath* or *hold ath*: Liebermann, *Gesetze*, i. 396–7; *Two Saxon Chronicles*, 246 (1115).

[84] For the king's rights, above, nn. 63–6. Heriots paid to sheriffs count for me as owed to the king. The 'wardship and marriage' and escheat mentioned by Maitland, *Domesday Book and Beyond*, 310, 314–15 are about church land.

dues and services owed to churches by fairly humble tenants are unlikely to derive from those that derived from the grant of land by kings or nobles to their noble followers. Since the rules laid down by Cnut about confiscation and heriots come in the part of his laws that seems to embody promises to rule less oppressively, most of them probably concern confiscations and heriots due to him.[85] I have to admit, however, that not all do so. While the order that lords should not take more than their right heriot may be directed at churches and others with relatively humble tenants, the rules about those who deserted their lords or fellows on campaign or who died on campaign with their lords look more feudo-vassalic. Nevertheless it may be a mistake to assume too easily that they must all be interpreted that way: the lord could have been merely the man's commander (perhaps earl or sheriff of his county), his patron, or his soke lord, rather than a lord who already had significant rights over property that he or a predecessor had originally granted to his follower. That is not to say that no relations before 1066 resembled those historians think characteristic of classical feudalism. Pushing them automatically into that mould, however, is not the best way of understanding them.

It may be that the power of the central government actually stimulated the growth of patronage, since people needed patrons to protect them and their property against its demands. The information in Domesday about restrictions on alienation suffered by people who may otherwise have had what were thought of as fairly complete rights in their property suggests the way that patronage could lead to what is called dependent tenure, but Domesday also makes it clear that relations of patronage ('commendation') were often separate from property relations. Patronage links sometimes formed hierarchies, but they corresponded with the social hierarchy, or hierarchy of power and influence, more closely than with any hierarchy of property rights in general in so far as one can be deduced. The same may have been the case after 1066. We have no reason, beyond historiographical tradition, to believe that all clientage then became attached to landholding. The reason that we hear less in the two centuries that followed Domesday Book about relations of patronage that were separate from landholding is that after 1086 they did not need to be recorded in the same way. At least some of the evidence of what is called 'bastard feudalism' in the later middle ages comes in the records of agreements that had probably not been written down hitherto or, if they were, have not survived. In 1086, however, King William's clerks needed to refer to relations of patrons and clients in order to explain the complications of rights, wrongs,

[85] Stafford, 'Laws of Cnut'.

and obligations that had been produced by twenty years of conquest and conflict.

## 8.4. *The Norman Conquest*

The Norman Conquest looms so large in accounts of English property law as well as of English feudalism that at the risk of some repetition it may be useful to discuss its impact before going on to consider the evidence about property in the twelfth and thirteenth centuries. Doing this has the additional advantage of separating what can reasonably be attributed to the conquest itself from what resulted from all the changes in economy, government, and law that took place in the twelfth century and later. I shall therefore consider here only the period between 1066 and 1100 and shall restrict myself as far as possible to evidence from that period. The traditional assumption that the Norman Conquest brought radical change to the rights and obligations of English property—and it is often not much more than an assumption—goes back to the seventeenth century, if not earlier. While Levellers and some lawyers then maintained that the Normans had subverted Anglo-Saxon liberties, Spelman and later historians saw the crucial import not as simple tyranny but as fiefs—'feuds and tenures', as Spelman called them, 'fees' or 'knights' fees' according to most later English usage.[86] The subject has been much debated in the past hundred years or so, but, especially since J. H. Round's essay on the introduction of knight service was published in 1891, the debate has generally been conducted on rather a narrow front. Even those who have rejected Round's picture of sudden and revolutionary change of military organization, and his assumption that this created sudden and revolutionary social change, have tended to focus primarily on the subjects of military service and a hierarchy of tenure or property rights.

Whatever the stages by which the lands William the Conqueror granted to his followers were 'subinfeudated' by them to their followers and divided into 'knights' fees', and whether or not anticipations of these arrangements are found before 1066, the focus of attention has been on the knight's fee as a distinctive form of landed property. Its essence is seen as its dependent or derivative character and its holder's obligation to serve as a fully equipped cavalryman. It thus fits neatly into the idea of feudal tenure traditionally based on a combination of the benefice of Carolingian legislation, Conrad II's ordinance of 1037, and inferences drawn from the later academic law of fiefs.[87] Recent arguments that English fiefs were not

---

[86] Spelman, *Reliquiae*, 4.     [87] Chapters 3.1 and 6.5, 8.

at first hereditary also seem to fit into the traditional view of an evolution towards inheritance, even if the chronology and circumstances of the supposed evolution in England are rather different.[88] Whatever the borrowings and comparisons, however, arguments about English feudalism remain distinctive, first in the emphasis on military obligations, and second in the form given to them by the peculiarity of the legal system that developed in England after the middle of the twelfth century. Although both aspects are largely explicable by genuine peculiarities in medieval England, they have also conditioned historical thinking in a way that makes comparisons both difficult and essential. If one looks not merely at military obligations and rights of inheritance but at the general obligations and rights of property, and if one looks at them against the background of obligations and rights in general both in pre-conquest England and in eleventh-century France (and elsewhere), many of the past arguments about the Norman Conquest and the introduction of feudalism seem a little blinkered.

The Normans seem to have been accustomed to fewer taxes and probably less formal military obligations, and to a closer link between property rights and jurisdiction, than were the English, but there is not much evidence that the conquest changed fundamental ideas about the rights and obligations of property in England very much.[89] All the references to the legal changes William I introduced imply a background of similar assumptions about custom and rights. The 'feudal law' by which, according to modern historians, William II wanted to judge the bishop of Durham when they quarrelled in 1088, seems in Symeon of Durham's account to have been simply secular law, whereas the bishop wanted to be judged according to canon law.[90] In so far as rights changed in practice it was to a large extent because of the turmoil of the times. Englishmen were expropriated in hundreds and thousands, but that was either because they rebelled or because the occupying forces were in a position to treat them as if they had. Domesday Book suggests that title to land in 1086 officially depended either on the title of one's predecessor at the time of King Edward's death or on a public investiture, carried out at royal command.[91] Later evidence about the succession to individual estates held after 1086 by those below the dangerous level of high politics suggests that a good many

---

[88] Chapters 3.4 and 5.5.

[89] Information about Normandy is scattered through the sections of chapter 5.

[90] Symeon of Durham, *Opera*, 170–95; cf. marginal note on p. 175; Barlow, *English Church, 1066–1154*, 282–4. On Symeon: Gransden, *Historical Writing*, 122 n.

[91] *Domesday Book*, e.g. i. 36a, 50a, 62b, 208b, ii. 174; Garnett, 'Coronation and Propaganda'; Holt, '1086', 62. On the reality behind the titles: Fleming, *Kings and Lords*, 107–214; Mortimer, 'Beginnings of the Honour of Clare'.

of them may have remained in the same families for some time. Where recorded forfeitures or losses were attributed to treason or lack of suitable heirs, that must surely imply a prima-facie right of inheritance—a right that had, after all, been recognized hitherto both in Normandy and England. Henry I's coronation charter recognized such a right—in principle.[92] The king's right to an inheritance due ('relief') was not supposed to amount to confiscation and resale.

Arguments that the principle of inheritance was not yet accepted seem to rely on several questionable premisses. First there are all the traditional presuppositions about feudalism, like the belief that under it all landowners except the king were 'merely tenants' and that feudal tenure was not originally hereditary.[93] Second, traditions of legal history have tended to foster the belief that what came before the foundation of the English common law in the twelfth and thirteenth centuries was not true law. As a result, the impression is sometimes conveyed that customary law was mere practice with no normative force.[94] But even if custom did not have the same kind of legal rules as were produced by later professional law its norms were probably no more conflicting and difficult to apply in practice. Methods of resolving disputes were different from what they would be under the common law, but that does not justify us in supposing that inheritance was not seen in terms of right before the common law provided remedies for those who thought their rights had been infringed or before it laid down rules about who should be the heir.[95] In many societies rights of inheritance do not include fixed rules of succession, while the derivation of rights from remedies seems to be an idiosyncrasy of relatively late common-law thinking.[96] Some of the evidence that has been used to argue about the inheritance of fiefs in the twelfth century, moreover, has concerned land held from churches. At best this is irrelevant to the heritability of other property. At worst it illustrates the troubles that the force of lay norms of inheritance caused to churches.[97] That is not, of course, to say

[92] Holt, 'Feudal Society II', 218.

[93] e.g. Thorne, 'English Feudalism', esp. 15–16, taking Ganshof's and Plucknett's brief remarks as authoritative. Cf. chapter 3.2.

[94] Thorne, 'English Feudalism', 16–18; Milsom, 'Inheritance by Women', 65 and *Legal Framework*, 120. On custom and norms, see chapter 3.3.

[95] On rules of inheritance: Milsom 'Inheritance by Women', 65. Distinctions between inheritance and succession or inheritance and succession by hereditary right do not seem to belong in the twelfth century: Holt, 'Rejoinder'.

[96] Jacob, *Law Dictionary*: Right, appears to have derived his rule basing rights on the existence of remedies at law from the index rather than the text of Vaughan, *Reports*, 38. Milsom, *Legal Framework*, and *Historical Foundations*, 4, 100, 107, 121–2, seems to imply a similar association, but cf. Pollock and Maitland, *History*, i. 360, 430.

[97] Apart from many entries about church land in *Domesday Book*: Robinson, *Gilbert Crispin*, 38; Galbraith, 'Episcopal Land-Grant', 372; *Cart. Mon. Ramseia*, no. 166; *Placita Anglo-*

that all lay property was heritable or that there were no disputes about it. If oral grants were as vague about terms and conditions as are the few charters that survive from before 1100, there must have been scope for many disputes afterwards. That some or many people got new charters confirming or regranting what their ancestors had received need not mean that they or their lords thought that they were not the true heirs of those ancestors. It shows only a sensible caution in a time of upheaval when written records were valued but record-keeping was poor. Altogether there seems no good reason to doubt that it was generally accepted that nobles and free men in England after the Norman Conquest, like nobles and free men before it both in England and Normandy, normally had a right to inherit their parents' land and to pass it on to their own children. In the conditions of conquest freedom of alienation and bequest may have been restricted in practice. That would presumably have affected the accumulation of custom, but the evidence, such as it is, does not suggest deliberate change. It also seems to me difficult to draw any hard and fast line between English wills and Norman post-obit gifts.[98] Some testators had always asked for royal approval of their bequests of land, and for a while some went on doing so.[99]

The first big change to ideas about property may have come from Domesday Book. It is the record itself and the way it is arranged that give, and may from the first have given, such a strong impression of a hierarchy of property and of a hierarchy created by grants. Some idea of a hierarchy of landholding (as well, of course, as a hierarchy of status and authority) may well have pre-dated Domesday. If ever there was a time when reality came near to the later myths of the origin of feudalism in royal grants, it was in post-conquest England, when a king really did give out estates wholesale to his nobles, or tell them that they could go and take them, and when they then in one way or another distributed smaller parcels to their followers.[100] Not all properties were given out as tidily as the myth requires, but there is abundant evidence that great men received great estates in return for their service and support and distributed smaller ones very quickly to followers over whom they presumably intended to retain authority. Nevertheless, any ideas of hierarchy would have been much vaguer before Domesday was compiled. The orders to produce

*Norm.* 114–17; *Reading Cart.* nos. 1, 27. Cf. Cheney, 'Litigation', and, on this and heritability in general, Hudson, 'Life-Grants'.

[98] Sheehan, *Will*, 267–74; Pollock and Maitland, *History*, ii. 326–31; cf. Holt, 'Feudal Society I', 197–8; Tabuteau, *Transfers*, 24–7.

[99] Stafford, *Unification and Conquest*, 159–61; Sheehan, *Will*, 19–21, 106–19, 267–74.

[100] Orderic Vitalis, *Hist. Eccl.* ii. 266.

information that went out at the beginning of 1086[101] must have been addressed to important people—*barones regis*, as the nearly contemporary geld accounts call them—rather than those who later became known as tenants in chief.[102] Geld (tax) lists would have said who owned (or had owned) estates, but, given the variety of ways in which property had been acquired, it may have been difficult, before the survey was made, to draw up complete and reliable lists of those who had received their land directly from the king. Any royal official who had tried to make one might, for a start, have been hard put to it to decide whether to include the lands of the great churches. Few of the church's lands had been granted to it by William, and some had not been granted by previous kings either. Great churches now generally appeared at the head of the lists of tenants in chief in each county, because, if church lands were to be listed, as they needed to be, the prestige of the church demanded that position.[103] At the other end of the lists came all those miscellaneous little people who had to be listed with the tenants in chief, either because they were royal servants or because they did not fit in anywhere else. All this fostered ways of looking at property rights that may have strengthened the king's hand when he made demands on his followers and subjects. William himself probably profited less from such conceptualizations than from the precedent of English royal rights, bolstered by hard military facts and hard political bargaining, but during the twelfth century negotiations about dues and obligations took place against the background of hierarchy set out in Domesday. That the hierarchy of 1086 appears so clearly as a hierarchy of property or 'tenure', as English legal historians like to call it, rather than one of status, authority, or jurisdiction, is to be explained partly by the sensitivity of titles to property in 1086.[104] Partly it was because the structure of local government before 1066 had separated jurisdiction from property more clearly than was the case in Normandy. Whether or not the Normans had yet fully realized the situation or were prepared to accept it, later readers have tended to read Domesday Book in the light of the still firmer separation that would be established in the course of the twelfth century.

Of all the anachronistic deductions that have been drawn from the arrangement and vocabulary of the survey since then, one of the most important is the belief that, because to us the word tenant implies restricted rights, holding in Domesday meant less than having or owning. R. H. C. Davis seemed to have focused on these implications of the word

---

[101] Galbraith, *Making of Domesday Book*, 121–2; Clarke, 'Domesday Satellites', 61.
[102] Williams, 'Geld Rolls', esp. 116 n. for a small divergence from the *Domesday Book* list.
[103] Though not e.g. York Abbey: *Domesday Book*, i. 298d, 305a, 314a.
[104] Holt, '1086'.

when he wrote that it was 'expounded on every page of Domesday Book [that] all land belonged to the king, and [that] the barons were merely his tenants or sub-tenants. In theory therefore they could not hold their lands by hereditary right.'[105] The theory, however, seems to be derived from one devised by those whom Maitland called 'severe feudalists of the seventeenth and later centuries' rather than being detectable in contemporary sources.[106] People who held land from the king seem to have been thought to have genuine rights over it that were defensible at law, just as did those who held land from them: Domesday, together with records of disputes from before 1154, suggests that the theory of the time, which seems to have survived much buffeting from practice, was that the rights both of tenants in chief and of those who held from them were supposed to be good even against the king, provided that the 'tenants' were loyal and paid their reliefs. There is, in short, no reason to suppose that the use of the verb *tenere* in itself implied less than what contemporaries thought of as full rights in eleventh-century England, any more than it did in France.[107] The alliterative association of having and holding, which is already found in Old English, survived into Middle English and beyond.[108] Perhaps it prompted the adoption of the Latin jingle *habendum et tenendum*, which had become entrenched in property deeds by 1200, without any suggestion that the two words had different meanings.[109] However that may be, the phrase 'to have and to hold' survived and was later transferred back into legal English, ultimately becoming enshrined in the marriage service of the Book of Common Prayer, where neither having nor holding implies a restricted tenure or one dependent on anyone—except God.[110] In Domesday Book most of the lists of those *tenentes terras* in each county are headed by King William, who *tenet* his individual manors just as King Edward *tenuit* his. Even 'holding from' someone else may not have implied an actual reduction of rights in England, any more than it did in France.[111] In the context of Domesday it sometimes does so, notably in the case of church land. In other cases those who 'held from' a lord may well have had their rights reduced or their obligations increased because of the bullying that accompanied conquest, while lessened rights or increased obligations may often have become embedded in custom, but that does not mean that reduced rights of property can be deduced from the use of the words. 'Holding from' in Domesday may sometimes have meant being under some kind of

---

[105] Davis, 'What Happened', 6. See also below, at n. 170.
[106] Pollock and Maitland, *History* ii. 5; and 2–6 in general.
[107] See index: *tenere*.     [108] *OED* vii. 16–17; *Middle Eng. Dict. G–H*, 535–6.
[109] Below, at n. 160. For an early example: *Regesta Regum Anglo-Norm.* i, no. 435.
[110] Cf. *Select Cases in Ecclesiastical Courts*, 104.
[111] See chapter 5, at nn. 19–25, 176–9.

authority or patronage, or indicated the derivation of the subordinate's title.

As for various forms of the word fief, they certainly occur in English sources for the first time soon after the conquest, but they are pretty rare before 1100 and carry much the same range of often non-committal senses as they did in contemporary France.[112] It seems equally misleading to suggest either that 'fief' or 'fee' was synonymous with 'knight's fee' or that the word already had its later connotation of heritability.[113] *Feu* and *feudum* are occasionally used in Domesday, most often in the sense, derived from French usage, of a superior estate or unit of authority.[114] The king's fief is mentioned at least once in Domesday and the fiefs of the queen and other lords more often.[115] Quite apart from the French analogy, this use surely excludes any suggestion of restricted or subordinate rights. Some lands of the bishops of London and Thetford were also called *feuda*: these seem to have been recent acquisitions that may not yet have been regarded as part of the endowments of their respective bishoprics.[116] Otherwise most properties that Domesday says were held *in feudo* or *ad feudum* seem to have been smallish and some paid rent. One manor in Middlesex (in circuit 3 of the survey) had been held for a while from King William *in feudo* for a rent *de firma* and had not been inherited.[117] Maybe the word was useful, as in France, because it was non-committal. In circuit 1, however, *in feudo* sometimes seems to mean much the same as *in alodio* or *in alodium*. *Alodiarii* here look rather like sokemen in other circuits. Some are explicitly said to have had the right to sell their land. Others lacked it, but they all look like people who may have had enough rights to create a presumption of free disposition.[118] Exceptions had to be noted. Though one would have thought that the property that Domesday describes as held *in alodio* or *in feudo* was on the lower border of what would have been called bookland before the conquest, it may be that Englishmen talking English would have called it that. In the twelfth century *on his boclande* was translated variously as *in feudo suo*, *in hereditate sua terra*, or *in alodio suo*; *bocland* as *terra testamentalis*, *alodium*, or *libera terra*; and *bocrihtes wyrthe* as *dignus*

[112] *Oxford Dict. Med. Latin.* Holt, 'Politics and Property', lists occurrences in charters. See chapter 5.5.
[113] e.g. Brown, *Origins*, 46.
[114] Maitland, *Domesday Book and Beyond*, 152–4; in addition to his examples: *Domesday Book*, e.g. i. 11a, 44d, 32d, 155c; ii. 175b, 176a–b.
[115] *Oxford Dict. Med. Latin*, 920. I owe the reference to the king's fief in *Domesday Book*, i. 158a, to John Blair.
[116] Taylor, 'Endowment of See of London'.
[117] *Domesday Book*, i. 129c.
[118] Darby and Campbell, *Domesday Geog. of SE England*, 254, 258, 382, 518; Maitland, *Domesday Book and Beyond*, 153–4.

*rectitudine testamenti sui.*[119] By then bookland was a memory, but, after all, there had never been an authoritative definition of it that had got lost.

Nor, for many years, would there be any authoritative definition of a fief or, in later legal usage, a fee. In 1088 the archbishop of Canterbury, defending the king's seizure of some of the bishop of Durham's lands, referred to the lands as the bishop's *feodum*, while the bishop called them his *episcopatus* or *episcopium*.[120] Both were probably arguing tendentiously, but it may well be that this bishop had lands apart from those of his see and that the distinction between the two estates was unclear. In 1093, when the quarrel was patched up, the king gave to God, St Cuthbert, and the church of Durham all the land that the bishop had hitherto held *in feodo*, so that he and his successors should thereafter hold it in alms as the church held the rest of its lands and benefices.[121] It is hard to tell whether *in feodo* here meant simply lay property or lay property owing specific services—military services?—and whether alms implied absence of all services. In 1166 the bishop's lands, which presumably counted as the property of the church, owed the service of ten knights.[122] Most fiefs probably consisted of land, because land was the most important kind of property, as well as the kind most likely to be recorded in surviving sources. Since the word fief was new here, one cannot find 'money fiefs' before 'land fiefs' in England as one can in Burgundy, but they need not have been a later or secondary development. Some soldiers who were not given land may very soon have received regular—or fairly regular—wages of the kind historians describe as 'money fiefs', while some Normans who received grants of land had to live at first off rents and dues from dependent peasants without any land for their direct cultivation:[123] the difference between grants of land and grants of rents may have been less clear than it looks in later theories of feudalism.

Practical changes in the rights and obligations of property in general, apart from the vast changes suffered by all those who lost part or all of what they owned, can be substantiated with varying degrees of certainty. Taxes continued to be levied on the old basis of assessment.[124] The only immediate change was that they became heavier and more frequent. In so far as great men gained exemption that may have been more because of royal

---

[119] Liebermann, *Gesetze*, i. 196–7, 294–5, 316–17, 444, 612.

[120] Symeon of Durham, *Opera*, 183–5.

[121] Craster, 'Contemporary Record', 36; Taylor, 'Endowment of See of London'.

[122] *Red Book*, 415–16.

[123] Harvey, 'Knight and Knight's Fee', 24; Searle, *Lordship and Community*, 48–65.

[124] There does not seem to be any reason to see the aids received by Westminster abbey from its *milites* (Robinson, *Gilbert Crispin*, 38) as prototype 'feudal aids': cf. *Cart. Shrewsbury*, no. 2, and below at nn. 185–8.

favour, and because the geld was such an appalling shock to Normans, than because those holding land directly from the king were identified from the first as a distinct legal category.[125] The forest laws look like a significant inroad on property rights. Whatever the regulations by which previous kings had protected their own hunting, the first evidence that subjects were restricted or prevented from hunting over their own land comes from this time. Complaints about the forest laws of the Norman kings cannot all be the effect of new records or yearning for a mythical golden age.[126] Early writs informing counties of grants, combined with the complaints in Domesday that grants had not been notified properly and with knowledge of later customs of livery of seisin, suggest that the traditional procedures of transferring property were not immediately or totally abandoned. Norman lords who granted land to their followers or to submissive Englishmen (or simply allowed submissive Englishmen to keep land) may well have also required a ceremony that symbolized subordination: that might explain how the rite that became known as homage became a normal requirement for some kinds of grant. Many Normans may also have been disconcerted by the ready-made structure of shire (county) and hundred courts and the way that they cut across lordships, but how far they deliberately ignored them and exercised anything like formal and separate jurisdiction over their free men within their lordships we do not know. If they did, then perhaps the Domesday enquiries gave them pause and encouraged their subjects to appeal beyond them to the county or the king. By Henry I's reign, if not before, some lords had learned that county and even hundred courts could not be ignored. Most of the evidence about seigniorial jurisdiction, however, comes from after 1100 and will be discussed later. For the time being I suggest merely that the idea that the Norman Conquest produced a significant shift to what is sometimes called private jurisdiction depends more on the imposition of models of feudalism than on hard evidence. It may have done but it is not proved that it did.

Where the argument about change has raged most fiercely is on the subject of military obligations. A good many historians might now agree that the evidence of immediate and systematic change looks weaker than J. H. Round maintained.[127] After much cogitation I think that the chief reason for looking for immediate and systematic change is the difficulty of aban-

[125] Green, 'Last Century'.
[126] Green, *Government of Henry I*, 124–30; chapter 5 at n. 51.
[127] Round, 'Introduction of Knight Service'. Hollister, *Military Organization*, surveys the evidence. Among more recent contributions to the vast literature: Gillingham, 'Introduction of Knight Service'; Holt, 'Introduction of Knight Service'.

doning a long and learned historiographical tradition.[128] The churches whose chroniclers—generally considerably later—complained about their sufferings under the Norman kings and the service they had to provide may have had to grant land to new men, some of them Normans, in order to get their service performed.[129] Some of them may have found it harder to argue about their customary obligations under the new regime than it had been. But none of them complained at all perspicuously about a change in the basis of their obligations in William I's reign. As usual, moreover, it is hard to transfer information about church land and its obligations to lay property. In the immediate aftermath of conquest traditional obligations must have often gone by the board. William must have needed all the service he could get from his own men while being prepared to take what his English servants told him was customarily owed by his English subjects— and a bit more when it seemed possible to get it. He may well have made new and explicit arrangements about the services that some—even many— of his followers would owe in respect of their new lands, but there is absolutely no evidence that a 'precise definition of service'[130] formed an automatic part of each grant.

When Henry II in 1166 initiated a great enquiry into the number of knights his immediate tenants had enfeoffed (*feodaverunt*) before and after 1135, some of the answers sent in by laymen, difficult as they are to interpret, suggest that, though some claimed to know the number of knights their ancestors had owed from the beginning, most, unlike the clergy, had no record of any agreed quota of service due. This is not improbable, given that the government's own records were apparently either non-existent or inadequate. In subsequent disputes it always apparently worked from the 1166 figures, not from any of its own. What laymen thought they owed was, it seems, what they thought that they and their predecessors had always owed and done.[131] Against the background of the apparent absence of records of numerical quotas of service in Normandy, the need for an occupying army to defend itself on its own terms, and the way that customary law was likely to work thereafter, the system we find in operation in 1166 looks less like the result of a new political and tenurial ideology than a response to the urgent needs of conquest that had then become fixed in custom. If it had been a deliberate introduction the new quotas might

---

[128] Gillingham, 'Introduction of Knight Service', and further conversation with John Gillingham have convinced me that what I said about this in 'Bookland, Folkland and Fiefs' was wrong.

[129] e.g. especially Douglas, 'Charter of Enfeoffment'.          [130] Stenton, *First Century*, 130.

[131] *Red Book*, e.g. 202–3, 210–11, 242–4, 299, 331–3, 340–1, 378–80, 401–2, 441; Keefe, *Feudal Assessments*, 65–7 *et passim*. Dr J. A. Green tells me that she thinks the government of Henry I had records of services owed. They may, however, have been less good by 1154.

have been recorded in Domesday Book. What was recorded in Domesday and the way it was recorded were nevertheless important in organizational terms. Whereas before 1066 most people with their own inherited property seem to have owed their service direct to the king and served county by county, the service recorded in 1066 was owed through the king's tenants in chief. Domesday Book's lists of those holding land directly under the king, county by county, may from early on have served pretty well for summoning those most worth summoning.

It is, moreover, pretty clear that those who owed military service did not form any more of a distinct category in terms of social or economic status than they had before 1066, and that property held by military service did not form a coherent category in terms of rights and obligations in general. In the earliest records that we have, the obligation to provide knights, both for field service and for garrison duty, was being shared by quite humble smallholders. 'Knights' fees' were not, as a category, marked off from other property by anything except the service that they owed, and not always by that. As early as the 1090s, and perhaps before, a fair number of those who owed knight service held only a fraction of a knight's fee. Some may have taken it in turn to serve, while some may always have contributed to costs instead. It was not unknown for smallholders to owe both rents and military service.[132] *Milites* were often contrasted with *pedites*, but apart from the fact that there had been *milites* in England before 1066 even if they had not customarily fought as cavalry, some men who did knight service may not, even with help from their fellows, have done it on the kind of expensive war-horses that implied a very noble life-style. Moreover, it is not clear that military obligation, whether on lay or ecclesiastical estates, was ever restricted to those who held by knight service, let alone to those whom we could even approximately call noble warriors.[133] William the Conqueror was believed to have imposed a duty on all free men in the kingdom to serve and defend him against his enemies both within and without England, while he and his successors all relied heavily on household troops and paid soldiers of one sort or another.[134] Englishmen, however recruited, were serving, however willingly or unwillingly, in royal armies by 1067. The obligations imposed on all free men in 1181 by the Assize of Arms may not have been totally in abeyance since 1066.[135] 'Feudal military service' was never the only military service owed, let alone performed, in post-conquest England, and those who served in royal armies were not all members of a noble élite.

[132] Lennard, *Rural England*, 112 n.
[133] Harvey, 'Knight and Knight's Fee'; *Red Book*, 210–11, 231–3; Mortimer, 'Land and Service'.          [134] Liebermann, *Gesetze*, i. 486; Prestwich, 'War and Finance'.
[135] Richardson and Sayles, *Governance*, 75–6.

352

## 8.5. *Words and concepts, 1100–1300*

During the first half of the twelfth century *feodum* became the normal form
of the word in English sources, replacing the *feudum, fevum,* or *feum* of
Domesday. By 1166 the answers to Henry II's enquiry were full of words
like *feodum militis, fefare, feofatus,* and *feodamentum.*[136] Perhaps they were
already being used as freely fifty or a hundred years before, though we have
no real reason to assume so. The words of 1166 may appear to have feudo-
vassalic connotations, but that is because these documents are about military obligations. In other contexts they suggest something rather different.
*Feodum,* while still used in its other older senses, had by now become the
normal word for what was thought of as full and free property, whether it
owed knight service or not. Land owing military service needed to be distinguished from other fees (*feoda*)—hence the expressions *feodum militis* or
*feodum militare.* Rent-paying land could be described as *feodum censuale* or,
more often, as granted or held in fee-farm (*in feodofirma, in fedfirmam, in
feufirmam,* etc.). In practice the distinctions were not always made so systematically: some land granted simply *in feodum* owed rent rather than military service.[137] Land held in fee (or 'in homage') was sometimes
contrasted with a lord's *dominium*: that is, with what a lord kept for himself. It was also, however, possible to envisage someone with *feoda militum*
on his *dominicum*—presumably because *feoda militum* here are units of
obligation rather than of property—and from the late twelfth century the
statement that someone was seised *in dominico suo sicut de feodo* became
standard in English law.[138] The range of senses attached to *dominus* and its
derivatives always needs caution: in the thirteenth century it could mean
the owner of inherited free property as well as his lord—whom some
modern writers confusingly tend to call his overlord.[139]

    As full and free property, fiefs were normally hereditary. By the
1120s charters issued by the king and laymen sometimes use the phrase *in
feodum et hereditatem* (or *in feodo et hereditate*).[140] Presumably when the

---

[136] Generally spelt thus in *Liber Niger* (the Little Black Book), which was made before the *Red
Book*: Poole, *Exchequer in the Twelfth Century,* 13–15.

[137] *Liber Niger,* i. 75; *Burton Chart.* 30–6; *Cart. Mon. Ramseia,* no. 255; Harvey, 'Abbot
Gervase'. There seems to be no reason to suppose that the distinction between *census* and *firma*
drawn in Richard fitz Nigel, *Dialogus,* 30, was generally accepted.

[138] *Chron. Henry II and Richard I,* i. 278; cf. *Red Book,* 212, and Harvey, 'Knight and Knight's
Fee', 22; *Glanvill,* 23, 149–51, 158, 164–6.

[139] *Britton,* i. 263; *Year Book 32–3 Edw. I,* 39.

[140] The earliest cases I have found in a quite casual search are *Regesta Regum,* ii, text no. 43
(1102×6, in the slightly different form *in feudum et jus hereditarium*); and then from the 1120s,
Stenton, *First Century,* 274 (no. 29); *Ancient Charters,* no. 10; *Book of Seals,* no. 528. Cf. *Oxford
Dict. Med. Latin,* 920 (5e).

combination was first used *feodum* was not absolutely clear on its own. By the middle of the century the phrase was probably tautologous, but it had already become such common form that it did not matter.[141] Some grants were also explicitly made for ever, but not, it seems, very many: specifying that a grant *in feodum et hereditatem* was made *imperpetuum* does not seem to have meant anything more than if *in feodum et hereditatem* stood on its own.[142] Because *feodum* increasingly implied full and heritable property the clergy were sometimes wary of it, denying that anyone holding property from their churches could hold it as a fief (in fee).[143] Since rents served as a regular reminder of the church's rights, some bishops and abbots may have thought that fee-farms were safer than other fiefs.[144] However that may be, some churches here as in other countries seem by the twelfth century to have abandoned the old safeguard of making grants for lives and were now granting full rights of inheritance. By mid century, if not before, some granted land in fief and inheritance, whether for rent (fee-farm) or otherwise.[145]

The books attributed to Glanvill and Bracton, which are thought to have been written respectively in the late 1180s and over several decades from about 1220, both take *feoda* pretty much for granted as units of free property. Both construct their work around the royal writs (orders in standard form directed generally to sheriffs, the parties, or the lord of the defendant) that from now on initiated and shaped the procedures of the king's courts. For Glanvill a free estate held *de feodo* or (as it was put in the writ of Mort d'Ancestor) *in dominico suo sicut de feodo suo* was permanent or inherited property as distinct from what was held *ut de vadio* or *ut de warda*. He then distinguished different kinds of fees or fiefs. Church property counted for him as *feoda*, and he may have seen *feoda* given in free alms as a subset of *feoda ecclesiastica*.[146] Among *laica feoda* there were several varieties, of which the most important were *feoda militaria* and free *sochagia*.[147] These last were the holdings of free sokemen (*sochemanni*), which,

---

[141] Tautology could of course serve for emphasis: *Ancient Charters*, no. 21 (*in feodum et hereditatem hereditarie omnem hereditatem* . . .); *Early Charters of St Paul's*, no. 163; *Docs. Danelaw*, no. 457.

[142] *Book of Seals*, no. 528; Stenton, *First Century*, 271–2; *Docs. Danelaw*, no. 457; Harvey, 'Abbot Gervase'.

[143] *Eng. Lawsuits*, no. 226; *Reading Cart.* nos. 1, 27; *Early Charters of St Paul's*, no. 163; Cheney, 'Inalienability'.

[144] Herbert of Bosham may have thought of fee-farms as unheritable: *Materials for Becket*, ii. 250.

[145] *Burton Chart.* 30–6; *Eng. Lawsuits*, 318, 325; *Early Yorks. Charters*, i, no. 265. On grants to a man and his (singular) heir: Lennard, *Rural England*, 173–4.

[146] *Glanvill*, 106, 137, 148, 150, 163; Kimball, 'Tenure in Frank Almoign'; Douglas, 'Frankalmoin'.

[147] *Glanvill*, 108, 149–50, 164.

unlike those of military tenants, were sometimes divided among all sons. We may deduce, though he does not say so, that whatever dues they owed—which might, to judge from other evidence, be merely token—excluded any formal obligation to military service. Socage for Glanvill thus seems to include what were sometimes called fee-farms, which, again, he does not mention, so that his socage already looks like what it had become by 1300, in Maitland's words: 'the great residuary tenure'.[148] Before then, however, there would be room for differences of opinion and terminology. Magna Carta distinguished fee-farm from socage, and even, confusingly, envisaged that some fee-farms might owe military service.[149] Glanvill also referred to *burgagia*, which probably covered most urban property. Last of his types of lay property came serjeanty, to which he made only passing reference. By the time of Bracton serjeanties formed an intermediate category that included a lot of inconvenient and mostly smallish holdings which did not seem to fit, or could be argued not to fit, either with military tenure or with socage.[150]

Bracton's categories are more complicated than Glanvill's, rather, it seems, because of intervening arguments about individual cases than because of any effort to reduce them to a system. The *De Legibus* is much concerned with the problem of deciding what property was free enough to be protected by the king's courts, but the concern did not produce a definition of *feoda* that would help to mark them off from unfree land.[151] For both authors (treating both for convenience as single), often as they refer to *feoda*, the more important category may have been free holdings (*libera tenementa*).[152] *Feodum* seems simply to have been a useful word: in neither treatise was it reified into a category that deserved discussion as such. Neither book, nor any English work before that of Spelman, can be called a treatise about fiefs in the sense that historians have since used the word.[153] What all this means is that neither the word *feodum* nor such words as *feoffare*, *feoffamentum* had any particularly feudo-vassalic connotation in England. They could be as well used for socages and burgages as for knights' fees or serjeanties.

During the thirteenth century the law of free property became ever

---

[148] Ibid. 71, 75–6, 82, 84–5, 108, 155; Pollock and Maitland, *History*, i. 294.

[149] Holt, *Magna Carta*, 326, 335 (1215, c. 37; 1225, c. 27).

[150] *Glanvill*, 108, 149–50, 164.          [151] Hyams, *Kings, Lords and Peasants*, 82–124.

[152] Bracton, *De Legibus*, ii. 126–7, explaining the anomalous position of leases for years, makes a passing distinction between a free holding and land held in fee.

[153] Littleton's *Treatise* is about fees, but fee simple, fee tail, etc. are not 'feudal tenures' in the sense in which historians or lawyers now use the words. For him the essence of fee simple is not that it is a dependent tenure but that it is for ever: *feodum idem est quod hereditas . . . et sic feodum simplex idem est quod hereditas legitima, vel hereditas pura*: Littleton, *Treatise*, 2–3, and cf. editor's preface, p. xi.

more dominated by the professional lawyers who argued about it in the king's courts. This produced further ways of subdividing *feoda*. One of the concerns of clients who employed skilled lawyers was to protect their property both against feckless widows or children, who might let land out of the family, and against the government, which might impose dues or take the whole estate over at a succession in one of the ways to be discussed below. One method of protection was to make what was then called a conditional gift, creating a *feodum talliatum* or fee tail as opposed to the fee simple of ordinarily inherited property. This system of entail was later partially superseded by the device of creating a use or trust, which entrusted the legal title to property to people who would now be called trustees. That developed too late for me to need to go into it, but the arcane complexities of the later English law of property were foreshadowed within my period by the appearance of the words *feodum simplex* and *feodum talliatum*.[154]

I have suggested that the idea of a permanent hierarchy of property created by grants of land may have originated in the arrangement of Domesday Book. However that may be, the idea probably became imprinted on people's minds by the practical differences made to people's obligations by their position in the hierarchy and, above all, by the demands made by the royal government on the king's direct tenants and passed on by them to those below. Henry I's grants to laymen did not regularly specify that the property was to be held from him. That may be just because it was taken for granted, but the way that a charter from near the end of his reign mentions it as an apparent afterthought suggests that the king and his advisers only gradually realized that it was important to make things absolutely clear.[155] It may already have become important to others. When people alienated knights' fees or fractions of a knight's fee they needed to pass on the obligation to military service imposed by the king. Pretty soon it must have become clear that the best and most profitable way to do that, whether or not one's own lord would have allowed one to do otherwise, was by way of what historians now call subinfeudation. This meant that one retained one's own obligations but demanded the equivalent (or, preferably, more) from the new owner, who would, in the terminology of the time, be one's tenant. By 1100, if not sooner, this meant that one also retained the right to relief, wardship, and so on. At least until the boundaries between knights' fees and socage had been worked out, and

[154] *Docs. Baronial Movement*, 88 (Pet. Bar. c. 27); *Statutes of the Realm*, i. 71 (13 Edw. I c. 1); Pollock and Maitland, *History*, ii. 11–29; Bean, *Decline*, 104–79.

[155] *Regesta Regum*, ii, texts from p. 305 on: no. 260, and cf. nos. 238, 256, 261, 300, and from earlier in the reign nos. 43, 53, 63. I have only gone through the charters transcribed here, not those abstracted. No. 300 is, incidentally, less clear than the abstract (catalogue, no. 1879) implies.

much—though not all—socage had been exempted from relief, wardship, and more than token rents, the same sort of considerations applied to most free property outside towns.[156] By the time that they no longer did so—or were less pressing—the common form and the conceptualizations that it reflected were established. By the middle of the century it may have been common, if not normal, for private charters to say that the land was to be held from someone, normally the donor or vendor.[157] My impression—though it is only an impression—is that this forms a marked contrast to the practice of the same period in northern France.

Charters concerning two kinds of property seem at first to have formed exceptions to the general rule. The first were those making or confirming grants to churches. As in other countries, and despite the appearance of the great churches in the Domesday hierarchy, the church was not apparently thought of much before the thirteenth century as holding its land from anyone. Given that so many surviving twelfth-century charters recorded grants or confirmations to churches, it cannot be accidental that they seem so seldom to have mentioned that the church concerned was to hold its land from the donor or anyone else.[158] By the thirteenth century, however, when the obligations of frankalmoin (free alms), as of other categories of property, had been more clearly worked out by the government and the courts, even land held in free alms was apparently often said to be held from someone—normally its donor.[159] The other sort of property that may at first not have been thought of as held from anyone in any sense that needed to be specified was urban property. Burgages on royal, ecclesiastical, or other estates (or sokes) and owing rents of some kind to the estate owner might be said to be held from the lord, especially if the lord were a church, but they were by no means the rule. In the twelfth century property in London and other towns could be subject to a complex of rents and payments, no doubt deriving from previous grants and investments, but the charters that set out these obligations did not as yet necessarily, or even perhaps generally, say that the property was to be held either from the donor or vendor or from anyone else. Later they said so more often. The first example of what became the common form of *habendum et tenendum* clause that I have seen comes in a London charter from between 1150 and

---

[156] See next section (8.6).

[157] Taking only the texts in Stenton, *First Century*, from p. 258 on, the statement is made in nos. 2, 6, 8, 15, 23–30, 32, 34–5, 39–41, 43, 47–8.

[158] This is purely impressionistic and not based on a thorough survey.

[159] Kimball, 'Tenure in Frank Almoign'. The first royal charter in free alms stating that the property is to be held from the king and his heirs on which I have happened is *Early Charters of St Paul's*, no. 52 (1199), but there may well be earlier cases.

1179.[160] London was a place where experienced drafters of charters were readily available. Maybe this charter was drafted by someone who thought it was the right thing to say even in the kind of grant of urban property from one layman to another that had not hitherto been thought to create a new layer of rights. The more or less standard clause that evolved in the thirteenth century for charters of all free property said that the new owner was to have and to hold to him and his heirs and assigns either from me (or us) and my (or our) heirs and assigns or from the chief lords of the fee.[161] From the end of the thirteenth century charters for property in London (and perhaps in other towns) often say simply that it is to be held from the chief lords of the fee, suggesting perhaps that no one knew who they were but that something had to be said.[162] The king's government and the lawyers who practised in his courts had created a unified law of free property that influenced legal practice even in towns with relative legal autonomy.

This survey of the reflection of ideas of tenurial hierarchy in twelfth- and thirteenth-century charters is based on a relatively small number of charters. But it may at least suggest that without much more work we should be cautious about assuming that all landowners after the Norman Conquest—or even all Norman landowners—took it for granted from the start that they held their land from the person from whom, or from whose predecessors, they had acquired it. The way that ideas of a hierarchy of property rights developed in England was different from the way that they developed in France, in Germany, in Sicily, or among the lawyers of north Italy. Kings of England after the Norman Conquest inherited a government that already exercised extensive controls over property. They then used the bureaucratic and legal skills that were becoming available to develop a new range of controls and obligations and tap new sources of wealth. Domesday Book shows the first stage. Thereafter the pattern of obligations that were imposed on those who held their land direct from the king and through them on their tenants became crystallized in other royal records, presumably by a series of negotiations and by tacit or explicit bargains that have themselves left little or no record. By the time of Magna Carta it was taken for granted that those who were most affected by royal exploitation were those who held their land directly from the king. In fact,

---

[160] *Early Charters of St Paul's*, no. 175. Cf. varying practice in nos. 67, 70, 82–3, 106–7, 111–12, 114–15, 121, 130, 134, 302.

[161] *Antrobus Deeds*, p. xxxvi, appendix no. 6 (before 1290): *habendum et tenendum eidem Ricardo le Gras heredibus et assingnatis suis de nobis et heredibus et assingnatis nostris*; no. 2 (before 1282), *habendum et tenendum eidem et Willemo et heredibus vel assignatis suis . . . de capitalibus dominis feodi illius.* For chief lords, below, at nn. 165–9.

[162] I am grateful to Dr Derek Keene for discussing this with me but he cannot be held responsible for my tentative generalizations.

that situation was already changing. The hierarchy of tenure had become
a premiss of legal thinking about property, not only in the minds of the
king's tenants in chief themselves, but in those of the professional lawyers
whose arguments in the royal courts shaped the development of the
English law of property. Meanwhile, however, by the thirteenth century
the government was finding the raising of taxes and armies through the
king's tenants in chief unprofitable and troublesome. Royal rights over the
king's tenants that had become established in custom nevertheless
remained well worth preserving, and were easier to preserve because lords
could be allowed to exercise corresponding—though severely restricted—
rights over those who held land from them. Relations with little or no jurisdictional content were thus preserved by a fiscal nexus. How far they were
preserved by the traditional affective force of feudo-vassalic ties is hard to
tell and needs more critical attention than it receives from historians who
cherish the tradition themselves. Some hints at points where the evidence
might be explored further will be suggested later when I discuss the obligations of military service and homage.

Consciousness of one's position in the hierarchy was preserved by the
undesirability of being a tenant in chief of the king: those who could show
they were not were exempt from the peculiarly fierce royal controls over
wards (under-age heirs), widows, and heiresses.[163] This had a terminological consequence. In the twelfth century people could be referred to as
'holding in chief', meaning directly, from any lord, as they were in
France.[164] What was held did not need to be any particular kind of property or imply anything that looks feudo-vassalic: when the burgesses of
Lincoln were allowed to hold their city from the king *in capite* they presumably hoped to account for their dues directly to the royal exchequer
(accounts office), not through the sheriff.[165] There is no reason to assume
that anyone thought that their city took on the rights and obligations of the
great barons who held their lands directly from the king or that the use of
the phrase *in capite* suggested any direct analogy with them. Throughout
the middle ages any immediate lord might be called a chief lord and land
might be said to be held from him *in capite*. A lord one rung above the chief
lord could be called a *superior dominus*. He might even be called a *superior
capitalis dominus*, which is confusing, though hardly more so than the habit
among modern historians of calling everyone from 'chief lords' to the king

---

[163] A claim to be one, made in 1177, seems unusual, if not unique: *Chron. Henry II and
Richard I*, i. 133.

[164] *Chron. Abingdon*, ii. 67. Cf. the use of *in capite* in thirteenth-century Lorraine: Parisse,
*Noblesse*, 539, 598.

[165] *Pipe Roll 31 Henry I*, 114. This has, however, received a 'feudal' interpretation: Tait,
*Medieval English Borough*, 158–9.

'overlords' and the tenants of every lord below the king 'subtenants'.[166] *Medius dominus* is cited from *c*.1208 and *medius* alone for a tenant from slightly later, but most of the vocabulary of 'mesne lords' and 'mesne tenants' seems to have been the creation of later lawyers.[167] In the middle ages most of the layers of property between the king and the immediate (chief) lord needed to be referred to comparatively rarely, while the political and fiscal significance of holding from the king, together with the ample records preserved about it, made it the most obvious form of tenure in chief.[168] By the seventeenth century 'tenures *in capite*' meant lands held directly from the king and, despite Thomas Madox, they have meant that ever since to most historians of medieval England.[169]

It is sometimes said that in post-conquest England all land really belonged to the king.[170] I have not been able to find any evidence that anyone in this period or indeed throughout the middle ages thought of property rights in this way. Domesday Book does not provide it unless its language and arrangement are wrenched out of their contemporary context. Even a weaker form of the contention, namely that all titles were envisaged as deriving from William the Conqueror, who had once held all property in the realm, and that this in some way made the titles of all subjects permanently incomplete, is undermined by Domesday's constant reference to the predecessors from whom the holders of property in 1086 claimed to derive their titles. The derivation was a fiction designed to cover violent expropriation, but that makes it all the more illuminating about the assumptions of the time. What the king had given his followers (or they had taken) depended ostensibly on what it had been lawful for him to confiscate. To the extent that what you got was what your predecessor had had, your title—in the theory implied in Domesday—depended on his as much as on the king's grant. Later on people often wrote as though the conquest had made a clean sweep, but it would be several centuries before anyone seems to have deduced that the rights of those who traced their titles to it were therefore more restricted or more conditional than property rights always are. In Henry II's reign Richard fitz Nigel, who was not backward in mythologizing the conquest and was certainly not one to play down royal authority, attributed the property rights of Englishmen, not Normans, after 1066 to royal generosity and mercy. Perhaps that was

[166] *Borough Customs*, i. 296 (13th cent.).
[167] Latham, *Revised Med. Latin Word-List*, 293–4; *OED* ix. 648.
[168] Pollock and Maitland, *History*, i. 233 n.
[169] Spelman, *Hist. of Sacrilege*, 131–2, and *Reliquiae*, 10–11; *Statutes of the Realm*, v. 259–66 (12 Chas. II c. 24); Madox, *Baronia*, 163–7.
[170] Not only in textbooks but by distinguished historians: above, at n. 105. But cf. Pollock and Maitland, *History*, ii. 4–5.

merely because he was not talking about Normans at the time, but there is
no reason to suppose that he thought rights created by William's grants to
be less good than rights to property granted by kings or lords in France.[171]
Thereafter long seisin was the best title.

In the thirteenth century, when kings and their lawyers began to argue
that all governmental authority was exercised by delegation from the king
and put the burden of proof of delegation on the holders of liberties or
franchises, they did not attempt to argue anything of the sort about rights
in land, as distinct from franchises over it. The earl who waved his rusty
sword in court and claimed that his ancestors had come with William the
Bastard and conquered their lands with the sword may, if the story is true,
have thought that his land was under attack along with his franchises, but
he was wrong. The theory of the delegation of governmental authority that
is implied in the Quo Warranto proceedings of thirteenth-century
England, and that had already been put forward at Roncaglia in 1158 and
perhaps in Sicily at about the same time, seems to have been quite distinct
in ideological character from the ideas about the source of noble property
that are supposed to be characteristic of feudalism.[172] Taken with the
strong line the law took about seisin, the story about the earl and his rusty
sword, tendentious as it is, suggests that, however nobles and free men in
the thirteenth century thought about land, they did not think that it all
really belonged to the king or even that their titles depended on some
original act of royal generosity. No doubt opinions differed and changed.
To some extent they may have become less clear and less susceptible of
simple rationalization during the thirteenth century, when the new legal
profession began to tie the English law of property into knots to suit the
hard cases they argued. But however anyone conceived of rights of property at the time, there seems to be very little evidence that they saw them
in the terms that seventeenth- and eighteenth-century antiquaries would
deduce from the *Libri Feudorum* and all the learned commentaries on it.
English common lawyers, after all, did not learn their law in the universities where the law of fiefs was studied.

## 8.6. *The obligations of property, 1100–1300*

My argument is that obligations to the king were a powerful determinant
of the way that the rules of property developed in England. It therefore
seems sense to start with obligations rather than with rights. Military

---

[171] Richard fitz Nigel, *Dialogus*, 54.

[172] Sutherland, *Quo Warranto*, 82 n., 182–9. See index: delegation, theory of. The theory
deserves more attention than it seems to have received from historians of medieval political
thought; cf. Reynolds, *Kingdoms and Communities*, 326–7.

service was a serious and toughly imposed obligation in twelfth- and thirteenth-century England, but the precise quantification of noble oblig- ations that seems to have distinguished England so strikingly from neigh- bouring kingdoms may always have been less important for military than fiscal purposes. I have already suggested that the numbers of knights owed by all tenants in chief may not have been known and agreed before 1166.[173] Great men who turned up with inadequate contingents no doubt got a cool reception and perhaps other unrecorded penalties, but that may have been a matter of politics rather than of formal, recorded, and agreed obligations attached to their property. Even after the great survey of 1166 there were still some doubts, while records of scutage (payments made by those who failed to serve in a particular campaign) apparently never included demands made for shortfalls in the contingents brought by royal tenants in chief who themselves turned up in person.[174] Nor is there any hard evi- dence about the period of service required by custom in the twelfth cen- tury. Campaigns in France inevitably required longer and more frequent service than mere defensive duties at home would have done, but they did not arouse recorded objections on the ground of exceeding any recognized period of service. The arguments that arose later about service overseas, like the recorded variations in the periods for which individual tenants in serjeanty had to serve, suggest that custom evolved towards definition through dispute and negotiation rather than starting from some generally accepted 'feudal custom'.[175]

How soon the king's tenants in chief were regularly allowed to pay rather than serve is uncertain. Contingents provided by the great churches that owed military service probably always tended to be poorly led and organized, and this would explain why some churches were paying scutage (or something like what later became known as scutage) as early as the reign of Henry I.[176] When Henry II took scutage for his Toulouse campaign in 1159 a respectful chronicler attributed the king's decision to his benevolent reluctance to burden country knights and the multitude of townspeople and peasants, but it made sound financial and military sense.[177] The per- sonal service of those owing one or two knights can never have been vital to royal armies. Their obligation nevertheless remained valuable and worth

[173] Above at nn. 128–31.
[174] Keefe, *Feudal Assessments*, 20, 35, 41, 46–7, 65–7, 78–80, 134; Dr J. A. Green, who thinks early twelfth-century records were better than I imply (though see above, n. 131), suggested to me that Norman kings may on occasion have required money as well as service even from those who served.
[175] Keefe, *Feudal Assessments*, 37–8; Kimball, *Serjeanty Tenure*, 69–81.
[176] Hollister, *Military Organization*, 121–2, 196–7; Green, *Government*, 76–7.
[177] Robert of Torigny, *Chron.* 202.

recording. Kings went on issuing the traditional summonses right through
the thirteenth century and beyond, and their greater subjects were
expected to turn up and pull their weight, but personal service was by then
more an obligation of social and political status than anything else. The
number of knights required had been progressively reduced and scutage
was becoming more trouble to collect than it was worth. The old rules had
become a strait-jacket. The government therefore tried to go over to
recruitment on the basis of wealth rather than tenure by knight service.
This was not an entire innovation. In 1181, if not before, all free men were
required to keep and bear arms, roughly in proportion to their status, in
the service of the king. In 1205 John called on everyone to defend the kingdom, including *servientes*, and by 1225 the regular responsibility to bear
arms in its defence was extended to the unfree. During the thirteenth century the government tried to make men with sufficient land become
knights, irrespective of the way they held their land. Those who were not
knights still had to have arms and might be called up, whether by royal officials or by their lords.[178] In the fourteenth century contracts with great
men and commissions of array made this wider recruitment more systematic and thorough.[179]

Meanwhile, when tenants by knight service who alienated land passed
on part or all of their obligation, this too was often a matter of money rather
than service. Many of those who owed military service to the king's tenants, or to their tenants, or the tenants of their tenants (and so on) owed
very small amounts. While their formal obligation could still make them
useful in castle garrisons, it was not likely to make them much more use in
field armies, whether lawfully making up their lord's obligations to his lord
and ultimately to the king (forinsec service[180]) or unlawfully supporting
their lord in rebellion, than were his tenants of comparable wealth who did
not hold by knight service. Rebellious lords were sometimes, though not
invariably, supported by their tenants, but precise legal obligations were
presumably less important in illegal activities than were general relations
of patronage and power. Peasant tenants might be easier to recruit than
people of higher status even if they were individually less useful. The bond
that linked lords and those who are recorded as following them in rebellions at different times cannot be assumed to have always been a feudo-
vassalic one.[181] Reserving military service on land was nevertheless

[178] Reynolds, *Kingdoms and Communities*, 270; Carpenter, 'English Peasants in Politics'.
[179] Sanders, *Feudal Military Service*, 59–67; Prestwich, *War, Politics, and Finance*, 69–91, and *Three Edwards*, 65–6.
[180] *Oxford Dict. Med. Latin*, 980 (4d).
[181] Holt, *Northerners*, 36–55, 61–78; Ault, *Private Jurisdiction*, 271; Carpenter, 'English Peasants in Politics'.

advantageous, since, as custom evolved and became fixed, that entitled the lord to relief, certain aids, and rights of wardship and marriage, as well as to scutage on all knights' fees and not just those needed to make up the lord's own quota of service. Even a fraction of a knight's fee would be held liable by definition to all these dues, while socage land would not.[182]

The most important and frequent tax taken during the earlier part of the twelfth century was not scutage but the traditional geld, now generally known as danegeld. It fell, at least in principle, equally on all levels and types of property, except that belonging to people with sufficient influence to get either exempted permanently or pardoned for a particular levy. Danegeld as such was not taken after 1162, but aids, gifts, or common assessments (*communes assise*) went on. These were imposed on counties, towns, and royal lands by the king's justices as they travelled around. Some of them may have been assessed on hides, like danegeld.[183] The association of some of these payments with *murdrum* (fines imposed on local peasants for—roughly speaking—unexplained deaths) and the later labelling of others as tallage make it likely that their main burden fell on people of low status, but it is not clear that all tenants by knight service, let alone all those who held fiefs (i.e. free heritable property), were always exempt.[184] They would not have been automatically exempt on the danegeld assessments. It is not known when (if ever) the separate taxation of the king's tenants in chief, assessed on knights' fees, became a deliberate policy designed to tap the wealth that pardons for danegeld, or the ending of danegeld, left untouched.

Scutage, as a payment made instead of performing military service, was probably raised on knights' fees from the start, but the evidence is by no means clear: the exchequer tried on occasion to get scutage or *auxilium militum* (which may have meant something different) from churches that owed no knight service. From the reign of Henry II scutage was regularly levied on the king's direct tenants according to knights' fees, though the returns to the enquiry of 1166 provided fuel for long arguments about the number of fees to be charged.[185] The first purpose to which the returns were put, however, and quite probably that for which the enquiry had been made, was not scutage. It was a levy imposed on all the king's tenants in chief ostensibly, at least, to pay for the marriage of his daughter.[186] This does not mean that it was imposed according to a long-established

[182] Mortimer, 'Land and Service', 190; Du Boulay, 'Gavelkind'; *Curia Regis Rolls*, xi, no. 1039; xii, nos. 419, 722; xv, no. 525; Madox, *Exchequer*, 472 n., 773 n. On scutage, below.
[183] Green, 'Last Century' and *Government*, 76; Richard fitz Nigel, *Dialogus*, 47–52, 108–9.
[184] Hoyt, *Royal Demesne*, 111–15.
[185] Green, *Government*, 76–7; Keefe, *Feudal Assessments, passim*.
[186] Keefe, *Feudal Assessments*, 13–14.

tradition by which noble vassals gave aid as a matter of course to their lord
for the marriage of his daughter, the knighting of his son, or his own ransom. Aids for these three purposes, and also for the lord's crusade, were by
now known in various parts of France but they were never taken from the
great nobles who in England are called the king's tenants in chief. Where
they were owed in France they were paid chiefly by people of fairly low status, including townspeople, and in some places at least they are known to
have derived from special agreements between lords and subjects.[187] In
England Henry I had taken a tax in 1110 for his daughter's marriage, but
it had apparently been assessed not only on his immediate tenants but, like
danegeld, on hides. Henry II's 'marriage aid' of 1168 was taken from the
king's tenants according to knights' fees, but it was also taken from towns
and from the king's own estates (what historians call the royal demesne),
with some bargaining about amounts.[188] Both Henry I and Henry II were
probably following precedents set by lesser lords in Anjou and Normandy.
What was new in 1110 was to tax great men, and what was new in 1168 was
to take the money from them as the king's tenants and according to the
knights' fees they held. Perhaps the reason why Henry II did not take an
aid for knighting his son was that no one thought of it. This kind of aid
from great men was not yet established in English custom.

By 1168, however, some subjects in England had for some time been following the French—including Norman—precedents in a more conven-
tional way. As early as 1125 the lord of Tutbury (Staffs.) had apparently
imposed an obligation to pay aids for his own ransom, his eldest daughter's
marriage, and the redemption of his honour.[189] Aids for knighting a lord
or his son were reported from various estates in 1170. They do not seem to
have been paid only by those owing military service or even perhaps only
by those whose property would in English terms have ranked as fiefs. Some
lords had also been taking aids for other purposes in the years before 1170,
including for paying their debts to Jews.[190] The abbot of Bury demanded
an aid from his knights in 1182 but had to argue about the amount and the
assessment.[191] Glanvill thought that a lord could take a variety of aids,
including for knighting his son and heir, marrying his eldest daughter, and
paying his own relief, provided that they were reasonable.[192] In 1183–4
what is apparently the first English reference linking the three aids that
would be recorded in Magna Carta (knighting, marriage, ransom) shows

---

[187] Chapter 7 at nn. 263–75.　　　　　[188] Mitchell, *Taxation in Medieval England*, 251–7.
[189] Stenton, *First Century*, 175.
[190] *Red Book*, pp. cclxvii–cclxxxi, nos. 20–4, 27–38, 45. Payments from knight's fees for scutage etc. seem to be separate: e.g. nos. 7, 12, 40–2, 45, 47–9, 51, 55–6. See Richardson, 'Anglo-
Norman Charter' and 'Anglo-Norman Return'.
[191] Jocelin of Brakelond, *Chron.* 27–8.　　　　　[192] *Glanvill*, 112.

them as owed by free men in general—and a church—on one midland estate.[193] Aids for the lord's crusade, although quite common in France, never apparently caught on in England. As for ransom aids, the only time they seem to have been recorded in practice (since it is not known if the lord of Tutbury ever took one) was when Richard I's ransom had to be paid. That was done by a combination of methods, including a tax of twenty shillings on each knight's fee and another assessed on hides like the old danegeld.[194] Magna Carta may be evidence that 'the three feudal aids' were by now well known in England, but the charter itself made them more widely known, as well as establishing their freedom from consent. Although its first allusion to them comes in a clause (1215 c.12) that otherwise mainly concerns military tenants, it refers to them elsewhere (c.15) simply as paid by free men. Since the charter was chiefly concerned to limit the obligations of the free, that does not exclude the possibility that they were sometimes paid by unfree peasants too. When the rates for knighting and marriage aids due to lords apart from the king were fixed in 1275 and those due to the king in 1352, they were fixed both for knights' fees and for socage.[195] Ransom aids seem meanwhile to have dropped out of view. One way and another it is possible to see why the English evidence has encouraged historians to think of the 'three feudal aids' in feudo-vassalic terms, but the association is not very convincing.

During the thirteenth century both scutage and the three aids became less important to kings. They took them when they could and when they could get nothing better, while royal officials and lawyers evidently thought it worth a good deal of argument to establish that some serjeanties owed scutage,[196] but other and more profitable taxes were taking over. A policy evolved of combining taxes that came to be raised through parliament and were assessed on the movable property of the population at large with taxes on particular categories of people who could make less trouble than the great nobles. The taxes on movables, although by definition not assessed on landed property as such, obviously fell on it indirectly. Categories of property were not distinguished: even the unfree paid if they had the bare minimum of assessable goods.[197] The poor indeed bore the greatest burden, since those who lived off rents came off lightly and the rich were best placed to sweeten both the assessors and those who commandeered goods on tough terms for government use. The ending of

[193] Stenton, *First Century*, 173–4, 276–7.
[194] Roger of Howden, *Chron.* ii. 210, 225; iv, pp. lxxxii–lxxxiv; William of Newburgh, *Hist.* 399–400; *Pipe Roll 5 Ric. I*, p. xxiii; *Rolls of King's Court, 1194–5*, pp. xxii–xxv.
[195] Bracton, *De Legibus*, ii. 116; *Statutes of the Realm*, i. 35, 322 (Stat. Westm. I, c. 36; 25 Edw. III, c. 11).
[196] Kimball, *Serjeanty Tenure*, 137–49.          [197] Maddicott, *English Peasantry*, 6–15, 19.

scutage must have been a sorrow to the king's tenants and those below
them who had given or sold land while reserving more military service on
it than they themselves owed. Still, both they and the king continued to get
other profits from lands held from them by knight service.

When the Norman kings took over the Old English custom of taking
heriots or succession dues on the death of nobles they abandoned the old
method of assessing them by the deceased's status or the size of his or her
estate. Perhaps this was impractical in the turmoil of the first decades after
1066. From 1086 Domesday's lists of those holding land directly from the
king provided information on the best pickings, while allowing the king's
tenants the quid pro quo of themselves taking dues, now called reliefs,
from some of the property that was no longer subject to royal heriot. Henry
I's coronation charter suggests that this system was in operation by 1100,
though just who had to pay reliefs and how much they owed would not be
fixed for a long time.[198] Glanvill thought that custom set the reliefs of a
knight's fee at five pounds and of socage at one year's value, but that the
heirs of baronies and serjeanties had to make their own terms.[199] The
Dialogue of the Exchequer took much the same line, though there is a hint
of past protest or negotiation behind its qualification that those who held
their land from baronies that had fallen into the king's hand (escheats) paid
at the rates fixed for knights' fees.[200] The general principle of a five-pound
relief may go back to the early twelfth century, though the method of
charging by each knight's fee may only have been worked out gradually.[201]
Disputes and bargains since Glanvill's time are reflected in Bracton's confused views on reliefs for socage: according to De Legibus they were taken
in some places, but wrongly: if they were taken they were not proper reliefs
but were more akin to the heriots paid by the unfree.[202] On the other hand
Bracton maintained that fee-farms (probably in effect socages that owed
more than token rents) owed reliefs that were to be fixed by mutual consent.[203]

Before Magna Carta barons' and earls' reliefs could be very high. Even
after it had fixed them at £100 for both groups there was still room for
argument about what constituted a barony, while some thought that if an

[198] Liebermann, *Gesetze*, i. 521 (c. 2).          [199] *Glanvill*, 108.
[200] Richard fitz Nigel, *Dialogus*, 95–7, 121. Both passages seem to me obscure. Holt, *Magna Carta*, 207, interprets them as meaning that the fixed rates applied only to tenants of escheats, but the author may perhaps mean that knight's fee rates applied to baronies in escheats and that only baronies held from the king were excepted.
[201] Green, *Government*, 83–5; Stenton, *First Century*, 163–4, 278; *Red Book*, p. cclxxix (no. 51).
[202] Bracton, *De Legibus*, ii. 244, 248, and cf. 110, 226: some of the confusion is probably due to additions by different authors.
[203] Ibid. 249; Pollock and Maitland, *History*, i. 293.

earl paid £100 an ordinary baron should pay 100 marks. This reduction was made in 1297, probably through a bureaucratic mistake.[204] One important difference between reliefs owed to the king and those owed to other lords may have emerged during the twelfth century. Henry I's charter says nothing about what came to be called 'primer seisin', but by the time of Glanvill the estates that Glanvill called 'chief baronies' were seized into the king's hand on the death of their owners and held until the reliefs were paid. Heirs of other lords, provided that there was no dispute about their inheritance, took possession straight away, before doing homage and paying relief.[205] By the thirteenth century, if not before, some lords were evidently trying to climb on the royal bandwagon of primer seisin, but, though this caused complaints for a while, they seem to have been frustrated. From 1267 heirs with complaints against lords who invaded their inheritances could get damages from them in the royal courts, whereas the king's tenants had to go on enduring the king's primer seisin.[206]

More important than relief, and in the long run the most important of all the features that marked off knights' fees from other free property, was the subjection of minor heirs to the lord's wardship and his control of their marriages and of the marriage of his tenants' widows. This too had pre-conquest precedents but developed fast and harshly under the Normans. Like reliefs and military service, it may have been easier to enforce, with the help of Domesday Book, on the king's own tenants than on anyone else. To judge from the promises Henry I made in 1100, William II, if not his father as well, had been interfering with the marriages of his barons' daughters and other female relatives even in the barons' lifetimes, in addition to disposing of their widows afterwards. The charter does not mention wardship as such.[207] Whatever Henry I promised, both he and the Angevin kings made large profits from their wardship and marriage rights, whether through direct exploitation by royal officials, through selling them, or through granting them on favourable terms to royal servants. Wardship and marriage aroused strong feelings. Their regulation followed reliefs, after the obligatory nod to the church, at the very beginning of Magna Carta.[208] As Henry I's charter and Magna Carta show, however, the king's rights over his tenants, like his right to relief, were balanced by their rights over their tenants. References to the exercise of their rights in the twelfth century seem to be rare, but by the thirteenth century it was generally accepted that only those holding by knight service and holding

---

[204] Reynolds, 'Magna Carta 1297'.                    [205] *Glanvill*, 82, 108, 110.
[206] Bracton, *De Legibus*, 245; Pollock and Maitland, *History*, i. 311; Waugh, *Lordship*, 66–7.
[207] Liebermann, *Gesetze*, i. 521–2 (c. 3, 4).
[208] Green, *Government*, 83–7; Holt, *Magna Carta*, 45–7, 107–8, 209–10, 316–20 (c. 2–3), 351–2 (c. 2–7).

greater serjeanties were rightly subject to wardship and marriage, while socage and burgage holdings and the smaller serjeanties were exempt. Urban property may have been exempt from very early, while the smaller serjeanties seem to have won their liberties by a slow process of oversight, adjustment, and argument.[209] The same probably applies to socage. Its exemption is traditionally explained by seeing wardship and marriage as the natural product of feudo-vassalic relations, but this seems implausible, given that socage tenants stood in terms of status midway between military tenants and the unfree, over whom similar rights were also exercised. Those churches that, to Bracton's displeasure, customarily exercised wardship and marriage rights over their socage tenants are more likely to have done so as part of wider controls over all their tenants than as a reflection of feudo-vassalic principles.[210]

However that may be, every other lord's rights in wardship and marriage were insignificant compared to the king's. Any minor heir whose father could be shown to have held any land at all direct from the king fell into the king's prerogative wardship, so that other lords were hard put to it to retain control over the lands he had held from them. Prerogative wardship, like primer seisin, was established by the time of Glanvill. Magna Carta prohibited royal wardship over heirs who might happen to hold land from other lords by knight service but from the king had only fee-farm, socage, or land held by trivial serjeanties. It also restricted royal rights over what was held from lordships that had come into the king's hand to what they would have been under another lord.[211] As the thirteenth century went on, royal administrators were confronted not only by the king's tenants wanting to regulate the system but by professional lawyers thinking of clever ways to help them evade it altogether. The details of both sides' efforts are relatively unimportant to my argument.[212] What matters to it is that, while there is no doubt that kings and other lords earlier in the middle ages had often claimed some supervisory rights over inheritance of land under their government, and thus sometimes over the minor heirs and widows of their subjects, the system of wardship and marriage as we see it in thirteenth-century England looks like the product of governmental methods, political conflicts, and legal arguments that were developed in the twelfth and thirteenth centuries. In so far as it had more distant origins, they can be related more plausibly to the already extensive powers of

---

[209] Kimball, *Serjeanty Tenure*, 167–98.
[210] *Glanvill*, 84; Bracton, *De Legibus*, ii. 226, 248–9; Pollock and Maitland, *History*, i. 321; *Curia Regis Rolls*, xi, no. 1039; Waugh, *Lordship*, 124–5; *Year Book 20–1 Edw. I*, 241, 361–5.
[211] Holt, *Magna Carta*, 326, 328 (c. 37, 43).
[212] Bean, *Decline*, 40–143; Waugh, *Lordship* is full of examples.

pre-conquest kings than to general ideas about the relations supposedly created when any lord accepted a man as his vassal and gave him land in return for service. There does not seem to be any evidence, for instance, that the king's rights in this field were seen as distinct from his other rights as king or were derived from a separate kind of authority—the authority of a 'feudal lord' over his 'vassals'. Although most kings enjoyed particularly close and personal relations with some of their tenants in chief (and with some subjects who were not their tenants) there is no evidence that this kind of interpersonal relation was thought to be the basis of their rights over their tenants in chief in general. A king's rights over his tenants were, apparently, from the start the rights of a king. Distinctive as they were, they were exercised through the same processes of administration and law as were his rights over his other subjects.

The obligation to perform homage for free property also poses rather more problems than simple models of feudo-vassalic relations imply. To start with, homage, as in France, was not done only when property owing military service was conveyed or there was a new lord or tenant. The oath taken to William I in 1086 looks rather like the general oaths of political subordination taken under the Carolingians and sometimes to pre-conquest kings or in times of stress in Normandy. When Henry I made his subjects take oaths to his son and heir in 1115–16 one chronicler uses the English words *manræden* and *hold athas* and another, using Latin, says that they pledged themselves to the young man by hands and oaths. This suggests both the ceremony of homage and an oath of fealty or fidelity, but the two ceremonies would not be regularly distinguished until lawyers got to work on them.[213] In England the dispute about the investiture of bishops did not focus on the difference between homage and fidelity as it did in Germany.[214] Even after we know that the ceremony of homage was reserved to people of higher status and others merely 'did fealty' (i.e. swore fidelity), manorial tenants were collectively called the homage when they made their presentment in the manor court.[215] There were many ways of being someone's man. Similarly, there were different reasons for swearing fidelity and it could mean different things: the form of the oath could be adjusted to the situation.[216] One of Henry II's motives for enquiring into knights' fees in 1166 was apparently to discover who among the tenants of

---

[213] *Two Saxon Chronicles*, 246; William of Malmesbury, *Gesta Regum*, ii. 495; Henry of Huntingdon, *Hist.* 239; Florence of Worcester, *Chron.* ii. 69; cf. Stevenson, 'Inedited Charter'; *Chron. Henry II and Ric. I*, i. 96–8, suggests they were not clearly distinguished in 1173; *Statutes of the Realm*, i. 227–8.
[214] Anselm, *Opera*, v. 333–4; Eadmer, *Hist. Novorum*, 186; chapter 9, at n. 51, and chapter 6, at nn. 141–2.
[215] *Oxford Dict. Med. Latin*, 1165 (7b).          [216] *Eng. Lawsuits*, no. 272.

his tenants in chief had not been registered as having gone through some kind of ceremony of allegiance (*ligantia*) to him. In 1170 enquiries were to be made in each county about those (of unspecified status) who ought to do homage to the king and had not done it. In 1176 royal justices were to take fealty (*fidelitates*) to the king from earls, barons, knights, free tenants, and peasants (*rustici*). They were to order those who had not done homage and allegiance to the king as to their liege lord (*homagium et ligantiam sicut ligio domino*) to get on and do it at the time appointed.[217] As all these orders suggest, new kings required affirmations of loyalty, under whatever name: to see it in the terms of an archaic *Herrenfall*, a relic from the time when the bonds of vassalage had supposedly only lasted for the lifetime of both parties, would be perverse. People who held land from several lords were supposed to regard one of them as what Richard fitz Nigel said was commonly called their liege lord (*dominus eius qui vulgo ligius dicitur*). Glanvill distinguished the liege lord as the one, whom he also calls the chief lord (*capitalis dominus*), from whom someone held his chief holding (*capitale tenementum*). This liege or chief lord need not be the king, but Glanvill implies that all homage, even that done *cum ligeancia*, reserved the faith that everyone owed to the king.[218] When discussing homage for land he felt constrained, as did Bracton after him, to note that homage for *dominium* alone was owed only to the king.[219] The obligation to be loyal to the king was in effect irrevocable except by exile, unless one was prepared to argue that one had been unfairly treated so that one could justly defy (*diffidare*) him.[220] The great and powerful sometimes found that worth trying for public relations purposes, but how far it worked may have depended more on political circumstances than on any generally accepted social norm.[221]

In the early twelfth century homage was no doubt often, perhaps normally, done when free land was conveyed but it does not seem ever to have been the only or most crucial ceremony. The public transfer of something symbolizing the property was equally or more important, and this 'livery of seisin' would later remain the essential dispositive ceremony in most circumstances, whether or not homage was done.[222] Those who derived

---

[217] *Red Book*, 412–13; Gervase of Canterbury, *Hist. Works*, i. 219; *Chron. Henry II and Ric. I*, i. 110.

[218] *Leges Henrici Primi*, 152 (43): the interpretation (ibid. 350) of *residens* as implying 'the special sense of feudal vassal' seems unjustified: cf. 148 (41. 2, 5); Richard fitz Nigel, *Dialogus*, 83; *Glanvill*, 103–4.

[219] *Glanvill*, 106; Bracton, *De Legibus*, ii. 231.

[220] William of Malmesbury, *Historia Novella*, 47; Arnold fitz Thedmar, *De Antiquis Legibus*, 63–5.

[221] *Pace* Bloch, 'Formes de la rupture'.

[222] *Eng. Lawsuits*, nos. 251, 270; Stenton, *First Century*, 262; Pollock and Maitland, *History*, ii. 90.

their title from inheritance could, at least by the time of Glanvill, take possession before doing homage, unless they held from the king, provided that they remained ready to do it and to pay their reliefs. Homage was also sometimes, if not always, demanded by new lords from new tenants after the accession of either of them. It seems likely that it was most likely to be required, whether on alienation or succession, where the lord or alienator reserved services or dues from the land. It was also especially useful to the clergy, who were in duty bound to keep control of their saints' property. Though St Augustine's, Canterbury, explicitly excused the king's steward from doing homage when they granted land to him in return for counsel and support, that must have been exceptional. It was surely a dangerous line to take.[223] As usual, what little evidence we have from before the later twelfth century concerns church property and it is hard to know how far it applies to relations between laymen. Homage for church land may have been particularly contentious since inheritance of church land raised particularly sensitive issues. A conscientious new bishop or abbot was much more likely to sweep a new broom through his church's tenants than was a lay heir through his father's. When Abingdon abbey had trouble getting military service from its tenants at the very beginning of the century, some of the recalcitrants apparently started by refusing to do homage to the new abbot.[224] Just as a tenant could refuse to pay homage, so an abbot or bishop could refuse to take it.[225] In practice, refusal of homage did not always keep out an heir or enable the abbot or bishop to eject a sitting tenant, but when Archbishop Thomas Becket refused to take the homage of John, the king's marshal, for Canterbury lands that John claimed by hereditary right, he then apparently went on to eject both John and other Canterbury tenants. It may have been this case that prompted Henry II and his counsellors to devise the new procedure of Novel Disseisin that set the pattern of the 'forms of action' that dominated the shape of English litigation about property for centuries to come.[226]

Glanvill's remarks about homage are in some ways puzzling. What he says about the mutual bond of fidelity that homage created between lord and man suggests that social norms lay behind his words, but the context and substance of the rules he lays down seem to have more to do with drawing nice distinctions for purposes of legal argument.[227] Since his rules

[223] *Reg. St Augustine's*, ii. 462: the text should read *absque umagio et fiantia* (cf. *Oxford Dict. Med. Latin*, i. 934: *fiantia*).

[224] *Chron. Abingdon*, ii. 128–9, 132–4.

[225] Not mentioned but probably implied: *Eng. Lawsuits*, no. 226; Matthew Paris, *Gesta Abbatum*, i. 159–66. Mentioned: *Eng. Lawsuits*, nos. 272, 316.

[226] Cheney, 'Litigation'.

[227] It is tempting to wonder whether his phraseology about the *mutua . . . dominii et homagii*

seem to reflect the changes that Novel Disseisin and Mort d'Ancestor had brought to the relations of lord and tenant, they cannot be very old. He makes homage more important to the lord than to the tenant: the tenant had to offer homage and relief but he was in possession meanwhile, while the lord could get no services, relief, or wardship until homage had been done.[228] This could well have been designed to stop any other ecclesiastical lord from treating his lay tenants as the archbishop had treated John Marshal. Perhaps the function that homage thereafter filled in procedures of inheritance had been influenced as much by the ways that churches had recently been using it to keep control of their endowments as by traditional bonds between lay nobles. By Bracton's time there was doubt whether socage owed homage, but if it did not, he said, it nevertheless owed fidelity, like villein (unfree) holdings. His arguments about homage for land were connected to his arguments about wardship and marriage: there was evidently a tendency to argue that these followed from homage.[229] It was clearly impossible to devise categories and rules that did not make nonsense of the long-established customs of one estate or another. This confirms the impression that rules about homage in the thirteenth century, like the distinction between homage and fidelity, have more to do with arguments between lawyers about particular cases than with traditional social norms. Homage remained especially important for those who held their land from the king, because they could not get possession of their lands until they had done it. It served a useful bureaucratic purpose.

One more obligation should be mentioned, though it will be dealt with more fully just below, where I discuss the corresponding right of fief-owners to jurisdiction over those who held land from them. Suit of court, the duty of attending one's lord's court, is rarely specified in twelfth-century charters or records of disputes. In the thirteenth century, as I shall mention, it became contentious. By 1275 tenants by knight service of at least some great landlords, along with some socage tenants, might be obliged to attend courts some distance from their holdings. Some of them were themselves lords of manors to which other free tenants, along with the unfree, normally owed suit.[230] As I shall argue, this obligation may also have become more widespread among free tenants since 1100.

---

*fidelitatis connexio* (*Glanvill*, 107) came from some other, more generally moralizing source. It was copied by Bracton (*De Legibus*, ii. 228). Cf. also John de Blanot (Acher, 'Notes', 149) and Beaumanoir (*Coutumes de Beauvaisis*, § 1735).

[228] *Glanvill*, 103–11.

[229] Bracton, *De Legibus*, ii. 110, 226, 248.

[230] Ault, *Private Jurisdiction*, 182–9, 216–23, 274, 323; *Docs. Baronial Movement*, 88–90 (c. 29); 144 (c. 16).

## 8.7. *The rights of property, 1100–1300*

So far as rights are concerned, I see no reason to suppose that it is any more anachronistic to talk in terms of property rights in early twelfth-century England than it is elsewhere in early medieval Europe or in many other societies with hierarchical social systems and customary law. In England, as in other countries of western Europe, it seems to have been assumed that a lord's rights in his lordship did not prevent people who held land within it from having rights that could be vindicated against him and against others. If it is wrong to call these 'proprietary rights' or 'rights good against the world',[231] that is because the phrases come from a different legal system. Records of disputes in early medieval Europe (including England) show people claiming or defending rights in land against third parties. If the third party was a church it might indeed claim to have granted the land under dispute and thus to be still its lord and ultimate owner, but laymen in denying such claims did not normally find it necessary to produce an alternative lord. Lords did not usually come into disputes as sources of rights in land but as figures of power or authority who might protect the rights of those subject to them: being subject was a matter of political, governmental authority, not of a relation that normally derived from a grant of land or implied reduced rights in land. In England in the twelfth and thirteenth centuries, it is true, we find a different kind of lordship. The custom of granting land to be held from its donor or vendor created or confirmed a lordship that consisted primarily of services or dues reserved on the conveyance and, if the land was held by knight service, of relief, wardship, and marriage rights. This kind of lordship, unless it was held by someone with other jurisdictional rights, entirely lacked the authority normally implied by lordship or *dominium*. Because donors or vendors were thus *ipso facto* lords, the obligation to warrant the new owner's title came to be considered an obligation of lordship.[232] In the circumstances it seems unlikely that this kind of lordship was the product of ancient and entrenched ideas of feudo-vassalic propriety, or that its holders automatically acquired the position of authority and reverence ascribed to lords in later theories of feudo-vassalic relations.

The argument that there were no true proprietary rights before Henry II's legal reforms gave them effective protection has concentrated primarily on the rights of inheritance and alienation as together constituting the essential elements of true property or 'ownership', and on seigniorial jurisdiction as evidence of their absence. I have already argued that lay

---

[231] As suggested e.g. by Milsom, *Legal Framework*, 37–40.     [232] Hyams, 'Warranty'.

property carried real rights of inheritance before Henry II's legal reforms.[233] In some ways his reign saw rights of inheritance reduced. Royal control over both sheriffs and royal castles was reasserted and extended: holding royal office or having custody of a royal castle became more distinct from holding either as part of one's inheritance.[234] In so far as the offices and castles were recognized to be royal, however, that did not affect the principle of the heritability of most free property. There seems no good reason to argue that grants made explicitly in fee and inheritance, and sometimes explicitly for ever, before the writ of Mort d'Ancestor was devised did not mean what they said. They surely imply that inheritance was thought of as a right that could be, or should be, vindicated at law. The new procedures that Henry provided did not confer more rights than his subjects were considered to have before, but offered them more immediate and routine methods of protecting their existing rights.

The issue of seigniorial jurisdiction is so important that it may be easier to discuss it before considering any other rights. S. F. C. Milsom, whose arguments about early twelfth-century property I am contesting, pointed out that when Henry II provided new procedures for the defence of property rights (though he did not describe them as such) those against whom royal protection was most needed were lords. That must often have been so, but whether the power of lords came from their possession of courts with jurisdiction over land held from them is more doubtful.[235] Milsom postulates a 'seigniorial world' in which, despite occasional royal interventions, the relations of lords and tenants were regulated by lordships that were in effect more or less sovereign before Henry II's legislation took effect.[236] F. M. Stenton drew a sympathetic picture of honorial or baronial courts doing justice between the peers of the courts. He maintained that courts 'which can only be described as feudal profoundly influenced the development of English society in the twelfth century' by evolving 'a coherent scheme of rights and duties out of the tangle of personal relationships produced by the sudden introduction of feudal tenure into England'.[237] I have no intention of trying to argue that there was no such thing as seigniorial jurisdiction or seigniorial courts of various kinds, but both Stenton's and Milsom's views of them seem to owe more to traditional premises of feudal historiography than to hard evidence. Not that the scarcity of the evidence, especially evidence of courts held by lay lords,

---

[233] At nn. 93–9, 140–5.

[234] *Bracton's Note-Book*, no. 1235; Warren, *Henry II*, 139–42.

[235] On the basis of seigniorial power: Biancalana, 'For Want of Justice', 505.

[236] Milsom, *Legal Framework*, 41, 179; the title of a paper he delivered in London in 1991 used the phrase 'seigniorial world'.

[237] Stenton, *First Century*, 45–6 and chap. 2 *passim*.

is evidence that they did not exist: their procedures would have been oral and unlikely to be recorded anyway. Besides, there is some evidence that lay lords did indeed have courts with some kind of authority over free men. Henry I envisaged that barons of his honour would deal with pleas between their *vavassores*, and what he said about the pleas makes it clear that the *vavassores* held land.[238] The *Leges Henrici Primi* say that every lord could summon his men and do right to them in his court.[239] This leaves some doubt about the nature of the cases and the status of the men. Manorial courts certainly had some civil and criminal jurisdiction over peasants, some of whom counted as free then and would still do so after more formal lines between free and unfree were drawn. Lords with extra franchises or liberties dealt with more, but few lay lords had the kind of franchises that gave them anything like enforceable jurisdiction over the free property of free men. There is no evidence that at this stage anyone who gave or sold land to be held from him was invariably assumed to have jurisdiction in disputes about it.

At least some of the lay lords whom we find dealing with disputes in the twelfth century seem to be earls or other great men, like the lord of a Sussex rape (a unit of local government) whose court was in effect a county court. Even the courts of great men like this, however, in the rare references to them look more often like assemblies held at their castles for the conduct of general business, including mediation and arbitration between their tenants or followers, than anything like lawcourts with enforceable or exclusive jurisdiction.[240] It is, moreover, not clear that royal orders to 'do right' always meant doing justice as a judge in a court. Henry I ordered someone to do full right to the abbot of Abingdon concerning the fief he claimed to hold from the abbot: that is, he was to act rightly according to the judgement of the abbot's court on him. When Gilbert de Ghent ordered anyone making a claim on anything in his lordship or granted by his alms (*aliquid de meo dominio vel de mea elemosina*) to come to him, so that he could do full right, he may have been intending to pre-empt lawsuits rather than preside over them.[241] We can infer from some of the writs

[238] See chapter 2 at nn. 21–2 and index: vavassors.
[239] Liebermann, *Gesetze*, i. 524 (c. 3); *Leges Henrici Primi*, 172–4 (55), though cf. Liebermann, *Gesetze*, i. 633 (9, 1–3).
[240] Stenton, *First Century*, 41–83: there was surely no reason why any consultation of a royal or other court should have been needed for the uncontentious family arrangement discussed on pp. 52–3, so it does not show any very striking independence: cf. Milsom, *Legal Framework*, 110; *Eng. Lawsuits*, nos. 162, 217, 198, 235, 252, 307, 343, 346. For simplicity I shall refer to this convenient collection where possible in this section rather than to the sources it reproduces. Evidence of the lord's disciplinary power (Milsom, *Legal Framework*, 25–7) seems to come mostly from after Henry II's legislation: Biancalana, 'For Want of Justice', 467, 483.
[241] *Reg. Regum*, ii, no. 974; cf. *Eng. Lawsuits*, nos. 227, 324. Cf. a reference to plaintiffs who, if the defendant is successful, *facient justiciam* to him in the emperor's court: *Dip. Frid. I*, no. 378.

ordering nobles to do right that some of them had courts, but in some cases the person to whom the writ was addressed was simply given authority to carry out the king's commands. That the king used the lord of one of the parties to execute an order is not surprising. 'Doing right' does not in itself imply a court.

Mary Cheney has suggested that early in his reign Henry II made a new and simplified procedure available for appealing to the king if one's lord had failed to do justice and that John Marshal made use of this against the archbishop of Canterbury in 1164.[242] Despite Henry I's expectations of baronial justice, however, people seem to have been complaining pretty freely to county assemblies and to the king from the beginning of the century. Early in Henry I's reign, knights who supported the lay custodian of Battle abbey's manor of Wye (Kent) in a dispute with the abbey claimed that they ought to do justice in their county, not in the abbey court, though they agreed that they would submit to the royal court.[243] About 1140 Roger de Mowbray gave a man called Uctred land which had belonged to Uctred's grandfather in fee and inheritance. Although Uctred was to hold his quarter-fee not from Roger but from one of Roger's tenants, Roger ordered that no one should implead Uctred except in his presence, because Uctred was his man and he was Uctred's defender (*quia inde homo meus est et ego ei presidium*).[244] This may mean that Roger envisaged hearing any plea himself, but he could perhaps have been thinking of being present in the county or king's court. A little later, Byland abbey appealed to him for help against people who were threatening the lands it held from him. On that occasion Roger did not apparently think of judging the case in his own court but interceded with powerful friends to delay the hearing in the king's court until he could return to England, ordering his mother and his officials to protect the abbey meanwhile.[245] There does not seem to be any evidence that people thought they ought to appeal through a hierarchy of tenure until this was suggested by one of Thomas Becket's biographers. The analogy with the hierarchy of ecclesiastical courts that had developed by then is suggestive.[246]

The courts of ecclesiastical lords may have been not merely better recorded in the surviving sources than those of lay lords but better established in reality. Some great churches had ancient sokes in which they

---

[242] Cheney, 'Decree'.

[243] *Eng. Lawsuits*, no. 174: presumably they meant the court of the rape rather than of the whole county of Sussex.

[244] *Charters of Honour of Mowbray*, no. 392.

[245] *Eng. Lawsuits*, no. 323: the story seems to make more sense if it was Roger rather than the abbot who wrote to friends at court.

[246] Cheney, 'Decree'; the courts in *Eng. Lawsuits*, no. 316 form at best an untidy hierarchy.

exercised a fairly wide jurisdiction over their humbler tenants and on to which further jurisdiction could be grafted. Some secured charters granting them exclusive first-instance jurisdiction over all their men, which in itself implies that all lords did not have it as a matter of course.[247] Yet both churches and their tenants were often, it seems, pretty ready to appeal outside their supposedly sovereign lordships. Even a church with exclusive first-instance jurisdiction seems to have accepted that it might have to demonstrate to the sheriff that it had done justice properly in its court.[248] Perhaps by the second half of the century the great churches were becoming less ready to recognize secular jurisdictions. Bishops and clergy were now judging or arbitrating, sometimes with lay lords but sometimes on their own, in a wide range of cases affecting church rights and property, quite apart from those concerning clerical crimes.[249] Provided they did so by royal command and under royal supervision the king might be happy to let them get on with it. If there were any courts that Henry II is likely to have regarded as threatening royal authority, they would be those of churches—and, to judge from John Marshal's case, not just their canon-law courts.

One way and another, then, there is not much evidence that rights of property in fees or fiefs, whether held by knight service or otherwise, automatically or normally included very much in the way of jurisdiction over free tenants, however they held their land. Few people who granted land to be held from them, and thus became in a sense lords of that land, may have had courts substantial enough for their jurisdiction to be infringed when Henry II's introduction of the writs of Novel Disseisin and Mort d'Ancestor enabled people with claims to free land to take their cases straight before royal judges.[250] Most of those whose courts were thus bypassed would be the bishops or abbots of great churches, great lay lords, or lords of manors. Lords of manors exercised regular jurisdiction over their peasant tenants, which was affected by the innovations in so far as the more free of their tenants wanted to use the new procedures and succeeded in doing so. Many early cases of Novel Disseisin seem to have concerned small properties belonging to what look like people of quite low status. As a result it became necessary to find criteria of freedom, and this produced the new law of villeinage.[251] Land judged to be free was protected by the royal courts. Villein land was not. Lords of manors thus lost exclusive

---

[247] Biancalana, 'For Want of Justice', 453 n. 81; cf. *Eng. Lawsuits*, no. 331.
[248] *Eng. Lawsuits*, no. 187.
[249] Biancalana, 'For Want of Justice', 474; *Eng. Lawsuits*, nos. 223, 233.
[250] Though see the comment of Guernes, *Vie de Saint Thomas*, 49 (ll. 1399–1400).
[251] Sutherland, *Novel Disseisin*, 11–12, 30–2, 48–50; Hyams, *Kings, Lords, and Peasants*.

jurisdiction, if they had hitherto thought of claiming it, over land held by free men or nobles within their manors. Above this level, the lords most likely to hold anything like regular courts would be lords with large and compact estates over which they had significant franchisal jurisdiction.

During the second half of the twelfth century, however, it became necessary for more lords than before to hold more regular courts. Anyone who took action that might infringe someone else's rights in free property was now liable to be asked to produce evidence that he or she had acted after a judgement.[252] The new writs therefore, combined with new rules about claims of default of justice and about essoins (i.e. about the amount of delay that was allowed), must have stimulated rather than stunted the development of seigniorial courts.[253] Lords needed more formal courts to produce judgements, and they needed to employ people with the new skills required to manipulate writs and arguments. The result might well be sharper ideas of both procedure and jurisdiction. In the thirteenth century people complained that lords were making new demands for attendance at their courts and were trying to insist that pleas of default of justice (and, apparently, false judgement) should trail through a hierarchy of seigniorial courts before going to the royal courts. Perhaps they were: the grievance may have arisen through genuinely new demands, not, as is sometimes thought, from a seigniorial reaction to the loss of old jurisdictions.[254] It is quite possible that the obligations of free men to attend lords' courts that were recorded in the late thirteenth century were being more regularly and formally imposed than they had been in the twelfth century.[255] The formal business done in such courts, apart from manorial business, cannot have been great, but then it may never have been. The 'great age of baronial jurisdiction'[256] in the twelfth century may be as insubstantial as many other golden ages in the unrecorded past.

How far pre-conquest rights of alienation were reduced by new ideas of a hierarchy of tenure and any new rights it gave to lords is hard to tell. Some charters to churches forbade alienation of church property, while the churches themselves sometimes imposed restrictions on what their tenants could do with their holdings, but that, of course, need not imply similar restrictions on property held from laymen.[257] At least some twelfth-century

---

[252] Biancalana, 'For Want of Justice', 467, 474, 482–4, 532 and n. 521.

[253] On essoins: Stenton, *English Justice*, 22–54.

[254] Matthew Paris, *Chron. Maj.* v. 545; *Docs. Baronial Movement*, 88–90 (c. 29). That this complaint also applied to false judgement is implied by ibid. 144 (c. 16).

[255] Ault, *Private Jurisdiction*; *Select Pleas in Manorial Courts*, pp. xli–lii; for royal grants of hundreds: Cam, *Liberties*, 67–9.        [256] Ault, *Private Jurisdiction*, 3.

[257] *Reading Cart.* nos. 1, 27; *Eng. Lawsuits*, no. 164; *Reg. St Augustine's*, ii. 462; Cheney, 'Inalienability'; most of the earlier examples in Waugh, 'Non-Alienation Clauses', concern church land. Much of Pollock and Maitland, *History*, i. 329–51, seems to me still valid.

laymen, however, if not most, secured the consent or confirmation of their lords to their gifts of land. Some lords may have made them pay for it. Norman practice may have been influential here, but it is impossible to know whether donors or vendors actually needed to get consent or whether they got it because the beneficiaries wanted them to as a matter of prudence. In conditions of customary law the distinction may be unreal: different lords had different levels of interest and right in different subordinate properties, especially before the boundary between free and unfree land had been worked out. Burgages were normally freely alienable, while socage land that owed few or no services may always have been easier to dispose of without consent. On the other hand the really prudent, or those dealing with property of which the title was likely to be doubtful, might get consent or confirmation from more people than the immediate lord. Anyone influential could be brought in. It might be worth paying for a royal charter of confirmation even though the land conveyed was not held directly from the king.[258] The records that Rochester cathedral kept of donations in the early years of the century included some with notes of consent by the donors' lords but some with only the consent of their wives and sons.[259] A casual search through a small number of charters suggests that family participation in gifts may have been as common as seigniorial participation, yet it has received much less notice from historians than it has in France.[260] Presumably the later development of succession law in the two countries explains the relative interest of legal historians, but it does not justify concluding that lords in early twelfth-century England had more rights in their tenants' land than their tenants' prospective heirs had. More work is needed before any reasonable conclusions about the necessity of permission to alienate at this period can be drawn.

Glanvill's concern about alienation was entirely with the rights of heirs, not of lords. He saw alienations in one's lifetime as at most undesirable but not wrong or prohibited. He thought that acquisitions could be freely disposed of, inside or outside the family, except that socage-holders under partible inheritance had to keep their sons' shares fair.[261] A good deal of what he said on the subject was conditioned by a taste for posing interesting hypothetical problems as well as by the changes made to the practice of inheritance by the Assize of Mort d'Ancestor, but his basic predilection

---

[258] Pollock and Maitland, *History*, i. 341; Hyams, 'Warranty', 447–51. Cf. chapter 5, at nn. 137–47.

[259] Tsurushima, 'Fraternity'.

[260] Consent of lord and kin: Stenton, *First Century*, 281–2, 284–5 (nos. 41, 46); *Early Yorks. Charters*, nos. 74–5; lord only: *Eng. Lawsuits*, no. 296 (p. 249); *Book of Seals*, no. 84; kin only: Stenton, *First Century*, 260, 278–9, 280 (nos. 5, 36, 38).

[261] *Glanvill*, 69–74.

for freedom to alienate need not have been new. The way he talks about acquisitions and the rights of heirs suggests that the security that Mort d'Ancestor gave to the single heir did not immediately wipe out older concerns.[262] If lords' rights had formerly been as clear and overriding as Milsom, for instance, thinks they were, Glanvill might perhaps have mentioned them, if only to dismiss them. Meanwhile Westminster abbey, for instance, still went on getting confirmations from the lords of donors just as it sometimes got them from the descendants of donors.[263] Rich abbeys took cautious advice.

Nevertheless, in spite of doubts about the position before Mort d'Ancestor, there is no doubt that, whatever it did to the claims of lords, it strengthened those of eldest sons against their siblings—except, of course, in the case of socage holdings with a recognized custom of division. Perhaps it was Mort d'Ancestor itself rather than any separate and deliberate royal enactment that effectively ended the bequest of land in England, except in towns.[264] At the same time the new procedures and rules of royal justice encouraged more formal family arrangements for endowing widows, daughters, and younger sons. Landowners who set aside land for these purposes might well want to restrict its alienation outside the family and retain a reversionary interest for their heirs. That could still be done by inserting appropriate clauses in the charters and did not affect the general principle that land was presumed to be alienable in the absence of special conditions.[265] Those who alienated land, whether inside or outside the family, were still supposed to see that services due to lords above them in the hierarchy (forinsec services) were done and that lords got their dues. By the early thirteenth century some lords at least were worried about losing their rights. A clause in the 1217 version of Magna Carta, repeated in the definitive version of 1225, forbade any free man from giving or selling so much land that he could not perform the service due to his lord.[266] The rule was ignored in a judgement of 1225, and on other occasions it was apparently taken as applying only to gifts in free alms.[267] Bracton favoured free alienation to the extent of arguing that a lord could be forced to accept the homage of someone who had acquired land from his

---

[262] Milsom, *Legal Framework*, 123 n. 3, cites cases which suggest that acquisitions were still thought more easily alienable than inherited property after Mort d'Ancestor should, one imagines, have made the distinction irrelevant.

[263] *Westminster Charters*, e.g. nos. 417, 420, 427, 433, 454, 456, 465, 485.

[264] A suggestion made to me by Professor J. Biancalana. Cf. Pollock and Maitland, *History*, i. 327; Sheehan, *Will*, 266–74.

[265] Waugh, 'Non-Alienation Clauses'.

[266] *Statutes of the Realm*, Charters of Liberties, 19, 24 (1217, c. 39, 1225, c. 32).

[267] *Curia Regis Rolls*, xii, no. 266; *Bracton's Note-Book*, no. 1248; *Cal. Pat. Rolls, 1232–47*, 234.

tenant.[268] Yet, despite this and despite some discussion of hypothetical layers of subinfeudation, the *De Legibus* does not explicitly draw attention to
the distinction between subinfeudation and substitution that seems so
obvious to legal historians. The lack of any clear appreciation of the distinction at the time is illustrated by the way that freely alienable urban
property was sometimes conveyed to be held from donors and sometimes
from chief lords, and sometimes was not to be held from anyone.[269] In any
case Bracton's ruling was not authoritative: lords did not always have to
accept new tenants, though they presumably had to do so when land was
conveyed by final concord as a result of a lawsuit, which seems quite often
to have been done by what we call substitution.[270] The old conflict of
sometimes incompatible rights had not been resolved by new rules of law,
nor were the rules themselves cast in the terms we might expect.

The most serious attacks on freedom of disposition came from the royal
government. From 1198, if not before, the government was interested in
making more use of its potential rights over serjeanties. One way it did this
was to control or tax the alienation of land held from the king by serjeanty.
When this became a regular policy from 1244 it was obviously intended
and applied to produce money.[271] Both John and Henry III also considered
restricting or licensing alienation by all their tenants in chief, and Henry
occasionally licensed leases and outright grants. Sometimes, as J. M. W.
Bean has suggested, this was done so as to secure the beneficiary's title, but
a total prohibition in 1256 on all unlicensed alienations by all who held
directly from the king was a deliberate piece of royal policy. Prominent
among the reasons given was the king's loss of wardships and escheats.[272]
Bullying serjeanty-tenants was one thing, however: making the baronage at
large pay fines was another. Edward I was in a stronger position than his
father, and during his reign both licences and pardons for unlicensed alienations began to be regularly issued and paid for.[273] In view of the parallel
developments in France and elsewhere, and in the context of English government and law in general, this looks less like the relic of a once general
restriction on all fiefs than a characteristic example of developing bureaucracy and taxation.[274] In 1290 the statute of Quia Emptores finally gave all
free men the right to sell free land and laid down that in future all such

---

[268] Bracton, *De Legibus*, ii. 140–3, 234–7; iii. 274.
[269] *Early Charters of St Paul's*, nos. 67, 70, 82–3, 106–7, 111–12, 114–15, 121, 130, 134, 302.
[270] Brand, 'Control of Mortmain', 29 n.; cf. Bean, *Decline*, 46–7; Pollock and Maitland,
*History*, i. 345.
[271] Kimball, *Serjeanty Tenure*, 208–41.
[272] Bean, *Decline*, 68–70; cf. Waugh, *Lordship*, 93; *Close Rolls, 1254–6*, 429.
[273] Bean, *Decline*, 71–9.
[274] Chapter 7, at nn. 211–15, chapter 6, at nn. 178, 286, 313–14, chapter 9, at nn. 308–22.

land would be held directly from the vendor's lord. Substitution, to use historians' terminology, thus finally replaced subinfeudation, though the statute, like the *De Legibus*, still did not use the words.[275] Even after 1290 lords could sometimes make things difficult for their tenants, so that tenants or those to whom they sold land would pay to be left in peace. The problems of securing good title cannot all, or even most of them, be attributed to the survival of old ideas of lordship.[276] Many arose from the methods that professional lawyers devised to protect their clients' interests against royal wardship, claims for dower, the possibly weak titles of those from whom they acquired land, their predecessors' settlements, or their descendants' efforts to escape from their own settlements.

Among the particular prohibitions on alienation that had appeared in some charters by 1200 was that on grants to churches—what became known as grants in mortmain. As the contrasting rules of tenure in free alms and by knight service were elaborated, so the disadvantage to lords of gifts that endangered their chance of service, reliefs, and wardship became more obvious.[277] But, even if knight service and its associated obligations derived from older social norms than I have argued they did, hostility to church property was not restricted only to lords with military tenants. The rulers of towns were unwilling to see too many burgages passing into the dead hand of the church.[278] Excessive church property was not feared because it undermined feudo-vassalic institutions but because it threatened the authority of secular government at every level. The story of how controls on mortmain were developed during the thirteenth century in the interest both of the crown and of other lords is both complicated and obscure. It seems that, well before the statute of mortmain was passed in 1279, laymen and clergy, litigants and judges had come to accept that churches should acquire land only with royal or seigniorial consent. When the statute was passed it seems, unlike the French ordinance of 1275, not to have been systematically used at first to produce revenue for the king.[279] Getting a licence apparently depended on first getting one from a lord or lords below the king. In this area therefore the central government does not seem, at least for a while, to have overridden its subjects' rights. To that extent the history of the rules on mortmain may seem not to support my argument. Perhaps this was partly because the government was already in a position to ignore, at least for a while, this particular source of income. In any case, the control of mortmain supports the general thrust of my

---

[275] *Rotuli Parl.* i. 41.  [276] Bean, *Decline*, 79–103.

[277] Kimball, 'Tenure in Frank Almoign'; Douglas, 'Frankalmoin'.

[278] Raban, *Mortmain Legislation*, 5–6, 13. The rest of this paragraph depends on Raban's chapter 1 and on Brand, 'Control of Mortmain'.

[279] Chapter 7, at n. 214.

argument in so far as it was a development of the thirteenth century that is easier to connect with other developments of that age of bureaucratic controls and close legal argument than with ancient social norms.

Lastly, in considering rights, we must glance at security against confiscation. The property of free men always had greater security than that of the unfree because the unfree were the easiest to bully. The difference was accentuated when it became easier for any free man, however low his social status, to appeal to royal justice. In so far as free land was normally that which, according to English terminology, was held *in feodum* one could say that fiefs had particular security, but that is playing with words. All confiscation was supposed to be subject to some kind of collective judgement. By the early twelfth century there seems to have been an idea that judgements should be made by the equals or peers of a defendant. In a lord's court this would presumably mean that the peers would be fellow tenants, but a link of local custom may have been as important as anything else.[280] The idea of judgement of peers at this stage thus seems more likely to have embodied the same general norm that lay behind Conrad II's ordinance of 1037 than to have been influenced either by it or by any supposedly new principles of feudal law brought in by the Normans.[281] Seigniorial courts do not seem to have been either the original home of the judgement of peers or more subject to their lords' will than other courts.[282] Under Henry II particular forms of collective judgement were preserved both in the assizes or juries that judged cases about free land in the king's court, and in the grand jury, which made accusations about serious crimes. Juries do not, however, seem to have been seen at first essentially as judgements by peers. Jurors were not chosen to match the status of litigants or their land. They were knights or free men who were supposed to represent the local community.

The idea that juries embodied the judgement of peers may derive from Magna Carta's requirement that the king should proceed against free men or their land only by lawful judgement of their peers or the law of the land (*per legale judicium parium suorum vel per legem terre*).[283] Perhaps peers got into Magna Carta, not from the traditional norms reflected in the earlier texts that have been mentioned, but from the academic law of fiefs. In letters to John and the rebellious barons in 1215 Innocent III referred to

---

[280] *Leges Henrici Primi*, 134 (31. 7); cf. Liebermann, *Gesetze*, i. 510; Stenton, *First Century*, 45, 55, 60–1, 91 n.
[281] See chapter 6.5 and index: peers.
[282] Milsom, *Legal Framework*, refers *passim* to decisions by lords in a way that gives the (perhaps unintended) impression that it was lords, rather than those present in their courts, who made them.
[283] Holt, *Magna Carta*, 326 (c. 39).

the barons as vassals—a word very rarely used in England—and to the need to do justice to them *per pares eorum* (or, in his letter to the barons, *vestros*) *secundum consuetudines et leges regni*.[284] The earls and barons who later came to be considered 'peers of the realm' soon started to claim judgement by their own peers, that is, by themselves alone, but for most of the population judgement of peers, enshrined in Magna Carta, came to mean trial by jury.[285] The reason why collective judgement survived into the age of professional law in England when it was gradually superseded elsewhere was surely that it was already fossilized in written forms established in the royal courts by the time that the legal profession took shape. English lawyers were trained on the writs that prescribed jury trial, so they had to live with them. But the protection of the lives and property of free men that juries provided can be only indirectly connected with the particular privileges of fiefholders that traditional ideas of feudo-vassalic relations suggest. Any connection that there was may have come from Innocent III and his knowledge of academic law.

Property continued to be confiscated for serious crimes after 1066, and indeed after 1215, but by the twelfth century only that of the king's tenants was supposed to go to him, while that of other criminals went to their lords.[286] Property that lacked an heir also went or, in what became the standard English expression, 'escheated' to its lord.[287] This was particularly valuable to lords before the rules of inheritance were established, before newly established Norman families had produced as many potential heirs as they would later, and before procedures were devised to enable heirs to claim their property in the royal courts. For the king the line between forfeiture and escheat for lack of heirs always remained a fine one that, in favourable political conditions, he could draw for himself.[288] By the later part of the twelfth century he also got the movable property of all those convicted of serious crimes and held their land for a year and a day before handing it over to their lords—possibly by then denuded of trees and houses.[289] After the loss of Normandy the king took all the English lands of those who had remained under French rule, irrespective of their position in the hierarchy of tenure. This may have been the origin of the rule by which only felons' lands went to their lords while traitors' lands

---

[284] Innocent III, *Selected Letters*, nos. 82–3. The 'unknown charter' says simply that the king promised not to take men *without judgement*: Holt, *Magna Carta*, 312 (c. 1). For Innocent and the law of fiefs, see below at nn. 308–12 and index: Innocent III.

[285] Reynolds, *Kingdoms and Communities*, 55–6; Keeney, *Judgment by Peers*, 84–110.

[286] e.g. *Eng. Lawsuits*, nos. 176, 183, 186, 317.

[287] Like most supposedly technical terms of feudalism, escheat originally had varying meanings: Niermeyer, *Lexicon*, 387.

[288] Green, *Government*, 58, 179–80; McFarlane, *Nobility*, 250–2.

[289] *Glanvill*, 90–1; Richard fitz Nigel, *Dialogus*, 97–8, 111–14.

went to the king.[290] Rules about escheats in towns varied: they were probably worked out in the thirteenth century and later as the king, the muni-
cipal authorities, or a local lord succeeded in creating precedents and laying
down custom.[291] In times of acute political conflict distinctions were not
always made with care or enforced with rigour. In 1265 the lands of those
who had supported the great baronial rebellion were supposed to be seized
into the king's hand, but some great lords who had ended up on the win-
ning side stepped in before the royal officials.[292] As it has not been established that all their seizures were of properties that were held from them,
their actions may illustrate the problems of law-enforcement in troubled
times rather than the strength of feudo-vassalic bonds. The protection
given by the king's courts to all free property, at least in principle and in
normal times, meanwhile restricted lords' powers in other ways. In the
twelfth century lords had sometimes been able to confiscate property when
services had not been done. Thereafter rules were gradually worked out so
that lords could take only movable property and hold it only pending the
resolution of the dispute.[293]

## 8.8. *English law and feudal law*

If feudal law means the academic law of fiefs that originated in twelfth-
century Italy and began to influence the practice of law in Germany and
France soon afterwards, then England was virtually without any feudal law
throughout the middle ages. If it means the customary law that governed
property that was called fiefs, then in twelfth- and thirteenth-century
England it was the law that governed all free and heritable property. If, as
those who talk of the introduction of feudal tenure at the Norman
Conquest suggest, feudal law or custom means law or custom about properties held by knight service, then there was even less distinction between
feudal law and other law. Rules about inheritance, confiscation, or rights of
alienation were different for people of higher status because all their rights
were better and their obligations were different, but until the late twelfth
century the rights and obligations of all classes were set and adjudicated by
the same fluid and more or less undifferentiated body of custom. The same
applies to matters that are often thought to have had peculiarly feudo-
vassalic connotations, like reliefs, wardship, or aids. As I have argued, the
rules about these subjects were not introduced to England as part of a

[290] Powicke, *Loss of Normandy*, 286–90; Pollock and Maitland, *History*, ii. 501–2.
[291] *London Eyre*, nos. 208–21; *Borough Customs*, i. 67–70.
[292] *Cal. Inq. Misc.* i, nos. 608–940.
[293] *Eng. Lawsuits*, no. 317; *Rot. Cur. Regis*, i. 62–3; *Docs. Baronial Movement*, 144, 146 (Prov.
Westm. 11, 17); *Statutes of the Realm*, i. 19–20, 23, 24 (Stat. Marlb. c. 1–4, 15, 21, 23–4).

coherent body of customs that were already prevalent among that undifferentiated mass of foreigners (mostly French) that the British like to call 'the Continent'. It is not just that the Normans did not introduce any different and coherent body of custom or law about property, but that rules about reliefs, wardship, or aids seem to have developed as part of the same body of customary law as governed all property. The rules in England were unusual in so far as an exceptionally powerful central government had already begun to enforce obligations on the property of people of high status before the conquest and went on doing so after it.

In so far as seigniorial courts, which are sometimes called feudal courts, had effective jurisdiction, the customary law that they used was presumably much the same—or should have been much the same—as that of the counties or hundreds in which they lay. Different honours or estates developed different customs on individual points, but that was normal and applied to other kinds of property too. Procedures in cases about fiefs— property held in fee—were at first no different from procedures about anything else. All judgements in all courts, even on peasants, were supposed to be produced by assemblies which represented the community whose customs were being applied.[294] When virtually all jurisdiction over free property passed to the king's courts this began to change. Argument soon became a matter for professional lawyers and judges, so that public participation was restricted to the members of assizes or juries, who were supposed only to answer the questions put to them under the terms of the writ.[295] What later came to be known as the common law of England was first of all royal law, and very soon became lawyers' law. The first stages of the process by which customary law became lawyers' law are revealed in Glanvill and Bracton. Both show the kind of interest in posing problems and making distinctions that was inculcated by academic education in the twelfth century and after. Both knew quite a lot about Roman law. S. E. Thorne concluded that Bracton had 'the principles and distinctions of Roman jurisprudence firmly in mind, using them throughout his work, wherever they could be used, to rationalize and reduce to order the results reached in the English courts'.[296] It is tempting to wonder whether either author could have seen any of the treatises that went to make up the *Libri Feudorum*. Chronologically this looks unlikely, especially for Glanvill, if one envisages them seeing them along with Roman-law texts, but a work on the law of fiefs could just possibly have been the source of Glanvill's

---

[294] Chapter 2.3; Reynolds, *Kingdoms and Communities*, 23–34, 51–9.
[295] Note the comments of the bishop of Winchester in 1233: ibid. 55.
[296] Bracton, *De Legibus*, i, p. xxxiii, see also pp. xxiv–xxxvii; *Glanvill*, pp. xxxvi–xxxviii; Barton, *Roman Law in England*.

remarks about the duty of a man not to attack or injure his lord, especially since he uses the tell-tale word *vassallus* at this point.[297] It could also explain his reference, taken up by Bracton, to a rule against inheritance by a direct ascendant that they both obviously found hard to justify.[298] Bracton's etymology of *vavassor*, however, does not suggest that he had used the *Libri*.[299] If, as I have suggested, a phrase from the law of fiefs came to England in Innocent III's reference to the judgement of peers, it did not apparently bring the rest of that law with it. According to the Oxford Dictionary the word vassal did not apparently enter the English language until late in the fifteenth century, when it was used in rather unspecific senses. In 1523 Coverdale told how Pope John XII 'did prescribe an othe unto Otho, in whiche Otho shold acknowlege him self to be the popes phasalle (as we do now cal it)'.[300]

By the thirteenth century the time for eclecticism in English legal learning was passing. In the twelfth century and early in the thirteenth land was sometimes said, in England as in France, to move from (*movere de*) its lord. Thereafter, while the expression became a technical term of the French law of fiefs, it seems to have faded out of English use.[301] For a while there was some overlap between common and canon lawyers, and in 1313 a royal justice suggested in passing during an argument that the law of the land was founded on Roman law (*la lei imperiele*).[302] As the procedure of the royal courts became more complex and esoteric, however, the training of the lawyers who worked in them became narrower and more technical so that they were less and less likely to have studied any law outside their own system. In so far as academic law encouraged an interest in categories or classification, Bracton himself came nearer to it than any of his immediate successors. Even he, however, was more interested in problems than in classification: although in various places he mentioned four different types of fee he did not really classify them into a 'scheme of tenures'. It was Maitland who did that.[303] As intellectual horizons narrowed this bias was accentuated. The training of lawyers who practised in the king's courts seems to have consisted largely in hearing cases, disputing points that

[297] *Glanvill*, 104–5. I have not searched the text for other references to *vassalli* but I have the impression that, like later English medieval lawyers, he does not use it generally.
[298] *Glanvill*, 73; Bracton, *De Legibus*, ii. 184; Lehmann, *Langobardische Lehnrecht*, 173. The analogy was noticed by Maitland in Pollock and Maitland, *History*, ii. 288.
[299] *De Legibus*, ii. 32; cf. Maitland, *Bracton and Azo*, 65.     [300] *OED* xix. 456.
[301] *Glanvill*, 27, uses it in a slightly different sense, but see, e.g. *Curia Regis Rolls*, viii. 67, 103. Later cases that I was kindly allowed to look up in the slips collected for the *Oxford Dictionary of Medieval Latin* by 1991 come from Gascon sources.
[302] *Year Book 1313*, 70; see also Brand, *Origins*, 155–6.
[303] Pollock and Maitland, *History*, i. 239–40. See above, at nn. 150–3.

arose, and studying the writs that initiated cases.[304] The categories of property and the rules about them thus became shaped by the different forms of action that developed from the different writs. This is illustrated by the rule that excluded leases for a term of years from the protection granted to fees or free holdings while leases for lives were protected.[305] The solution to what was clearly felt to be an anomaly was not to redefine the categories or change the rule but to provide a separate action for lessees.[306] Meanwhile many properties never came to court and so never needed to be fitted into any categories, however ramshackle. A fourteenth-century set of model entries for court rolls gives a specimen announcement of the death of a tenant called John Frankeleyne, who had held a virgate of land freely for five shillings a year. The lord—probably St Albans abbey— was to have a heriot of a horse with bridle, saddle, and sword, and wardship of John's son, who was afterwards to give a relief and do *feoditatem*—presumably fidelity.[307] Lawyers might have called John a tenant in socage, but the obligations of his heir could have given rise to argument, quite apart from the breach of Magna Carta involved in asking for a relief after wardship. The effect of the cases that did come to court, meanwhile, was to produce an ever widening gap between property law in England and elsewhere, and between the English fee—whether fee simple or fee tail— and the fief of the academic law of fiefs, not merely in terminology and concepts but in the rights and obligations that could be protected and enforced at law.

As yet the gap posed less of a problem in arguing the king's case in disputes outside England than one might imagine. King John's troubles in France and with the pope came, of course, when all legal systems were still inchoate.[308] When he surrendered his kingdoms of England and Ireland to Innocent III in 1213 he received them back as the pope's *feodatarius* or *feodarius*, swearing fidelity, promising to do homage to Innocent in person if he could get there, and committing himself and his heirs to an annual tribute of 1,000 marks.[309] He subsequently did the promised homage to the papal legate in England. In 1213–14 Innocent expressed the new relations in various ways: John had put himself and his land under apostolic governance (*apostolice . . . ditioni*), submitting himself and his kingdom

---

[304] Brand, *Origins*, 110–15, 117–19.

[305] The rule may not have been as old as Novel Disseisin: *Curia Regis Rolls*, i. 400 (*pace* the comment of Milsom, *Legal Framework*, 22 n.).

[306] Simpson, *History of Land Law*, 71–8; Challis, 'Are Leaseholds Tenements?'

[307] *Court Baron*, 103–4; Hyams, *Kings, Lords, and Peasants*, 77–9.

[308] See chapter 7, at nn. 83–5.

[309] Rymer, *Foedera*, i (1), 111–12, 115. The pope used the form *feodarius*: Innocent III, *Selected Letters*, no. 67.

temporally to him to whom he and it were already subject spiritually. England now belonged specially or by special rights (*speciali jure*), *in jus et proprietatem* or *in racione dominii* to the Roman church. This suggests that Innocent may have thought of England as what Italian historians call a *feudo oblato*, like those created by Hadrian IV in 1157.[310] In the letter in which he condemned Magna Carta the pope said that the king had received England and Ireland back *in feudum* and referred to the rebels as *vassali* conspiring against their lord and *milites* conspiring against their king.[311] Together with the pope's reference to the judgement of peers, his use of the word *vassali* may imply a knowledge of the academic law of fiefs. If so, it provided him with nothing more than useful words. His condemnation of the baronial rebels and the charter was made much more as the Vicar of Christ than as John's secular lord. One hardly needs a knowledge of feudo-vassalic principles or of any particular system of law to understand the relations that John's surrender set up between the pope and the kingdom of England. Like similar relations that had been formed between popes and other kings earlier,[312] it was an adaptation of ways of dealing with ecclesiastical—rather than lay—property to the needs of international power politics, that was expressed in the vocabulary available at the time. Despite differences in local law both English and Italians probably understood it in much the same way.[313] When John was dying he made the papal legate whom Innocent had sent him the first executor of his will and the first protector of his son. One does not need to postulate any universal feudal custom about wardship in order to understand why Innocent's successor took over responsibilities towards John's heir.[314] The tribute that was owed by the kings of England under the settlement of 1213, and that the pope referred to as a *census*, does not fit the model of feudo-vassalic relations.[315] It was asked for from time to time and paid occasionally for about a century after Henry III's minority.[316] Thereafter the special relationship set up in 1213 seems to have been more or less forgotten.

     The claims of English kings to rule Wales were facilitated by the fact that Wales was not a kingdom, so that the Welsh arguably lacked the right to separate laws and independent government that were associated with

---

[310] Chapter 6, at n. 218.
[311] Innocent III, *Selected Letters*, nos. 53–5, 60, 67, 80, 82.          [312] Chapter 6.7.
[313] Cheney, *Pope Innocent III*, 332–7, 382–6; Lunt, *Financial Relations*, 130–40.
[314] Rymer, *Foedera*, i (1), 144. Seigniorial wardship is not mentioned in Lehmann, *Langobardische Lehnrecht*. Honorius III's references to his *pupillus* suggest Roman law: Sayers, *Papal Government*, 162–7 (*Liber Censuum*, i. 356–7, cited there, does not seem to mention papal responsibility for widows and children who had taken oaths of fidelity).
[315] *Census* does not appear in the index of Lehmann, *Langobardische Lehnrecht*.
[316] Lunt, *Financial Relations*, 141–72; Sayers, *Papal Government*, 165.

kingdoms.[317] A series of treaties from the time of Henry II on whittled away the Welsh princes' independence.[318] By the mid thirteenth century English law was defined enough to be useful and there were lawyers to give advice, if necessary, on how to use it advantageously. In 1241 David, prince of Gwynedd, had to do homage to Henry III and grant him the homages of all the nobles of Wales. He had also to agree that he held in chief from Henry the lands that were left to him and that if he withdrew his faithful service all his lands would be forfeit to the king and his heirs for ever.[319] Each settlement thereafter involved further jurisdictional concessions until the Statute of Wales declared in 1284 that the land of Wales, which had formerly been subject to the king *jure feodali*, had now been annexed outright to the crown.[320] There is no need to look outside the English law of the time to find the meaning of *jure feodali*: although the princes of Wales had not been explicitly said to hold their principality *in feodum*, the English government had assimilated their rights to the property rights of subjects. Now they were forfeit, as any subject's rights might be and as the treaty of 1241 had envisaged they might be.

Scotland, being a kingdom, posed more problems in principle as well as in practice. In 1174 King William the Lion became Henry II's liege man (*homo ligius*) for Scotland and all his other lands (*de Scotia et de omnibus aliis terris suis*) and did fidelity to him as to his liege lord and as Henry's other men were accustomed to do it. It is not explicitly stated that he did homage to Henry, but he did it to Henry's son and agreed that any of his men from whom Henry wanted homage and fidelity should do them to him.[321] In 1237 a marriage treaty recognized that Alexander II and his heirs should hold the three northern counties of England, to which he laid claim, *in dominico* for a token rent payable to the king of England. The treaty did not use the phrase *in feodum*, but it makes clear that, although Alexander's liberties in the counties would be extensive, the area would remain part of the kingdom of England.[322] When Edward I adjudicated in the Scottish succession dispute of 1290–2 as *superior dominus* (or, in French, *sovereyn seignour*) of the kingdom of Scotland, one of the claimants, Robert Bruce, asked to be judged by the natural law (*dreit naturel*) by which kings reign, probably because he thought that the rules of succession hitherto followed either in Scotland or in England would not suit his case. Edward's counsellors, including some who were probably trained in canon and Roman law, agreed that imperial or written law would not be suitable and that

---

[317] Reynolds, *Kingdoms and Communities*, 256–61, 320–4.
[318] Davies, *Age of Conquest*, 290–307, 335–56.
[319] *Littere Wallie*, nos. 4–5.
[320] *Statutes of the Realm*, i. 55.
[321] *Anglo-Scottish Relations*, no. 1.
[322] Ibid. no. 7.

English law should be used. It is not clear that the choice of laws made any difference to the outcome.[323]

In 1301, after the Scots had begun their long war of independence, they secured the support of Boniface VIII. In his bull *Scimus fili* the pope produced the slightly surprising information that Scotland belonged by right to the Roman church. It was not and had not been feudally subject to the kings of England (*progenitoribus tuis regni Anglie regibus sive tibi feudale non extitit nec existit*).[324] It is difficult to translate *feudale* here. Boniface may have meant simply temporal subjection—subjection by secular law. If he had been thinking in terms of the feudal law that was based on the *Libri Feudorum* he might have thought of recalling that England too was a fief of the Roman church. He did not do so, though a civil lawyer who advised Edward I may have thought that he did. Master William of Sardinia was afraid that, if the pope were allowed to judge in temporal matters and concerning a lay fee, he might assert that the king of England was his vassal. If the pope thought that the king had renounced his vassalage (*negasse vassalagium suum*) he might make judgements about the fief that he says (*dicit*) the king holds from the church.[325] William concentrated otherwise on points of legal and diplomatic procedure rather than on the substance of feudal or other relations. The answer Edward actually sent, on the advice of other Roman lawyers and notaries as well as William, started with a firm statement that the kings of England had from ancient times ruled over (*prefuerunt*) the kingdom of Scotland and its kings in temporal matters, *jure superioris et directi dominii*—a phrase which suggests both academic Roman and feudal law (*directum dominium*) and perhaps English law (cf. *superior dominus*) as well.[326] This claim was supported by a historical survey from the time of Brutus to that of the last Scottish king, John Baliol, who, having rendered the customary homage and sworn fidelity, attended parliament as a subject (*tanquam noster subditus*) of Edward's kingdom. The precedents from more recent history that Edward cited were true enough, however tendentiously used.

The real problem with Scotland if one were to talk about fiefs and vassalage would be to fit a kingdom into one's argument, whether under the

---

[323] *Edward I and the Throne of Scotland*, i. 121, ii. 167, 170, 205, 212–13; Barrow, *Robert Bruce*, 42–3.

[324] *Anglo-Scottish Relations*, no. 28.

[325] Ibid. no. 29: although most of this passage deals with hypothetical claims that the pope might make, *dicit* suggests that William thought the pope actually did claim that England was a papal fief. *Libri Feudorum* does not refer to denying vassalage in those terms, though cf. Lehmann, *Langobardische Lehnrecht*, 165.

[326] *Anglo-Scottish Relations*, no. 30. The parallel letter sent by the English barons says the kings of England *superius et directum dominium regni Scotie habuerunt et in possessione vel quasi superioritatis et directi dominii ipsius regni Scotie . . . extiterunt*: Rymer, *Foedera*, i (2), 927.

*Libri Feudorum* or under any body of customary law. The Scots indeed argued that by common law (*droit commun*) one kingdom should not be subject to another.[327] By common law they may have meant generally accepted law and custom—perhaps what Robert Bruce had meant by natural law. Past homages (or some of them) had been done for lands in England, not for the kingdom of Scotland.[328] The force of their arguments about the essential independence of kingdoms was recognized tacitly in Edward's ordinance for the government of Scotland in 1305, which referred to it throughout as a land, not a kingdom. Ideas about kingdoms were too strong for Edward: he ordered the people of this mere land or non-kingdom to elect representatives of their community to come to his parliament to discuss arrangements with a parallel panel of Englishmen. The laws of Scotland were to be revised and reformed, but they remained the laws of Scotland. No real attempt was made to deny that Scotland was a separate political entity.[329] Edward never seems to have called Scotland a fief any more than Henry II had done. Once again, ideas of feudo-vassalic relations are not needed to understand what was going on here. Modern imperialist ideas may be as relevant, especially when one considers the growing contempt for Welsh, Irish, and Scottish law shown by the English of the time.[330]

## 8.9. *Conclusion*

English property law never displayed the contrast between fief and alod that is presupposed by ideas of classic feudalism. It is no accident that English has no phrase for the *fief de reprise*. In reality, however, outside the terminology of lawyers, it was not so much that there were no alods in England after 1066 as that English fees were never quite like the classic fiefs—any more than were most fiefs elsewhere. The property of nobles and free men in pre-conquest England was very similar to Frankish alodial property. However, perhaps because ideas about property were less developed in England when the church arrived than they were in Gaul, church property influenced the development of lay property in England differently. The division between bookland and other property before the tenth century seems to be unique, while the rules about properties held by laymen from churches did not have such a wide effect on lay property in England as they did in the Frankish empire. Partly this may have been

[327] British Library, MS. Cott. Vesp. F. vii, fo. 16, translated in Barrow, *Robert Bruce*, 117–18. Cf. Petot, 'Droit commun'.
[328] British Library, MS. Cott. Vesp. F. vii, fos. 15–16.
[329] *Anglo-Scottish Relations*, no. 33; on the laws: Barrow, *Robert Bruce*, 135–6.
[330] Davies, *Domination and Conquest*, 114–15.

because English churches did not acquire such vast estates, so that, though English kings made use of church lands, they were not in a position to set up anything on the scale of the Carolingian benefices *verbo regis*. Partly it was because, just when the central government collapsed in France and local rulers were having to control local property as best they could, the kings of a united England were imposing military service and taxes on all their subjects. Like earlier Frankish kings and emperors, they could afford to allow property-owners relative freedom of alienation and bequest.

If, as long tradition asserts, feudalism was introduced into England by the Norman Conquest, then, whether it is seen in military terms as a matter of knights' fees and knight service or in jurisdictional terms as a matter of seigniorial courts, it was a pretty fugitive affair which barely outlasted its first century. If it is seen as already developing before 1066 then it might be said to have lasted longer, but the arguments for that, whether in terms of military service or of a tenurial hierarchy, seem hard to sustain. The introduction of the word fief and a new concept of a hierarchy of property rights seem to be genuine consequences of the conquest. The concept of a hierarchy of property rights probably owes a good deal to Domesday Book, although it only came to be articulated during the twelfth century, when rights and obligations were worked out and enforced according to the way they had been set down in 1086. The very word hierarchy may, however, be misleading: property rights were arranged in layers, but the top layer did not have most rights. Most of the rights of property, including the fundamental rights to use, management, and receipt of the income, were enjoyed, as they were elsewhere, by those at the lowest layer above that of unfree peasants. Except in the case of property held by military service by heiresses or minor heirs, the rights of a lord in the layer above were restricted to certain dues and services: the king, of course, did better, but it still remains true that more rights of property belonged to those who came to be called tenants in demesne than to either the king or any other lord.

Properties that were called fiefs or fees in England fit the pattern of classic feudalism only in the roughest of ways. *Feodum* in England did not mean knight's fee any more than it did in France. It meant all free and heritable property. One kind of fief or fee, the socage holding, had in fact a good many of the characteristics of the alod of twelfth- and thirteenth-century France. The power of the English government meant that all English fees in the twelfth and thirteenth centuries were to some extent precarious, but the same power also protected free property from anyone except the government. Since kings before the conquest had confiscated property fairly freely—in fact probably more freely than they could by the thirteenth century—there is no reason to suppose that rights in the fees or fiefs of post-conquest England were any more partial and conditional than rights in property had been in pre-conquest England or than they are in most societies. The rights and obligations of property in England had something in common with those of France and other countries that shared the same general background of rural economy, hierarchical government, and ideas of custom and justice, but they differed because political circumstances differed and custom evolved in different ways. Some of the English rules, like those about military service, reliefs, aids, and wardship, went to make up the picture of feudo-vassalic institutions that was composed in later centuries. My look at the way those rules actually developed and worked, however, suggests that the composition is a palimpsest over medieval realities.

# 9

# THE KINGDOM OF GERMANY

## 9.1. *The problems*

THE kingdom of Germany is taken here to cover all the territory included in the great kingdom, whatever it was called at different times before 1300, that developed out of the eastern part of the Carolingian empire. The chapter will include some material on Lotharingia, but touches on the kingdoms of Burgundy and Provence only in the twelfth century. Some of the material on the former middle kingdom has already been used in the chapters on France: to some extent the untidiness and overlaps reflect an untidy historical situation and overlapping historiographical traditions. My coverage of a huge and varied area is in any case so patchy that overlaps or omissions on the edges seem relatively unimportant. Like every other chapter, this one ignores a mass of regional and local variations. It is not that I believe them to have been insignificant: my hypothesis is, as usual, rather that the traditional interpretation of regional differences has been postulated on a premiss about the nature of political and property relations that needs to be revised before the differences can be evaluated.

During the nineteenth century the prevailing view seems to have been that *Lehnswesen* (that is, feudalism in its supposedly more precise sense) developed in Germany from the Carolingian age much as it did in France, if rather more slowly. In this century more attention was paid until recently to phenomena that seemed more peculiarly German than *Lehnswesen*. Feudo-vassalic institutions contributed less to medieval Germany, it was thought, than did the ancient, pre-feudal Germanic *Treue* and the ethnic or national communities of the 'tribes' (*Stämme*) represented by the great duchies.[1] While neither *Treue* nor *Stämme* now look as convincing as they did,[2] a latent conflict of opinion about the development of feudo-vassalic institutions remains unresolved. On the one hand, words like *Lehen* (or *Lehn*) and *Vasall* are used of the entire period of the middle ages, while the rules of feudal law are often stated as if they can be assumed

[1] See e.g. Mitteis, 'Land und Herrschaft'; Kienast, *Fränkische Vasallität*.
[2] Graus, 'Über die sogenannte germanische Treue' and 'Herrschaft und Treue'; Wenskus, 'Probleme'; Kroeschell, 'Verfassungsgeschichte' (and cf. Reynolds, *Kingdoms and Communities*, 236–7, 252–6, 289–90).

to have been in existence throughout.[3] On the other, some historians see
feudo-vassalic relations and institutions as spreading into Germany from
France relatively late, so that Germany only became fully feudalized from
the twelfth century.[4] The issue seems not to have aroused open controversy, perhaps because feudo-vassalic terminology and institutions in
Germany have attracted less attention recently than they have elsewhere,
except from legal historians working on later medieval jurisdiction. For
them it is natural to start from the premiss that *Lehnrecht* was a system of
rules that existed from the beginning of their period, having grown naturally out of the *Lehnswesen* of the earlier middle ages. Given my doubts
about the whole idea of a package of feudo-vassalic relations with its own
technical terms, it might be expected that I should consider a relative lack
of new interest in the stages of its development to be no loss. It does, however, mean that I have been able to find fewer surveys and discussions of
the development of supposedly feudo-vassalic institutions and vocabulary
in post-Carolingian centuries of the sort that have provided useful guides
to the sources elsewhere.

Some of the problems with which German medieval historians have
been more preoccupied are highly relevant to my subject, such as the
ancient Germanic or merely feudal character of fidelity or *Treue*, the relation between nobility and freedom, the change from government through
interpersonal links to territorial government, and the origin of the 'territorial states' of late medieval Germany. I have found some difficulties
in making use of the learning devoted to them. The words used, *Herrschaft* and *Gefolgschaft*, *Altfreie*, *Edelfreie*, *Königsfreie*, and *Gemeinfreie*,
*Personenverbandsstaat* and *Flächenstaat*, are peculiar to German history,
and, as I pointed out at the beginning of the last chapter, the use of different terminologies for different countries makes comparisons difficult.
These words, moreover, now carry so much historiographical baggage that
it is quite hard for someone brought up in the very different (and also idio-
syncratic) British tradition to understand what is under discussion, let
alone to evaluate the arguments.[5] The use of mid-North-Sea formations
like 'stem-duchy' or 'tradition' (for a gift or conveyance) seems to me to
compound the problems. I shall therefore use ordinary modern English

---

[3] The use of *Lehen* goes back to the nineteenth century: e.g. headings to royal charters in the
MGH *Diplomata*. For the rules, see e.g. *Handwörterbuch*, ii. 203–5, 465–7, 1698–1701, 1704–10,
1714–17, 1731, 1725–34.

[4] e.g. Schulze, *Grundstrukturen*, i. 63–7, though cf. e.g. Maurer, *Herzog*, 137–48.

[5] Reuter, 'New History' and *Germany*, and Freed, 'Reflections', explain some of the background to the problems while Reuter, 'Imperial Church System', bridges the gap on one subject.
Cf. Kroeschell, 'Verfassungsgeschichte'. Articles in *Handwörterbuch* on the words used above
provide short guides to some of the arguments, though from inside the tradition.

words as far as possible, adding the German words that I am trying to translate in order to enable the reader to see what I am doing. In order to facilitate comparisons I shall, for instance, translate *imperium* and *regnum* as empire and kingdom rather than as *Reich*, and refer loosely but, I hope, comprehensibly to charters (as I do in other chapters) rather than to diplomata. One word I have not felt able to translate is *ministerialis*. Because the category of people described as *ministeriales*, that is non-menial servants and administrators who were classified during the eleventh and twelfth centuries as unfree, had no exact parallel in the other countries I am concerned with, there seems to be no word for it in other languages than Latin or German (*Dienstmänner*, *Ministerialen*). 'Ministerial' is sometimes used, but it is not a current word in English and does not seem very helpful.[6]

## 9.2. *Before 911*

Most of what needs to be said here for my purposes about political and property relations in the kingdom of the East Franks before 911 has been said in chapter 4. The Franks east of the Rhine came less and later under Roman influence, including the influence of the church, than those in Gaul, but by the eighth century, when information about them becomes less inadequate, their practices and norms do not seem to have been radically different. As for the other peoples who became part of Louis the German's kingdom in 843, the problem is that almost all the relevant information about them, whether in law-codes or charters, comes from a period when they had already come under Frankish domination or influence, so that it is dangerous to argue back to earlier conditions.[7] Without in any way implying that there were no substantial differences in the customs and polities of the Alemanni, Bavarians, Saxons, Thuringians, and Frisians, and indeed of other local groups between and among them,[8] it seems nevertheless possible to deduce that all their societies and their ideas of property fell within the same broad category that seems to have covered the other societies of early medieval Europe that have so far been discussed. That is to say, they formed predominantly agricultural societies which were highly unequal but in which both nobles and lesser free men—and sometimes women—could have rights in land that the society regarded as similar and similarly deserving of protection.

To take the point about stratification first, all the societies in what later became the kingdom of Germany about which we have any relevant information seem to have recognized different ranks that could roughly be ren-

---

[6] For English readers: Arnold, *German Knighthood*; Freed, 'Nobles, Ministerials'.
[7] Schott, 'Stand des Leges-Forschung'.      [8] Reuter, *Germany*, 51–69.

dered as nobles, free men, and the unfree, with probably a good many grey areas in between. The Saxons may have placed a particularly wide gulf between nobles and free men in terms of wergeld (the value placed on someone's life), but the ninth-century story that intermarriage between classes was punishable in Saxony by death looks a little improbable, at least as a generally enforced rule.[9] On the other hand, whereas the Saxons seem to have formed a kind of aristocratic republic, the Thuringians had been a kingdom before they were conquered by the Franks in the sixth century and the Bavarians continued to have a duke who was very like a king until the end of the eighth. The eighth-century Bavarian polity also included *grafiones*, presumably serving under the duke, who looked like counts to Paul the Deacon.[10] In 769 the duke had servants (*servi principis*) called *adalscalhae*.[11] Whether they were the same as the counts or *grafiones*, included them, or were entirely separate, is unclear. We may guess that they constituted the kind of bodyguard or following that customarily evokes ideas of vassalage or of the Germanic retinue or war-band (*Gefolgschaft*). Their duties may have been military or administrative or both. The men whom a Frankish chronicler called Duke Tassilo's *vassi* in 788 may have been *adalscalhae*, but that does not mean that their position and duties were the same as those of royal *vassi* in the much larger and more highly organized Frankish kingdom.[12] Even if they had been, what we know of Frankish *vassi* makes it misleading to deduce that any properties that *adalscalhae* (or, for the matter of that, any other Bavarian nobles) enjoyed were fiefs (*Lehensgüter*) granted by the duke.[13]

The meagre evidence of laws and early charters suggests that inherited property that deserved the full protection of the law was envisaged in all these societies as belonging to an apparently quite wide section of the population, not merely to nobles, let alone to the duke or king, if any. The duties that people owed, whether explicitly in respect of their property or not, probably varied according to status. Nobles and free men probably owed some kind of military service. Those at the bottom end of freedom or semi-freedom may have had more menial and heavier obligations, but

[9] *Leges Saxonum*, 52–6 (c. 14–17); Ruodolfus, *Translatio*, 675.
[10] Paul, *Hist. Langobardorum*, 200 (V. 36).
[11] *Concilia*, ii (1), no. 15, c. 7 (for the date: Störmer, *Früher Adel*, 15). Störmer, 16–18, suggests that *adalscalhae* may have been the same as the *barschalken* referred to elsewhere, but, apart from the puzzling use of *servi*, they look superior to them. Unless surely misleading analogies with much later developments in the status of *ministeriales* are brought in, the prefix *adal* suggests that *servi* here may mean servants, without any connotation of personal unfreedom as apparently understood in this period.
[12] *Ann. Regni Francorum*, 80. Tassilo's relations with the Franks are discussed in chapter 4 (index: Tassilo).
[13] Störmer, *Früher Adel*, 16.

this did not necessarily mean that they thereby lost all rights of inheritance and protection by law and custom.[14] By the eighth century the word alod was used occasionally in non-Frankish areas.[15] Whatever word was used for land in Latin—*alodium, proprium, proprietas, res*, or anything else—it seems to have been thought of, like Frankish alods, as normally belonging to an individual or a small group of close kin, like brothers or a father and his sons, who had inherited it. The rules of inheritance probably varied both between different societies and according to the judgement of those concerned in individual cases. So did rules about the alienation of land. The laws emphasize gifts to the church as the most obvious and likely form of alienation, but sales to others are mentioned in the Saxon and Bavarian codes and could be inferred from the Thuringian laws.[16] The problem posed by gifts and sales in all these societies, as in others like them, was to reconcile the rights of the current owner and the good of his soul with the rights of his heirs or joint owners. Dividing the inheritance of which part was to be alienated was the answer put forward in some of the laws. Another, presumably, was to get the consent of possible heirs. Although there may have been differences between the different societies in the degree of freedom to alienate that they allowed at any one period, the variations in what the surviving codes allow may have less to do with differences between established norms in each society than with the cases that happened to provoke the recorded legislation. Property that the donors had acquired rather than inherited is mentioned occasionally in early Bavarian records of church lands, but they do not necessarily imply that it was more freely alienable.[17]

Although clerical influence must have lain behind statements that any free man could give his land to the church without let or hindrance, requests made by churches to whatever person or persons seemed best suited to protect their property may explain the many ducal consents to gifts in the early records of the bishoprics of Salzburg and Freising. The duke's permission is not invariably recorded for all the gifts from nobles and free men that were listed at Salzburg in the late eighth century.[18] Whether it was nevertheless given or was considered necessary it is impossible to say. If it was, what has already been said about the development of traditions of

[14] *Concilia*, ii (1), no. 15, c. 5; *Lex Baiwariorum*, 286–90, 352, 402, 442–5 (I. 13, VII. 5, XII. 8, XVI. 17).
[15] *Mittellateinisches Wörterbuch*, i. 493–6.
[16] *Leges Alamannorum*, 24 (I. 1, II); *Lex Baiwariorum*, 268–70, 351–2, 402, 428–45 (I, VII. 5, XII. 8, XV. 9–10, XVI); *Leges Saxonum*, 71–4, 78–81 (c. 41–8, 61–4); *Lex Thuringorum*, 123–33, 138 (c. 26–30, 32–4, 54).
[17] e.g. *Trad. Freising*, nos. 77, 136, 336; *Salzburger UB*, i, pp. 19–20, 35.
[18] *Salzburger UB*, i, pp. 1–52.

consent-giving elsewhere suggests that that need not imply that the property of either nobles or free men constituted anything that it is useful to call ducal fiefs. The ruling by a council of 769 that what was given by the prince to nobles should remain with them and be under their power for them to leave to their descendants presumably meant just that: it became their full property and part of their inheritance.[19] Some free Bavarians may nevertheless have had less control over their property than others. Among the Salzburg donors listed in about 790 some, including some not explicitly noted as noble, were said to be *potestativi*.[20] What greater validity, if any, this gave to their grants, or what, if anything, it implies about the nature of the rights and obligations attached to the property before they gave it, is unclear. In the Saxon laws a free man who had been under the *tutela* of a noble, and was then sent into exile and needed to sell his inheritance, had to give first refusal to his *tutor*. If the law reflects conditions before the Frankish conquest it may indicate that some nobles in republican Saxony had acquired the kind of control over lesser free men and their property that elsewhere might more probably belong to a king.[21]

If both nobles and free men enjoyed what were thought of as complete rights over their property (subject to the rights of their heirs), that does not mean that it was not confiscatable. Predictably, given the obvious authority of the duke in Bavaria, the crimes for which someone's property could be forfeit to him (*res eius infiscentur in publico*) were carefully specified. In the eighth century the duke also apparently got property that was left without heirs.[22] The Bavarian ruling of 769 that the wife of a noble should not lose her property for her husband's treason illustrates the difficulty of interpreting legislation under the conditions of customary law. It was just the sort of rule that might have been accepted in principle anywhere in medieval Europe: Otto II would legislate to the same effect for all his faithful subjects (*subditi nostri fideles*) two hundred years later.[23] The principle was probably enunciated in 769 and 976 because influential women (or women belonging to influential families) had recently suffered. In practice rulers in many countries and at whatever level must often have ignored it.

By the ninth century all these polities were incorporated into the Frankish empire and thereby subjected to many of the same political pressures. The variation in local economies and traditions must have affected relations between kings and nobles, whether indigenous or immigrants,

[19] *Concilia*, ii (1), no. 15, c. 8.
[20] *Salzburger UB*, i, pp. 1–52, discussed in Störmer, *Früher Adel*, 13–28.
[21] *Leges Saxonum*, 81 (c. 64); cf. 62 (c. 25–6) for the killing of one's lord.
[22] *Lex Baiwariorum*, 291–3, 430 (II. 1, XV. 10); cf. *Leges Alamannorum*, 84–5 (c. 23–4); *Concilia*, ii (1), no. 15, c. 9.
[23] *Concilia*, ii (1), no. 15, c. 11; *Dip. Otto II*, no. 130.

and between nobles and lesser free men, but the evidence suggests that political and property relations fell within the general pattern sketched in chapter 4. Great nobles might serve the king as counts or margraves while lesser men served as *vassi*. The normal form of property for both remained what they had inherited or otherwise acquired with what were thought of as full rights, while some held land as one of the various forms of benefice discussed in chapter 4. As I argued there, a count's benefice seems to have consisted of his office and the royal land, probably or mainly in his county, that he looked after ex officio. Both office and land were entrusted to him on quite different terms from those on which small estates on church or royal land were granted to *vassi*. East of the Rhine the areas within which counts officiated are obscure,[24] but however they were defined and whether or not they changed from time to time, counts were presumably expected to do much the same work as they did in the rest of the empire: that is, they were supposed to look after royal property and royal interests, raise forces for the emperor or king, and preside over the more important local assemblies.

Louis the German's lands suffered from the same divided loyalties and interests as the rest of the divided empire, but in some ways his problems were less acute than those of his brothers. His long external frontiers offered as many possibilities of tribute-taking and conquest as of hostile invasion. The problems of internal control and communication that confronted him and his successors may have been exacerbated by the presence of a smaller pool of literate servants than there was in Italy or the western kingdom, but it is not clear that that was so.[25] Writing was in any case only one tool of government and not the most important. The potential tension between royal and comital authority may be implied in the anger that confronted Louis when he had the *vassus* of a count blinded, but it was apparently the king's sons, not the count, who protested.[26] Whatever the rights and wrongs of that case, there must often have been times when the enterprise and ability that counts needed to display might seem a threat to their king. Louis dismissed counts on occasion, and so, despite their greater difficulties, did some of his Carolingian successors.[27] The capitulary of Quierzy (877) is often cited as a step on the path, supposedly so damaging to royal authority, that turned counties into hereditary fiefs, but even if it had established the inheritance of counties by right (which it did not), it applied only to Charles the Bald's kingdoms. In the east counts and margraves presumably continued to regard themselves as royal officials, even

---

[24] Reuter, *Germany*, 27, 92–3.
[25] Ibid. 89–90; McKitterick, *Carolingians and the Written Word*, 59 n. 82, 232–5.
[26] *Annales Fuldenses*, 73.          [27] Krah, *Absetzungsverfahren*, 193–248.

if they were left to themselves for much of the time and reckoned, all things being well, to pass on their offices to their sons. Those who by the end of the century called themselves dukes may have got control over counts in what they considered their duchies in a way that could prove a threat to the king, but their position was as yet barely established and their independence would soon be challenged. Some supervision of counts and of local affairs in general still went on. In Louis the Child's reign a count might refer for judgement in the royal court a dispute about royal property in his county that was claimed by some of his *vassalli*, while a margrave might be told to hold a royal enquiry into the allegedly unjust taking of tolls.[28]

## 9.3. *Government and jurisdiction from 911 to the early twelfth century*

In the eastern half of the former empire, unlike the western, the structure of Carolingian government did not break down in the tenth century. The political conditions in which nobles and free men held property and served their king, count, bishop, or anyone else changed, but they changed more slowly and less drastically than they did in the west. That being so, it seems improbable that the eastern kingdom, and even the more recently acquired parts of it, lost the traditions and values of the ninth century to such an extent as to become what German historians call a *Personenverbandsstaat*—a state (or kingdom or society) held together merely or primarily by interpersonal bonds among the nobility. Some general reasons for doubting the appropriateness of this model for any of the early medieval kingdoms with which I am concerned have been mentioned in chapter 2.2. It seems especially unsuitable for a kingdom of the size and power of the East Frankish kingdom. Apart from probabilities, whether one sees the *Personenverbandsstaat* as decentralized and bound together primarily by mutual bonds between nobles with their own pre-existing rights, or as formally centralized, with nobles still enjoying their original rights but accepting that they had gained them by grants from the king, it does not seem to fit the evidence.[29] The decisions to preserve the kingdom that were taken by at least some of its great men in 900, 911, and 918–19, and that apparently did not need to be taken for centuries thereafter, suggest some sense of collective or public solidarity. Although the kingdom seems to have remained without an official name for two hundred years, its subjects can hardly have

---

[28] *Dip. Germ. Karol.* Louis the Child, no. 76; *Capit.* no. 253.
[29] These formulations are taken from Mayer, 'Ausbildung', 463, which seems, though the idea of the *Personenverbandsstaat* has been used and developed since, to be the basic text.

been unaware of its existence.[30] Its victories and the imperial glory of its king must have given those who fought in its armies some kind of collective pride.

Expressions like *res publica* or *reus majestatis* came into more frequent use in chronicles and charters in the eleventh century and later, but there does not seem to be much reason, except for historiographical traditions based on nineteenth-century ideas of social evolution, to suppose that the notions of public welfare and of the heinousness of rebellion against the king who represented it were new to laymen at that time.[31] Nor is there any reason to suppose that the distinction between the property a king had as a member of a family and that which belonged to the kingdom was drawn first by intellectuals rather than by laymen, though it probably only came to notice when a new king was not the obvious and unchallenged heir of the last.[32] While the period between one king's death and another's election or coronation was always liable to be dangerous, there is no evidence that classically inspired ideas of 'transpersonal' government emerged for the first time in the eleventh century, before which the period was normally accepted as a free-for-all in which the kingdom did not exist.[33] New kings were elected to an existing kingdom. Solidarity and public spirit were, of course, never universal and unshaken: apart from all the peasants who neither knew nor cared how much of the dues and services they paid were passed on to the central government, the very power and glory of the king provoked rivalry and rebellion.[34] But this kind of rebellion was quite different from the 'feudal anarchy' of an area where local lords were virtually independent. It is perverse to suppose that the inhabitants of Germany, whether powerful or not, owed obedience to their king only as the 'feudal lord' at the head of a hierarchy of interpersonal links of 'vassalage'.

The word *vassus* seems to have been generally used in tenth-century German documents much as it had been in Carolingian ones—that is, for laymen, apparently of free but not usually very high status, who undertook

---

[30] When I discussed the issue of solidarity in *Kingdoms and Communities*, 289–97, I had not read Müller-Mertens, *Regnum Teutonicum*, on the issue of the name, which I now find very cogent.

[31] Widukind, *Libri*, 95 (II. 36) refers to *res publica* (cf. for the ninth century: Nelson, 'Legislation and Consensus', 219 n. 80); Thietmar, *Chronicon*, 342 (VI. 54) has *reus majestatis* (cf. *Capit.* no. 98, c. 3); cf. Reuter, 'Unruhestiftung', 319–20; Coing, *Römisches Recht*, 35, 95.

[32] Mayer, *Fürsten und Staat*, 215–17; Wadle, *Reichsgut*, 49–57, 100–23, and *Annales Sancti Disibodi*, 23; cf. chapter 8 at n. 34. The distinction was not always observed after 1125: Metz, *Staufische Güterverzeichnisse*, 138–9.

[33] Cf. Beumann, 'Zur Entwicklung'.

[34] Leyser, *Rule and Conflict*, 9–42; Bruno, *Buch*, 25–30.

military and governmental duties for their lords.[35] There is some indication, however, that the words *vassi, vassalli,* or *vasalli*[36] acquired more prestige here, as they did in Italy. The description of vassals as noble in local documents may imply only that they were big fishes in small pools, but at least two tenth-century counts were referred to as *vassi*.[37] During the eleventh century the word became less common in royal charters, though it continued to be used in church records for the lay servants or followers of bishops and abbots. By that time the kind of people who would earlier have been called *vassi* were increasingly often called the *milites, satellites, clientes,* and—of course—the *fideles* of those they served, but that does not mean that all these words meant the same: they focused on different characteristics or functions, not all of which need have been shared by all the people denoted by one or more of the words.[38] Albert of Aachen, telling the story of the first crusade some time after 1119, described how Godfrey of Bouillon was not merely adopted as the son of the Byzantine emperor Alexius, but, with hands joined, made himself Alexius's vassal (*sed etiam in vassalum junctis manibus reddidit*) along with all the other western leaders present.[39] This evokes the traditional historians' concept of vassalage and homage very well, but it is difficult to see how Albert, let alone the crusaders themselves in the 1090s, could have had in mind all the connotations that historians associate with the word and ceremony. For Albert a *vassalus* was probably a subordinate or servant whose entry into service was characteristically marked by a rite involving joined hands, though he does not (for what it is worth) happen to mention an oath. Beyond that, the nature of the relation is quite unclear: rites involving hands were used in many circumstances. One thing seems clear about all uses of the words *vassi, vassallus,* et cetera, at this stage. Though some *vassi* or *vassalli* held property granted to them on various restricted terms none of the words yet seems in itself to imply landholding in such a way as to justify translating it as fiefholder or *Lehnsmann.*

Feudo-vassalic terminology and concepts are peculiarly inappropriate when applied to dukes, margraves, and counts. No doubt many of them felt

---

[35] As I have not found any detailed studies of the use of the words in Germany (though see e.g. Fleckenstein, 'Entstehung') and my own search of the sources has had to be very sketchy, this paragraph must be taken as particularly provisional and tentative.

[36] The spelling with one s, though not, of course, uniform, seems to have begun fairly early in German documents.

[37] *Salzburger UB,* i, no. 15; *Urkunden Eichstätt,* i, no. 4; *Dip. Otto I,* nos. 33, 198; Freed, 'Formation', 76 n.

[38] Among many examples of variant uses, Lampert, *Opera,* 61, calls Count Dietmar's subordinate who accused him of treason his *miles* while Adam of Bremen, *Gesta,* 149, calls him his *satelles.*

[39] Albert, *Historia,* 311 (II. 16).

the kind of personal loyalty that goes with high office and close personal connections and that medieval historians tend to characterize as vassalic or feudal—though, to judge from their rebellions, some evidently did not.[40] The conditions on which they held their benefices, however, are more likely to have approximated, at least at first, to those of their predecessors under the Carolingians than to those that would be worked out later under the influence of academic and professional law.[41] To claim that counts' benefices were offices rather than fiefs or *Lehen* in the sense of late medieval law does not mean that they were part of a closely supervised bureaucracy or that their holders had no rights. Kings with their eyes fixed on conquests in the east or the old middle kingdom, and above all on the imperial crown, were prepared to leave their dukes and counts a pretty free hand. Many dukes and counts were allowed to pass on their offices to their sons, so that some came to think of them as theirs by hereditary right, but even in the mid eleventh century a duke might have to get royal approval of plans for his son's succession.[42] Throughout the tenth and eleventh centuries both dukes and counts who stepped too far out of line were liable to dismissal.[43] The principle that counts and even dukes exercised their authority by delegation was, it seems, not questioned as a principle any more than it was explicitly stated, however much individuals objected to what they saw as royal injustice or tyranny in dismissing individuals from their duchies or counties.[44] The tradition by which the king handed over a banner as a symbol of ducal authority seems to have been established by the beginning of the eleventh century.[45] Counts were presumably appointed with less ceremony but may well have taken some sort of oath and undergone some sort of rite, perhaps very like that which would by the twelfth century be called *hominium* or *homagium*.[46] All these rites were symbols of the delegation of authority in which it is anachronistic to find meanings that they would acquire under a feudal law that would be formulated later in different political circumstances.

Although royal charters that identify land by (among other things) the count in whose county it lay suggest that counts functioned within discrete units of territory, it is not clear that they did. With the passage of time

---

[40] Leyser, *Rule and Conflict*, 9–42; Reuter, *Germany*, 199–208.

[41] Benefices as such are discussed later (9.5).

[42] *Annales Altahenses Maiores*, 799; Hermann of Reichenau, *Chronicon*, 124.

[43] Krah, *Absetzungsverfahren*, 249–372; for Henry IV's reign (not covered by Krah), e.g. Lampert, *Opera*, 113, 124, 149–50; *Dip. Hein. IV*, nos. 386, 388.

[44] Bruno, *Buch*, 25, 30.

[45] Thietmar, *Chronicon*, 245, 278 (V. 2, VI. 3); Bruckauf, *Fahnlehen*, surveys the evidence thereafter.

[46] *Annales Altahenses Maiores*, 801, 804; Scheyhing, *Eide*, surveys the evidence, while fitting it more neatly into later models than I would do.

whatever pattern of counties there had ever been east of the Rhine must have become increasingly complex.[47] One source of complication was the grant of immunities to churches. The grant of whole counties to bishops, on the other hand, presumably made less difference to the pattern, while any impediment to ultimate royal control involved in the permanence and formality of church rights was presumably not very significant until the troubles of the Investiture Contest and its aftermath.[48] Until then bishops and abbots, like lay nobles, held their offices and lands under royal authority, though on rather different terms.[49] Under the Carolingians bishops, like counts, had held their offices as royal benefices. When bishops were appointed to their bishoprics, and presumably *a fortiori* when they were given counties, they probably took oaths and underwent rites of appointment rather like those of their lay colleagues: until the boundary between the spiritual and temporal aspects of their authority came to be argued about, and the nature and implications of rites of appointment were debated and defined, there was nothing particularly secular, let alone 'feudal', about the oaths and ceremonies involved.[50] The arguments about whether bishops should do homage (*hominium*) that developed in Germany early in the twelfth century were about homage done to the king or emperor for what were, for good reason, called *regalia*.[51] Fitting them into the later feudal law as if bishops were a kind of vassal and the king was merely a 'feudal lord' is anachronistic. The debate about the homage or fidelity owed by bishops may well have contributed to the debates of academic lawyers about the obligations of fiefholders, but while the two debates could have started at about the same time in Italy, the debate about bishops surely started first in Germany.

Other changes to counties, however, were by the beginning of the twelfth century making them more suitable to be fitted into ideas of feudal anarchy and of kings as 'mere feudal lords'—when such ideas came to be developed. Formal grants of exemption from comital jurisdiction do not seem to have been made to lay lords before the twelfth century—though that, of course, may be because the charters, if any, have disappeared.[52] Newly settled land, however, whether cleared from forests or conquered from Slavs, was not, it seems, always brought within existing counties. Instead, the lords of such lands sometimes seem to have exercised what was

---

[47] Among the vast literature, e.g. Reuter, *Germany*, 92–3; *Handwörterbuch*, i. 1775–95.
[48] Reuter, 'Imperial Church System'.
[49] For the terms, see the next two sections (9.4–5).
[50] Ekkehard, *Continuatio*, 141; see index: homage; investiture.
[51] Classen, 'Wormser Konkordat'; Fried, 'Regalienbegriff'.
[52] Stengel, *Immunität*, 510, 514, 590, *et passim*, seems to imply that all grants were to churches, though *Dip. Arnulf*, no. 32 is a rare earlier grant to a layman.

effectively comital jurisdiction over their tenants, presumably without formal delegation, in what are sometimes called alodial counties (*Allodialgrafschaften*). Counts—or margraves or dukes—who were accustomed to dividing their own lands between their children might as a matter of course divide their offices when they passed them on too. Count (*Graf*) was thus becoming no more than a title held by nobles who exercised authority, not merely over more or less unfree tenants on their own estates, but over free men within whatever area they could dominate. The counties held by this new kind of count seem not to have been called benefices,[53] while other counties (presumably of the older, royal kind), along with duchies and margravates, continued to be so. So far as people thought about the distinction, they would presumably have seen it, not as one between fief and alod, in the sense that historians use the words, but as between those who held royal office and those who did not. How soon or how far anyone saw a possible threat to royal power in the dichotomy (if they noticed it at all) is unclear. Given the expansion of settlement and the preoccupations of counts on the one hand, and the size of the kingdom and the preoccupations of kings on the other, a good deal may have passed unnoticed. Lords always had some jurisdiction over their less free tenants and subjects and there was no firm dividing line between such tenants and some of the people who normally came under comital authority. By the time the danger to royal authority over counties in general became obvious, the anomalous new counties or quasi-counties may have been sanctified by custom. That may help to explain why historians have had such difficulty in explaining the origin of what they see as a new kind of 'territorial lordship' (*Territorialstaat, Landesherrschaft*) that was coming into existence in the twelfth century. Some of the units of government and jurisdiction that emerge into historical view then and later were based on older counties or the ecclesiastical immunities over which laymen had secured control as advocates of the churches concerned; some were based on authority that nobles were able to exercise over tenants on their 'alodial property' with little contradiction; most, like the similar lordships of France or Italy, probably derived from varied origins, helped by some bullying and fighting along the way. All were as yet very undefined, with plenty of overlaps and sources of conflicts both between rival lords and between lords and subjects.[54] Until the twelfth century, however, the

[53] I deduce this from the references to *Allodialgrafschaften* and the arguments about them that I have read.

[54] e.g. Arnold, *Count and Bishop* and *Princes and Territories*; Heinrich, *Die Grafen von Arnstein*, 245–77; Mitterauer, 'Formen'; Patze, *Entstehung*; Schulze, 'Adelsherrschaft'; Störmer, *Früher Adel*, 392–414, 424–61; Freed, 'Reflections', especially 564–6, 575.

underlying conflict between ideas of delegation and ideas of inherited rights and custom was not, so far as we know, confronted, except, at the very end of the eleventh century, during the conflict over investitures, in relation to the rights of bishops and their churches. If some laymen worried about the validity of their own rights and others worried more about claims made against them, no rules had yet been formulated and recorded by which to decide disputes.

How much kings in the tenth and eleventh centuries were concerned about controlling and supervising their dukes, counts, and margraves, about doing justice among their subjects, or about the internal order of their kingdom in general, is difficult to know. The lack of surviving administrative records, combined with the application of stereotypes about feudal government and about Germany's inevitable disunity, may have created an exaggerated impression of local government as entirely unsupervised by a totally unbureaucratic royal government. It is likely that relatively few records were made and kept before 1100, but there is no reason why the list of forces summoned to Italy by Otto II between 980 and 983 should have been the only one ever made or why it should have been made entirely from unwritten memory.[55] If no records of royal land had been kept for centuries then the amount of it that remained to be recorded in a survey that survives from (probably) the 1130s is remarkable.[56] Grants of royal land suggest that tabs of some sort, whether written or not, had been kept on it: throughout the tenth and eleventh centuries royal charters normally identified properties by *villa*, *pagus*, and the count in whose county it lay. The occasional grant by separate charters of scattered properties that had formerly belonged to one person might even imply that separate reports (whether oral or written) were received from each county or *pagus* before the grant was made.[57] Much royal property had passed into the hands of counts by the twelfth century, but some at least had done so not by embezzlement but by royal grants.[58] Whether or not historians consider such grants to have been royal mistakes, the process looks different from that by which counts in France took over royal property because they became in effect independent rulers of whatever territory they could dominate. However little the counts of Germany had been supervised from the start, and however far royal control slipped in the troubles of the late

---

[55] *Constitutiones*, i, no. 436; cf. Werner, 'Heeresorganisation'; Reuter, 'Imperial Church System', 364 n. In addition to the evidence cited by Werner, ibid. 834–5, *Dip. Frid. I*, no. 44 suggests some record of obligation. On chancery records: Stengel, *Immunität*, 132, 264–82, 335–8.

[56] *Constitutiones*, i, no. 440; Brühl, *Fodrum*, 181–94.

[57] e.g. *Dip. Hein. III*, nos. 157–9, 305, 310–11; cf. *Dip. Otto I*, no. 54.

[58] e.g. *Dip. Hein. I*, no. 36; *Dip. Otto I*, nos. 33, 40, 56, 65, 78, 311, 370; *Dip. Otto III*, nos. 19, 320; Thietmar, *Chronicon*, 228 (V. 7).

eleventh century, the situation here looks quite different. The suggestion that the reason why German kings relied on bishops and abbots for support and service, and made use of unfree servants (*ministeriales*) as soldiers and administrators, was that they could not rely on their great nobles is over-simplified and implausible.[59] They certainly leant heavily on churches, but the services of the clergy were no substitute for those of laymen, while *ministeriales* were useful in war and peace precisely because kings were active and powerful enough to need full-time servants near at hand as well as representatives with more independent responsibility in the localities.[60] The transfer of royal estates from the care of counts to that of *ministeriales* may have been intended to offset the loss of control over counts that is discernible by 1100, but it also foreshadowed the increasing specialization of administration that would appear later in other kingdoms.[61]

What is clear, and contrasts strongly with the situation in France, is that royal assemblies continued to attract the presence of great men, though obviously, given their own responsibilities and the size of the kingdom, not of all great men all the time. Consultation was a sign of power not of weakness.[62] Having to consult one's potential commanders before going to war was normal in the middle ages, just as it was normal to consult them before dismissing any of them from counties or duchies, making large grants, or taking any decision that they would have to help one carry out.[63] Being able to appoint or dismiss dukes or counts did not mean being able to do it without consultation. Since there was an element of election or collective approval in all office-holding, local opinion might need to be considered as well as that of the princes or great men of the realm. Annoying as any of this was to individual kings whose decisions were thwarted,[64] it did not, according to the ideas of the time, detract from royal authority. If German kings were sometimes exceptionally dependent on their great men in order to get elected in the first place, that did not, in this period, seem to hamper them much once they were elected.

Royal assemblies in Germany were primarily concerned with great affairs, including the disciplining of great men and the adjudication of their disputes, but there does not seem to have been any rule that limited royal

---

[59] Bosl, 'Reichsministerialität', 75; cf. Arnold, *German Knighthood*, 209–12; Freed, 'Reflections', 568–9.

[60] Cf. the 'men raised from the dust' in early twelfth-century England: Orderic, *Hist. Eccl.* vi. 16.

[61] Arnold, *Princes and Territories*, 54.     [62] Reynolds, *Kingdoms and Communities*, 302–5.

[63] Krause, 'Königtum'; Krah, *Absetzungsverfahren*, 361–3, suggests that the need for consultation increased in the eleventh century, but the evidence for it as a new norm does not seem strong.

[64] *Mon. Hist. Ducatus Carinthiae*, iii, no. 250.

jurisdiction to such matters. Pleas and complaints could apparently be brought to the king by anyone who could get his ear or the ear of someone with influence.[65] Most justice, however, whether we would call it civil or criminal, was done locally. As a result it followed customs that varied from time to time and from place to place. Differences between the duchies or other old provinces may have been less significant than they would appear when they were written down and argued about later. Categories in customary law were malleable and depended on what was being discussed at the time: sometimes the contrast was between the custom of one lordship or village and another, sometimes between kingdoms, sometimes between what applied to individuals of different status or reputed origin. To see any of this as involving what historians would later call the principle of 'personal' as against 'territorial' law, or a conflict between the two, is overstrained. People of different status were naturally treated differently, while individuals who claimed to live according to customs different from those of the locality they were in were sometimes allowed to follow their own, most often perhaps in matters of inheritance. All the same, since customary law worked through meetings and judgements that held good, so far as they did, for areas of government, it was fundamentally territorial, whether the territory was that of a kingdom, a county, or a village.

Justice concerning free men and their free property should, on Carolingian precedents, have been done in courts or assemblies held by counts or their deputies. Very little is known about such assemblies at this time, but that does not mean that they were not held. So long as counts were in some sense royal officers, they would have needed meetings of some kind to pass on royal orders, raise royal forces and dues, and give a colour of legality to royal confiscations. The judgements of *scabini*, which Otto I's charters, for instance, sometimes cite in justification of confiscations, were presumably made in local assemblies and reported back by counts, even if the vaguer references to 'lawful judgements' in other charters are less easy to pin down.[66] In 1027 disputes about the property of Moosburg abbey were investigated by counts holding *placita* and relying on the verdicts of *scabini* given in the public assembly (*in mallo publico*).[67] At least one German county was identified in the eleventh century not by its count but by what was presumably its meeting-place.[68] As the old counties broke up and new lordships of various sorts appeared, new courts or assemblies were presumably summoned and, if the new unit survived,

[65] Reuter, *Germany*, 215, cites some examples.
[66] A public *mallus* is mentioned in *Dip. Otto I*, nos. 54, 207, a *mallus* held by a church in nos. 85, 100. For other judgements, nos. 52, 59–60, 78, 80, 107, etc.
[67] *Constitutiones*, i, no. 439; cf. *Monumenta Boica*, xxviii (2), no. 116; *Cart. Gorze*, no. 106.
[68] *Handwörterbuch*, i. 1781–2.

became rooted in custom.[69] Given what we know of the procedures of medieval government it seems highly likely that all these meetings dealt with a variety of business, both administrative and judicial, civil and criminal.

Though counts' courts in their Carolingian or post-Carolingian form had been more recently established in Germany than in France, there does not seem to be any evidence that they were less well established and effective or had less control over nobles than they did in the western kingdom. It is true that German charters contain fewer references to local assemblies than do those from France, but this may be because in Germany the great churches that preserved the records which provide our evidence continued to rely for protection on the king. They therefore got their charters from him, even when he was merely confirming grants, exchanges, or other agreements that had been made locally. If dukes and counts had been more independent, churches might have got more charters from them and we might then have witness lists that would have provided as plausible evidence of noble attendance at comital *placita* as we have from France. How effectively dukes, counts, and their officials kept the peace, whether on their own account or as royal officials, we do not know, but, even if kings of Germany did not worry much about local conflicts and disorders that did not threaten their power directly,[70] they must have worried a bit. Enthusiasm for the 'peace movement' of the eleventh century has led some historians to write as if the ideal of peace was invented by the French clergy of the time and as if the 'feudal nobility' constituted its chief enemies.[71] But all agricultural societies need peace, and all rulers of such societies need a measure of law and order if they are to maintain their authority. Eleventh-century German kings on occasion explicitly enjoined peace on their subjects. Even when they did not use the word, they may have been as successful in frightening wrongdoers into behaving themselves as any 'peace movement' without royal authority could be. Feuds and self-help, whether among nobles or commoners, were not peculiar to Germany or, so far as we know, more destructive of peace there than elsewhere.

Part of the difficulty of deciding how far nobles were outside any effective jurisdiction and control comes from the impossibility of defining status groups in this period. People of relatively high status and local power are always harder to control and bring to court. Nobles who had their own counties, or exercised a comparable jurisdiction over church land

[69] For *placita* in the first half of the twelfth century, e.g. *Cod. Dip. Sax. Reg.* pt. 1, i, no. 60; *Reg. Dip. Thuringiae*, ii, no. 55; *Urkundenbuch Magdeburg*, no. 264; *Chron. Saint-Mihiel*, no. 89; *Monumenta Boica*, i, pp. 53–5; Franz, *Quellen*, no. 80; cf. Wibald, *Epistolae*, no. 167 (p. 284).
[70] Reuter, 'Unruhestiftung' and *Germany*, 215–16.
[71] A view cogently challenged by Martindale, 'Peace and War'.

as advocates, may well have refused to attend other courts in the area or submit to their jurisdiction. Only the king's court could deal with the really big offenders. There does not, however, seem to be any contemporary evidence to suggest either that the nobility was more defined and privileged in Germany than elsewhere or that everyone who belonged to families that historians now call the high nobility (*Hochadel*) was automatically free of comital jurisdiction. Such ideas derive from applying to this period rules about nobility and freedom that would only be worked out later in different legal and political conditions.[72]

So far as jurisdiction over property is concerned, it seems likely that the less free peasants had to take their disputes to their lords' courts, while the more free, including those whom historians might classify as the lesser nobility, went on going in the first instance to whatever court or assembly seemed to hold authority in the area, whether it was held by a duke, margrave, count, advocate, or his deputy. In 1135 the monk Ortlieb told how Count Rudolf, the father of one of the founders of Ortlieb's abbey of Zwiefalten in Swabia, had acquired a piece of property some time around the middle of the eleventh century.[73] The owner, who was paralysed, had given it to Rudolf, to whom he was apparently related, on condition that Rudolf looked after him as his son until his death. A sister of the invalid later turned up and put in a claim to the land. According to Ortlieb it was out of sheer mercy that Rudolf gave her a bit of her brother's land, although, he says, according to those skilled in law she had lost her hereditary rights through leaving her husband. Rudolf, it seems, intended the gift to be only for the sister's life, for he left the whole estate to his sons as part of his own inheritance and *proprietas*. No one, according to Ortlieb, raised any objection at the time in any meeting of dukes or counts (*nullo reposcente in quovis colloquio ducum aut comitum*). The story can be interpreted in various ways. Ortlieb was concerned to defend Rudolf's title, on which that of Zwiefalten depended, and his account shows a count getting away with what may well have been sharp practice. His reference to assemblies is vague: perhaps there were no regular courts with anything like adequate jurisdiction for Rudolf to worry about. On the other hand, Ortlieb's justification, however disingenuous, would not have worked even for himself if it was unenvisageable that complaints about free property should be brought against powerful people like Rudolf and his sons to assemblies held by the duke or by a count or counts. Complaints against less

[72] Particularly rigid divisions of German society are suggested e.g. by Bloch, *Feudal Society*, 180, 336, though cf. 268–9; Leyser, 'Frederick Barbarossa', 167; Freed, 'Origins', 213. They might be inferred from Ficker, *Vom Heerschilde*, but note 215–24; cf. Mitteis, *Lehnrecht und Staatsgewalt*, 437–8.
[73] Ortlieb, *Zwiefalter Chroniken*, 22–4.

413

powerful people with free property would presumably be brought rather more readily to the same sort of assembly.

The argument put forward here is not that the Saxon and Salian kings ruled a peaceful and well-ordered kingdom, with everyone doing what the king told them. No medieval kingdom was like that. But these kings would not have had the reputation they had, or raised the armies they did, if they had had no control over their dukes and counts, or if that control had gone no further than the dukes and counts. For many people of middle rank, including the soldiers or servants of great men whom historians call their vassals, relations with immediate superiors must have been more important than any they had with the king, but that was a matter of fact rather than of obligation. Whether or not general oaths were regularly taken locally from free men, as they were supposed to be taken under the Carolingians, the oaths sworn to a new king at his coronation look as though they were thought of as taken by great men and others present as representatives of the people at large.[74] Everyone owed fidelity to the king.

Kings on occasion exercised jurisdiction over those whom historians call their under-vassals (*Aftervasallen*) as well as over dukes and counts. When Otto I's brother Henry got him to reverse his punishment of Henry's *vassi*, the king's right to impose the punishment in the first place seems to have been implicitly accepted.[75] When the margrave Gero's *milites* insulted a bishop, Henry II made Gero purge himself by oath and ordered the trial and punishment of the guilty.[76] If dukes were left to appoint counts within their duchies, the counts may have been encouraged to feel more dependent on them than on the king, but it did not always work like that. Duke Ernest of Swabia failed to carry the counts of Swabia with him in rebellion against Conrad II, apparently because the faith they had promised to him was against everyone except the king and they thought their duty to the king was paramount.[77] Godfrey of Lotharingia, in his effort to secure his father's duchy, is said to have imposed an oath for three years on all the men of his land to support him against anyone he wanted.[78] Presumably this included supporting him against the king, against whom he was rebelling, but it was as yet probably more usual either to assume, as the counts of Swabia did, that one's duty to the king was excepted from an oath to anyone else, or to except it explicitly.[79] The *militia* of Bamberg who excused themselves anxiously for not answering Henry IV's summons to

---

[74] Widukind, *Libri*, 34, 63–4; *Dip. Hein. II*, no. 34; Wipo, *Opera*, 24; Scheyhing, *Eide*, 70, 78.
[75] *Dip. Otto I*, nos. 59, 135.     [76] Thietmar, *Chronicon*, 388, 390 (VI. 96–8).
[77] Wipo, *Opera*, 40. Maurer, *Herzog*, 147–8 called the counts Ernest's *Vasallen* and Conrad's *Aftervasallen*, while Bosl, *Frühformen*, 277–8, translated the faith they had promised as *Lehenstreue*.
[78] *Annales Altahenses Maiores*, 801.     [79] *Urkundenbuch mittelrhein. Terr.*, no. 394.

military service may have been disingenuous in their reasons, but their need to make excuses implies a direct obligation to the king.[80]

In 1119 William of Champeaux told Henry V that he was sure that Henry would suffer no diminution of his kingdom if he gave up investing bishops. When William had become bishop of Châlons he had, he said, received nothing from the hand of the king of France but he nevertheless served his king faithfully.[81] Hesso Scholasticus, who tells the story, suggests that William's argument was conclusive, but, however much royal power over the church in Germany had suffered in the past fifty years, emperors still exerted more authority over the appointment of more bishops in the kingdom of Germany and got more service from them than Louis VI did in France. Even if the muddle of more or less autonomous local jurisdictions was now rather like that of France, the later recovery of royal authority in France shows that that need not have impeded something similar in Germany. However that may be, and whatever one makes of the changes in central and local government that can be dimly seen in the records of the tenth and eleventh centuries, it is not very illuminating to characterize them as either a progress or a descent to feudalism. At no point between 900 and the mid twelfth century will the kingdom fit models of 'feudal anarchy' that are based either on France in the same period or on late medieval Germany. The most important evidence against the dominance of feudo-vassalic values and relations must come, however, from an investigation of the rights and obligations of free and noble property.

## 9.4.  *Full property from 911 to the early twelfth century*

It has long been taken as a fundamental fact of German medieval history that much noble property was alodial.[82] While it is almost certainly right that most nobles, and indeed most free men, held their land, at least until the twelfth century, with what were then thought of as full rights, the characterization of such rights as alodial suggests that their constitutional significance has been assessed in the light of later law and still later historiography. The contrasting categories of alod and fief only began to be applied to noble property in Germany in the twelfth century and the distinction gained its full constitutional importance later in the middle ages. The idea that kings of Germany based their power over their greater

[80] *Briefsammlung der Zeit Heinrichs IV*, no. 35.          [81] *Libelli de Lite*, iii. 21–2.

[82] *Handwörterbuch*, i. 121; Gillingham, *Kingdom of Germany*, 13. 'Alod' and 'alodial' now normally have double l in both German and English. My choice of spelling is explained in chapter 3 n. 1.

subjects on the position of supreme feudal lord (*oberster Lehnsherr*), so that
'alodholders' were more or less independent, can be deduced from pre-
twelfth-century sources only by reading them in the light of later theories.
The word alod was used in Germany during this period, but less often than
*proprietas, proprium*, or *hereditas*. All four, along with *possessio, predium, pat-
rimonium*, and even *dos*, were explained as *eigen, eigin*, et cetera in early
glosses. As late as 1286 *allodium* was enough of a foreign (or lawyer's) word
in Saxony for *liberum allodium* to be explained in a charter as *ain friez aigen*.
How many of the increasingly frequent references to alods from the twelfth
century are attributable to the influence of academic and professional law
and how much to the multiplication of documents it is impossible to say.
The two are in any case closely connected. The varying range of connotations that can be found in later medieval sources show that the coming of
more professional law did not impose uniformity of usage.[83]

Two historians have argued recently that in the tenth and eleventh centuries *hereditas* and *proprietas* sometimes represented rather different categories of property. H. C. Faussner maintained that from the reign of
Henry I royal grants made *jure hereditario* to great nobles conveyed something less than the rights they enjoyed in the estates they had inherited *jure
proprietatis*, though something more than attached to a normal benefice. An
estate granted *jure hereditario* would be inherited, but subject (under what
Faussner called *jus beneficiarium*[84]) to possible reversion and need for confirmation at the death of both the king and the grantee.[85] Karl Leyser also
thought that royal grants gave, or sometimes gave, less than what nobles
held in their own inheritances, though he referred to such grants as made
'in propriety' and stressed slightly different restraints: though the beneficiary would be able to alienate what came from the king more freely than
he could his inherited land, he was also more liable to forfeiture, while
inheritance was more restricted so that reversions were more likely.[86]
Some of the implications of these arguments for specific rights and obligations will be discussed below, but both, as they stand, seem to depend too
much on subtle and consistent distinctions for an age of customary law.
How long the origins of individual estates were remembered, and how far
memories agreed, is unknown.[87] Whatever the variations in the rights and

---

[83] *Deutsches Rechtswörterbuch*, i. 486–502, ii. 1321–7; *Mittellateinisches Wörterbuch*, i. 482–96.
Cf. Köbler, 'Eigen', and Ebner, *Das freie Eigen*.

[84] Faussner, 'Verfügungsgewalt', 347 n. and 'Herzog und Reichsgut', 23, 26–7.

[85] Faussner, 'Verfügungsgewalt', especially 347–55, 403, 416–19.

[86] Leyser, 'Crisis', especially 414, 426–40. The evidence for distinction between *hereditas* and
*proprietas* in p. 427 n. 1 is not clear to me. If the point is that the property remained in some way
the king's *after* the grant, that is not what the documents quoted say.

[87] See e.g. Störmer, *Früher Adel*, 277.

obligations of what was thought of as full property, they are unlikely to have been reflected at the time in the consistent use of particular words for what were then consistently recognized as separate categories.[88] Devising categories that are similar to those found later in a more academic legal culture (though not quite the same), and postulating the existence of unrecorded rules about them, makes the sources of this period harder rather than easier to understand. Occam's law is against it.

Before considering the general rights and obligations of what looks like full property, it may be useful to consider two kinds of property that have often been considered as special and were indeed in different ways special at the time. The first is royal property. In principle the title of the king or emperor to estates that he held was better than anyone else's: not only was there no one to confiscate it or demand services from it, but he was—if not quite the sole ultimate judge of title—a powerful president over those who were supposed to judge. Restraints on the king's power to dispose of property are mentioned, but in rhetorical or controversial contexts: polemic produced by the Investiture Contest cannot be taken as statements of recognized and agreed law. All the same, when Guy of Ferrara suggested that each king's grants of secular property needed to be renewed by his successors, he was using for his own purposes an idea that, however often it was rejected in practice, had been around for a long time. Otto III (or Gerbert on his behalf) alluded to it in 998.[89] In 1001 another of Otto's charters mentioned the need for consultation about royal gifts. Whether this applied only to property of the kingdom (*Reichsgut*) as opposed to that of the royal family (*Hausgut*) is not made clear here but looks clear in a charter of 1020.[90] So long as those who needed to be consulted were as loosely defined as they were in this period, however, a competent king would usually be able to get adequate consent. Using the *Reichsgut/Hausgut* distinction might be a convenient way round particular objections, but the application of the distinction to particular properties may have been arguable anyway. The suggestion that exchanges were used to overcome serious restrictions on alienation by ensuring that the royal estate remained undiminished is implausible: the vast majority of exchanges made by royal charter, if not all of them, were of ecclesiastical, not royal, property. The record of royal grants shows that royal property, including *Reichsgut*, was not inalienable in practice and that it could be granted with apparently full

[88] *Hereditare* and *proprietare* both seem to have the sense of giving (with apparently full rights) in *Dip. Hein. II*, no. 370: it is tempting to see their combined use here as designed for elegant variation.

[89] *Libelli de Lite*, i. 564–5; *Constitutiones*, i, no. 23.

[90] *Dip. Otto III*, no. 390; *Dip. Hein. II*, no. 433; this distinction was taken up by Gerhoh of Reichersburg: *Libelli de Lite*, iii. 152.

rights to a wide range of individual lay persons as well as to churches.[91] If there was a principle or norm of inalienability, then it was so often breached in grants made in the most formal way that one must suppose the existence of a contrary and more widely accepted principle or norm—and whatever the conflict of norms, the king was in a good position to decide which to apply.[92]

Consideration of church property in Germany has been complicated by the concept of the 'proprietary church' (*Eigenkirche*). Whether it is applied to parish churches, or to monasteries (*Eigenklöster*), or is extended to the king's rights over bishoprics (*Eigenbistümer*),[93] the concept depends on the interpolation into a quite different society of a crude form of nineteenth-century ideas of property and power.[94] The premiss seems to be that all power is based on property rights and that property rights form a single, self-defining entity. But when people granted a whole church, or rights in it, *in proprium* or *in proprietate*, when churches were bought and sold, or when Abbo of Fleury objected to people calling a church theirs,[95] they were surely none of them thinking in these terms. The rights that kings and lords had over churches do not seem to have been envisaged as the same as those they had over secular property, any more than the rights they had in castles were the same as those they had over unfree tenants or servants, despite the use of the word *proprietas* in connection with any of them. Chapels inside people's houses were no doubt 'theirs' in a relatively obvious sense, but the control exercised over most so-called proprietary churches was more like that of a ruler than an owner, with the additional flavour that the ruler often saw himself as a benefactor and was supposed to be the special protector of the beneficiary. Powerful benefactors and protectors in any society are inclined to loom over their benefactions: appointing subordinates is an obvious exercise of benevolent authority that may easily slide into making use of the appointment for patronage and profit.[96] Taking some of the income one has generously made available (which may, on second thoughts, look unnecessarily large), especially during a vacancy, may seem no more than a reasonable return for one's generosity and trouble. All this applies equally to the benefactors of charities in modern society and to relations of power and protection in many societies. It does not need to be explained in terms of either Germanic or feudal values or of anything else peculiar to the early middle ages. The

[91] Cf. the contrary arguments of Faussner, 'Verfügungsgewalt', 366–78.
[92] *Monumenta Boica*, xxviii (2), no. 116, suggests a policy of preserving the royal estate rather than a rule against alienation.
[93] Tellenbach, *Church*, 76–81, 288–9; cf. Reuter, 'Imperial Church System', 351.
[94] See chapter 3.2–3.      [95] Abbo, *Apologeticus*, 465–6.
[96] Southern, *Making of the Middle Ages*, 124.

concept of the proprietary church, like that of feudalism itself, with which it is often closely connected,[97] discourages the investigation of a wide range of relations of property and power.

The Carolingian system by which counts looked after the property of great churches and the emperor borrowed bits of it for the defence of the realm was inherited by the kings of the East Franks or Germans. One of the most striking signs of the survival of Carolingian ideas and Carolingian power in the eastern kingdom is the way that kings continued to grant church property to their followers in much the same kind of benefices *verbo regis* as the Carolingian emperors had used.[98] If the conditions of such grants were less well recorded it was perhaps partly because they were assumed. The practice was open to abuse, as it had always been: beneficiaries kept land longer than the church wanted or, perhaps, than the king may have intended, while dukes and counts granted benefices on church land for their own purposes as well as the king's.[99] None of this meant that churches and their lands belonged to the king in the same way as either his personal property or the lands he held as king. Nor did occasional references to the benefices (i.e. benefits or favours) granted to churches by kings mean that bishops, abbots, or their churches held their lands and jurisdictions as what historians call benefices or fiefs.[100] The first reference to the property of bishoprics or abbeys as fiefs was said in 1901 to date from the thirteenth century.[101] I have happened on one possible reference before then: in 1165 the bishop of Cambrai said that he held a certain fief by hereditary right from the count of Hainaut. Whether this means that he held it as bishop rather than as an individual is unclear.[102] The fidelity that bishops and abbots owed to the king and the oaths they took to him did not imply that they held their land with less than the normal full rights. Kings might loom over churches and abuse their authority over church property, but that property still belonged to God and his saints with as full rights as it was possible to envisage. It was normally granted *in proprietate* or *in proprium* and for ever—so much for ever that it must not be alienated. The

[97] e.g. Pöschl, *Regalien*, 93–6; Auer, 'Kriegdienst', 50, 60; Werner, 'Heeresorganisation', 840–1; Tellenbach, *Church*, 81.
[98] *Urkundenbuch Hersfeld*, i, no. 37; *Dip. Otto I*, nos. 122, 287; *Dip. Otto II*, no. 57; *Urkundenbuch mittelrhein. Terr.*, i, no. 382; Bruno, *Buch*, 103. See also below, at n. 179.
[99] *Dip. Otto II*, no. 57; *Chron. St-Mihiel*, 30; *Dip. Hein. III*, no. 157; Bloch, 'Urkunden S. Vanne', no. 56.
[100] e.g. *Dip. Otto I*, no. 286. On the varied use of the word: Lesne, 'Diverses Acceptions'; *Mittellatein. Wörterbuch*, i. 1433–41.
[101] Boerger, *Belehnung*, 45–53. Scheyhing, *Eide*, 84–9, counters this by asserting the identity of benefice and fief.
[102] *Dip. Frid. I*, no. 493: at this date and in this context *feodum* could be used without implications of restricted rights.

rule of canon law that church property should not be permanently alienated was much clearer than any rule that kings should not alienate the property they held as kings:[103] hence all the exchanges of church property that the king, as protector of the church, solemnly confirmed.[104]

The rights and obligations that normally attached to the property of free lay people look in some respects fairly like those in other countries, though, as usual, there are some differences. Again as usual, both similarities and differences in the evidence may be more clearly seen when it is compared with the evidence from elsewhere rather than interpreted in the light of assumptions about what it ought to say according to the rules of feudalism. Here I have to discuss rights and obligations in general terms, ignoring the mass of local variations of custom almost entirely, but my impression is that the variations were more often those of detail and borderline rather than of substantive norms. I start from the premiss that obligations were at first owed to the king, and shall, for the sake of simplicity, treat them as such throughout. It should, however, be borne in mind that, in so far as counts were left unsupervised, obligations owed to them as representatives of the king might come to be owed to them on their own accounts. As counties broke up and counts became in effect hereditary lords of more or less independent lordships the tendency was accelerated. Lesser landowners who by the twelfth century had come under the jurisdiction of a local lord (whatever his title) may thus have suffered from some erosion of their rights, as well as increase in their burdens, as they did in similar circumstances elsewhere. As in France, local lords may have felt more pressure to control the alienation of their subjects' property than a king would do, and may have enjoyed more freedom to confiscate it than they did when the subjects could appeal to an assembly outside the lord's control. Such evidence as I have seen, however, suggests that, even if the boundaries between the old categories of property shifted, they remained more distinct than they did in much of France.

Royal charters that granted land *in proprium* or *in proprietatem* do not always say that it was granted for ever or that it was to be inherited, but many give the beneficiary free power to have, give, sell, and do what he wishes with it.[105] Given the apparent lack of a formulary by which charters were drawn up, it seems to be a reasonable inference that this was the intention of most. The point was surely to stress that what was given was given. As far as the king was concerned it was no longer his property.[106] It

[103] See index: church property.
[104] In 1034 *antiqua jura* were said to require royal authority for confirmation of its exchange: *Dip. Konrad II*, no. 213.
[105] Gladiss, 'Schenkungen', 101–2.
[106] e.g. *Dip. Otto I*, nos. 8, 33, 40, 49, 52, 56–7, 64–5, 69, 71, etc. and especially no. 198.

was still under his royal authority, as was everyone's property, but the belief that what was granted by a king remained more under his authority than what was inherited from time immemorial (whenever that was) seems to be derived from later models of feudalism rather than from contemporary evidence.[107] Otto I even gave to the *servus* of a nunnery full power to inherit, alienate, et cetera the estate that Otto said he transferred as completely as he could from his own right and lordship into that of the *servus* (*in proprium et a jure nostro et dominio in jus eius et dominationem prout juste et legaliter possumus*).[108] Rather than taking this as devaluing the freedom of disposition mentioned in charters to free persons, we may deduce that Otto, for whatever reason, intended this particular *servus* (whatever legal status the word implied) to have as good rights in this estate as he could give him.[109] Grants *in proprium* and *in proprietatem* that were intended to last only for one or more lives are not unknown: the more explicit of these suggest that the intention was to give the beneficiary freedom of disposition—for instance, to choose the second life—during the period of the grant.[110] Anomalous as such grants seem, they suggest that freedom of disposition was seen as part of the full rights normally associated with grants *in proprium* or *in proprietatem*.

In practice, though royal authority to alienate might be useful to the immediate beneficiary, it may not have been long remembered. The real impediment to alienation came from the current owner's potential heirs. Though their rights were, here as elsewhere, less rigorous and inescapable under customary law than historians have sometimes made them appear, there is ample evidence that, if the consent of fairly close relatives was not secured first, they might make trouble for the new owners later.[111] Despite occasional references in charters to property that had been acquired by the donor rather than inherited, it is not generally made clear that acquisitions, whether from the king or anyone else, were in principle considered to be more freely alienable, as they were in France. They may have been, however, and perhaps custom varied.[112] Another difference from France was

[107] e.g. Störmer, *Früher Adel*, 277; Leyser, 'Crisis'; Weitzel, *Dinggenossenschaft*, 1180–6.

[108] *Dip. Otto I*, no. 147, discounted by Gladiss, 'Schenkungen', 102.

[109] Krause, 'Königtum', 51; Mitterauer, 'Formen', 284–6.

[110] *Salzburger UB*, i, nos. 36, 46; *Dip. Konrad I*, no. 917; possibly *Dip. Hein. IV*, no. 137. It is not clear (*pace* Leyser, 'Crisis', 432–3), even from *Dip. Hein. II*, no. 89, that the grant to Esico in *Dip. Otto III*, no. 320 was intended from the first to be only for life.

[111] Ortlieb's allegation that *leges saeculi* made it impossible to leave one estate away from the heirs is obviously designed to justify the precautions then taken, which he admitted were dishonest: *Zwiefalter Chron.* 28 (I. 5). He did not mention the same impediment to the gift of other inherited properties to his abbey.

[112] *Handwörterbuch*, i. 964–5, mentions the distinction only in connection with later town law (though cf. *Urkunden-Buch Enns*, ii, no. 371, for 1210). Leyser, 'Crisis', 426, 429, may be arguing on analogy with France.

that, presumably because the churches which preserved records for us still relied on the king for protection, they did not get local lords to authorize the gifts they received. This must be the reason why the evidence for seigniorial consents to gifts to churches is so slight. Even in the early twelfth century, when such consent was becoming compulsory as well as desirable in France, it is much easier to find churches in Germany getting the consent of kin than of a lord, and to find trouble being made later, if they had not done so, by kinsmen than by lords, counts, or king.[113] Dukes and counts sometimes gave consent, probably because they were asked to do so by great churches, and helped the churches get royal consent, but it is not clear how far this impinged on the traditional freedom of full property.[114] When Henry V gave St Florian (Upper Austria) general permission to acquire property from free men the point seems to have been to extend royal protection over the abbey's future acquisitions rather than to allow people to make gifts that they could not otherwise make.[115] The most important requirement for the valid gift or sale of free property, even more important than getting the agreement of possible claimants, was a full public transfer or investiture, preferably if not invariably made before an appropriate local official and assembly, normally by handing over a symbolic object.[116]

All property of laymen seems to have been liable to confiscation for crime, and notably for infidelity—in effect, treason or rebellion.[117] The evidence that what had been inherited time out of mind could be forfeit is what makes implausible the suggestion that what was granted by the king was intended to be particularly vulnerable. Nor is there any evidence that what was remembered or recorded as granted by a king was more likely to be taken back in default of heirs than what was not:[118] a charter of 967 implies that any land without heirs would belong to the kingdom.[119] There might be fewer descendants of recent grantees to claim an inheritance, but

---

[113] e.g. *Mainzer UB*, i, nos. 527, 571; *Urkundenbuch Magdeburg*, no. 264; Ortlieb, *Zwiefalter Chron.* 24, 28 (I. 5). The permission given by the count of Grüningen, ibid. 38 (I. 7), may not have been for gifts of land or land held with full rights.

[114] *Dip. Konrad III*, no. 245; Faussner, 'Herzog', gives examples of varying patterns of consent, though, as already suggested, I find his deductions from them over-subtle.

[115] *Urkunden-Buch Enns*, no. 91.

[116] e.g. *Cart. Gorze*, no. 106; *Salzburger UB*, no. 35; *Dip. Otto I*, nos. 78, 207; *Actes des comtes de Namur*, no. 1; *Osnabrücker UB*, i, no. 138: on investiture here *digito suo*, cf. *Sachsenspiegel Lehnrecht*, 48 (26. 1, 53), probably reflecting procedures for transfer of full rights; these are not described in *Landrecht*, but cf. 132 (II. 4. 1); *Cod. Dip. Sax. Reg.* pt. 1, ii, no. 255. Ficker, *Vom Heerschilde*, 34, noted the non-feudal use of 'investiture'.

[117] Infidelity or perfidy: *Dip. Otto I*, nos. 115, 189.

[118] See Leyser, 'Crisis', 430. Only a few of the cases of 'royal inheritance' listed there in p. 435 n. 5 seem to support the suggestion clearly. Some allege supposedly voluntary gifts to the king.

[119] *Dip. Otto I*, no. 343.

there is no evidence that the general rules of inheritance were any different. What all confiscations needed—or were supposed to need—was a
proper judgement.[120] That does not mean that they always got it or that
people did not fear arbitrary forfeiture.[121] The principle was nevertheless
clear. Kings were supposed to consult before taking the property of their
subjects, just as they were supposed to consult about all matters of substance. Lesser lords must, if anything, have been under stronger pressure
to consult, whether or not they did. Who should be consulted depended on
the status of the alleged criminal and of his land. Before taking anything,
whether inheritance or benefice, from one of his great men or princes, the
king would do well to consult the other great men.[122] For lesser people representatives of local communities like *scabini* would be appropriate and
adequate. Eleventh-century statements of custom suggest that even the
unfree expected and might be granted the right to appeal to collective
judgement, sometimes explicitly that of their fellows or peers, when they
were accused of offences.[123] When Conrad II promised those who held
benefices on royal or church land in Italy that they would not be evicted
without judgement of their peers he was presumably promising what was
accepted, at least by laymen, as right in Germany.[124] If it was accepted for
benefices it was surely accepted for what was held *in proprium* and by inheritance, whether from time out of mind or under a remembered grant. A
judgement to justify taking a benefice was no doubt easier to get than one
to take full property, and perhaps one to resume a recent grant was also relatively easy, while full property was more likely to be returned to its heirs
than were benefices. That, however, seems to have been a matter of royal
favour rather than of right. There is, incidentally, no evidence as yet of any
*Leihezwang* or rule that kings had to give away what they had confiscated,
such as developed later in Germany. They seem quite often to have given
it to churches, but that may have been a good way of forestalling later pleas
from disgruntled heirs.

Among obligations, military service is often supposed to have become
'feudalized' in this period, so that the old Germanic or Carolingian obligation on all free men was replaced by one that was restricted to the holders of benefices or fiefs, who owed their services to their immediate lords
rather than to the king.[125] This presupposes seeing the obligations of

---

[120] Above, at n. 66.　　　　　　　　　　　　　　[121] Lampert, *Opera*, 151.
[122] The dismissal of counts from their benefices was discussed in the previous section.
[123] *Constitutiones*, i, no. 423; *Mon. Bambergensia*, no. 25; *Urkundenbuch mittelrhein. Terr.*, i,
no. 382; other references to judgement of peers: *Constitutiones*, i, no. 424; *Chron. Saint-Mihiel*,
no. 50; *Dip. Konrad III*, no. 74.
[124] See chapter 6.5.
[125] Werner, 'Heeresorganisation', 805, 840; Auer, 'Kriegdienst', 321, 50–3.

counts and bishops to the king in feudo-vassalic terms, which I have argued is misleading. As Werner demonstrated, the contingents required from part of the kingdom in the *Indiculus loricatum* of 980–3 suggest that the army was raised roughly within the traditional units of duchies or *regna*, though, as one might expect in an age both of customary law and of frequent musters, the units had been adjusted to suit political change.[126] The numbers of soldiers owed by the bishops, abbots, dukes, counts, and other individuals who are listed were presumably also based on past custom, but would have been liable, and gone on being liable, to change over time as a result of favour, bargaining, and changes in the pattern of landholding.[127] Great churches with comital authority organized the royal service (*heribannum*) due from free men within their immunities, presumably including some free men who had full property rights.[128] Most service owed by bishops and abbots was, however, probably owed in respect of the property that belonged with full rights to their churches. Although the churches' amenability to royal pressure may have made their quotas larger, the chief reason they owed as much as they did was that they held great estates. Dukes and counts presumably figure in the *Indiculus* partly as royal officials who organized the military service of the areas under their care, but there is no reason to assume that they did not owe some obligations in respect of their own full property. The other lay nobles listed separately in the *Indiculus* were perhaps those who were rich and powerful enough to be worth negotiating with individually. Again, the bulk of their property was surely held with full rights and their obligations were presumably assessed more or less in proportion to its extent. In practice, whatever careful assignment of obligations to particular estates may have been made at one time or another would have got overlaid in time by custom and negotiation. How much kings or their servants fussed about quotas, and how good were the records to enable them to do so, we cannot now say, but it seems possible that great kings engaged on such great operations as were the kings of Germany would not quarrel about administrative details so long as they got adequate forces. What seems reasonably clear is that by and large kings during this period got adequate forces: whether or not individual dukes or counts are recorded as taking part in individual expeditions, it is difficult to believe either that royal armies could have achieved what they did in Italy without support from the lay nobility as a whole, or that the great nobles in general would have wanted to be left out from such opportunities for glory and loot.

It might be argued that the system, so far as we can discern it, was

[126] Werner, 'Heeresorganisation'; *Constitutiones*, i, no. 436.
[127] *Dip. Arnulf*, no. 155; *Dip. Otto I*, no. 92.    [128] *Dip. Otto III*, no. 104.

'feudal' in so far as the great lords, lay and ecclesiastical, who were summoned by the king were 'tenants in chief' who were responsible for the service of contingents made up of their tenants. There are several objections to this. There does not seem to be any reason except historiographical tradition to suppose that the relations involved were envisaged in terms of a pyramidal hierarchy of property rights. They look more like a rather untidy hierarchy of responsibility that evolved for political and military convenience and gradually became embedded in custom. It seems impossible to explain, for instance, why some monasteries dealt directly with the king (or, in German historical usage, were *reichsunmittelbar*[129]) and others were 'mediatized', that is, were left under local nobles. The very effort to put them into such categories and then to make sense of the varying patterns of obligations from each category—so far as the categories can be defined and divided, which is not very far[130]—reflects the preoccupations of a later age. For great royal expeditions across the Alps, it made sense to raise relatively small contingents of well-armed and more professional soldiers, rather than call on the mass of free men, and to get those who were likely to be reliable commanders to be responsible for raising as many of them as possible.

Counts, bishops, and abbots had inherited a system of granting benefices (whether on royal or church estates) in order to supply soldiers. The holders of this kind of benefice, especially if they were unfree and therefore more tightly bound to service, could make a useful nucleus, though we have no reason to believe that landowners, and especially lay landowners, did not make up numbers with household troops and paid soldiers. To assume that all, or even most, eleventh-century *milites* were benefice-holders is to beg several questions.[131] Many people referred to in the sources, either individually or in groups, as *milites* may have been owners of full property or of none. We know most about the ecclesiastical contingents of beneficed and sometimes unfree soldiers, because they are best recorded, but we do not know that they made up most of the royal armies. How the rest were raised and why most of them served is largely a matter of guesswork. When kings called up forces in any area (for there is some evidence that call-ups might, for practical reasons, be regional[132]) some may have responded because they wanted adventure and loot; some because they thought they were obliged to do so as loyal and upstanding subjects; while some may have lain low for all kinds of reasons.[133] If it is

[129] A word not apparently found before the fifteenth century: *Handwörterbuch*, iv. 799–801.
[130] Auer, 'Kriegdienst', 56–64.       [131] Johrendt, '"Milites" und "Militia"', e.g. 427.
[132] Auer, 'Kriegdienst', 66–7; Reuter, 'Imperial Church System', 365.
[133] e.g. Bruno, *Buch*, 26–7, 37 (c. 21–2, 35).

possible or likely that some were pressed to serve because they owned enough property to enable them to equip themselves and fight competently, then they, along with the churches that owed service for their lands, must raise doubts in our minds about seeing the armies as based on feudo-vassalic obligations. If we nevertheless decide that beneficed soldiers probably came to predominate, and that the needs of Italian expeditions contributed to this change, we are landed with a paradox: whereas in Germany the needs of long-distance expeditions provoked what is seen as the feudalization of military service, in England similar needs rather later are held to have had the opposite effect. The answer is surely that in both cases customary obligations were adapted to provide fewer but better-equipped and more willing soldiers for longer periods.[134] Labelling them feudal or non-feudal is simply fitting the evidence into the categories we have imposed.

What is clear is that, however armies for Italy were raised, an obligation to some kind of local military service was not restricted to those whom historians see as immediate tenants of the king and their benefice-holders. Some kind of obligation to the king or to whatever privileged church or local lord had taken over royal rights in an area, whether by royal grant or gradual usurpation, seems to have been much more widely dispersed and enforced. In practice it probably lay primarily on landholders, the free presumably owing it generally in respect of land held with what were thought of as full rights and the less free in respect of their less protected and more burdened holdings.[135] Some or all of the obligations of smallholders may have been often or always fulfilled by money payments. In Saxony at least, however, the building, repairing, and guarding of fortresses seems to have continued to be a practical obligation:[136] those who laboured on building and supplying forts may have generally been the servants or tenants of greater landowners, as well as of the king, but some of those who guarded them might, as in other countries, be better classified as middle-ranking free men, with their own land, than as nobles. Military service was not the prerogative of nobles any more than it was of benefice-holders: the boundary between noble and peasant was too wide and too uncertain for that to be possible. Men whom well-equipped cavalrymen might despise socially and militarily could be called on to bear arms in defence of fortresses and

---

[134] The evidence about a fixed length of service is distinctly weak: Auer, 'Kriegdienst', 55 (though his inference that the Saxon withdrawal in Widukind, *Libri*, 104–5 (III. 2) was caused by the end of their obligation rather than by winter and illness seems unjustified).

[135] On the connection (or lack of connection) between freedom and military service: Schulze, 'Rodungsfreiheit'.

[136] *Dip. Otto I*, no. 287; *Dip Hein. II*, no. 189; Widukind, *Libri*, 48–51 (I. 35); *Dip. Konrad III*, no. 119; Reuter, *Germany*, 142–3.

kingdom on occasion. In a moment of danger in 1066, according to a monk
of Lorsch writing about a hundred years later, the abbot assigned hundreds
of armed soldiers to each of the abbey's twelve holders of military
benefices, known in the vernacular as *hereschilt*, in proportion to the sizes
of the benefices.[137] It is tempting to guess that the rank and file may have
constituted the *Heerbann*, in contrast to the élite *Heerschild*, but that may
suggest too consistent and schematic a use of language.[138] The Lorsch
scribe seems to have used *hereschilt* to mean the military strength that his
abbey owed to the king. The point here is that, though we do not know
how the extra armed men were raised or who they were, they are less likely
to have been considered noble by any standards than were the twelve
benefice-holders. Though the wearing of swords by peasants could be considered pretentious and dangerous, the practical needs of official defence
and policing, as well as of self-defence, make any idea of an exclusively
'noble' army and a totally unarmed peasantry anachronistic.[139]

Other services and dues owed by free landowners in this period are even
more obscure, but that does not justify the conclusion that full property
was in its nature exempt from any. On Carolingian precedents, and bearing in mind the general medieval norms of collective government and
responsibility, one would expect that landowners were expected to attend
the local assemblies held by counts or their deputies. Great men with land
in several counties probably reserved their energies for the king's court or
the courts over which they presided as counts, but they may have sometimes been represented in other counties by whoever had charge of their
land there. The problems and implications of attendance at comital or
other courts were touched on in the previous section: so little is known that
they are not worth further consideration here. The exemptions that
churches and, later, towns secured from the obligation to provide lodging
for the royal court on its travels or for royal soldiers suggest that earlier on
it may have lain on the public at large. Royal and ecclesiastical estates may
always have borne most of the burden, but that could be an illusion of the
sources: Lampert of Hersfeld attributed Henry IV's shameful need to buy
daily necessities with cash to the refusal of *aliae publicae dignitates*, as well
as bishops and abbots, to fulfil their customary duties.[140] If the public officials who seem to be referred to here were counts they may have normally

---

[137] *Qui communicato 12* [sic in printed text] *illustrium fidelium suorum consilio, qui numero etiam beneficialis summa militaris clipei, qui vulgo dicitur hereschilt, Laureshamensis ecclesiae adtinens includitur, singulis pro quantitate beneficii centenos milites armatos ut traditur assignavit: Chron. Laureshamense,* i. 415, and cf. ibid. 423; *Dip. Konrad III*, no. 167.
[138] *Deutsches Rechtswörterbuch*, v. 530–2.
[139] Bruno, *Buch*, 34 (c. 31); *Casuum S. Galli Cont. II*, 161.
[140] Lampert, *Opera*, 173; Brühl, *Fodrum*, 116–219.

supplied what they did from royal land, but they may also have relied on contributions from lesser landowners. It seems reasonable to suppose that from the start any dues and services that greater landowners owed to counts, apart from military service, would be passed on to their tenants, but this does not mean that the property of nobles was in itself exempt, only that those with few or no tenants would feel more of the brunt. The distinction would have been sharpened when counties broke up and counts became more independent. Those who fell under the jurisdiction of the ban rather than imposing it on others would presumably go on paying old dues and may have confronted new ones as well.

By the twelfth century the custom that had accumulated around local authority that had been delegated or usurped would have made it difficult for the king to regain his old dues or impose new ones. Henry V, on the suggestion of his father-in-law, the king of England, apparently horrified his great men by a proposal to raise a general tax.[141] Nevertheless, the fact—or allegation—that he considered it is a reminder of the continued prestige and authority of the monarchy: the ability of twelfth-century emperors to raise armies is another. So long as property-owners could, one way or another, be got to provide military service and supplies, direct taxes could be dispensed with.

## 9.5. *Benefices and fiefs from 911 to the early twelfth century*

The use of the word *beneficium* both for the offices and appurtenant lands of counts, dukes, and bishops and for the relatively small holdings used by kings and churches to support soldiers has already been mentioned in this chapter. It continued to be used throughout this period for these offices and lands, and also for others that were granted with less than full rights but on apparently rather different terms from those that by custom attached to peasant holdings. Though *beneficium* was much more common, *precarium* (or *precaria*) continued to be used occasionally for a temporary grant made by a church. In 1015 the bishop of Paderborn gave a small estate for life, not, he said, *in precariam* but *in beneficium*, to someone who had given property to his new monastery.[142] Perhaps he meant that the donor had not asked for the grant but, whatever distinction was intended, there is no reason to see it as either generally accepted or as implying different rights and obligations. The first recorded occurrence of the word *feo* or *feus*, from which *feodum* or *feudum* derives, comes from the south-western edge of what became the kingdom of Germany at the end of the

[141] Otto of Freising, *Chronica*, 332–3.     [142] *Reg. Hist. Westfaliae*, i, no. 86.

eighth century, when it was used in charters of St Gall for annual rents.[143] It does not seem to have spread northwards from there, at least for some time. The first known use of *feodum* in Germany after that comes from Lotharingia early in the eleventh century, when it was applied to small, rent-paying peasant holdings on the archbishop of Trier's estate.[144] By the early twelfth century it had become fairly common west of the Rhine, presumably under the influence of French terminology.[145] Since *beneficium* was the usual word in documents from the kingdom of Germany as a whole until the twelfth century, and indeed well on into it, discussion of the introduction and use of *feodum* is postponed to the next section.

In German the usual word for property that scribes called *beneficia* was *lehen* or *len*. A royal charter of 1013 refers to *ereditarium beneficium quod vulgo erbelehen dicitur*, and the Lorsch cartulary, in an account of events of about 1107 written some seventy years later, talks of Lorsch's *principalia beneficia quod vulgo appellantur vollehen*.[146] That does not imply either that *lehen* or *beneficium* always denoted the same kind of property or that *lehen* meant what it would mean to lawyers and historians later. If counts' benefices, the benefices of free men or *ministeriales* owing military service, and the small holdings of peasants could all on occasion be called *len* or *lehen*, then the word did not denote a category of property with consistent status, rights, or obligations. The conditions on which benefices or *lehen* were held must have varied, partly according to the status of the holder, partly according to local custom, and partly according to the purpose of the grant. The only common characteristic of property held in benefice was that rights in it were dependent and incomplete because it had been granted by someone who retained superior rights over it quite apart from any pre-existing governmental authority. This is made clear by all the charters by which tenth- and eleventh-century kings gave to people *in proprietatem* what they had formerly held *in beneficium*, and by the many documents that attest to the determination of abbots and bishops to preserve the superior and ultimate rights of their churches over what they granted as benefices.[147]

In order to establish more about the connotations of the word *beneficium* (or, very occasionally in the later part of the period, those of *feodum*) when used in connection with property, we need, as usual, to investigate the

---

[143] *Urkundenbuch S. Gallen*, nos. 105, 133; Schneider, *Annales du Midi*, 80 (1968), 480–1.

[144] *Urkundenbuch mittelrhein. Terr.*, i, no. 287. No serious work seems to have been done on the subject since Krawinkel, *Feudum*, whose method does not seem designed to show the first occurrence of any form. His 1018 document (p. 46) is interpolated: cf. *Handwörterbuch*, ii. 1729.

[145] Parisse, *Noblesse lorraine*, 531–4; *Gesta abbatum Trudon.*, 284.

[146] *Dip. Hein. II*, no. 271; *Codex Laureshamensis*, i. 423.

[147] e.g. *Dip. Otto I*, no. 286; *Dip. Otto III*, nos. 19, 320; Thietmar, *Chronicon*, 228–9 (V. 7); *Salzburger UB*, nos. 36–7; *Osnabrücker UB*, i, no. 138; *Urkundenbuch mittelrhein. Terr.*, i, no. 338; *Urkundenbuch Niederrhein*, i, no. 192; *Trad. Freising*, no. 1536; *Dip. Konrad III*, no. 137.

rights and obligations attached to the property. Again as usual, the difficulty is that most of the evidence concerns benefices held from churches: the difficulty is in fact greater than usual here, since my inevitably brief trawl through the sources has produced even less about the terms on which benefices in Germany before the twelfth century were held from any lay lord apart from the king than I have found elsewhere. As I have argued in previous chapters, churches had different preoccupations in exploiting their estates from laymen and were governed by different rules. The conditions attached to benefices on lay estates cannot be assumed to be the same as those on church estates.

The most prized and most contested rights that might attach to benefices were probably inheritance and security against confiscation. I have already discussed the way that counts' benefices came to be inherited as counties were broken up and as counts assimilated their offices and ex officio lands to their family property. In earlier chapters I have also suggested that kings and other lay lords may often have been willing to allow those to whom they granted small estates in return for military and other services to pass on to their heirs, provided that those heirs were reasonably loyal and capable. The *ereditarium beneficium quod vulgo erbelehen dicitur* that Henry II gave to the bishop of Merseburg in 1013 may be evidence of this: whether the bishop allowed the father and son who had held it from the king to stay in possession we do not know.[148] Churches in Germany, as elsewhere, were willing to allow peasants, even more or less free peasants, to inherit their land: those whose status was low enough to mean that they owed regular rents and services were profitable enough to be allowed to pass on church land to their children, especially when, as seems to have sometimes at least been customary, the children had to pay a due in kind or money before taking up their holdings.[149] Grants to free men and nobles were another matter. Most bishops and abbots preferred to restrict any grants they made to free men and nobles *in precario* or *in beneficio* to a specified number of lives.[150] It was not impossible to recover land after it had been left with a locally powerful family for several generations but it was difficult.[151] That was one reason why some donors and prelates tried to prevent land from being granted in benefice by churches, as if that amounted to outright alienation.[152]

<hr/>

[148] *Dip. Hein. II*, no. 271.    [149] *Cart. Gorze*, nos. 115, 119; *Constitutiones*, i, no. 428.
[150] e.g. *Salzburger UB*, pp. 143–4, no. 82; *Cart. Gorze*, no. 106; *Urkundenbuch mittelrhein. Terr.*, i, nos. 338, 382, ii, no. 235; Bloch, 'Älteren Urkunden', no. 56; *Dip. Konrad III*, no. 63.
[151] *Dip. Hein. III*, no. 302; Franz, *Quellen*, no. 80.
[152] *Urkundenbuch mittelrhein. Terr.*, i, no. 168; *Dip. Hein. II*, no. 433; *Dip. Konrad II*, no. 129; *Urkundenbuch Niederrhein*, i, no. 192; *Trad. Regensburg*, nos. 653, 787; *Reg. Hist. Westfaliae*, no. 198.

By the twelfth century great churches in Germany, like great churches in other countries, were finding it difficult to hold out against the accumulation of lay custom and lay objections to temporary inheritance. The equivocal position of the German *ministeriales* on the boundary between servility and honour contributed some peculiar features to the process by which ecclesiastical claims were ultimately defeated here. When the bishop of Worms recorded the customs that governed the unfree persons who constituted his *familia* (that is, in this context, presumably those who directly supported his *familia* or household) in the 1120s, he allowed them to inherit without paying dues.[153] The fact that he mentioned this suggests that it was a new concession. If so, it may have been won on the initiative of the *ministeriales* who were numbered among the *familia*, held responsible offices in the bishop's household, and owed service for him in the royal army. To judge from the customs granted to similar *ministeriales* in the service of other churches later in the eleventh century and in the twelfth, these unfree but increasingly indispensable soldiers and servants were well placed to build up group solidarity, pass on information from group to group, and bargain with their lords.[154] The holdings of the Worms *ministeriales* were not referred to in the customs of the 1020s as benefices, but the word was used around 1060 when the *ministeriales* of the bishop of Bamberg secured a similar set of customs, though not one that exempted them from inheritance dues.[155] It is just possible that by now *beneficia*—or *lehen*—were beginning to carry some connotations of guaranteed rights, at least when they were connected with military service:[156] soldiers who served in Conrad II's army in 1037, when he promised that *milites* with benefices on royal or church land could pass on their holdings to their sons and were not to be evicted without judgement of their peers, may have brought the news home for themselves and their fellows to mull over.[157] Though Conrad made his concession for short-term purposes and directed it primarily at the tenants of the archbishop of Milan, the content of his charter—in effect a charter of liberties—may not have seemed too unreasonable to him or to his counts and other lay subjects. It would, however, have worried conscientious bishops and abbots when they came to realize its impact, and it may have contributed to the heritability that, as we shall see, seems to have been a widely accepted feature of *jus beneficiale* quite early in the twelfth century.

---

[153] *Constitutiones*, i, no. 428, c. 3, 11.

[154] *Dip. Hein. IV*, no. 125; Arnold, *German Knighthood*, 76–99; Freed, 'Formation' and 'Reflections'.                              [155] *Monumenta Bamberg.*, no. 25.

[156] For earlier uses, see *Trad. Freising*, no. 1244. See also index: benefices, especially references there to chapter 4.

[157] *Dip. Konrad II*, no. 129. See chapter 6.5.

When land was granted for several lives the persons whose lives were involved were generally specified. Benefices held by *ministeriales* in return for services would go to sons or others who could perform the service. Restricting those who could inherit would increase the chance of a reversion in the event of their failure.[158] How far either the king or other lay lords prescribed the rules of inheritance to their benefices in this period seems to be unknown. The king would no doubt get royal benefices left without heirs, just as he got full property, and other lords probably claimed theirs back if they had records of them. If either they or the king took succession dues from the heirs to their benefices, the evidence of church practice here as in France suggests they more probably took them from any unfree *ministeriales* to whom they gave benefices than from free tenants. As for *Herrenfall*, that is the lapse of benefices on a change of lord, there does not seem to be any evidence that kings made an issue of it, but some of the bishops or abbots who tried to revoke their predecessors' grants may have maintained, as Otto III did in 998, that no grant by a prelate could bind his successor.[159] Whether benefice-holders in general, apart from the holders of important offices, were normally expected to seek formal investiture to renew their rights, either on their own succession or on that of their lords, seems slightly unlikely. If they had been, there would not have been so many disputes about properties that churches claimed were benefices but that the families which had held them for generations claimed were their full property. That is not to say that some benefices, apart from important offices, were not occasionally renewed by ceremonies similar to those by which they had originally been granted.

These ceremonies are likely to have involved a less formal and public version of the kind of rite that was used for the conveyance of full property. Some acknowledgement of the grantor's continuing rights and the tenant's obligations was also likely to be required. That means that although, as I have repeatedly argued, there was nothing exclusively feudo-vassalic about homage or oaths of fidelity, lords probably often made their new tenants swear to be faithful and admit that they were in some sense their grantors' men. In 1142 a benefice held from the margrave of Vohburg was said to be held *jure hominii*.[160] To judge from the number of disputes about benefices granted long before, even churches, which by the eleventh

---

[158] For reversions, not only from *ministeriales*: *Urkundenbuch mittelrhein. Terr.*, i, no. 394; *Codex Laureshamensis*, i. 423; *Dip. Konrad III*, no. 125.

[159] *Constitutiones*, i, no. 23, discussed in chapter 6 at n. 76.

[160] *Dip. Konrad III*, no. 79; cf. *Codex Laureshamensis*, i. 423; *Urkundenbuch Magdeburg*, no. 298.

century were beginning to keep increasingly careful records, did not note all their grants at the time they were made.[161]

Security against eviction was closely linked to inheritance. Like inheritance it may more often have been a worry for tenants of churches than for those of the king or lay lords. When counts or dukes were dismissed, replaced, or won new lands from each other or from churches, the adherents of the old regime no doubt suffered, but secular lords who took on tenants from their fathers or other relatives may often have taken their tenure for granted. If they wanted to confiscate a benefice they were accustomed to the norms of collective judgement and could often reckon well enough on shared values, as well as power, to be able to swing a judgement in their own favour. The ordinance of 1037 may not therefore have represented a significant innovation or threat to them. On the other hand, the accumulation of custom about the rights of benefices may have made it increasingly desirable to record the judgements of other benefice-holders on the eviction of a free benefice-holder, just as it had long been desirable to record those on the confiscation of full property.

The situation of ecclesiastical lords and their tenants was different. A bishop or abbot was more likely to be saddled with totally unwanted tenants installed by an unrelated, and perhaps unknown, predecessor than was a secular lord. If he was energetic and conscientious he might feel a duty to try to recover property that had been granted in benefice to a predecessor's kinsmen or to someone foisted on the church by a king, duke, or count.[162] Some benefice-holders on church land were protected by lay friends in high places, if not by the king himself, but others presumably lost their holdings when the church's influence prevailed at court.[163] A prelate who saw the property of God and his saints lost to a layman would be reluctant to have his church's claim judged by the layman's lay peers. All the same, the clergy were accustomed to having their tenants' crimes judged by the judgement of peers, while the same forces as strengthened the claim of benefice-holders to inheritance—that is, the accumulation of custom, perhaps reinforced by knowledge of the 1037 ordinance—pressed them towards acceptance, however unwilling, of the judgement of peers when they wanted to take back benefices. The abbot of St Maximin, Trier, in his long struggle to get rid of a tenant wished on him by Henry II, in the

---

[161] Krause, 'Königtum', 65, says that royal charters of enfeoffment (*Belehnungen*) start under Henry V (which, in the absence of printed charters for Henry V, I have not checked), except for one from 1071. This charter (*Dip. Hein. IV*, no. 242; *Constitutiones*, i, no. 441), however, which dealt with a complex political situation, is a doubtful case. Gislebert of Mons, *Chronique*, 11–13, writing over a century later, sees it in what are surely anachronistic terms.

[162] For benefices *verbo regis*, above, n. 98.

[163] Gerhard, *Vita S. Oudalrici*, 416; *Dip. Otto I*, nos. 121, 180; *Dip. Otto II*, nos. 57, 97.

end got a judgement of the peers of the original tenant's successor in the 1080s. Imperial intervention once again precluded total victory, but the abbey got part of the land back and imposed an agreed rent on the rest.[164] Benefice-holders whose unfree status made it difficult for them to appeal beyond their lord's court would be particularly vulnerable to forfeiture. The earliest customs conceded to *ministeriales* which explicitly mention confiscation seem to be those of Cologne, granted in the 1160s. Even then benefices as such are not mentioned, and the customs give the *ministerialis* whose goods are seized the mere right to appeal to the nobles of the land, especially the officials of the archbishop's court, to intercede for him.[165] Earlier customs, however, gave *ministeriales* the right to judgement of their peers when accused of offences. As *ministeriales* raised their status by their military service and general usefulness, and as the rights of benefice-holders or fiefholders came to be recognized as distinctive, the security against eviction that now seemed to go with benefices and fiefs is likely to have been one of the advantages that they claimed.

It may be that some customary restriction on the alienation of benefices is implied by the grants of land *in proprium* for restricted periods that were mentioned in the previous section, but the only real evidence I have found of rules about their alienation before 1136 concerns those that were held by *ministeriales*. It was presumably a corollary of the unfree status of *ministeriales* that their property should be what became known as *Inwartseigen*, that is, property that may be conveyed only to others within the same estate.[166] The impact of Lothar III's Roncaglia decree of 1136, prohibiting *milites* from alienating their benefices, will be discussed later, but it certainly does not imply that alienations had been unknown or rare hitherto.[167] Since the reason given for the ordinance was that alienations impeded the raising of imperial armies, and since the bulk of the army was raised north of the Alps, there had presumably not been any effective rule against them there.

Because military obligations to the king and kingdom remained a reality in Germany and because grants of property on restricted terms were apparently widely used to secure it, it seems probable that more properties held from churches, and perhaps from laymen, of the sort known as benefices (or, later, fiefs) owed military service here than did in Italy or France. The use of benefices by those who owed service because of their own free property in order to help them fulfil their obligations was dis-

---

[164] *Urkundenbuch mittelrhein. Terr.*, i, no. 382.    [165] Weinrich, *Quellen*, no. 70, c. 3.
[166] *Trad. Freising*, no. 1244; *Constitutiones*, i, no. 438, c. 6. In 1142 some free settlers were required only to give their lord first refusal if they wanted to sell: *Hamburg UB*, no. 165.
[167] *Dip. Lothar III*, no. 105; see chapter 6 at nn. 102–3.

cussed in the previous section. Military service was not all that such benefices owed. *Ministeriales*, for instance, who held benefices owed other services as well. Some properties called benefices (or fiefs) never carried military obligations. Some owed rents. As late as *c.*1100 some of the *beneficiales* of Carden abbey, who must have been people of low status, had to repair hedges as well as paying annual rents.[168] Some benefice-holders owed nothing because that was agreed when the grant was made, or came to owe nothing because nothing was got from them for so long that any original agreement was overlaid by practice.[169] When churches granted land in benefice to powerful neighbours they often hoped for friendship, favour, and some kind of protection rather than for formal service. In 1095, in return for the fidelity, devoted service, and sure and certain help that the count of Luxemburg promised and swore to the archbishop of Trier, the archbishop granted him six hundred manses (units of property) *in beneficium* as soon as they should fall vacant. For the first three hundred the count would owe nothing beyond the assurance of service and aid that he had sworn. He would have to pay a hundred marks for the rest but would not thereafter owe any specific services.[170] Someone who gave valuable estates to a church might even be granted an annual rent along with a life benefice of the gift or of other church property, so that in effect the lord was paying a rent to the tenant, rather than the other way round.[171]

When military service was owed it was presumably by the same sort of agreement as other services. The primary and fixed obligation (so far as any obligation under customary law was fixed) lay on the landowner: it was up to him or her to fulfil it as it could best be fulfilled, whether by grant of benefices or otherwise, though the terms made would inevitably be conditioned by custom and would themselves contribute to the further development of custom. It is possible that all or most small benefices granted to individual potential soldiers started from fairly standard terms of service, but we have no evidence that they did. Even if they had, variations in royal demands and in the lord's own demands for local service would have gradually altered them. The details about the provision of horses and arms, the payment of expenses, and the length of service recorded in customs granted to *ministeriales* in the twelfth century may therefore testify rather to the multiplication of arguments and records than to a breakdown of formerly uniform and accepted obligations.[172] Some lords preferred to make

---

[168] *Urkundenbuch mittelrhein. Terr.*, i, no. 400; cf. ibid. ii, no. 235; *Cart. Gorze*, no. 106; *Osnabrücker UB*, i, no. 138; *Reg. Hist. Westfal.* no. 198; *Urkundenbuch Niederrhein*, i, no. 371.

[169] *Trad. Freising*, no. 1536; *Gesta abbatum Trudon.* 284: *Codex Laureshamensis*, i. 423.

[170] *Urkundenbuch mittelrhein. Terr.*, i, no. 394.

[171] *Urkundenbuch Niederrhein*, i, no. 192.

[172] *Dip. Konrad II*, no. 140 (confected before 1125); *Constitutiones*, i, no. 447 (*c.*1160:

bulk contracts to fulfil their obligations. In 1052 the archbishop of Trier made a *conventionem sive precariam* with the count of Arlon by which, with the consent of the king, the count received various estates *in precariam* for the lives of himself, his wife, and his two sons in return for providing forty armed men (*scutati*) for service this side of the Alps or twenty if the archbishop or the king made an expedition beyond.[173] As the abbey of Lorsch (Hesse) found, however, it could be dangerous to have all one's eggs in one basket.[174]

Other obligations of benefice-holders are obscure. If they were supposed to attend their lord's court it may often have been because their lord, whether count, bishop, or advocate, held a court anyway for those under his more general authority. One advantage that the holders of some smaller benefices gained from the agreements made about their holdings may have been that they were let off some of the duties that fell on their neighbours, like providing horses and hospitality. As this suggests, and as I shall argue in the next section, benefices by the early twelfth century were beginning to be attractive to people of relatively low social status. Nobles could enlarge their estates, at least for a time, by securing property from churches or from each other in benefice, but for them benefices would always be second best. In the event of a dispute over his benefice a noble or prosperous free man would hope that his political and social standing would secure him the same kind of judgement by his fellows as he would get about his own inherited property. Most of the people whom we shall see trying to get their land or office counted as benefices or fiefs in the first half of the twelfth century were in a quite different position. They were *ministeriales* or others who probably stood on the border between freedom and unfreedom. Whether they were affected by any prestige that attached to the word benefice (or *lehen*) because it was used for the benefices of counts and other great men seems doubtful: the difference between counts' benefices and those of most people who pressed for *beneficiale jus* was too great. What the would-be benefice-holders wanted was the rights of inheritance and security and the defined and restricted services that were coming to be associated with benefices or fiefs. For people of low status the advantage of a benefice was that it ought to give them some of the rights that great men took for granted.

Disputes about benefices were not apparently judged by a particular sort of law that was any more uniform than any other law, nor were they decided in separate courts and by different procedures. There is no

apparently about the service of free benefice-holders as well as *ministeriales*); Weinrich, *Quellen*, no. 70. Ortlieb, *Zwiefalter Chron.* 48 (I. 9) seems to be about escort rather than military service.

[173] *Urkundenbuch mittelrhein. Terr.*, i, no. 274.     [174] *Codex Laureshamensis*, i. 423.

evidence that the later distinction between *Landrecht* (the general law of a province or lordship) and *Lehnrecht* (feudal law or the law of fiefs) had yet been drawn.[175] The first stage in claiming a benefice would be to go to the landowner from whom one claimed to hold it, who probably held courts or assemblies that dealt with other matters too, whether those that pertained to comital jurisdiction or merely the affairs of his less free peasant tenants. Either side seems to have then been allowed to appeal to whatever superior authority could be got to pay attention. Ecclesiastical lords sometimes sought support against their tenants from their superiors in the church and sometimes went to a count or duke or straight to the king.

To fit these cases into a theory of appeals through the layers of a feudo-vassalic hierarchy is to fit them into the theories that would be worked out to explain a system of law that had not yet been invented and explained. That does not mean that there was no hierarchy of property rights along-side the social, political, and ecclesiastical hierarchies. There was, and sometimes the different hierarchies coincided, but they did not do so in the systematic way that models of the 'feudal pyramid' suggest. Later lawyers would fit churches into the 'hierarchy of tenure' and still later historians would talk of the 'feudalization of the church'. At this period, however, as I have argued, churches held their property with full rights, not as fiefs.[176] Where bishops had rights over abbeys or demanded services from them it was as diocesans or perhaps counts rather than as 'feudal lords'.[177] In the more formal records, and perhaps the more formal procedures, of the twelfth century, whole series of past grants of the property being conveyed might be cited.[178] It is easy to assume that these past grants represented layers of property rights so that each past grantor had retained some kind of right over what he had granted. In some cases he or she probably had, especially where past grants are explicitly said to have been made in benefice, but in others, especially where the property seems to be held with full rights, that looks unlikely. Past grants and surrenders of rights may be mentioned because anyone who had once held property, on whatever terms, and had passed it on, or their relatives, might put in a claim to it. Prudent rulers of churches that received land found it best to get consents

---

[175] Köbler, 'Land und Landrecht'. The reference in 1133 to King Arnulf's grant *beneficario more potius quam jure locus* (*Dip. Lothar III*, no. 54) seems to be drawing a slightly different dis-tinction from the later one.

[176] Above, at nn. 100–4, and index: church property.

[177] *Dip. Otto I*, no. 92; *Dip. Otto II*, no. 57; Bloch, 'Älteren Urkunden', no. 56; *Urkunden Eichstätt*, i, no. 4; *Urkundenbuch mittelrhein. Terr.*, i, no. 382; *Monumenta Boica*, xiii, pp. 141–6; *Actes des évêques de Metz*, no. 54. One monastery could also have rights over the property of another: e.g. *Dip. Konrad III*, nos. 182, 245.

[178] *Actes des évêques de Metz*, no. 54; *Dip. Konrad III*, nos. 74, 99, 260: on the last of these see Faussner, 'Verfügungsgewalt', 367–8.

or surrenders from all possible claimants, or make the new charter serve as a register of past titles and their supersession. If this sounds vague and untidy, that reflects how things probably were under customary law, before anyone had tried to fit the varying relations of property and government into a neat system or devise a theory to accommodate them.

The advocacies of churches illustrate how difficult it sometimes is to say who held what from whom, what it means to say it, and how to fit the parties into a feudo-vassalic framework. Some lay advocates who acted for churches, particularly in the exercise of criminal jurisdiction, were appointed by kings, which suggests that their offices had some of the advantages, from the king's point of view, of Carolingian benefices *verbo regis*. Some churches indeed granted their advocacies as benefices, though they became wary of allowing this when the rights of benefices became more established. Even before then—or before the evidence of established rights becomes clear—some advocacies were not recorded as benefices: they were simply advocacies, did not need to be further defined, and would not have been usefully defined by being called benefices.[179] An advocate, as well as being an officer of his church and whoever chose him, was supposed to receive his office from the hand of the king, which at best confuses the shape of the hierarchy and at worst might imply the 'multiple vassalage' that so shocks historians of feudalism.[180] The advocate of St Maximin was to receive the 'service' of a meal from the abbey, which would not fit very well with the position of a feudal tenant who ought to owe services to his lord rather than receive them.[181] Since the model had not yet been invented, and advocates had not been fitted into it, however, that did not matter.

It may be that the claims to hold in benefice or fief that appear in the twelfth century were not a new phenomenon but one that is revealed then by the multiplication of records. Since it seems to derive from a link between military service, benefice-holding, security of tenure, and social status that developed during the tenth and eleventh centuries, it may well have developed then. It cannot be explained simply as part of the general 'rise of the knights', a phenomenon about which, as it is usually characterized, I expressed some doubts in chapter 2. What we have in Germany seems rather different from anything I have found in the other areas studied in this book. It is a claim, not merely to higher social status, but to greater property rights, and it seems to be based, not on merely being a

[179] e.g. *Dip. Hein. III*, no. 372; *Mainzer UB*, i, no. 527; *Dip. Konrad III*, no. 245. The analogy with benefices *verbo regis* is suggested by Parisse, *Noblesse lorraine*, 59–62.
[180] Stengel, 'Land und lehnrechtliche Grundlagen', 299. See index: multiple vassalage.
[181] *Dip. Hein. III*, no. 372; *Dip. Konrad III*, no. 245.

'knight', wearing a sword, being able to fight on horseback, and so on, but on an obligation to military service that required horses, arms, and the property to support them. Such claims were provoked by two phenomena that seem peculiar to Germany. First there was the nature of the military service that had long been demanded by emperors and would-be emperors. Those who, whether originally free or unfree, were granted land to enable them to provide service with horses and arms for imperial service as the *Heerschild* of their lords were inevitably, if unintentionally, invited to consider their status as more noble than that of their neighbours whose obligations were more demeaning. The second phenomenon was the development of a class of unfree servants, the *ministeriales*, whose employment as responsible household administrators and professional or semi-professional soldiers must have made them feel entitled to the privileges of freedom and even nobility.[182] In the long run they secured those privileges, but bishops and abbots who had already learnt the disadvantages of granting land in benefice to free men were not going to let their unfree servants get the corresponding advantages if they could help it. When dealing with *ministeriales* and peasants the clergy could expect the support of the lay authorities. But while the demands of *ministeriales* gave an extra edge to the arguments about *jus beneficiale* or *jus feodale* that developed in the twelfth century, the legal significance that benefices had acquired was not, as I shall argue, important only to them. It affected free men too.

According to the argument of this book the question whether Germany was more or less feudalized than France by 1100 is meaningless. Nevertheless, if one wants to ask it, and if one takes one of the defining characteristics of feudalism as an obligation to military service from fief- or benefice-holders, then Germany looks distinctly more feudal than France. Military service here was more defined and more often connected to benefices (or fiefs) than it seems to have been in most of France. If one takes feudalism in the sense favoured by legal historians outside England, as implying conformity to the law of fiefs as it developed from the twelfth century on, a case could again be made for saying that by 1150, if not by 1100, Germany was the more feudal of the two kingdoms. By then benefices and fiefs had begun to constitute something more like a category of property with more consistent—though far from totally consistent—rights and obligations than they yet constituted in France. On the other hand, there is no evidence, apart from the dubious case of Hainaut in 1071, that converting properties into fiefs was used as a means of political control. Churches, of course, often granted benefices to those who gave them

---

[182] *Casuum S. Galli Cont. II*, 161; Ortlieb, *Zwiefalter Chron.* 48 (I. 9).

property or surrendered property to them after disputes, but that was an old tradition that did not derive from feudo-vassalic ideas and practices. Whether because the king and other great men could assert their authority well enough without making their subjects surrender their property and receive it back as fiefs, or because they simply had not thought of doing so, there is no evidence as yet in Germany of what is called in French *la reprise de fief* or in German *Lehnsauftragung* or *Auftragungen von Eigengut zu Lehn*.

## 9.6. *Words, concepts, and law: the twelfth century*

Though some allowance is made for influence on procedures from canon law and for a quasi-professional influence from notaries on the drafting of official documents, it seems to be generally accepted that German secular law did not become the preserve of anything like a legal profession until the appearance of Roman lawyers trained in German universities in the fifteenth century.[183] Little emphasis also seems to be placed on the development of more professional administration in government and estate management at every level. To a foreign historian studying the evidence of property law in twelfth- and thirteenth-century Germany that is surprising. While government here did not become bureaucratic in the way that it did in Italy or England, and professional law did not develop as it did alongside the bureaucracies in either of those countries, there is some evidence of the trend towards more systematic and literate administration that seems to have characterized most of western Europe at the time. There is also some evidence of the associated trend towards a more expert and more esoteric kind of law. Though most records apart from charters have disappeared, more were being made and kept both by the royal government and by those of lesser lay lordships and estates.[184] The *ministeriales*, as an existing and captive nucleus of administrators, may have been well suited to pick up an adequate level of functional literacy and then make use of it.[185]

One aspect of the new government here, as in France and Italy, was the sorting out of something like a network of jurisdictions from the mass of overlapping and conflicting claims to local power and dues that had developed over the centuries.[186] The way that this happened and that the word

[183] Coing, *Römisches Recht*; Stelzer, *Gelehrtes Recht*; Moraw, 'Gelehrte Juristen'; Trusen, *Anfänge des gelehrten Rechts*; Burmeister, *Studium* (including the law of fiefs as part of learned law, pp. 131–3) and 'Anfänge des Notariats'; Diestelkamp, *Lehnrecht*, 116–27; Weitzel, *Dinggenossenschaft*, 961–78, 1139–51, 1248–50.

[184] *Ältesten Lehnsbücher*; *Codex Falkensteinensis*; *Eppsteinschen Lehensverzeichnisse*; Metz, *Staufische Güterverzeichnisse*; Patze, *Entstehung der Landesherrschaft*, 524, 533–7; Diestelkamp, *Lehnrecht*, 45, 116–27.

[185] Metz, *Staufische Güterverzeichnisse*, 2, 140–2.

[186] Hirsch, *Hohe Gerichtsbarkeit* and works cited in n. 54 above.

'ban' was used suggests that the immunities and jurisdiction granted earlier to great churches formed a model that helped to cast a veil of legitimacy over the jurisdictions of some of the newer emerging lordships.[187]
Germans who knew about the declaration apparently made at Roncaglia in
1158 that all jurisdiction was derived from the emperor may not have
found it very controversial.[188] Two years earlier the emperor had declared
that no one in the new duchy of Austria was to exercise any jurisdiction
(*aliquam justiciam*) without the duke's permission.[189] However royal jurisdiction was conceptualized and justified, the appeals to the royal court
recorded in Frederick I's charters and thereafter in the printed
*Constitutiones* suggest that its authority was recognized at least to the extent
that appeals were made to it and that its procedures were becoming rather
more regular and formal.[190] Most of these appeals came from ecclesiastical
lords, but that may be partly because churches were better than laymen at
keeping the charters that recorded royal judgements. That most of the
appeals concerned what the editors of the texts considered feudal law may
be rather more significant. The law about what were coming to be called
fiefs and the rights of fiefs (*jus feodale, jus beneficiale*, etc.) was becoming a
matter of argument—argument that is likely to have required a certain
development of legal expertise about the rules that were formulated and
the way that they could be manipulated.

The significance of the spread in Germany of the word *feodum* (or
*feudum*, though this seems at first less common) during the twelfth century
is difficult to assess. The usual assumption that it signals the spread of
feudo-vassalic ideas and practices from France needs to be examined.
Quite apart from the difficulty of fitting the contemporary French evidence
into the traditional feudo-vassalic model, the assumption involves a confusion of words and phenomena.[191] It also ignores the possibility of influence
from Italy. Though *feodum*, rather than *feudum*, looks more French than
Italian, it is not impossible that *feodum, feodale jus*, and the verb *infeovdare*
(*sic*) may have got into a Bamberg charter of 1123 partly at least under
Italian influence.[192] Much more work on the subject is needed, but in the
mean time it is not at all clear that *feudum* or *feodum* was widely used in
Germany before the reign of Frederick I, when, as I shall argue, influences
from Italian academic law cannot be ruled out. Whatever difference of
meaning, if any, the scribes of documents intended by using *feodum* instead

[187] Hirsch, *Hohe Gerichtsbarkeit*, 173–80, 221–3.          [188] *Dip. Frid. I*, no. 238.
[189] Ibid. no. 151.
[190] For royal jurisdiction on crime: *Constitutiones*, i, nos. 74, 140, 277, 318; ii, nos. 196, 319,
371–2.
[191] See chapter 1 at nn. 33–5.          [192] *Monumenta Boica*, xiii, pp. 141–6.

of *beneficium*, the distinction was presumably irrelevant to German-speakers, since both words seem to have been translations of *lehen, len*, et cetera. Evidence that *beneficium* was a translation of *lehen* has already been mentioned.[193] By the thirteenth century *feodum* was being explained in the same way.[194] *Lehen* could also be translated as *mansa*, that is, a unit of property once thought of as a typical household's holding but by now generally much subdivided. A royal charter of 1162 referred to eighty manses *qui Frankonica lingua lehen appellantur*, that the margrave of Meissen held from the emperor and empire *in beneficium*. Here the *lehen* seem to be relatively small units that, while forming part of the margrave's benefice, may not all have been held from him with the same or even similar rights and obligations. The same applies to the sixty *novalia* (newly cleared lands) *que vulgo dicitur lehn* that the margrave gave to a church in 1173.[195]

*Feodum* seems to occur in royal charters for the first time after 1100. Most of the occurrences in the first half of the century are in charters dealing with Italy, Provence, and the southern or western edges of the kingdom of Germany proper, where Italian or French influence may be responsible, so that they may simply reproduce the terminology of the requests from these areas without implying that the royal chancery, let alone the emperor himself, noticed any political significance in it.[196] A judgement made in Conrad III's presence at Liège in 1140 ruled that the *ministeriales* of Stavelot abbey could not, as they claimed, hold village offices as hereditary fiefs (*per feodum et hereditario jure*), but this need not mean that Conrad heard or used the word: the German word *len* or *lehen* was presumably the one used in court.[197] If Conrad knew or noticed that the charter issued in his name rendered *lehen* as *feodum*, rather than the more familiar *beneficium*, that may not have struck him as having any bearing on the grander kind of *lehen* or benefice with which he would more usually be concerned. I have found only three cases where *feodum* or a derivative was used in connection with a count's benefice before 1162. In 1142 Duke Matthew of Lotharingia referred to property as having passed into his predecessors' fief (*in feodum antecessorum meorum*), but this French usage seems to have been unknown further east. On the French analogy it

---

[193] Above, n. 146.     [194] *Deutsches Rechtswörterbuch*, viii. 881.
[195] *Dip. Frid. II*, nos. 349, 600.
[196] Though Henry V's charters are not available in print, *Dip. Lothar III*, no. 23 repeats it from one of them. Also (omitting charters about Italy) *Dip. Lothar III*, no. 70; *Dip. Konrad III*, nos. 30, 40, 74, 132, 143, 146, 152, 193; *Dip. Frid. I*, no. 76. *Dip. Frid. I*, no. 382 suggests that Conrad III's chancery did not always scrutinize the contents of charters very carefully. Cf., as late as 1218, the use of *movere* (which seems to have been commoner in France than Germany) in *Constitutiones*, ii, no. 64.
[197] *Dip. Konrad III*, no. 40; cf. Wibald, *Epistolae*, no. 150 (p. 235).

probably meant that the land had come under his lordship or government, without implying that his rights in the lordship were in any way limited or dependent.[198] A charter of Conrad III, issued in 1147, referred to what a count in Carinthia possessed *jure feodi* in land and unfree servants (*mancipia*).[199] That the use of the word for royal benefices of high status was spreading into the rest of the kingdom may be suggested by Frederick Barbarossa's confirmation in 1154 of an exchange of land between the bishop of Speyer and the count of Württemberg: the count's land was said to have been held from the count palatine who had held it from the royal majesty *in feodum*.[200] But although *feodum* was becoming common at all levels, *beneficium* remained equally or more common. What is thought to be the original Latin version of the *Sachsenspiegel Lehnrecht* uses it throughout, and never *feodum*.[201]

A significant distinction between the two terms has been found in the episode when Pope Hadrian IV, writing to Frederick Barbarossa in 1157, referred to the *beneficia* that Frederick had received from the papacy.[202] According to a Cologne chronicler, what caused offence was that the word was interpreted (which clearly means translated) as *feodum*: Frederick asked indignantly whether the cardinals who brought the letter saw what the emperor had from God alone as the grant of the favour of a fief (*pro feodi beneficio computant*).[203] The problem with this story is that the translation of the pope's words presumably produced the word *lehen*, so that the distinction between *beneficium* and *feodum* would have been lost on the emperor and his lay magnates. The pope may not have realized this when he afterwards tried to smooth things over. What he had meant by *beneficium*, he said, was not *feudum* but *bonum factum*—a good deed or benefaction.[204] That Hadrian should introduce the word *feudum* here was not surprising: academic and professional lawyers in Italy were now using it and *beneficium* interchangeably in their discussions of subordinate property. While the two words were interchangeable in those contexts, *feodum* lacked the other, more anodyne connotations that *beneficium* had and to which Hadrian drew attention. In the very same year his chancery was using *feudum* in a charter so as to imply political subordination to the papacy.[205] It is easy enough, without postulating any essentially feudo-vassalic ideas or supposedly technical feudal usages as current in Germany, to see why the German court had objected in the first place. The point was

---

[198] *Chron. Saint-Mihiel*, no. 89, and cf. the *feudum advocati* in no. 50. See chapter 5.5.
[199] *Dip. Konrad III*, no. 193.                                [200] *Dip. Frid. I*, no. 76.
[201] Eike von Repgow, *Auctor Vetus*; *Handwörterbuch*, iv. 1230.
[202] Heinemeyer, '"beneficium"', citing earlier literature.        [203] *Chron. Reg. Colon.* 94.
[204] Otto and Rahewin, *Gesta Friderici*, 176–7, 196.
[205] *Liber Censuum*, no. 102; see chapter 6, at n. 219.

that Frederick did not regard the empire as bestowed on him by the pope in any sense that implied that his rights in it were subordinate.

Much more significant than the use of the word *feodum* on its own were the references that multiply from the 1120s on to *jus beneficiarium, jus beneficiale, jus feodale,* et cetera. From that time on (if not earlier) such expressions were used in documents that strongly suggest that the rights attached to a benefice or fief were seen to be desirable for the tenant. In a good many cases on which I have happened the desirable feature at issue was heritability. A significant number of the documents record disputes between churches and their *ministeriales* or other people of apparently quite modest status. Others, even if they are not about actual disputes, make it clear that such people wanted the rights, notably inheritance and security of tenure, that were, it seems, associated with benefices or fiefs. In some cases holding *in beneficium* is explicitly contrasted with being merely permitted or allowed to occupy property or with holding *in villicationem*. Either alternative, it seems, would allow the church to evict tenants in a way that would be more difficult if their holdings were recognized as benefices.[206] The Stavelot case of 1140 that has already been mentioned illustrates this. Despite royal judgements against them that were said to go back to the reign of Henry V, some of the *ministeriales* who administered the abbey's estate had been claiming for years to hold their offices (*ministeria, id est judiciarias et villicationes*) by fief and inheritance. Confronted by an abbot in good standing at the royal court they were bound to lose in the end. It was judged that no village official (*nullus judex qui vulgo scultetus dicitur, nullus villicus qui vulgariter maior dicitur*) could pass on his office to his son or hold it longer than the abbot wished.[207]

As I have already argued, the demands of military service and the use of unfree servants to perform it had created anomalies of status in Germany. *Ministeriales* who offended their monastic masters by swaggering about with swords in the manner of nobles were liable to start claiming the rights associated with the kind of fiefs or benefices that normally belonged to people who bore arms and rode fine horses.[208] In 1165 Frederick Barbarossa confirmed a judgement of the bishop of Naumburg that those who held benefices from the abbot of St Georgenkloster, Naumburg, and falsely called themselves *herscilt* could not, whatever they called them-

[206] *Dip. Konrad II*, no. 140 (thought to have been composed in the 1120s); *Reg. Hist. Westfaliae*, no. 192; *Casuum S. Galli Cont. II*, 161; *Urkundenbuch Niederrhein*, i, nos. 317, 370; *Mainzer UB*, i, no. 549; *Trad. Regensburg*, no. 792; *Trad. Freising*, no. 1536; *Dip. Lothar III*, nos. 35, 93; *Dip. Konrad III*, nos. 40, 167, 266; *Hamburg UB*, no. 189; *Dip. Frid. I*, no. 138; *Urkundenbuch Magdeburg*, no. 298.
[207] *Dip. Lothar III*, nos. 35, 93; *Dip. Konrad III*, no. 40; Wibald, *Epistolae*, no. 150 (p. 235); *Dip. Frid. I*, no. 1.
[208] *Casuum S. Galli Cont. II*, 161.

selves, have any feudal or other rights (*nullam feodalem justiciam nec ali-quam justiciam*) except those that the bishop's own beneficed men had.[209] In this case the benefice-holders are not called *ministeriales* or said to have been unfree, but they may have been people of rather moderate status: they could not stand up to an abbot who was backed by his bishop and king. Nor on this occasion was the issue seen as one of benefice or no benefice: it was possible to envisage a sort of benefice that had not acquired fully privileged status. There was still plenty of room for inconsistency and for drawing boundaries where the particular case and the status and influence of the parties required. In 1151 Conrad III and his court had confirmed a judge-ment by the advocate of the nunnery of Kitzingen against someone who had claimed tithes as held from Kitzingen by inheritance in benefice (*jure paterno in beneficio*). The advocate ruled, and the royal court confirmed, that none of the church's lay tenants could hold *de jure beneficiale* because the church did not have the *regalia* known as *herscilt*—which presumably meant that it did not owe military service.[210] In 1165, however, while Frederick was visiting Kitzingen, he ordered that neither the bishop of Bamberg nor anyone else was to intrude on the abbey's property; that in future the abbess was not to invest anyone with benefices that had reverted to the church through lack of heirs; but that those who held the church's benefices in the mean time should have them in peace and pass them on to their legitimate sons as their heirs.[211] It looks as if, *Heerschild* or no *Heerschild*, Kitzingen's benefice-holders were now allowed something like the *jus paternus* that had been at issue in 1151.

The lower boundary of benefice-worthy status was controversial, but not because benefices were the characteristic holdings of nobles. Except when they occupied royal offices or held land or advocacies from churches, nobles normally held property not in benefice but as *proprietas* carrying full and independent rights. At one time their rights in royal or church offices or lands had been determined more by the nature of the office and the sta-tus of the office-holder than by the connotations of the word benefice. To some extent, as the outcome of the cases about people of lower status shows, status was still very important, but *jus feodale* or *beneficiale* was now acquiring a definition that cut across the divisions of status. Churches had to be wary of using the word benefice (or fief) for advocacies as well as for humbler offices. In 1121 the bishop of Bamberg insisted that the advocate of his new monastery of Bosau was not to have *beneficiale jus*: if he did not

---

[209] *Urkundenbuch Naumburg*, i, no. 252; *Dip. Frid. I*, no. 475.

[210] *Dip. Konrad III*, no. 266; Krieger, *Lehnshoheit*, 160–1. Fried, 'Regalienbegriff', 465 n., cites this charter, but neither he nor Ott, 'Regalienbegriff', I think, discusses it.

[211] *Dip. Frid. I*, no. 489.

do his job (*si inutilis esse voluerit*) the monks could replace him.[212] In 1160 the bishop of Brixen granted the advocacy of Polling *feodale jure* to Henry the Lion, duke of Saxony and Bavaria. Henry would have been a hard person to cross whatever the bishop's reluctance to give lay advocates too much security of tenure. The best that could be got, probably, was the duke's promise that neither he nor his heirs would grant the advocacy to subadvocates *beneficiali jure*.[213] It was not just advocacies that could be lost to a church by the rights its tenants could claim in their benefices. The archbishop of Magdeburg arranged that a canon of his cathedral and the canon's mother were not to hold *ex jure beneficii* the properties he allowed them: they were simply to have the profit or income (*redditus*) for their lives, and when they died the properties were to revert to the church.[214]

All this argument about the rights of benefices or fiefs evokes the contemporary development of academic law in Italy. I have already suggested that rumours of Conrad II's 1037 ordinance may have reached Germany and influenced the development of custom there. Just how soon and how much the lines of argument used in Germany were influenced by those of Italian lawyers would no doubt become clearer with more study of more documents. In the mean time, while Italian influences in the first half of the twelfth century cannot be ruled out, German arguments about the rights or benefices could have been prompted by German conditions without any input from outside. By the second half of the century the likelihood of Italian influence, however slight, is greater. Abbot Markward of Fulda (1150–65) told how, under his negligent predecessors, laymen who held *villicationes* took the abbey's best manses and passed them on to their heirs *pro beneficiali jure* and how princes in different regions took the abbey's estates there and had them as if they had been benefices. As for the church's unfree tenants at home, they were exposed to every thief who told them: 'You are mine: I have acquired you in benefice.' Meanwhile the impoverished church still had to serve the king and the pope. If an abbot wanted to argue with all these laymen at law he was met by ingenious and cunning arguments about their rights, which they called *lehenreht*.[215] At first sight it is tempting to wonder if ingenious and cunning arguments came, at whatever remove, from Italian lawyers, but there must have been many German laymen sharp enough to work out the implications of developing custom about benefices for themselves, and then to work out arguments about it that were good enough to seem shockingly cunning to their opponents.

The temptation to suspect contact with professional lawyers is stronger

[212] *Urkundenbuch Naumburg*, no. 123.       [213] *Urkunden des Heinrichs des Löwen*, no. 43.
[214] *Dip. Konrad III*, no. 125.              [215] Franz, *Quellen*, no. 80.

in the case of the imperial *ministerialis* Werner of Bolanden (d. *c.*1190). In
1166 Werner made an exchange of property with the bishop of Metz under
which the bishop granted him one estate *in beneficium* and granted another
to the king's son, Henry, from whom Werner was to hold it *jure beneficii*.
Werner's rights in both were to be the same. As the charter says, they
exceeded the *jus beneficiale*—that is, presumably, the normal rights of
benefices. He was not to be obliged to do any service outside the area
(which is described), except if it should be necessary to go to the imperial
court, and could pass the property on to daughters if he had no sons and
to any agnates (including women) if he had neither. He was not to be summoned at law about *jus beneficiale* or anything else thought up by sharp
practice (*nec jure beneficii nec aliqua arte male excogitata unquam in causam
deberet vocari*). The provision that if he or his heirs delayed for several
years in claiming their benefice it was not to imperil their rights suggests
that Werner—who was presumably responsible for the terms—may have
had Frederick I's Roncaglia decrees of 1154 and 1158, or one of them, in
mind.[216] All this suggests a lawyerlike approach that turned *jus beneficiale*
from being merely the rights of fiefs into something more like feudal law
or law about fiefs. Werner later made (or had made) his list of the 'fiefs,
that is benefices' that he held from the kingdom and other lords and of
those that others held from him. In it he noted that he owed no service at
all for the benefices in the 1166 charter. About another of his many properties he noted that the identity of the alodholder was nothing to him, for
he installed a benefice-holder on it and required his dues from him as if he
were himself lord of the alod.[217] The forty-five lords from whom Werner
held benefices are evidence less of the 'multiple vassalage' or 'multiple allegiance' which is supposed to show the decline of old values than of the way
that he and others were able to use the developing conventions of property
law to build up their estates.[218]

  By the second half of the century there were plenty of ways in which
people like Werner could have picked up information about the new sort
of law. The texts of the Roncaglia decrees of 1136, 1154, and 1158 are preserved in Italian rather than German sources, so it is hard to say how
widely they were known in Germany, but some Germans who were at
Roncaglia in 1158 must have noticed them and some may have met lawyers
and talked to them. Some German students who attended Italian schools
may have brought back some knowledge of the law of fiefs along with their

[216] *Dip. Frid. I*, no. 517; see chapter 6.9.
[217] *Ältesten Lehnsbücher*, 19, 21, 24 and n. 191. For its date and the date of Werner's death:
Eckhardt, 'Das älteste Bolander Lehnbuch'.
[218] Cf. *Codex Falkensteinensis*, no. 2.

canon law.[219] Some of those who spent time as administrators or soldiers in Italy may have been helped or hindered by lawyers using the law of fiefs and may have brought their experience home with them. Provence was another early source of information about canon law, and other forms of academic law seem to have been studied there too.[220] In 1161 a charter from Frederick I to the bishop of Avignon allowed the bishop to confiscate fiefs from those who did not come after three summonses to answer his complaints against them, and also fiefs that were not claimed within the officially fixed time (*infra tempus legibus statutum*) of a year and a day.[221] These provisions strongly suggest a knowledge of the Roncaglia legislation that may well have gone along with a wider knowledge of the academic law of fiefs.[222] Taken with the provisions about the rules of inheritance that are also included in the charter, the impression is of a care to provide for eventualities that is surely the product of a new way of thinking about the administration and control of property. It may not be coincidental that the charter gave the bishop permission to appoint a notary.

Envisaging ways in which knowledge of academic law could have come into Germany is not the same as showing that it did or that, if it did, it made much impact on practice. It is well known that occasional phrases of Roman law got into royal charters at this time without altering the practice of the law.[223] One Roman phrase that does not seem to have been noticed—*pro tribunali sedere*—appears occasionally both in royal and other charters: there is no reason to suppose that the new knowledge and skills were restricted to people in the emperor's service.[224] To judge from my quite unsystematic searches, the words *vassalli* and *pares*, which may be pointers to knowledge of the texts of the law of fiefs, seem to be rare in the twelfth century.[225] The similarity between the judgement of peers and the traditional practices of collective judgement in any case makes it hard to know if the use of the phrase *judicium parium* implies any significant change in procedure.[226] Some movement towards more regular and formal procedures nevertheless seems to be discernible. The need for three summonses

[219] Coing, *Römisches Recht*, 12, 14–44.
[220] Classen, *Studium*, 39–40; Stelzer, *Gelehrtes Recht*, 33, 190–1; Gouron, *La Science juridique*, 32–6, 64–6.
[221] *Dip. Frid. I*, no. 329 (cf. 195). For evidence of jurists in Avignon slightly later: Giordanengo, *Droit féodal*, 81 n., 97–8, 139, 141, 147–8.
[222] Cf. also *Dip. Frid. I*, nos. 187, 634.
[223] Coing, *Römisches Recht*, 28–9; Appelt, 'Einleitung', 123–9.
[224] *Cod. Dip. Sax. Reg.* pt. 1, ii, no. 60 (1120); *Dip. Frid. I*, nos. 91, 242, 305, 752, 760, 762, 987; *Urkundenbuch Magdeburg*, no. 345; *Corpus Iuris Civilis*, i. 79, 629 (*Dig.* IV. 1, XXXVIII. 15).
[225] Vassals occur in *Dip. Frid. I*, nos. 300, 988; *Cod. Dip. Sax. Reg.* pt. 1, iii, no. 12. Peers: *Dip. Konrad III*, no. 74 (*compares*); *Dip. Frid. I*, no. 378 (battle with a peer), 493; Gislebert, *Chron.* 189, 251.
[226] Though *Constitutiones*, i, no. 367 may imply argument about new rules.

to court of a defendant is mentioned in the 1080s and may have been traditional, but the alternative of a single peremptory summons, which is
occasionally mentioned, clearly derived, as has been pointed out, from
Roman law.[227] Customary law was being stated in writing, elaborated, and
applied to different kinds of case.[228] Royal charters announcing judgements made in the king's court did not yet follow a regular form.
Occasionally in the twelfth century, however, and more often later in the
thirteenth, they show a trend towards a distinctive pattern that may reflect
more formal—and certainly distinctive—procedures in reaching judgement.[229] The appellant is identified, his request is stated, and sometimes
the emperor is said to have appointed a prince to give the judgement on
behalf of all. This practice, by which the judgement (*sententia*) was not
given by the president of the court himself, whenever it started and wherever it came from, would be mentioned in the *Sachsenspiegel* and seems to
have been followed, at least on occasion, in the later thirteenth century.[230]
My impression that by 1200 judgements were perhaps more often issued
in the form of normative rules is based on very few cases. Even if it were
right, the rules seem to have been freely manipulated to produce the
desired results, while the discussions that preceded judgements were presumably pretty unsystematic: if any expert or semi-professional legal
advisers were around they must have been in the background. All the same,
they may have been there.

The practice of government was changing, though again the evidence of
academic influence is slight and inconclusive. The first reference I have
found to the conversion of full property to benefices to be held from the
empire *jure beneficii* comes in Frederick I's peace ordinance of 1152, where
it served as a mitigated form of confiscation.[231] This is not very like the earlier creations of *fiefs de reprise* in southern France and Italy. Frederick's
agreement in the same year to allow the duke of Zähringen to have
Burgundy and Provence did not mention benefices, while his charter
establishing the duchy of Austria in 1156 refers to the duchy as held in
benefice only, it seems, in the traditional sense in which all duchies were
benefices.[232] The arrangements about inheritance in this case were not,

---

[227] Heinemeyer, 'Prozess', 53–5.
[228] *Urkundenbuch mittelrhein. Terr.*, i, no. 382; *Urkundenbuch St. Stephan*, no. 114; *Dip. Frid. I*, nos. 111 (Italy), 329 (Avignon), 774, 795, 934; *Annales Reichespergenses*, 472; *Annales Palidenses*, 94; *Monumenta Boica*, xii. 345 (peasants); *Constitutiones*, i, no. 372.
[229] *Dip. Frid. I*, nos. 304, 338, 475, 634, 795, 840; *Constitutiones*, i, no. 328.
[230] Eike von Repgow, *Sachsenspiegel Lehnrecht*, 93, 95 (67. 4, 10); Franklin, *Reichshofgericht*, ii. 268–70, lists some twelfth-century examples from 1124. For later, e.g. *Constitutiones*, iii. 72, 308, 477, 557. [231] *Dip. Frid. I*, no. 125.
[232] Ibid. nos. 12, 151; cf. Otto of St Blasius, *Chron.* 30. Ibid. 28–9 seems to involve a rather different kind of transaction.

however, traditional: not only was the duchy to be formally inherited, it was to pass to both sons and daughters. If Duke Henry and his wife died without children it would go to whoever they chose. One of the advantages of benefices that would emerge as the law became more standardized was that, given the lord's agreement, the grant of land in benefice or fief allowed the normal rules of inheritance to be circumvented in the interests of either party.[233]

It has been suggested that a charter of 1157 is evidence that Frederick had already started a policy of 'feudalizing' Germany. The charter quashes the grant of a benefice that the city of Marseille had made to the count of Provence although the city held the benefice from the archbishop of Arles and had not got either his or the emperor's consent.[234] The reason given for the quashing was that what was held from the empire ought to be possessed *jure feodali*, so that it could not be alienated without the consent of the lord. This may be connected with the Roncaglia ordinance of 1136 that Frederick had confirmed in 1154 and would confirm again in 1158. The charter's allusion to *jus feodale* cannot, however, have meant that the rules about fiefs were being extended to property (or noble property) in general.[235] Great lords and others continued to have other property alongside their benefices, as we can see when only the duchy of Saxony, and not his other inherited property, was confiscated from Henry the Lion in 1180. If Frederick had already introduced a blanket feudal law, or even significantly extended its competence, there would have been no point in his later agreements with the counts of Bar and Hainaut, which turned their alods into fiefs. These look like the same kind of transaction, designed to secure a measure of political subordination, that we have seen elsewhere.[236] It is significant that both counties were in sensitive border areas: presumably *reprises de fiefs* (*Lehnsauftragungen*) of this kind would have been unnecessary within the heart of Germany, where Frederick seems to have only made one grant in fief at all.[237] Some of his subjects were, however, already finding such transactions useful in dealing with their rivals, subjects, or potential subjects. The landgrave of Thuringia accepted a property and regranted it in benefice, *feodali iure*, before 1172, and Werner of Bolanden adopted the same method for building up his estate.[238] Some at least of the smaller properties that Werner granted back in benefice to those from whom he had acquired them, however, may not have enjoyed the full

---

[233] Krieger, *Lehnshoheit*, 48–52.                                    [234] *Dip. Frid. I*, no. 169.
[235] *Handwörterbuch*, ii. 1731.
[236] Grosdidier, *Comté de Bar*, 678–80; *Dip. Frid. I*, no. 857.      [237] *Dip. Frid. I*, no. 316.
[238] *Cod. Dip. Sax. Reg.* pt. 1, ii, no. 412; Patze, *Entstehung*, 303; *Ältesten Lehnsbücher*, 29, 31, 33–6.

*beneficiale jus* that counts on the borders of the kingdom would demand and receive.

When it was a matter of claiming property without heirs, or confiscating it—which could sometimes come to much the same thing—Frederick's policy was probably not very different from that of his Saxon and Salian predecessors, and not very different from that of his more powerful princes either.[239] But he, and even more his princes and lesser lords in the kingdom, may have had to pay more attention to forms, like the rules about the summonses that must be issued to potential victims, than had been paid in the previous century. This is illustrated above all in the proceedings against Henry the Lion in 1179–80.[240] The Gelnhausen charter that announced the forfeiture of the duchy of Saxony mentioned the threefold summons required under feudal law (*sub feodali jure*) and Henry's contempt, as well as the unanimous sentence of the princes, presumably because this sort of formality and detail mattered.[241] A century and a half earlier Conrad II had had to take to his bed and then lie on the floor crying in order to get the agreement of his son and the other princes to his confiscation of the duchy of Carinthia, but there was apparently no fuss about formalities: all that mattered was general consent, for which the princes wanted the presence of the king's son and heir.[242] That was a matter of prudent politics, not of formal legal rules. Not, of course, that rules had replaced politics by 1180: whatever the rules that would be deduced later from Frederick's regrant to others of the lands he had taken from Henry, the reason why he gave them to his supporters was surely political. There does not seem to have been any law or custom that forbade him to retain them.[243] Nor is there any indication in the Gelnhausen charter that, in dividing the spoils among his supporters, Frederick either formally or informally recognized anything new about the status of his great men or princes or that they had now become his tenants according to feudal law.[244]

## 9.7. Words, concepts, and law: the thirteenth century

Foolhardy as it may seem for an outsider to enter a field as well worked as that of Eike von Repgow's *Sachsenspiegel*, it is unavoidable.[245] Both parts of the work seem to have been written in the 1220s: the *Lehnrecht*, with

---

[239] For Henry the Lion: Helmold, *Cronica*, 201–2; Hüttebräuker, *Erbe*, 40, 58.
[240] Heinemeyer, 'Prozess', citing earlier work.             [241] *Dip. Frid. I*, no. 795.
[242] *Mon. Hist. Duc. Carinthiae*, no. 250.
[243] Goez, *Leihezwang*; Krause, 'Sachsenspiegel'.
[244] Cf. e.g. Mitteis, *Lehnrecht und Staatsgewalt*, 431–2, 435; Freed, 'Origins', 228.
[245] In the following section I shall cite the *Landrecht*, *Lehnrecht*, and *Auctor vetus* (the Latin version) using simply those titles, with book and paragraph numbers without an author or page numbers. All three, with the modern German translation, which I found extremely helpful

which I shall be primarily concerned, deals with the law about fiefs (*len*), while the much longer *Landrecht* deals with Saxon law in general, occasionally alluding to matters of *Lehnrecht*, so that there are a fair number of overlaps.[246] To an outsider who approaches it from the background so far sketched in this book and especially with the Italian and English law tracts in mind, the *Lehnrecht* does not give the impression of being a straight statement of customary law, whether new or archaic. Although it is not an academic discussion in the sense that the texts of the *Libri Feudorum* are, it occasionally refers to disagreements,[247] and throughout pays much attention to details of procedure that were surely not uncontroverted traditional practice. If it is right that Eike wrote the *Lehnrecht* first, and wrote first in Latin, he may have done so because the law about benefices cried out for discussion—discussion of a kind that would appeal to the literate. That makes sense in view of the twelfth-century material that has been cited. As it is put at the beginning of the Latin text, which is thought to be his own first version, he was writing to give instruction about *jus beneficialis*, which he later translated as *lenrecht*.[248] If it is also right that Eike could have learned most of his law through attending assemblies and listening to discussions and judgements,[249] that also supports the hypothesis, based on the twelfth-century material, that there were by now people around who combined Latin literacy with an intelligent and informed interest in practical points of the law of property. There was plenty for them to argue about—and in a rather different way from the way members of local assemblies would have argued a hundred years before. Trying to reconcile new rules and the new practice of rulers with traditional custom must have been difficult, especially when an assembly was confronted with written records that hindered compromise. It may also have been intellectually stimulating—stimulating enough to encourage Eike to write down the result, no doubt favouring his own views, and combine it into some kind of system.

Seen like this, the *Lehnrecht* suggests that particularly interesting subjects, around which a good deal of case-law had built up, were the borderline between benefices (or fiefs, though the Latin text never uses the word *feodum*) that deserved to be protected by *lenrecht* and those that did not; summons, whether to courts or armies; grants of reversions (i.e. grants to

(though I have checked everything I have cited against the original), are listed in the bibliography under Eike von Repgow.

[246] For a general account: *Handwörterbuch*, iv. 1227–37. Overlaps: Droege, *Landrecht*, 25–6; Krause, 'Sachsenspiegel', 49.

[247] *Lehnrecht*, 10. 1, 22. 1, 68. 7, 78. 1.

[248] *Auctor vetus*, I. 1.

[249] Ignor, *Allgemeine Rechtsdenkung*, 210.

take effect after the present tenant's death); some aspects of alienations; rules about inheritance, investiture, and homage; and the circumstances in which a lord could seize fiefs. Against the twelfth-century background that has been sketched, the first of these (the problem of the borderline between protected and unprotected fiefs) needs no explanation: it is the primary concern, as I shall argue shortly, of the opening discussion of the *Heerschild* and probably lies behind the sections at the end of the *Lehnrecht* that deal with fiefs in towns, fiefs consisting of village offices, and fiefs for—presumably rather low-status—soldiers (*borchlen, burmesterscap, sciltlen*). The interest in reversions may be explained by Frederick II's grants of them— though others, of course, may have been making similar grants.[250] Royal attempts between 1179 and 1227 to seize property in Saxony when its owner died, even on occasions when a brother was still available to inherit it, may account for some of the interest in what ought to happen on the death of a fiefholder, while the request that a new fiefholder should identify the fief with which he was to be invested looks like part of the systematic exploitation of property and power that one might expect at this period.[251] Arguments about both investiture and alienation may also have arisen because of information derived, directly or indirectly, from the royal ordinances of 1136, 1154, and 1158, and the legal learning they had provoked in Italy. The much discussed paragraphs in both the *Lehnrecht* and the *Landrecht* about not granting away or dividing jurisdictions (*gerichte, geruchte*) are strongly reminiscent of Lothar III's ordinance, repeated by Frederick I and embodied in the *Libri Feudorum*, on the alienation of imperial benefices.[252] The rule that required investiture and/or homage within a year and six weeks could come from Frederick's decrees, with six weeks added to the year and a day to allow for due summons.[253] It is of course possible that a year and a day was already traditional, but the extension looks like the result of argument. As for the rider that the permitted delay was multiplied by the number of layers of fiefs between the tenant and the king, that looks like a triumph of ingenuity provoked by a particular case or cases.[254] It may have been allowed on occasion, but one wonders how often and in how many lordships. The rule that a son and heir must do homage, although he automatically came into full possession of his father's

---

[250] Goez, *Leihezwang*, 92.

[251] Krause, 'Sachsenspiegel', 97–9, and cf. Henry the Lion's apparently similar policy, above, n. 239; *Lehnrecht*, 24. 2–3. On identification of fiefs: Krieger, *Lehnshoheit*, 105, and index: fiefs, recognition.

[252] *Landrecht*, III. 53. 3; *Lehnrecht*, 71. 3; cf. *Auctor vetus*, II. 68; Krause, 'Sachsenspiegel'.

[253] *Lehnrecht*, 10. 5, 22. 1; cf. *Auctor vetus*, I. 32. *Lehnrecht*, 13. 1–2 is linked with these. Eckhardt drew attention to its similarity to Lehmann, *Consuetudines Feudorum: Antiqua*, 23 (VII. 5).

[254] *Lehnrecht*, 25. 3–4.

fief so that he did not require formal investiture, draws a nice distinction that was presumably partly conditioned by political circumstances:[255] in England, while the same rule applied to property held from other lords, the king took over what was held directly from him until homage was done. It is difficult to believe that these details—and all the others—were agreed all over Saxony, let alone all over Germany, but it seems quite likely that the issues, and others like them, were widely discussed.

The *Sachsenspiegel* demonstrates the extent to which the law about fiefs or benefices had become a separate branch of law. It could be discussed separately and had some distinctive rules and practices, but it was not yet perceived as a separate system of law, as the overlaps between *Landrecht* and *Lehnrecht* show. The law about fiefs must often have been seen in any area as part, if a rather special part, of the general law of that area—the law of the land, the *Landrecht*. Nor did the *Lehnrecht* always have separate courts.[256] The first recourse in a matter concerning it must be to the lord from whom the fief was held, but anyone appealing further normally went to the *overe herre* (Latin: *superior dominus*), who looks in at least some references like the local prince or ruler whose court or assembly would also judge cases about full property and much else.[257] If the fief was held from someone with full property (*egen*; Latin: *proprietas*), however, they went straight to the king—though the way Eike justifies this raises some doubts about it as a regular practice.[258] Although the rules about summons may have sometimes meant holding special meetings to deal with cases about fiefs, it seems highly improbable that meetings dealing with different sorts of cases were regularly kept separate. Eike maintains that, though a fiefholder need not answer to the supreme lord (*deme oversten herren*) so long as he answers his immediate lord, he is none the less the man of the supreme lord.[259] Eike may use 'man' here in the general sense of subject rather than in the traditionally feudo-vassalic sense, but either way his view was different from that which John de Blanot would later adopt.[260]

There is much else in the *Sachsenspiegel* that deserves discussion in the context of my subject but cannot have it here. The *Heerschild*, however, which Eike discusses near the beginning of both his treatises, must be mentioned.[261] The account of the *Heerschild* in the *Landrecht* follows a

[255] *Lehnrecht*, 6, 22. See index: primer seisin.

[256] They were still not, or not always, clearly separate in the later middle ages: Diestelkamp, *Lehnrecht*, 265–6; Krieger, *Lehnshoheit*, 511–55.

[257] *Lehnrecht*, 15. 1, 38. 1, 48. 2, 49. 1, 76. 2 (where *vor sime lantrichtere* (*in judicio* in *Auctor vetus*) is translated by Schott as *vor seinem Lehenrichter*).

[258] *Lehnrecht*, 65. 4, 69. 8.

[259] Ibid. 14. 3.                                          [260] Chapter 7, at nn. 116–18.

[261] *Landrecht*, I. 3. 1–2; *Lehnrecht*, 1, 2. 4–6; *Auctor vetus*, I. 2–3. For earlier uses of the word, above at nn. 137–8, 209–10.

description of the seven ages of the world, so that the seven ages are paralleled by the seven layers or orders of society, of which Eike lists six: first, the king; second, bishops, abbots, and abbesses; third, lay princes; fourth, free lords; fifth, free people of standing in court (*scepenbare lude*) and the men of the free lords; and lastly their men. He seems to have tried to supply the missing seventh by alluding to the way that princes were now the men of bishops, as they had not been formerly, but as he had already put bishops and lay princes into different levels it does not work. The trouble with the whole scheme was that Eike was trying to match it with the seven ages, which were then intellectually fashionable. In the first Latin version of the *Lehnrecht* the point of introducing the *Heerschild*—there called *beneficialis clipeus*—seems, as one might expect from twelfth-century disputes, to have been to define those who had the right to protected tenure. Fundamentally that was generally a matter of status, but Eike, like the author of the first tract of the *Libri Feudorum*, found it difficult to disentangle social from political status and both from property relations, and then to fit the muddle of real life into his scheme.[262] The tangle is illustrated by the case of the bishop of Lausanne. After Frederick I had allowed the duke of Zähringen to have the right of investing three bishops in his area with their *regalia*, the bishop of Lausanne, who was one of them, was no longer summoned to royal assemblies and felt a loss of status.[263] He would have been in the wrong place in Eike's scheme. That the king sometimes held land from others would also have seemed an anomaly to Eike if he had known or thought about it in this context.[264] Like much else, it only became an anomaly when an intellectual—for Eike must be counted as such, even if he was not an academic—tried to make rules and build them into a system. So far as the *Heerschild* is concerned, the important point— or what started as the important point—was that people within the ranks of the *Heerschild* had *beneficiale jus* and those below it did not. The layers that later came to represent such a beautiful example of 'feudal hierarchy' have a distinctly intellectual and theoretical character. As their position in the *Landrecht* implies, they represented an ideal pattern of social and political relations in general, not just those created by fiefholding. Many people were under the jurisdiction or authority of someone, who was often, though not invariably, in a higher order by Eike's ranking, without holding a fief from him or her. Taking the scheme as a hierarchy of property rights, with the corollary that the links between the ranks were normally

---

[262] See chapter 6.8.      [263] *Constitutiones*, i, no. 281.
[264] *Dip. Frid. I*, nos. 577, 954. Many other supposed anomalies have been pointed out, e.g. Ficker, *Vom Heerschilde*, 37–51; Freed, *Counts of Falkenstein*, 63.

created by the grant of property by people in higher ranks to people in lower ranks, compounds the problem that Eike himself created when he tried to fit everyone—or everyone who mattered—into seven orders to match the seven ages.

If it is right that Eike's account of *Lehnrecht* reflects both changes in practice and closer and more co-ordinated habits of argument about law, then its rapid diffusion and adaptation in other areas suggests that the changes were not confined to Saxony and that practices and arguments elsewhere were sufficiently similar to make his work seem relevant. A charter issued in 1222 by Frederick II's son Henry, king of the Romans, suggests that some of the same problems were being confronted in Lotharingia.[265] The charter resolves some of them in the same way as Eike and others differently.[266] One difference concerned the qualifications for taking part in judgement. There had always been a potential conflict between respect for status and authority on the one hand and the right of underdogs to be judged by their peers on the other. Eike went for status: no one could judge anyone of higher status than himself and princes could judge anyone.[267] The 1222 ruling was that any *ministerialis* with a fief (anywhere or only within the same lordship?[268]) could judge about the fiefs of nobles and *ministeriales*, though not about those of princes.[269] Perhaps the inferiority of *ministeriales* was offset from the point of view of their lords by their official position. In Augsburg, meanwhile, a problem arose about the kind of property that could claim the protection of the feudal law. In 1225 the royal court ruled that furs, winter boots, and similar gifts could not: the abbot of St Ulrich could give them at his pleasure but his officials and servants had no right to demand them.[270]

While the details of the law about fiefs were being hammered out, its scope was being enlarged by the conversion of full property to fiefs. In 1231, for instance, the bishop of Münster and the count of Cleve made an agreement by which the count received back five estates *in feodo* that he had formerly held as his *proprietas*: the obligations on the property were unchanged and male and female inheritance would be allowed. The point was to confirm an alliance of mutual aid, counsel, and defence against everyone except the emperor and the church of Cologne.[271] In 1235 Otto, the grandson of Henry the Lion, was reconciled with the emperor by surrendering to him his own castle of Lüneburg which in German was called

---

[265] *Constitutiones*, ii, no. 279.
[266] Apart from the point discussed below, cf. c. 3 with *Lehnrecht*, 65. 4.
[267] *Lehnrecht*, 71. 20; cf. 12. 1, 69. 1–2.
[268] Cf. *Constitutiones*, i, no. 367; *Auctor vetus*, II. 57; *Lehnrecht*, 69. 1.
[269] *Constitutiones*, ii, no. 279, clause 1; cf. no. 196.   [270] Ibid. ii, no. 288.
[271] *Westfalisches UB*, iii. 292.

his *Eigen (proprium castrum suum Luneburch quod idiomate Theutonico vocatur eygen)*. Frederick then formally granted it to the empire along with the city of Brunswick, which he had just bought for the purpose—that is, in modern terms, he converted it all from his personal or family property (*Hausgut*) to that of *Reichsgut*. He then made Lüneburg and Brunswick into a duchy, which Otto, as duke and prince, was to hold as a fief of the empire, to be inherited by sons and daughters.[272] The charter exemplifies not only the new clarity of categories but the way that duchies and counties, which had long been known as benefices, were being integrated into the new law of benefices or fiefs.[273]

In contrast with most of the great nobles of France, however, the lay princes of Germany seem to have generally retained some estates that were not reckoned as fiefs: the contrast may be testimony not only to the relative weakness of the German monarchy by the end of the thirteenth century but to its earlier strength. Whereas the category of full or alodial property had more or less disintegrated in the western kingdom, the maintenance of government had preserved it in Germany into the time when legal and political conditions made a general redefinition impracticable. But although princes were not brought entirely within the scope of the new feudal law, it provided a vocabulary and framework for their relations with the monarchy which kings found helpful when the civil wars of the thirteenth century eroded their traditional authority. The principle that all jurisdiction had to be delegated from the emperor, enunciated by Frederick I and confirmed in 1234, 1274, and 1283, looked less unreal in the context of Eike's *Heerschild* than it would otherwise have done by the late middle ages.[274] The position of great churches and their property also made sense against the background of the new feudal law. Like duchies and counties, bishoprics and abbeys had long been thought of as royal benefices, bishops were invested with their *regalia* by the king, and their property was under royal protection so that gifts and exchanges were confirmed by royal charters. In the multiplying copies and adaptations of the *Sachsenspiegel* bishops and abbots appeared immediately below the king in the *Heerschild*. It is not surprising that in the thirteenth century church property began to be called fiefs and integrated into the feudal law.[275]

Within principalities and lesser lordships, rulers used the same method

---

[272] *Constitutiones*, ii, no. 197.
[273] Cf. Calmet, *Hist. Lorraine*, ii, preuves, col. 481–2; *Urkundenbuch Niederrhein*, ii, no. 646; *Constitutiones*, iii, nos. 476–8, iv, nos. 195, 479–82, 995, though the categories were not always clear: e.g. *Trad. Oberaltaich*, no. 127, and below, on Pomerania.
[274] *Constitutiones*, ii, no. 319, iii, nos. 27, 347.
[275] Boerger, *Belehnung*, 43–53. For a stage in this transformation: *Verdener Geschichtsquellen*, ii, no. 35.

of binding nobles and free men—particularly those with castles—to them by making property into fiefs.[276] Some, and some lesser lords, used it to extend their control over quite small properties. Some of these small new fiefs, although held by people who look little if anything more than peasants, were apparently held by feudal law, though one wonders if all were: the word fief continued to be used sometimes for peasant properties in Germany, as it was elsewhere, in ways that later lawyers and historians would not approve.[277] The creation of fiefs was probably less important to the maintenance or extension of most princes' powers than it was to the king's powers over princes, though this varied from place to place. Many *fiefs de reprise* are said to have been created in Hainaut and elsewhere near the French border, but the elimination of large alodial properties there may also have happened more insidiously, as it did over the border, where noble property in general came to be reckoned as fiefs from the thirteenth century.[278] In Austria, on the other hand, though some noble property was converted to fiefs, a good deal was not.[279] In Frisia it was not apparently until the fifteenth century that noble properties were turned into fiefs by new rulers who thought that that was what they ought to be—though the change made then did not affect rights and obligations significantly.[280] The stage at which rulers began to use the creation of fiefs and the feudal law to strengthen their hands and the ways they did it clearly varied. In the principality of Cologne a hybrid category, the *ligium allodium* of St Peter (the patron saint of the archbishopric), is referred to in 1254, when it was used to justify bringing lordships of the count of Jülich under the archbishop's jurisdiction.[281]

Pomerania suggests the way that categories could be adapted and rules made that may seem wrong to a modern legal historian but served the purposes of rulers and apparently made sense to their subjects. By the later thirteenth century churches there seem generally to have held their lands *in proprietate* and laymen to have held theirs *in feodo* from a church, the duke, or another lord. What churches had in other lordships, however, seems not to have been considered *in proprietate*, while lay property, if

---

[276] Caesarius, *Wundergeschichten*, iii. 243–4; *Westfalisches UB*, iii, nos. 618–20; *Urkunden Eichstätt*, i, nos. 73, 87; Diestelkamp, *Lehnrecht*, 57 n., 91–3, 138; Parisse, *Noblesse lorraine*, 553–66, 589, 604, 725. Ficker and Puntschart, *Vom Reichsfürstenstande*, ii, contains many references but not all are equally convincing.

[277] *Eppsteinschen Lehensverzeichnisse*, nos. 39, 60, 105, 206, 270.

[278] Didier, *Droit des fiefs*, 41–3; *Coutumes de Hainaut*, 1–3; Génicot, *Économie rurale*, i. 74–88, ii. 26; chapter 7.3.

[279] Brunner, *Land und Herrschaft*, 355, 371 (Eng. trans. 202, 305).

[280] Diestelkamp, 'Lehnrecht und Territorien', 79–80.

[281] *Urkundenbuch Niederrhein*, ii. no. 410.

exempted from dues, could be held *cum omni jure et proprietate*.[282] In 1332 the duke as lord of the fief confirmed the sale from one citizen of Stettin to another, who intended to give the property to a church, of *proprietatem totam seu directum dominium* of ten manses, with jurisdiction.[283] The estate does not seem to have been turned from fief to *proprietas* simply in anticipation of the gift: the two categories seem not to have been always mutually exclusive, for there are other occasions on which what was sold *cum omni jure et proprietate* seems to have been held from a church.[284] There are problems in the terminology of the Pomeranian charters, including the varied connotations that seem to attach to *proprietas*, but they cannot be solved by assuming that the draftsmen were inexpert bunglers.[285] There is no reason why they should have used words in the ways that contemporary Italian academics or later lawyers would think appropriate. Working out what they meant needs more study of the rights and obligations of Pomeranian property without forcing it into the categories that we think appropriate. The dukes of Pomerania and princes of Rügen seem to have had competent servants who had a clear idea of what they were about as they made records and collected dues, including presumably the dues (*lenware*) that seem to have been owed on the registration of conveyances between subjects.[286] Some of them may have had some knowledge of academic law: the first charter to mention *dominium utile et directum*, which was issued in 1269, was drawn up by a ducal chaplain who was also a notary.[287] The word vassal occurs fairly often. Though it sometimes seems to mean official or servant rather than fiefholder, there may be a faint echo of the academic texts in a charter of 1249 (not a ducal charter), which granted property *jure feodali*, when it refers to the fidelity which vassals owe to lords (*fidelitatem quam vasalli dominis tenentur*).[288] Expressions like *pheodum verum et legale* also have a quasi-professional ring.[289] The relatively free hand that colonial conditions gave to those who set up a legal and governmental system may, however, have contributed as much to the rules of property-holding that developed in Pomerania as any book-learning that some of the rulers' servants had acquired.

Without arguing that there was a regular legal profession engaged in secular law it is possible to suggest that there are hints elsewhere in

---

[282] The exceptions: *Pommersches UB*, nos. 5104; 1808, 3750, 4257, 4755, 4952. Cf. Benl, *Gestaltung*, 148, 298–342, *et passim*.

[283] *Pommersches UB*, no. 4959.                     [284] Ibid. nos. 1808, 3750, 4755.

[285] Cf. Benl, *Gestaltung*, 304–15, 350, and 202–3, 343–66.

[286] *Pommersches UB*, nos. 894, 2367, 3441–2, 3750, 4547–8, 5282.          [287] Ibid. no. 894.

[288] Ibid. no. 500; cf. e.g. Lehmann, *Consuetudines: Antiqua*, 26 (VIII. 11). Vassal occurs earlier in *Pommersches UB*, ii than the index says. Vol. i has no *index verborum*.

[289] e.g. *Pommersches UB*, nos. 377, 1046, 1877, 3418.

Germany at the presence of what might be called legal experts: that is, people who may or may not have attended formal schools, but who drafted charters, gave advice, or spoke for their clients, not only from general experience of local custom and the ways of the world, but with fairly specialized knowledge of the procedures and arguments that were likely to be useful in preserving and enlarging their property. The spokesman (*vorspreke, prolocutor*) and the advisers that Eike allowed a fiefholder to have with him in court had to hold fiefs from the same lord, which makes them look unprofessional, though they might be as wily and experienced as Eike himself.[290] The requirement, however, like the insistence in the 1222 rulings about procedures in Lotharingia that an advocate or *patronus cause* must be a fiefholder of the duke, suggests that the point was controversial:[291] few things are more suggestive of professional law than distrust of its practitioners. In 1274 King Rudolf issued a number of orders about the working of the royal court. Among these were regulations of the fees charged and a warning to advocates to compose differences amicably and not demand more than was due from those whose advocates they were.[292]

Some, even all, of these advocates may have been primarily canon lawyers, but professional boundaries, like academic boundaries, were less jealously marked than they would be later.[293] Hostiensis (d. 1271) mentions the rule of inheritance to fiefs as he saw it applied in Germany when he was there. Since he cites the *Consuetudines Feudorum* (that is, presumably, what I call the *Libri Feudorum*) on a related point he may have discussed it with his German colleagues.[294] As late as 1371 an opinion or *consultacio* about the obligations of homage that was written for the rulers of Hanover was, it said, drawn *ex legibus et canonibus*—*legibus* here probably including the tenth section of the Novellae, that is, the *Libri Feudorum*.[295] The word vassal seems to be used more frequently as the thirteenth century goes on, difficult as it is to assess the significance of this at a time of greater documentation. Sometimes, though by no means always, it is used in the sense of fiefholder. It is especially suggestive of influence from academic law when it is used in rulings that conform to the requirements of the law of fiefs, as when judgements are made or ordered to be made by fellow vassals or peers.[296] While most of the documents con-

---

[290] *Lehnrecht*, 67. 4–6, 10.  [291] *Constitutiones*, ii, no. 279.

[292] Ibid. iii, no. 72; cf. Rockinger, *Briefsteller*, 998–9.

[293] Stelzer, *Gelehrtes Recht*, 124, 145–236, though in her discussion of the diffusion of texts, pp. 101–4, 109, she does not mention those of the law of fiefs.

[294] Hostiensis, *Summa Aurea*, fo. 154.

[295] *Urkundenbuch Braunschweig*, iv, no. 118. See chapter 6.8.

[296] *Constitutiones*, iii, nos. 438, 542, 557, 585, 586; iv, no. 63; *Urkundenbuch Niederrhein*, ii, no. 646; *Urkunden Eichstätt*, i, no. 209.

cerning property in a collection of thirteenth- and early fourteenth-century formularies concern ecclesiastical property, any notary who could cope with these would have to understand a good deal about lay property too, for which a few forms are given.[297] Some information in the textbooks was wrong, like the statement that privileges to lay people were not granted for ever, while the listing of documents according to the nature of the transfer (*de titulo vendicionis, de donacione inter vivos*), however useful for actual drafting, is unilluminating about categories of property. More was probably learned by training on the job, whether in writing charters or listening to arguments.

However they acquired it, some Germans were surely acquiring a certain practical expertise in the law connected with secular government and estate management, and some were using it to earn at least part of their living, whether in the service of rulers and property-owners or as advisers to those who had to go to court. The wide dispersal of governmental authority and jurisdiction, just as it made for variations in the law to be learned and practised, also prevented anything like a single profession developing, let alone the kind of élite that appeared where more business was concentrated in fewer courts. The use of German in charters and records suggests the workaday and practical level at which much legal work was done. Nevertheless, it looked for a while in the thirteenth century as though the royal court might develop a more extensive jurisdiction in which the law about fiefs would often be involved. Although in practice feudal law varied from place to place, the arguments it had provoked since the early twelfth century had invited appeals for authoritative resolution in a way that the law of full property apparently did not. As knowledge, however indirect, of the academic background filtered through, the stimulus to argument and appeal was increased and so was the tendency, however slight as yet, towards professionalism.

## 9.8. *The rights and obligations of property, 1100–1300*

To describe the rights and obligations of fiefs, full property, and peasant property all over Germany during this period would be a vast task, especially as I have not found many local studies of rights and obligations to guide me. All that will be attempted here will be a brief and summary sketch, largely ignoring local variations, of the ways in which the rules seem to have changed.

As we have seen, twelfth-century laymen thought of the rights of

---

[297] Rockinger, *Briefsteller*, 262–5, 294, 334, 337–9, 380–4, 938–48, 981, 1018.

beneﬁces or ﬁefs as including heritability.[298] While most property held in
ﬁef or in beneﬁce was from now on inherited, however, not all of it was.
One of the advantages of beneﬁces in Germany was that their conditions
could be varied by individual agreements—agreements that were now
much more often recorded in writing and were therefore more likely to
remain in force. Eike's disapproval of the opinion that ﬁefs could be
granted for ﬁxed terms suggests that some were but that their status was in
doubt.[299] Some churches still made grants for life or lives. Sometimes
these served as recompense for a gift or as a compromise after a dispute,
but at least two churches in Pomerania were making three-life grants of the
old sort at the very end of the thirteenth century and beyond.[300] The duke
of Pomerania also made a grant for life, called a *precaria*, to his chaplain in
1324. Other lords may well have made similar grants, whatever their clerks
called them.[301] Some of the grants of reversions to ﬁefs at present held by
others, which were common enough to interest Eike, may imply that the
current holder had only a life interest, though others could have depended
on the absence of heirs.[302] The seizure, or attempted seizure, of ﬁefs by the
king and by churches when heirs failed is amply attested.[303] It was, however, probably during this period that kings lost the right to seize full property when it lacked heirs. The combination of more written records, more
formal legal argument, and, by the end of the period, declining power was
against them. Princes and other lords meanwhile probably claimed heirless
ﬁefs with increasing regularity. That was especially useful where all or
most lay property was now counted as ﬁefs, as seems to have been the case
in Hainaut under French inﬂuence or in Pomerania in conditions of conquest.[304] Because of the contractual nature of most German ﬁefs, their use
to conﬁrm political alliances, and the continuing variety of German law,
however, it was possible for a lord to agree that a ﬁef would be inherited
for ever without falling to him.[305]

Failure of heirs depended on the rules of inheritance. It is sometimes
said that inheritance to ﬁefs was originally restricted to sons and was only

[298] *Dip. Konrad III*, nos. 121, 123, do not seem to me (*pace* Faussner, 'Verfügungsgewalt',
351) to show a general rule against inheritance.
[299] Eike von Repgow, *Sachsenspiegel Lehnrecht*, 78. 1 and *Auctor vetus*, III. 21.
[300] *Urkundenbuch Niederrhein*, i, no. 371; *Dip. Konrad III*, no. 63; *Urkundenbuch St. Stephan*,
no. 208; *Urkunden Eichstätt*, i, no. 81; *Pommersches UB*, nos. 1567, 1780, 1808, 3237, 4895, 5216.
[301] *Pommersches UB*, no. 3765.
[302] *Dip. Konrad III*, no. 123; *Urkunden Eichstätt*, no. 50; Goez, *Leihezwang*, 76–94.
[303] e.g. Krause, 'Sachsenspiegel', 97–9; Ficker and Puntschart, *Vom Reichsfürstenstande*, 225;
*Constitutiones*, ii, no. 351, iv, nos. 59–63; *Epistolae Saec. XIII*, ii, no. 592; Arnold, *Count and
Bishop*, 157–62. Cf. for peasant holdings: *Urkundenbuch Halberstadt*, no. 308.
[304] *Pommersches UB*, no. 3669; for other lay rulers as recorded later: Diestelkamp, *Lehnrecht*,
257–8; Brunner, *Land und Herrschaft*, 371 (Eng. trans. 305).
[305] *Westfälisches UB*, no. 485. The same intention may lie behind *Dip. Frid. I*, no. 517.

later widened. The rule was often enunciated or assumed in this period, but there is no evidence that it had ever been generally accepted or that it was regularly observed now. Both statements of the principle and exceptions to it were made throughout the twelfth and thirteenth centuries.[306] While one advantage of fiefs—for both parties—was that they embodied *ad hoc* contracts, full property still set the standard, so that the practice of inheritance to fiefs tended to approximate as closely to that for full property as lords would allow. This can be seen not only in provisions for inheritance by daughters if there were no sons but in the joint tenure of fiefs and their division between sons.[307] Even where rulers were able to make most or all lay property above peasant level into fiefs, it did not result in a general exclusion of women.

My general impression is that more rules about the right to alienate property were now being formulated, but what types of property they were intended to cover or how consistently they were applied in practice seems to become more problematical the closer one looks. The impact of the Roncaglia ordinances of 1136, 1154, and 1158 on Germany is uncertain. The 1136 ordinance was apparently intended to prevent alienation by the tenants of counts and bishops, rather than any grants that they themselves made. Since it was designed to preserve military service to the king it may well have been intended to apply to Germany—unless something of the sort was already supposed to apply there.[308] The prohibition on the division of counties et cetera in Frederick Barbarossa's second reissue of the ordinance suggests a new concern with the responsibilities of delegated authority which implies that the rules were intended to apply to counts as well as to their tenants.[309] Occasional revocations of grants made by lay nobles in Germany seem to reflect this preoccupation, but it seems highly unlikely that such revocations were made in conformity with generally recognized and enforced rules about the alienation or subinfeudation of all fiefs as such.[310] In 1296 the unlicensed alienation of fiefs by Otto of Burgundy entailed not merely the revocation of his grants but the confiscation of all his fiefs and all his other property, movable and immovable.[311] Rules that were invoked or manipulated in exceptional political circumstances need not have reflected generally accepted norms.

[306] Wibald, *Epistolae*, no. 104; *Dip. Frid. I*, nos. 151, 158, 200, 329, 489, 517, 857, 522; Weinrich, *Quellen*, no. 70; *Coutumes de Hainaut*, 3–4; *Constitutiones*, ii, nos. 197, 298, 310; iii, no. 585; iv, nos. 59, 62; *Urkundenbuch Niederrhein*, ii, nos. 173, 646; *Cart. Metz*, no. 163; *Westfälisches UB*, iii, nos. 618–19; *Urkunden Eichstätt*, i, no. 73; Kern, *Acta imperii*, no. 171.
[307] Eike von Repgow, *Sachsenspiegel Landrecht*, I. 17. 1, *Lehnrecht*, 8, 29, 32, 71. 4.
[308] *Dip. Lothar III*, no. 105.                                         [309] *Dip. Frid. I*, no. 241.
[310] Ibid. no. 634; *Constitutiones*, ii, no. 160; iii, no. 347, though iii, no. 26 seems more general.
[311] Ibid. iii, no. 557.

The application of the twelfth-century ordinances to ecclesiastical property is equally unclear. Efforts to control alienations by bishops and
abbots—including the grant of benefices or fiefs—were an old story and
one that was by no means over.[312] In 1223 prelates who did not receive
investiture from the emperor and did not have what was commonly called
*heerschilt* were forbidden to grant perpetual fiefs.[313] What case may have
provoked this ruling is unknown, but it may have been designed to protect
churches against their tenants rather than restrict their own powers. The
Roncaglia ordinances, or the law of fiefs in which they were incorporated,
may have provided a convenient justification for revocations of grants in
particular cases, but sometimes the reasons given for restricting or revoking a bishop's grants were different from those implied in the ordinances.[314] In any case, all these restrictions were surely applied very
selectively. Bishops and abbots clearly did not get royal consent for their
own grants of benefices as a matter of course, nor did they probably enforce
the 1136 restrictions regularly on alienations by the tenants. In 1228 the
bishop of Bamberg made a grant to his dear friend the count palatine of the
Rhine and duke of Bavaria under feudal law, but subject to an agreement
(*hoc pacto interposito*) that the count-duke and his heirs were not to pledge,
sell, nor in any way alienate the property from the church without special
permission. A grant by the bishop of Metz ten years later conveys the same
impression that prohibitions on alienation had to be specially noted and
emphasized.[315]

What we are seeing is more rule-making, more recording of rules and
agreements, and more efforts by lords to control the disposition of property, all probably taking place against a more active land market. It was easier to justify controlling fiefs than full property. Some of the controls on
fiefs may have been developed by churches on the analogy of those they
imposed on peasant holdings.[316] *Ministeriales*, like peasants, could be forbidden, for instance, to sell their property to anyone outside the estate, or
perhaps required to give the lord the first refusal. Though these restrictions applied most clearly to what they held in benefice, some of them
apparently found it wise to secure permission to sell or give away what they
held with supposedly full rights.[317] In Pomerania, it looks as though con-

---

[312] Above, n. 152. Outright alienation could still be contemplated in the thirteenth century:
Rockinger, *Briefsteller*, 338–9 (no. 101).

[313] *Constitutiones*, ii, no. 94: though issued at Capua, the reference to *heerschilt* shows it applied
to Germany. See index: *Heerschild*.

[314] *Dip. Frid. I*, no. 329; *Constitutiones*, i, no. 328; ii, nos. 150, 277.

[315] *Monumenta Boica*, xii. 374–5; *Cart. Metz*, no. 163.       [316] Cf. chapter 5, at nn. 115–16.

[317] *Dip. Konrad III*, no. 81; *Dip. Frid. I*, no. 138; *Verdener Geschichtsquellen*, no. 33;
*Hamburgisches UB*, nos. 165, 313; *Cod. Dip. Sax. Reg.* pt. 1, iii, no. 330; *Constitutiones*, ii, no. 172;
cf. Patze, *Entstehung*, 508–9.

veyances of all free property were supposed to be registered with the duke
or the relevant ecclesiastical lord if they were to carry full rights.[318] In the
early fourteenth century a church there forbade someone who acquired
perpetual property under it to alienate to any knight, squire (*armiger*), or
other person of a different condition from himself.[319] Restrictions on gifts
or sales to churches seem to have started relatively late in Germany, first,
it seems, in town charters during the later thirteenth century.[320] In 1297
the royal court, in answer to a question from the abbess of Essen, ruled that
any vassal or *ministerialis* holding a fief from her church and with no
ascending or descending heirs could give or leave the fief to the church,
provided that it was not held jointly with others.[321] The moment was
hardly appropriate for enunciating a rule that would be as unwelcome to
churches as were the kinds of restrictions on gifts that rulers elsewhere
were imposing, but it would have been a difficult one for any thirteenth-
century German king to consider. As the abbess's case suggests, the biggest
impediment to alienation may in many cases have come from the relatives
and potential heirs of the would-be donor or vendor rather than from his
or her lord. References to the consent of wives and family or to their objections are very common in conveyances of full property and can occasionally be found in those of fiefs too.[322] The first unambiguous reference to
greater freedom of disposition for acquired property that I have found for
Germany comes from 1210.[323] It is apparently stated as a rule in late
medieval town customs.[324]

While it was easier to construct legal arguments for imposing controls
on fiefs than on *proprietas*, the formal categories were probably less important than political circumstances and the status of the property-holder.
The 1158 ordinance said that a lord was not to transfer a fief without the
consent of his vassal. Consents of fiefholders (not, of course, normally
called vassals in Germany) can be found occasionally before then, probably illustrating the greater formality and better record-keeping that are discernible quite early in the twelfth century. Irrespective of the ordinance,
they were particularly necessary when the fief- or benefice-holder was
someone of importance.[325] Whether any such rule applied to all who held

[318] *Pommersches UB*, nos. 894, 1948, 2367, 3728, 3750, 3819, 5282, 5323.
[319] Ibid. no. 3310, and cf. no. 4352. [320] *Handwörterbuch*, i. 148–50.
[321] *Constitutiones*, iii, no. 585.
[322] e.g. *Mainzer UB*, i, no. 571; *Urkundenbuch Magdeburg*, no. 264; *Cart. Gorze*, no. 189; *Cod. Dip. Sax. Reg.* pt. 1, iii, nos. 30, 304, 316; *Urkunden Eichstätt*, i, no. 312. Fiefs: *Pommersches UB*, no. 1697; *Constitutiones*, iii, no. 585; Eike von Repgow, *Sachsenspiegel Lehnrecht*, 8. 1.
[323] *Urkunden-Buch Enns*, ii, no. 371.
[324] *Handwörterbuch*, i. 964–5: I infer that it is not thought to have been generally recognized elsewhere.
[325] *Dip. Konrad III*, nos. 74, 79, 99; *Dip. Frid. I*, nos. 350, 373.

benefices in the old sense or came to be generally recognized as part of the law of fiefs is doubtful. Rules had to be made and adapted as cases arose and legal arguments were elaborated. The bishop of Lausanne resented being put under the duke of Zähringen in 1152 but he did not appeal to any rule of feudal law against the transfer.[326] In 1216, however, when two abbesses objected to being transferred from the empire (i.e. presumably the direct government of the emperor) to the bishop of Regensburg, the royal court declared that no principality could or ought to be transferred from the empire to anyone else without the consent of its prince.[327] This may have come later to be considered a rule of the law of fiefs, but bishoprics and abbeys, though benefices in an older sense, were not properties that would have needed to come under the protection of the feudal law as it had begun to develop in the twelfth century. Their lands were as yet reckoned to be full property, not fiefs.

All things being equal, fiefs were easier to confiscate than full property during this period, but all things were not always equal. Both forms of property—and even the hereditary property of peasants—were supposed to be protected by due process, but whether or how that protection worked depended on political conditions and the status of the parties. The most important element of due process was collective judgement, which was the norm in the royal court and in provincial and local assemblies applying general law (*Landrecht*) as much as in the particular form of the judgement of peers that was laid down in the academic law of fiefs.[328] The same norm applied to legislation as well as judgement: neither princes nor other lords, according to a ruling of 1231, ought to introduce new laws without consulting the better and greater men of the land.[329] It may well have been arguments based on knowledge, however slight, of the law of fiefs that brought the distinction between being judged by one's equals and fellow fiefholders and by the better and greater people present in a wider assembly into general notice and discussion.[330] Although the distinction does not always seem to have been clear in the later middle ages, it may have been partly as a result of such discussion that it came to be a rule in Germany that neither the king nor any other lord ought to preside in cases in which he was concerned.[331] All forms of collective judgement were liable to come under threat with the advent of professional and learned law. The enshrinement of judgement of peers in the learned texts did not enable it

[326] *Constitutiones*, i, no. 281; cf. Theoderic, *Libellus*, 65–6.
[327] *Constitutiones*, ii, no. 57.
[328] Otto and Rahewin, *Gesta*, 50–1; Brunner, *Land und Herrschaft*, 237 (Eng. trans. 197); Arnold, *Count and Bishop*, 146; Weitzel, *Dinggenossenschaft*, 941–65, 1152.
[329] *Constitutiones*, ii, no. 305.       [330] Above, nn. 225, 267–9, 296.
[331] Diestelkamp, *Lehnrecht*, 267–8; *Constitutiones*, iii, no. 72; Krieger, *Lehnshoheit*, 511–16.

to survive in Italy, but it seems to have survived in Germany, at least in some courts, into the seventeenth century.[332]

Although all property was supposed to be protected by due process the rules for confiscation varied. Frederick Barbarossa's peace ordinance of 1152 decreed that inheritances (i.e. property held with full rights) forfeited by peace-breakers was to go to their heirs. Benefices would presumably go to their lords, as they were to do under legislation of 1230 which similarly ordered that the heirs of heretics were to get their full property (*bonis . . . deberent hereditariis ac patrimonio gauderent*).[333] This rule was not followed precisely at the confiscation of Henry the Lion's benefices in 1180, when his inheritance was apparently left to him rather than to his heirs, but that was a very special case. It was followed on at least one occasion in the thirteenth century, but full property was not apparently always spared.[334] Confiscations from dukes and counts were always a matter of politics rather than of the strict letter of the law. During the thirteenth century, kings could use the feudal law, argued by legal experts and administered by government servants, to make threats of forfeiture against princes and others of doubtful allegiance or with doubtful claims to their lordships who failed to claim investiture.[335] In the long run the debilitating effect of contested elections and civil war on royal power would make it more or less impossible for kings to confiscate anything from princes, but the combination of diminished royal power with the use and elaboration of the law of fiefs explains the later belief that princely alods were absolute property, unconfiscatable and subject to no obligations. When the king or other lord confiscated fiefs according to law there seems, at least before 1300, to have been no normative rule requiring him to grant them to anyone else.[336] Heirs may have tried to claim them, perhaps by analogy with their claims to forfeited full property, and others no doubt put in claims that might be politically hard to resist, but these claims were not yet recognized as rights. The *Leihezwang* awaited the creativity of historians of feudalism.[337]

The most important duty laid on most fiefs, which distinguished them

[332] Theuerkauf, *Land und Lehnswesen*, 84; though cf. Weitzel, *Dinggenossenschaft*, 1081.

[333] *Dip. Frid. I*, no. 25 (but cf. no. 774); *Constitutiones*, ii, no. 308.

[334] Caesarius, *Wundergeschichten*, iii. 271; *Constitutiones*, iii, no. 557. The different categories of property do not seem to be mentioned in connection with Frederick II's ultimately unsuccessful attempt to confiscate the duchy of Austria, perhaps because Frederick did not intend to recognize the duke's female heirs: *Constitutiones*, ii. 201–2; Hermann, *Annales*, 392–3; *Cont. Sancrucensis*, 638; Ficker, *Herzog Friedrich*, 47–88.

[335] Ficker and Puntschart, *Vom Reichsfürstenstande*, ii. 225; Huillard-Bréholles, *Hist. Diplom.* i (2), 821–2; *Urkundenbuch Niederrhein*, ii, nos. 173, 1005; *Constitutiones*, ii, nos. 154, 359, iii, nos. 72, 111, 122 c. 8, 282, 557–8 (A c. 4, B c. 3), iv, nos. 51–4; *Asseburger UB*, nos. 275, 278.

[336] *Constitutiones*, ii, nos. 323, 359; iii, nos. 557–8 (A c. 4, B c. 3); iv, no. 62; Goez, *Leihezwang*, 182–9, 207–9, 223–4.

[337] Krause, 'Sachsenspiegel', 25–9.

most clearly from other forms of property, was the fiefholder's need to seek formal investiture. Count Siboto IV of Neuburg-Falkenstein (d. 1166) was anxious that all the benefices he held from different lords should be claimed after his death for his children, but whether this meant claiming them within a fixed time is unclear: his worry may imply uncertainty about the rules at this stage rather than a need to obey them exactly.[338] By the time of the *Sachsenspiegel* time limits were precise but subject to close argument, and all fiefholders had to be formally invested both on their own accession to the property and on a change of lord—though whether Eike envisaged this as the succession of a lord by inheritance as well as transfer is not always clear.[339] The rules that existed by then were surely a reflection less of old norms than of deliberate attempts by lords to preserve their rights in face of those that new ideas of *jus beneficiale* had bestowed on fiefholders.[340] In the long run many lords did more than preserve their rights. As rules were elaborated they extended them, in some cases demanding and getting the sort of succession dues that before the twelfth century had probably been taken only or chiefly from people of low status.[341] The right of lords to confiscate fiefs that were not formally claimed within a year and a day was confirmed by the royal court in 1234.[342] Royal use of the requirement of investiture according to the feudal law in the thirteenth century has already been mentioned in connection with the rules for confiscation. By the fifteenth century less important people with royal fiefs could lose them outright if they were not invested at the right time.[343] Meanwhile, though those who were concerned with applying the feudal law or arguing about it naturally discussed homage and oaths of fidelity only in the context of fiefs, both words and phenomena had wider uses.[344] The reservation of fidelity to the king was not regularly mentioned in oaths to lesser lords, but it would be rash to assume that it was never taken for granted before royal power over the princes had dwindled in practice and been argued away by lawyers in theory.[345]

---

[338] *Codex Falkensteinensis*, no. 2; Freed, *Counts of Falkenstein*, 62–3.

[339] Eike, *Sachsenspiegel Lehnrecht*, 20–1, 30, 32–3, 74, 76 (2. 2, 7; 11. 1–3; 13. 2; 56. 1; 57. 4; 71. 14) and above at nn. 253–5.

[340] e.g. Poly, *Provence*, 151 n. 119.

[341] Above, at n. 153; *Mainzer UB*, i, no. 571; Wibald, *Epistolae*, no. 140; *Dip. Frid. I*, no. 517; *Monuments de Neuchatel*, i, no. 31; *Westfälisches UB*, viii, no. 510; *Pommersches UB*, no. 4933; Didier, *Droit des fiefs*, 220–3; Génicot, *Économie rurale*, i. 58 n., 60, 72, 156; Krieger, *Lehnshoheit*, 451–63.

[342] *Constitutiones*, ii, no. 323.

[343] Krieger, *Lehnshoheit*, 465–6; for other lordships, e.g. Diestelkamp, *Lehnrecht*, 140.

[344] *Deutsches Rechtswörterbuch*, vi. 34–8 (*Hulde*), ix. 154–8 (*Mannschaft*).

[345] Wibald, *Epistolae*, no. 163; *Westfälisches UB*, iii, no. 292; *Constitutiones*, ii, no. 372; *Chron. Hildesheimense*, 867–8; *Urkundenbuch Braunschweig*, iv, no. 118; cf. Krieger, *Lehnshoheit*, 394, 557–9.

There is ample evidence from the twelfth century that great churches then owed service on royal expeditions to Italy much as they had done earlier, negotiating alterations to their obligations on occasion. The same seems to apply to dukes and counts.[346] Most of the evidence that we have about how contingents were made up comes from this century. It looks as though *ministeriales* generally owed service in proportion to the size of their benefices. The archbishop of Cologne's *ministeriales* with the smallest holdings were allowed to pay an army tax (*herstura*, modernized as *Heersteuer*) instead.[347] Such payments, analogous to the English scutage, were also taken elsewhere, but bishops themselves could not get away with them: when the archbishop of Salzburg tried to do so he found himself in trouble with Frederick Barbarossa.[348] By the thirteenth century, however, emperors were finding it harder to enforce obligations on the princes. As for the services of those who held fiefs or benefices from them it may be that from now on they were simply owed to the princes on their own account, rather than to the emperor through the princes. In so far as they had been owed for royal expeditions to Italy, however, they may have gradually become forgotten. Some of those who are often called the 'feudal nobility' (*Lehnsadel*) and who served alongside paid soldiers in later medieval armies may have done so because the obligation was thought to go with their fiefs. If that was so, it seems, in view of the evidence about military service earlier, rather unlikely that their obligations had survived from much earlier. Late medieval organization of armies on supposedly feudal principles probably owed more to the creative use of the law of fiefs and the social and political ideas of the time than to archaic survivals.

Garrisons, meanwhile, were increasingly provided by people who held property in the fortified towns that could be brought under feudal law as *Burglehen*.[349] Feudal law also helped in the control of castles. Although it seems to have been generally accepted that no one—irrespective, apparently, of the nature of his or her property—ought to build a castle without the consent of the count in whose county it stood, the rule was obviously hard to enforce in the thirteenth century.[350] One of the most compelling reasons that princes and other lords had for getting the castles within their

[346] *Dip. Konrad III*, nos. 167, 245; Otto and Rahewin, *Gesta Friderici*, 113 (II. 12); *Dip. Frid. I*, nos. 12, 151, 578.

[347] *Dip. Konrad II*, no. 140; *Constitutiones*, i, no. 447; Gislebert of Mons, *Chronique*, 13–14; Weinrich, *Quellen*, no. 70, c. 4.

[348] *Dip. Frid. I*, nos. 318, 327, 341–2, 346 (and *Constitutiones*, i, nos. 198, 201), 578.

[349] Diestelkamp, 'Lehnrecht und Territorien', 72–4. For *Burglehen*: Eike, *Sachsenspiegel Lehnrecht*, 106–8, 110–12 (71. 9–20, 72. 2, 4–9); Krieger, *Lehnshoheit*, 58–64.

[350] *Dip. Frid. I*, no. 854; *Constitutiones*, ii, no. 304, iii, nos. 261, 506, and cf. 549.

spheres of government or influence turned into fiefs was that it became customary to include in the negotiations not only that the castle-owner would make an oath of fidelity in return for confirmation of his rights of inheritance and so on, but that he would agree to open his castle to his lord when the lord might need it.[351]

Services that had always been owed by people, including peasants, who did not hold fiefs were also transferred from the king to their immediate lords. References to general duties in defence of the country (*lantwere*) and in building or manning fortifications continue to occur in twelfth- and thirteenth-century documents.[352] When Frederick I, in the proclamation of peace at the beginning of his reign, ordered judges to impose a fine on any peasant (*rusticus*) who carried arms, including a sword or lance, he seems to have intended it as part of a general prohibition on the carrying of unnecessary arms. Peasants were nevertheless supposed to keep the arms they might need whenever they were called on to help in policing, even though they were not to carry them about.[353] The peace ordinance of 1152 may signal the beginning of a trend to disarm the lower classes, but if so it was an early signal of what would be a slow and halting trend.[354] A good many of the military obligations both of fiefholders and others were probably by 1300, if not sooner, converted into money payments but, when traditional obligations to *lantwere*, bridge-work, and fortification-work were transferred to Pomerania, the duties remained real and necessary—though sometimes commutable to money dues—into the fourteenth century.[355] Those who were supposed to serve the duke of Pomerania with a war-horse and harness (*dextrarius phalleratus*) in the early fourteenth century owed what was reckoned as one vassal service (*servicium vasallicum*).[356] This terminology seems more likely to indicate knowledge of the feudal law than the survival of old feudo-vassalic traditions, while the forces promised by the duke to the margrave of Brandenburg in 1278 were surely owed because of the treaty they then made rather than as a feudo-vassalic duty.[357] Lists from the 1320s, arranged by advocacies (local government areas), show some individuals (some of them called *milites* or *domini*) owing

[351] Gislebert of Mons, *Chronique*, 74–5; *Cart. Metz*, no. 163; *Urkundenbuch Niederrhein*, ii, no. 410; *Eppsteinschen Lehensverzeichnisse*, nos. 200–1; Brunner, *Land und Herrschaft*, 371 (Eng. trans. 305); Schulze, *Grundstrukturen*, 70.

[352] *Hamburgisches UB*, nos. 404, 613, 645–6, 648, 651, 805; Brunner, *Land und Herrschaft*, 301–3, 360 (Eng. trans. 247–8, 297); *Deutsches Rechtswörterbuch*, viii. 689–94.

[353] *Constitutiones*, i, nos. 140 c. 12–15, 277 c. 14.          [354] Fehr, 'Waffenrecht'.

[355] *Pommersches UB*, nos. 67, 894, 1908, 2367, 5104.

[356] Ibid. nos. 3418, 3721, 4901, 4933. Some of the horses owed in Pomerania were for carrying rather than military service: ibid. nos. 716, 3165, 3277; Benl, *Gestaltung*, 366 n., 369.

[357] *Pommersches UB*, no. 1096 and cf. no. 4320; Benl, *Gestaltung*, 366. For fiefs in Pomerania, above, at nn. 282–9.

service to the prince of Rügen with one horse each, or more in a few cases, while some seem to have been grouped together to provide a cavalryman between them.[358] In 1905 the editor of the text indexed some of these groups as noble families. Perhaps, long after their deaths, they had been pressed into service as ancestors in the genealogies of eighteenth- and nineteenth-century nobles. Irrespective of whether they held their lands *in feodum*, they may not have been very noticeably noble when they were alive.[359]

Most benefices or fiefs that owed regular rents were the smallholdings of peasants which people who studied and used the feudal law would probably not have considered fiefs at all, but greater men sometimes owed money rents—and, of course, did not always owe military service.[360] Various dues and services were owed to princes and other lords as rulers rather than as lords of fiefs, like the *grevenbede* paid to counts and many other forms of *bede* (modern German: *Bitte*; Latin: *petitio, precaria*).[361] Exemptions could be granted from all of them, so that most probably fell principally on people at the bottom, whether they were tenants of those with full property or fiefs or whether they had supposedly full rights in their own holdings. It has sometimes been said that the so-called 'feudal aids' were rarely if ever owed in Germany, but this may be because historians were looking for them in feudo-vassalic contexts.[362] Twelfth- and thirteenth-century charters granted to towns in the western part of the kingdom sometimes mention that the townspeople either will or will not have to pay aids for the lord's ransom, the knighting of his son (or sons, and sometimes that of himself and a brother as well), and the marriage of his daughter (or daughters and sisters). The idea of these aids may have come from France, but royal demands may have prompted negotiations between bishops and their cities about the rules for special aids to start independently of the French precedents. By 1156 the bishop of Augsburg was allowed to take an aid when he was summoned to the imperial court or when he went to Rome with the emperor or for his consecration. Other lords, both lay and ecclesiastical, sometimes took aids to cover the expenses of attending the imperial court or serving in the imperial army.[363] The

---

[358] *Pommersches UB*, nos. 3441–2.

[359] Cf. Bilow, *Abgabenverhältnisse*, 154–65, esp. 157.

[360] *Trad. Freising*, no. 1536; *Dip. Frid. I*, no. 378; *Urkundenbuch St. Stephan*, no. 209; *Urkunden-Buch Enns*, ii, no. 371; *Salzburger UB*, i. 832–3 (no. 120).

[361] Zeumer, *Deutsche Städtesteuern*, 5–35; Patze, *Entstehung*, 521; Brunner, *Land und Herrschaft*, 293 (Eng. trans. 240–1); *Deutsches Rechtswörterbuch*, i. 1336–9.

[362] Mitteis, *Lehnrecht*, 615; Ganshof, *Feudalism*, 92; Bloch, *Feudal Society*, 223; *Handwörterbuch*, v. 964.

[363] Stephenson, 'La Taille dans les villes d'Allemagne', 3, 4 n., 5, 8 n., 9, 11, 17, 27–33; Zeumer, *Deutschen Städtesteuern*, 29, 32–6, 44, 49–52; *Dip. Frid. I*, no. 147.

town charters suggest that where these special aids were taken they were raised, as they were in France, from the population at large, that is from peasants and ordinary townspeople, and sometimes served as a compromise between complete freedom from exceptional taxes and taxes taken whenever the lord wanted.[364] As in France there seems to be no reason to suppose that they originated from what historians would traditionally consider vassalic obligations.[365]

During the twelfth century, after Henry V's alleged plan of raising a general tax was abandoned, emperors managed pretty well without one. In the thirteenth century the moment for imposing anything of the kind was past or passing, though the account of 1241 shows that Frederick II was still able to raise a fair amount from urban communities, Jews, and others who probably had customary obligations towards the support of the royal court.[366] Princes and other lords were, however, beginning to raise taxes, presumably from anyone sufficiently under their control and jurisdiction to be made to pay. In the 1180s the count of Hainaut was, according to Gislebert of Mons, regretfully compelled by his debts to oppress his land with tallages. Duke Frederick II of Austria was said to have taken sixty pence from every manse in his duchy.[367] Landowners doubtless passed the burden of these taxes, and others like them, to their peasant tenants, but there is no particular reason to suppose that they weighed on one kind of property more than another.


## 9.9. *Conclusion*

There is much more evidence of the practice of courts after 1300 than before, so that legal historians have been able to show the feudal law in action then in a way that is impossible earlier.[368] From the later fourteenth century there were universities in Germany. From the fifteenth lawyers trained in Roman law, some of whom must have picked up some knowledge of the law of fiefs as part of their Roman law, were practising in royal and princely courts.[369] From now on German 'feudists' (academic stu-

---

[364] e.g. *Urkundenbuch Niederrhein*, ii, no. 265.

[365] Zeumer, *Deutschen Städtesteuern*, 56–7, pointed this out, though his reasons for rejecting an origin in the *Lehnsverbande* seem to me weak.

[366] *Constitutiones*, iii, pp. 1–5; Metz, *Staufische Güterverzeichnisse*, 98–116; Brühl, *Fodrum*, 214–17.

[367] Gislebert, *Chronique*, 193–4; *Cont. Sancrucensis*, 638; Zeumer, *Deutschen Städtesteuern*, 16–17.

[368] Krieger, *Lehnshoheit*; Diestelkamp, *Lehnrecht*.

[369] Coing, *Römisches Recht*; Burmeister, *Studium*; Trusen, *Anfänge des gelehrten Rechts*; Moraw, 'Gelehrte Juristen'; Krieger, *Lehnshoheit*, 517; Diestelkamp, *Lehnrecht*, 126–7, 274–7.

dents of the law of fiefs) would elaborate the principles and categories of feudal law. The political and jurisdictional situations that they justified or argued about were those of their own time, which were in many ways different from those of the period before 1200. When historians began to study the middle ages through the feudal law they saw it, here as in other countries, as a reflection of conditions that they thought had obtained throughout the middle ages.[370] Feudalism, they thought, meant a weak monarchy and a divided nation. If feudalism had started with the Carolingians, as they came to think it had, then the seeds of division were sown early. As in other countries, historians have accepted many of the assumptions of the seventeenth- and eighteenth-century scholars, while drawing further distinctions and elaborating further categories that, however heuristically helpful they may seem, impose the characteristics of academic and professional law on to the customary law of the earlier middle ages. The Lotharingian *fief de danger* was an invention of the fifteenth century, while the first example of the word *Aktivlehen* (a fief granted out) in the *Deutsches Rechtswörterbuch* comes from 1919.[371]

If one starts, on the basis of what I have argued about France and Italy, by questioning the idea that the substance of the feudal law (*Lehnrecht*) was already in existence in the twelfth century as a natural emanation of earlier feudo-vassalic relations (*Lehnswesen*), the relations of king and nobles, nobles and their free subjects look rather different. My conclusions must be extremely tentative and need testing against much more evidence, but such as I have found suggests to me that the benefices of the period before 1100 were different from the *Lehen* of the later middle ages. They belonged in a legal and political context in which most of the rules of the later jurisprudence had not been made and into which they would not have fitted. I am less tentative in suggesting that the evidence of arguments about the rights of benefices and fiefs in the early twelfth century is striking and thought-provoking. How much influence there was on German law from the Italian law of fiefs before 1300 is difficult to say, but—tentatively—the development of feudal law between 1100 and 1300 suggests that there was more legal expertise and bureaucratic administration about in Germany than seems generally to have been noticed. The full development of feudo-vassalic institutions in Germany, however, came still later. The records of law and government after 1300 show that the creation of fiefs and the

---

[370] Theuerkauf, *Land und Lehnswesen*, 88–124, especially 121 n. (Vultejus); Brunner, 'Feudalismus, feudal', ii. 340 (Justi).

[371] Coudert, 'Fief de danger', 162; *Deutsches Rechtswörterbuch*, i. 472; the volume including *Passivlehen* (a fief received) was not yet available to me when this was written, though Ficker, *Vom Heerschilde*, 48, referred to *das passive Lehnsverhältniss* in 1862.

exaction of obligations from fiefholders were an important aspect of the 'administrative states' (*Verwaltungsstaaten*) of the late middle ages. The *Verwaltungsstaat* was not the successor of the feudal state: the two developed together—or rather, were the same.

# IO

# CONCLUSION

A GOOD deal of this book has been rather negative in tone. Many sentences have begun with 'It is not clear that . . .', 'There is no evidence for . . .', 'There is no reason to believe . . .', and similar phrases. That has been inevitable. My purpose has been to compare the medieval evidence of property relations and political relations with the concepts of the fief and of vassalage as they are used by medieval historians. I started with some doubts about fiefs and considerable scepticism about vassalage, but I have found much less evidence to support the traditional picture of either, and of their connection and development, than I expected in my most sceptical moments. I hope that I have not overstated my case and understated the evidence. I have tried not to do so.

My first—still negative—conclusion is that the evidence I have found and have set out in the course of the book does not suggest that the relation between rulers and nobles in the later middle ages had evolved out of that between early medieval war-leaders and their followers in the way that accounts of non-Marxist feudalism suggest. They did not start from the 'personal' vassalage of the war-band and then become 'territorialized' through the grant of fiefs. Nor did fiefs then gradually become hereditary while obligations to military service, aid, counsel, and so on remained attached to them. The idea of this development derives ultimately from a small piece of conjectural history put forward in the early twelfth century by one of the Lombard lawyers whose little treatises were soon after combined into the *Libri Feudorum*. Since the sixteenth century an elaborated version of his story has been combined with myths of national origins in the so-called Age of Migrations to create a paradigm of such wide appeal, flexibility, and compelling force that it has been able to absorb centuries of amendment, adaptation, and elaboration without losing its shape. The myth made good sense against a background of ideas of the history of Europe and of social evolution in general that developed at the time that it took shape. Between the fall of the Roman empire and the development of what was seen as civilized modern government, Europe had, it was thought, relapsed into a state of barbarism in which ideas of public welfare, public spirit, and rational law were kept alive only by the church. In this

475

reversion to the primitive the only values that laymen could appreciate were those of kinship and personal loyalty.

As I argued in chapter 2.2, this picture of 'primitive society' is incompatible with modern knowledge, while some of the evidence in subsequent chapters has, I hope, suggested that early medieval society was held together by more than interpersonal bonds. I have not thought it necessary to argue that the picture of the whole middle ages as dominated by unruly barons and knights who made war on each other and tyrannized over hapless peasants from their castles is inadequate, because no medieval historians now see the period in that way. It is not just that the number of castles is in many areas a poor guide to the number of totally or even largely independent lordships, let alone to the number of sieges and battles fought around them. People who were called knights and barons were brought up to admire the military values of courage and loyalty or at least to pay lipservice to them, but a fair number never marched (or rode) in armies and even fewer fought in battles. Talk of unruly barons or knights and hapless peasants, moreover, implies a dividing line that, as I argued in chapter 2.3, is very hard to draw, particularly in the earlier middle ages. Almost all, if not all, medieval societies were extremely unequal and authoritarian, but they were divided by many gradations rather than by a single gulf between nobles and peasants. Like other stratified, authoritarian, agricultural societies they were held together partly by coercion but partly also by values and norms that, so far as we can see, were probably quite widely shared. The study of different societies that has gone on since the model of feudalism was invented suggests that many societies do, by and large, hold together, and not merely because of either interpersonal relations or fierce government from the top. Analogies prove nothing but they are suggestive.

In chapter 2.3 I suggested some of the values and norms that held the societies of medieval western Europe together. Members of the ruling classes of unequal societies may find more and different reasons for rivalries and disputes than those they rule, and may be subject to fewer countervailing sanctions, but they are also the most likely to subscribe to the society's publicly pronounced values. Medieval values laid great stress on authority and especially on the authority of kings. Kingdoms were seen as communities and so were lesser lordships within them. Within each community responsibility lay on those who were often referred to as its better and wiser members—that is, the richer and more established. What held noble society together therefore, so far as it was held together, was the same values that held the rest of society together, reinforced by the need of solidarity against inferiors and outsiders. Interpersonal relations were not the whole story nor even most of the story. On grounds both of evidence and

476

of plausibility the relationship that medieval historians call vassalage was much less important than models of non-Marxist feudalism suggest.

From this negative conclusion about vassalage I pass to more positive conclusions that I draw from the evidence I have presented about changing forms of property. The fiefs of the twelfth century and later, from which sixteenth- and seventeenth-century ideas of feudal law were derived, formed a fundamentally different category of property from either the kind of holdings that had earlier been called fiefs or the earlier properties of nobles, which had not generally been called fiefs. The nearest precedents that I have been able to find from before the twelfth century for most of the rules about the rights and obligations of fiefs as we know them from later records are practices that great churches adopted for dealing with their property. This may be partly because so much of our information about the earlier period has to come from records that churches preserved, but we should at least consider the implications of using the relations of bishops or abbots with their tenants as evidence of those between kings and lay nobles or between the nobles and their own followers. In any case, as I hope I have shown, enough evidence about the relations between kings or lay lords and their followers survives to show that they were quite different from what is implied in traditional accounts of the evolution of feudo-vassalic institutions. Nobles and free men did not generally owe military service before the twelfth century because of the grant of anything like fiefs to them or their ancestors. They normally held their land with as full, permanent, and independent rights as their society knew, and they owed whatever service they owed, not because they were vassals of a lord, but because they were subjects of a ruler. They owed it as property-owners, normally in rough proportion to their status and wealth. Inheritance dues (reliefs, *rachats*, etc.) seem to have originated, not as signs of the originally temporary nature of grants made by lords to their vassals, but in the dues taken by churches from their peasant tenants. The earliest evidence of 'feudal aids', on the other hand, comes from lay estates, but is no earlier than the late eleventh century. These aids were first taken, it seems, by lords in west France from people who held land within their lordships without any indication of a feudo-vassalic relationship. Aid and counsel (*auxilium et consilium*) was a neat phrase that at first had no feudo-vassalic connotations but was adopted when written records multiplied and standard phrases became useful.[1]

When fiefs are mentioned in the thirteenth century and later they cover a much wider category of property than earlier (except in England, where

[1] See index: aid and counsel, aids, succession dues.

the word had from the twelfth century been used even more widely). The category was enlarged not merely because individual alods had been surrendered and turned into fiefs, but because the word fief was now applied to much noble property without any formal surrender and conversion. Property in the thirteenth century and later was subject to dues and services, and sometimes to general taxes, that depended on records kept by literate, numerate, more or less professional administrators, and it was classified and argued about by a new kind of lawyers employing a new kind of expertise. The records were not always accurate and the arguments deployed about rights and obligations by both sides were sometimes tendentious, but the flaws were those of systems different from any generally used before about 1100. They were systems that begin to have at least some of the characteristics that Max Weber associated with bureaucracy, little as he may have associated bureaucracy with the middle ages.[2] Whatever the regional variations in its timing and in the systems that resulted, the change from the immanent, variable, and flexible customary law of the earlier middle ages to the more esoteric, rigid, and expert law of the later was one of profound significance that profoundly affected the rights and obligations of property. It was not just that, as is sometimes said, feudal obligations and feudal law became more precise in the twelfth century. The new law was a different kind of law and so relationships and institutions within it were fundamentally altered. Carolingian government had relied on literate servants, and English government in the century before the Norman Conquest had already become, by the standards of the time, remarkably bureaucratic, but the law that each administered was not professional law. It cannot make sense to envisage the Carolingian benefice and the thirteenth- or fourteenth-century fief as embodying the same legal institution—not because the names were different but because they existed within different legal systems.[3] A good many references to fiefs in the later middle ages often reflect lawyer's law rather than the norms and values of lay society at large, but in so far as they reflect wider values it seems reasonable to start from the assumption that what they reflected were the values of the time. Because social norms still stressed the validity of custom as well as the duties of obedience, both rulers and subjects, like lawyers, tended to claim the sanction of ancient custom and to moralize about the duties of loyal and grateful subjects. That does not mean that the obligations of property-holders which were then justified or contested were in reality archaic survivals.

My first positive conclusion therefore is that, in so far as anything like

---

[2] Weber, *Social and Economic Organization*, 329–33.
[3] Cf. Ganshof in *Handwörterbuch*, i. 369.

feudo-vassalic institutions existed, they were the product not of weak and unbureaucratic government in the early middle ages but of the increasingly bureaucratic government and expert law that began to develop from about the twelfth century. Given the evidence of early bureaucracy in England and of the development of a legal profession soon after, it may be thought that I am applying to other countries a model constructed from English evidence. I hope that I am not applying it as a model in the sense of forcing the evidence for other countries into it: I do not suggest that either bureaucratic or legal developments in other kingdoms were the same as those of England. On the other hand, one of the uses of comparisons is to take ideas or insights from one area of enquiry to others. The English evidence may have been useful in drawing attention to possible implications of the evidence of record-keeping and new sorts of legal argument in other countries.

My remaining conclusions concern matters for possible investigation and methods of investigation. First, there is the need for comparison. The model of non-Marxist feudalism that has been constructed out of the later medieval evidence is grossly over-simplified and schematic even for the later middle ages. Political conditions and legal systems differed and the rights and obligations of property, however it was classified, differed accordingly. Calling the traditional model an ideal type and pointing to variations as exceptions or anomalies that do not affect its validity has, as I argued in chapter 1, discouraged historians from investigating either uniformities or variations. Reliance on the model allows them to work within their separate national traditions with a minimum of comparisons, using the model to fill in gaps in their own evidence while explaining what does not fit it as the result of Germanic or Roman survivals, national character, or other circumstances that look special because they do not fit the model. Since modern historiographical traditions have by and large grown up within the boundaries of modern states, the variations within what is seen as feudal law and feudal society consequently appear to have done the same, though local or regional historians can please local patriots by using the general model with its national modifications and then finding further local variations of their own. Some of the apparent differences between national histories derive from the varying nature of the sources available and some from real differences in the phenomena, but it is difficult to judge which so long as national and regional histories are fitted into a composite model. The traditional account connects the rise of feudo-vassalic institutions with the weakness of government, especially of royal government in the post-Carolingian centuries. This can be explained only by the preoccupation of those who created the model with the history of France. The

479

monarchies of Germany and England were far from weak at the time. A connection with disunity and 'feudal anarchy' can be made to explain the postponement of full feudalization in Germany to the later middle ages, but that line of argument ignores the significant differences in government and law between the two periods that I have already mentioned. England contributes much the best evidence of a connection between fiefs and military service and of the hierarchy of property rights—indeed the only evidence of either that fits the model without heavy interpretation. It also supplies the only evidence of reliefs and aids owed by great nobles to kings and by tenants (the word vassal being used here even less than elsewhere) right through the 'feudal hierarchy'. Yet England fits the model in other respects very badly. Feudal hierarchy and feudal obligations go here with an exceptionally strong and bureaucratic central government, while the very word *feodum* very soon acquired very different connotations from those it had in areas influenced—as England was not—by the academic feudal law.

Reliance on the model as a substitute for comparison of the evidence of actual phenomena has obscured similarities as well as differences. One example of possible similarity that might be further investigated is the way that lordships became established with more fixed borders and fixed jurisdictions during the eleventh and twelfth centuries. National traditions seem to operate very separately here, largely perhaps because each is so teleologically focused on the structures of the Ancien Régime that grew out of late medieval jurisdictions. Looking more closely at the nature of early medieval government, the ideas of authority and custom that prevailed then, and the increase in record-keeping and changes in methods of government and law at the stage when jurisdictions were established, suggests possibilities for comparisons that might be illuminating. An example of an apparently unnoticed difference may be taken from rules about the alienation of acquired property. When, after writing my chapters on France, I started on Italy, I discovered that the rule that allowed property that the alienator had acquired for himself to be alienated more freely than what he had inherited did not seem to apply there as it did in France. I later discovered that references to it in Germany only seemed to occur from about 1200. What I had accepted as a natural and common-sense rule that presumably applied everywhere and that I had read into the earliest references to acquisitions in Frankish sources, may not have been anything of the sort. It needs more investigation than I have given it. The same applies to a good many of my findings.

Another suggestion about method concerns the study both of political relations and of property rights. Both have been hampered by the use of

CONCLUSION

naïve concepts and naïve assumptions about the relation between concepts, words, and phenomena.[4] Concentration on vassalage has obscured the difference between a whole range of different social and political relations. In studying property relations concentration on words, such as alod, benefice, or fief, needs to be replaced or supplemented by a search for a whole range of separate rights or obligations—as many of each as one can think of. Plodding through the uncertain evidence of the rights and obligations of property in different areas is not a particularly exciting form of research but it seems to throw up conclusions that suggest significant changes to our picture of medieval society. A similar method might be helpful in discussing the much larger and, in my view, more important subject of relations between lords and their unfree or less free peasants, which I have had to exclude from this book. Much has already been learned during this century about medieval serfdom, but the subject could be advanced still further if attention was broadened from the issue of freedom or unfreedom as seen at the time, or the particular disabilities that became controversial at particular moments, to a wider range of rights and obligations. The kind of check-list of rights and obligations that I proposed in chapter 3.2 might be useful if applied both to supposedly free and supposedly unfree peasants.[5] The check-list should then certainly include the rights to exclude others from one's property and to have access to the property of others, which were omitted from it in this book. The erosion of common rights, as commons and wastelands came to be regarded as the property of the lord rather than as resources of the community under his lordship, formed one more example of the way that property law was changed once professional lawyers took it over.[6]

Finally, I suggest that the emphasis on interpersonal relations implied in the feudo-vassalic model has obscured the problem of the reasons for change. The history of feudo-vassalic institutions tends to be ethos-led. Even the desire for land felt by the vassals or knights that provoked the 'territorializing' of the relation of lord and vassal, the growth of 'multiple vassalage', and so on, sometimes seems to reflect a change or weakening of ethos rather than anything else. If we are to understand changes in political relations and the rights and obligations of property we need to pay more attention to other factors. First there are high politics and actual events. *Histoire événementielle* affects relations of property and power. The ambitions, rivalries, and wars of individual kings and other rulers explain, for

[4] See chapter 1.2.
[5] I found the comparison of unfreedom in two different societies with different economies, legal systems, etc. in Kolchin, *Unfree Labor*, extremely thought-provoking.
[6] Thompson, *Customs in Common*, 159–68.

481

instance, a great deal of the difference between what happened to the western and eastern halves of the Carolingian empire, while the foreign ambitions of German and English kings explain the systems of military service that they preserved or developed at a stage when the kings of France did not. The evidence I have found suggests to me that, so far as changes in attitudes and ethos can be found, they may have resulted from varying political developments rather than causing them.

The ambitions and wars of rulers produced demands for men and money that had a great deal to do with the development of the new sort of government and law that I maintain produced the supposedly feudo-vassalic institutions that can be found in the middle ages. But bureaucracy and professional law were only made possible by much more profound changes in society—the growth of population, of economies, and of the supply of silver, coined and uncoined, and the spread of literacy and academic education. Despite regional variations in all these and in political conditions, evidence of them all (and of other striking changes, such as those in art and architecture), and of their impact on government, estate man- agement, and law, appears everywhere at roughly the same time—that is, during what one might call a very long twelfth century. The coincidence, however imprecise, poses a question that is often considered separately by economic, ecclesiastical, and intellectual historians, and that political and legal historians tend to consider separately within their respective tradi- tions of national history. Why did all these kinds of change happen some time around the twelfth century, and how were they connected? Posing another question—or posing an old question in a new or slightly different context—may not seem a very good way of presenting a positive conclu- sion to my argument, but it seems to be the conclusion to which my argu- ment leads. In any case all my conclusions, whether negative or positive, substantial or methodological, are put forward rather as hypotheses to be tested, refined, and falsified, than as firm conclusions. I have no wish to create a new model into which evidence is to be fitted as it has been fitted for centuries into the model of feudalism.

# *Appendix*

## Early Treatises on the Law of Fiefs

Without having done more than study Lehmann's printed texts fairly cursorily in the course of writing chapter 6 (Italy) I have not felt competent to question his division of the Antiqua (i.e. the compilation made, probably at Milan, soon after 1150) into separate treatises, but I suggest that his dating of the treatises (and of one or two other early treatises that were not incorporated in the *Libri Feudorum*) might be questioned. I follow Lehmann's numbering of the different treatises.[1]

1a (*Ant.* 8–13: I, II[2]) must have been written after (or during) the time of Urban II. Whatever constitution of whatever pope the author was following, he presumably thought he was referring to Urban II not Urban I (*Ant.* 12: II. 6). I do not, however, follow Lehmann's argument that 1a must have been written after 1d: there does not seem to be any reason why the *antiqui sapientes* of 1a should be the *sapientes* of 1d. An appeal to the good old law of wise men in the past was too much a matter of course at the time to make any derivation of one from the other necessary. Moreover, the view of 1a's wise men of old (who, if the writer knew or noticed the dates of his sources, were before the time of Rothari) concerned the grades of kinship, which are not mentioned in the 'constitution of Lothar' in 1d, which seems to be a version of the 1037 ordinance.

1b (*Ant.* 13–15: III–V) was dated after 1a by Lehmann for various reasons none of which seem conclusive to me. In particular the suggestion that the inheritance of duchies and counties (*Ant.* 14) makes it late seems questionable: 1c's remarks (*Ant.* 16, cf. 34) give a different view of the same situation rather than of an earlier one. The trend towards inheritance had been completed long before any of the treatises. In spite of the differences of terminology that Lehmann noted, parts of 1b are so close to 1a as to suggest a common source at least in the sense of shared discussion or common attendance at the same lectures. On the other hand there seems to be a slight difference of opinion between them about the limitation of grades of kinship (*Ant.* 9, 13). Perhaps it was a subject that was discussed at the time.

---

[1] As set out in *Consuetudines*, 2–4.

[2] Hereafter I shall give references by citing the printed text of Lehmann, *Consuetudines Feudorum*, i: *Compilatio Antiqua*, as *Ant.*, with the page number, or giving the number of the title and section within it (e.g. I. 2), or both.

I do not know why Lehmann thought that the author of 1b favoured the church, and favoured it, he implies, more than 1a.[3]

1c (*Ant.* 34–5: IX and 16–18: VI. 1–6[4]). IX is attributed in the manuscripts to Hugh of Gambolo, which puts it into the early twelfth century, though it is difficult to be sure how near it needs to be to the time (1112) when he is recorded as *judex* and consul in Pavia. Although generally included in earlier recensions, it was omitted from the vulgate *Libri Feudorum*.[5] Lehmann suggested that VI. 1–6 should also be attributed to Hugh, but it is possible to suggest tentative reasons against this. There are slight differences of terminology and a slight suggestion of difference of opinion between it and IX, which, taken together with the very close correspondence at other points, makes me wonder whether one part may not be, or include, a reworking of the other by a different hand and mind.[6]

1d (*Ant.* 18–21: VI. 7–14[7]) was the earliest in Lehmann's view. His only reason seems to have been its supposed priority over 1a, which I have questioned above. As a rough paraphrase of what seems to be the 1037 decree (misattributed to a King Lothar, apparently through taking the wrong heading from the *Lombarda* or *Liber Papiensis*), interspersed with additions, it is in some ways rather close to Ariprandus's work (see below), which Lehmann put relatively late.

I have no wish to question Lehmann's conclusion that all these tracts, with 1e (*Ant.* 21–4: VII), are earlier than Obertus's letters, and are probably to be connected with Pavia rather than Milan. I also think that he was probably right to deduce that the absence of any reference to Lothar III's ordinance of 1136 means that they were all written before 1136. The Pisa constitution of 1160 (or maybe, originally, a bit earlier[8]) does not allude to Lothar's prohibition on alienation either, but then Pisa was much farther away from Roncaglia than Pavia was, and the 1160 constitutions are not concerned with the kind of fiefs with which Lothar was concerned.[9] Presumably academic Pavian (or Milanese) lawyers writing after 1136 would have known of the ordinance and have taken it into account. Must they necessarily have cited it directly? If, as Classen seems to have thought (see below), Anselminus's remarks about alienation under *investitura* were

---

[3] Both allowed successors of ecclesiastical grantors more freedom than those of lay grantors (I. 5; IV. 2; cf. also 1a at II. 6). 1b invalidated grants to churches without seigniorial consent (V. 3).

[4] I do not know why Lehmann put VI. 6 into 1d: it seems to me, on his reasoning, to belong with 1c and I have therefore included it there.

[5] Weimar, 'Handschriften', 32–3, 35–6, 46.

[6] Terminology: VI. 1–6 uses *senior* and *beneficium*, whereas IX uses *dominus* and both *feudum* and *beneficium*. Opinion: IX. 3 puts in a suggestion of personal opinion that is not in VI. 3.

[7] For the beginning of 1d see n. 4 above.  [8] Classen, *Studium*, 85–8.

[9] Bonaini, *Statuti*, ii. 963: Pisans could alienate fiefs to other Pisans without consent of their lords.

concerned with the same sort of property as benefices or fiefs, the answer might be No.

One—very tentative—reason for wondering whether all these tracts might be dated slightly later than Lehmann thought (though they could still be before 1136) is the possibility, mentioned in chapter 6, that the lists of reasons for the confiscation of fiefs or benefices that some of them give could just possibly have been influenced by the troubles that Albert of Sambonifacio (d. 1135), marquis of Verona, seems to have had with his followers. A *tractatus de dictamine* composed in north Italy, probably in the 1130s, contains a letter which the author attributes to Albert—the man, incidentally, whose death allowed the chapter of Verona to reclaim Cerea.[10] The letter makes Albert complain to Lothar III about his treatment by the *capitanei et valvasores et cuncti satellites* of the house of the countess Matilda of Canossa (d. 1115). They had persuaded him to become their lord and he had rewarded them handsomely—though he does not actually mention lands in his list of rewards. Then, after he had no more to give, they craftily enticed (*seduxerunt*) his wife and took her to Canossa and held her and it violently.[11] This need not have involved sexual relations: another letter, attributed to the *capitanei et valvasores*, puts a very different light on the affair, but if anything at all like this really happened—and the details of the letter fit fairly well into the political circumstances of the time—the story must have lost nothing in being told around north Italy. This story would, of course, account for only two of the offences listed in the tracts, while none of the tracts mentions capture of the lord's sons, which Albert also alleged. On balance it seems unlikely that it can have been responsible for making lawyers think about offences deserving confiscation, so that it is not a serious argument for dating them after 1125.

Obertus's letters must have been written about the middle of the century.[12] The letter that appears first in the book (VIII. 1–15, 17–29[13]) may have been written first, but there need not have been any significant difference in dates. Both letters cite Lothar III's ordinance (VIII. 5, 15; X. 10) but neither refers to either of Frederick I's, which should put them between 1136 and 1154. Classen thought they were more probably written in the 1140s than the 1150s.[14] One consideration might be how quickly one thinks that lawyers devised a way of evading Lothar's ordinance by making conveyances *per libellum*, referred to in VIII. 15 (*Ant.* 28). It is tempt-

[10] For the Sambonifacio and Cerea, see chapter 6.5.
[11] Wattenbach, 'Iter Austriacum', 83–6; cf. Simeoni, 'Origini', 108–10.
[12] For his career see chapter 6.8 and Classen, *Studium*, 50–68.
[13] I follow Lehmann's attribution to him of the whole of tit. VIII except 16.
[14] Classen, *Studium*, 59–60.

ing to wonder whether Obertus, who served as an imperial *missus* and was obviously a lawyer of high repute in Milan, may have been one of the emperor's advisers for the legislation of 1154.

Anselminus de Orto's treatise *Super contractibus* was presumably written not much later, if, as seems probable, it was written by the son to whom Obertus addressed his letters. Perhaps it was written on the basis of Anselmus's (or Anselminus's) studies in Roman and Lombard law, before his father's letters were written.[15] Incidentally, Anselminus allows alienation of property held under *investitura* without consent of the lord. If by *investitura* he means something like a fief or benefice, which seems likely, then Lehmann's arguments about the other treatises would suggest that it was written before 1136, which seems improbable.[16]

Lehmann thought that Ariprandus's commentary on the *Lombarda* and his *Summula* were written around the middle of the century, after Obertus's letters.[17] The commentary says that investiture should be sought within a year, but the *Summula* allows a *privatus* to delay for a year and a day and a knight for a year and a month.[18] Lehmann concluded that Ariprandus had seen both 1d (VI. 11), which allows a year and a month, and Obertus's second letter (*Ant* 36: X. 2), which allows a year and a day. He also thought that the *Summula*'s reference to fuller reasons for confiscation of fiefs enumerated *in feudorum consuetudines* meant that Ariprandus had seen the Antiqua. I do not think that these conclusions are necessary. There may well, however, have been differences of opinion before Obertus about the time to be allowed for investiture. The compromise Ariprandus found by giving different deadlines for *miles* and *privatus* was entirely his own anyway. Ariprandus had evidently seen some tract on the customs of fiefs but it need not have been the whole Antiqua. The precise dating of Ariprandus's work is impossible, and, I suggest, like the precise dates of the other tracts, is of secondary importance. Whenever they were written, Ariprandus's works, in their brevity and their close relation to the *Lombarda*, seem nearer to 1a–e than they are to the more Romanist and more sophisticated letters of Obertus. That is why I have discussed them along with the pre-Obertian treatises in chapter 6.

[15] Classen, *Studium*, 64–5.    [16] On *investitura*, see chapter 6, n. 61.

[17] Anschütz, *Lombarda-Commentare*; Lehmann, *Consuetudines: Antiqua*, 4. There are also glosses attributed to Ariprandus in early MSS of the Antiqua, including on later books (listed by Lehmann on the page before his preface), but these seem to be opinions attributed to him rather than evidence that he saw the actual texts to which they are attached.

[18] Anschütz, *Lombarda-Commentare*, 195, 196. Anschütz printed the further qualifications in the *Summula* in square brackets. It is not clear what this means. The passages of the *Summula* which he put in square brackets do not all correspond to its differences from the commentary but he does not suggest that they were later additions. The explanation on p. xix would not apply to this text.

# List of Works Cited

ABBREVIATIONS

| | |
|---|---|
| *AESC* | *Annales: Économies, Sociétés, Civilisations* |
| *AHR* | *American Historical Review* |
| *ANS* | *Anglo-Norman Studies* |
| *BEC* | *Bibliothèque de l'Ecole des Chartes* |
| *BIHR* | *Bulletin of the Institute of Historical Research* |
| *BISIME* | *Bullettino dell'istituto storico italiano per il medio evo* |
| *BJRL* | *Bulletin of the John Rylands Library* |
| *BSBS* | *Bollettino storico-bibliografico subalpino* |
| CNRS | Centre National de Recherches Scientifiques |
| *DA* | *Deutsches Archiv für Erforschung des Mittelalters* |
| *EHR* | *English Historical Review* |
| FSI | Fonti per la storia d'Italia |
| *HJ* | *Historische Jahrbuch* |
| *HZ* | *Historische Zeitschrift* |
| *MA* | *Le Moyen Age* |
| *MEF* | *Mélanges d'archéologie et d'histoire de l'école française de Rome: (moyen âge et temps modernes)* |
| MGH | Monumenta Germaniae Historica |
| *MGH Scriptores* | Monumenta Germaniae Historica: *Scriptores*: folio series |
| MGH SRG | Monumenta Germaniae Historica: Scriptores Rerum Germanicarum |
| *MIÖG* | *Mitteilungen des Instituts für österreichische Geschichtsforschung* |
| *PBA* | *Proceedings of the British Academy* |
| *PL* | *Patrologia Latina*, ed. J. P. Migne and others (Paris, 1844–1903) |
| *QFIA* | *Quellen und Forschungen aus italienischen Archiven und Bibliotheken* |
| RCI | Regesta Chartarum Italiae |
| *Revue belge* | *Revue belge de philologie et d'histoire* |
| *RH* | *Revue historique* |
| *RHDFE* | *Revue historique de droit français et étranger* |
| *RHGF* | *Recueil des historiens des Gaules et de la France* |
| RIS | Rerum Italicarum Scriptores |
| RS | Rolls Series |
| *Settimane* | *Settimane di studio del Centro italiano di studi sull'alto medioevo* |
| *SM* | *Studi medievali* |

| | |
|---|---|
| *TRHS* | *Transactions of the Royal Historical Society* |
| *VF* | *Vorträge und Forschungen* |
| *ZRG GA* | *Zeitschrift der Savigny-Stiftung für Rechtsgeschichte: Germanistische Abteilung* |
| *ZRG KA* | *Zeitschrift der Savigny-Stiftung für Rechtsgeschichte: Kanonistische Abteilung* |

### 1. MANUSCRIPTS

| | |
|---|---|
| British Library MS Cott. Claudius E3 | fos. 3–158: Ralph Diceto's *Abbreviatio Chronicorum* |
| MS Cott. Vespasian F. vii | fos. 15–16: Scottish arguments against Edward I, 1301 |
| Public Record Office C 47/27–8 | Chancery miscellanea, diplomatic documents |
| SC 1/48 | Special Collections, ancient correspondence |

### 2. ALL OTHER WORKS, BOTH PRIMARY AND SECONDARY (PRINTED, MICROFICHE, AND TYPESCRIPT)

Abbo of Fleury, *Apologeticus*, in *PL* 139, 461–71.

Abels, R. P., *Lordship and Military Obligation in Anglo-Saxon England* (Berkeley, 1988).

Acher, J., 'Notes sur le droit savant au moyen âge', *RHDFE* 30 (1906), 125–78.

*Acta imperii inedita*, ed. E. Winkelmann (Innsbruck, 1880).

*Actes de Guillaume le conquérant et de la reine Mathilde pour les abbayes caennaises*, ed. L. Musset (Caen, 1967).

*Actes des comtes de Flandre, 1071–1128*, ed. F. Vercauteren (Brussels, 1938).

*Actes des comtes de Namur, 946–1196*, ed. F. Rousseau (Brussels, 1937).

*Actes des évêques de Metz: Étienne de Bar*, ed. M. Parisse (Nancy, no date: since 1970?).

*Actes du Parlement de Paris*, ed. E. Boutaric (Paris, 1863–7).

*Actes et documents anciens intéressant la Belgique*, ed. C. Duvivier, ii (Brussels, 1903).

Adam of Bremen, *Gesta Hammaburgensis Ecclesiae Pontificum*, ed. B. Schmendler (MGH SRG 2, 1917).

Airlie, S., 'The Political Behaviour of the Secular Magnates in Francia, 829–79' (Oxford D.Phil. thesis, 1985): typescript.

Albert of Aachen, *Historia Hierosolymitana* in *Recueil des historiens des croisades: historiens occidentaux* (Paris, 1841–95), iv. 265–713.

Alessandro di Telese, *De Rebus Gestis Rogerii libri quattuor* in *Cronisti e Scrittori*, ed. G. del Re (Naples, 1845), 81–156.

Alfred, *King Alfred's Version of St Augustine's Soliloquies*, ed. T. A. Carnicelli (Cambridge, Mass., 1969).

*Ältesten Lehnsbücher der Herrschaft Bolanden*, ed. W. Sauer (Wiesbaden, 1882).

Amato di Montecassino, *Storia de' Normanni*, ed. V. de Bartholomeis (FSI 76, 1935).

*Ancient Charters*, ed. J. H. Round (Pipe Roll Society, 1888).

Andreas de Isernia, *In usus feudorum commentaria* (Naples, 1571).

*Anglo-Scottish Relations, 1174–1328*, ed. E. L. G. Stones (2nd edn., Oxford, 1970).

*Annales Altahenses Maiores*, in *MGH Scriptores*, xx. 782–824.

*Annales de Saint-Bertin*, ed. F. Grat and others (Paris, 1964).

*Annales Fuldenses*, ed. F. Kurze (MGH SRG 7, 1891).

*Annales Palidenses*, in *MGH Scriptores*, xvi. 48–98.

*Annales Regni Francorum*, ed. F. Kurze (MGH SRG 6, 1895).

*Annales Reichespergenses*, in *MGH Scriptores*, xvii. 443–76.

*Annales Sancti Disibodi*, in *MGH Scriptores*, xviii. 4–30.

Anschütz, A., *Die Lombarda-Commentare des Ariprandus und Albertus* (Heidelberg, 1855).

Anselm of Canterbury, *Epistolae*, in *PL* 158–9.

—— *Opera Omnia*, ed. F. S. Schmitt, ii (Rome, 1940).

Anselminus de Orto, *Super contractibus emphiteosis et precarii et libelli atque investitura*, ed. R. Jacobi (Weimar, 1854).

*Antrobus Deeds before 1625*, ed. R. B. Pugh (Wiltshire Archaeol. Soc. Records Branch, 3, 1947).

Appelt, H., 'Einleitung' to *Dip. Frid. I* (MGH, 1990).

—— 'Friedrich Barbarossa und das römische Recht', in *Kaisertum, Königtum, Landesherrschaft* (Vienna/Cologne/Graz, 1988), 61–80; reprinted from *Römische Hist. Mitteilungen*, 5 (1962), 18–34.

Arbois de Jubainville, H. d', 'Document sur l'obligation de la résidence imposée aux barons', *RHDFE* 5 (1861), 68–70.

—— *Histoire des ducs et des comtes de Champagne* (Paris, 1859–66).

*Archives historiques de Poitou*, xiii (1883).

Arnold fitz Thedmar, *De Antiquis Legibus Liber: Cronica Maiorum et Vicecomitum Londoniarum*, ed. T. Stapleton (Camden Society, ser. 1, 34, 1846).

Arnold, B., *Count and Bishop in Medieval Germany* (Philadelphia, 1991).

—— *German Knighthood* (Oxford, 1985).

—— *Princes and Territories in Medieval Germany* (Cambridge, 1991).

Arnulf, *Gesta archiepiscoporum Mediolanensium*, in *MGH Scriptores*, viii. 1–31.

*Asseburger Urkundenbuch*, ed. J. von Bocholtz-Asseburg (Hanover, 1876–1905).

Asser, *Life of King Alfred*, ed. W. H. Stevenson (Oxford, 1904).

Aston, T. H., 'The Origins of the Manor in England', *TRHS* ser. 5, 8 (1958), 59–83.

Atto of Vercelli, *Epistolae*, in *PL* 134, 95–124.

*Auctor vetus de beneficiis*: see Eike von Repgow.

Auer, L., 'Der Kriegdienst des Klerus unter der sächsischen Kaisern', *MIÖG* 79 (1971), 316–407; 80 (1972), 48–70.

Ault, W. O., *Private Jurisdiction in England* (New Haven, Conn., 1923).

Azo, *Quaestiones*, ed. E. Landsberg (Freiburg, 1888).

Bachrach, B. S., 'A Study in Feudal Politics: Relations between Fulk Nerra and William the Great', *Viator*, 7 (1976), 111–22.

Baldus, *In usus feudorum commentaria [Opus aureum]* (Lyon, 1550).

Baldwin, J. W., *The Government of Philip Augustus* (Princeton, NJ, 1986).

Balon, J., *Les Fondements du régime foncier au Moyen Âge* (Louvain, 1954).

—— *Ius Medii Aevi: la Structure et la gestion du domaine de l'église au Moyen Age dans l'Europe des Francs* (Namur, 1959).

Barlow, F., *The English Church, 1066–1154* (London, 1979).

Barroux, R., 'L'Abbé Suger et la vassalité du Vexin en 1124', *MA* 64 (1958), 1–26.

Barrow, G., *The Kingdom of the Scots* (London, 1973).

—— *Robert Bruce* (3rd edn., Edinburgh, 1988).

Barthélemy, A. de, 'Étude sur les lettres d'anoblissement', *Revue historique nobiliaire et biographique*, NS 5 (1869), 193–208, 241–52.

Barthélemy, D., 'La Mutation féodale a-t-elle eu lieu?', *AESC* 47 (1992), 767–77.

Barton, J. L., *Roman Law in England* (*Ius Romanum Medii Aevi*, v. 13. a: Milan, 1971).

Bates, D., *Normandy before 1066* (London, 1982).

Baumel, J., *Histoire d'une seigneurie du midi de la France: naissance de Montpellier (985–1213)* (Montpellier, 1969).

Bautier, R. H. (ed.), *La France de Philippe Auguste* (Colloques Internationaux du CNRS, 602, Paris, 1982).

Bean, J. M. W., *The Decline of English Feudalism* (Manchester, 1968).

Beaumanoir, Philippe de Remi, Sire de, *Coutumes de Beauvaisis*, ed. A. Salmon (Paris, 1900); commentary by G. Hubrecht in vol. 3 (Paris, 1974).

Becker, L. C., *Property Rights: Philosophical Foundations* (London, 1977).

Bede, *Historia Ecclesiastica*, ed. C. Plummer (Oxford, 1896).

Beech, G. T., *A Rural Society in Medieval France* (Baltimore, 1964).

Behrends, F., 'Kingship and Feudalism according to Fulbert of Chartres', *Mediaeval Studies*, 25 (1963), 93–9.

Bémont, C., *De Johanne cognomine sine terra* (Paris, 1884).

Bendix, R., and Berger, B., 'Images of Society and Problems of Concept Formulation in Sociology', in L. Gross (ed.), *Symposium on Sociological Theory* (New York, 1959), 92–118.

Benedetto di S. Andrea del Soratte, *Chronicon*, ed. G. Zucchetti (FSI 55, 1920).

*Benedicti Regula*, ed. R. Hanslik (Vienna, 1960).

Benjamin, R., 'A Forty Years War: Toulouse and the Plantagenets, 1156–96', *Historical Research*, 61 (1988), 270–85.

Benl, R., *Die Gestaltung der Bodenrechtsverhältnisse im Pommern vom 12. bis zum 14. Jahrhundert* (Cologne, 1986).

Benton, J. F., 'Philip the Fair and the Jours of Troyes', *Studies in Medieval and Renaissance History*, 6 (1969), 281–344.

Bergengruen, A., *Adel und Grundherrschaft im Merowingerreich* (Wiesbaden, 1958).

Berman, H. J., *Law and Revolution* (Cambridge, Mass., 1983).

Bertrand de Bar-sur-Aube, *Girart de Vienne*, ed. W. van Emden (Paris, 1977).

Beumann, H., 'Zur Entwicklung transpersonaler Staatsvorstellung', *VF* 3 (1956), 185–224.

Biancalana, J., 'For Want of Justice: Legal Reforms of Henry II', *Columbia Law Review*, 88 (1988), 433–536.

Bilow, F. von, *Geschichtliche Entwicklung der Abgabenverhältnisse in Pommern und Rügen* (Greifswald, 1843).

Bisson, T. N., *Assemblies and Representation in Languedoc in the Thirteenth Century* (Princeton, 1964).

—— *Medieval France and her Pyrenean Neighbours* (London, 1989), 153–78: 'Feudalism in Twelfth-Century Catalonia' (also in *Structures féodales*, 173–92).

Blackstone, W., *Commentaries on the Laws of England*, ed. J. T. Coleridge (London, 1825).

Bloch, H., 'Die älteren Urkunden des Klosters S. Vanne', *Jahrbuch der Gesellschaft für lothringische Geschichte*, 14 (1902), 48–150.

Bloch, Marc, *Feudal Society*, trans. L. A. Manyon (London, 1965); *La Société féodale* (Paris, 1939).

—— *Mélanges Historiques* (Paris, 1963), i. 189–209: 'Les Formes de la rupture de l'hommage'.

Bloch, Maurice, *Marxist Analysis and Social Anthropology* (London, 1975), 203–28: 'Property and the End of Affinity'.

—— *Ritual, History and Power* (London, 1989).

Bocchi, F., 'Regulation of the Urban Environment by the Italian Communes from the Twelfth to the Fourteenth Century', *BJRL* 72 (1990), 63–78.

Bock, F., 'Some New Documents Illustrating the Early Years of the Hundred Years War', *BJRL* 15 (1931), 60–99.

Boerger, R., *Die Belehnung der deutschen geistlichen Fürsten* (Leipzig, 1901).

Bognetti, G. P., 'Gli Arcivescovi interpreti della realtà e il crescere dei minori ordini feudali', in *Storia di Milano*, ii (Milan, 1954), 845–62.

Bonaini, F. (ed.), *Statuti inediti della città di Pisa* (Florence, 1854–7).

Bonnassie, P., *La Catalogne du milieu du x*^e *à la fin du xi*^e *siècle* (Toulouse, 1975).

*Book of Seals, Sir Christopher Hatton's*, ed. L. C. Loyd and D. M. Stenton (Oxford, 1950).

Bordone, R., 'Società e potere in Asti e nel suo comitato fino al declino dell'autorità regia', *BSBS* 73 (1975), 357–439.

*Borough Customs*, ed. M. Bateson (Selden Society, 18–19, 1904, 1906).

Bosl, K., *Frühformen der Gesellschaft im mittelalterlichen Europa* (Munich, 1964).

—— 'Die Reichsministerialität', in T. Mayer (ed.), *Adel und Bauern* (Leipzig, 1943), 74–108.

Bosworth, J., and Toller, T. N., *Anglo-Saxon Dictionary* (Oxford, 1898).

Bouchard, C. B., 'The Origins of the French Nobility', *AHR* 86 (1981), 501–52.

Boulet-Sautel, M., 'Le Droit romain et Philippe Auguste', in Bautier, *La France de Philippe Auguste* (q.v.), 489–501.

Bournazel, E., *Le Gouvernement capétien au xii*^e *siècle* (Paris, 1975).

Boussard, J., 'L'Enquête de 1172 sur les services de chevalier en Normandie', *Recueil de travaux offert à M. Clovis Brunel* (Paris, 1955), i. 193–208.

Boutruche, R., *Seigneurie et féodalité* (Paris, 1968).

—— *Une société provinciale en lutte contre le régime féodal* (Paris, 1947).

Bracton, Henry de, *De Legibus et Consuetudinibus Angliae*, ed. G. E. Woodbine and S. E. Thorne (Cambridge, Mass., 1968–77).

*Bracton's Note-Book*, ed. F. W. Maitland (London, 1887).

Brancoli Busdraghi, P., 'La Formazione storica del feudo lombardo come diritto reale', *Studi senesi*, 76 (1964), 53–114, 224–280, 431–500. Also published in book form (Quaderni di Studi Senesi, ii, 1965).

Brand, P. A., 'The Control of Mortmain Alienation in England, 1200–1300', in J. H. Baker (ed.), *Legal Records and the Historian* (London, 1978), 29–40.

—— *The Origins of the English Legal Profession* (Oxford, 1992).

*Briefsammlung der Zeit Heinrichs IV*, ed. C. Ardmann and N. Fickermann (MGH, Briefe der deutschen Kaiserzeit, 5, 1950).

*Britton*, ed. F. M. Nichols (Oxford, 1865).

Brooks, N. P., 'Anglo-Saxon Charters', *Anglo-Saxon England*, 3 (1974), 210–31.

—— 'Arms, Status and Warfare in Late Saxon England', in D. Hill (ed.), *Ethelred the Unready* (Oxford, 1978), 81–103.

—— 'The Development of Military Obligations in Eighth and Ninth Century England', in P. Clemoes and K. Hughes (eds.), *England before the Conquest* (Cambridge, 1971), 69–84.

—— *Early History of the Church of Canterbury* (Leicester, 1984).

Brown, E. A. R., '*Cessante Causa* and the Taxes of the Last Capetians', *Studia Gratiana (Post Scripta)*, 15 (1972), 565–87.

—— *Customary Aids and Royal Finance in Capetian France* (Cambridge, Mass., 1992).

—— 'Customary Aids and Royal Fiscal Policy under Philip VI', *Traditio*, 30 (1974), 192–258.

—— '*Franks, Burgundians, and Aquitanians' and the Royal Coronation Ceremony in France* (Trans. Am. Philos. Soc. 82 (2), 1992).

—— 'The Tyranny of a Construct: Feudalism and Historians of Medieval Europe', *AHR* 79 (1974), 1063–88.

Brown, R. A., *Origins of English Feudalism* (London, 1973).

Brown, S. D. B., 'Military Service and Monetary Reward in the Eleventh and Twelfth Centuries', *History*, 74 (1989), 20–38.

Bruckauf, J., *Fahnlehen und Fahnbelehnung im alten deutschen Reiche* (Leipzig, 1907).

Brühl, C., *Fodrum, Gistum, Servitium Regis* (Cologne, 1968).

Brunner, H., *Deutsche Rechtsgeschichte*, ii (2nd edn., Leipzig, 1928).

Brunner, O., '"Feudalismus": ein Beitrag zur Begriffsgeschichte', in L. Kuchenbuch (ed.), *Feudalismus* (Frankfurt, 1977), 155–95.

—— 'Feudalismus, feudal', in O. Brunner and others (eds.), *Geschichtliche Grundbegriffe*, ii (Stuttgart, 1975), 337–50.

—— *Land und Herrschaft* (Darmstadt, 1973): trans. H. Kaminsky and J. van H. Melton as *Land and Lordship* (Philadelphia, 1992).

Bruno of Magdeburg, *Buch vom Sachsenkrieg*, ed. H. C. Lohmann (MGH Kritische Studientexte, 1937).

Brussel, N., *Nouvel examen de l'usage général des fiefs en France* (Paris, 1750).

Budriesi Trombetti, A. L., 'Prime ricerche sul vocabulario feudale italiano', *Atti dell'Accademia delle scienze dell'Istituto di Bologna: classe di scienze morali . . . Rendiconti*, 62 (1973–4), 277–401.

—— *Vassalli e feudi a Ferrara e nel Ferrarese dall'età precomunale alla signoria estense* (Atti e mem. della dep. prov. ferrarese di storia patria, ser. 3, 28, 1980).

Bueno da Mesquita, D. M., 'Ludovico Sforza and his Vassals', in E. F. Jacob (ed.), *Italian Renaissance Studies* (London, 1960), 184–216.

Bullough, D. A., 'Europae Pater', *EHR* 85 (1970), 59–105.

*Bündner Urkundenbuch*, i, ed. E. Meyer-Marthaler and F. Perret (Chur, 1955).

Bur, M., 'Aux origines du fermage: l'exemple du chapitre cathédral de Meaux', *Revue du Nord*, 49 (1967), 5–21.

—— *La Formation du comté de Champagne* (Nancy, 1977).

Burmeister, K. H., 'Anfänge und Entwicklung des öffentlichen Notariats bis zur Reichsnotariatsordnung vom 1512', *Festschrift für F. Elsener*, ed. L. Carlsen and F. Ebel (Sigmaringen, 1977), 77–90.

—— *Das Studium der Rechte im Zeitalter des Humanismus im deutschen Rechtsbereich* (Wiesbaden, 1974).

*Burton Chartulary*, ed. G. Wrottesley (*William Salt Arc. Soc. Collections*, 5, 1884).

Caesarius of Heisterbach, *Die Wundergeschichten*, ed. A. Hilka, iii (Bonn, 1937).

Caetani, G. (ed.), *Documenti dell'archivio Caetani: Regesta Chartarum*, i (Perugia, 1922).

Cahen, C., *Le Régime féodal de l'Italie normande* (Paris, 1940).

*Calendar of Inquisitions Miscellaneous*, i (London, 1916).

*Calendars of Patent Rolls, 1226–1516* (London, 1901–39).

Calmet, A., *Histoire ecclésiastique et civile de Lorraine* (Nancy, 1728).

Cam, H. M., *Liberties and Communities in Medieval England* (London, 1963).

Cammarosano, P., *Le Campagne nell'età comunale* (Turin, 1976).

—— 'Le Strutture feudali nell'evoluzione dell'Occidente mediterraneo: note su un colloquio internazionale', *SM* ser. 3, 22 (1981), 837–69.

Campbell, J., 'Observations on English Government from the Tenth to the Twelfth Century', *TRHS* ser. 5, 25 (1975), 39–54.

*Capitularia Regum Francorum*, ed. A. Boretius (MGH Legum Sect. 2, 1883–1901).

Carpenter, D. A., 'English Peasants in Politics, 1258–67', *Past & Present*, 136 (1992), 3–42.

*Carte dello archivio capitolare di Asti*, ed. F. Gabotto and N. Gabiani (Pinerolo, 1907).

*Carte latine di abbazie Calabresi provenenti dall'archivio Aldobrandini*, ed. A. Pratesi (Vatican City, 1958).

*Cartulaire d'Apt*, ed. N. Didier (Paris, 1967).

*Cartulaire de Béziers*, ed. J. Rouquette (Paris/Montpellier, 1918).

*Cartulaire de Château-du-Loir*, ed. E. Vallée (Archives historiques du Maine, Le Mans, 1905).

*Cartulaire de l'abbaye de Beaulieu*, ed. M. Deloche (Paris, 1859).

*Cartulaire de l'abbaye de Conques*, ed. G. Desjardins (Paris, 1879).

*Cartulaire de l'abbaye de Gorze*, ed. A. Herbomez (Paris, 1898).

*Cartulaire de l'abbaye de la Trinité de Vendôme*, ed. C. Métais (Paris/Vendôme, 1893).

*Cartulaire de l'abbaye de Montiéramey* (Collection des principaux cartulaires du diocèse de Troyes, ed. C. Lalore, 7, Paris, 1890).

*Cartulaire de l'abbaye de Saint-Aubin d'Angers*, ed. B. de Broussillon (Angers, 1896–9).

*Cartulaire de l'abbaye de Saint-Corneille de Compiègne*, ed. C. Morel (Montdidier, 1904–9).

*Cartulaire de l'abbaye de Saint-Trond*, ed. C. Piot (Brussels, 1870).

*Cartulaire de l'abbaye de Saint-Victor de Marseille* (Paris, 1857).

*Cartulaire de l'abbaye de Saint-Vincent du Mans*, ed. R. Charles and Menjot d'Elbenne (Mamers, 1886–1913).

'Cartulaire de la Seigneurie de Fontjoncouse', ed. G. Mouynès, *Bulletin de la Commission Arch. et Litt. de l'arrondissement de Narbonne*, i (1877), 107–346.

*Cartulaire de l'évêché de Metz*, ed. P. Marichal (Paris, 1903–8).

*Cartulaire de Maguelone*, ed. J. Rouquette and A. Villemagne (Montpellier, 1912–23).

*Cartulaire de Marmoutier pour le Vendômois*, ed. A. de Trémault (Paris, 1893).

*Cartulaire de Molesme*, ed. J. Laurent (Paris, 1911).

*Cartulaire de Richerenches*, ed. marquis de Ripert-Monclar (Avignon, 1907).

*Cartulaire des abbayes de Saint-Pierre de la Couture et de Saint-Pierre de Solesmes* (Le Mans, 1881).

*Cartulaire de Saint-André-le-Bas de Vienne*, ed. C. U. J. Chevalier (Lyon, 1869).

*Cartulaire de Saint-Étienne, Limoges*, ed. J. de Font-Réaulx (Bulletin de la société arch. et hist. du Limousin, 69 (1921) [titlepage has 68 (1919)]).

'Cartulaire de Saint-Maur-sur-Loire', in *Archives d'Anjou*, ed. P. Marchegay (Angers, 1843), 293–429.

*Cartulaire de Saint-Vincent de Mâcon*, ed. M. C. Ragut (Mâcon, 1864).

*Cartulaire de Vierzon*, ed. G. Devailly (Paris, 1963).

*Cartulaire du prieuré de Paray-le-Monial*, ed. C. U. J. Chevalier (Montbéliard, 1891).

*Cartulaire générale de Paris*, ed. R. de Lasteyrie (Paris, 1887).

*Cartulaire lyonnais*, ed. M. C. Guigue (Lyon, 1885).

*Cartulaires de l'église cathédrale de Grenoble dits cartulaires de Saint Hugues*, ed. J. Marion (Paris, 1869).

*Cartulaires du Bas-Poitou*, ed. P. Marchegay (Les Roches-sur-Yon, 1877).

*Cartularium Monasterii de Ramseia*, ed. W. H. Hart and P. A. Lyons (RS 79, 1884–93).

*Cartulary of Shrewsbury Abbey*, ed. U. Rees (Aberystwyth, 1975).

Caspar, E., *Roger II* (Innsbruck, 1904).

*Casuum Sancti Galli Continuatio II*, in *MGH Scriptores*, ii. 148–63.

*Catalogus Baronum*, ed. E. M. Jamison (FSI, 1972).

Cavallari, V., 'Il Conte di Verona fra l'xi ed il xii secolo', *Atti e memorie dell'Accademia di agricoltura scienze e lettere di Verona*, ser. 6, 20 (1968–9), 203–74.

Certain, E. de (ed.), *Miracles de Saint Benoît* (Paris, 1858).

Challis, H. W., 'Are Leaseholds Tenements?', *Law Quarterly Review*, 6 (1890), 69–71.

Chaplais, P., 'The Anglo-Saxon Chancery: from the Diploma to the Writ', *Journal of the Society of Archivists*, 3 (1965–9), 160–76.

—— 'English Arguments concerning the Feudal Status of Aquitaine', *BIHR* 21 (1946–8), 203–13.

—— 'Le Traité de Paris de 1259 et l'inféodation de la Gascogne allodiale', *MA* 61 (1955), 121–37; 'Le Duché-Pairie de Guyenne', *Annales du Midi*, 69 (1957), 5–38, and 70 (1958), 135–60; 'La Souveraineté du roi de France et le pouvoir législatif en Guyenne au début du xiv$^e$ siècle', *MA* 69 (1963), 449–67: all repr. in *Essays in Medieval Diplomacy and Administration* (London, 1981).

*Chartae Latinae Antiquiores*, xiii, ed. H. Atsma and J. Vezin (Zurich, 1981).

*Charters of the Honour of Mowbray*, ed. D. E. Greenway (London, 1972).

'Chartes de Saint-Étienne de Nevers', ed. R. de Lespinasse, *Bulletin de la Société nivernaise des lettres, sciences et arts*, ser. 3, 12 (1908), 51–130.

*Chartes et documents pour servir à l'histoire de l'abbaye de Saint-Maixent*, ed. A. Richard (Archives historiques de Poitou, 16: Poitiers, 1886).

*Chartularium del monastero di S. Benedetto di Conversano*, ed. D. Morea (Montecassino, 1892).

Chédeville, A., *Chartres et ses campagnes (xi$^e$–xiii$^e$ s.)* (Paris, 1973).

Cheney, C. R., *Pope Innocent III and England* (Stuttgart, 1976).

Cheney, M., 'A Decree of Henry II on Defect of Justice', *Tradition and Change: Essays in Honour of Marjorie Chibnall*, ed. D. Greenway and others (Cambridge, 1985), 183–93.

—— 'Inalienability in Mid-Twelfth-Century England', *Proceedings of the Sixth International Congress of Medieval Canon Law* (Monumenta Iuris Canonici, ser. C: Subsidia, 7, Vatican, 1985), 467–78.

—— 'The Litigation between John Marshal and Archbishop Thomas Becket in 1164', in J. A. Guy and H. G. Beale (eds.), *Law and Social Change in British History* (London, 1984), 9–26.

Chénon, E., *Étude sur l'histoire des alleux en France* (Paris, 1888).

—— 'Le Rôle juridique de l'*osculum* dans l'ancien droit français', *Mémoires de la Société nationale des antiquaires de France*, 76 (1924), 124–55.

Cheyette, F. L., 'The "Sale" of Carcassonne to the Counts of Barcelona', *Speculum*, 63 (1988), 826–64.

Chittolini, G., *La Formazione dello stato regionale e le istitutioni del contado* (Turin, 1979), 36–100: 'Infeudazioni e politica feudale nel ducato visconteo-sforzesco'; also in *Quaderni storici*, 19 (1972).

*Chronica Regia Coloniensis*, ed. G. Waitz (MGH SRG 18, 1880).

*Chronicle of the reigns of Henry II and Richard I*, ed. W. Stubbs (RS 49, 1867).

*Chronicon Casauriense*, in *Rerum Ital. Scriptores*, ed. L. A. Muratori, ii (2) (Milan, 1726), 775–1018.

*Chronicon Hildesheimense*, in *MGH Scriptores*, vii. 845–73.

*Chronicon Laureshamense*, in *MGH Scriptores*, xxi. 334–453.

*Chronicon Monasterii de Abingdon*, ed. J. Stephenson (RS 2, 1858).

*Chronique de Morigny*, ed. L. Mirot (Paris, 1912).

*Chronique de Saint-Pierre de Bèze*, in *Chronique de Saint-Bénigne de Dijon*, ed. E. Bougard and J. Garnier (Dijon, 1875), i. 231–503.

*Chronique de Saint-Pierre-le-Vif de Sens*, ed. R. H. Bautier and M. Gilles (Paris, 1979).

*Chronique et cartulaire de l'abbaye de Bergues-Saint-Winoc*, ed. A. Pruvost (Bruges, 1875).

*Chronique et chartes de l'abbaye de Saint-Mihiel*, ed. A. Lesort (Paris, 1909–12).

Clarke, H. B., 'The Domesday Satellites', in P. H. Sawyer (ed.), *Domesday Book: a Reassessment* (London, 1985), 50–70.

Classen, P., 'Fortleben und Wandel spätrömischen Urkundenwesens im frühen Mittelalter', *VF* 23 (1977), 13–54.

—— *Studium und Gesellschaft im Mittelalter* (Schriften der MGH, 29, 1983).

—— 'Die Verträge von Verdun und von Coulaines 843 als politische Grundlagen des Westfränkischen Reiches', *HZ* 196 (1963), 1–35.

—— 'Das Wormser Konkordat in der deutschen Verfassungsgeschichte', *VF* 17 (1973), 411–60.

Claude, D., 'Untersuchungen zum frühfränkischen Comitat', *ZRG GA* 81 (1964) 1–79.

*Close Rolls of the Reign of Henry III* (London, 1902–72).

*Codex Astensis*, ed. Q. Sella (Rome, 1880).

*Codex Diplomaticus Cajetanus* (Monte Cassino: Tabularium Casinensis, 1887–91).

*Codex Diplomaticus Cremonae*, ed. L. Astegiano, i (Turin, 1896).

*Codex Diplomaticus Fuldensis*, ed. E. F. J. Dronke (1850: repr. Aalen, 1962).

*Codex Diplomaticus Nassoicus*, ed. K. Menzel and W. Sauer (Wiesbaden, 1885).

*Codex Diplomaticus Saxoniae Regiae*, pt. i, ed. O. Posse (Leipzig, 1882–9).

*Codex Falkensteinensis*, ed. E. Noichl (Munich, 1978).

*Codex Laureshamensis*, ed. K. Glöckner (Darmstadt, 1929–36).

*Codex Legum Antiquarium*, ed. F. Lindenbrog (Frankfurt, 1613).

*Codice diplomatico della repubblica di Genova*, i (FSI 77, 1936).

*Codice diplomatico del monasterio di Bobbio*, ed. C. Cipolla (FSI 52–4, 1918).

*Codice diplomatico Longobardo*, ed. L. Schiaparelli and C. R. Brühl (FSI 62–6, 1929–73).

*Codice diplomatico Normanno di Aversa*, i, ed. A. Gallo (Naples, 1926).

*Codice diplomatico Padovano*, ed. A. Gloria (Venice, 1881).

Cohen, M. R., *Law and the Social Order* (New York, 1933).

Cohen, R., and Middleton, J. (eds.), *Comparative Political Systems* (Austin, Texas, 1967).

Coing, H., *Römisches Recht in Deutschland* (*Ius Romanum Medii Aevi*, v. 6: Milan, 1964).

Coke, E., *Institutes, part I*, ed. F. Hargrave and C. Butler, iii (London, 1794).

'Comptes et enquêtes d'Alphonse, comte de Poitou', *Archives Historiques de Poitou*, 8 (1879), 1–160.

*Concilia Aevi Karolini* (MGH Concilia ii (1), 1906).

Constable, G., 'Nona et Decima', *Speculum*, 35 (1960), 224–50.

*Constitutiones et Acta Publica Imperatorum et Regum* (MGH Legum Sectio 4, 1893–1906).

*Consuetudines Feudorum*, in Lehmann, *Das Langobardische Lehnrecht* (q.v.).

Contamine, P., *La Noblesse au moyen âge* (Paris, 1976).

Conti, E., *La Formazione della struttura agraria moderna nel contado fiorentino* (Rome, 1965).

*Continuatio Sancrucensis II*, in *MGH Scriptores*, ix. 637–46.

'Conventum inter Guillelmum Aquitanorum comitem et Hugonem Chiliarchum', ed. J. Martindale, *EHR* 84 (1969), 528–48.

Conze, W., 'Adel', in O. Brunner and others (eds.), *Geschichtliche Grundbegriffe*, i (Stuttgart, 1972), 1–48.

*Corpus Iuris Canonici*, ed. A. Friedberg (Graz, 1955).

*Corpus Iuris Civilis*, ed. T. Mommsen and others (Berlin, 1954).

*Correspondance administrative d'Alfonse de Poitiers*, ed. A. Molinier (Paris, 1894).

Coss, P. R., 'Literature and Social Terminology', in T. H. Aston (ed.), *Social Relations and Ideas* (Cambridge, 1983), 109–50.

Coudert, J., 'Le Fief de danger en Lorraine jusqu'à la rédaction des coutumes', *Mémoires de la société pour l'histoire de droit*, 29 (1968–9), 159–95.

*The Court Baron*, ed. F. W. Maitland (Selden Society, 4, 1891).

*Coutumes de Toulouse (1286) et leur premier commentaire (1296)*, ed. H. Gilles (Toulouse, 1969).

*Coutumes du pays et comté de Hainaut*, ed. C. Faider (Brussels, 1871–8).

*Coutumiers de Normandie*, ed. E. J. Tardif (Rouen, 1881–96).

Craig, T., *Jus Feudale Tribus Libris Comprehensum* (London, 1655).

—— *Scotland's Soveraignty Asserted* (London, 1695).

Craster, H. H., 'A Contemporary Record of the Pontificate of Ranulf Flambard', *Archaeologia Aeliana*, ser. 4, 7 (1930), 33–56.

Cuozzo, E., *Catalogus Baronum: Commentario* (FSI 101**, 1984).

—— '"Milites" e "testes" nella contea normanne di Principato', *BISIME* 88 (1979), 121–63.

*Curia Regis Rolls* (London, 1923– ).

Cuttino, G. P., 'Another Memorandum Book of Elias Johnston', *EHR* 63 (1948), 90–104.

Darby, H. C., and Campbell, E. M. J., *Domesday Geography of South-East England* (Cambridge, 1962).

David, M., *Le Patrimoine foncier de l'église de Lyon* (Lyon, 1942).

Davies, R. R., *The Age of Conquest: Wales 1063–1415* (Oxford, 1991): first pub. as *Conquest, Coexistence and Change* (Oxford, 1987)

—— *Domination and Conquest* (Cambridge, 1990).

Davies, W., and Fouracre, P. (eds.), *The Settlement of Disputes in Early Medieval Europe* (Cambridge, 1986).

Davis, R. H. C., 'What Happened in Stephen's Reign', *History*, 49 (1964), 1–12.

Daviso, M. C., 'La Carta di Tenda', *BSBS* 47 (1949), 131–43.

Dean, T., *Land and Power in Late Medieval Ferrara* (Cambridge, 1988).

*Deutsches Rechtswörterbuch* (Preussische (later Deutsche) Akademie der Wissenschaften, Weimar and Berlin, 1912– ).

Devailly, G., *Le Berry du x$^e$ siècle au milieu du xiii$^e$ siècle* (Paris, 1973).

Devic, C., and Vaissete, J., *Histoire générale de Languedoc* (Toulouse, 1872–1904).

Devisse, J., 'Essai sur l'histoire d'une expression qui a fait fortune: *consilium et auxilium* au ix$^e$ siècle', *MA* 74 (1968), 179–205.

Dhondt, J., *Études sur la naissance des principautés territoriales en France* (Bruges, 1948).

Didier, N., *Le Droit des fiefs dans la coutume de Hainaut* (Paris, 1945).

Diestelkamp, B., *Das Lehnrecht der Grafschaft Katzenelnbogen* (Aalen, 1969).

—— 'Lehnrecht und spätmittelalterliche Territorien', *VF* 13 (1970), 65–96.

Dilcher, H., *Die Sizilische Gesetzgebung Kaiser Friedrichs II* (Cologne, 1975).

Dillay, M., 'Le "service" annuel en deniers des fiefs de la région angevine', *Mélanges P. Fournier* (Paris, 1929).

*Dip.* followed by the name of a king or emperor: see *Diplomata Karolinorum, Diplomata Regum et Imperatorum Germaniae, Diplomata Regum Germaniae ex stirpe Karolinorum.*

*Diplomata Belgica*, ed. M. Gysseling (Brussels, 1950).

*Diplomata Karolinorum*, i (MGH, 1906): cited as *Dip. Karol.* i, with charter number; iii (MGH, 1966), cited as *Dip. Karol.* iii, with name of king and charter number.

*Diplomata Regum et Imperatorum Germaniae* (MGH, 1879– ): cited as *Dip.* with name of king or emperor and charter number.

*Diplomata Regum Francorum e stirpe Merowingica*, ed. K. Pertz (MGH, 1872).

*Diplomata Regum Germaniae ex stirpe Karolinorum*, i–iv (MGH, 1932–60): cited as *Dip. Germ. Karol.* with name of king and charter number.

*Diplomatic Documents preserved in the Public Record Office*, ed. P. Chaplais (London, 1964).

*Diplomi di Berengario I*, ed. L. Schiaparelli (FSI 35, 1903).

*Diplomi italiani di Lodovico III e di Rodolfo II*, ed. L. Schiaparelli (FSI 37, 1910).

*Documenti dell'archivio comunale di Vercelli*, ed. G. Colombo (Pinerolo, 1901).

*Documenti per la storia della città di Arezzo*, ed. U. Pasqui (Florence, 1899–1937).

'Documenti Terracinesi', ed. I. Giorgi, *BISIME* 16 (1895), 55–92.

*Documents historiques inédits*, i, ed. M. Champollion Figeac (Paris, 1841).

*Documents Illustrative of the Social and Economic History of the Danelaw*, ed. F. M. Stenton (London, 1920).

*Documents of the Baronial Movement of Reform and Rebellion*, ed. R. E. Treharne and I. J. Sanders (Oxford, 1973).

Dodwell, B., 'East Anglian Commendation', *EHR* 63 (1948), 289–306.

*Domesday Book* (London: Record Commission, 1783–1816): vol. 1 cited by folio, with recto columns as a and b, verso as c and d; vol. 2 recto as a, verso as b.

*Domesday Book Studies*, ed. A. Williams (London, 1987).

Donahue, C., 'The Future of the Concept of Property Predicted from its Past', *Nomos*, 22 (1980), 28–68.

Donizo, *Vita Mathildis*, ed. L. Simeoni (RIS 5 (2), Bologna, 1930).

Douglas, A. W., 'Frankalmoin and Jurisdictional Immunity', *Speculum*, 53 (1978), 26–48.

Douglas, D. C. 'A Charter of Enfeoffment under William the Conqueror', *EHR* 42 (1927), 245–7.

—— (ed.), *Feudal Documents from the Abbey of Bury St Edmunds* (London, 1932).

Droege, G., *Landrecht und Lehnrecht im hohen Mittelalter* (Bonn, 1969).

Dubled, H., 'La Notion de propriété en Alsace du viiie au xe siècle', *MA* 65 (1959), 429–52.

Du Boulay, R., 'Gavelkind and Knight's Fee in Medieval Kent', *EHR* 77 (1962), 504–11.

Duby, G., *Hommes et structures du moyen âge* (Paris, 1973).

—— 'Recherches sur l'évolution des institutions judiciaires pendant le xe et le xie siècles dans le sud de la Bourgogne', *MA* 52 (1946), 149–94; 53 (1947), 15–38.

—— *La Société aux xie et xiie siècles dans la région mâconnaise* (2nd edn., Paris, 1971).

Du Cange, C. du Fresne, seigneur, *Glossarium mediae et infimae Latinitatis*, ed. L. Favre (Paris, 1883–7).

Duchesne, F. (ed.), *Historiae Francorum Scriptores*, iv (Paris, 1641).

Dudo of St Quentin, *De Moribus et Actis Primorum Normanniae Ducum*, ed. J. Lair (Caen, 1865).

Dufournet, J., *Cours sur la Chanson de Roland* (Paris, 1972).

Dumas, A., 'Encore la question: fidèles ou vassaux?', *RHDFE* 44 (1920), 159–229, 347–90.

Du Moulin, C., *Opera* (Paris, 1681).

Dunbabin, J., *France in the Making, 843–1180* (Oxford, 1985).

Duparc, P., 'La Commendise ou commende personnelle', *BEC* 119 (1961), 50–112.

—— 'Libres ou hommes liges', *Journal des savants* (1973), 81–98.

Dupont, A., 'L'Aprision et la régime aprisionnaire', *MA* 71 (1965), 179–213, 375–99.

Dupuy, P., *Histoire du différend d'entre le pape Boniface VIII et Philippe le Bel* (Paris, 1655).

Eadmer, *Historia Novorum*, ed. M. Rule (RS 81, 1884).

*Early Charters of St Paul's*, ed. M. Gibbs (Royal Hist. Soc. Camden Series 3, 58, 1939).

*Early Yorkshire Charters*, i, ed. W. Farrer (n.p., 1914).

Ebner, H., *Das freie Eigen* (Klagenfurt, 1969).

Eckhardt, A., 'Das älteste Bolander Lehnbuch', *Archiv für Diplomatik*, 22 (1976), 317–44.

Eddius Stephanus, *Life of Bishop Wilfrid*, ed. B. Colgrave (Cambridge, 1927).

*Edward I and the Throne of Scotland*, ed. E. L. G. Stones and G. G. Simpson (Oxford, 1978).

Eike von Repgow, *Auctor vetus de beneficiis*, ed. K. A. Eckhardt (MGH, Fontes iuris Germanici antiqui, NS 2 (1), 1964): cited by book and paragraph.

—— *Sachsenspiegel Landrecht* and *Sachsenspiegel Lehnrecht*, ed. K. A. Eckhardt (MGH, Fontes iuris Germanici antiqui, NS 1 (1–2), 1973): the *Landrecht* is cited by book, paragraph, and, where necessary, subsection, the *Lehnrecht* by paragraph and subsection.

—— *Sachsenspiegel*, ed. C. Schott, trans. R. Schmidt-Wiegand and C. Schott (Zürich, 1984).

Einhard, *Epistolae*, in *Epistolae Karolini Aevi*, iii (MGH, 1899).

Eisenstadt, S. N., and Roniger, L. (eds.), *Patrons, Clients and Friends* (Cambridge, 1984).

Ekkehard, *Casuum Sancti Galli Continuatio I*, in *MGH Scriptores*, ii. 74–147.

*English Historical Documents*, ed. D. C. Douglas, i (London, 1955).

*English Lawsuits from William I to Richard I*, ed. R. C. van Caenegem, i (Selden Society, 106, 1990).

*English Medieval Diplomatic Practice*, ed. P. Chaplais (London, 1982).

*Enquêtes administratives d'Alfonse de Poitiers*, ed. P. F. Fournier and P. Guébin (Paris, 1959).

*Epistolae Karolini Aevi*, ii (MGH, 1895).

*Epistolae Saeculi XIII . . . Selectae*, ii (MGH, 1887).

*Eppsteinschen Lehensverzeichnisse und Zinsregister des XIII. Jahrhunderts*, ed. P. Wagner (Wiesbaden, 1927).

Ermold le Noir, *Poème sur Louis le Pieux*, ed. E. Faral (Paris, 1932).

*Établissements de Saint Louis*, ed. P. Viollet (Paris, 1881).

Eudes de Saint-Maur, *Vie de Bouchard le vénérable*, ed. C. Bourel de la Roncière (Paris, 1892).

Evergates, T., *Feudal Society in the Bailliage of Troyes under the Counts of Champagne, 1152–1284* (Baltimore, 1975).

'Ex gestis Ambasiensium Dominorum', in *RHGF*, x. 238–42.

Fasoli, G., 'Città e feudalità', in *Structures féodales* (q.v.), 365–85.

—— 'Note sulla feudalità canossiana', *Atti e memorie della deputazione di storia patria per le antiche provincie modenesi*, ser. 9, 3 (1963), 217–29; also in *Studi Matildici* (Modena, 1964), 69–81.

—— 'Ricerche sulla legislazione antimagnatizia nei comuni dell'alta e media Italia', *Rivista di storia del diritto italiano*, 12 (1939), 86–133, 240–309.

—— *Scritti di storia medievale* (Bologna, 1974), 49–77: 'Castelli e signorie rurali', reprinted from *Settimane*, 13 (1966), 531–67.

Faussner, H. C., 'Herzog und Reichsgut im bairisch-österreichischen Rechtsgebiet im 12. Jahrhundert', *ZRG GA* 85 (1968), 1–58.

—— 'Die Verfügungsgewalt der deutschen Könige über weltlicher Reichsgut im Hochmittelalter', *DA* 29 (1973), 345–449.

Favier, J., *Philippe le Bel* (Paris, 1978).

Favre, E., *Eudes, Comte de Paris et roi de France* (Paris, 1893).

Feenstra, R., 'L'Emphytéose', in *La Formazione storica del diritto moderno in Europa* (Atti del terzo congresso internaz. della soc. ital. di storia del diritto, Florence, 1977), 1295–1320.

—— 'Les Origines du dominium utile chez les glossateurs', *Flores Legum H. J. Scheltema oblati* (Gröningen, 1971), 49–93.

Fehr, H., 'Das Waffenrecht der Bauern im Mittelalter', *ZRG GA* 34 (1914), 111–211; 38 (1917), 1–114.

Feuchère, P., 'Pairs de principauté et pairs de château', *Revue belge*, 31 (1953), 973–1002.

Ficker, A., *Herzog Friedrich II der letzte Babenberger* (Innsbruck, 1884).

Ficker, J., *Forschungen zur Reichs- und Rechtsgeschichte Italiens* (Innsbruck, 1868–74).

—— *Vom Heerschilde* (Innsbruck, 1862).

—— and Puntschart, P., *Vom Reichsfürstenstande*, ii (Innsbruck, 1911–23).

Fischer, D. H., *Historians' Fallacies* (London, 1971).

Flach, J., *Les Origines de l'ancienne France* (Paris, 1886–1917).

Fleckenstein, J., 'Die Entstehung des niederen Adels und das Rittertum', in J. Fleckenstein (ed.), *Herrschaft und Stand* (Göttingen, 1977), 17–39.

Fleming, R., *Kings and Lords in Conquest England* (Cambridge, 1991).

—— 'Monastic Lands and England's Defence in the Viking Age', *EHR* 100 (1985), 247–65.

Flodoard, *Les Annales de Flodoard*, ed. P. Lauer (Paris, 1905).

—— *Historia Remensis Ecclesiae*, in *MGH Scriptores*, xiii (1881), 405–599.

Florence of Worcester, *Chronicon*, ed. B. Thorpe (London, 1848–9).

Flori, J., *L'Essor de la Chevalerie* (Geneva, 1980).

*Formulae Merovingici et Karolini Aevi*, ed. K. Zeumer (MGH Legum Sect. 5, 1886).

Fossier, R., 'Chevalerie et noblesse en Ponthieu aux xi$^e$ et xii$^e$ siècles', in *Études de civilisation médiévale. Mélanges offerts à E. R. Labande* (Poitiers, 1974).

—— *L'Enfance de l'Europe* (Paris, 1982).

—— *La Terre et les hommes en Picardie* (Paris, 1968).

Fournier, G., *Le Peuplement rural en Basse Auvergne durant le haut moyen âge* (Paris, 1962).

Fournier, M., *Histoire de la science du droit en France*, iii (Paris, 1892).

Franklin, O., *Das Reichshofgericht im Mittelalter* (Weimar, 1867–9).

Franz, G. (ed.), *Quellen zur Geschichte des deutschen Bauernstandes im Mittelalter* (Berlin, 1967).

Freed, J. B., *The Counts of Falkenstein: Noble Self-Consciousness in Twelfth-Century Germany* (Trans. Am. Philos. Soc. 79 (6), 1984).
—— 'Reflections on the medieval German nobility', *AHR* 91 (1986), 553–75.
—— 'The Formation of the Salzburg Ministerialage in the Tenth and Eleventh Centuries', *Viator*, 9 (1978), 67–102.
—— 'Nobles, Ministerials, and Knights in the Archdiocese of Salzburg', *Speculum*, 62 (1987), 575–611.
—— 'The Origins of the European Nobility: the Problem of the Ministerials', *Viator*, 7 (1976), 211–41.
Fried, J., 'Der Regalienbegriff von 11. und 12. Jahrhundert', *DA* 29 (1973), 450–528.
Frier, B. W., *Landlord and Tenant in Imperial Rome* (Princeton, 1980).
Fulbert of Chartres, *Letters and Poems*, ed. and trans. F. Behrends (Oxford, 1976).
—— *Tractatus contra Judaeos*, in *PL* 141, 306–18.
Funck-Brentano, F., *Philippe le Bel en Flandre* (Paris, 1897).
Fustel de Coulanges, N. D., *La Monarchie franque* (Paris, 1888).
—— *Les Origines du système féodal* (Paris, 1890).
Galbert of Bruges, *Histoire du meurtre de Charles le bon*, ed. H. Pirenne (Paris, 1891).
Galbraith, V. H., 'An Episcopal Land-Grant of 1085', *EHR* 44 (1929), 353–72.
—— *The Making of Domesday Book* (Oxford, 1961).
*Gallia Christiana*, ed. D. de Sainte-Marthe and others (Paris, 1715–1865).
*Gallia Christiana Novissima*, ed. J. H. Albanès (Montbéliard, 1895–1920)
Ganshof, F. L., 'Benefice and Vassalage in the Age of Charlemagne', *Cambridge Hist. Journal*, 6 (1939), 147–75.
—— 'Charlemagne et le serment', in *Mélanges d'histoire du moyen âge dédiés à la mémoire de L. Halphen* (Paris, 1951), 259–70.
—— 'Charlemagne et les institutions de la monarchie franque', in W. Braunfels (ed.), *Karl der Grosse* (Düsseldorf, 1965–8), i. 349–93; translated by B. and M. Lyon in *Frankish Institutions under Charlemagne* (Providence, RI, 1968).
—— 'Le Droit urbain en Flandre au début de la première phase de son histoire (1127)', *Revue d'histoire du droit*, 19 (1951), 387–416.
—— *Feudalism*, trans. P. Grierson (London, 1964 edn.).
—— 'Les Liens de vassalité dans la monarchie franque', *Recueils de la Société Jean Bodin*, 1 (1958), 153–69.
—— 'Note sur la concession d'alleux à des vassaux sous le règne de Louis le Pieux', *Storiografia e Storia: Studi in onore di E. Duprè Theseider* (Rome, 1974), 589–99.
—— 'Note sur l'apparition du nom de l'hommage', *Aus Mittelalter und Neuzeit. Gerhard Kallen sum 70. Geburtstag*, ed. J. Engel (Bonn, 1957).
—— 'Note sur les origines de l'union du bénéfice avec la vassalité', in *Études d'histoire dédiées à la mémoire de Henri Pirenne* (Brussels, 1937), 173–97.
—— 'L'Origine des rapports féodo-vassaliques', *Settimane*, 1 (1954), 27–69.
—— *Recherches sur les tribunaux de châtellenie en Flandre* (Antwerp, 1932).

—— 'Les Transformations de l'organisation judiciaire dans le comté de Flandre', *Revue belge*, 18 (1939), 43–61.

—— 'Zur Entstehungsgeschichte und Bedeutung des Vertrages von Verdun', *DA* 12 (1956), 313–30.

Garaud, M., *Les Châtelains de Poitou et l'avènement du régime féodal* (Poitiers, 1967).

Garnett, G., 'Coronation and Propaganda', *TRHS* ser. 5, 36 (1986), 91–116.

Gattola, E., *Ad historiam abbatiae Cassinensis Accessiones* (Venice, 1734).

Gaudemet, J., 'Les Tendances à l'unification du droit en France dans les derniers siècles de l'ancien régime', *La Formazione storica del diritto moderno in Europa* (Atti del terzo congresso internaz. della società italiana di storia del diritto, Florence, 1977), 157–94.

Gaufredus Malaterra, *De Rebus Gestis Rogerii . . . et Roberti Guiscardi*, ed. E. Pontieri (RIS 5 (1), 1928).

Geary, P., *The Aristocracy in Provence* (Stuttgart, 1985).

Geertz, C., *Negara* (Princeton, 1980).

Génicot, L., *L'Économie rurale namuroise au bas moyen âge* (Louvain, 1943– ).

—— 'Trois thèses d'histoire régionale', *Revue d'hist. ecclés.* 70 (1975), 439–62.

Gerbert of Reims, *Briefsammlung*, ed. F. Weigle (MGH, Briefe der deutschen Kaiserzeit, ii, 1966).

Gerhard, *Vita sancti Oudalrici episcopi*, in *MGH Scriptores*, iv. 377–428.

Gervase of Canterbury, *Historical Works*, ed. W. Stubbs (RS 73, 1879–80).

*Gesta Abbatum Trudonensium*, in *MGH Scriptores*, x. 213–448.

*Gesta Domni Aldrici Cenomannicae Urbis*, ed. R. Charles and L. Froger (Mamers, 1889).

Gillingham, J., 'The Introduction of Knight Service into England', *ANS* 4 (1982), 53–64.

—— *The Kingdom of Germany in the High Middle Ages* (London, 1971).

Giordanengo, G., *Le Droit féodal dans le pays de droit écrit* (Rome, 1988).

—— '*Epistola Philiberti*', *MEF* 82 (1970), 809–53.

—— 'Vocabulaire et formulaires féodaux en Provence et en Dauphiné (xiie–xiiie siècles)', in *Structures féodales* (q.v.), 85–107.

—— 'Vocabulaire romanisant et réalité féodale en Provence', *Provence historique*, 25 (1975), 255–73.

Gislebert of Mons, *Chronique*, ed. L. Vanderkindere (Brussels, 1904).

Gladiss, D. von, 'Die Schenkungen der deutschen Könige zu privatem Eigen (800–1137)', *DA* 1 (1937), 80–137.

*Glanvill: The Treatise on the Laws and Customs of England commonly called Glanvill*, ed. G. D. G. Hall (Edinburgh, 1965).

Gluckman, M., *The Ideas in Barotse Jurisprudence* (Manchester, 1972).

—— *Politics, Law and Ritual in Tribal Society* (Oxford, 1965).

Godefroy, F., *Dictionnaire de l'ancienne langue française* (Paris, 1880–1902).

Goez, W., *Der Leihezwang* (Tubingen, 1962).

Goffart, W., 'From Roman Taxation to Mediaeval Seigneurie', *Speculum*, 47 (1972), 165–87, 373–94.

Goffart, W., *The Le Mans Forgeries* (Cambridge, Mass., 1966).

—— 'Old and New in Merovingian Taxation', *Past & Present*, 96 (1982), 3–21.

Goffman, E., *Interaction Ritual* (London, 1967).

Goody, J., 'Against "Ritual": Loosely Structured Thoughts on a Loosely Defined Topic', in S. F. Moore and B. Myerhoff (eds.), *Secular Ritual* (Amsterdam, 1977), 25–35.

—— *Death, Property and the Ancestors* (Stanford, 1962).

—— 'Feudalism in Africa?', *Journal of African History*, 4 (1963), 1–18.

—— *The Logic of Writing and the Organization of Society* (Cambridge, 1986).

Gouron, A. 'Autour de Placentin à Montpellier', *Studia Gratiana*, 19 (1976), 339–54.

—— 'Les Étapes de la pénétration du droit romain au xii<sup>e</sup> siècle dans l'ancienne Septimanie', *Annales du Midi*, 69 (1957), 103–20.

—— *La Science juridique française aux xi<sup>e</sup> et xii<sup>e</sup> siècles* (*Ius Romanum Medii Aevi*, I. 4. d, e: Milan, 1978).

Gransden, A., *Historical Writing in England c. 550 to c. 1307* (London, 1974).

Graus, F., 'Herrschaft und Treue', *Historica*, 12 (1966), 5–44.

—— 'Über die sogenannte germanische Treue', *Historica*, i (1959), 71–121.

Green, D. H., *The Carolingian Lord* (Cambridge, 1965).

Green, J. A., *The Government of England under Henry I* (Cambridge, 1986).

—— 'The Last Century of Danegeld', *EHR* 96 (1981), 241–58.

Gregory of Tours, *Libri Historiarum X* (MGH Scriptores Rerum Merowingicarum, i, 1951).

Gregory VII, *Register*, ed. E. Caspar (MGH Epistolae Selectae, ii, 1955).

Grey, T. C., 'The Disintegration of Property', *Nomos*, 22 (1980), 69–85.

Grosdidier, M., *Le Comté de Bar des origines au traité de Bruges* (Paris, 1922).

Grossi, P., 'Problematica strutturale dei contratti agrari nella esperienza giuridica dell'alto medioevo italiano', *Settimane*, 13 (1966), 487–529.

Guébin, V., 'Les Amortissements d'Alphonse de Poitiers, 1247–70', *Revue Mabillon*, 15 (1925), 80–106, 133–44, 293–304; 16 (1926), 27–43.

Guernes de Pont-Sainte-Maxence, *Vie de Saint Thomas*, ed. E. Walberg (Lund, 1922).

Guilhiermoz, P. E., *Essai sur l'origine de la noblesse* (Paris, 1902).

Guillaume de Jumièges, *Gesta Normannorum Ducum*, ed. J. Marx (Rouen, 1914).

Guillaume le Breton, *Gesta Philippi Augusti*, in *Œuvres de Rigord et de Guillaume le Breton*, ed. H. F. Delaborde (Paris, 1882–5), i. 168–333; *Philippidos* in ibid. ii.

Guillot, O., *Le Comte d'Anjou et son entourage au xi<sup>e</sup> siècle* (Paris, 1972).

Guillotel, H., 'La Dévolution de la seigneurie de Dol-Combour aux xi<sup>e</sup> et xii<sup>e</sup> siècles', *RHDFE* ser. 4, 53 (1975), 190.

Guyotjeannin, O., *Episcopus et comes* (Mémoires et documents publiés par la Société de l'École de Chartes, 30: Geneva, 1987).

Haillan, B. de Girard, seigneur du, *L'Histoire de France* (Paris, 1576).

Hall, J. W., 'Feudalism in Japan: a Reassessment', in J. W. Hall and M. B. Jansen (eds.), *Studies in the Institutional History of Modern Japan* (Princeton, NJ, 1968).

Hallam, H., *View of the State of Europe during the Middle Ages* (London, 10th edn., 1853).

Halphen, L., 'La Lettre d'Eude de Blois au roi Robert', *RH* 97 (1908), 287–96.

—— 'La Place de la royauté dans le système féodal', *RH* 172 (2) (1933), 248–56.

*Hamburgisches Urkundenbuch*, i, ed. J. M. Lappenberg (Hamburg, 1842).

*Handwörterbuch zur deutschen Rechtsgeschichte*, ed. A. Erler and E. Kauffmann (Berlin, 1964– ).

Hariulf, *Vita sancti Arnulfi*, in *PL* 174, 1367–1438.

Harmer, F. E. (ed.), *Anglo-Saxon Writs* (Manchester, 1952).

Harvey, B. F., 'Abbot Gervase de Blois and the Fee-Farms of Westminster Abbey', *BIHR* 40 (1967), 127–42.

Harvey, P. D. A., 'Rectitudines Singularum Personarum and Gerefa', *EHR* 108 (1993), 1–22.

Harvey, S., 'The Knight and Knight's Fee in England', *Past and Present*, 49 (1970), 1–43.

Haskins, C. H., *Norman Institutions* (Cambridge, Mass., 1918).

Haverkamp, A., *Herrschaftsformen der Frühstaufer in Reichsitalien* (Stuttgart, 1970).

Heinemeyer, K., 'Der Prozess Heinrichs des Löwen', *Blätter für deutsche Landesgeschichte*, 117 (1981), 1–60.

Heinemeyer, W., '"beneficium—non feudum sed bonum factum": der Streit auf dem Reichstag zu Besançon 1157', *Archiv für Diplomatik*, 15 (1969), 155–236.

Heinrich, G., *Die Grafen von Arnstein* (Cologne, 1961).

Helmold, *Cronica Slavorum*, ed. B. Schmeidler (MGH SRG 32, 1937).

*Hemingi Chartularium*, ed. T. Hearne (Oxford, 1723).

Henry of Huntingdon, *Historia Anglorum*, ed. T. Arnold (RS 74, 1879).

Herlihy, D., 'Church Property on the European Continent, 701–1200', *Speculum*, 36 (1961), 81–105; repr. in his *The Social History of Italy and Western Europe, 700–1500* (London, 1978).

Hermann, *Altahensis Annales*, in *MGH Scriptores*, xvii. 381–416.

Hermann of Reichenau, *Chronicon*, in *MGH Scriptores*, v. 67–133.

*Hessisches Urkundenbuch: Zweite Abteilung*, i (Stuttgart, 1891).

Hincmar, *De Villa Novilliaco*, in *MGH Scriptores*, xv (2), 1167–9.

—— *Pro Ecclesiae Libertatum Defensione*, in *PL* 125, 1035–70.

Hirsch, *Die hohe Gerichtsbarkeit im deutsche Mittelalter* (Prague, 1922).

*Historiae Patriae Monumenta: Chartarum*, ii (Turin, 1853).

*Historiae Tornacenses*, in *MGH Scriptores*, xiv. 327–52.

*Historia gloriosi regis Ludovici, Ludovici Filii*, printed in Suger, *Vie de Louis le Gros*, ed. A. Molinier (Paris, 1887), 147–78.

Hoffmann, H., 'Ivo von Chartres und die Lösung des Investiturproblem', *DA* 15 (1959), 393–440.

—— 'Der Kirchenstaat im hohen Mittelalter', *QFIA* 57 (1977), 1–45.

Hoffmann, H., 'Langobarden, Normannen, Päpste', *QFIA* 58 (1978), 137–80.

Hohfeld, W. C., *Fundamental Legal Conceptions* (New York, 1919).

Hollister, C. W., *Military Organization of Norman England* (Oxford, 1965).

—— 'Normandy, France and the Anglo-Norman *Regnum*', *Speculum*, 51 (1976), 202–42.

Hollyman, K. J., *Le Développement du vocabulaire féodal en France pendant le haut moyen âge* (Paris, 1957).

Holt, J. C., '1086', in J. Holt (ed.), *Domesday Studies* (Woodbridge, 1987), 41–64.

—— 'Feudal Society and the Family in Early Medieval England: I', *TRHS* ser. 5, 32 (1982), 193–212.

—— 'Feudal Society and the Family in Early Medieval England: II', *TRHS* ser. 5, 33 (1983), 193–220.

—— 'The Introduction of Knight Service into England', *ANS* 6 (1983), 89–106.

—— *Magna Carta* (Cambridge, 1965).

—— *The Northerners* (Oxford, 1961).

—— 'Politics and Property in Early Medieval England', *Past and Present*, 57 (1972), 1–52; 'A Rejoinder', ibid. 65 (1974), 127–35.

Honoré, A. M., 'Ownership', in A. G. Guest (ed.), *Oxford Essays in Jurisprudence* (Oxford, 1961), 107–47.

Hostiensis (Henry de Susa), *Summa Aurea* (Lyon, 1548).

Hoyt, R. D., *The Royal Demesne in English Constitutional History* (Ithaca, NY, 1950).

Hudson, J., 'Life-Grants of Land and the Development of Inheritance in Anglo-Norman England', *ANS* 12 (1989), 67–80.

Huillard-Bréholles, J. L. A. (ed.), *Historia Diplomatica Friderici Secundi* (Paris, 1852–61).

Huppert, G., *The Idea of Perfect History* (Chicago, 1970).

Hüttebräuker, L., *Das Erbe Heinrichs des Löwen* (Göttingen, 1927).

Hyams, P. R., *Kings, Lords, and Peasants in Medieval England* (Oxford, 1980).

—— 'Warranty and Good Lordship in Twelfth-Century England', *Law and History Review*, 5 (1987), 437–503.

Ignor, A., *Über das allgemeine Rechtsdenkung Eikes von Repgow* (Paderborn, 1984).

Imbart de la Tour, P., 'Les Colonies agricoles et l'occupation des terres désertes à l'époque Carolingienne', in *Mélanges P. Fabre* (Paris, 1902).

Innocent III, *Selected Letters concerning England*, ed. C. R. Cheney and W. H. Semple (London, 1953).

*Inquisitio Eliensis*, ed. N. E. S. A. Hamilton (London, 1876).

Irsigler, F., *Untersuchung zur Geschichte des frühfränkischen Adels* (Bonn, 1969).

Ivo of Chartres, *Epistolae*, in *PL* 162.

Jackson, R. A., 'Peers of France and Princes of the Blood', *French Historical Studies*, 7 (1971), 27–46.

Jacob, G., *A New Law Dictionary* (9th edn., London, 1772).

[Jacques d'Ableiges], *Le Grand Coutumier de France*, ed. F. Laboulaye and R. Dareste (Paris, 1868).

Jacques de Révigny, *Œuvres*, ed. P. de Tourtoulon (Paris, 1899).

James, E., *The Franks* (Oxford, 1988).

—— *The Origins of France* (London, 1982).

Jamison, E. M., 'Additional Work on the *Catalogus Baronum*', printed at the end of *Catalogus Baronum* with sep. pagination or in *BISIME* 83 (1971), 1–65.

—— 'The Administration of the County of Molise in the Twelfth and Thirteenth Centuries', *EHR* 44 (1929), 529–59; 45 (1930), 1–34.

—— 'The Norman Administration of Apulia and Calabria', *Papers of the British School at Rome*, 6 (1913), 211–480.

—— 'The Sicilian Norman Kingdom in the Mind of Anglo-Norman Contemporaries', *PBA* 24 (1938), 237–85.

Jeffcott, C., 'The Idea of Feudalism in China', in Leach, *Feudalism* (q.v.), 155–74.

Jocelin of Brakelond, *Chronicle*, ed. H. E. Butler (Edinburgh, 1949).

John of Salisbury, *Letters*, ed. W. J. Millor and C. N. L. Brooke, ii (Oxford, 1979).

John, E., *Land Tenure in Early England* (Leicester, 1960).

—— *Orbis Britanniae* (Leicester, 1966).

Johrendt, J., '"Milites" und "Militia" im 11. Jahrhundert in Deutschland', in A. Borst (ed.), *Das Rittertum im Mittelalter* (Darmstadt, 1976).

Joinville, Jean, sire de, *Histoire de Saint Louis*, ed. N. de Wailly (Paris, 1878).

Jones, G., *History of the Vikings* (London, 1968).

Jordan, K., 'Das Eindringen des Lehnswesens in das Rechtsleben der römischen Kurie', *Archiv für Urkundenforschung*, 12 (1931–2), 13–110.

'Journal des conférences d'Avignon, 1344', in J. Froissart, *Œuvres*, ed. Kervyn de Lettenhove (Paris, 1874).

Kaplan, A., *The Conduct of Enquiry* (Scranton, Pa., 1964).

Keefe, T. K., *Feudal Assessments and the Political Community under Henry II and his Sons* (Berkeley, 1983).

Keeney, B. C., *Judgment by Peers* (Cambridge, Mass., 1949).

Kehr, P., *Die Steuer in der Lehre der Theologen des Mittelalters* (Berlin, 1927).

Keller, H., 'Die soziale und politische Verfassung Mailands', *HZ* 211 (1970), 34–64.

Kelley, D. R., *Foundations of Modern Historical Scholarship* (New York, 1970).

—— and Smith, B. G., 'What was Property? Legal Dimensions of the Social Question in France (1789–1848)', *Proc. Am. Philos. Soc.* 128 (1984), 200–30.

Kennedy, A. G., 'Disputes about *Bocland*: the Forum for their Adjudication', *Anglo-Saxon England*, 14 (1985), 175–95.

Kern, F. (ed.), *Acta imperii Angliae et Franciae (1267–1313)* (Tübingen, 1911).

Kienast, W., *Deutschland und Frankreich in der Kaiserzeit, 900–1270* (Stuttgart, 1974).

—— *Die fränkische Vasallität* (Frankfurt, 1990).

Kimball, E. G., *Serjeanty Tenure in Medieval England* (New Haven, Conn., 1936).

—— 'Tenure in Frank Almoign and Secular Services', *EHR* 43 (1928), 341–53.

Köbler, G., 'Eigen und Eigentum', *ZRG GA* 95 (1978), 1–33.

—— 'Land und Landrecht im Frühmittelalter', *ZRG GA* 86 (1969), 1–40.

Koeppler, H., 'Frederick Barbarossa and the Schools of Bologna', *EHR* 54 (1939), 577–607.

Kolchin, P., *Unfree Labor* (Cambridge, Mass., 1987).

*Konstitutionen Friedrichs II*, ed. H. Conrad and others (Cologne, 1973).

Krah, A., *Absetzungsverfahren als Spiegelbild von Königsmacht* (Aalen, 1987).

Krause, H. G., 'Königtum und Rechtsordnung in der Zeit der sächsischer und salier Herrscher', *ZRG GA* 82 (1965), 1–98.

—— 'Der Sachsenspiegel und das Problem des sogenannten Leihezwangs', *ZRG GA* 93 (1976), 21–99.

Krawinkel, H., *Feudum* (Schriften der Akad. für deutschen Recht: Forschungen zum deutschen Recht, ii (2), Weimar, 1938).

Krieger, K. F., *Die Lehnshoheit der deutschen Könige im Spätmittelalter* (Aalen, 1979).

Kroeschell, K., *Deutsche Rechtsgeschichte* (Opladen, 1980).

—— 'Die Treue in der deutschen Rechtsgeschichte', *SM* ser. 3, 10 (1969), 465–89.

—— 'Verfassungsgeschichte und Rechtsgeschichte des Mittelalters', in *Gegenstand und Begriffe der Verfassungsgeschichtsschreibung* (Berlin, 1983).

Lafaille, G., *Annales de la ville de Toulouse* (Toulouse, 1687–1701).

La Fontaine, J., 'Land and the Political Community in Bugisu', in W. A. Shack and P. S. Cohen (eds.), *Politics in Leadership* (Oxford, 1979).

Lambert, bishop of Ardres, *Epistolae*, in *RHGF* xv. 178–206.

Lambert of Ardres, *Historia comitum Ghisnensium*, in *MGH Scriptores*, xxiv. 550–642.

Lambert Waterlos, *Annales Cameracenses*, in *MGH Scriptores*, xvi. 509–54.

Lampert of Hersfeld, *Opera*, ed. O. Holder-Egger (MGH SRG 38, 1894).

*Landrecht*: see Eike von Repgow.

Landulph Senior, *Mediolanensis Historiae Libri Quatuor*, ed. A. Cutolo (RIS 4 (2), Bologna, 1942).

Langlois, C. V., *Le Règne de Philippe III* (Paris, 1887).

Laplanche, J. de, *La Réserve coutumière dans l'ancien droit français* (Paris, 1925).

Larner, J., *Italy in the Age of Dante* (London, 1980).

Laspeyres, E. A., *Ueber die Entstehung und älteste Bearbeitung der Libri Feudorum* (Berlin, 1830).

Latham, R. E., *Revised Medieval Latin Word-List* (London, 1965).

Lavisse, E. (ed.), *Histoire de France*, ii (1) (Paris, 1911).

Lawson, M. K., 'The Collection of Danegeld and Heregeld in the Reigns of Aethelred and Cnut', *EHR* 99 (1984), 721–38.

*Layettes du trésor des chartes*, ed. A. Teulet and others (Paris, 1863–1909).

Leach, E., and others (eds.), *Feudalism: Comparative Studies* (Sydney, 1985).

Le Bras, G., *Institutions ecclésiastiques de la Chrétienté médiévale* (A. Fliche and V. Martin (eds.), *Histoire de l'Église*, xii, Paris, 1959).

—— and others, *Histoire du droit et des institutions de l'église en occident* (Paris, 1958– ).

Le Cacheux, P., 'Une charte de Jumièges', *Mélanges de la société de l'histoire de Normandie*, 11 (1927), 205–16.

*Leges Alamannorum*, ed. K. A. Eckhardt (Göttingen, 1958–62).

*Leges Burgundionum*, ed. L. R. de Salis (MGH Legum Sect. 1, ii (1), 1892).

*Leges Henrici Primi*, ed. L. J. Downer (Oxford, 1972).

*Leges Langobardorum*, ed. F. Beyerle (2nd edn., Witzenhausen, 1962).

*Leges Saxonum*, ed. K. von Richthofen, *MGH Leges* (folio), v. 1–102.

Le Goff, J., *La Civilisation de l'Occident médiéval* (Paris, 1977).

—— 'Le Rituel symbolique de la vassalité', in *Pour un autre moyen âge* (Paris, 1977), 349–420, trans. A. Goldhammer as 'The Symbolic Ritual of Vassalage', *Time Work and Culture in the Middle Ages* (Chicago, 1980), 237–87.

Lehmann, C., *Consuetudines Feudorum*, i: *Compilatio Antiqua* (Göttingen, 1892) and *Das Langobardische Lehnrecht* (Göttingen, 1896): reprinted together as *Consuetudines Feudorum*, ed. K. A. Eckhardt (Aalen, 1971), with both old and new pagination. Both are cited by their original names and pagination.

*Lehnrecht*: see Eike von Repgow.

Leicht, P. S., 'Il feudo in Italia nell'età carolingia', *Settimane*, 1 (1954), 71–107.

—— *Scritti vari di storia del diritto italiano* (Milan, 1943–9), i. 183–97: 'Gasindii e vassalli'; ii (2), 89–146: 'Livellario nomine'.

—— *Storia del diritto italiano: il diritto privato*, iii (2nd edn., Milan, 1948).

Lemarignier, J. F., 'La Dislocation du "pagus" et le problème des "consuetudines" (x^e–xi^e siècles)', in *Mélanges d'histoire du moyen âge dédiés à la mémoire de L. Halphen* (Paris, 1951), 401–10.

—— *La France médiévale* (Paris, 1970).

—— *Le Gouvernement royal aux premiers temps capétiens* (Paris, 1966).

—— *Recherches sur l'hommage en marche et les frontières féodales* (Lille, 1945).

Lennard, R., *Rural England* (Oxford, 1959).

Lesne, E., 'Les Bénéficiers de Saint-Germain-des-Prés au temps de l'Abbé Irminon', *Revue Mabillon*, 12 (1922), 73–89, 209–18.

—— 'Les Diverses Acceptions du terme "beneficium" du viii^e au ix^e siècle', *RHDFE* ser. 4, 3 (1924), 5–56.

—— *Histoire de la propriété ecclésiastique en France* (Paris, 1910–43).

Levillain, L., 'Les Nibelungen historiques et leurs alliances de famille', *Annales du Midi*, 49 (1937), 337–408; 50 (1938), 5–66.

Levine, N., 'The German Historical School of Law and the Origins of Historical Materialism', *Journal of the History of Ideas*, 48 (1987), 431–51.

Levy, W., *West Roman Vulgar Law: the Law of Property* (Philadelphia, 1951).

Lewis, A. R., *The Development of Southern French and Catalan Society, 718–1050* (Austin, Texas, 1965).

—— 'Seigneurial Administration in Twelfth Century Montpellier', *Speculum*, 22 (1947), 562–77.

Lewis, I. M., *Social Anthropology in Perspective* (2nd edn., Cambridge, 1985).

*Lex Baiwariorum*, ed. E. de Schwind (MGH Legum Sect. 1, v, 1888).

*Lex Frisionum*, ed. K. A. and A. Eckhardt (MGH Fontes iuris Germanici antiqui 12, 1982).
*Lex Ribuaria*, ed. F. Beyerle and R. Buchner (MGH Legum Sect. 1, iii (2), 1951).
*Lex Thuringorum*, ed. K. F. von Richthofen, *MGH Leges* (folio), v. 103–44.
Leyser, K., 'The Crisis of Medieval Germany', *PBA* 69 (1983), 409–43.
—— 'Frederick Barbarossa and the Hohenstaufen Polity', *Viator*, 19 (1988), 153–76.
—— *Rule and Conflict in an Early Medieval Society* (London, 1979).
*Libelli de Lite Imperialium et Pontificum* (MGH, 1891–7).
*Libellus querulus de miseriis ecclesiae Pennensis*, in *MGH Scriptores*, xxx (2), 1461–7.
*Liber Censuum de l'église romaine*, ed. P. Fabre and L. Duchesne (Paris, 1905–10).
*Liber Consuetudinum Mediolani*, ed. E. Besta and G. L. Barni (Milan, 1949).
*Liber Eliensis*, ed. E. O. Blake (Royal Hist. Soc. Camden Series 3, 92, 1962).
*Liber Instrumentorum Memorialium: Cartulaire des Guillems de Montpellier*, ed. A. Germain (Montpellier, 1884–6).
*Liber Niger Scaccarii*, ed. T. Hearne (London, 1774).
*Liber Papiensis* and related texts (including rubrics etc. from the *Lombarda*), in *MGH Leges* (folio), iv. 289–640.
*Libro Verde della chiesa d'Asti*, ed. G. Alessandria (Pinerolo, 1904–7).
Lieberman, D., *The Province of Legislation Determined* (Cambridge, 1989).
Liebermann, F. (ed.), *Die Gesetze der Angelsachsen* (Halle, 1916).
*Littere Wallie*, ed. J. G. Edwards (Cardiff, 1940).
Littleton, T., *Lyttleton His Treatise of Tenures*, ed. T. E. Tomlins (London, 1841).
Littré, M. P. E., *Dictionnaire de la langue française* (Paris, 1956–8).
*Livre d'Agenais*, ed. G. P. Cuttino (Toulouse, 1956).
*Livres de Jostice et de Plet*, ed. P. N. Rapetti (Paris, 1850).
Lloyd, C., *Explanation in Social History* (Oxford, 1986).
Lloyd, P. C., 'The Political Structure of African Kingdoms', in M. Banton (ed.), *Political Systems and the Distribution of Power* (London, 1968), 63–112.
Loisel, A., *Institutes coustumieres*, ed. M. Reulos (Paris, 1935).
—— *Mémoires de Beauvais et Beauvaisis* (Paris, 1617).
*London Eyre of 1244*, ed. H. M. Chew and M. Weinbaum (London Record Society, 6, 1970).
Longnon, A. (ed.), *Documents relatifs au comté de Champagne et de Brie, 1172–1361* (Paris, 1901).
Lot, F., *Fidèles ou vassaux?* (Paris, 1904).
—— 'Quelques mots sur l'origine des pairs de France', *RH* 54 (1894), 34–59.
—— 'Les Tributs aux Normands et l'Église de France au ixe siècle', *BEC* 85 (1924), 58–78.
—— and Fawtier, R., *Histoire des institutions françaises au moyen âge*, ii (Paris, 1958).
Loud, G. A., *Church and Society in the Norman Principality of Capua* (Oxford, 1985).
—— 'Monarchy and Monastery in the Mezzogiorno: the Abbey of St Sophia,

Benevento, and the Staufen', *Papers of the British School at Rome*, 59 (1991), 283–318.

Lowrie, R. H., 'Incorporeal Property in Primitive Society', *Yale Law Journal*, 37 (1928), 551–68.

Loyn, H. S., 'Kinship in Anglo-Saxon England', *Anglo-Saxon England*, 3 (1974), 197–209.

Loyseau, C., *Œuvres* (Lyon, 1701): incl. *Cinq livres des offices* and *Livre des seigneuries*, each with separate pagination.

Luchaire, A., *Histoire des institutions monarchiques de la France* (Paris, 1883–5), including vol. iii: *Études sur les actes de Louis VII.*

—— *Louis VI le Gros* (Paris, 1890).

Luhmann, N., *The Differentiation of Society* (New York, 1982).

Lunt, W. E., *Financial Relations of the Papacy with England to 1327* (Cambridge, Mass., 1939).

Lyon, B., *From Fief to Indenture* (Cambridge, Mass., 1957).

Lyons, J., *Semantics* (Cambridge, 1977).

McFarlane, K. B., *The Nobility of later Medieval England* (Oxford, 1973), 248–69: 'Had Edward I a Policy towards the Earls?'; also in *History*, 50 (1965), 145–59.

McKitterick, R., *The Carolingians and the Written Word* (Cambridge, 1989).

—— *The Frankish Kingdoms under the Carolingians* (London, 1983).

Mackrell, J. Q. C., *The Attack on Feudalism in Eighteenth-Century France* (London, 1973).

Maddicott, J. R., *The English Peasantry and the Crown, 1294–1341* (Past & Present Supp. no. 1, 1975).

Madox, T., *Baronia Anglica* (London, 1736).

—— *History and Antiquities of the Exchequer* (London, 1711).

Magnou, E., 'Note sur le sens du mot *fevum* en Septimanie et dans la marche d'Espagne à la fin du x$^e$ et au début du xi$^e$ siècle', *Annales du Midi*, 76 (1964), 141–52.

Magnou-Nortier, E., 'Fidélité et féodalité méridionales d'après les serments de fidélité', *Annales du Midi*, 80 (1968), 457–84.

—— *Foi et fidélité: recherches sur l'évolution des liens personnels chez les francs du vii$^e$ au ix$^e$ siècle* (Toulouse, 1976).

*Mainzer Urkundenbuch*, ed. M. Stimming and P. Acht (Darmstadt, 1968–72).

Mair, L., *Introduction to Social Anthropology* (Oxford, 1965).

Maitland, F. W. (ed.), *Bracton and Azo* (Selden Society, 8, 1895).

—— *Collected Papers* (Cambridge, 1911).

—— *Constitutional History of England* (Cambridge, 1946).

—— *Domesday Book and Beyond* (Cambridge, 1907).

—— *Township and Borough* (Cambridge, 1898).

Major, J. R., '"Bastard Feudalism" and the Kiss', *Journal of Interdisc. Hist.* 17 (1987), 509–35.

Manaresi, C. (ed.), *Atti del comune di Milano fino all'anno MCCXVI* (Milan, 1919).

Mansi, J. D. (ed.), *Sacrorum Conciliorum Nova et Amplissima Collectio* (Venice, 1757–98: repr. Graz, 1960–1).

Maquet, J., *Power and Society in Africa* (London, 1967).

Marca, P. de, *Marca Hispanica* (Paris, 1688).

Martin, O., *Histoire de la coutume de la prévôté et vicomté de Paris* (Paris, 1922–30).

Martindale, D., 'Sociological Theory and the Ideal Type', in L. Gross (ed.), *Symposium on Sociological Theory* (New York, 1959), 57–91.

Martindale, J., 'The Kingdom of Aquitaine and the "Dissolution of the Carolingian Fisc"', *Francia*, 11 (1984), 131–92.

—— 'Peace and War in Early Eleventh-Century Aquitaine', in C. Harper-Bill and R. Harvey (eds.), *Ideals and Practice of Medieval Knighthood*, iv (1992), 147–76.

Mason, P., *Patterns of Dominance* (Oxford, 1970).

*Materials for the History of Thomas Becket*, ed. J. C. Robertson and J. B. Sheppard (RS 67, 1875–85).

Matthew Paris, *Chronica Majora*, ed. H. R. Luard (RS 57, 1872–83).

—— *Gesta Abbatum*, ed. H. T. Riley (RS 28d, 1867–9).

Maurer, H., *Der Herzog von Schwaben* (Sigmaringen, 1978).

Mauss, M., *The Gift*, trans. I. Cunnison (London, 1970).

Mayer, T., 'Die Ausbildung der Grundlagen des modernen deutsches Staat im hohen Mittelalter', *HZ* 159 (1938–9), 457–87.

—— *Fürsten und Staat* (Weimar, 1950).

Meijers, E. M., *Études d'histoire du droit* (Leiden, 1956–73).

Ménager, L. R., 'La Législation sud-italienne sous la domination normande', *Settimane*, 16 (1960), 439–96.

Merryman, J. H., 'Ownership and Estate', *Tulane Law Review*, 48 (1974), 916–45.

Metman, J., 'Les Inféodations royales d'après le "Recueil des actes de Philippe Auguste"', in Bautier, *La France de Philippe Auguste* (q.v.), 503–17.

Metz, W., *Das karolingische Reichsgut* (Berlin, 1960).

—— *Staufische Güterverzeichnisse* (Berlin, 1964).

—— *Zur Erforschung des karolingischen Reichsgutes* (Darmstadt, 1971).

*Middle English Dictionary*, ed. H. Kurath and others (Ann Arbor, 1952– ).

Milsom, S. F. C., *Historical Foundations of the Common Law* (2nd edn., Cambridge, 1981).

—— 'Inheritance by Women in the Twelfth and early Thirteenth Centuries', in M. S. Arnold and others (eds.), *The Laws and Customs of England* (Chapel Hill, 1981), 60–89.

—— Introduction to Pollock and Maitland, *History of English Law* (Cambridge, 2nd edn. reissued 1968).

—— *The Legal Framework of English Feudalism* (Cambridge, 1976).

Minogue, K. R., 'The Concept of Property', *Nomos*, 22 (1980), 3–27.

Mitchell, S. K., *Taxation in Medieval England* (New Haven, Conn., 1951).

Mitteis, H., *Deutsche Rechtsgeschichte*, ed. H. Lieberich (16th edn., Munich, 1981).

—— 'Land und Herrschaft' (review article), *HZ* 163 (1941), 255–81, 471–89.

—— *Lehnrecht und Staatsgewalt* (Weimar, 1933).

—— *The State in the Middle Ages*, trans. H. F. Orton (Amsterdam, 1975) from *Der*

*Staat des hohen Mittelalters* (4th edn., Munich, 1953).

*Mittellateinisches Wörterbuch*, ed. O. Prince and J. Schneider (Munich, 1967– ).

Mitterauer, M., 'Formen adeliger Herrschaftsbildung im hochmittelalterlichen Österreich', *MIÖG* 80 (1972), 265–338.

Monboisse, R., *L'Ordre féodal des 'Montagnes d'Auvergne' du xii<sup>e</sup> au xv<sup>e</sup> siècle* (Aurillac, 1966).

Montesquieu, C. de Secondat, baron de, *De l'esprit des lois*, in *Œuvres* (Lyon, 1792).

Montorzi, M., *Diritto feudale nel basso medioevo* (Turin, 1991).

*Monumenta Bambergensia* (*Bibliotheca Rerum Germanicarum*, Berlin, 1864–9), ed. P. Jaffé, v.

*Monumenta Boica* (Munich, 1763–1954).

*Monumenta Historica Ducatus Carinthiae*, ed. A. von Jaksch, iii (Klagenfurt, 1904).

*Monuments de l'histoire de Neuchâtel*, ed. G. A. Matile (Neuchâtel, 1844–8).

Moore, B., *Injustice: the Social Basis of Obedience and Revolt* (White Plains, NY, 1978).

Moore, S. F., *Law as Process* (London, 1978).

—— *Social Facts and Formations* (Cambridge, 1986).

—— and Myerhoff, B. (eds.), *Secular Ritual* (Amsterdam, 1977).

Mor, C. G., *L'Età feudale* (Milan, 1951–2).

Moraw, P., 'Gelehrte Juristen im Dienst der deutschen Könige des späteren Mittelalters', *Die Rolle der Juristen bei der Entstehung des modernen Staates*, ed. R. Schnur (Berlin, 1986).

Mortimer, R., 'The Beginnings of the Honour of Clare', *Proc. of Battle Conference*, 3 (1980), 119–41.

—— 'Land and Service: the Tenants of the Honour of Clare', *ANS* 8 (1986), 177–97.

Müller-Mertens, E., *Regnum Teutonicum* (Vienna, 1970).

—— *Karl der Grosse, Ludwig der Fromme und die Freien* (Berlin, 1963).

—— 'Zur Feudalentwicklung im Okzident und zur Definition des Feudalverhältnisses', *Zeitschrift für Geschichtswissenschaft*, 14 (1966), 52–73.

Munzer, S. R., *A Theory of Property* (Cambridge, 1990).

Muratori, L. A. (ed.), *Antiquitates Italicae Medii Aevi* (Milan, 1738–40).

—— *Rerum Italicarum Scriptores* (Milan, 1723–51).

Murray, A. C., *Germanic Kinship Structure* (Toronto, 1983).

Musset, L., 'Huit essais sur l'autorité ducale en Normandie', *Cahier des annales de Normandie*, 17 (1985), 3–148.

—— 'Réflexions sur *alodium* et sa signification dans les textes normands', *RHDFE* ser. 4, 47 (1969), 606.

Navel, H., 'L'Enquête de 1133 sur les fiefs de l'évêché de Bayeux', *Bulletin de la société des antiquaires de Normandie*, 42 (1934), 5–80.

Nelson, J. L., *Charles the Bald* (London, 1992).

—— 'A King across the Sea: Alfred in Continental Perspective', *TRHS* ser. 5, 36 (1986), 45–68; 'Charles the Bald and the Church', *Studies in Church Hist.* 16

(1979), 103–18; 'The Church's Military Service in the Ninth Century', ibid. 20 (1983), 15–30; 'Legislation and Consensus in the Reign of Charles the Bald', in P. Wormald and others (eds.), *Ideal and Reality in Frankish and Anglo-Saxon Society* (Oxford, 1983); 'Public *Histories* and Private History in the Work of Nithard', *Speculum*, 60 (1985), 251–93: all repr. in *Politics and Ritual in Early Medieval Europe* (London, 1986).

—— 'Kingship and Empire', in J. H. Burns (ed.), *Cambridge History of Medieval Political Thought* (Cambridge, 1988), 211–51.

Niermeyer, J. F., 'Remarques sur la formation du vocabulaire institutionnel médiolatin', *Archivum Latinitatis Medii Aevi*, 28 (1958), 253–61.

—— and Kieft, C. van de, *Mediae Latinitatis Lexicon Minus* (Leiden, 1976).

Nithard, *Histoire des fils de Louis le Pieux*, ed. P. Lauer (Paris, 1926).

Nobili, M., 'Vassalli su terra monastica fra re e "principi": il caso di Bobbio', *Structures féodales* (q.v.), 299–309.

*Notitia de Servitio Monasteriorum*, in *Corpus Consuetudinum Monasticarum*, ed. K. Hallinger and others, i (Siegburg, 1963), 485–99.

*Novum Glossarium mediae Latinitatis* (Copenhagen, 1959– ).

Noyé, G., 'Féodalité et habitat fortifié en Calabre', *Structures féodales* (q.v.), 607–28.

Odegaard, C. E., 'Carolingian Oaths of Fidelity', *Speculum*, 16 (1941), 284–96.

—— *Vassi and Fideles in the Carolingian Empire* (Cambridge, Mass., 1955).

Odo of Cluny, *Vita sancti Geraldi Aurillacensis comitis*, in *PL* 133, 639–704.

*Les Olim*, ed. A. A. Beugnot (Paris, 1839–48).

Olivier-Martin, F., *Histoire du droit français* (Paris, 1948).

*Oorkonden der Graven van Vlaanderen (1191–1206)*, ed. W. Prevenier (Brussels, 1964–71).

Orderic Vitalis, *Historia Ecclesiastica*, ed. M. Chibnall (Oxford, 1969–80).

*Ordonnances des roys de France de la troisième race*, ed. E. de Laurière and others (Paris, 1733–1847).

Ortlieb, *Die Zwiefalter Chroniken Ortliebs und Bertholds*, ed. L. Wallach (Sigmaringen, 1978).

*Osnabrücker Urkundenbuch*, ed. F. Philippi (1892; repr. Osnabrück, 1969).

Ott, I., 'Der Regalienbegriff im 12. Jahrhundert', *ZRG KA* 66 (1948), 234–304.

Otto Morena, *Historia Frederici I*, ed. F. Güterbock (MGH SRG NS 7, 1930).

Otto of Freising, *Chronica sive Historia de Duabus Civitatibus*, ed. A. Hofmeister (MGH SRG 40, 1912).

—— and Rahewin, *Gesta Friderici Imperatoris*, ed. G. Waitz (MGH SRG 46, 1912).

Otto of St Blasius, *Chronica*, ed. A. Hofmeister (MGH SRG 47, 1912).

Ourliac, P., 'L'Esprit du droit méridional', in *Droit privé et institutions régionales: études historiques offertes à J. Yver* (Paris, 1976), 577–94.

—— *Études d'histoire du droit médiéval* (Paris, 1979).

—— 'Législation, coutumes et coutumiers au temps de Philippe Auguste', in Bautier, *La France de Philippe Auguste* (q.v.), 471–88.

Overmann, A., *Gräfin Mathilde von Tuscien* (Innsbruck, 1895).

*Oxford Dictionary of Medieval Latin from British Sources* (Oxford, 1975– ).

*Oxford English Dictionary* (2nd edn., Oxford, 1989).

*Pactus Legis Salicae*, ed. K. A. Eckhardt (MGH Legum Sect. 1, iv (1), 1962).

Painter, S., 'The Lords of Lusignan in the Eleventh and Twelfth Centuries', *Speculum*, 32 (1957), 27–47.

Panikkar, K. N., 'A Historical Overview', in Sarvepalli Gopal (ed.), *Anatomy of a Confrontation* (New Delhi, 1991), 22–37.

Parieu, E. de, 'Étude sur la pratique dorée de Pierre Jacobi', *Revue de législation et de jurisprudence*, 20 (1844), 417–52.

Parisse, M., *La Noblesse lorraine, xi$^e$–xiii$^e$ siècle* (Lille, 1976).

Patruccio, C. E. (ed.), 'Le più antiche carte dell'abbazia di Caramagna', *Miscellanea Saluzzese*, i (Pinerolo, 1902), 55–157.

Patze, H., *Die Entstehung der Landesherrschaft in Thüringen* (Cologne, 1962).

Paul the Deacon, *Historia Langobardorum*, ed. G. Waitz (MGH SRG 48, 1878).

Perrin, C. E., *Recherches sur la seigneurie rurale en Lorraine* (Paris, 1935).

Pertile, A., *Storia del diritto italiano*, iv (2nd edn., Turin, 1893); vi (Turin, 1900).

Pescatore, G., 'Die Stellungnahme des Irnerius zu einer lehnrechtlichen Frage', *Mélanges Fitting* (Paris, 1908), ii. 163–4.

Petit-Dutaillis, C., *Les Communes françaises* (Paris, 1947).

—— *Le Déshéritement de Jean sans Terre* (Paris, 1925).

—— *Studies and Notes supplementary to Stubbs' Constitutional History*, trans. W. E. Rhodes and W. T. Waugh (Manchester, 1911–14).

Petot, P., 'Le Droit commun en France selon les coutumiers', *RHDFE* ser. 4, 38 (1960), 412–29.

—— 'L'Ordonnance du 1$^{er}$ mai 1209', in *Recueil de travaux offerts à C. Brunel* (Paris, 1955).

—— 'L'Origine de la mainmorte servile', *RHDFE* ser. 4, 19 (1940–1), 275–309.

Peyvel, P., 'Structures féodales et frontière médiévale', *MA* 93 (1987), 51–83.

*Pipe Roll 31 Henry I*, ed. J. Hunter (London, 1833).

*Pipe Roll 5 Ric. I* (Pipe Roll Soc. NS 3, 1927).

Pirenne, H., *Mohammed and Charlemagne*, trans. B. Miall (London, 1939).

Pithou, P., *Opera* (Paris, 1609).

*Placita Anglo-Normannorum*, ed. M. M. Bigelow (London, 1879).

*Placiti del 'regnum Italiae'*, ed. C. Manaresi (FSI 92, 96–7, 1955–60).

Pocock, J. G. A., *The Ancient Constitution and the Feudal Law* (Cambridge, 1957).

Pollock, F., and Maitland, F. W., *History of English Law* (2nd edn., Cambridge, 1911).

Poly, J. P., *La Provence et la société féodale, 879–1166* (Paris, 1976).

—— 'Vocabulaire "féodo-vassalique" et aires de culture durant le haut moyen âge', in *La Lexicographie du latin médiéval* (Colloques internationaux du CNRS, 589, Paris, 1981), 167–90.

—— and Bournazel, E., 'Couronne et mouvance; institutions et représentations mentales', in Bautier, *La France de Philippe Auguste* (q.v.), 217–36.

Poly, J. P., and Bournazel, E., *La Mutation féodale: x$^e$–xii$^e$ siècles* (Paris, 1980).

*Polyptyque de Saint-Bertin*, ed. F. L. Ganshof and others (Paris, 1975).

*Pommersches Urkundenbuch*, ed. R. Klempin and others (Stettin, 1868–Cologne, 1962; vol. i repr. Cologne, 1970)

Poole, R. L., *The Exchequer in the Twelfth Century* (Oxford, 1912).

Pöschl, A., *Die Regalien der mittelalterlichen Kirchen* (Graz, 1928).

Pothier, R. J., *Œuvres* (Paris, 1845–6), ix. 101–265: 'Traité du droit de domaine de propriété'; ibid. 493–783: 'Traité des fiefs'.

Power, E., 'On Medieval History as a Social Study', *Economica*, NS i (1934), 13–29.

Powicke, F. M., *The Loss of Normandy* (Manchester, 2nd edn., 1961).

Prestwich, J. O., 'War and Finance in the Anglo-Norman State', *THRS* ser. 5, 4 (1954), 19–43.

Prestwich, M., *The Three Edwards* (London, 1980).

—— *War, Politics, and Finance under Edward I* (London, 1972).

Prou, M., 'De la nature du service militaire dû par les roturiers aux xie et xiie siècles', *RH* 44 (1890), 313–27.

Raban, S., *Mortmain Legislation and the English Church* (Cambridge, 1982).

Ralph Diceto, *Opera Historica*, ed. W. Stubbs (RS 68, 1876).

*Ratherii episcopi Veronensis Vita*, in *PL* 136, 27–142.

Ratherius, *Briefe*, ed. F. Weigle (MGH Briefe der deutschen Kaiserzeit, i, 1949).

*Reading Abbey Cartularies*, ed. B. R. Kemp (Royal Hist. Soc. Camden Series 4, 92, 1962).

*Recueil d'actes relatifs à l'administration des rois d'Angleterre en Guyenne au xiiie siècle* (*Recogniciones Feodorum in Aquitania*), ed. C. Bémont (Paris, 1914).

*Recueil des actes de Charles le Chauve*, ed. G. Tessier (Paris, 1943–5).

*Recueil des actes de Charles le Simple*, ed. P. Lauer (Paris, 1949).

*Recueil des actes d'Eudes, roi de France*, ed. R. H. Bautier (Paris, 1967).

*Recueil des actes de Henri II, roi d'Angleterre et duc de Normandie, concernant les provinces françaises et les affaires de France*, ed. L. Delisle and E. Berger (Paris, 1906–27).

*Recueil des actes de Louis II, Louis III et Carloman II*, ed. F. Grat (Paris, 1978).

*Recueil des actes de Pépin I et Pépin II, rois d'Aquitaine*, ed. L. Levillain (Paris, 1926).

*Recueil des actes de Philippe I*, ed. M. Prou (Paris, 1908).

*Recueil des actes de Philippe Auguste*, ed. H. F. Delaborde and others (Paris, 1916– ).

*Recueil des actes des comtes de Pontieu*, ed. C. Brunel (Paris, 1930).

*Recueil des actes des ducs de Normandie (911–1066)*, ed. M. Fauroux (Caen, 1961).

*Recueil des actes des ducs normands d'Italie*, ed. L. R. Ménager, i (Bari, 1980).

*Recueil des chartes de l'abbaye de Cluny*, ed. A. Bernard and A. Bruel (Paris, 1876–1903).

*Recueil des chartes de l'abbaye royale de Montmartre*, ed. E. de Barthélemy (Paris, 1883).

*Recueil des chartes de Saint-Nicaise de Meulan*, ed. E. Houth (Paris, 1924).

*Recueil des historiens des Gaules et de France*, ed. M. Bouquet, L. Delisle, and others (Paris, 1869–1904).

*Red Book of the Exchequer*, ed. H. Hall (RS 99, 1896).

Redon, O., 'Seigneurs et communautés rurales dans la contado de Sienne au xiii$^e$ siècle', *MEF* 91 (1979), 149–96, 619–57.

Reeve, A., *Property* (London, 1986).

*Regesta Alsatiae*, ed. A. Bruckner, i (Strasbourg, 1949).

*Regesta Chartarum Pistoriensium: Vescovado*, ed. N. Rauty (Pistoia, 1974).

*Regesta Diplomatica Historiae Thuringiae*, ed. O. Dobenecker (Jena, 1896–1939).

*Regesta Historiae Westfaliae*, ed. H. A. Erhard (Münster, 1847–51).

*Regesta Regum Anglo-Normannorum*, ed. H. W. C. Davis and others (Oxford, 1913–69).

*Regesto di Farfa*, ed. I. Giorgi and U. Balzani (Rome, 1879–1914).

*Regesto Mantovano*, ed. P. Torelli (RCI 12, 1914).

*Regesto Sublacense*, ed. L. Allodi and G. Levi (Rome, 1885).

*Regii Neapolitani Archivi Monumenta* (Naples, 1845–61).

Regino of Prüm, *Chronicon*, ed. F. Kurze (MGH SRG 50, 1890).

*Register of St Augustine's Canterbury*, ed. G. J. Turner and H. E. Salter (London, 1924).

*Registrum Magnum del comune di Piacenza*, ed. E. Falcone and R. Peveri (Milan, 1984–8).

Reulos, M., *Étude sur l'esprit, les sources, et la méthode des Institutes Coutumières d'Antoine Loisel* (Paris, 1935).

Reuter, T., 'The End of Carolingian Military Expansion', in P. Godman and R. Collins (eds.), *Charlemagne's Heir* (Oxford, 1990).

—— *Germany in the Early Middle Ages* (London, 1991).

—— 'The "Imperial Church System" of the Ottonian and Salian Rulers', *Journal of Eccles. Hist.* 33 (1982), 347–74.

—— 'A New History of Germany', *History*, 6 (1981), 440–4.

—— 'Unruhestiftung, Fehde, Rebellion, Widerstand', in S. Weinfurth and H. Seibert (eds.), *Die Salier und das Reich* (Sigmaringen, 1991), iii. 297–325.

Reynolds, S., 'Bookland, Folkland and Fiefs', *ANS* 14 (1992), 211–27.

—— *Kingdoms and Communities in Western Europe, 900–1300* (Oxford, 1984).

—— 'Magna Carta 1297 and the Legal Use of Literacy', *Historical Research*, 62 (1989), 233–44.

—— 'Medieval *Origines Gentium* and the Community of the Realm', *History*, 68 (1983), 375–90.

—— 'More about Feudalism', *Peasant Studies*, 14 (1987), 250–9.

—— 'Towns in Domesday Book', in J. C. Holt (ed.), *Domesday Studies* (Woodbridge, 1987), 295–309.

—— 'What do we mean by Anglo-Saxon and Anglo-Saxons?', *Journal of British Studies*, 24 (1985), 395–414.

Richard, J., *Les Ducs de Bourgogne et la formation du duché du xi$^e$ au xiv$^e$ siècle* (Paris, 1954).

Richard, J., *Saint Louis* (Paris, 1983).

Richard fitz Nigel, *Dialogus de Scaccario*, ed. C. Johnson and others (Oxford, 1983).

Richardot, H., 'A propos des personnes et des terres féodales', in *Études d'histoire du droit privé offertes à P. Petot* (Paris, 1959), 463–71.

—— 'Le Fief roturier à Toulouse aux xiie et xiiie siècles', *RHDFE* ser. 4, 14 (1935), 305–59, 495–569.

—— 'Franc-fiefs', *RHDFE* ser. 4, 27 (1949), 28–63, 229–73.

Richardson, H., 'An Anglo-Norman Return to the Inquest of Sheriffs', *BJRL* 27 (1942–3), 179–81.

—— 'A Twelfth-Century Anglo-Norman Charter', *BJRL* 24 (1940), 168–72.

Richardson, H. G., and Sayles, G. O., *The Governance of Medieval England* (Edinburgh, 1963).

Richer, *Histoire de France*, ed. R. Latouche (Paris, 1937).

Riesenberg, P. N., *Inalienability of Sovereignty in Medieval Political Thought* (New York, 1956).

*Rigestum comunis Albe*, ed. E. Milano (Pinerolo, 1903).

Rigord, *Gesta Philippi Augusti*, in *Œuvres de Rigord et de Guillaume le Breton*, ed. H. F. Delaborde (Paris, 1882–5), i. 1–167.

Rippe, G., 'Commune urbaine et féodalité en Italie du nord: l'exemple de Padoue', *MEF* 91 (1979), 659–97.

—— 'L'Evêque de Padoue et son réseau de clientèles', *Structures féodales* (q.v.), 413–28.

—— '*Feudum sine fidelitate*. Formes féodales et structures sociales dans la région de Padoue à l'époque de la première commune', *MEF* 87 (1975), 187–239.

Robert of Torigny, *Chronica*, in *Chronicles of the Reigns of Stephen etc.*, ed. R. Howlett (RS 82, 1884–90), iv. 81–315.

Robertson, A. J. (ed.), *Anglo-Saxon Charters* (Cambridge, 1956).

Robinson, J. A., *Gilbert Crispin* (London, 1911).

Rockinger, L. (ed.), *Briefsteller und Formelbücher* (Munich, 1863).

Rodger, A., *Owners and Neighbours in Roman Law* (Oxford, 1972).

Rodulfus Glaber, *Historiarum Libri Quinque*, ed. N. Bulst, trans. J. France (Oxford, 1989).

Roffe, D., 'Domesday Book and Northern Society', *EHR* 105 (1990), 310–36.

—— 'From Thegnage to Barony', *ANS* 12 (1989), 157–76.

Roger of Howden, *Chronica*, ed. W. Stubbs (RS 51, 1871).

Roger Wendover, *Flores Historiarum*, ed. H. G. Hewlett (RS 84, 1886–9).

Rogozinski, J., 'Ennoblement by the Crown and Social Stratification in France, 1285–1322', in W. C. Jordan and others (eds.), *Order and Innovation in the Middle Age*s (Princeton, NJ, 1976).

*Rôles gascons*, ed. C. Bémont: *Supplément au tome premier* (Paris, 1896).

*Rolls of the King's Court, 1194–5*, ed. F. W. Maitland (Pipe Roll Soc. 14, 1891).

Rota, A., 'L'Apparato di Pillio alle consuetudines feudorum', *Studi e memorie per la storia dell'università di Bologna*, 14 (1938), 1–170.

Roth, P., *Feudalität und Unterthanverband* (Weimar, 1863).

—— *Geschichte des Beneficialwesens* (Erlangen, 1850).

*Rotuli Curiae Regis*, ed. F. Palgrave (London: Record Commission, 1835).

*Rotuli Parliamentorum* (London: Record Commission, 1783).

Round, J. H., *Feudal England* (London, 1895), including at 182–245: 'The Introduction of Knight Service into England'; repr. with small alterations from *EHR* 6 (1891), 417–43, 625–45; 7 (1892), 11–24.

—— 'Introduction to the Hertfordshire Domesday', in W. Page (ed.), *Victoria History of Hertford*, iii (Westminster, 1902), 263–99.

Rumble, A. R., 'Old English *Boc-Land* as an Anglo-Saxon Estate-Name', *Leeds Studies in English*, 18 (1987), 219–30.

Ruodolfus and Meginhardus, *Translatio sancti Alexandri, MGH Scriptores*, ii. 673–81.

Rymer, T. (ed.), *Foedera* (2nd edn., London: Record Commission, 1816–30).

Sachsenspiegel: see Eike von Repgow.

Sagnac, P., and Caron, P. (eds.), *Les Comités des droits féodaux, 1789–93* (Paris, 1907).

Sainct Julien, P. de, *De l'Origine des Bourgognons* (Paris, 1581).

Saltman, M., 'Feudal Relationships and the Law: a Comparative Enquiry', *Comparative Studies in Society and History*, 29 (1987), 514–32.

*Salzburger Urkundenbuch*, ed. W. Hauthaler and F. Martin (Salzburg, 1910–23).

Sanders, I. J., *Feudal Military Service* (London, 1956).

Sautel, G., 'Note sur la formation du droit royal d'amortissement', *Études d'histoire du droit canonique dédiées à G. le Bras* (Paris, 1965), 689–704.

Sautel-Boulet, M., 'Le Rôle juridictionnel de la cour des pairs aux xiii^e et xiv^e siècles', *Recueil des travaux offert à M. Clovis Brunel* (Paris, 1955), ii. 507–20.

Sawyer, P. H., *Anglo-Saxon Charters* (London, 1968).

—— '1066–1086. A Tenurial Revolution', in P. H. Sawyer (ed.), *Domesday Book: a Reassessment* (London, 1985).

Sayers, J. E., *Papal Government and England during the Pontificate of Honorius III* (Cambridge, 1984).

Scheyhing, R., *Eide, Amtsgewalt und Bannleihe* (Cologne, 1960).

Schioppa, A. P., 'Le Rôle du droit savant dans quelques actes judiciaires italiens des xi^e et xii^e siècles', *Confluence des droits savants et des pratiques juridiques. Actes du colloque de Montpellier* (Milan, 1979).

Schlatter, R., *Private Property: the History of an Idea* (London, 1951).

Schmidt, S. W. and others (eds.), *Friends, Followers and Factions* (Berkeley, 1977).

Schmitz, P., *Histoire de l'ordre de Saint Benoît* (Gembloux, 1942–56).

Schneider, J., contribution to discussion printed in *Annales du Midi*, 80 (1968), 480–1.

Schneidmüller, B., *Nomen Patriae: die Entstehung Frankreichs in der politische-geographischen Terminologie* (Sigmaringen, 1987).

Schott, C., 'Der Stand des Leges-Forschung', *Frühmittelalterliche Studien*, 13 (1979), 29–55.

Schulze, H. K., *Adelsherrschaft und Landesherrschaft* (Cologne, 1963).

—— *Grundstrukturen der Verfassung im Mittelalter*, i (2nd edn., Stuttgart, 1990).

Schulze, H. K., 'Rodungsfreiheit und Königsfreiheit', *HZ* 219 (1975), 529–50.

Scott, J. C., *Domination and the Arts of Resistance* (New Haven, Conn., 1990).

Searle, E., *Lordship and Community: Battle Abbey and its Banlieu* (Toronto, 1974).

—— *Predatory Kinship and the Creation of Norman Power, 840–1066* (Berkeley, 1988).

*Select Cases in Ecclesiastical Courts of the Province of Canterbury, c. 1200–1301*, ed. N. Adams and C. Donahue (Selden Soc. 95, 1981).

*Select Pleas in Manorial Courts*, ed. F. W. Maitland (Selden Soc. 2, 1895).

Sestan, E., 'Problemi sulle origini e sviluppi del feudalesimo con particolare riguardo all'Italia', *Critica storica*, 23 (1986), 6–120.

Sheehan, M., *The Will in Medieval England* (Toronto, 1963).

Sigonio, C., *Opera Omnia* (Milan, 1732).

Simeoni, L., 'Le Origini del comune di Verona', *Nuovo Archivio Veneto*, NS 25 (1913), 49–145.

—— 'Per la genealogia dei conti di Sambonifacio', *Nuovo Archivio Veneto*, NS 26 (1913), 302–23.

Simpson, A. W. B., *A History of the Land Law* (Oxford, 1986).

Smith, A., *Lectures in Jurisprudence*, ed. R. L. Meeks and others (Oxford, 1978).

Smith, D. B., 'Sir Thomas Smith, Feudalist', *Scottish Historical Review*, 12 (1915), 271–302.

Smith, J. C., 'The Concept of Native Title', *Univ. of Toronto Law Journal*, 24 (1974), 1–16.

*Song of Roland*, ed. G. J. Brault (University Park, 1978).

Southern, R. W., *Making of the Middle Ages* (London, 1953).

—— *Saint Anselm* (Cambridge, 1990).

Spagnesi, E., *Wernerius Bononiensis Iudex* (Florence, 1970).

Spelman, H., *History and Fate of Sacrilege*, ed. C. F. S. Warren (London, 1895).

—— *Reliquiae Spelmanniae*, ed. E. Gibson (London, 1723).

Spufford, P., *Money and its Use in Medieval Europe* (Cambridge, 1988).

Stafford, P., *The East Midlands in the Early Middle Ages* (Leicester, 1985).

—— 'The Laws of Cnut and the History of Anglo-Saxon Royal Promises', *Anglo-Saxon England*, 10 (1982), 173–90.

—— *Unification and Conquest* (London, 1989).

*Statuta civitatis Mutine anno 1327 reformata*, ed. C. Camponi (Parma, 1864).

*Statutes of the Realm* (London: Record Commission, 1810–28).

*Statuti della provincia romana*, ed. F. Tomasetti and others, i (FSI 48, 1910).

*Statuti di Bologna dell'anno 1288*, ed. G. Fasoli and P. Sella (Vatican City, 1937–9).

Stein, P., *Regulae Juris* (Edinburgh, 1966).

Stelzer, W., *Gelehrtes Recht in Österreich* (Vienna, 1982).

Stengel, E. E., 'Fuldensia V', *Archiv für Diplomatik*, 8 (1962), 12–67.

—— *Die Immunität in Deutschland bis zum Ende des 11. Jahrhunderts* (Innsbruck, 1910).

—— 'Land und lehnrechtliche Grundlagen des Reichsfürstenstandes', *ZRG GA* 66 (1948), 294–342.

Stenton, D. M., *English Justice between the Norman Conquest and the Great Charter* (London, 1965).

Stenton, F. M., *First Century of English Feudalism* (Oxford, 1961).

—— *Latin Charters of the Anglo-Saxon Period* (Oxford, 1955).

—— 'St Benet of Holme and the Norman Conquest', *EHR* 37 (1922), 225–35.

Stephenson, C., *Mediaeval Feudalism* (Ithaca, NY, 1942).

—— *Medieval Institutions* (Ithaca, NY, 1954), 1–40: 'Aids of French Towns', translated and revised from *MA* ser. 2, 24 (1922), 274–328; 41–103: 'The Origin and Nature of the *Taille*', from *Revue belge*, 5 (1926), 801–70; 156–83: 'Commendation and Related Problems in Domesday', from *EHR* 59 (1944), 289–310; 205–33: 'The Origin and Significance of Feudalism', from *AHR* 46 (1941), 788–812.

—— 'La Taille dans les villes d'Allemagne', *MA* ser. 2, 26 (1924), 1–43.

Stevenson, W. H., 'An Inedited Charter of King Henry I', *EHR* 21 (1906), 505–9.

Störmer, W., *Früher Adel* (Stuttgart, 1978).

Strayer, J. R., *The Administration of Normandy under Saint Louis* (Cambridge, Mass., 1932).

—— and Taylor, C. H., *Studies in Early French Taxation* (Cambridge, Mass., 1939).

*Structures féodales et féodalisme dans l'Occident méditerranéen* (Collection de l'École française de Rome, 44, 1980).

Stutz, U., *'Romerwergeld' und 'Herrenfall'* (Berlin, 1934).

Suger, *Œuvres*, ed. A. Lecoy de la Marche (Paris, 1867).

—— *Vie de Louis VI le Gros*, ed. H. Waquet (Paris, 1964).

Sutherland, D. W., *The Assize of Novel Disseisin* (Oxford, 1973).

—— *Quo Warranto Proceedings in the Reign of Edward I* (Oxford, 1963).

Symeon of Durham, *Opera omnia*, ed. T. Arnold (RS 75, 1882–5).

Tabacco, G., 'L'Allodialità del potere nel medioevo', *SM* 11 (1970), 565–615.

—— 'La costituzione del regno italico al tempo di Federico Barbarossa', *Relazioni e comunicazioni al XXXIII congresso storico Subalpino* (Turin, 1970), 163–77.

—— 'Dai possessori dell'età carolingia agli esercitali dell'età langobarda', *SM* ser. 3, 10 (1969), 221–68.

—— 'Fief et seigneurie dans l'Italie communale', *MA* 75 (1969), 5–37, 203–18.

—— 'I Liberi del re nell'Italia carolingia e postcarolingia': partly published in *SM* ser. 3, 5 (1964), 1–65, 6 (1) (1965), 1–70 (also in full in book form, Spoleto, 1966, which I have not seen).

—— *The Struggle for Power in Medieval Italy*, trans. R. B. Jensen (Cambridge, 1989).

*Tabularium Casinensis: Codex Diplomaticus Cajetanus* (Monte Cassino, 1887–1960).

Tabuteau, E. Z., 'Definition of Feudal Military Obligations in Eleventh-Century Normandy', in M. S. Arnold and others (eds.), *On the Laws and Customs of England* (Chapel Hill, 1981).

—— *Transfers of Property in Eleventh-Century Normandy* (Chapel Hill, 1988).

Tait, J., *The Medieval English Borough* (Manchester, 1936).

Tangheroni, M., 'La Sardegna prearagonese', in *Structures féodales* (q.v.), 525–6.

Tardif, J. (ed.), *Monuments historiques* (Paris, 1866).

Taviani, H., 'Pouvoir et solidarités dans la principauté de Salerne', in *Structures féodales* (q.v.), 587–606.

Taylor, P., 'The Endowment and Military Obligations of the See of London', *ANS* 14 (1992), 287–312.

Tellenbach, G., *The Church in Western Europe from the Tenth to the Early Twelfth Century*, trans. T. Reuter (Cambridge, 1993).

Theoderic, *Libellus de libertate Epternacensi*, in *MGH Scriptores*, xxiii. 64–72.

Theuerkauf, G., *Land und Lehnswesen vom 14. bis zum 16. Jahrhundert* (Cologne, 1961).

Thietmar of Merseburg, *Chronicon*, ed. F. Kurze (MGH SRG 54, 1889).

Tholin, G., and Fallières, O. (eds.), 'Hommages des seigneurs de l'Agenais au comte de Toulouse en 1259' and 'Prise de possession de l'Agenais au nom du roi de France en 1271', *Recueil des travaux de la société d'agriculture, sciences et arts d'Agen*, ser. 2, 13 (1897), 11–120.

Thomas, P., 'Notes sur Galbert de Bruges', *Mélanges d'histoire offerts à H. Pirenne* (Brussels, 1926), 515–17.

Thompson, E. P., *Customs in Common* (London, 1991).

Thorne, S. E., 'English Feudalism and Estates in Land', *Cambridge Law Journal*, 1959, 193–209; repr. in *Essays in English Legal History* (London, 1985), 13–30.

Tiraboschi, G., *Storia dell'augusta badia di S. Silvestro di Nonantola* (Modena, 1784–5).

Tirelli, V., 'Osservazioni sui rapporti tra sede apostolica, Capua e Napoli durante i pontificati di Gregorio VII e Urbano II', *Studi sul medioevo Cristiano offerti a R. Morghen* (Rome, 1974), 961–1010.

Toubert, P., 'Les Statuts communaux et l'histoire des campagnes lombardes au xiv<sup>e</sup> siècle', *MEF* 72 (1960), 297–508.

—— *Les Structures du Latium médiéval* (Paris, 1973).

*Traditionen des Hochstifts Freising*, ed. T. Bitterauf, i (Munich, 1905).

*Traditionen des Hochstifts Regensburg*, ed. J. Widemann (Munich, 1943).

*Traditionen des Klosters Oberaltaich*, i, ed. C. Mohr (Munich, 1979).

Trusen, W., *Anfänge des gelehrten Rechts in Deutschland* (Wiesbaden, 1962).

Tsurushima, H., 'The Fraternity of Rochester Diocese', *ANS* 14 (1992), 313–37.

Tucoo-Chala, P., *Gaston Fébus et la vicomté de Béarn* (Bordeaux, 1960).

—— *La Vicomté de Béarn et le problème de sa souveraineté* (Bordeaux, 1961).

*Two Saxon Chronicles Parallel*, ed. C. Plummer and J. Earle (Oxford, 1892).

Ughelli, F., *Italia Sacra* (Venice, 1717–22).

Ugo Falcando, *Liber de regno Sicilie*, ed. G. B. Siracusa (FSI 22, 1897).

*Urkundenbuch der Abtei Sanct Gallen*, ed. H. Wartmann and others (Zürich, 1863–50).

*Urkundenbuch der Benedikter-Abtei St. Stephan in Würzburg*, i, ed. F. J. Bendel and others (Leipzig, 1912).

*Urkundenbuch der . . . mittelrheinischen Territorien*, ed. H. Beyer, i (Coblenz, 1860).

*Urkundenbuch der Reichsabteien Hersfeld*, i, ed. H. Weirich (Marburg, 1936).

*Urkundenbuch des Erzstifts Magdeburg*, ed. F. Israel and W. Möllenberg (Magdeburg, 1937).

*Urkundenbuch des Hochstifts Halberstadt*, ed. G. Schmidt (Leipzig, 1883–9).

*Urkundenbuch des Hochstifts Naumburg*, i, ed. F. Rosenfeld (Magdeburg, 1925).

*Urkunden-Buch des Landes ob der Enns*, ed. Museum Francisco-Carolinum, ii (Linz, 1856).

*Urkundenbuch für die Geschichte des Niederrheins*, ed. T. J. Lacomblet (Düsseldorf, 1840–58).

*Urkundenbuch zur Geschichte der herzöge von Braunschweig und Lüneburg*, ed. H. Sudendorf (Hanover, 1859–83).

*Urkunden des Heinrichs des Löwen*, ed. K. Jordan (MGH Deutschen Geschichtsquellen, 1949).

*Urkunden des Hochstifts Eichstätt* (*Monumenta Boica*, 49–50, Munich, 1910, 1932).

Vale, M., *The Angevin Legacy and the Hundred Years War* (Oxford, 1990).

Valous, G. de, *Le Temporel et la situation financière des établissements de l'ordre de Cluny du xii^e au xiv^e siècle* (Paris, 1935).

Van Caenegem, R., 'Government, Law and Society', in J. H. Burns (ed.), *Cambridge History of Medieval Political Thought* (Cambridge, 1988), 174–210.

Van de Kieft, C., 'De feodale maatschappij der middeleeuwn', *Bijdragen en Mededelingen betreffende de geschiedenis der Nederlanden*, 89 (1974), 193–211.

Van Houtts, E. M. C., 'The Ship List of William the Conqueror', *ANS* 10 (1987), 159–83.

Van Luyn, P., 'Les Milites dans la France du xi^e siècle', *MA* 77 (1971), 5–51, 193–238.

Vaughan, J., *Reports and Arguments* (London, 1706).

Venezky, R. L., and Healey, A. di P., *Microfiche Concordance to Old English* (Toronto, 1980).

*Verdener Geschichtsquellen*, ed. W. von Hodenberg, ii (Celle, 1857).

Verhein, K., 'Studien zu den Quellen zum Reichsgut der Karolingerzeit I', *DA* 10 (1953–4), 313–94; and 'Studien . . . II', *DA* 11 (1954–5), 333–93.

Verriest, L., *Le Régime seigneurial dans le comté de Hainaut du xi^e à la révolution* (Louvain, 1917–56).

Vidal, H., 'Le *feudum honoratum* dans les cartulaires d'Agde et de Béziers', *Hommages à André Dupont* (Montpellier, 1974).

Violante, C., *La Società milanese nell'età precomunale* (Bari, 1953).

*Vita Bertulfi*, in *MGH Scriptores*, xv. 633–41.

*Vita Hludowici imperatoris*, in *MGH Scriptores*, ii. 604–48.

Vollrath-Reichelt, H., *Königsgedanke und Königtum bei den Angelsachsen* (Cologne, 1971).

Vuitry, A., *Études sur le régime foncier de la France avant la révolution de 1789* (Paris, 1878).

Wace, *Le Roman de Rou*, ed. A. J. Holden (Paris, 1970–3).

Wadle, E., *Reichsgut und Königsherrschaft unter Lothar III* (Berlin, 1969).

Wallace-Hadrill, J. M., *The Frankish Church* (Oxford, 1988).

—— *The Long-Haired Kings* (London, 1962).

Ward, J. O., 'Feudalism: Interpretative Category or Framework of Life in the Medieval West?', in Leach, *Feudalism* (q.v.), 40–67.

Warlop, E., *The Flemish Nobility before 1300*, trans. J. B. Ross and H. Vandermoere (Kortrijk, 1975).

*War of Saint-Sardos: Gascon Correspondence and Diplomatic Documents*, ed. P. Chaplais (Royal Hist. Soc. Camden Series 3, 87, 1954).

Warren, W. L., *Henry II* (London, 1973).

Watkins, J. W. N., 'Ideal Types and Historical Explanation', in H. Feigl (ed.), *Readings in the Philosophy of Science* (New York, 1953), 723–43.

Wattenbach, W., 'Iter Austriacum, 1853', *Archiv für Kunde österreichischer Geschichts-Quellen*, 14 (1855), 1–94.

Waugh, S. L., *The Lordship of England* (Princeton, NJ, 1988).

—— 'Non-Alienation Clauses in Thirteenth-Century English Charters', *Albion*, 17 (1985), 1–14.

Weber, M., *Economy and Society*, trans. G. Roth and C. Wittich (New York, 1968).

—— *From Max Weber*, trans. H. H. Gerth and C. Wright Mills (London, 1948).

—— *Theory of Social and Economic Organization*, trans. A. M. Henderson and T. Parsons (New York, 1964).

Weigle, 'Ratherius von Verona im Kampf um das Kirchengut', *QFIA* 28 (1937–8), 1–35.

Weimar, P., 'Die Handschriften des Liber feudorum und seiner Glossen', *Rivista internazionale di diritto comune*, 1 (1990), 31–98.

—— 'Die legistische Literatur der Glossatorenzeit', in *Handbuch der Quellen und Literatur der neueren europäischen Privatrechtsgeschichte*, i: *Mittelalter*, ed. H. Coing (Munich, 1973), 129–260.

Weinberger, S., 'Les Conflits entre clercs et laïcs dans la Provence du xie siècle', *Annales du Midi*, 92 (1980), 269–79.

—— 'Precarial Grants: Approaches of the Clergy and Lay Aristocracy to Landholding and Time', *Journal of Medieval History*, 11 (1985), 163–9.

Weinrich, L. (ed.), *Quellen zur deutschen Verfassungs-, Wirtschafts- und Sozialgeschichte bis 1250* (Darmstadt, 1977).

Weitzel, J., *Dinggenossenschaft und Recht* (Cologne, 1985).

Wenskus, R., 'Probleme der germanische-deutschen Verfassungs- und Sozialgeschichte im Lichte der Ethnosoziologie', in *Historische Forschungen für W. Schlesinger*, ed. H. Beumann (Cologne, 1974), 19–46.

Werner, K. F., 'Heeresorganisation und Kriegführung im deutschen Königreich des 10. und 11. Jahrhunderts', *Settimane*, 15 (1967), 791–843.

—— 'Kingdom and Principality in Twelfth-century France', in T. Reuter (ed.), *The Medieval Nobility* (Amsterdam, 1978), 243–90.

—— 'Missus—Marchio—Comes', in W. Paravicini and K. F. Werner (eds.), *Histoire Comparée de l'Administration (ive–xviiie siècles)* (Beihefte der *Francia*, 9, 1980), 191–245.

*Westfalisches Urkunden-Buch*, iii, ed. R. Wilmans; viii, ed. R. Krumbholtz (Münster, 1859, 1913).

*Westminster Abbey Charters*, ed. E. Mason (London Rec. Soc. 25, 1988).

Whelan, F. G., 'Property as Artifice', *Nomos*, 22 (1980), 3–27.

White, S. D., *Custom, Kinship, and Gifts to the Saints* (Chapel Hill, 1988).

Wibald of Stablo, *Epistolae*, in *Bibliotheca Rerum Germanicarum* (Berlin, 1864–9), ed. P. Jaffé, i. 76–616.

Wickham, C., *Early Medieval Italy* (London, 1981).

—— 'Economic and Social Institutions in Northern Tuscany in the Eighth Century', in *Istituzioni ecclesiastiche della Toscana medioevale* [no editor named] (Lecce, 1980), 7–26.

—— 'Land Disputes and their Social Framework in Lombard-Carolingian Italy', in Davies, *Settlement* (q.v.), 105–24.

—— *The Mountains and the City: the Tuscan Appennines in the Early Middle Ages* (Oxford, 1988).

Widukind, *Rerum Gestarum Saxonicarum Libri Tres*, ed. P. Hirsch (MGH SRG 60, 1935).

Willard, J. F., *Parliamentary Taxes on Personal Property, 1290–1334* (Cambridge, Mass., 1934).

William Durandus, *Speculum Juris* (Frankfurt, 1668).

William of Malmesbury, *Gesta Regum*, ed. W. Stubbs (RS 90, 1887–9).

—— *Historia Novella*, ed. K. R. Potter (Edinburgh, 1955).

William of Newburgh, *Historia Rerum Anglicarum*, in R. Howlett (ed.), *Chronicles of the Reigns of Stephen etc.* (RS 82, 1884–90), i. 1–409, ii. 409–53.

Williams, A., 'How Land was Held Before and After the Norman Conquest', in A. Williams (ed.), *Domesday Book Studies* (London, 1987), 37–8.

—— 'Introduction, Text, and Translation of the Dorset Geld Rolls', *Victoria History of the County of Dorset*, iii, ed. R. B. Pugh (Oxford, 1968), 115–49.

Willoweit, D., 'Dominium und proprietas', *HJ* 94 (1974), 131–56.

Wipo, *Opera*, ed. H. Bresslau (MGH SRG 61, 1915).

Wood, C. T., *The French Apanages and the Capetian Monarchy, 1224–1328* (Cambridge, Mass., 1966).

Wood, I., 'Disputes in Late Fifth- and Sixth-Century Gaul', in Davies, *Settlement* (q.v.), 1–22.

Wormald, P., 'The Age of Bede and Aethelbald', in James Campbell (ed.), *The Anglo-Saxons* (Oxford, 1982).

—— *Bede and the Conversion of England* (Jarrow, 1984).

—— 'Charters, Law and the Settlement of Disputes in Anglo-Saxon England', in Davies, *Settlement* (q.v.), 149–68.

*Year Book 20–1 Edward I*, ed. A. J. Horwood (RS 31, 1866).

*Year Book 32–3 Edward I*, ed. A. J. Horwood (RS 31, 1864).

*Year Book 1313*, ed. W. C. Bolland (Selden Society 36, 1918).

Yver, J., 'Les Châteaux forts en Normandie jusqu'au milieu du xii⁰ siècle', *Bulletin de la Société des Antiquaires de Normandie*, 53 (1955–6), 28–115.

Yver, J., 'Les Premières Institutions du duché de Normandie', *Settimane*, 16 (1969), 299–366.

—— '"Vavassor", note sur les premiers emplois du terme', *RHDFE* 52 (1974), 548–9.

Zdekauer, L., 'La *carta libertatis* e gli statuti della Rocca Tintinnano', *Bullettino senese di storia patria*, 3 (1896), 327–76.

Zerbi, P., 'Il termine "fidelitas" nelle lettere di Gregorio VII', *Studi gregoriani*, 3 (1948), 129–48.

Zeumer, K., *Die deutschen Städtesteuern* (Leipzig, 1878).

# Index

INDEX

Pavia 215, 235, 484
peace of God 412
peasants (general): 15, 29, 37–47, 476–7
  in England 326, 340, 366, 371, 376, 378
  in France 130–1, 133, 153, 169, 279, 315
  in Germany 404, 426, 437, 470–2
  in Italy 186–7, 194, 213, 250, 253
peasants (particular aspects):
  bearing arms 39–42, 363, 426–7, 470; see also
    military service
  property 42, 48, 57, 63, 481; Frankish 77–8,
    80–1, 91, 95, 100–1, 106; in England 325–7,
    331, 334–5, 349, 362–3, 378; in France after
    1100: 130, 151–2, 154, 156, 175, 295, 297,
    304; in Germany 428–30, 458, 464, 466, 471;
    in Italy 186, 196, 203, 205, 221, 232, 244, 254
  see also freedom; homme de poosté; rustici;
    vilenages
peers 17, 44, 274, 375
  judgement of 4–5, 21, 37, 51–2; among
    Franks 103–4; in England 384, 388, 390;
    in France 132–3, 294, 304–6; in Germany
    423, 431, 433–4, 448, 456, 460, 466–7; in
    Italy 200, 202–4, 221, 224–6, 228, 233,
    236–7, 252–3, 255
  of kingdoms 42–3, 305–6, 385
Penna (Abruzzi), bishop of 212–13
Périgord 301
Peter, count of Mauguio 135, 140
Peter Jacobi 321–2
Petit-Dutaillis, C. 274
Philip I, king of France 141–2, 144, 166–7
Philip II, Augustus, king of France 119, 228,
  259, 266–7, 270–8, 288, 292, 296–7,
  299–300, 309, 315, 320
Philip III, king of France 302, 316
Philip IV, the Fair, king of France 293, 303,
  310–11, 316–17
Philip VI, king of France 318
Philip de Beaumanoir, see Beaumanoir
Piacenza 233
Pilius, glossator 227
Pippin I, king of the Franks 86, 89, 96, 98, 160
Pirenne, H. 299
Pisa 204, 217, 222–3, 233, 237, 239, 260, 484
Placentinus, Roman lawyer 260
Poitou 139, 156, 274, 279
  count of 139, 147, 158, 163; see also Aquitaine
Polling (Bavaria) abbey 446
Poly, J. P. 118
Pomerania and dukes of 458–9, 462, 464–5, 470
Ponthieu, counts of 267, 276, 298
Pontoise (Val d'Oise), church of Saint-Melon
  142
popes, papacy, and papal lands 135–6, 195,
  209–14, 233–4, 239, 241, 250, 390, 392,
  443–4, 446

see also Alexander II, Boniface VIII, Gerbert,
  Gregory VII and IX, Hadrian IV,
  Honorius III, Innocent III, John XII, Leo
  IX, Nicholas II, Urban I and II
possessio 183, 416
Pothier, R. J. 319
praepositi 218
praestaria 143, 186
precaria 48
  Frankish 78–9, 89–91, 96, 103–4
  in England 329
  in France after 900: 143–4, 161
  in Germany 428, 430, 436, 462, 471
  in Italy 186, 198, 200, 213, 249
primer seisin 368–9
private, see public
privatus contrasted with knight 220
property:
  communal 57 n., 75, 76, 183; see also
    common rights, inheritance rules, towns
  documentary title, see alienation (written
    records), church property (records)
  ecclesiastical, see church property
  full property ('ownership') 53–4, 59–65, 68,
    71, 73, 477; among Franks 75–7, 79, 96,
    100, 105–11, 398; in England 325–31,
    333–41, 343–8, 353–61, 374–5, 384–6,
    394–5; in France: 900–1100: 122, 125, 133,
    145–60, 166–7, 180, after 1100: 258, 260,
    267–8, 271–6, 281, 284, 289, 295–320; in
    Germany: before 1100: 399–402, 413–29,
    432, 435, after 1100: 445, 450, 454, 457,
    461, 463, 465–7; in Italy 182–5, 206–10,
    237, 241–5
  see also alod, hereditas, proprietas
  general ideas about 4–6, 14–16, 45, 48–74;
    Frankish 81–2, 107–8, 114; in England
    326–7, 331, 343, 346, 360–1, 374–5, 394–5;
    in France after 900: 152, 178, 259, 280,
    294–5, 319; in Germany 398, 416–18, 461;
    in Italy 182–3, 194, 205
  inheritance of, see inheritance
  obligations 56; see aids, military service,
    rents, succession dues, taxes
  proprietary churches, see Eigenkirchen
  reversionary rights 55, 69; in England 329,
    340, 344, 356, 367, 381–2, 385–6; in France
    143, 158, 292, 296–7, 319; in Germany
    401, 416, 422–3, 432, 435, 445–6, 451–3,
    462, 467; in Italy 185, 209
  security/confiscation 5, 44, 49–50, 55–6,
    60–2; among Franks 78–81, 91, 98, 102–4,
    106, 401–2; in England 325, 328, 332, 334,
    336, 341, 343–4, 349, 360, 384–6, 391,
    394–5; in France 122, 137, 157–8, 171,
    180, 273–5, 279, 292, 304, 319; in
    Germany; before 1100: 401–2, 406, 411,

540

INDEX

Saint-Maur-sur-Loire (Maine-et-Loire) abbey 139, 158
St Maximin, *see* Trier
Saint-Médard (Soissons, Aisne) abbey 141
Saint-Winoc (Nord) abbey 298
Saladin tithe 315
sale or purchase of land 57
　before 900: 76, 184, 186, 400
　900–1100: 149, 175, 221, 334, 337, 348
　after 1100: 222, 254, 261, 264, 279, 290–1,
　　301, 313, 374, 382–3, 457, 464
　*see also* alienation; money economy
Salzburg, archbishop of 469
　bishopric 400–1
Sambonifacio, counts of 197–8, 204
　*see also* Albert, Hubert
Sancerre (Cher), count of 266
Sardinia 182
Saxony and Saxons 108, 326, 398–400, 426,
　453–4, 456
　duchy 450–1
　duke of, *see* Henry
　law, *see* law (Saxon)
*scabini* 411, 423
*Schwabenspiegel* 7, 37, 71
Scotland 7–8, 324, 391–3
　kings of, *see* Alexander II, John, William I
scutage 362
　*see also* military service (payments)
Seneca 217
*senior* 36, 200
Septimania 97, 108
serjeanties 355, 362, 369, 382
sheriffs 337, 340 n., 341, 354, 359, 375, 378
shires, *see* counties
Siboto IV, count of Neuburg–Falkenstein 468
Sicily, kingdom of 12, 182, 209, 242–9, 252,
　254, 358, 361
　king of 246–9, 255; *see also* Charles, Roger II,
　William I or II, Frederick II
　*see also* Normans
Sigonio, C. 181
Simon de Montfort, count of Toulouse 310
Slavs 407
Smith, A. 7–9
Smith, Sir T. 7
socage 354–7, 364, 367, 369, 373, 380–1, 389, 394
Soissons, *see* Saint-Médard
sokes and sokemen 336, 338–41, 348, 354, 357,
　377
Soncino (Lombardy) 231–2
sovereignty 22, 26, 36, 287–8, 293, 391
　inalienability 72
Spain 15, 85, 109
　Spaniards 97, 108–10
Spelman, Sir H. 7, 323, 342, 355
Speyer, bishop of 443

*sporla* 298
　see also *Herrenfall*
Stabilis, alleged serf of Fleury 40–2
state:
　categories of state 26, 397, 403, 408, 474
　idea and phenomenon 20–2, 26–7, 34, 397
Stavelot (Belgium) abbey 442, 444
Stenton, F. M. 375
Stephen, count of Blois 135
Stephen, count of Meaux and Troyes 134
Stephen the marshal 266–7
Stettin 459
*subditi, sousgis* 36, 284, 310, 314, 392, 401
subinfeudation 100, 207, 222, 244, 250, 289,
　300, 303, 342, 356, 382–3, 463
　*see also* hierarchy
substitution, *see* subinfeudation
subvassals or subtenants, *see* rear
succession dues 49, 61, 63–4, 65, 69 , 477, 480
　in England: before 1100: 144, 334 n., 336–8,
　　340–1, 344, 347; after 1100: 247, 356–7,
　　364, 367–8, 372–4, 383, 386–7, 389, 395
　in France 132, 144, 279, 297–300, 318, 320
　in Germany 203, 430–2, 468
　in Italy and Sicily 200, 203, 230, 247, 254
Suger, abbot of Saint-Denis 270–2, 275, 292
summons (to court etc.): rules 200, 235, 245,
　318, 376, 379, 448–51, 453–4
Sussex 376
suzerainty 36
Swabia 413–14
　duke of, *see* Ernest II
Sylvester II, pope, *see* Gerbert
Symeon of Durham 343

Tabuteau, E. 175
Tacitus 24
tallage 364, 472; *see also* taxes
Tassilo, duke of Bavaria 86, 98, 399
taxes 53, 56–7, 61, 65–6, 70, 327, 478
　Frankish 80–2, 92, 106, 153
　in England 336–7, 343, 345, 349–50, 360,
　　364–8, 394
　in France 294, 302, 312–18, 327
　in Germany 428, 469, 471–2
　in Italy 185, 245, 247, 254
　*see also* aids; alienation (licenses); geld; military
　　service (payment); succession dues; tallage
Teduin, count 195, 197
Templars 281, 298
temporary grants 461, 477
　at will of lord 5, 78, 83, 172, 229, 254, 325
　ex officio holdings 62; among Franks 82–3,
　　93–8, 107, 111–13, 402; in England
　　329–30, 337; in France after 900: 134–5,
　　138–40, 161, 172–3; in Germany 402, 406,
　　445; in Italy 187–8, 191, 193, 207–8

542